Genetic Programming II

Complex Adaptive Systems
John H. Holland, Christopher Langton, and Stewart W. Wilson, advisors

Adaptation in Natural and Artificial Systems: An Introductory Analysis with Applications to Biology, Control, and Artificial Intelligence
John H. Holland

Toward a Practice of Autonomous Systems: Proceedings of the First European Conference on Artificial Life
edited by Francisco J. Varela and Paul Bourgine

Genetic Programming: On the Programming of Computers by Means of Natural Selection
John R. Koza

From Animals to Animats 2: Proceedings of the Second International Conference on Simulation of Adaptive Behavior
edited by Jean-Arcady Meyer, Herbert L. Roitblat, and Stewart W. Wilson

Intelligent Behavior in Animals and Robots
David McFarland and Thomas Bösser

Advances in Genetic Programming
edited by Kenneth E. Kinnear, Jr.

Genetic Programming II: Automatic Discovery of Reusable Programs
John R. Koza

Also Available:
Genetic Programming: The Movie
John R. Koza and James P. Rice

Genetic Programming II Videotape: The Next Generation
John R. Koza and James P. Rice

Genetic Programming II

Automatic Discovery of
Reusable Programs

John R. Koza

A Bradford Book
The MIT Press
Cambridge, Massachusetts
London, England

Second printing, 1998

© 1994 Massachusetts Institute of Technology

Set in Palatino by Proteus Typography, Palo Alto, California.

Printed and bound in the United States of America.

Library of Congress Cataloging-in-Publication Data

Library of Congress Catalog Card Number 94–76375

to my mother and father

CONTENTS

Detailed Table of Contents

Preface

ORGANIZATION OF THE BOOK

Chapter 1 introduces the eight main points to be made, with section 1.1 providing an overview of the book.

Chapter 2 provides a brief tutorial on the conventional genetic algorithm, the LISP programming language, genetic programming, and sources of additional information on the entire field of evolutionary computation. (The reader who is already familiar with these subjects may decide to skip this chapter entirely.)

Chapter 3 discusses the three-step hierarchical problem-solving process.

Chapter 4 lays the groundwork for all the problems to be described later. Using a simple problem (the two-boxes problem), section 4.2 illustrates how genetic programming without automatically defined functions is applied to a problem. (This section may be skipped by a reader who is already familiar with the process.) Sections 4.4 and 4.5 introduce the ideas of subroutines and automatically defined functions (ADFs). Section 4.6 illustrates the preparatory steps for applying automatically defined functions to a problem. Section 4.8 explains structure-preserving crossover and the branch typing technique used throughout the first three-quarters of this book. Section 4.10 explains how the size (average structural complexity) of the genetically evolved solutions to problems is measured. Section 4.11 explains the methodology used for measuring the number of fitness evaluations (the computational effort) required to yield a solution to a problem with a probability of 99%.

Chapters 5 through 25 solve a variety of problems from a variety of fields, both with and without automatically defined functions.

Sections 6.7 and 6.8 introduce the ideas of multiple automatically defined functions and hierarchical automatically defined functions.

Chapter 17 introduces certain computational issues in molecular biology.

Section 18.1 introduces transmembrane domains in proteins.

Section 18.3 discusses memory and states in genetically evolved programs.

Section 18.4 introduces the idea of restricted iteration in genetic programming.

Section 19.1 contains background on omega loops in proteins.

Appendix A is a list of the special symbols used in the book.

Appendix B is a list of special functions defined in the book.

Appendix C is a list of type fonts used in the book.

Appendix D contains the default parameters used to control the runs of genetic programming reported in this book.

Appendix E contains Common LISP computer code for implementing automatically defined functions.

Appendix F is an annotated bibliography on genetic programming.

Appendix G contains information on an electronic mailing list, public resository, and FTP site for genetic programming.

VIDEOTAPE ASSOCIATED WITH THIS BOOK

A color VHS videotape entitled *Genetic Programming II Videotape: The Next Generation* by John R. Koza and James P. Rice is available from The MIT Press. This videotape provides an overview of this book and a visualization of actual computer runs for many of the problems discussed in this book. The videotape is available in three formats: NTSC (ISBN 0-262-61099-X), PAL (ISBN 0-262-61100-7), and SECAM (ISBN 0-262-61101-5). The videotape may be ordered by mail from The MIT Press, 55 Hayward Street, Cambridge, Massachusetts 02142 USA; by telephone at 617-625-8569 or 800-356-0343; by electronic mail at `mitpress-orders@mit.edu`; or by FAX at 617-625-9080. In addition, the 1992 book *Genetic Programming: On the Programming of Computers by Means of Natural Selection* by John R. Koza (ISBN 0-262-11170-5) and the 1992 videotape *Genetic Programming: The Movie* by John R. Koza and James P. Rice (ISBN 0-262-61084-1 for NTSC format, ISBN 0-262-61087-6 for PAL format, and ISBN 0-262-61088-4 for SECAM format) are also available from The MIT Press.

Acknowledgments

James P. Rice of the Knowledge Systems Laboratory at Stanford University brought his exceptional knowledge in programming LISP machines to the programming of the problems in this book. In addition, he created all the artwork for the figures in this book and made innumerable helpful comments and suggestions on this book.

Martin A. Keane of Keane Associates in Chicago, Illinois conceived the impulse response problem and made numerous helpful suggestions to improve this book.

Douglas L. Brutlag of the Biochemistry Department of Stanford University was helpful in explaining various issues concerning biochemistry and molecular biology.

Stewart W. Wilson of the Rowland Institute for Science in Cambridge, Massachusetts provided continuing encouragement for the work here.

I am indebted for many helpful comments and suggestions made by the following people concerning various versions of the manuscript:

- David Andre of Canon Research Center of America, Palo Alto, and the Computer Science Department, Stanford University

- Peter J. Angeline of Loral Federal Systems Company, Owego, New York

- Jason Bluming of Enterprise Integration Technologies, Palo Alto, California

- Scott Clearwater of Xerox PARC, Palo Alto, California

- Robert J. Collins of USAnimation, Inc., Los Angeles

- Patrik D'haeseleer of LSI Logic, Mountain View, California

- Justin Gray of Alysis Software Corporation, San Francisco

- Frederic Gruau of the Laboratoire de l'Informatique du Parallélisme, Ecole Normale Supèrieure de Lyon in Lyon, France

- Simon Handley of the Computer Science Department, Stanford University

- David A. Hinds of the Department of Cell Biology, Stanford University

- Kent Hoxsey of Haiku, Hawaii

- Hitoshi Iba of the Machine Inference Section of the Electrotechnical Laboratory of Japan

- Jan Jannink of the Computer Science Department, Stanford University
- Christopher Jones of Cornerstone Research, Menlo Park, California
- Chin H. Kim of Rockwell International, Downey, California
- Kenneth E. Kinnear, Jr. of Adaptive Computing Technology, Boxboro, Massachusetts
- Tod Klingler of the Section on Medical Informatics of the Biochemistry Department of Stanford University
- W. B. Langdon of the Computer Science Department of University College, London
- Martin C. Martin of Carnegie Mellon University
- Sidney R. Maxwell III of Borland International, Scotts Valley, California
- Melanie Mitchell of the Santa Fe Institute, Santa Fe, New Mexico
- Nils Nilsson of the Computer Science Department, Stanford University
- Thomas Ngo of Interval Research, Palo Alto
- Howard Oakley, Institute of Naval Medicine, United Kingdom
- Tim Perkis of Antelope Engineering, Albany, California.
- John Perry of Cadence Design Systems, San Jose, California
- Craig W. Reynolds of Electronic Arts, San Mateo, California
- Justinian Rosca of the Computer Science Department, University of Rochester
- Malcolm Shute of the University of Brighton, England
- Eric Siegel of the Computer Science Department, Columbia University
- Jerry Tsai of the Department of Cell Biology, Stanford University
- Walter Alden Tackett of Hughes Missile Systems
- Rao Vemuri of the Department of Applied Science, University of California, Davis

John R. Koza
Computer Science Department
Stanford University
Stanford, CA 94305 USA
E-MAIL: Koza@Cs.Stanford.Edu

Genetic Programming II

1 Introduction

Genetic Programming: On the Programming of Computers by Means of Natural Selection (hereafter referred to as *Genetic Programming*) proposed a possible answer to the following question, attributed to Arthur Samuel in the 1950s:

How can computers learn to solve problems without being explicitly programmed? In other words, how can computers be made to do what is needed to be done, without being told exactly how to do it?

Genetic Programming demonstrated a surprising and counterintuitive answer to this question: computers can be programmed by means of natural selection. In particular, *Genetic Programming* demonstrated, by example and argument, that the domain-independent genetic programming paradigm is capable of evolving computer programs that solve, or approximately solve, a variety of problems from a variety of fields.

To accomplish this, genetic programming starts with a primordial ooze of randomly generated computer programs composed of the available programmatic ingredients, and breeds the population using the Darwinian principle of survival of the fittest and an analog of the naturally occurring genetic operation of crossover (sexual recombination). Genetic programming combines a robust and efficient problem-solving procedure with powerful and expressive symbolic representations.

This book extends the results in *Genetic Programming* to larger and more difficult problems. It focuses on exploiting the regularities, symmetries, homogeneities, similarities, patterns, and modularities of problem environments by means of automatically defined functions.

An *automatically defined function (ADF)* is a function (i.e., subroutine, procedure, module) that is dynamically evolved during a run of genetic programming and which may be called by a calling program (e.g., a main program) that is simultaneously being evolved. Automatically defined functions were conceived and developed by James P. Rice of the Knowledge Systems Laboratory at Stanford University and myself (Koza and Rice 1992b).

As will be seen, genetic programming with automatically defined functions may solve regularity-rich problems in a hierarchical way.

Regularities appear in many problem environments.

- Designers of microprocessor chips reuse certain standard circuits (cells), each performing the same elementary function throughout the chip.

- Biologists have observed that many mechanisms for performing certain functions in living things are reused, in identical or similar form, to perform other functions in the same organism or in other organisms.

- In designing a house, architects use certain basic constructions over and over again in identical or almost identical ways.

- The same techniques are reused at different stations along an assembly line to weld different parts together.

- Different clerks apply the same procedures of double-entry bookkeeping to process different streams of transactions.

- Computer programmers invoke a similar process of reuse when they repeatedly call a subroutine from a calling program.

Complicated systems in the real world typically contain massive amounts of regularity. Understanding, designing, and constructing large systems requires, as a practical matter, the leverage gained from the exploitation of regularity, modularity, and symmetry. For example, writing computer programs would be utterly impractical if programmers had to reinvent, from scratch, the code for the square root, cosine, array-access, file-handling, and printing on each separate occasion when they needed those functions.

Similarly, design of a microprocessor chip containing thousands of occurrences of a standard cell would be impractical if the chip designer had to start from the first principles of electronic design and separately think through the design of each such cell.

The natural world abounds with instances where the same structure or behavior recurs in identical or similar form. Cells of living things contain millions of identical copies of thousands of different function-performing proteins. Humans contain trillions of such cells, but the entire structure is specified by chromosomes containing only a few billion bits of information. The three-dimensional coordinates for each atom, of each protein, of each copy of a protein, of each cell is not explicitly listed in the chromosomes. Instead, there is a hierarchical arrangement of structures and substructures and massive reuse of certain basic constructions.

Problems from complex, regularity-rich environments can often be solved by applying a three-step hierarchical process. This three-step process may be viewed in a top-down way and a bottom-up way.

In the top-down way of describing the *hierarchical problem-solving process*, one first tries to find a way to decompose a given problem into subproblems. Second, one tries to solve each of the subproblems. Third, one tries to solve the original overall problem by using the now-available solutions to the subproblems. If this process is successful, one ends up with a hierarchical and modular solution to the problem. The popular technique of *divide and conquer* is an example of this three-step problem-solving process.

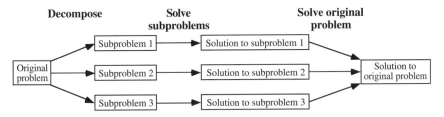

Figure 1.1   Top-down way of viewing the three-step hierarchical problem-solving process.

Figure 1.1 depicts the top-down way of viewing this three-step hierarchical process. The original overall problem is shown at the left. In the step labeled "decompose" near the top left of the figure, the original problem is decomposed into three subproblems. In the step labeled "solve subproblems" in the top middle of the figure, the three subproblems are solved. Finally, in the step labeled "solve original problem" near the top right, the solutions of the three subproblems are invoked and assembled into a solution to the overall problem.

In practice, certain subproblems may be difficult enough to warrant a recursive reinvocation of the entire three-step process in order to solve them.

Computer programmers constantly use this three-step problem-solving process. In the terminology of computer programming, the process starts when the programmer analyzes the overall problem and divides it into parts. Second, the programmer writes subprograms (subroutines, procedures, functions) to solve each part of the problem. Third, the programmer writes a calling program (e.g., the main program) that solves the overall problem by calling the subprograms. The main program assembles the results produced by the subprograms into a solution to the overall problem.

Sometimes the task to be performed by a subprogram is itself so complex that the programmer will choose to reapply the entire three-step problem-solving process to that task. In that event, a subprogram might call one or more sub-subprograms. The subprogram is then written so as to assemble the solutions to its sub-subprograms and thereby perform its task.

This three-step process may be beneficial in two ways. The total effort required to decompose the problem into subproblems, solve the subproblems, and assemble the solutions to the subproblems into a solution of the overall problem often proves to be less than the effort required to solve the original problem without the aid of the hierarchical process. In addition, if the decomposition has been done astutely, the solutions to the subprograms will often be reusable many times (either identically or with a slight variation) in building up the solution to the overall problem. Reuse may lead to simpler and smaller (more parsimonious) solutions. Of course, if a beneficial decomposition cannot be found or there are no opportunities for reuse, the three-step process is counterproductive.

In the bottom-up way of describing the hierarchical three-step problem-solving process, we first try to discover useful regularities and patterns at the

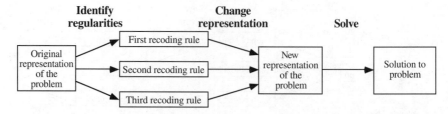

Figure 1.2   Bottom-up way of viewing the hierarchical three-step problem-solving process.

lowest (given) level of the problem environment. Second, we change the representation of the problem and restate it in terms of its inherent regularities and patterns, thus creating a new problem. Third, we solve the presumably more tractable recoded problem. If this process of finding regularities and recoding is successful, one ends up with a hierarchical solution to the problem.

The recoding of the original problem is a *change of representation* from the original representation of the problem to a new representation.

Regularities and patterns are, of course, most useful if they reappear many times in the problem environment.

Previously non-obvious regularities often become apparent when there is such a change of representation. In practice, the process of discovering a solution to the recoded problem may itself require further discovery of regularities and patterns and additional recoding.

As before, this hierarchical process is considered productive only if the total effort required to identify the regularities, change the representation, and solve the new problem is less than the effort required to solve the original problem without the aid of the three-step process.

Figure 1.2 shows the original representation of a problem, three recoding rules for changing the representation of the problem, the new representation of the problem, and a solution to the problem. The step labeled "identify regularities" near the top left of the figure identifies three recoding rules that can be applied to the problem environment. The step labeled "change representation" in the top middle of the figure recodes the original problem using the three just-discovered recoding rules and creates a new representation of the problem. Finally, the step labeled "solve" near the top right solves the problem as restated in terms of the new representation.

I believe that the goal of getting computers to solve problems without being explicitly programmed requires the exploitation of regularities and modularities in a hierarchical way. Large complex problems are generally not solved by individually crafting each minute part of the overall solution. Automatic programming seems unlikely to be realized for large problems if each part of the overall solution to a problem is handled as a unique event that is never to be seen again. Hierarchical organization and reuse seem to be required if automatic programming is ever to be scaled up from small problems to large problems.

The hierarchical three-step problem-solving process described above offers an alluring way to gain the leverage that is needed to solve large problems. However, the question immediately arises as to how can one go about implementing this process in an *automated* and *domain-independent* way.

Implementation of the top-down approach to the hierarchical process calls for answers to the following:

- How does one go about decomposing a problem into subproblems?
- Once the subproblems have been identified, how does one solve the subproblems?
- Once the subproblems have been identified and solved, how does one assemble the solutions of the subproblems into a solution to the original overall problem?

The bottom-up approach requires answers to these implementation issues:

- How does one go about finding regularities at a low level of the problem environment?
- Once the regularities have been identified, how does one recode the original problem into a new problem in terms of these regularities (i.e., how does one change the representation)?
- Once the regularities have been identified and the recoding has been done, how does one solve the original problem as now framed in terms of the new representation?

The reader of *Genetic Programming* will recognize that the discovery of a solution to a subproblem (i.e., the second step of the top-down approach) can often be accomplished by means of genetic programming. Indeed, *Genetic Programming* demonstrated that a broad range of problems can be solved, or approximately solved, by genetically breeding a population of computer programs over a period of many generations.

But what about the other steps of the process? How are they to be performed in an automated and domain-independent way? More important, even if the individual steps can be performed separately, how are they to be *integrated* with one another?

The surprising and counterintuitive result that will be demonstrated in this book is that, for a variety of problems, *all three steps* of the hierarchical problem-solving process can be performed, *automatically and dynamically*, within a run of genetic programming when automatically defined functions are added to the toolkit of genetic programming.

The technique of automatically defined functions enables genetic programming to automatically discover useful functional subunits dynamically during a run. The concurrent evolution of functional subunits and calling programs enables genetic programming to realize (in an implicit manner) the entire three-step hierarchical problem-solving process described above automatically within a run of genetic programming.

Starting from a primordial ooze of randomly generated compositions of programmatic ingredients, genetic programming with automatically defined functions simultaneously evolves the functional subunits and coadapted call-

ing programs by employing the Darwinian principle of survival and reproduction of the fittest and genetic crossover. As in *Genetic Programming*, programming is done by means of natural selection; the program structure that
solves the problem arises from fitness.

The realization by genetic programming of the three-step hierarchical problem-solving process occurs concurrently, not temporally (as the phrase "three
steps" might suggest). More precisely, one can *interpret* the results produced
by genetic programming with automatically defined functions as a realization
of the three-step process. Genetic programming with automatically defined
functions does not, in fact, explicitly perform any of the three steps (either of
the top-down or bottom-up formulation). That is, there is no explicit decomposition of the original problem into subproblems; there is no separate solution of subproblems; and there is no explicit assembly of solutions to
subproblems into a solution to the overall problem. Similarly, there is no
explicit search or discovery of patterns, no change of representation, and no
separate solution of any new problem expressed in any higher level representation. Instead, hierarchical decomposition and changed representation
are emergent properties that we impute to the results produced by genetic
programming with automatically defined functions.

If it is indeed possible to solve a problem by simultaneously evolving a
calling program and one or more subroutines, the question immediately arises
as to whether this process delivers any benefits in terms of the amount of
computation necessary to discover the solution or in terms of the parsimony
of the evolved solutions.

The evidence, provided by examples and argument in this book, supports
the following eight main points:

Main point 1: Automatically defined functions enable genetic programming to solve a variety of problems in a way that can be interpreted as a
decomposition of a problem into subproblems, a solving of the subproblems,
and an assembly of the solutions to the subproblems into a solution to the
overall problem (or which can alternatively be interpreted as a search for
regularities in the problem environment, a change of representation, and a
solving of a higher level problem).

Main point 2: Automatically defined functions discover and exploit the
regularities, symmetries, homogeneities, similarities, patterns, and modularities of the problem environment in ways that are very different from the style
employed by human programmers.

Main point 3: For a variety of problems, genetic programming requires
less computational effort to solve a problem with automatically defined functions than without them, provided the difficulty of the problem is above a
certain relatively low problem-specific breakeven point for computational
effort.

Main point 4: For a variety of problems, genetic programming usually
yields solutions with smaller overall size (lower average structural complexity) with automatically defined functions than without them, provided the
difficulty of the problem is above a certain problem-specific breakeven point
for average structural complexity.

Main point 5: For the three problems herein for which a progression of several scaled-up versions is studied, the average size of the solutions produced by genetic programming increases as a function of problem size at a lower rate with automatically defined functions than without them.

Main point 6: For the three problems herein for which a progression of several scaled-up versions is studied, the computational effort increases as a function of problem size at a lower rate with automatically defined functions than without them.

Main point 7: For the three problems herein for which a progression of several scaled-up versions is studied, the benefits in terms of computational effort and average structural complexity conferred by automatically defined functions increase as the problem size is scaled up.

Main point 8: Genetic programming is capable of simultaneously solving a problem and evolving the architecture of the overall program.

1.1 OVERVIEW

The general approach of this book is to produce evidence supporting the eight main points by solving a number of illustrative problems from various fields, with and without automatically defined functions.

Chapter 2 provides a brief tutorial on the conventional genetic algorithm, the LISP programming language, and genetic programming. Section 2.4 itemizes sources of additional information for the field of evolutionary computation. (The reader who is already familiar with these subjects may decide to skip this chapter.)

Chapter 3 further explains the three-step hierarchical problem-solving process.

Chapter 4 lays the groundwork for all the problems to be described later using a simple illustrative problem. The two-boxes problem presents the opportunity to define a useful functional subunit and to use that subunit twice in solving the problem.

Sections 4.2 and 4.3 illustrate the successful application of genetic programming without automatically defined functions to solve the two-boxes problem. (This review of genetic programming may be skipped by the reader who is already familiar with the process.)

Sections 4.4 and 4.5 introduce the ideas of subroutines and automatically defined functions.

Section 4.6 describes the preparatory steps for applying automatically defined functions to a problem.

Section 4.7 explains the method of creating the initial random population with automatically defined functions.

Section 4.8 explains structure-preserving crossover and the branch typing technique used throughout the first 20 chapters of this book.

Section 4.9 shows the results with automatically defined functions. This section shows that it is possible to simultaneously evolve both a functional subunit and a coadapted calling program dynamically during a run in order to solve a problem. In other words, genetic programming works with automatically defined functions. If automatically defined functions work at all for this problem, one naturally begins to wonder whether they yield some economy in terms of the computational burden necessary to solve a problem.

Section 4.10 explains the measure of average structural complexity, $\overline{S}$, used to measure the size of the solutions produced by genetic programming.

Section 4.11 explains the methodology used in creating the performance curves for measuring the number of fitness evaluations required to yield a solution (or satisfactory result) for a problem with a satisfactorily high probability (say 99%). The performance curves permit calculation of a measure of computational effort, E, for a problem.

One of the reasons why it is desirable to solve a problem using automatically defined functions is to avoid repetitively solving and re-solving identical or similar subproblems. Unfortunately, when the performance of genetic programming is compared, with and without automatically defined functions, for the two-boxes problem in chapter 4, we are disappointed to find that genetic programming with automatically defined functions is a distinct disadvantage both in terms of the number of fitness evaluations required to yield a solution with 99% probability and the average size of the evolved solutions. The reason for this disappointing result for this particular problem appears to be that the two-boxes problem offers the opportunity for only the barest amount of reuse (only one reuse of only one subroutine) and only the barest amount of reused code within the subroutine (only two multiplications).

The tide turns in chapter 5. We show there that automatically defined functions can indeed reduce the computational effort required to solve a problem. This chapter compares a simple version and a scaled-up version of four different problems. The problems illustrate four different dimensions for scaling: the order of a polynomial, the number of arguments to a Boolean function, the number of harmonics of a sinusoidal function, and the frequency of use of π in an algebraic expression. All eight versions are solved both with and without automatically defined functions, thus producing 16 series of runs. Genetic programming is able to solve all eight versions, both with and without automatically defined functions.

When we analyze the 16 sets of results, we find that automatically defined functions are disadvantageous as measured by computational effort for the simpler version of each problem, but become advantageous for the scaled-up version of the same problem. The reason appears to be that the simpler versions of the four problems are *too simple* to overcome the overhead associated with automatically defined functions. There is insufficient regularity in the simpler versions of the four problems to make automatically defined functions beneficial. In contrast, the scaled-up version of each problem is sufficiently difficult to benefit (often just slightly) from automatically defined functions. Each of these four problems apparently straddles a breakeven point in computational effort.

The problems in the remaining chapters are distinctly on the beneficial side of the breakeven point for computational effort.

Chapter 6 considers the problem of symbolic regression of the Boolean even-parity function with a progressively increasing number of arguments.

In sections 6.3 through 6.6, a baseline is established for solving the even-3-, 4-, 5-, and 6-parity problems without automatically defined functions using a fixed population size of 16,000.

Section 6.7 introduces the idea of multiple automatically defined functions and section 6.8 introduces the hierarchical version of automatically defined functions.

The even-3-, 4-, 5-, and 6-parity problems are then solved with automatically defined functions. The substantial symmetry and modularity of this problem environment means that there are considerable opportunities for decomposing the problem into subproblems, solving the subproblems, and assembling the solutions to the subproblems into a solution of the problem as a whole. Automatically defined functions prove to be beneficial in terms of computational effort in solving this progression of problems.

Even though the even-6-parity problem without automatically defined functions was never solved with a population size of 16,000, the advantages of automatically defined functions enable the even-7-, 8-, 9-, 10-, and 11-parity problems to be solved using a population of only 4,000.

Automatically defined functions usually prove to be beneficial in terms of the parsimony of the solutions produced by genetic programming.

As the even-parity problem is scaled up from 3, to 4, to 5, and to 6 arguments, the growth in the average size of the solutions is only about half as large with automatically defined functions as without them. As the even-parity problem is scaled up, the growth in the computational effort is also considerably less with automatically defined functions than without them.

In all of the problems mentioned above, we chose the number of automatically defined functions and the number of arguments that they would each possess in the overall program. There are a number of practical techniques that can be used in making these architectural choices. The reader might wonder whether such initial architectural choices are important in determining whether genetic programming is capable of solving a problem.

In chapter 7, we solve the even-5-parity problem using 15 different combinations of the number of automatically defined functions and the number of arguments. The result is that genetic programming solves the problem regardless of the choice of architecture. The required computational effort varies somewhat among the 15 architectures; however, the computational effort with automatically defined functions is less for all 15 architectures than the computational effort without automatically defined functions.

The origin of the illustrative problems presented in this book is worth mentioning. Finding problems suitable for exploring the question of how to discover and exploit regularities of problem environments proved to be a difficult, but necessary preliminary task to doing the experimental research described in this book. There are two reasons for this.

First, ever-present considerations of available computer time played a dominant role in the selection and formulation of problems. When we talk about computer time, we are not talking merely about the time required to make one run of a problem. The general approach of this book is to compare the average performance in solving a problem, both with and without automatically defined functions. Consequently, a problem is suitable for this book only if it is solvable within a certain maximum number of generations, both with and without automatically defined functions. Because genetic programming is a probabilistic algorithm and not every run is successful within the allowed maximum number of generations, getting a successful run usually takes more than one run. Again, because genetic programming is probabilistic, measuring performance requires that multiple, successful runs must be produced, both with and without automatically defined functions. The controlling constraint is the time required for the multiple, successful runs for whatever version of a problem proves to be the slowest (which, in practice, usually turns out to be when automatically defined functions are not being used). Runs of problems in this book can be very slow indeed (often requiring several days each). Indeed, the runs documented in this book took about four years of computer time.

In addition, we wanted at least some of the problems in this book to be scalable along some dimension. Our desire to study scaling experimentally further increased our requirements for computer time. We needed problems for which *multiple, successful* runs, *both* with and without automatically defined functions, for *a progression of several scaled-up versions* of the problem could be made within a reasonable amount of computer time. We were only able to find three problems for which we could make a range of comparisons within a reasonable total amount of computer time: the even-3-, 4-, 5-, and 6-parity problems (chapter 6); the lawnmower problem with lawn sizes of 32, 48, 64, 80, and 96 (chapter 8); and the bumblebee problem with 10, 15, 20 and 25 flowers (chapter 9).

Of course, there is nothing unusual about the fact that the phenomena under study are barely detectable with the available instrumentation. Each enhancement in the power of telescopes, microscopes, particle accelerators, and virtually every other scientific instrument has enabled new questions to be experimentally examined. The new questions are, of course, usually at the edge of what is detectable by the latest piece of equipment.

A second reason for the difficulty in finding suitable benchmark problems concerns the scope of recent work in the fields of machine learning, artificial intelligence, and neural networks. Many of the problems in *Genetic Programming* were benchmark problems that had been the focus of considerable previous research. This is not the case in this book. Only the Boolean parity and symmetry problems have an extensive history; only a few other problems in this book have even a modest history (e.g., the artificial ant problem of chapter 12). In most instances, we had to construct suitable problems. The reason for this is that existing paradigms from the fields of machine learning, artificial intelligence, and neural networks have generally not proved to be capable of discovering and exploiting regularities and symmetries in the way that automatically defined functions do. Consequently, researchers in those fields have usually given a blind eye to regularity-rich problems. Such problems have only rarely appeared as benchmark problems in these fields. The seeming exception (the Boolean parity problem) is the exception that proves the rule. The parity problem usually appears in the literature not because its problem environment is replete with regularities, but because it difficult to learn (since changing any one input always toggles the output). Published solutions to the parity problem usually do not solve the problem by discovering and exploiting the interesting regularities in this problem environment. Instead, the parity problem is typically used to show that a particular paradigm is powerful enough to overcome the difficulties of the problem and to solve it (usually without discovering or exploiting very symmetry that makes the problem interesting to us).

For these reasons, we found it necessary to construct several additional regularity-rich problems for testing automatically defined functions. The first of these (the lawnmower problem in chapter 8) was specifically designed to

- be much faster to run than the parity problem (it can be run with a population size of only 1,000, rather than 16,000 or 4,000),
- have exploitable regularities,
- be hard enough to have interesting hierarchical decompositions,
- have a sufficiently rich and varied function set to enable the problem to be solved in many distinctly different ways, using many district programming styles and motifs
- be on the beneficial side of the breakeven point for computational effort,
- be on the beneficial side of the breakeven point for average structural complexity,
- be scalable in some dimension, and
- be so much faster to solve that we could say, in spite of all of the uncertainties inherent in measuring wallclock time, that this problem is clearly on the beneficial side of the breakeven point for wallclock time when automatically defined functions are used.

In the lawnmower problem, the goal is to find a program for controlling the movement of a lawnmower so that the lawnmower cuts all the grass in a homogeneous, unobstructed yard. The lawnmower problem is scaled in terms of the size of the lawn. Lawn sizes of 32, 48, 64, 80 and 96 are considered.

In addition to demonstrating scaling, the lawnmower problem of chapter 8 illustrates another interesting aspect of hierarchical computer programming. In chapters 4 through 7, information is transmitted to the genetically evolved reusable subprograms solely by means of explicit arguments. The automatically defined functions are usually repeatedly invoked with different instantiations of these explicit arguments. When transmitted values are received by an automatically defined function, they are bound to dummy variables (formal parameters) that appear locally inside the function. An alternative to this explicit transmission of information to a subprogram is the implicit transmission of information by means of side effects on the state of a system. In the lawnmower problem considered in this chapter, one of the two automatically defined functions takes no explicit arguments.

Genetic programming is capable of solving the lawnmower problem, both with and without automatically defined functions for all five sizes of lawn (sections 8.3 through 8.7 and sections 8.9 through 8.13). Section 8.14 consolidates the experimental evidence and shows that, for any of the given lawn sizes, substantially less computational effort is required with automatically defined functions than without them. Moreover, the average size of the programs that successfully solve the problem is considerably smaller when using automatically defined functions than when not using them.

Section 8.15 considers the specific numerical amounts by which genetic programming with automatically defined functions outperforms genetic programming without automatically defined functions. When the problem size is scaled up from 32, through 48, 64, and 80, and eventually to 96, the average size of the programs that successfully solve the lawnmower problem appears to be a linear function of problem size, both with and without automatically defined functions. However, the two linear relationships are different. The average size without automatically defined functions seems to be a substantial linear multiple of the problem size. However, the average size of the programs that successfully solve the problem with automatically defined functions seems to consist of a substantial fixed overhead plus a very small linear multiple of the problem size.

When the problem size is scaled between 32 and 96, the computational effort required for the lawnmower problem without automatically defined functions increases at an explosively nonlinear rate. However, with automatically defined functions, there appears to be only a linear growth in the required computational effort.

The above-mentioned measure of computational effort based on the number of fitness evaluations required to solve a problem with a satisfactorily high probability is only one possible way to measure the computational burden associated with a problem-solving algorithm. Section 8.16 shows that less wallclock time is required with automatically defined functions than without them.

Chapter 9 considers the bumblebee problem. This problem is scaled along the axis representing the number of flowers that the bee has to visit. The bumblebee problem provides an example of a problem in the domain of floating-point numbers. Four progressively more difficult versions of this problem are run, each with and without automatically defined functions. Automatically defined functions again prove to be beneficial in terms of the computational effort required to solve the problem and the average structural complexity of the evolved solutions.

The progression of four bumblebee problems is similar to the progression of parity problems and lawnmower problems in that the computational effort grows rapidly with problem size without automatically defined functions, but appears to grow more slowly with automatically defined functions. Similarly, the average structural complexity appears to grow more slowly with automatically defined functions than without them.

The bumblebee problem illustrates another aspect of genetic programming with automatically defined functions. In the parity problem and the lawnmower problem, we were able to understand the genetically evolved regularities by analyzing the solutions evolved by genetic programming. Even though the bumblebee problem was designed to contain a considerable amount of exploitable regularity and modularity, we were unable to understand any discovered regularity by looking at either the genetically evolved program or the trajectory of the bee. Nonetheless, we believe that regularities exist in the genetically evolved solutions employing automatically defined functions because the comparative statistics provide indirect evidence of the discovery and exploitation of some regularity (not necessarily one contemplated by us) in the problem environment.

Chapter 10 shows that for the parity problem, the lawnmower problem, and the bumblebee problem, the advantages in terms of computational effort and parsimony conferred by automatically defined functions increase as the problem size is scaled up. In other words, genetic programming with automatically defined functions is scalable automatic programming for the particular problems and ranges of problem sizes that were studied.

Chapter 11 shows how information can be transmitted between a calling program and a subprogram in yet another way, namely implicit transmission through a global variable. The problem is to find the impulse response function for a linear time-invariant system. The fact that the subprograms are real-valued functions of a single variable permits the genetically evolved automatically defined functions to be visualized graphically. The genealogical audit trails in section 11.7 illustrate the way that crossover works to evolve improved programs in a population. The impulse-response problem provides another example of a problem in the domain of floating-point numbers.

The artificial ant problem considered in chapter 12 shows a problem that can be solved using subprograms with no explicit arguments. In all of the previous problems, at least some information is transmitted to the reusable subprograms by means of explicit arguments. The subprograms in these problems are then repeatedly invoked with different instantiations of the arguments. In this problem, the state of the system is available to both the subroutine and the calling program and side-effecting operations alter the state of a system. Information is transmitted between the subroutine and calling program implicitly by means of the current state of the system. Since the effect of each side-effecting operation depends on the current state of the system, the state of the system acts as the implicit arguments to the operation.

The Boolean even-parity problem (chapters 6 and 7), the lawnmower problem (chapter 8), and the bumblebee problem (chapter 9) all contained a considerable amount of exploitable regularity. In contrast, the artificial ant problem in chapter 12 shows that the amount of regularity required in the problem environment for automatically defined functions to be beneficial can be very modest (consisting of a common inspecting motion applied in only two directions).

The problem of the obstacle-avoiding robot considered in chapter 13 is similar to the lawnmower problem; however, in this problem obstacles prohibit the straightforward exploitation of the regularities present in the problem environment.

The minesweeper problem of chapter 14 is similar to the problems of the lawnmower and the obstacle-avoiding robot; however, in this problem, the obstacles are lethal. Consideration of the lethality of the obstacles in the minesweeper problem is so important that it dominates the considerations required to find a solution to the problem.

Both the problem of the obstacle-avoiding robot and the minesweeper problem demonstrate the benefits of automatically defined functions in an environment that is more complicated and less homogeneous than the lawnmower problem.

Chapters 15 through 20 present problems that, when solved using automatically defined functions, illustrate the simultaneous discovery of initially-unknown detectors and a way of combining the just-discovered detectors. The detectors that are dynamically discovered during the run of genetic programming are then repeatedly used in solving the problem.

Chapter 15 considers the problem of identifying the letters I and L on a 6-by-4 pixel grid. The evolved programs consist of hierarchical combinations of five local detectors. The five automatically defined functions perform local sensing of a nine pixel subarea of the overall grid. The main part of the overall program moves the detectors around the overall grid and integrates the local sensory input provided by the five detectors.

Section 15.6 studies the genealogical audit trail of a solution to this problem and illustrates the way that crossover works to evolve improved programs in a population. In section 15.7, the same problem is solved using a mixture of differently sized detectors. Section 15.8 considers a translation invariant version of the problem.

Chapter 16 illustrates the automatic discovery of initially unknown detectors for the problem of deciding whether a five-card hand from a pinochle deck is a flush or a four-of-a-kind. Correlation is introduced in section 16.2 as a way to measure the fitness of a predicting program (and further discussed in subsection 18.5.2). This problem paves the way for the subsequent four chapters (17 through 20) on computational problems in molecular biology and biochemistry.

The problems of analyzing data associated with the growing databases in the field of molecular biology appear to be an especially promising area in which to apply genetic programming.

Complex relationships in data from the real world can often only be expressed by a combination of mathematical operations of different types. Some of the underlying relationships in empirical data may be simple linear relationships; others can be captured only with polynomials, rational polynomials, or other classes of functions. Conditional operations may be required to segment parts of the space from one another and to create alternative disjoint models of the data. Calculations involving iterations and memory may also be required to recognize the patterns and relationships in empirical data. In short, modeling complex empirical data requires the flexibility of computer programs.

Existing methods for pattern recognition, classification, and data mining usually require that the user commit to the nature of the model before the modeling process begins. In contrast, in genetic programming, the size and shape as well as the content of the computer program that models the data is open to evolution.

I believe that genetic programming with automatically defined functions is especially well suited to problems of discovering patterns and relationships in empirical data because its expressiveness and flexibility enable it to find solutions consisting of complex combinations of mathematical operations, conditional operations, iteration, memory, and hierarchical decision-making. Moreover, since genetic programming evolves the size and shape as well as the content of the computer program that solves the problem, it has the potential to discover unanticipated relationships in empirical data.

Chapter 17 contains an introduction to some of the major current computational issues in biochemistry and molecular biology. Section 17.1 introduces chromosomes and DNA. The discussion then turns to the role of proteins in living things (section 17.2), transcription and translation (section 17.3), and amino acids and protein structure (section 17.4). The primary, secondary, tertiary, and quartenary structures of proteins are introduced in sections 17.5, 17.6, 17.7, and 17.8, respectively. Section 17.9 contains references to the growing number of recent applications of conventional genetic algorithms to molecular biology and biochemistry.

Chapter 18 considers the problem of predicting whether protein segments are transmembrane domains or non-transmembrane areas of a protein. Our solution to this problem incorporates the automatic discovery of initially unknown detectors, restricted iteration, and memory.

Section 18.1 contains background on transmembrane domains in proteins.

Section 18.2 defines the set-creating version of the problem of predicting whether a protein segment is a transmembrane domain or a non-transmembrane area of a protein.

Mathematical calculations typically employ iterations and memory. Section 18.3 discusses settable variables, memory, state, and setting functions in genetically evolved programs.

Section 18.4 introduces the idea of restricted iteration in genetic programming. Restricted iteration is a practical way of introducing iteration into populations of genetically evolved computer programs.

The set-creating version of the transmembrane problem in sections 18.5 through 18.9 illustrates the use of settable variables, memory, state, setting functions, and restricted iteration.

The best predicting program evolved by genetic programming for the set-creating version of the transmembrane problem with automatically defined functions has a slightly better error rate than four other published results. This genetically evolved program is an instance of an algorithm produced by an automated technique which is superior to that written by human investigators.

The above version of the transmembrane problem was motivated by and patterned after recent work on this problem employing set formation. However, absent this other work, it would have been more natural to approach this problem with computer programs composed of the ordinary arithmetic operations of addition, subtraction, multiplication, and division and ordinary conditional operations. Sections 18.10 and 18.11 present the arithmetic-performing version of the transmembrane problem. Again, the predicting program evolved by genetic programming for this second version of the transmembrane problem with automatically defined functions has a slightly better error rate than the same four other benchmark results.

Chapter 19 extends the techniques of the transmembrane problem to another problem of molecular biology. The problem here is to predict whether or not a given protein segment is an omega loop. Omega loops are an irregular kind of secondary structure in proteins. Section 19.1 provides background on them. There is a set-creating version of the problem (section 19.3) and an arithmetic-performing version (section 19.5).

Chapter 20 extends the two versions of the transmembrane problem from chapter 18 to a more difficult version of the problem in which the goal is to predict whether an *individual* amino acid lies in a transmembrane domain or a non-transmembrane area. A partial parsing of the entire protein sequence is employed in this version of the problem using a lookahead technique.

Chapters 21 through 25 deal with the evolutionary determination of the architecture of genetically evolved programs.

Prior to these chapters, whenever we applied genetic programming with automatically defined functions to a problem, we first determined the number of function-defining branches of the overall program that is to be evolved and the number of arguments possessed by each function-defining branch. If there was more than one function-defining branch, we also determined the nature of the hierarchical references (if any) allowed between the function-defining branches. Four different ways of making these architectural choices are used (as described in chapter 7): prospective analysis of the nature of the problem, seemingly sufficient capacity, affordable capacity, and retrospective analysis of the results of actual runs. Chapter 7 shows that regardless of which of 15 architectures is employed, genetic programming with automatically defined functions is capable of solving the even-5-parity problem and, in addition, that less computational effort is required for all 15 architectures with automatically defined functions than without them. Nonetheless, the user may, for some problems, be unable or unwilling to use any of these four techniques.

Chapter 21 shows that the architecture of the overall program can be evolutionarily selected within a run of genetic programming while the problem is being solved. In the evolutionary method of determining the architecture of the overall program, the architecture of the overall program is not prespecified. Instead, the initial random population contains programs with a variety of architectures. The architecture of the eventual solution is evolutionarily selected by a competitive fitness-driven process that occurs during the run at the same time as the problem is being solved. Because the population is architecturally diverse, the technique of branch typing described in section 4.8 would hamstring the crossover operation. An alternative, called point typing, is explained in section 21.2. Structure-preserving crossover with point typing permits robust recombination while simultaneously guaranteeing that architecturally different parents will sire syntactically and semantically valid offspring.

Section 21.3 presents results for the even-5-parity problem using the evolutionary method of determining the architecture of the overall program. Sections 21.4 and 21.5 present results for the even-4- and 3-parity problems, respectively.

In the previous chapters, the user of genetic programming determined a sufficient set of primitive functions from which the yet-to-be-evolved programs are composed. Suppose that we did not know what set of primitive functions is sufficient to solve a problem or, for some reason, did not want to make the decision of determining the set of primitive functions for a problem. One approach might be to choose a set of primitive functions from a large, presumably sufficient superset. However, suppose we wanted to evolve a set of primitive functions, rather than merely home in on a subset of primitive functions within a prespecified superset.

Chapter 22 explores the question of whether a sufficient set of primitive functions (expressed in some elementary way) can be evolutionarily determined during a run at the same time that genetic programming is solving the problem and selecting the architecture of the overall program. Section 22.2 presents results for the even-5-parity problem using the evolutionary method of determining a sufficient set of primitive functions and selecting the architecture of the overall program. Section 22.3 presents results for the Boolean 6-multiplexer. It is interesting to consider whether only one primitive function is sufficient for solving a problem. Section 22.4 revisits both problems with the constraint that only one primitive function be used.

In order to evolve a computer program capable of producing the desired output for a given problem, it is necessary to have access to a set of inputs that are at least a superset of the inputs necessary to solve the problem (that is, the terminals must be sufficient for the problem). In all the previous chapters, the user of genetic programming determined a sufficient set of terminals from which the yet-to-be-evolved programs are composed.

Chapter 23 considers the question of whether it is possible for genetic programming to determine the terminal set of a problem (in the sense of enabling genetic programming to select the inputs of the yet-to-be evolved program from a sufficient superset of available inputs) during a run at the same time that genetic programming is evolving a sufficient set of primitive functions, evolutionarily selecting the architecture, and solving the problem. Section 23.1 shows that this is possible for the even-5-parity problem.

Every function in the function sets of all the foregoing problems has satisfied the closure requirement in that it has been able to accept, as its arguments, any value that may possibly be returned by any function in the function set that may appear as its arguments and any value that may possibly be assumed by any terminal in the terminal set of the problem that may appear as its arguments.

Chapter 24 considers the question of whether it is possible for genetic programming to evolve a set of primitive functions satisfying the closure requirement at the same time that genetic programming is evolving a sufficient set of primitive functions, determining the architecture of the overall program, and solving the problem. Sections 24.1 and 24.2 respectively show that this is possible for the even-4-parity problem and the even-5-parity problem, respectively.

Chapters 21 through 24 demonstrated that genetic programming is capable of evolving (selecting), in various separate combinations, the solution to a problem, the architecture of the overall program, the primitive functions, and the terminals while satisfying the sufficiency requirement and the closure requirement.

Chapter 25 pulls the techniques of the chapters 21 through 24 together and shows that genetic programming can evolve the architecture, primitive functions, sufficiency, terminals, and closure, all at the same time as it solves a problem. Section 25.1 presents results for the even-4-parity problem. Section 25.2 presents results for the even-5-parity problem.

Chapter 26 explores the role that representation plays in facilitating or thwarting the solution of problems. Specifically, programs with automatically defined functions provide a different way of viewing a problem space than programs without automatically defined functions. To do this, this chapter revisits various problems from this book in terms of the distribution of values of fitness for one set of 1,000,000 randomly generated programs with automatically defined functions and a second set of 1,000,000 randomly generated programs without them. For these problems, there is a difference between the two distributions in terms of their outliers. Since the generation of these 1,000,000 programs does not, of course, involve either the Darwinian operation of reproduction or the genetic operation of crossover, the difference in distributions is a reflection solely of the way points in the search space of the problem are represented. The difference is a reflection solely of the chosen representation scheme. The representation chosen to view the points in the search space of the problem is a kind of lens through which the system views its world. It appears that a computer program incorporating automatically defined functions provides a better lens for viewing problems whose environment is regular, symmetric, homogeneous, and modular than does a computer program composed of similar ingredients without automatically defined functions. We call this difference the "lens effect."

The organization and style of this book has been dictated by the fact that our conclusions depend on experimental evidence. This book does not provide any mathematical proof that genetic programming with automatically defined functions can always be successfully used, much less advantageously used, to solve all problems of every conceivable type. It does, however, provide empirical evidence to support its observations. The ability of an independent researcher to replicate the results is therefore crucial. To facilitate replication by other researchers, each chapter has been organized in a uniform style that clearly identifies the key details of the problem, identifies the preparatory steps that must be taken to apply genetic programming to the problem, and presents the results of our actual runs. I believe that sufficient information is provided for each experiment described herein to allow it to be independently replicated so as to produce substantially similar results (within the limits inherent in any process involving probabilistic operations and subject to minor details of implementation).

The conclusion (chapter 27) recapitulates the eight main points that are supported by the evidence from the various problems in this book.

2 Background on Genetic Algorithms, LISP, and Genetic Programming

This chapter contains a brief explanation of the conventional genetic algorithm, a brief introduction to the LISP programming language, a brief introduction of the basic ideas of genetic programming, and pointers to sources of additional information about evolutionary computation. The purpose of this chapter is to provide background which will make this book a self-contained explanation of genetic programming with automatically defined functions. *Genetic Programming* contains considerable additional detail on the subjects of this chapter.

Readers already familiar with genetic programming may decide to skip this chapter.

2.1 BACKGROUND ON GENETIC ALGORITHMS

John Holland's pioneering book *Adaptation in Natural and Artificial Systems* (1975, 1992) showed how the evolutionary process can be used to solve problems by means of a highly parallel technique that is now called the *genetic algorithm*.

The *genetic algorithm* transforms a *population* of individual objects, each with an associated value of *fitness*, into a new *generation* of the population, using the Darwinian principle of survival and reproduction of the fittest and analogs of naturally occurring genetic operations such as *crossover* (sexual *recombination*) and *mutation*.

Each possible point in the search space of a problem is encoded, using a problem-specific representation scheme, as a fixed-length character string (i.e., as a chromosome) or other mathematical object. The genetic algorithm attempts to find the best (or at least a very good) solution to the problem by genetically breeding the population of individuals over a number of *generations*.

There are four major preparatory steps required to use the conventional genetic algorithm on fixed-length character strings to solve a problem, namely determining

(1) the representation scheme,

(2) the fitness measure,

(3) the parameters and variables for controlling the algorithm, and

(4) a way of designating the result and a criterion for terminating a run.

In the conventional genetic algorithm, the individuals in the population are usually fixed-length character strings patterned after chromosome strings. Specification of the representation scheme in the conventional genetic algorithm starts with a determination of the string length L and the alphabet size K. Often the alphabet is binary, so K equals 2. The most important part of the representation scheme is the mapping that expresses each possible point in the search space of the problem as a particular fixed-length character string (i.e., as a chromosome) and each such chromosome as a point in the search space of the problem.

A precondition for solving a problem with the genetic algorithm is that the representation scheme satisfy the *sufficiency* requirement in the sense that it is capable of expressing a solution to the problem.

Finding a representation scheme that facilitates solution of a problem by the genetic algorithm often requires considerable insight into the problem and good judgment.

The evolutionary process is driven by the fitness measure. The fitness measure assigns a fitness value to each fixed-length character string that it encounters in the population. The fitness measure should satisfy the requirement of being *fully defined* in the sense that it is capable of evaluating any fixed-length character string that it encounters in any generation of the population. The nature of the fitness measure varies with the problem.

The primary parameters for controlling the genetic algorithm are the population size, M, and the maximum number of generations to be run, G. Populations can consist of hundreds, thousands, tens of thousands or more individuals. There can be dozens, hundreds, thousands, or more generations in a run of the genetic algorithm. In addition, there are a number of secondary quantitative and qualitative control variables that must be specified in order to run the genetic algorithm (as enumerated in *Genetic Programming*, table 27.8).

Each run of the genetic algorithm requires specification of a termination criterion for deciding when to terminate a run and a method of result designation. The *termination criterion* for a run of the genetic algorithm usually consists of either satisfying a problem-specific *success predicate* or completing a specified maximum number of generations to be run, G.

The success predicate depends on the nature of the problem and the user's goal. For example, the success predicate may consist of achieving a result that exceeds a certain threshold. Sometimes it is possible to recognize a 100%-correct solution to a problem when it is discovered (even though one did not know the answer before the result was encountered). One frequently used method of *result designation* for a run of the genetic algorithm is to designate the best individual obtained in any generation of the population during the run (i.e., the *best-so-far* individual) as the result of the run. Another method involves designating the best individual obtained in the generation on which the run terminated as the result of the run.

Once the four preparatory steps for setting up the genetic algorithm have been completed, the genetic algorithm can be run.

The three steps in executing the genetic algorithm operating on fixed-length character strings are as follows:

(1) Randomly create an initial population of individual fixed-length character strings.

(2) Iteratively perform the following substeps on the population of strings until the termination criterion has been satisfied:
   (a) Assign a fitness value to each individual in the population using the fitness measure.
   (b) Create a new population of strings by applying the following three genetic operations. The genetic operations are applied to individual string(s) in the population selected with a probability based on fitness (with reselection allowed).
      (i) Reproduce an existing individual string by copying it into the new population.
      (ii) Create two new strings from two existing strings by genetically recombining substrings using the crossover operation at a randomly chosen crossover point.
      (iii) Create a new string from an existing string by randomly mutating the character at one randomly chosen position in the string.

(3) Designate the string that is identified by the method of result designation (e.g., the best-so-far individual) as the result of the genetic algorithm for the run. This result may represent a solution (or an approximate solution) to the problem.

The genetic algorithm is a probabilistic algorithm. Probabilistic steps are involved for creating the initial population, selecting individuals from the population on which to perform each genetic operation (e.g., reproduction, crossover), and choosing a point (i.e., a crossover point or a mutation point) within the selected individual at which to perform the selected genetic operation. Additional probabilistic steps are often involved in measuring fitness. Thus, anything can happen and nothing is guaranteed in the genetic algorithm.

In practice, it is usually necessary to make multiple independent runs of the genetic algorithm in order to obtain a result that the user considers successful for a given problem. Thus, the above three steps are, in practice, embedded in an outer loop representing separate runs.

Figure 2.1 is a flowchart of one possible way of implementing the conventional genetic algorithm. Run is the current run number. N is the maximum number of runs to be made. The variable Gen refers to the current generation number. M is the population size. The index i refers to the current individual in the population. The sum of the probability of reproduction, p_r, the probability of crossover, p_c, and the probability of mutation, p_m, is one.

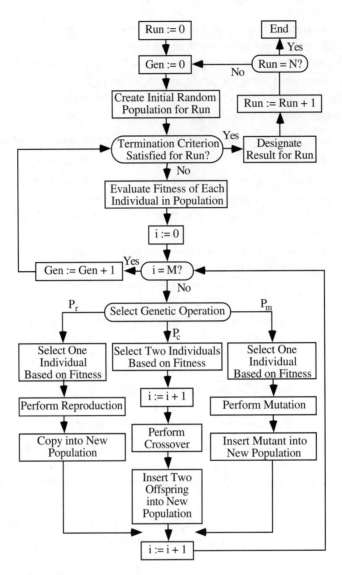

Figure 2.1 Flowchart of the conventional genetic algorithm.

The best individual produced by looping over i is the *best-of-generation* individual; the best individual produced by looping over Gen is the *best-of-run* individual; and the best individual produced by looping over Run is the *best-of-all* individual. If there is a tie for any of these classes of best individual, the single individual that first produced the best result is arbitrarily designated as the best.

The genetic operation of *reproduction* is based on the Darwinian principle of reproduction and survival of the fittest. In the reproduction operation, an individual is probabilistically selected from the population on the basis of its fitness (with reselection allowed) and then the individual is copied, without change, into the next generation of the population. The

Table 2.1 Two parental strings.

Parent 1	Parent 2
011	110

Table 2.2 Two crossover fragments.

Crossover fragment 1	Crossover fragment 2
01-	11-

Table 2.3 Two remainders.

Remainder 1	Remainder 2
--1	--0

Table 2.4 Two offspring produced by crossover.

Offspring 1	Offspring 2
010	111

selection is done in such a way that the better an individual's fitness, the more likely it is to be selected.

The genetic operation of *crossover* allows new individuals to be created and new points in the search space to be tested. The operation of crossover starts with two parents independently selected probabilistically from the population on the basis of their fitness (with reselection allowed). As before, the selection is done in such a way that the better an individual's fitness, the more likely it is to be selected. The crossover operation produces two offspring. Each offspring contains some genetic material from each of its parents.

Individuals from the population can be selected *and, in general, are selected* more than once during a generation to participate in the operations of reproduction and crossover. Indeed, the differential rates of survival, reproduction, and participation in genetic operations by more fit individuals is an essential part of the genetic algorithm.

Tables 2.1 through 2.4 illustrate the crossover operation being applied to the two parental strings 011 and 110 of length $L = 3$ over an alphabet of size $K = 2$. Table 2.1 shows the two *parents*.

The crossover operation begins by randomly choosing a number between 1 and L–1 using a uniform probability distribution. There are L–1 = 2 interstitial locations lying between the positions of a character string of length $L = 3$. In the crossover operation, one of these interstitial locations (say the second) is randomly chosen and becomes the *crossover point*. Each parent is then split at this crossover point into a crossover fragment and a remainder. Table 2.2 shows the *crossover fragments* of parents 1 and 2.

The part of each parent that remains after the crossover fragment is identified is called the *remainder*. Table 2.3 shows the remainders of parents 1 and 2.

The crossover operation combines crossover fragment 1 with remainder 2 to create offspring 1. Similarly, the crossover operation combines crossover fragment 2 with remainder 1 to create offspring 2. Table 2.4 shows the two *offspring*.

The two offspring are usually different from their two parents and different from each other. Crossover is a creative operation that produces new individuals that are composed entirely of genetic material from their two parents. Intuitively, if a character string represents a somewhat effective approach to solving a given problem, then some values at some positions of that character string probably have some merit. More important, some combinations of values situated at two or more positions probably have some merit when they are present together in the character string. By recombining randomly chosen parts of somewhat effective character strings, a new character string that represents an even more fit approach to solving the problem may be produced.

In the special case where the two parents selected to participate in crossover are identical, the two offspring will be identical to each other and identical to their parents, regardless of the crossover point. This incestuous case occurs frequently because of the Darwinian selection of individuals to participate in the reproduction and crossover operations on the basis of their fitness. Consequently, identical copies of a highly fit individual may come to dominate a population. *Premature convergence* occurs when an individual becomes dominant in a population but is not the global optimum of the search space.

The operation of *mutation* begins by probabilistically selecting an individual from the population on the basis of its fitness. A *mutation point* along the string is chosen at random, and the single character at that point is randomly changed. The altered individual is then copied into the next generation of the population. Mutation is potentially useful in restoring genetic diversity that may be lost in a population because of premature convergence. Mutation is used very sparingly in most genetic algorithm work.

In implementing the genetic algorithm on a computer, the reproduction, crossover, and mutation operations are performed on copies of the selected individuals. The selected individuals remain unchanged in the population until the end of the current generation. More fit individuals generally are usually reselected many times to participate in the operations.

The Darwinian selection of individuals to participate in the operations of reproduction, crossover, and mutation on the basis of their fitness is an essential aspect of the genetic algorithm. When an individual is selected on the basis of its fitness to be copied (with or without mutation) into the next generation of the population, the effect is that the new generation contains the characteristics it embodies. These characteristics consist of certain values at certain positions of the character string and, more importantly, certain combinations of values situated at two or more positions of the string. When two individuals are selected on the basis of their fitness to be recombined, the new generation contains the characteristics of both of these parents.

The probabilistic selection used in the genetic algorithm is an essential aspect of the algorithm. The genetic algorithm allocates every individual, however poor its fitness, some chance of being selected to participate in the operations of reproduction, crossover, and mutation. That is, the genetic algorithm is not merely a greedy hillclimbing algorithm. Instead, the genetic algorithm resembles simulated annealing (Kirkpatrick, Gelatt, and Vecchi 1983; Aarts and Korst 1989; van Laarhoven and Aarts 1987) in that individuals that are known to be inferior are occasionally selected. In fact, simulated annealing resembles a genetic algorithm with a population size, M, of 1.

The fact that the genetic algorithm operates on a population of individuals, rather than a single point in the search space of the problem, is an essential aspect of the algorithm. The advantage conferred by the existence of a population is not merely the obvious benefit of dropping 1,000 parachutists, rather than one, onto the fitness landscape. The population serves as the reservoir of the probably-valuable genetic material that the crossover operation needs to create new individuals with probably-valuable new combinations of characteristics.

The genetic algorithm works in a domain-independent way on the fixed-length character strings in the population. The genetic algorithm searches the space of possible character strings in an attempt to find high-fitness strings. The space may be highly nonlinear and its fitness landscape may be very rugged. To guide this search, the genetic algorithm uses only the numerical fitness values associated with the explicitly tested strings. Regardless of the particular problem domain, the genetic algorithm carries out its search by performing the same disarmingly simple operations of copying, recombining, and occasionally randomly mutating the strings.

In practice, the genetic algorithm is surprisingly rapid in effectively searching complex, highly nonlinear, multidimensional search spaces. This is all the more surprising because the genetic algorithm does not have any knowledge about the problem domain except for the information indirectly provided by the fitness measure.

Genetic algorithms superficially seem to process only the particular individual character strings actually present in the current generation of the population. However, *Adaptation in Natural and Artificial Systems* (Holland 1975, 1992) focused attention on the remarkable fact that the genetic algorithm implicitly processes, in parallel, a large amount of useful information concerning unseen Boolean hyperplanes (schemata). A *schema* (plural: *schemata*) is a set of points from the search space of a problem with certain specified similarities. A schema is described by a string over an extended alphabet consisting of the alphabet of the representation scheme (e.g., 0 and 1 if the alphabet is binary) and a *don't care symbol* (denoted by an asterisk).

The genetic algorithm creates individual strings in the new generation of the population in such a way that each schema can be expected to be automatically represented in proportion to the ratio of its *schema fitness* (i.e., the average of the fitness of all the points from the search space that are contained in the schema) to the *average population fitness* (i.e., the average of the fitness of all the points from the search space that are contained in the population).

An important conclusion in *Adaptation in Natural and Artificial Systems* (Holland 1975, 1992) is that the growth rate for each schema in the genetic algorithm is an approximately optimal use of the available information in maximizing the payoff from the genetic algorithm over a period of generations.

The success of the genetic algorithm in solving problems also arises from the creative role of the crossover operation. Indeed, a once-controversial point in *Adaptation in Natural and Artificial Systems* (Holland 1975, 1992) concerns the preeminence of the crossover operation and the relative unimportance of mutation in the evolutionary process in nature and in solving artificial problems of adaptation using the genetic algorithm. The genetic algorithm relies primarily on crossover. The role of mutation is comparatively insignificant.

Figure 2.2 presents a geometric interpretation of the crossover operation as applied to the same illustrative problem for which $L = 3$ and $K = 2$. It shows the parental strings 011 and 110 that produce the string 111 as one of their offspring. Each point in the search space is represented by a chromosome string of length L over the binary alphabet. The $2^L = 8$ vertices of a hypercube of dimensionality $L = 3$ represent the points in the search space of the problem. The population of chromosomes is a subset of the vertices of the hypercube. The two parents 011 and 110 participating in the crossover are points in the search space of the problem and are thus represented by two vertices of the hypercube. The offspring 111 produced by the crossover of 011 and 110 is represented as another vertex of the hypercube. All three of these individuals are shown in the figure as solid black circles.

Crossover fragment 11– may be thought of as the set containing all the strings of length L from the search space that have 1 in their first position, have 1 in their second position, and have either 0 or 1 in their third position (i.e., "don't care" about the third position). In other words, the crossover fragment 11– can be viewed as the associated schema 11*. Schemata are explained in detail in *Genetic Programming* (section 3.2), although a detailed understanding of schemata is not necessary to follow the argument being made here. The schema 11* is the set of strings of length 3 from the search space that have a 1 in their first positions and a 1 in their second positions. The * in the third position of schema 11* indicates that we don't care what symbol (0 or 1) is in that position of the strings. Thus, this schema (set) has two members, namely the points 110 and 111 from the search space of the problem. The geometric interpretation of this set of two points is the straight line (hyperplane of dimensionality 1) along the

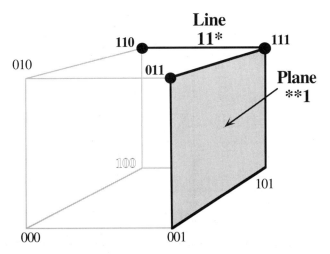

Figure 2.2 Geometric interpretation of the crossover operation recombining parents 011 and 110 to produce 111 as an offspring.

top of the hypercube. One of the points in the schema, namely 110, is necessarily one of the parents participating in the crossover.

Similarly, the remainder −−1 may be viewed in terms of its associated schema **1. The schema **1 contains all strings that have either 0 or 1 in their first position (i.e., "don't care" about the first position), either 0 or 1 in their second position (i.e., "don't care" about the second position), and have a 1 in their third position. The remainder −−1 may be viewed as the schema (set) **1 containing the four members 001, 101, 011, and 111. The geometric interpretation of this set of four points is the plane (hyperplane of dimensionality 2) on the right of the hypercube incorporating the four points 001, 101, 011, and 111. As before, one of the points, namely 011, is necessarily one of the parents participating in the crossover.

The important feature of the crossover operation is that the offspring 111 produced by the crossover operation lies at the intersection of the two schemata (sets). Specifically, the offspring 111 is at the intersection of the straight line represented by the schema 11* and the plane represented by the schema **1.

Each of the 2^L points in the search space of a problem (i.e., each vertex of the hypercube of dimensionality L) belongs to 2^L sub-hyperplanes (schema) of dimensionality between 0 and L. For example, when $L = 3$, each vertex of the hypercube of dimensionality 3 belongs to $2^L = 8$ hyperplanes of dimensionality between 0 and 3. Specifically, each vertex belongs to one hyperplane of dimensionality 0 (i.e., the point itself), three straight lines (i.e., hyperplanes of dimensionality 1), three planes (i.e., hyperplanes of dimensionality 2), and one hypercube of dimensionality 3 (i.e., the whole search space).

When a particular point in the search space is observed to have a certain fitness value, this observed fitness can serve as an estimate of the fitness of all of the 2^L sub-hyperplanes to which the particular point belongs. In other words, the fitness of a single point can be attributed to each of the 2^L sub-hyper-

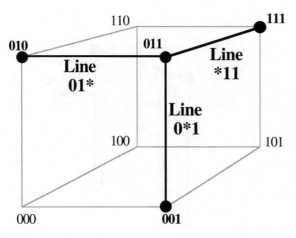

Figure 2.3 Geometric interpretation of the mutation operation operating on parent 011 to produce 001, 010, or 111 as an offspring.

planes to which the point belongs. This estimate is admittedly rough and sometimes incorrect. Indeed, the correct fitness of a sub-hyperplane of dimensionality $j < L$ is the average of the fitness values for all 2^j points in the sub-hyperplane. In practice, the population size, M, employed in the genetic algorithm is very small in relation to the 2^L points in the search space and is also very small in relation to the 2^j points in a hyperplane of dimensionality j (for all but the smallest values of j). Consequently, there are usually only a few members of the population (only one member in this example) from which to estimate the hyperplane fitness. Nonetheless, if only this small number, M, of points from the search space have been explicitly measured for fitness, this admittedly rough and sometimes-incorrect estimate of the hyperplane fitness is the best available estimate.

The two parents are selected to participate in the crossover operation on the basis of their fitness. In practice, this usually means that both parents have relatively high fitness. If we attribute the fitness of the two observed parental points to all the points in the straight line 11* and to all the points in the plane **1, we see that the offspring point 111 at the intersection of this straight line and this plane **1 shares two independent estimates that it has relatively high fitness. In other words, when the crossover operation creates a new offspring individual, there are two independent pieces of evidence, both admittedly rough and sometimes incorrect, suggesting that the new individual may have relatively high fitness. Thus, the crossover operation directs the future search by the genetic algorithm into areas of the overall search space that tend to have higher and higher fitness.

In contrast, when the mutation operation is applied to a single individual in the population selected on the basis of fitness, the newly created mutant is a point at the end of one of the straight lines (hyperplanes of dimensionality 1) radiating away from the single parental individual. The mutant lies in various schemata (a line, two planes, and the entire search space) to which the single individual belongs; however, the only one piece of evidence suggesting that the mutant has relatively high fitness is the original selection of the single parent.

Figure 2.3 presents a geometric interpretation of the mutation operation operating on the parental string 011. The three points in the search space at a Hamming distance of 1 (i.e., 010, 111, or 001) are the offspring that may potentially be produced by the mutation operation. The parental string and the three potential offspring are all shown as solid black circles.

The fact that there is independent corroborating evidence in favor of the offspring produced by crossover is one reason that crossover is more important than mutation in driving the genetic algorithm toward the successful discovery of a global optimum point in the search space.

2.2 BACKGROUND ON LISP

Any computer program – whether it is written in FORTRAN, Pascal, C, C++, assembly code, or any other programming language – can be viewed as a sequence of applications of functions (operations) to arguments (values). Compilers use this fact by first internally translating a given program into a parse tree and then converting the parse tree into the more elementary machine code instructions that actually run on the computer. However this important commonality underlying all computer programs is obscured by the large variety of different types of statements, operations, instructions, syntactic constructions, and grammatical restrictions found in most programming languages.

Genetic programming is most easily understood if one thinks about it in terms of a programming language that overtly and transparently views a computer program as a sequence of applications of functions to arguments.

Moreover, since genetic programming initially creates computer programs at random and then manipulates the programs by various genetically motivated operations, genetic programming may be implemented in a conceptually straightforward way in a programming language that permits a computer program to be easily manipulated as data and then permits the newly created data to be immediately executed as a program.

For these two reasons, the LISP (LISt Processing) programming language is especially well suited for genetic programming. However, it should be recognized that genetic programming does not require LISP for its implementation and is not in any way based on LISP.

For the purpose of this discussion, we can view LISP as having only two types of entities: atoms and lists. The constant 7 and the variable TIME are examples of *atoms* in LISP. A *list* in LISP is written as an ordered collection of items inside a pair of parentheses. (A B C D) and (+ 1 2) are examples of lists in LISP.

Both lists and atoms in LISP are called *symbolic expressions* (*S-expressions*). The S-expression is the only syntactic form in pure LISP. There is no syntactic distinction between programs and data in LISP. In particular, all data in LISP are S-expressions and all programs in LISP are S-expressions.

The LISP system works by evaluating (executing) whatever it sees. When seen by LISP, a constant atom, such as 7, evaluates to itself, and a variable atom, such as TIME, evaluates to the current value of the variable. When LISP sees a list, the list is evaluated by treating the first element of the list (i.e., whatever is just inside the opening parenthesis) as a function. The function is then applied to the results of evaluating the remaining elements of the list. That is, the remaining elements of the list are treated as arguments to the function. If an argument is a constant atom or a variable atom, this evaluation is immediate; however, if an argument is a list, the evaluation of such an argument involves a recursive application of the above steps.

For example, in the LISP S-expression (+ 1 2), the addition function + appears just inside the opening parenthesis. The S-expression (+ 1 2) calls for the application of the addition function + to two arguments, namely the constant atoms 1 and 2. Since both arguments are atoms, they can be immediately evaluated. The value returned as a result of the evaluation of the entire S-expression (+ 1 2) is 3. Because the function + appears to the left of the arguments, LISP S-expressions are examples of *prefix notation*.

If any of the arguments in an S-expression are themselves lists (rather than constant or variable atoms that can be immediately evaluated), LISP first evaluates these arguments. In Common LISP (Steele 1990), this evaluation is done in a recursive, depth-first way, starting from the left. We use the conventions of Common LISP throughout this book. The S-expression

```
(+ (* 2 3) 4)
```

illustrates the way that computer programs in LISP can be viewed as a sequence of applications of functions to arguments. This S-expression calls for the application of the addition function + to two arguments, namely the sub-S-expression (* 2 3) and the constant atom 4. In order to evaluate the entire S-expression, LISP must first evaluate the sub-S-expression (* 2 3). This argument (* 2 3) calls for the application of the multiplication function * to the two constant atoms 2 and 3, so it evaluates to 6 and the entire S-expression evaluates to 10.

Other programming languages apply functions to arguments somewhat differently. For example, the FORTH programming language uses *postfix notation*. For example, the above LISP S-expression would be written in FORTH as

```
2 3 * 4 +
```

FORTH first evaluates the subexpression

```
2 3 *
```

by applying the multiplication function * to the 2 and the 3 to get 6. The function * appears to the right of the two arguments, 2 and 3, in FORTH. It then applies the addition function + to the intermediate result, 6, and the 4 to get 10.

FORTRAN, Pascal, and C use ordinary *infix notation* for two-argument functions, so the above LISP and FORTH programs would be written as

```
2*3 + 4
```

in those languages. Here the multiplication function * appears between the arguments 2 and 3 to indicate that the * is applied to the arguments 2 and 3. Similarly, the addition function + is applied to the intermediate result, 6, and the 4 to get 10.

The term "computer program," of course, carries the connotation of the ability to do more than merely perform compositions of simple arithmetic operations. Among the connotations of the term "computer program" is the ability to perform alternative computations conditioned on the outcome of intermediate calculations, to perform operations in a hierarchical way, and to perform computations on variables of many different types. Unlike most other programming languages, LISP goes about all these seemingly different things in the same way: LISP treats the item just inside the outermost left parenthesis as a function and then applies that function to the remaining items of the list.

For example, the LISP S-expression

```
(+ 1 2 (IF (> TIME 10) 3 4))
```

illustrates how LISP views conditional and relational elements of computer programs as applications of functions to arguments. The three-argument addition function + at the top level calls for the application of the addition function to its three arguments: the constant atom 1, the constant atom 2, and the sub-S-expression (IF (> TIME 10) 3 4). In the sub-sub-S-expression (> TIME 10), the relation > is viewed as a function. The > is applied to the variable atom TIME and the constant atom 10. The sub-subexpression (> TIME 10) then evaluates to either T (true) or NIL (false), depending on the current value of the variable atom TIME. The conditional operator IF is viewed as a function and is then applied to three arguments: the logical value, T or NIL, returned by the subexpression (> TIME 10), the constant atom 3, and the constant atom 4. If the first argument of an IF evaluates to T (more precisely, anything other than NIL), the function IF returns the result of evaluating its second argument (i.e., the constant atom 3), but if the first argument evaluates to NIL, the function IF returns the result of evaluating its third argument (i.e., the constant atom 4). The S-expression as a whole evaluates to either 6 or 7, depending on whether the current value of the variable atom TIME is or is not greater than 10.

Most other programming languages use different syntactic forms and statement types for operations such as *, >, and IF. Operator precedence rules and parentheses are used in such languages to ensure the correct association of arguments to operators. LISP performs all of these operations with a common syntax.

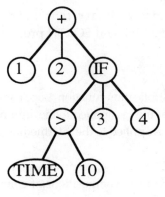

Figure 2.4   LISP S-expression depicted as a rooted, point-labeled tree with ordered branches.

One of the advantages of prefix or postfix notation is that a *k*-argument function (such as the three-argument addition function above) is handled in a more consistent and convenient fashion than is the case with ordinary infix notation.

Any LISP S-expression can be graphically depicted as a rooted point-labeled tree with ordered branches. Figure 2.4 shows the tree corresponding to the S-expression (+ 1 2 (IF (> TIME 10) 3 4)). This tree has nine *points* (i.e., functions and terminals).

In this graphical depiction, the three internal points of the tree are labeled with functions +, IF, and >. The root of the tree is labeled with the function appearing just inside the leftmost opening parenthesis of the S-expression (i.e., the +). The six external points (leaves) of the tree are labeled with terminals (the variable atom TIME and the constant atoms 1, 2, 3, 4, and 10). The branches are ordered because the order of the arguments matters for many functions (e.g., IF and >). Of course, the order does not matter for commutative functions such as +.

This tree form of a LISP S-expression is equivalent to the parse tree that the compilers of most high level programming languages construct internally, unseen by the programmer, to represent the program being compiled.

An important feature of LISP is that all LISP computer programs have just one syntactic form (the S-expression). The programs of the LISP programming language are S-expressions, and an S-expression is, in effect, the parse tree of the program. Moreover, data is also represented in LISP by S-expressions. For these reasons, we use LISP throughout this book for presenting computer programs and for explaining the genetic operations. However, it is important to note that virtually any programming language is capable of representing and implementing these programs and genetic operations. It is not necessary to implement genetic programming in LISP. Indeed, since the publication of *Genetic Programming*, versions of genetic programming have been implemented in C, C++, Pascal, FORTRAN, Mathematica, Smalltalk, and other programming languages.

2.3   BACKGROUND ON GENETIC PROGRAMMING

Genetic programming is an extension of the conventional genetic algorithm described in section 2.1 in which the structures undergoing adaptation are hierarchical computer programs of dynamically varying size and shape.

Genetic programming is an attempt to deal with one of the central questions in computer science: How can computers learn to solve problems without being explicitly programmed? In other words, how can computers be made to do what needs to be done, without being told exactly how to do it?

The search space in genetic programming is the space of all possible computer programs composed of functions and terminals appropriate to the problem domain.

In applying genetic programming to a problem, there are *five major preparatory steps*. These five steps involve determining

(1)   the set of terminals,

(2)   the set of primitive functions,

(3)   the fitness measure,

(4)   the parameters for controlling the run, and

(5)   the method for designating a result and the criterion for terminating a run.

The first major step in preparing to use genetic programming is to identify the *terminal set* for the problem. The terminals correspond to the inputs of the as-yet-undiscovered computer program.

The second major step in preparing to use genetic programming is to identify the *function set*. The functions may be standard arithmetic operations, standard programming operations, standard mathematical functions, logical functions, or domain-specific functions. The functions may perform their work by returning one or more values or by performing side effects (e.g., on the state of a system).

Each computer program (i.e., mathematical expression, LISP S-expression, parse tree) is a composition of functions from the function set, $\mathcal{F}$, and terminals from the terminal set, $\mathcal{T}$. The set of terminals (along with the set of functions) are the ingredients from which genetic programming attempts to construct a computer program to solve, or approximately solve, the problem.

A precondition for solving a problem with genetic programming is that the set of terminals and the set of functions satisfy the *sufficiency* requirement in the sense that they are together capable of expressing a solution to the problem.

Each of the functions in the function set should be able to accept, as its arguments, any value that may possibly be returned by any function in the function set and any value that may possibly be assumed by any terminal in the terminal set. A function set and terminal set that together satisfy this requirement are said to satisfy the *closure* requirement.

These first two major steps correspond to the step of specifying the representation scheme for the conventional genetic algorithm. The remaining three major steps for genetic programming correspond exactly to the last three major preparatory steps for the conventional genetic algorithm.

The evolutionary process is driven by a *fitness measure* that evaluates how well each individual computer program in the population performs in its problem environment. The fitness measure should satisfy the requirement of being *fully defined* in the sense that it is capable of evaluating any computer program that it encounters in any generation of the population.

The *primary parameters* for controlling a run of genetic programming are the population size, M, and the maximum number of generations to be run, G. In addition, there are a number of *secondary parameters* (quantitative and qualitative control variables) that must be specified in order to control a run of genetic programming (as identified in appendix D).

Each run of genetic programming requires the specification of a *termination criterion* for deciding when to terminate a run and a method of *result designation*. We usually designate the best-so-far individual as the result of a run.

Once the five major steps for preparing to run genetic programming have been completed, a run can be made.

In genetic programming, populations of thousands of computer programs are bred genetically. This breeding is done using the Darwinian principle of survival and reproduction of the fittest along with a genetic crossover operation appropriate for mating computer programs. As will be seen, a computer program that solves (or approximately solves) a given problem may emerge from this combination of Darwinian natural selection and genetic operations.

Genetic programming starts with an initial population of randomly generated computer programs composed of functions and terminals appropriate to the problem domain. The creation of this initial random population is, in effect, a blind random search of the search space of the problem as represented by the computer programs. Because a population is involved, genetic programming may be viewed as a parallel search algorithm.

The nature of the fitness measure varies with the problem.

For some problems, the fitness of a computer program can be measured by the error between the result produced by the computer program and the correct result. The closer this error is to zero, the better the computer program. Typically, the error is not measured over just one combination of possible inputs to the computer program. Instead, error is usually measured as a sum (or average) over a number of representative combinations of the inputs to the program (i.e., values of an independent variable). That is, the fitness of a computer program in the population is measured over a number of different *fitness cases*. The fitness cases may be chosen at random over a range of values of the independent variables or in some structured way (e.g., at regular intervals over a range of values of each independent variable). For example, the fitness of an individual computer program in the population may be measured in terms of the sum, over the fitness cases, of the absolute value of the differences between the output produced by the program and the correct answer to the problem (i.e., the *Minkowski distance*) or in terms of the square root of the sum of the squares (i.e., *Euclidean distance*).

For many problems, fitness is not computed directly from the value returned by the computer program but instead is determined from the consequences of the execution of the program. For example, in a problem of optimal control, the value returned by the controller affects the state of the system. The fitness of a program is based on the amount of time (fuel, distance, or money, etc.) it takes to bring the system to a desired target state. The smaller the amount of time (fuel, distance, or money, etc.), the better. The fitness cases in problems of control often consist of a sampling of different *initial conditions* of the system.

For problems involving a task, fitness may be measured in terms of the amount of points scored (food eaten, work completed, cases correctly handled, etc.).

If one is trying to recognize patterns or classify examples, the fitness of a particular program may be measured by some combination of the number of instances handled correctly (i.e., true positives and true negatives) and the number of instances handled incorrectly (i.e., false positives and false negatives). For example, correlation may be used as the fitness measure in pattern recognition and classification problems. The fitness cases consist of a representative sampling of patterns or items to be classified.

If the problem involves finding a good randomizer, the fitness of a given program might be measured by entropy.

For some problems, it may be appropriate to use a *multi-objective fitness measure* incorporating a combination of factors such as correctness, parsimony, or efficiency.

In each of the foregoing examples, fitness was computed explicitly. However, fitness may be computed implicitly by permitting programs to interact (usually in a simulation) with their environment or among themselves in a situation where certain behavior leads to survival (and, consequently, the opportunity to reproduce and recombine) where certain other behavior does not.

The computer programs in the initial generation (i.e., generation 0) of the process will generally have exceedingly poor fitness. Nonetheless, some individuals in the population will turn out to be somewhat more fit than others. These differences in performance are then exploited.

Both the Darwinian principle of reproduction and survival of the fittest and the genetic operation of crossover are used to create a new offspring population of individual computer programs from the current population of programs.

The reproduction operation involves selecting a computer program from the current population of programs on the basis of its fitness (i.e., the better the fitness, the more likely the individual is to be selected) and allowing it to survive by copying it into the new population.

A crossover operation capable of operating on computer programs (described below) is used to create new offspring computer programs from two parental programs selected on the basis of their fitness. The parental programs typically differ from one another in size and shape. The offspring programs are composed of subexpressions (subtrees, subprograms, subroutines, building blocks) from their parents. These offspring programs are typically of different sizes and shapes than their parents. If two computer programs are somewhat effective in solving a given problem, then some of their parts probably have some merit. Recombining randomly chosen parts of somewhat effective programs may yield a new computer program that is even more fit at solving the problem.

The mutation operation may also be used in genetic programming.

After the genetic operations are performed on the current population, the population of offspring (i.e., the new generation) replaces the old population (i.e., the old generation).

Each individual in the new population of computer programs is then measured for fitness, and the process is repeated over many generations.

At each stage of this highly parallel process, the state of the process will consist only of the current population of individuals.

The force driving this process consists only of the observed fitness of the individuals in the current population in grappling with the problem environment.

As will be seen, this algorithm produces populations of computer programs which, over many generations, tend to become increasingly fit at grappling with their environment.

The hierarchical character of the computer programs that are produced is an important feature of genetic programming. The results of genetic programming are inherently hierarchical. In many cases the results produced by genetic programming are default hierarchies, prioritized hierarchies of tasks, or hierarchies in which one behavior subsumes or suppresses another. The dynamic variability of the population of computer programs that are developed along the way to a solution is also an important feature of genetic programming.

Another important feature of genetic programming is the absence or relatively minor role of preprocessing of inputs and postprocessing of outputs. The inputs, intermediate results, and outputs are typically expressed directly in terms of the natural terminology of the problem domain. The computer programs produced by genetic programming consist of functions that are natural for the problem domain. The postprocessing of the output of a program, if any, is done by a *wrapper* (*output interface*).

Finally, the structures undergoing adaptation in genetic programming are active. They are not passive encodings of the solution to the problem. Given a computer on which to run, the structures in genetic programming are active structures which usually can be directly executed in their current form.

In summary, genetic programming breeds computer programs to solve problems by executing the following three steps:

(1) Generate an initial population of random compositions of the functions and terminals of the problem (computer programs).

(2) Iteratively perform the following substeps until the termination criterion has been satisfied:

    (a) Execute each program in the population and assign it a fitness value using the fitness measure.

    (b) Create a new population of computer programs by applying the following two primary operations. The operations are applied to computer program(s) in the population selected with a probability based on fitness (with reselection allowed).

       (i) Reproduce an existing program by copying it into the new population.

      (ii) Create two new computer programs from two existing programs by genetically recombining randomly chosen parts of two existing programs using the crossover operation applied at a randomly chosen crossover point within each program.

(3) Designate the program that is identified by the method of result designation (e.g., the best-so-far individual) as the result of the run of genetic programming. This result may represent a solution (or an approximate solution) to the problem.

Figure 2.5 is a flowchart that implements the above three steps of the genetic programming paradigm. Run is the current run number. N is the maximum number of runs to be made. The variable Gen refers to the current generation number. M is the population size. The index i refers to the current individual in the population. The sum of the probability of reproduction, p_r, and the probability of crossover, p_c, is one.

Mutation is not used for any of the runs reported in this book for reasons discussed in *Genetic Programming* (subsection 6.5.1). However, if mutation were used, there would be a third branch flowing out of the sausage labeled "Select Genetic Operation" (as in figure 2.1).

Crossover operates on two parental computer programs selected with a probability based on fitness and produces two new offspring programs consisting of parts of each parent.

For example, consider the following computer program (shown here as a LISP S-expression):

`(+ (* 0.234 Z) (- X 0.789)),`

which we would ordinarily write as

$$0.234z + x - 0.789.$$

This program takes two inputs (X and Z) and produces a floating point output.

Also, consider a second program:

`(* (* Z Y) (+ Y (* 0.314 Z))),`

which is equivalent to

$$zy(y + 0.314z).$$

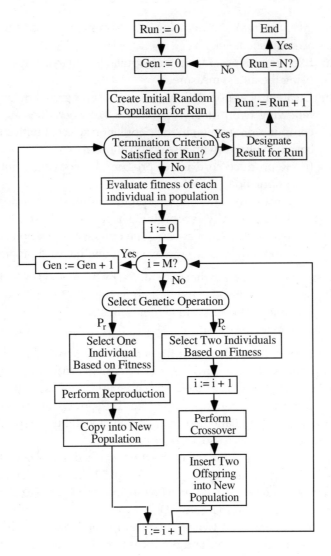

Figure 2.5 Flowchart for genetic programming.

In figure 2.6, these two *parents* are depicted as rooted, point-labeled trees with ordered branches. Internal points (i.e., nodes) of the tree correspond to functions (i.e., operations) and external points (i.e., leaves, endpoints) correspond to terminals (i.e., input data). The numbers beside the function and terminal points of the trees appear for reference only.

The *crossover* operation creates new offspring by exchanging subtrees (i.e., subroutines, sublists, subprocedures, subfunctions) between the two parents. The subtrees to be exchanged are chosen at random. The two parents are typically of different sizes and shapes. Suppose that the points of both trees are numbered in a depth-first, left-to-right way starting at the top. Further suppose that the point 2 (out of seven points of the first parent) is randomly

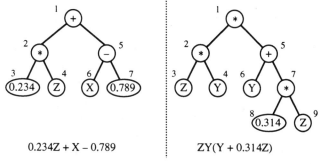

0.234Z + X − 0.789   ZY(Y + 0.314Z)

Figure 2.6   Two parental computer programs.

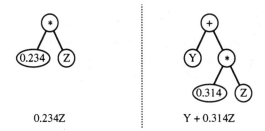

0.234Z   Y + 0.314Z

Figure 2.7   Two crossover fragments.

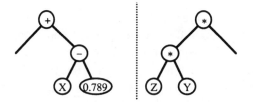

Figure 2.8   Two remainders.

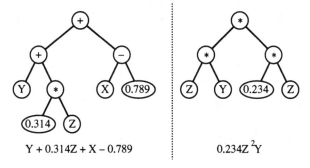

Y + 0.314Z + X − 0.789 $0.234Z^2Y$

Figure 2.9   Two offspring programs.

chosen as the *crossover point* for the first parent and that the point 5 (out of nine points of the second parent) is randomly chosen as the crossover point of the second parent. The crossover points in the trees above are therefore the multiplication (*) in the first parent and the addition (+) in the second parent. The two *crossover fragments* are the two subtrees rooted at the chosen crossover points as shown in figure 2.7.

These two crossover fragments correspond to the underlined subprograms (sublists) in the two parental computer programs above.

The *remainder* is the portion of a parent remaining after the deletion of its crossover fragment.

Figure 2.8 shows the two remainders after removal of the crossover fragments from the parents.

The first offspring is created by inserting the second parent's crossover fragment into the first parent's remainder at the first parent's crossover point. The second offspring is created by inserting the first parent's crossover fragment into the second parent's remainder at the second parent's crossover point.

The two offspring resulting from crossover are

```
(+ (+ Y (* 0.314 Z)) (- X 0.789))
```

and

```
(* (* Z Y) (* 0.234 Z)).
```

The two *offspring* are shown in figure 2.9.

The crossover operation creates two new computer programs using parts of existing parental programs. Because entire subtrees are swapped and because of the closure requirement on the function set and terminal set, this crossover operation always produces syntactically valid programs as offspring regardless of the choice of the two crossover points.

Because programs are selected to participate in the crossover operation with a probability based on their fitness, crossover allocates future trials of the search for a solution to the problem to regions of the search space whose programs contain parts from promising programs.

The crossover operation described above is the basic version of crossover for mating computer programs in genetic programming. Implementation of automatically defined functions requires structure-preserving crossover as described in section 4.8.

2.4   SOURCES OF ADDITIONAL INFORMATION

The field of evolutionary computation includes genetic algorithms, *evolutionsstrategie*, evolutionary programming, classifier systems, and genetic programming.

Additional information on genetic algorithms can be found in Goldberg 1989; Davis 1987, 1991; Michalewicz 1992; and Buckles and Petry 1992. Conference proceedings in the field of genetic algorithms include Grefenstette 1985, 1987; Schaffer 1989; Belew and Booker 1991; Forrest 1993; Rawlins 1991;

and Whitley 1992. Stender 1993 describes parallelization of genetic algorithms. Davidor 1992 describes application of genetic algorithms to robotics. Schaffer and Whitley 1992 and Albrecht, Reeves, and Steele 1993 describe work on combinations of genetic algorithms and neural networks. Bauer 1994 describes applications of genetic algorithms to investment strategies.

Much of the ongoing work of the Santa Fe Institute in New Mexico, as reported in technical reports and other publications, is related to genetic algorithms.

Recent work on *evolutionsstrategie* is emphasized in Schwefel and Maenner 1991 and Maenner and Manderick 1992.

Conference proceedings in the field of evolutionary programming include Fogel and Atmar 1992, 1993. Fogel 1991 describes the application of evolutionary programming to system identification.

Genetic classifier systems (Holland 1986; Holland et al. 1986) employ credit-allocation algorithms along with the genetic algorithm to create a set of if-then rules to solve problems. Forrest 1991 describes the application of genetic classifier systems to semantic nets.

There are many papers on evolutionary computation in conference proceedings from the fields of artificial life (Langton et al. 1989; Langton et al. 1991; Langton 1994), emergent computation (Forrest 1990), and the simulation of adaptive behavior (Meyer and Wilson 1991; Meyer, Roitblat, and Wilson 1993).

The three journals *Adaptive Behavior, Artificial Life,* and *Evolutionary Computation,* published by The MIT Press, contain articles on various aspects of evolutionary computation.

Kinnear 1994a is an edited collection of papers reporting on recent advances in genetic programming.

The proceedings of the IEEE World Conference on Computational Intelligence in Florida on June 26 to July 2, 1994, contain another large group of papers on genetic programming.

An annotated bibliography of genetic programming appears in appendix F.

Appendix G contains information on an electronic mailing list, public respository, and FTP site for genetic programming.

3   Hierarchical Problem-Solving

The goal of automatically solving problems has been a continuing theme since the beginning of the fields of automatic programming, machine learning, and artificial intelligence (Nilsson 1980; Winston 1981; Shirai and Tsujii 1982; Rich 1983; Charniak and McDermott 1985; Laird, Rosenbloom, and Newell, 1986a, 1986b; Tanimoto 1987; Barr, Cohen, and Feigenbaum 1989; Rosenbloom, Laird, and Newell 1993).

In the top-down formulation of the three-step hierarchical problem-solving process, the first step is the identification of the way of decomposing the overall problem into one or more subproblems. The second step is the solving of the subproblem(s). The third step is the solving of the overall problem using the now-available solutions to the subproblems.

We can illustrate additional aspects of the three-step hierarchical problem-solving process in its top-down formulation with four related examples from the field of elementary calculus.

Introductory textbooks on differential calculus usually show how to directly differentiate elementary functions such as x^2 or $\sin x$ by calling on first principles and the definition of the derivative as the limit, as Δx approaches zero, of a ratio of the changes, Δy and Δx. However, as soon as the function $y(x)$ to be differentiated becomes slightly more complicated (e.g., when $y(x)$ is the product of two functions), it requires considerable effort to manipulate the cumbersome algebraic expressions required to find the limiting value of $\Delta y / \Delta x$.

3.1   HIERARCHICAL DECOMPOSITION

Suppose that problem 1 is to differentiate the function $y(x)$, where $y(x)$ is the product

$$y(x) = x^2 \sin x.$$

Although it is possible to differentiate a product of two elementary functions by calling on basic definitions and first principles, it is easier to employ the three-step hierarchical problem-solving process.

First, one decomposes the problem of differentiating the product, $x^2 \sin x$, into two subproblems, namely the subproblem of differentiating the first factor, x^2, and the subproblem of differentiating the second factor, $\sin x$.

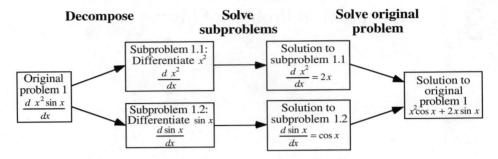

Figure 3.1 Three-step top-down hierarchical approach applied to problem 1 of differentiating $y(x) = x^2 \sin x$.

Second, one separately solves the two subproblems. As already mentioned, it is relatively easy to differentiate elementary functions such as x^2 or $\sin x$ separately using first principles; the derivatives are $2x$ and $\cos x$, respectively.

Then, in the third step of the hierarchical problem-solving process, one assembles the solutions to the two subproblems into a solution to the original problem. When differentiating a product, the assembly involves one addition and two multiplications. Specifically, the derivative of the product is found by multiplying the first factor, x^2, by the derivative of the second factor (i.e., the solution, $\cos x$, to the second subproblem) and then adding the result of this first multiplication to the result of multiplying the second factor, $\sin x$, by the derivative of the first factor (i.e., the solution, $2x$, to the first subproblem). Thus, one obtains

$$\frac{dy(x)}{dx} = x^2 \cos x + 2x \sin x$$

as the solution to problem 1.

Figure 3.1 shows the application of the three-step top-down hierarchical approach applied to problem 1. The first step is labeled "decompose" and produces the boxes containing the two subproblems 1.1 and 1.2. The second step is labeled "solve subproblems" and leads to the boxes containing the solutions to subproblems 1.1 and 1.2. The third step is labeled "solve original problem." Solving the original problems requires that one "assemble" the solutions to the two subproblems into the solution to the overall problem.

The three steps of this problem-solving process are not necessarily obvious or easy to perform. In particular, the step labeled "decompose" requires the insight that factoring the given expression in a particular way is productive. Many decompositions yield subproblems that are much harder to solve than the original problem. The step labeled "solve subproblems" requires actual differentiation by computing the limiting values of $\Delta y / \Delta x$ for two expressions. This step requires some effective mechanism for actually solving problems. The step labeled "solve original problem" requires finding a way to assemble the now-available solutions to the subproblems using the available primitive operations, such as multiplication and addition. Like the second step, this step requires an effective mechanism for actually solving problems.

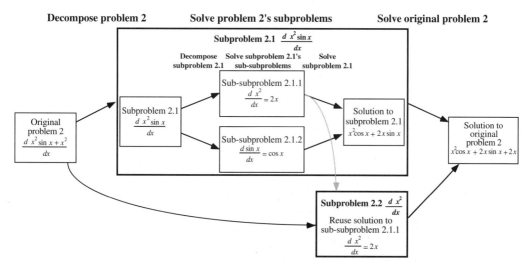

Figure 3.2   Three-step top-down hierarchical approach applied to problem 2 of differentiating $f(x) = x^2 \sin x + x^2$.

Reduction in the overall effort required to solve a problem is a motivating reason for using the three-step hierarchical problem-solving process. If the decomposition is done astutely, less overall effort is required to do the decomposition, solve the subproblems, and assemble the solutions to the subproblems into an overall solution than is required to solve the original problem directly. The net savings accrues even though the process requires three separate steps and requires the solution of more separate problems. The problem of differentiating the product $x^2 \sin x$ entails solving four different problems using the hierarchical process. One must do the decomposition; one must separately differentiate the two elementary functions, x^2, and $\sin x$; and one still must solve the overall problem (by assembling the overall solution by applying one addition and two multiplications to the now-available derivatives of x^2 and $\sin x$). Nevertheless, less total effort is required to grapple with all four of these separate problems than would be required to apply first principles and the definition of the derivative to solve the overall problem. Because of this, *hierarchical decomposition* can be a way of reducing the total effort needed to solve an overall problem.

3.2 RECURSIVE APPLICATION AND IDENTICAL REUSE

Now let us consider problem 2 requiring the differentiation of the following two-term sum:

$$f(x) = x^2 \sin x + x^2.$$

In applying the three-step hierarchical problem-solving process to problem 2, we first decompose the problem of differentiating the sum into subproblem 2.1 of differentiating the first addend, $x^2 \sin x$, and subproblem 2.2 of differentiating the second addend, x^2, as shown in figure 3.2.

Second, we solve these two component subproblems. Suppose we were seeing subproblem 2.1 requiring the differentiation of the product $x^2 \sin x$ for the first time (i.e., we had not just encountered it as problem 1 above). Subproblem 2.1 is sufficiently difficult that it should be solved by invoking the entire three-step hierarchical problem-solving process as if it were itself an original problem. Recursive invocation of the entire three-step hierarchical problem-solving process is another way of reducing the total effort needed to solve an overall problem.

When we recursively invoke the entire three-step process on subproblem 2.1, we find that subproblem 2.1 decomposes into sub-subproblem 2.1.1 (differentiating x^2) and sub-subproblem 2.1.2 (differentiating $\sin x$). We solve these two sub-subproblems and assemble their solutions into a solution of subproblem 2.1, $x^2 \cos x + 2x \sin x$.

If we are alert as we start to solve subproblem 2.2 (differentiating x^2), we will notice that we already differentiated x^2 as part of the process of solving subproblem 2.1 (i.e., as sub-subproblem 2.1.1). It would be much more efficient to reuse the already-obtained solution to this sub-subproblem than to solve it again. This *identical reuse* is another way to reduce the total effort needed to solve an overall problem.

The third step in solving problem 2 is to solve the overall problem by assembling the solutions to subproblems 2.1 and 2.2 into a solution to the overall problem. When differentiating a sum, the assembly consists of adding the derivative of the first addend to the derivative of the second addend. Thus,

$$\frac{df(x)}{dy} = x^2 \cos x + 2x \sin x + 2x.$$

is the solution to problem 2 of differentiating the sum $f(x) = x^2 \sin x + x^2$.

Figure 3.2 shows the application of the three-step top-down hierarchical approach applied to problem 2 of differentiating the sum $f(x) = x^2 \sin x + x^2$. The decomposition creates subproblems 2.1 (differentiating the first addend $x^2 \sin x$) and 2.2 (differentiating the second addend x^2). This first step is labeled "decompose problem 2" near the top left of the figure and gives rise to the two large boxes that dominate the middle of the figure. In the second step of solving problem 2, subproblems 2.1. and 2.2 are solved. This step is labeled "solve problem 2's subproblems" near the top middle of the figure. The third step of solving problem 2 involves assembling the solutions to subproblems 2.1 and 2.2 into an overall solution. This step is labeled "solve original problem 2" near the top right.

Subproblem 2.1 (the largest box of figure 3.2) can be most efficiently solved by recursively invoking the entire three-step problem solving process on it. Thus, we insert all three steps shown in figure 3.1 inside the large box labeled "solve subproblem 2.1." These steps are now relabeled "decompose subproblem 2.1," "solve subproblem 2.1's sub-subproblems," and "solve subproblem 2.1." The decomposition of subproblem 2.1 gives rise to sub-subproblem 2.1.1 (differentiating x^2) and sub-subproblem 2.1.2 (differentiating $\sin x$).

The solving of subproblem 2.2 (differentiating x^2) can be entirely avoided by reusing, without modification, the derivative of x^2 already obtained in the process of solving sub-subproblem 2.1.1. This reuse of an already-solved sub-subproblem is indicated by the gray arrow between "sub-subproblem 2.1.1" and "subproblem 2.2."

The solution to problem 2 is produced by assembling the solutions to subproblems 2.1 and 2.2. This step is labeled "solve original problem 2" near the top right of figure 3.2. This step involves solving the original problem by assembling the now-available solutions to the subproblems.

3.3   PARAMETERIZED REUSE AND GENERALIZATION

Now consider problem 3 of differentiating the sum

$g(x) = x^3 + x^4.$

If we were to proceed unthinkingly in applying the three-step hierarchical problem-solving process to problem 3, we would first decompose the problem into the two subproblems of differentiating the two addends. Subproblem 3.1 would require the differentiation of x^3; and subproblem 3.2 would require the differentiation of x^4. In this treatment, subproblems 3.1 and 3.2 are two entirely unrelated subproblems.

Figure 3.3 shows the application of the three-step top-down hierarchical approach applied to problem 3 of differentiating $y(x) = g(x) = x^3 + x^4$ in which there are separate subproblems for differentiating x^3 and x^4. The first step is labeled "decompose" and produces the boxes containing the two subproblems 3.1 and 3.2. The second step is labeled "solve subproblems" and leads to the boxes containing the solutions to subproblem 3.1 (differentiating x^3) and subproblem 3.2 (differentiating x^4). The third step is labeled "solve original

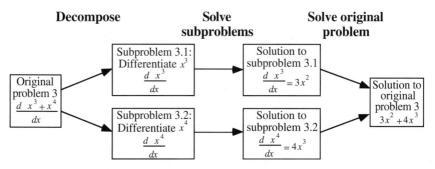

Figure 3.3   Three-step top-down hierarchical approach applied to problem 3, differentiating $y(x) = g(x) = x^3 + x^4$, in which there are separate subproblems for differentiating x^3 and x^4.

problem." This step involves assembling the solutions to subproblems 3.1 and 3.2 to obtain $3x^2 + 4x^3$ as the solution to the overall problem.

However, if we are alert, we will notice that the subproblems 3.1 and 3.2 are similar; they differ only in that the power of x to be differentiated is 3, rather than 4. It would be preferable to have a general problem-solving mechanism for differentiating x^m and then invoke this one general mechanism on two occasions to differentiate x^3 and x^4. On each of the two invocations, the general differentiator for x^m would take into account the particular power of x involved (i.e., 3 or 4). That is, the first invocation of the general problem-solving mechanism for differentiating x^m would be instantiated with the argument 3, and the second invocation would be instantiated with the argument 4.

If a general mechanism is to exploit similarities among subproblems, it is first necessary to identify the differences between the similar subproblems to be solved by the general mechanism. Second, it is necessary to communicate the identified difference to the general mechanism. This is called *instantiation*. Third, the general mechanism must appropriately use the communicated information to solve the particular instance of the class of similar problems. In this example, the difference between the two subproblems consists of the single numerical argument (3 versus 4). The value of this argument is the information that must be communicated. Upon receipt of this information, the general mechanism for differentiating x^m will use the numerical argument (3 or 4) to produce the appropriate answer, $3x^2$ or $4x^3$. This process of *parameterized reuse* illustrates yet another way to reduce the overall effort needed to solve a problem. Parmetrized reuse corresponds to a *generalization* of the problem-solving mechanism.

Figure 3.4 shows the application of the three-step top-down hierarchical approach applied to problem 3 of differentiating $g(x) = x^3 + x^4$ in which there is a general mechanism for differentiating x^m. The first step is labeled "decompose" and produces one subproblem (labeled 3.3) (differentiate x^m), rather than the two subproblems shown in figure 3.3. The second step is labeled "solve subproblem 3.3" and yields a general mechanism for differentiating x^m. The two subproblems 3.1 and 3.2 of figure 3.3 are solved in figure 3.4 by means of a parameterized reuse of the general mechanism for differentiating x^m. When this general mechanism is instantiated with 3, it produces the derivative of x^3; and when it is instantiated with 4, it produces the derivative of x^4. The labeled arrows in figure 3.4 show these instantiations. The third step is labeled "solve original problem" and assembles (by adding) the derivative of x^3 and the derivative of x^4 to create the solution to the overall problem.

In the terminology of computer programming, the two subproblems of differentiating x^3 and x^4 are parameterized by m. The differentiating mechanism is a subroutine. The calling program invokes the subroutine with a particular value of the parameter, m. The particular value of the parameter is communicated to the subroutine as a transmission of the

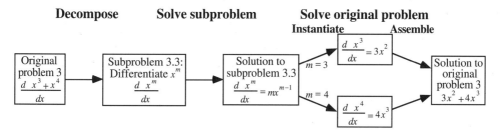

Figure 3.4 Three-step top-down hierarchical approach applied to problem 3, differentiating $y(x) = g(x) = x^3 + x^4$, in which there is a general mechanism for differentiating x^m.

parameter. The subroutine is written in terms of a dummy variable (formal parameter) and uses the dummy variable in an appropriate way to produce its result.

3.4 ABSTRACTION

Now consider problem 4 of differentiating, with respect to the independent variable x, the four-term sum

$$h(x) = x^2 \sin x + x^2 + x^3 + \Omega(t),$$

where the independent variable t and the function $\Omega(t)$ do not depend on x, and are not correlated with x in any way. In applying the three-step hierarchical problem-solving process to problem 4, we first decompose the problem of differentiating this four-term sum into the four subproblems of differentiating the four addends. $\Omega(t)$ makes no contribution to the overall mathematical function that expresses the way $h(x)$ changes in response to changes in the independent variable x. Accordingly, when we solve the fourth subproblem, we will find that $d\,\Omega(t)/dx$ is zero. The independent variable t and the function $\Omega(t)$ make no contribution to the derivative because they are completely irrelevant to x. When certain variables can be identified as being irrelevant to the solution to a subproblem, the subproblem can be solved without regard to the values of these irrelevant variables. If we have a mechanism for differentiating x^m that applies to all values of x and m, that mechanism also applies for all combinations of values of x, and m, and t (where t is an irrelevant variable). Once a certain variable is identified as being irrelevant to the solution to a subproblem, the mechanism for solving that subproblem becomes reusable on all the combinations of the three variables (x, m, and t). The process of excluding irrelevant information (the *abstraction* of a problem out of an environment containing irrelevant variables) makes a solution to a subproblem applicable to more situations and thereby facilitates reuse of the solutions to already-solved subproblems and may result in less total effort being required to solve an overall problem.

The calculus examples above illustrate the five reasons why the hierarchical problem-solving approach is beneficial.

First, when a complex problem is decomposed astutely, less overall effort is required to decompose a problem into subproblems, solve the subproblems, and finally assemble the solutions to the subproblems into a solution to the original problem than is required to solve the original problem directly. This is the benefit associated with *hierarchical decomposition*.

Second, the ability to recursively invoke the hierarchical problem-solving process within the second step of the process brings the benefits of the entire process to bear within the second step so that a subproblem can be solved with less effort than if it were solved directly. This is the benefit associated with *recursive application* of the hierarchical approach.

Third, if the problem environment contains regularities, and if the decomposition is done astutely so that a subproblem corresponds to such a regularity, the solution to the subproblem becomes potentially reusable. When a particular subproblem repeatedly occurs in an identical way in a problem environment, the subproblem need not be separately solved each time that it occurs. Instead, the solution to the subproblem can be reused, without modification, on each identical recurrence of the subproblem. This is the benefit associated with *identical reuse*.

Fourth, if the problem environment contains regularities, the solution to a subproblem becomes potentially reusable if a solution to a subproblem can be constructed that solves not just one particular subproblem, but instead solves a class of similar subproblems. When the differences between multiple similar occurrences of a particular subproblem can be identified so that the solution to the subproblem becomes reusable merely by taking the identified differences into account, the solution to the subproblem becomes a *generalization*. This is the benefit associated with *reuse with modification* or *parameterized reuse*. Generalization is a consequence of parameterized reuse. The method of communicating the identified differences may be direct or indirect. In the direct method of communication, the differences associated with an occurrence of a subproblem are explicitly expressed as free parameters and the particular values of the parameters are explicitly communicated to the mechanism for solving the subproblem. In the indirect method of communication, the differences associated with an occurrence of a subproblem are embodied in the current state of the system and the mechanism for solving the subproblem merely deals with the state of the system that it encounters. In the indirect method, communication to the mechanism for solving the subproblem is implicit through the current state of the world.

Fifth, to the extent that certain variables of the system can be identified as being irrelevant to the solution of a subproblem, then a solution of a subproblem can be reused on every combination of the irrelevant variables. Each solution to a subproblem (whether applicable only to identical situations or a broader set of similar situations) becomes reusable on a large number of combinations of variables of the system. This may result in less overall effort being required to solve the problem. This is the benefit associated with *abstraction*.

In summary, the five ways that the hierarchical problem-solving approach reduces the overall effort required to solve a problem arise from the

- efficiency associated with the process of *hierarchical decomposition,*
- efficiency gained by *recursive application* of the process of hierarchical decomposition,
- *identical reuse* of solutions to already-solved subproblems,
- *parameterized reuse* (reuse with modification) or *generalization* of solutions to similar, but different, subproblems, and
- *abstraction* of irrelevant variables broadens the applicability of the solutions to subproblems.

The five benefits of the hierarchical problem-solving approach offer promising ways to gain the leverage that is needed if methods of automatic programming are ever to be scaled up from small "proof of principle" problems to large problems.

The alluring benefits of the hierarchical three-step problem-solving process raise the practical question: How does one go about implementing this process in an automated and domain-independent way?

From the top-down point of view:

- How does one go about decomposing a problem into subproblems?
- Once the subproblems have been identified, how does one solve the subproblems?
- Once the subproblems have been identified and solved, how does one invoke and assemble the solutions of the subproblems into a solution to the original overall problem?

A similar set of practical questions arises in connection with implementing the hierarchical three-step problem-solving process from the bottom-up point of view:

- How does one go about finding regularities at the lowest level of the problem environment?
- Once the regularities have been identified, how does one recode the original problem into a new problem in terms of these regularities (i.e., how does one change the representation)?
- Once the regularities have been identified and the recoding has been done, how does one solve the original problem as now framed in terms of the new representation?

3.5 SOAR AND EXPLANATION-BASED GENERALIZATION

SOAR (an acronym for "State, Operator, And Result") is one approach to applying the three-step hierarchical problem-solving process. SOAR was developed in the early 1980s at Carnegie Mellon University by John Laird (now at the University of Michigan), Paul Rosenbloom (now at the University of Southern California), and the late Allen Newell (Laird, Rosenbloom, and Newell, 1986a, 1986b; Rosenbloom, Laird, and Newell 1993).

SOAR is an architecture for general problem solving. It is inspired by its inventors' views on human cognition processes. The SOAR architecture has been used to control autonomous agents. Such agents use available knowledge, solve problems, increase their knowledge by remembering solutions that they find, and interact with their environment. In addition, SOAR attempts to provide a unified theory of human cognition and a way to model cognitive data.

The SOAR architecture formulates all goal-oriented behavior of autonomous agents as a search in a problem space. A *problem space* consists of a set of states and a set of operators that cause changes in state of the autonomous agent. A *goal* is formulated as the task of reaching a desired state (or states). Satisfying a goal involves starting at the initial state and applying a sequence of operators that results in reaching the desired state(s). Interaction with the external environment may occur by means of perceptual input (e.g., from a vision system) and motor commands (e.g., to control a robot arm).

Knowledge is represented as a set of if-then production rules. When the condition part of an if-then rule matches the current state of the system, the rule fires. When knowledge is incomplete, there may be no rule that applies. In that event the system will not know what operator to apply and the system will not know how to proceed. When such an *impasse* occurs, a subgoal is generated to resolve the impasse. SOAR processes the subgoal as a new problem space. Further impasses may arise in the new problem space causing the generation of still more subgoals and problem spaces. The result is a hierarchy of subgoals, each with an associated problem space. In the SOAR literature, this process is known as *universal sub-goaling*.

Subgoals become satisfied when some problem-solving technique solves the problem. SOAR works in conjunction with various domain independent methods for solving problems (so-called *weak methods*). Laird, Rosenbloom, and Newell 1986a enumerate 17 different weak methods that can be used with SOAR. These weak methods include *generate and test* (blind random search), simple hillclimbing, steepest ascent hillclimbing, various search techniques (e.g., depth-first search, alpha-beta search, iterative-deepening search), various techniques of artificial intelligence (e.g., means-end analysis, constraint satisfaction, unification), and other techniques. Eventually, the available weak method may solve the subproblem in the newly created problem space, thereby satisfying the subgoal.

When a subgoal is satisfied, the solution produced by the weak method is summarized and remembered in an additional new set of if-then rules, called *chunks*. That is, SOAR remembers (caches, learns) the way of satisfying the subgoal (solving the subproblem). Note that in the SOAR community the word "learn" has the everyday meaning of "remembering" the solution of a subproblem, whereas in the machine learning community the word "learn" has the specialized meaning of "finding" or "discovering" the solution. The chunks that SOAR has learned (remembered) are then available for subsequent reuse. Both identical reuse and parameterized reuse are contemplated by SOAR. That is, SOAR can be programmed to do generalization and abstraction. If the system ever again arrives in a state where the rules of a chunk are applicable, no impasse is generated on this occasion. Consequently, no subgoal and no new problem space is generated. Instead, the applicable if-then rules of the chunk fire and the previously discovered solution to the subgoal is applied to the current situation.

SOAR is a variant of explanation-based generalization (DeJong 1981; DeJong 1983; Winston et al. 1983; Mitchell, Keller, and Kedar-Cabelli 1986; Rosenbloom and Laird 1986; Minton 1990).

In addition, the pioneering work on search and macros (Fikes, Hart, and Nilsson 1972; Korf 1980, 1985a, 1985b) serves as an underpinning for some of the techniques of SOAR. Fikes, Hart, and Nilsson (1972) proposed a process for saving a generalized version of a plan called "macrops." These plans, constructed by the STRIPS planning system, were represented in a tabular format that linked the preconditions of each operator in the plan with other operators in the plan that established those preconditions. The format allowed either all or just part of the saved plan to be easily accessed for future use. Additionally, the plans were generalized by replacing constants that were specific to the original use of the plan by variables that could be bound differently in subsequent uses. Their generalization process foreshadowed explanation-based generalization.

Consider the eight-puzzle in which there are eight numbered tiles and one hole within a 3-by-3 grid. The system begins with the eight tiles and one hole in initial locations within the grid (the initial state). The goal is to relocate the eight numbered tiles and one hole to the desired locations (the desired state). The four available operations for changing the current state of the system involve moving a tile to the left, right, up, or down into the adjacent hole (thereby causing the hole to end up to the right, left, down, or up, respectively). A solution to the problem consists of a sequence of moving operations that causes all eight tiles and the hole to end up in their desired locations.

The eight-puzzle can now serve to show how SOAR directly and explicitly implements the three-step hierarchical problem-solving process. First, the problem is explicitly decomposed by the user into separate subproblems. Solving the eight-puzzle in SOAR begins with a clever serial decomposition (Korf 1985a, 1985b) in which the problem is explicitly decomposed into an ordered sequence of six subproblems (subgoals). Subproblem k involves moving the tile numbered k to its final desired location with each lower-numbered tile remaining at (or being restored to) its respective desired location. When the solutions to these six subproblems are executed in consecutive order, the overall effect is that the first six tiles become properly located and the remaining two tiles and hole are also necessarily in their proper locations.

Second, each subproblem is separately solved by a weak method, such as iterative-deepening search (Korf 1985b). The solution to a subproblem of properly locating tile k consists of a sequence of sliding operations discovered by the weak method.

Third, the overall problem is solved by assembling the solutions to the six subproblems. The assembly consists of executing the six subproblem solutions, once each, in the predetermined consecutive order.

As will be seen starting in the next chapter, the approach for hierarchical problem-solving used in this book is very different from SOAR, explanation-based generalization, and other techniques of symbolic artificial intelligence.

4 Introduction to Automatically Defined Functions – The Two-Boxes Problem

This chapter will use a simple illustrative problem, the two-boxes problem, to lay the groundwork for the methods that will be used throughout this book.

The two-boxes problem will be stated in section 4.1.

The preparatory steps necessary to solve the two-boxes problem using genetic programming *without* automatically defined functions will be presented in section 4.2 and the problem will be solved in section 4.3. (These sections review the way of applying genetic programming to a problem and may be skipped by readers already familiar with genetic programming).

Section 4.4 will describe the idea of a subroutine. The idea of automatically defined functions will be introduced in section 4.5.

The additional preparation necessary to solve the two-boxes problem using genetic programming *with* automatically defined functions will be presented in section 4.6.

Section 4.7 describes how the initial random population is generated with automatically defined functions. Section 4.8 describes structure-preserving crossover and the typing required with automatically defined functions.

The two-boxes problem is then solved in section 4.9 using automatically defined functions.

Section 4.10 will present the methodology for computing the average structural complexity, $\bar{S}$, of the solutions produced by genetic programming. Then, the average structural complexity without automatically defined functions, $\bar{S}_{without}$, will be compared with the average structural complexity with automatically defined functions, $\bar{S}_{with}$, for the two-boxes problem.

Section 4.11 will present the methodology for calculating the computational effort, E, for measuring the number of fitness evaluations required to yield a solution to a problem with a satisfactorily high probability. Then, the computational effort without automatically defined functions, $E_{without}$, will be compared with the computational effort with automatically defined functions, E_{with}, for the two-boxes problem.

4.1 THE PROBLEM

The two-boxes problem has six independent variables, called L_0, W_0, H_0, L_1, W_1, and H_1, and one dependent variable, called D.

Table 4.1 shows 10 fitness cases for the two boxes problem, each consisting of a combination of the six independent variables and the associated value of the dependent variable. The values of the six independent variables appear in the first six columns of each row. The last column of each of row contains the value of the dependent variable, D, that is produced when some as-yet-unknown mathematical expression is applied to the given values of the six independent variables. For example, the first row of this fitness-case table shows that when $L_0 = 3$, $W_0 = 4$, $H_0 = 7$, $L_1 = 2$, $W_1 = 5$, and $H_1 = 3$, then the value of the dependent variable, D, is 54.

The two-boxes problem involves finding a computer program (i.e., mathematical expression, composition of primitive functions and terminals) that produces the observed value of the single dependent variable as its output when given the values of the six independent variables as input. We call problems of this type *symbolic regression* because we are seeking a mathematical expression, in symbolic form, that fits, or approximately fits, a given sample of data. A symbolic regression problem may also be called a *symbolic system identification* problem or a *black box* problem.

Symbolic regression differs from conventional linear regression, quadratic regression, exponential regression, and other conventional types of regression where the nature of the model is specified in advance by the user. In conventional linear regression, for example, one is given a set of values of various independent variable(s) and the corresponding values for the dependent variable(s). The goal is to discover a set of numerical coefficients for a linear expression involving the independent variable(s) that minimizes some measure of error (such as the square root of the sum of the squares of the differences) between the values of the dependent variable(s) computed with the linear expression and the given values for the dependent variable(s). Similarly, in quadratic regression the goal is to discover a set of numerical

Table 4.1 Fitness-case table for the two-boxes problem showing the value of the dependent variable, D, associated with the values of the six independent variables, L_0, W_0, H_0, L_1, W_1, and H_1.

Fitness case	L_0	W_0	H_0	L_1	W_1	H_1	D
1	3	4	7	2	5	3	54
2	7	10	9	10	3	1	600
3	10	9	4	8	1	6	312
4	3	9	5	1	6	4	111
5	4	3	2	7	6	1	−18
6	3	3	1	9	5	4	−171
7	5	9	9	1	7	6	363
8	1	2	9	3	9	2	−36
9	2	6	8	2	6	10	−24
108	1	10	7	5	1	45	

coefficients for a quadratic expression that minimizes the error. It is left to the user to decide whether to do a linear regression, a quadratic regression, an exponential regression, or whether to try to fit the data points to some other type of function. But often, the real problem is deciding what type of model most appropriately fits the data, not merely computing the appropriate numerical coefficients after the model has already been chosen. Symbolic regression searches for both the functional form and the appropriate numeric coefficients that go with that functional form.

A mere glance at table 4.1 will not disclose the mathematical relationship between the six independent variables and the one dependent variable. The relationship is not at all obvious. In fact, the relationship is nonlinear and cannot be discovered merely by applying conventional linear regression. Genetic programming provides a way to find a mathematical relationship (i.e., a computer program) that fits, or approximately fits, this given sample of data. In fact, the relationship is

$$D = W_0 H_0 L_0 - W_1 H_1 L_1.$$

Figure 4.1 shows two boxes. The relationship among the variables in table 4.1 represents the difference, D, in volume between a first box whose length, width, and height are L_0, W_0, and H_0, respectively, and a second box whose length, width, and height are L_1, W_1, and H_1, respectively.

A human programmer writing a computer program to compute the difference in these two volumes in a programming language such as FORTRAN might write a main program something like

```
D = W0*L0*H0 - W1*L1*H1
PRINT D
```

If it were understood that the last value computed by a program is its output, then there would be no need for the explicit PRINT statement in the above FORTRAN program. Similarly, in the LISP programming language, it is sufficient merely to write the S-expression

```
(- (* L0 (* W0 H0)) (* L1 (* W1 H1)))
```

and evaluate the S-expression for its value.

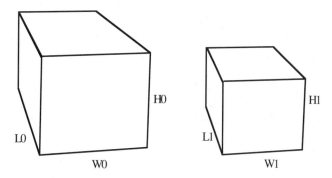

Figure 4.1 Two boxes.

Introduction to Automatically Defined Functions – The Two-Boxes Problem

The FORTRAN statement and the S-expression are each a symbolic solution to this system identification problem.

The above computer programs are, of course, very simple in that they produce only a single value. In general, computer programs can return a set of values, side-effects on a system, or a combination thereof.

4.2 PREPARATORY STEPS WITHOUT ADFs

This section applies genetic programming without automatically defined functions to the two-boxes problem.

As already mentioned, the five major preparatory steps in applying genetic programming to a problem involve determining

(1) the set of terminals,

(2) the set of primitive functions,

(3) the fitness measure,

(4) the parameters for controlling the run, and

(5) the method for designating a result and the criterion for terminating a run.

The first major step in preparing to use genetic programming is to identify the set of terminals. The terminals can be viewed as the inputs to the as-yet-undiscovered computer program. The terminals from the terminal set, along with functions from the function set, are the ingredients from which genetic programming attempts to construct a computer program to solve, or approximately solve, the problem. The terminals for this problem are the six independent variables and the terminal set, $\mathcal{T}$, is

$\mathcal{T} = \{\texttt{L0}, \texttt{W0}, \texttt{H0}, \texttt{L1}, \texttt{W1}, \texttt{H1}\}$.

The second major step in preparing to use genetic programming is to identify the set of functions that are to be used to generate the mathematical expression that attempts to fit the given finite sample of data. A reasonable choice might be the function set consisting of the ordinary two-argument arithmetic operations of addition, subtraction, and multiplication along with a version of division that is protected against divisions by zero. The *protected division function* % takes two arguments and returns the number 1 when division by 0 is attempted (including 0 divided by 0), and, otherwise, returns the normal quotient. Therefore, the function set, $\mathcal{F}$, for this problem is

$\mathcal{F} = \{+, -, *, \%\}$.

An argument map is associated with each set of functions. The *argument map* of a set of functions is the list containing the number of arguments required by each function. Thus, the argument map for the function set, $\mathcal{F}$, is

$\{2, 2, 2, 2\}$.

The protected division function ensures, as a practical matter, that the function set, $\mathcal{F}$, satisfies the closure requirement for this particular problem. However, the potential of an overflow or underflow always exists whenever any arithmetic operation (including addition, subtraction, or multiplication) is performed on a computer (as discussed further in section 11.2).

Each computer program is a composition of functions from the function set, $\mathcal{F}$, and terminals from the terminal set, $\mathcal{T}$. In this problem, the output of any program composed of these functions and terminals is intended to correspond directly to the value of the dependent variable, D, of this problem. Therefore, there is no need for a *wrapper* (output interface) to further modify the output of the program for this problem.

The third major step in preparing to use genetic programming is identifying the fitness measure. Fitness is typically measured over a number of different fitness cases. There are 10 fitness cases for this problem, each consisting of a combination of the six independent variables, L_0, W_0, H_0, L_1, W_1, and H_1, and the associated value of the dependent variable, D.

In defining fitness for a problem, we start with a definition of *raw fitness* stated in terms natural to the problem domain. The raw fitness for this problem is the sum, taken over the 10 fitness cases, of the absolute value of the difference (error) between the value produced by a program for the six given values of the independent variables and the correct value for the dependent variable D. The closer this sum of errors is to 0, the better the program. *Standardized fitness* (described in detail in *Genetic Programming*, subsection 6.3.2) is the zero-based fitness measure actually used by genetic programming. Since better programs have a smaller value of raw fitness and since a 100%-correct program would have a raw fitness of 0 for this problem, standardized fitness is the same as raw fitness for this problem.

Since every computer program in the population returns a numerical value, it is always possible to compute the fitness of any program. Therefore, this fitness measure satisfies the requirement of being fully defined for any program that might arise in the population.

The *hits* measure for this problem counts the number of fitness cases for which the numerical value returned by the program comes within a small tolerance (called the *hits criterion*) of the correct value. The hits criterion for this problem is 0.01.

The fourth major step in preparing to use genetic programming involves determining the values of certain parameters to control the runs.

The two *major parameters* for controlling a run of genetic programming are the population size, M, and the maximum number of generations to be run, G. The default value for the population size, M, is 4,000 for this book and the default value for the maximum number of generations to be run, G, is 51 (i.e., generation 0 with 50 additional generations). Depending on the complexity of the problem, populations of 1,000, 8,000, or 16,000 are used for some problems. A few problems are run for only 21 generations because of time constraints.

In addition to the two major parameters for controlling runs, 19 additional *minor parameters* control runs of genetic programming. The default values for the minor parameters are detailed in appendix D.

The fifth major step in preparing to use genetic programming involves specifying the method for designating a result and the criterion for terminating a run. The termination criterion for a problem is triggered either by running the specified maximum number of generations, G, or by the satisfaction of a problem-specific success predicate by at least one program in the population. The success predicate for this problem is that a program scores the maximum number of hits (i.e., 10). This occurs when each of the 10 values returned by a genetically evolved program for the 10 combinations of the six independent variables comes within 0.01 of the associated value of the dependent variable, D. In other words, this success predicate considers an approximate solution to be a *satisfactory result* for this problem. If we had specified that the success predicate consisted of achievement of a value of standardized fitness of exactly 0, then only an exact *solution* would be considered to be a satisfactory result. We designate the best-so-far individual as the result of a run of genetic programming.

The function set for a problem should be chosen so that it is capable of solving the problem. Mathematical expressions composed of addition, subtraction, multiplication, and division are certainly capable of approximating a given set of numerical data. Since this problem requires finding a program that approximately fits the given data (reflected by the success predicate merely requiring the scoring of 10 hits), it is reasonable to believe that the function set, $\mathcal{F}$, satisfies the sufficiency requirement. However, in general, the sufficiency of a function set depends on both the function set and the success predicate for the problem. For example, if the success criterion for the problem required attainment of a value of standardized fitness of exactly zero (thus requiring an algebraically correct solution to the problem), then we would be less certain that the function set, $\mathcal{F}$, satisfies the sufficiency requirement (absent additional knowledge about the characteristics of the source of the given data).

Table 4.2 summarizes the key features of the two-boxes problem when automatically defined functions are not being used. We call this table (and the 15 similar tables in this book) the *tableau without ADFs* for the problem. Each such tableau without ADFs summarizes the main choices made while applying the five major preparatory steps of genetic programming. A supplementary tableau with ADFs will be presented later.

The second and third rows of each tableau without ADFs correspond to the first and second major preparatory steps for genetic programming and summarize the choices for the terminal set and function set, respectively, for the problem. The choice of the terminal set and function set determines whether a wrapper (shown in the eighth row) is needed for a particular problem.

The fourth through seventh rows of each tableau without ADFs relate to the third major preparatory step and present the choices made concerning the fitness measure for the problem.

Table 4.2   Tableau without ADFs for the two-boxes problem.

Objective:	Find a program that produces the observed value of the single dependent variable, *D*, as its output when given the values of the six independent variables as input.
Terminal set without ADFs:	The six actual variables of the problem, L0, W0, H0, L1, W1, and H1.
Function set without ADFs:	+, -, * and %.
Fitness cases:	10 combinations of random integers between 1 and 10 for the six independent variables L0, W0, H0, L1, W1, and H1.
Raw fitness:	The sum, over the 10 fitness cases, of the absolute value of the error between the value returned by the program and the observed value of the dependent variable.
Standardized fitness:	Same as raw fitness.
Hits:	The number of fitness cases (out of 10) for which the absolute value of the error is less than 0.01 (the hits criterion).
Wrapper:	None.
Parameters:	$M = 4,000$. $G = 51$. Different fitness cases are chosen for each run.
Success predicate:	A program scores the maximum number (i.e., 10) of hits.

The ninth row of each tableau without ADFs corresponds to the fourth major preparatory step and presents the control parameters for the problem. This row always includes the two major parameters of population size, *M*, and the maximum number of generations to be run, *G*. The 19 minor numerical and qualitative control parameters are generally not specifically mentioned in the tableau unless they differ from the default values (appendix D). For this particular problem, a different set of randomly created fitness cases is created for each separate run.

The tenth row of each tableau without ADFs relates to the fifth major preparatory step. The method of result designation used throughout this book is the best-so-far method. The termination criterion used throughout this book is a disjunction based on completing the maximum number of generations to be run, *G*, and satisfaction of a problem-specific success predicate. Only the success predicate is specifically mentioned in the tableau.

4.3   RESULTS WITHOUT ADFs

Now that we have completed the five major steps for preparing to use genetic programming, we will describe a run of genetic programming without automatically defined functions for the two-boxes problem.

A run of genetic programming for this problem starts with the creation of a population of 4,000 random computer programs, each composed from the available functions (+, -, *, and %,) from the function set, *F*, and the available terminals (L0, W0, H0, L1, W1, and H1) from the terminal set, *T*. The process of creating the initial random generation is specified by means of a computer program in appendix E of this book and described in detail in *Genetic Programming* (section 6.2).

The 4,000 randomly generated individuals found in the initial generation of the population are, in effect, a blind random search of the space of computer programs representing possible solutions to this problem.

The results of such a blind random search are not very good. The *worst-of-generation* program in the population for generation 0 has the enormous error (fitness) of 3,093,623. This is an average deviation of 309,362 between the value produced by this computer program and the correct value of *D* (whose average magnitude is only 173.4 in table 4.1). This individual is shown below:

```
(* (* (+ (* H1 W0) (* H1 W0)) (+ (* H0 W1) (* H1 H1))) (- (* (% L1
L1) (- L0 W1)) (* (* W1 W1) (- W0 H1)))))
```

However, even in a randomly created population of programs, some individuals are better than others.

The *average fitness of the population* as a whole (the *mean*) for generation 0 is 1,195,092 (only about a third of the fitness of the worst). The mean for generation 0 can reasonably be viewed as a *baseline* value for a blind random search of the program space of this problem.

The fitness of the *median* (2,000th best) individual of the population for generation 0 has a fitness of 1571.8 and is

```
(% (- L1 W0) (+ (* W1 H0) W1))
```

which is equivalent to

$$\frac{L_1 - W_0}{W_1 + W_1 H_0}.$$

The fitness of the median individual for this problem is considerably better (i.e., smaller) than the average fitness of the population as a whole because the average is significantly raised by a few extremely unfit individuals in the poorest percentiles of the population.

The best individual from generation 0 has a standardized fitness of 783. The average error between the correct value of *D* and the value of the output, *D*, produced by this program is 78.3. This average error is about 45% of the average magnitude (173.4) of the 10 values of *D* in table 4.1, so the performance of this best individual from generation 0 must be viewed as being very bad; nonetheless, this error is better than the error produced by the other 3,999 random individuals in generation 0.

The *best-of-generation* program in generation 0 of the population (hereafter often referred to as *the best* of the specified generation) is

```
(* (- (- W0 L1) (- W1 H0)) (+ (- H0 H0) (* H0 L0))).
```

This program has seven functions and eight terminals and thus has 15 *points*. It is equivalent to

$$H_0 L_0 (W_0 + H_0 - W_1 - L_1) \ .$$

This expression bears little resemblance to the correct mathematical expression for solving the two-boxes problem. Like many randomly generated individuals, this program is blind to several of the independent variables which are needed to solve the problem correctly. This individual does not contain H1.

Throughout this book, we frequently display individuals and present statistics from generation 0 in order to show the prohibitive difficulty of finding the solution to the problem at hand merely by means of blind random search and in order to give the reader a sense of the general appearance of random computer programs that are composed of the available primitive functions and terminals for the particular problem domain.

The Darwinian reproduction operation is then applied a certain number of times to single individuals selected from the population on the basis of their fitness (with reselection allowed). In addition, the genetic crossover operation is then applied to a certain number of pairs of parents selected from the current population on the basis of their fitness (with reselection allowed) to breed a new population of programs. Throughout this book, the number of reproduction operations performed for each generation is equal to $p_r = 10\%$ of the population size (i.e., 400 for a population of size 4,000). The number of crossover operations is equal to $p_c = 45\%$ of the population size (i.e., 1,800 crossovers involving 3,600 individuals and producing 3,600 offspring).

The vast majority of the offspring in the newly created generation 1 are, like their parents from generation 0, highly unfit. However, some of the offspring may be slightly more fit than their parents.

Figure 4.2 presents the *fitness curves* for this run showing, by generation, the standardized fitness of the best-of-generation program, the standardized fitness of the worst-of-generation program, and the average of the standardized fitness for the population as a whole. The figure starts at generation 0 and ends at the generation on which a 100%-correct solution was evolved on this particular run (i.e., generation 11). Standardized fitness is shown here on a logarithmic scale since the standardized fitness of both the worst-of-generation program and the average of the standardized fitness for the population as a whole are typically very large for problems of symbolic regression. Since the standardized fitness of the 100%-correct program evolved in generation 11 is zero, the final point is not plotted on this logarithmically scaled graph.

As a run of genetic programming continues from generation to generation, we typically observe a generally monotonic improvement (i.e., a decrease) in the average standardized fitness of the population as a whole and in the standardized fitness of the best-of-generation individual. For example, the standardized fitness of the best-of-generation program progressively improves to 778, 510, 138, 117, 53, and 51 between generations 2 and 7 of this run.

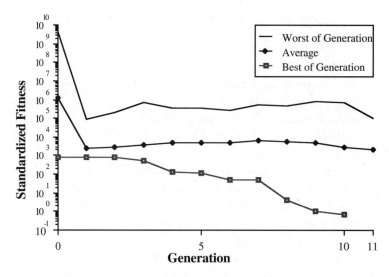

Figure 4.2 Fitness curves for the two-boxes problem without ADFs.

In generation 8, the standardized fitness of the best-of-generation program improves to 4.44, so the average error is now only 0.444 per fitness case (versus 78.3 per fitness case for the best of generation 0). This average error is only 0.2% of the average magnitude of the 10 values of D in table 4.1. This program has 27 points and is

```
(- (- (* (* W0 H0) L0) (* (* L1 H1) W1))
  (% (+ W0 L0) (- (- L0 W1) (+ (+ W1 L1) (* L1 W1))))).
```

This individual is equivalent to

$$W_0 H_0 L_0 - W_1 H_1 L_1 - \frac{W_0 + L_0}{L_0 - 2W_1 - L_1 - L_1 W_1}.$$

As can be seen, the first two terms of this expression correspond to what we know to be an algebraically correct solution to this problem, while the third term is an extraneous and erroneous term.

In generations 9 and 10, standardized fitness further improves to 1.10 and 0.65, respectively.

In generation 11, the best-of-generation program achieves a standardized fitness of 0. This 11-point program is

```
(- (* (* W0 H0) L0) (* (* L1 H1) W1))
```

which is equivalent to

$$W_0 H_0 L_0 - W_1 H_1 L_1.$$

This program (which we can recognize as an algebraically correct solution to the problem) scores 10 hits because its error is less than 0.01 (the hits criterion) for all 10 fitness cases. A program that scores 10 hits satisfies the success predicate of this problem and causes this run to be terminated at generation 11

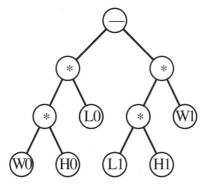

Figure 4.3 100%-correct best-of-run program from generation 11 for the two-boxes problem without ADFs.

(rather than continuing on to generation 50). This best-of-generation program is, therefore, also the best-of-run program and the best-so-far program.

Figure 4.3 shows this 100%-correct best-of-run individual from generation 10 as a rooted, point-labeled tree with ordered branches.

The best of generation 8 differs from the best of generation 11 by the erroneous and extraneous subtractive term. This similarity does not mean that the best of generation 8 is necessarily one of the (up to) eight ancestors of the best of generation 11; a genealogical audit trail can be used to determine this.

We define the *variety* of a population at a given generation to be the fraction of the programs in that population that are different from every other program in the population. Variety is determined by using the LISP function EQUAL, which considers two programs to be the same if they have exactly the same tree structure and the exactly same labeling of the points of the tree with functions and terminals. A value of variety of 100% indicates that all programs in the population are different.

Figure 4.4 shows the *variety curve* for the population for the two-boxes problem. Variety starts at 1.00 at generation 0 because duplicates are eliminated when the initial random population is created. Variety fluctuates around 0.85 for most of this particular run.

The solution that evolved in this particular run of this simple problem happened to be an algebraically correct and parsimonious solution to the problem at hand. However, genetic programming does not, in general, produce such solutions in problems of symbolic regression. Instead, genetic programming typically evolves relatively large programs that are good approximations to the data.

4.4 THE IDEA OF SUBROUTINES

A human programmer writing a program for the two-boxes problem would probably notice the symmetry and regularity of the mathematical expression

$W_0 H_0 L_0 - W_1 H_1 L_1$.

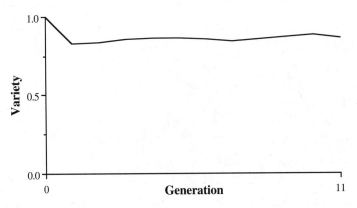

Figure 4.4 Variety curve for the two-boxes problem without ADFs.

This expression contains a multiplication of three numbers in two places. The physical interpretation of this regularity is as a computation of volume.

Regularities and symmetries in a problem environment can often be exploited in solving a problem. An alternative way of writing the program for the two-boxes problem involves first writing a subroutine (defined function, subprogram, procedure) for the common calculation and then repeatedly calling the subroutine from a main program. The six lines of code below in the LISP programming language contain a two-line defined function and a one-line main program:

```
1    ;;;- definition of the three-argument function "volume"-
2    (progn (defun volume (arg0 arg1 arg2)
3           (values (* arg0 (* arg1 arg2))))
4    ;;;- main program for computing the difference
5    ;;;  of two volumes-
6           (values (- (volume L0 W0 H0) (volume L1 W1 H1))))
```

Lines 1, 4 and 5 contain comments (indicated by semicolons) informing us that a subroutine called `volume` follows on lines 2 and 3 and that a result-producing main program follows on line 6.

Lines 2 and 3 contain the definition of a function (called a `defun` in LISP). A `defun` declaration does four things.

First, the `defun` (line 2) assigns a name, `volume`, to the function being defined. The name permits subsequent reference to the function by a calling program (line 6).

Second, the `defun` (line 2) identifies the *argument list* of the function being defined. In this `defun`, the argument list is the list, (`arg0 arg1 arg2`), containing the three *dummy variables* `arg0`, `arg1`, and `arg2`. These three dummy variables (also known as *formal parameters*) are entirely local to the function being defined (lines 2 and 3) and do not appear at all in the result-producing main program (line 6).

Third, the `defun` contains a *body* (line 3) that performs the work of the function. The work here consists of the multiplication of the three dummy variables, `arg0`, `arg1`, and `arg2`, using two invocations of the two-argument primitive function of multiplication (*). The body of the function being defined does not have access to the actual variables of the problem, `L0`, `W0`, `H0`, `L1`, `W1`, and `H1`. Instead, it operates only with the three dummy variables that are local to the function definition.

Fourth, the `defun` identifies the value to be returned by the function. In this example, the single value to be returned (i.e., the product of the three dummy variables `arg0`, `arg1`, and `arg2`) is highlighted with an explicit invocation of the `values` function (line 3). LISP programmers do not ordinarily use the `values` function in this overt manner; however, we use it throughout this book to highlight the value(s) being returned by each defined function (and the result-producing main program). Some programming languages have a statement called `return` for identifying the value to be returned by a subroutine; others require the programmer to assign the value to be returned to a special variable with the same name as the function.

Line 6 contains the result-producing main program. The main program calls the defined function `volume` twice and then assembles the values returned by the two invocations of the defined function `volume`. Specifically, the assembly consists of subtracting the two values returned by the function `volume`. The main program does not have access to the dummy variables `arg0`, `arg1`, and `arg2`; they are entirely local to the defined function `volume`. Instead, the main program calls the function `volume` using the actual variables of the problem. When the main program calls `volume` the first time, the three dummy variables, `arg0`, `arg1`, and `arg2`, are instantiated with the particular values, `L0`, `W0`, and `H0`, respectively, of the *actual variables* of the problem. Then, when the main program calls `volume` the second time, the three dummy variables are instantiated with the values, `L1`, `W1`, and `H1`, respectively. Finally, the body of the main program performs the work of subtracting the two volumes. The single value to be returned by the main program in line 6 is highlighted with an explicit invocation of the `values` function.

The Common LISP function `progn` evaluates each of its arguments sequentially and returns the result of evaluating its last argument. When the six lines above are evaluated in LISP, the `progn` on line 2 causes the sequential evaluation of the *function-defining branch* (lines 2 and 3) and the *result-producing branch* (line 6). The `progn` starts by evaluating its first argument, namely the function-defining branch. When a `defun` is evaluated in LISP, the function involved becomes defined and the `defun` returns the name (i.e., `volume`) of the function just defined. Since the `progn` returns only the result of the evaluation of its last argument, the value returned by the `defun` in the first branch is lost (inconsequentially). The `progn` now evaluates its second branch, namely the result-producing branch. The result-producing branch calls the now-defined function `volume` twice and does a subtraction. Since this second branch is the last argument of the `progn`, the value returned by the overall six-line program consists of the numerical value returned by the `values` function associated with the result-producing branch. For this reason, the result-producing branch may also be referred to as the *value-returning branch*.

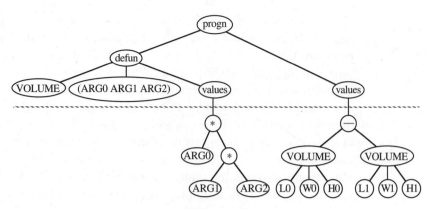

Figure 4.5 An overall program consisting of a function-defining branch for the function volume and a result-producing branch that computes the difference between the volumes of two boxes.

Figure 4.5 shows the overall structure of the above six-line program for the two-boxes problem. The function-defining branch (containing the `defun`) appears in the left part of this figure and the result-producing branch (the main program) appears on the right. The bodies of the two branches appear below the horizontal dotted line.

The above illustrative defun for volume has three dummy variables, returns only a single value, has no *side effects* (i.e., does not change the state of any system), and refers only to its three local dummy variables (i.e., it does not refer to any of the actual variables of the overall problem). However, in general, defined functions may have any number of arguments (including no arguments), may return multiple values (or no values at all), may or may not perform side effects, and may or may not explicitly refer to the actual variables of the overall problem.

Different names are used to describe the idea of a defined function in different programming languages. In FORTRAN, a subroutine is called a *function* or *subroutine* depending on whether or not a single value is returned. In Pascal, a subroutine is labeled as a *function* or *procedure* based on this same distinction. In LISP, no such distinction is made and all subroutines are called *functions* and defined by means of a `defun`. Reusable code can appear in computer programs in several other ways. For example, in some programming languages, such as FORTRAN, single-valued functions consisting of only a simple arithmetic calculation may be defined as an *in-line function* within a program without creating an external subroutine or function. These functions can then be referenced repeatedly within the particular program or subprogram in which they are defined. In LISP, the `let` construction can be used to bind the value returned by some expression to a variable that can then be repeatedly referenced within the region of a program delineated by the `let`. In addition, the `flet` and `labels` constructions can be used to establish local definitions of functions.

When a programmer writes a subroutine for `volume`, the function definition is usually not composed of a particular combination of the actual variables of the problem. Instead, a function definition is *parameterized* by dummy variables (formal parameters), such as `arg0`, `arg1`, and `arg2`. The function definition is a general, reusable method for computing volume. The dummy variables are usually instantiated with a different combination of the actual variables of the problem on each occasion when `volume` is invoked. However, in spite of the different instantiations, `volume` carries out its work in terms of the dummy variables in precisely the same way on each occasion. For example, `volume` may be called with `L0`, `W0`, and `H0` on one occasion by

```
(volume L0 W0 H0).
```

In addition, `volume` may be called with `L1`, `W1`, and `H1` on another occasion by

```
(volume L1 W1 H1).
```

In addition, the dummy variables can be instantiated with expressions consisting of a composition of functions and terminals, rather than mere terminals. For example, `volume` might be called with `(- L0 L1)`, `(- W0 W1)`, and `(- H0 H1)` as its arguments by

```
(volume (- L0 L1) (- W0 W1) (- H0 H1)).
```

However, in spite of the different instantiations, `volume` multiplies the current value of its three dummy variables and returns that product as its result.

What is gained by writing the program for the two-boxes problem using a defined function?

First, once the function `volume` is defined, it may then be repeatedly called with different instantiations of its arguments from more than one place in the main program. Defined functions exploit the underlying regularities and symmetries of a problem by obviating the need to tediously rewrite lines of essentially similar code. In this example, we first call the function `volume` with `L0`, `W0`, and `H0` as instantiations of its three dummy arguments and we then call it with `L1`, `W1`, and `H1`. Of course, a mere two calls to a function whose work is as trivial as `volume` does not create a compelling need for a defined function. However, there is a considerable advantage to a defined function when a more complicated calculation must be performed numerous times.

Second, the use of function definitions and calls may improve the parsimony (i.e., decrease the size) of an overall computer program. One of the ways by which parsimony may be measured is in terms of the size of the overall program (i.e., the number of points in the parse tree of the program). The two illustrative programs above for the two-boxes problem do not exhibit any advantage in terms of parsimony since the simple main program without the `defun` (e.g., the program evolved by generation 11 in section 4.3) contains fewer points than the combination of the main program and the `defun` for `volume`. However, if the work of the `defun` were less trivial, there generally is a considerable improvement in parsimony of the overall program from the use of a defined function.

Third, if automated learning is involved, the ability to extract a reusable subroutine may obviate the need to relearn the same behavior or concept on each separate occasion that it is needed. Function definitions may reduce the computational burden required to yield a solution to a problem with a satisfactorily high probability.

Fourth, the process of defining and calling a function, in effect, decomposes a given problem into a hierarchy of subproblems. In the two-boxes problem, the decomposition consists of identifying the subproblem of computing volume. This subproblem is solved by multiplying three numbers. The solution to the overall problem is obtained by calling the subroutine with two different instantiations of its three dummy variables and assembling the results by subtraction.

In practice, a human programmer might or might not choose to encode a solution to this particular problem using a subroutine because the common calculation is so simple (merely the product of three numbers), because there are only two invocations of the common calculation, and because the main program is so simple (merely a subtraction of the result of the two calls to the subroutine). However, if the repeated calculation were more substantial (e.g., solving a quadratic equation or computing a Taylor series approximation for the exponential function), virtually every programmer would choose to write a subroutine, rather than tediously rewrite the code for the common calculation. Furthermore, when an overall program is large, many programmers prefer to write subroutines to modularize their programs even if no calculations are repeated.

When the main program is executed, the subroutine `volume` is called twice. Each of the two-argument multiplications contained in the subroutine is executed twice so that there is a total of four multiplications. Note that this number, four, is the same whether or not a subroutine is used. That is, decomposing the problem into subroutines and then repeatedly calling the subroutines does not, in itself, reduce the total number of elementary operations that must be performed in order to execute an already-known solution to a problem. In fact, because calling a subroutine in most programming languages usually introduces a certain number of additional operations as overhead, there is usually a slight increase in the total number of machine instructions performed.

Nonetheless, one beneficial effect of writing subroutines is the generally smaller size of the overall program required to solve the problem. Such savings are particularly significant when the subroutines are non-trivial. Another beneficial effect of writing subroutines is that it may take the human programmer less time and effort to create the program to solve the program. One can speculate that the analog of this latter benefit in the domain of automated problem-solving is that it might take less computation to learn the solution to a problem with subroutines than without them.

The three-step hierarchical problem-solving process described in chapter 3 is involved whenever a programmer chooses to write a subroutine.

4.5   THE IDEA OF AUTOMATICALLY DEFINED FUNCTIONS

Genetic programming provides a way to bring the benefits of the three-step hierarchical process described in the previous section to bear on solving problems.

Genetic programming provides a way to solve a subproblem (i.e., the second step of the top-down approach). But what about the other steps of this three-step problem-solving process? How are they to be performed in an automated and domain-independent way? And, even if the individual steps can be performed separately, how are they then to be integrated with one another?

One answer appears to be to automate the entire process of writing sub-routines and the programs that call them. Figure 4.5 showed an overall program consisting of a defined function called `volume` and a calling program that computed the difference between the volumes of two boxes. Our approach is to use genetic programming to simultaneously evolve functions (automatically defined functions) and calling programs during the same run. When we talk about "automatically defined functions," we mean that we intend that genetic programming will *automatically* and *dynamically* evolve, by means of natural selection and genetic operations, a combined structure containing automatically defined functions and a calling program capable of calling the automatically defined functions. During the run, genetic programming will genetically breed a population of programs, each consisting of a definition of a function definition in its function-defining branch and a main program in its result-producing branch. The bodies of both the function-defining branches and the result-producing branch are each determined by the combined effect, over many generations, of the selective pressure exerted by the fitness measure and by the effects of the Darwinian reproduction and the crossover operations. The function defined by the function-defining branch of a particular individual in the population is available for use by the result-producing branch of that individual. The manner and the number of times, if any, that the automatically defined function of an individual in the population will actually be called by the result-producing branch of that particular individual is not predetermined, but is instead determined by the evolutionary process.

The concurrent evolution of functional subunits and calling programs would enable genetic programming to realize the entire three-step hierarchical problem-solving process described above, automatically and dynamically within a run of genetic programming.

The program in figure 4.5 is an example of a constrained syntactic structure (*Genetic Programming*, chapter 19). Each program in the population contains one function-defining branch and one result-producing branch. The result-producing branch may call (but is not required to call) the function-defining branch.

Figure 4.6 shows the overall structure of an individual program consisting of one function-defining branch and one result-producing branch. The

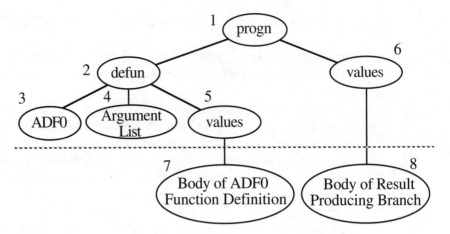

Figure 4.6 An overall program consisting of one function-defining branch and one result-producing branch.

function-defining branch appears in the left part of this figure and the result-producing branch appears on the right.

This overall program has eight different *types* of points. The first six types are *invariant* and we place them above the horizontal dotted line in the figure to indicate this. The last two types are *noninvariant* and constitute the bodies (work) of the two branches; they appear below the horizontal dotted line. The eight types are as follows:

(1) the root of the tree (which consists of the place-holding `progn` connective function),

(2) the top point, `defun`, of the function-defining branch,

(3) the name, `ADF0`, of the automatically defined function,

(4) the argument list of the automatically defined function,

(5) the `values` function of the function-defining branch identifying, for emphasis, the value(s) to be returned by the automatically defined function,

(6) the `values` function of the result-producing branch identifying, for emphasis, the value(s) to be returned by the result-producing branch,

(7) the body of the automatically defined function `ADF0`, and

(8) the body of the result-producing branch.

Each overall program in the population has its own result-producing branch and its own function-defining branch. Note that each reference to an automatically defined function in the result-producing branch of an overall program in the population refers to the particular automatically defined function belonging to that overall program (and not to any other identically-named automatically defined function belonging to some other program in the population).

If more than one value is to be returned by the overall program, there are multiple arguments to the `values` function of the result-producing branch (point 6 in figure 4.6). That is, the result-producing branch consists of multiple subbranches under the `values` function. When the `progn` evaluates its last argument (i.e., the `values` at point 6 associated with the result-producing branch), the multiple values returned by the subbranches of the result-producing branch are returned as the output of the overall program.

The result-producing branch typically contains the actual variables of the problem. The actual variables of the problem usually do not appear in the function-defining branches, although they may be made directly available to such branches.

In general, a program may contain more than one function-defining branch. The number of different types of points in programs involving automatically defined functions is always at least eight (as shown in figure 4.6; however, there may be more than eight types if there is more than one function-defining branch. If a program has more than one function-defining branch, each such branch may potentially refer to the others. For example, a function-defining branch might be permitted to refer hierarchically to any function that has already been defined by an earlier function-defining branch. Potentially, a function-defining branch may recursively refer to itself. However, we do not discuss recursion in this book.

When storing a program having the above structure in a computer, we do not actually create a LISP S-expression containing the invariant points of types 1 through 6 (i.e., the points above the horizontal dotted line in figure 4.6). In practice, only the bodies of the function-defining branch(es) and the bodies of the result-producing branch of an overall program (i.e., the points of types 7 and 8 in figure 4.6) are actually created and explicitly stored. These bodies are gathered together as arguments to a top-level `LIST` function. The overall program represented by the list of bodies created by this `LIST` function is then interpreted in a manner semantically equivalent to the structure described above (i.e., as if all the points above the horizontal dotted line were present). Appendix E presents details on the implementation of automatically defined functions on a computer in LISP.

As will be seen, an automatically defined function can

- perform a calculation similar to that which a human programmer might use,
- perform a calculation unlike anything a human programmer would ever use,
- redundantly define a function that is equivalent to a primitive function that is already present in the function set of the problem,
- ignore some of its dummy variables,
- be entirely ignored by every potential calling branch,

- define a constant value (i.e., a value that is independent of all of the dummy variables and any other variables that may be available to the automatically defined function),
- return a value identical to one of the dummy variables (so that the automatically defined function redundantly defines a terminal that is already present in the terminal set of the problem), or
- call another automatically defined function with a subset of, or a permutation of, its dummy variables.

The need for reusable subroutines appears in every area of artificial intelligence and machine learning, and neural networks.

Many existing paradigms for machine learning, artificial intelligence, and neural networks automatically and dynamically define functional subunits during runs (the specific terminology being, of course, specific to the particular paradigm). However, automatically defined functions operate differently than the functional subunits one sometimes encounters in such paradigms. We illustrate this point with an example from the field of pattern recognition.

Consider the problem of learning to recognize a pattern presented as an array of pixels in which the same feature appears in two different places within the overall pattern. Specifically, suppose a feature consisting of a vertical line segment within a 3-by-3 pixel region appears in both the upper middle of a 9-by-5 array of pixels and the lower middle of the same array.

Figure 4.7 shows the 3-by-3 pixel feature defining a vertical line segment.

Figure 4.8 shows the 3-by-3 feature from figure 4.7 in two different locations within the overall 9-by-5 array of pixels. The two occurrences of the 3-by-3 feature are framed in the figure.

Many existing paradigms from the fields of artificial intelligence, machine learning, and neural networks are capable of learning to recognize the overall pattern described above. These paradigms are able to efficiently discover the 3-by-3 feature among the nine pixels p_{11}, p_{12}, p_{13}, p_{21}, p_{22}, p_{23}, p_{31}, p_{32}, and p_{33} in the upper middle of the 9-by-5 array. They are also able to independently rediscover this same feature among the nine pixels p_{51}, p_{52}, p_{53}, p_{61}, p_{62}, p_{63}, p_{71}, p_{72}, and p_{73}, in the lower middle of the array. But most existing paradigms generally do not provide a way to discover this common feature *just once*, to generalize the detector of the feature so that it is not hardwired to particular pixels (but is, instead, parameterized), and then reuse the generalized feature detector in a parameterized way to recognize occurrences of this common feature in different 3-by-3 pixel regions within the overall array.

Specifically, let us consider the way that neural networks (Rumelhart, Hinton, and Williams 1986; Hinton 1989) and genetic classifier systems (Holland 1986; Holland et al. 1986) might treat this problem of pattern recognition.

We first consider neural networks.

Figure 4.9 shows the 9-by-5 array of pixels, two occurrences of the same 3-by-3 feature, and two neurons, each capable of recognizing the 3-by-3 feature.

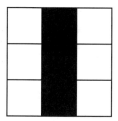

Figure 4.7 A 3-by-3 pixel feature consisting of a vertical line segment.

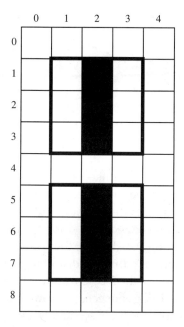

Figure 4.8 Two identical 3-by-3 pixel features in a 9-by-5 array of pixels.

Various different neural network architectures and training paradigms can be successfully used to train a 45-input neural network to recognize the 3-by-3 feature located at pixels p_{11}, p_{12}, p_{13}, p_{21}, p_{22}, p_{23}, p_{31}, p_{32}, and p_{33} within the 9-by-5 array of pixels. The learning necessary to recognize this 3-by-3 feature might be embodied in the simple subassembly consisting of a single neuron shown at the top right of figure 4.9. There are nine weighted connections between this neuron and its nine inputs, p_{11}, p_{12}, p_{13}, p_{21}, p_{22}, p_{23}, p_{31}, p_{32}, and p_{33}. Negative weights (–1) are assigned to the connections from the pixels p_{11}, p_{13}, p_{21}, p_{23}, p_{31}, and p_{33} and positive weights (+1) are assigned to the connections from pixels p_{12}, p_{22}, and p_{32}. The sum of the nine products of the weights and inputs is +3. Since this sum equals this neuron's threshold of 3, the neuron emits an output of +1 indicating recognition of the 3-by-3 feature. Thus, the subassembly consisting of this first neuron and these weights is capable of recognizing the first occurrence of the 3-by-3 feature.

The neural network can also learn to recognize the occurrence of this same 3-by-3 feature located at pixels p_{51}, p_{52}, p_{53}, p_{61}, p_{62}, p_{63}, p_{71}, p_{72}, and

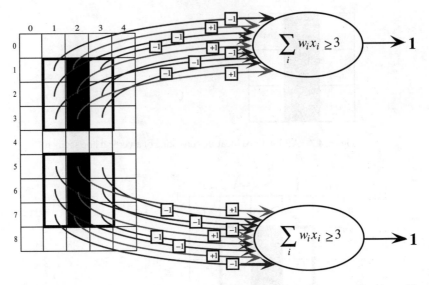

Figure 4.9 Two neurons recognizing a vertical line segment located in two places in an 9-by-5 array of pixels.

p_{73} within the 9-by-5 array. The learning necessary to recognize the second occurrence of the feature might be embodied in the subassembly consisting of the second neuron shown at the bottom right of figure 4.9. This second neuron has nine weighted connections –1 for p_{51}, p_{53}, p_{61}, p_{63}, p_{71}, and p_{73} and +1 for p_{52}, p_{62}, and p_{72}). As before, the sum of the weighted inputs is +3 and equals this neuron's threshold, so the neuron emits an output of +1 indicating recognition of the 3-by-3 feature. However, with the usual implementations of most existing connectionist paradigms, this second set of nine weights would be learned entirely separately and independently from the first set of nine weights. This is true even though the "same" 3-by-3 feature is involved and even though the same sets of nine weights can recognize the feature.

In contrast, a human programmer writing a computer program to recognize this 3-by-3 feature would write a general nine-argument subroutine *just once* and then call the reusable subroutine twice (instantiating the first call with the actual variables p_{11}, …, p_{33} as arguments and instantiating the second call with the actual variables p_{51}, …, p_{73}). The writing of a single reusable subroutine by the human corresponds to the neural network doing its learning just once; embodying its learning in a subassembly; making a copy of the already-learned subassembly; positioning the copy in a new location in the overall neural net; connecting nine *different* pixels as inputs to the copy of the subassembly in its new location; and consolidating the outputs of the two subassemblies in the same output neuron (not shown).

When a set of weights is discovered enabling a particular neuron in a neural network to perform some subtask (e.g., recognize the 3-by-3 features above, detect an edge, perform the behavior of the exclusive-or function, etc.), the training process can be viewed as a process of defining a function (i.e., creating a function taking the values of the specific inputs to that neuron as arguments and producing a binary output signal whose value is determined by whether or not the threshold of the neuron is exceeded). Moreover, a process of abstraction occurs when this neural function is used in that all other inputs to the neural network that are not connected (or are connected with a zero or negligible weight) to the neuron involved play no role in computing the value of the neural function being defined (i.e., in producing the output signal).

The neural function thus defined differs from the automatically defined functions that we have been discussing. The neural function is called only once from within the neural network and it is called only by the specific part of the neural net where it is created. Moreover, this neural function is called only with the one particular fixed set of inputs that happens to be hardwired to a specific neuron. Conceivably the subtask performed by the neuron might be useful elsewhere in the neural network. That is, the same set of weights, thresholds, and biases that enable the neural function to perform its calculation might be useful elsewhere in the neural network to perform a similar calculation. However, the usual implementations of most existing paradigms for training neural networks do not provide a way to reuse the set of connection and weights that are discovered in one part of the network in other parts of the network where a similar subtask must be performed on a different set of inputs. That is, there is no propagation of a generalized structure; there are no dummy variables that are capable of being instantiated with different sets of inputs; there is no reuse of a useful neural function in more than one place. Instead, the training algorithm for the neural net has to independently rediscover the useful combination of weights, thresholds, and biases for every neuron that needs to perform the same calculation on its particular inputs.

The above description greatly simplifies the way most modern neural networks work. For example, a subassembly for detecting a feature would typically be far more complicated than one neuron in an actual neural network; the multiple neurons involved would probably be arranged in layers creating a hierarchy; the weights would probably be floating-point values, rather than just –1 and +1; and sigmoidal signals would probably be used. Nonetheless, the above example correctly makes the point that a particular subassembly for recognizing a feature is usually hardwired to a particular nine pixels in the usual implementations of the most popular neural network architectures and training paradigms.

The field of neural networks is vast and some researchers have attempted to deal with the discovery of modular features in neural networks. For example, the neocognitron (Fukushima and Miyake 1982; Fukushima, Miyake, and Takatuki 1983; Fukushima, 1989) is a multilayer neural network that can recognize a displaced or distorted pattern. In some neural network architectures, some weights are common to groups of neurons belonging to a receptor field, so that something that is learned in one part of the field is available to the other neurons of the group.

P00	P10	P20	P30	P40	P50	P60	P70	P80
*****	*010*	*010*	*010*	*****	*****	*****	*****	*****

Figure 4.10 Condition part of classifier system rule for recognizing the first occurrence of the 3-by-3 feature.

Le Cun et al. (1990) describes this *weight sharing* architecture as follows:

A fully connected network with enough discriminative power for the task would have far too many parameters to be able to generalize correctly. Therefore a restricted connection-scheme must be devised, guided by our prior knowledge about shape recognition. There are well-known advantages to performing shape recognition by detecting and combining local features. We have required our network to so this by constraining the connections in the first few layers to be local. In addition, if a feature detector is useful on one part of the image, it is likely to be useful on other parts of the image as well. One reason for this is that the salient features of a distorted character might be displaced slightly from their position in a typical character. One solution to this problem is to scan the input image with a single neural that has a local receptive field, and store the states of this neuron in corresponding locations in a layer called a *feature map*. This operation is equivalent to a convolution with a small size kernel, followed by a squashing function. The process can be performed in parallel by implementing the feature map as a plane of neurons whose weight vectors are constrained to be equal. That is, units in a feature map are constrained to perform the same operation on different parts of the image. An interesting side-effect of this *weight sharing* technique, already described in Rumelhart, Hinton, and Williams 1986, is to reduce the number of free parameters by a large amount, since a large number of units share the same weights. ... In practice, it will be necessary to have multiple feature maps, extracting different features from the same image.

In addition, recent work on cellular encodings (Gruau 1992a, 1992b, 1993a, 1993b, 1994a, 1994b; Gruau and Whitley 1993a, 1993b) has applied genetic programming to evolve neural networks that exploit regularities in the problem environment (see subsection F.4.1 in appendix F). Nonetheless, the above example correctly reflects the usual implementation of the most popular neural network architectures and training paradigms.

We now consider genetic classifier systems.

Genetic classifier systems learn sets of if-then rules capable of solving problems. An if-then rule consists of a *condition* (*if-part*) and an associated *action* (*then-part*). A genetic classifier system with 45 environmental inputs is, in principle, capable of recognizing the two occurrences of the 3-by-3 feature within the 9-by-5 array of pixels in figure 4.8.

A classifier system might learn to recognize the first (upper) occurrence of the feature by creating an if-then rule whose condition has the 45 symbols shown in figure 4.10. This condition is satisfied when pixels p_{11}, p_{13}, p_{21}, p_{23}, p_{31}, and p_{33} are all 0 and when pixels p_{12}, p_{22}, and p_{32} are all 1. The don't care

P00	P10	P20	P30	P40	P50	P60	P70	P80
*****	*****	*****	*****	*****	*010*	*010*	*010*	*****

Figure 4.11 Condition part of classifier system rule for recognizing the second occurrence of the 3-by-3 feature.

symbols (*) appearing in the other 36 positions cause the values of the other 36 pixels to be ignored. The satisfaction of the condition fires the rule and triggers an action that represents recognition of the 3-by-3 feature in the upper part of the 9-by-5 array of pixels.

Similarly, the classifier system might learn to recognize the second occurrence of the feature by creating a rule whose condition is shown in figure 4.11. This condition is satisfied when pixels p_{51}, p_{53}, p_{61}, p_{63}, p_{71}, and p_{73} are all 0 and when pixels p_{52}, p_{62}, and p_{72} are all 1.

A reusable subroutine for recognizing the two occurrences of the 3-by-3 feature operates very differently from the way that a classifier system operates. The creation of a reusable subroutine would correspond to an ability on the part of the classifier system to do the learning just once; to embody its learning in a first rule whose condition has nine active positions associated with pixels p_{11}, p_{12}, p_{13}, p_{21}, p_{22}, p_{23}, p_{31}, p_{32}, and p_{33}; to make a copy of the condition of the first rule; to add the copy of the first rule to the classifier system's set of if-then rules; to modify the copy by moving the rule's nine active positions to a different nine positions within the 45 positions so that the modified rule is capable of identifying the feature when it appears in pixels p_{51}, p_{52}, p_{53}, p_{61}, p_{62}, p_{63}, p_{71}, p_{72}, and p_{73} within the 9-by-5 array; and to give the second if-then rule the same action as the first rule.

4.6 PREPARATORY STEPS WITH ADFs

In section 4.2, we applied the five major preparatory steps of genetic programming to the two-boxes problem and set up the problem as shown in table 4.2, the tableau without ADFs. We then applied genetic programming to the problem using a population size of 4,000 and obtained the following 100%-correct solution:

```
(- (* (* W0 H0) L0) (* (* L1 H1) W1)).
```

This solution can be viewed as a main program whose inputs are L0, W0, H0, L1, W1, and H1. The output of the program is the single value returned by the entire expression.

Before applying genetic programming with automatically defined functions to the two-boxes problem, it is first necessary to choose the number of function-defining branches that are to be available and the number of arguments possessed by each automatically defined function. If there is more than one automatically defined function involved, it is also necessary to determine the nature of the references (if any) allowed between the defined functions. This group of architectural choices (required because automatically defined functions are being used) constitutes the *sixth major step* in preparing to use genetic programming. In practice, this sixth major step is performed first when automatically defined functions are involved, (i.e., this step is performed before the usual five major preparatory steps).

The sixth major step in preparing to use genetic programming may require some analysis of the problem. Since the two-boxes problem involves boxes of dimensionality 3, we decided that 3 is an appropriate choice for the number of arguments for a defined function for this problem. We also decided to employ one defined function for this problem. Consequently, each individual overall program in the population will consist of one three-argument function-defining branch (defining a function named ADF0). For many problems, considerations of available computer resources (i.e., computer time and memory) will, as a practical matter, drive these choices. Chapter 7 summarizes the four methods we usually use to make these architectural choices. However, chapters 21 through 25 demonstrates that even these choices can, if desired, be left to the evolutionary process.

Once the sixth major step has been performed, it is also necessary to specify the terminal set for the result-producing branch, the function set for the result-producing branch, the terminal set for each function-defining branch, and the function set for each function-defining branch. That is, it is necessary to perform the first and second major steps for each branch of the overall program.

We first consider the result-producing branch.

The purpose of the yet-to-be-evolved computer program is to take the six inputs and produce one output. Thus, the result-producing branch should be a program whose input consists of the six actual variables of the problem, L0, W0, H0, L1, W1, and H1, and whose output represents the value of the single dependent variable of the problem. Thus, the terminal set, T_{rpb}, for the result-producing branch is

$$T_{rpb} = \{\text{L0, W0, H0, L1, W1, H1}\}.$$

The function set of the result-producing branch will contain the four arithmetic operations of addition, subtraction, multiplication, and protected division % (section 4.2). Since automatically defined functions are being used, the function set of the result-producing branch also contains the automatically defined function ADF0. Thus, the function set, F_{rpb}, for the result-producing branch is

$$F_{rpb} = \{\text{ADF0}, +, -, *, \%\}$$

with an argument map for this function set, F_{rpb}, of

$$\{3, 2, 2, 2, 2\}.$$

The result-producing branch of each individual program in the population is a composition of primitive functions from the function set, F_{rpb}, and terminals from the terminal set, T_{rpb}.

This problem illustrates a frequently useful way of constructing the terminal set and function set for the result-producing branch. Specifically, when automatically defined functions are being used, the terminal set, $\mathcal{T}_{rpb}$, of the result-producing branch is the same as the terminal set, $\mathcal{T}$, that would have been used if automatically defined functions were not involved. The function set, $\mathcal{F}_{rpb}$, of the result-producing branch is the union of the available automatically defined functions (just ADF0 here) and the function set, $\mathcal{F}$, that would have been used if automatically defined functions were not involved.

We now apply the first and second major steps to the function-defining branch.

Since the function-defining branch defines a function in terms of three dummy variables, the terminal set, $\mathcal{T}_{adf}$, for the function-defining branch is

$\mathcal{T}_{adf} = \{\texttt{ARG0}, \texttt{ARG1}, \texttt{ARG2}\}$.

The function set, $\mathcal{F}_{adf}$, for the function-defining branch is

$\mathcal{F}_{adf} = \{+, -, *, \%\}$

with an argument map for set, $\mathcal{F}_{adf}$, of

$\{2, 2, 2, 2\}$.

The function-defining branch of each individual program in the population is a composition of primitive functions from the function set, $\mathcal{F}_{adf}$, and terminals from the terminal set, $\mathcal{T}_{adf}$.

This problem also illustrates a frequently useful way of constructing the terminal set and function set for the function-defining branch. When automatically defined functions are being used, the terminal set, $\mathcal{T}_{adf}$, of the function-defining branch consists of as many dummy variables as there are arguments for the automatically defined function involved. Since the automatically defined function here has three arguments, $\mathcal{T}_{adf}$, consists of ARG0, ARG1, and ARG2. The function set, $\mathcal{F}_{adf}$, of the function-defining branch is the same function set, $\mathcal{F}$, that would have been used if automatically defined functions were not involved.

The third, fourth, and fifth major preparatory steps in solving the two-boxes problem are the same with automatically defined functions as without them.

Table 4.3 is called the *tableau with ADFs* for the problem and is the first of 16 such tableaux in this book. This tableau supplements the tableau without ADFs (table 4.2) for this problem with the information specifically applicable to the use of automatically defined functions. The tableau with ADFs relates to the architecture of the overall program and the terminal set and function set of each branch of the overall program (i.e., the sixth major preparatory step).

The second row of the tableau with ADFs reflects the choice of the architecture of the overall programs for the problem. The architecture includes the number of function-defining branches and the number of arguments possessed by each automatically defined function. If there were more than one

Table 4.3 Tableau with ADFs for the two-boxes problem.

Objective:	Find a program that produces the observed value of the single dependent variable, D, as its output when given the values of the six independent variables as input.
Architecture of the overall program with ADFs:	One result-producing branch and one three-argument function-defining branch defining a three-argument automatically defined function ADF0.
Parameters:	Branch typing (described in section 4.8).
Terminal set for the result-producing branch:	The six actual variables of the problem, L0, W0, H0, L1, W1, and H1.
Function set for the result-producing branch:	+, -, *, and %, and the one three-argument automatically defined function ADF0.
Terminal set for the function-defining branch ADF0:	The three dummy variables ARG0, ARG1, and ARG2.
Function set for the function-defining branch ADF0:	The four primitive functions of the problem, +, -, *, and %.

automatically defined function, the architectural information would also specify whether the automatically defined functions may, or may not, make reference to one another in a hierarchical way.

The third row identifies the values of any parameters relating to the use of automatically defined functions. This row identifies the chosen way of assigning types to the noninvariant points of an overall program (i.e., branch typing or point typing as described in section 4.8).

The fourth and fifth rows specify the terminal set, $\mathcal{T}_{rpb}$, and function set, $\mathcal{F}_{rpb}$, for the result-producing branch.

The sixth and seventh rows specify the terminal set, $\mathcal{T}_{adf}$, and function set, $\mathcal{F}_{adf}$, for the first function-defining branch (defining ADF0).

There may be more than seven rows in a tableau with ADFs if there is more than one automatically defined function. The tableau contains additional rows in the event that there is more than one kind of automatically defined function (e.g., automatically defined functions with different terminal sets, different function sets, or different argument maps).

4.7 CREATION OF THE INITIAL RANDOM POPULATION

When automatically defined functions are being used, the initial random generation of the population must be created so that each individual overall program in the population has the intended constrained syntactic structure (e.g., one function-defining branch and one result-producing branch for the two-boxes problem). Specifically, every individual program in generation 0 for

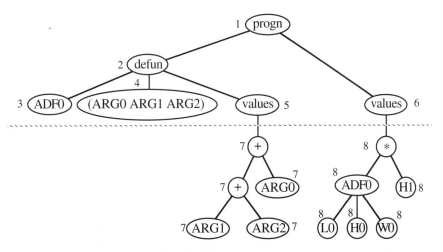

Figure 4.12 A randomly created program from generation 0 for the two-boxes problem with ADFs.

the current example must have (or behave as if it has) the invariant structure represented by the six points of types 1 through 6 shown above the dotted line in figure 4.6. Each function and terminal in the function-defining branch of the current example is of type 7. The function-defining branch is a random composition of functions from the function set, $\mathcal{F}_{adf}$, and terminals from the terminal set, $\mathcal{T}_{adf}$. Each function and terminal in the result-producing branch of the current example is of type 8. The result-producing branch is a random composition of functions from the function set, $\mathcal{F}_{rpb}$, and terminals from the terminal set, $\mathcal{T}_{rpb}$.

Figure 4.12 shows a randomly created program from generation 0 for the two-boxes problem consisting of one function-defining branch and one result-producing branch. In this program ADF0 computes the sum of its three dummy variables. The result-producing branch computes $H_1(L_0 + W_0 + H_0)$.

4.8 STRUCTURE-PRESERVING CROSSOVER AND TYPING

In the crossover operation, a crossover point is randomly chosen in each of two parents and genetic material from one parent is then inserted into a part of the other parent to create an offspring. When automatically defined functions are involved, each program in the population conforms to a constrained syntactic structure. Crossover must be performed in a structure-preserving way so as to preserve the syntactic validity of all offspring.

As already mentioned, every point in an overall program is assigned a type. Some of the points in an overall program are invariant over the entire population. For example, every program in the population with one function-defining branch and one result-producing branch as described above must have the invariant structure represented by the six points of types 1 through 6 shown above the dotted line in figures 4.6 and 4.12. More complex overall programs typically have more than six such invariant points.

Introduction to Automatically Defined Functions – The Two-Boxes Problem

Structure-preserving crossover never alters the invariant points of an overall program, so none of these invariant points are ever eligible to be crossover points in structure-preserving crossover. Instead, structure-preserving crossover is restricted to the noninvariant points shown below the dotted line in figures 4.6 and 4.12. As previously mentioned, the invariant points of programs with automatically defined functions are not actually created, stored, or manipulated in our computer implementation of this process.

Every noninvariant point in the overall program is also assigned a type. The basic idea of structure-preserving crossover is that any noninvariant point anywhere in the overall program is randomly chosen, without restriction, as the crossover point of the first parent. Then, once the crossover point of the first parent has been chosen, the crossover point of the second parent is randomly chosen from among points of the same type. The typing of the noninvariant points of an overall program constrains the set of subtrees that can potentially replace the point and the subtree below it. This typing is done so that the structure-preserving crossover operation will always produce valid offspring.

The following two ways of assigning types to the noninvariant points of an overall program are employed in this book:

- *Branch typing* assigns a different type uniformly to all the noninvariant points of each separate branch of an overall program. There are as many types of noninvariant points as there are branches in the overall program.

- *Point typing* assigns a type to each individual noninvariant point in the overall program. The type assigned reflects the function set of the branch where the point is located, the terminal set of the branch where the point is located, the argument map of the function set of the branch where the point is located, and any syntactic constraints applicable to the branch where the point is located.

Branch typing is the default choice for the way of assigning types. It is used on the two-boxes problem.

Branch typing can be illustrated using the program shown in figure 4.12. In branch typing, a first type (type 7) is assigned to all five points in the body of the function-defining branch and a second type (type 8) is assigned to all six points in the body of the result-producing branch. When structure-preserving crossover is performed, any noninvariant point anywhere in the overall program (i.e., any of the 11 points of type 7 or 8) may be chosen, without restriction, as the crossover point of the first parent. However, the crossover point of the second parent must be chosen only from among points of this same type. In the context of this example, if the crossover point of the first parent is from the function-defining branch (type 7), the crossover point of the second parent is restricted to its function-defining branch (its type 7 points); if the crossover point of the first parent is from the result-producing branch (type 8), the crossover point of the second parent is restricted to its result-producing branch (its type 8 points). In other words, structure-preserving crossover will either exchange a subtree from a function-defining branch only with a subtree from another function-defining branch or it will exchange a subtree from a result-producing branch only with a subtree from another result-producing branch. The restriction on the choice of the crossover point of the second parent ensures the syntactic validity of the offspring.

Point typing is used when the architecture of the overall program is being evolved during the run. It will be described in detail in chapter 21 where it is first used and then illustrated in chapters 21 through 25. (Another approach, like-branch typing, is discussed in section 15.4, but not used in this book).

There is a fundamental difference between a crossover occurring in a function-defining branch versus one occurring in the result-producing branch. Since the result-producing branch usually contains multiple references to the function-defining branch(es), a crossover occurring in the function-defining branch is usually leveraged in the sense that it simultaneously affects the result-producing branch in several places. In contrast, a crossover occurring in the result-producing branch provides no such leverage.

4.9   RESULTS WITH ADFs

We now examine one actual run of genetic programming with automatically defined functions for the two-boxes problem.

The run starts with the creation of a population of 4,000 random programs; the program shown in figure 4.12 is typical of such programs.

As one would expect, the 4,000 randomly generated individuals found in generation 0 are not very good. The fitness of the worst individual program in the population for generation 0 has the enormous error (standardized fitness) of 3.07×10^{38}. This baffling program invokes its defined function ADF0 seven times in its result-producing branch and is shown below:

```
(progn (defun ADF0 (ARG0 ARG1 ARG2)
          (values (- (* (* (% ARG2 ARG0) (+ ARG0 ARG1)) (+ (*
          ARG1 ARG1) (- ARG0 ARG1))) (* (* (* ARG0 ARG0) (-
          ARG2 ARG0)) (% (+ ARG2 ARG2) (- ARG1 ARG2)))))
       (values (ADF0 (% (- (% W0 L0) (+ W0 L1)) (- (- W0 H0) (*
          W0 H0))) (* (ADF0 (* W1 W0) (% W0 H1) (ADF0 L1 W1 L0))
          (ADF0 (ADF0 H0 W0 H0) (- H0 W1) (* H1 H0))) (* (- (ADF0
          L0 H0 H1) (ADF0 H1 L0 H0)) (% (* H1 H1) (- W0 L1))))))).
```

The average fitness of the population as a whole for generation 0 is 3.54×10^{34}.

The median individual in the population for generation 0 has a fitness of 1538.5 and is

```
(progn (defun ADF0 (ARG0 ARG1 ARG2)
          (values (+ (% (* ARG2 ARG1) (+ ARG1 ARG2)) (% (% ARG2
          ARG2) (- ARG0 ARG0)))))
       (values (+ (- (+ W1 H1) (ADF0 H0 W0 W0)) (* (* W1 W0) (-
          W0 W0))))))).
```

Using the fact that the protected division function % returns 1 for an attempt to divide by 0, we see that the defined function ADF0 is equivalent to

$$\frac{Arg1 Arg2}{Arg1 + Arg2} + 1.$$

Although ARG0 appears twice in ADF0, it plays no role in the value returned by ADF0 because (- ARG0 ARG0) is 0 and (% <<X>> 0) returns <<X>> for all <<X>>.

Substituting this expression into the one occurrence of ADF0 in the result-producing branch, we see that the result-producing branch is equivalent to

$$W_1 + H_1 - \frac{W_0 W_0}{W_0 + W_0} - 1 + W_1 W_0 (W_0 - W_0) = W_1 + H_1 - \frac{W_0^2}{2 W_0} - 1.$$

As can be seen, this expression bears little resemblance to the correct mathematical expression for the solution to this problem. Indeed, as is typical for random individuals, this individual is partially blind and does not even use three of the six independent variables that we know are needed to express a solution to the problem.

The fourth best individual from generation 0 has a fitness of 1,153 and is

```
(progn (defun adf0 (ARG0 ARG1 ARG2)
          (values (* (- ARG1 ARG2) (% ARG2 ARG2))))
       (values (* (ADF0 H1 W0 W1) (* L0 W1)))))).
```

The automatically defined function here ignores one of its dummy variables (ARG0). Since ADF0 is equivalent to (- ARG1 ARG2), the result-producing branch is equivalent to

$$L_0 W_1 (W_0 - W_1).$$

The best of generation 0 has a standardized fitness of 1,142 and is

```
(progn (defun adf0 (ARG0 ARG1 ARG2)
          (values (% (* (% (- ARG2 ARG0) (% ARG2 ARG2)) ARG0) (*
            (* (- ARG1 ARG0) (+ ARG2 ARG1)) ARG2))))
       (values (- (* W1 W1) (* W1 (* (- H1 H0) L1))))))).
```

This program has 16 terminals and 14 functions in the body of its function-defining branch and its result-producing branch and has 30 points.

This best-of-generation individual for generation 0 does not invoke ADF0 in the result-producing branch, so the result produced by the program is equivalent to

$$W_1^2 - W_1 L_1 (H_1 - H_0).$$

Although this best-of-generation program bears little resemblance to the correct mathematical expression for solving the problem, this program is better than the other 3,999 programs of generation 0.

The standardized fitness of the best-of-generation program progressively improves to 1,101, 909, 823, 699, 697, and 96 between generations 1 and 6.

In generation 6, the best-of-generation program has 34 points, invokes its ADF0 twice, and is

```
(progn (defun ADF0 (ARG0 ARG1 ARG2)
          (values (- (- ARG0 ARG0) (* (* ARG0 ARG1) (% ARG2 (%
          ARG2 ARG2))))))
       (values (- (+ (- (ADF0 L1 W1 H1) (ADF0 W0 H0 L0)) L0)
                   (+ (- H1 H1) (- (% L0 L0) H1)))))).
```

The definition of ADF0 for this individual is equivalent to

$$-Arg_0 Arg_1 Arg_2$$

and is the *negative volume* of a box of dimensions ARG0, ARG1, and ARG2.

The result-producing branch for the best of generation 6 is equivalent to

$$W_0 H_0 L_0 - L_1 W_1 H_1 + L_0 - 1 + H_1.$$

As it happens, the standardized fitness of the best of generation 7 is also 96; however, this individual scores the same value of fitness in a very different way. This 34-point individual invokes its ADF0 twice and is

```
(progn (defun ADF0 (ARG0 ARG1 ARG2)
          (values (- (- ARG1 ARG0) (* (* ARG0 ARG1) (% ARG2 (%
          ARG2 ARG2))))))
       (values (- (+ (- (ADF0 L1 W1 H1) (ADF0 W0 H0 L0)) L0)
                   (+ (- H1 H1) (- (% L0 L0) H1))))))).
```

The function definition for this ADF0 for this individual from generation 7 is equivalent to

$$Arg_1 - Arg_0 - Arg_0 Arg_1 \frac{Arg_2}{\left(\dfrac{Arg_2}{Arg_2}\right)} = Arg_1 - Arg_0 - Arg_0 Arg_1 Arg_2$$

The result-producing branch for the best of generation 7 is equivalent to

$$W_1 - L_1 - \frac{L_1 W_1}{H_1} - H_0 - W_0 - \frac{W_0 H_0}{L_0} + L_0 - 1 + H_1.$$

In contrast to ADF0 from the best of generation 6 (which was an interpretable formula for negative volume), this ADF0 from the best of generation 7 is a complex expression that has no obvious interpretation in the context of the problem. Nonetheless, this ADF0, along with this result-producing branch, is just as good as the easier-to-understand, equally-fit program from generation 6.

The trajectory of programs produced in the successive generations of a run of genetic programming (viewed, say, from the perspective provided by the best-of-generation programs) is considerably different from the trajectory of versions of programs that a human programmer would produce in the process of creating and debugging a program.

The best-of-generation programs from generations 6 and 7 are both typical, in their own ways, of the intermediate results that are usually produced by genetic programming. Both of these two intermediate results are approximately correct. The first two of the five terms of the best of generation 6, in fact, represent an algebraically correct solution to the problem, while the last three terms are extraneous and erroneous. The program from generation 7 is typical of the opaque programs often evolved by genetic programming.

Genetically produced intermediate results from successive generations are often closer and closer approximations to the 100%-correct solution to the problem. They generally exhibit better and better fitness when measured in terms of the fitness measure being used on the problem.

An improved program in a later generation of genetic programming is not the consequence of the application of any logically sound or mathematically valid rules of inference to any program from an earlier generation. Similarly, a later program is not the result of an intellectual diagnosis of the deficiencies or bugs in a previous program. None of the intermediate expressions produced by genetic programming would probably ever appear in a debugging sequence created by a human programmer. An intermediate version of a program produced by a human programmer is typically syntactically close to the immediately preceding version (perhaps just a few keystrokes away). Moreover, intermediate versions typically are syntactically close to the correct answer. However, successive versions of a program produced by a human programmer are typically very distant when measured in terms of a fitness measure based on the sum of the absolute errors between the results produced by the program and the correct answer. For example, a typical intermediate version of a program in a debugging sequence produced by a human programmer might have an erroneous plus sign (instead of a minus sign) or an incorrect reference to some incorrect variable, such as H1 (instead of W1).

In generation 13, the best-of-generation individual has 24 points, has a standardized fitness of 0.0, and scores 10 (out of 10) hits. This 100%-correct individual is

```
(progn (defun ADF0 (ARG0 ARG1 ARG2)
          (values (- (* ARG2 ARG0) (* (+ ARG0 (* ARG0 ARG1)) (%
           ARG2 (% ARG2 ARG2)))))) 
       (values (- (ADF0 L1 W1 H1) (ADF0 W0 H0 L0)))))).
```

The 15-point ADF0 in this program contains one subtraction, one addition, three multiplications, and two divisions and eight terminals. It can be simplified to

$$-Arg_0 Arg_1 Arg_2.$$

In other words, ADF0 is a calculation of the negative volume of the box of dimensions ARG0, ARG1, and ARG2. The result-producing branch then invokes this useful calculation twice and does a subtraction (in what a human programmer would consider to be "reverse" order) to produce a 100%-correct solution to the problem.

An examination of ADF0 for this best-of-run program from generation 13 shows that it is the same as ADF0 of the best of generation 6.

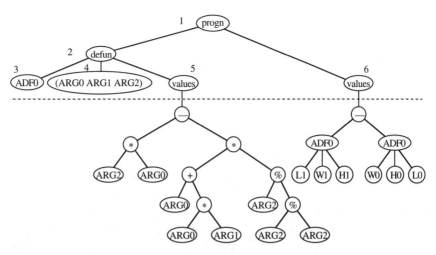

Figure 4.13 100%-correct best-of-run program from generation 13 for the two-boxes problem with ADFs.

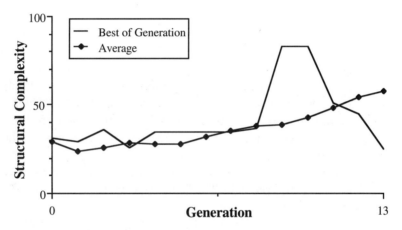

Figure 4.14 Structural complexity curves for the two-boxes problem with ADFs.

Figure 4.13 shows the 100%-correct best-of-run individual from generation 13 of this run with automatically defined functions as a rooted, point-labeled tree with ordered branches. The function-defining branch is on the left of this figure and the result-producing branch is on the right. The six points of types 1 through 6 above the horizontal dotted line are invariant. The body of the function-defining branch appears beneath the `values` of the function-defining branch (point 5). All of the 15 points in the body of the function-defining branch are of type 7. The body of the result-producing branch appears beneath the `values` of the result-producing branch (point 6). All of the nine points of the body result-producing branch are of type 8.

Structural complexity measures the size of a program. The *structural complexity* of a program is a count of the number of times that the functions from the function set and the terminals from the terminal set appear in a program.

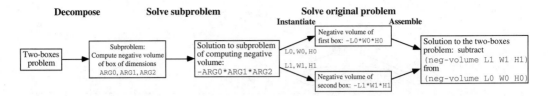

Figure 4.15 Three-step top-down hierarchical approach applied to the two-boxes problem in which there is a general mechanism for computing the negative volume of a box.

This count excludes invariant points (such as the points of types 1–6 in figures 4.6, 4.12, and 4.13 that are above the dotted line). There are 24 points in the 100%-correct best-of-run program from generation 13 shown in figure 4.13. The smaller the size of a program, the more parsimonious it is.

Figure 4.14 shows the *structural complexity curves* for this run of the two-boxes problem with automatically defined functions. The figure shows, by generation, the structural complexity in the best-of-generation program and the average of the values of structural complexity for all the programs in the population.

The above 100%-correct solution evolved with automatically defined functions can be interpreted in the light of the three-step problem-solving process. Genetic programming decomposed the overall problem into the simpler subproblem of computing negative volume. Genetic programming then solved the problem of computing negative volume (in ADF0). Finally, genetic programming solved the overall problem in the result-producing branch by using subtraction to assemble the two negative volumes into the difference of the two volumes.

Figure 4.15 shows the application of the three-step top-down hierarchical process to this problem. The first step is labeled "decompose" and produces the subproblem of finding the negative volume of a box of dimensions ARG0, ARG1, and ARG2. The second step is labeled "solve subproblem" and yields a general mechanism for finding the negative volume (taking the negative of the product of ARG0, ARG1, and ARG2). When this general mechanism is instantiated with the actual variables, L0, W0, and H0, of the first box (shown with the labeled arrow), it produces the negative volume of the first box. Similarly, when it is instantiated with the actual variables, L1, W1, and H1, for the second box, it produces the negative volume of the second box. The third step is labeled "solve original problem" and solves the overall problem by invoking the general mechanism for finding the negative volume twice and by assembling (using subtraction) the negative volume of the second box and the negative volume of the first box.

The above solution to the two-boxes problem illustrates three of the five ways in which the hierarchical problem-solving approach can be beneficial: hierarchical decomposition, parameterized reuse, and abstraction.

First, hierarchical decomposition is manifested by the fact that the overall program for solving the problem consists of a subroutine for computing the negative volume and a result-producing branch.

Second, the two occasions on which the subroutine ADF0 is invoked with different instantiations of values for its three dummy variables illustrate parameterized reuse of the solution to the subproblem of computing the negative volume. The function ADF0 is a general way of determining negative volume and may be reused on *any* combination of values or expressions. Generalization occurs whenever parameterized reuse occurs.

Third, each occasion when ADF0 is invoked with three particular actual variables of the problem by the result-producing branch, abstraction is occurring. The exclusion of information that is irrelevant to solving the subproblem currently under consideration is an important aspect of the process of decomposing an overall problem into subproblems. During the time that the subroutine ADF0 is computing the negative volume of the first box with the dimensions of the first box using L0, W0, and H0, the three other actual variables of the problem, L1, W1, and H1, are momentarily irrelevant. The subroutine identifies a subset of the information available from the overall problem environment as being relevant to the solution of the subproblem and excludes all the remaining available information. There are an infinite number of combinations of the three momentarily irrelevant dimensions, L1, W1, and H1, of the second box, but none of them is relevant to the computation of the negative volume of the first box. The problem of computing the negative volume of the first box is a problem within a three-dimensional subproblem subspace of the overall six-dimensional space of the overall problem. The three-dimensional problem of computing the negative volume of the first box is abstracted from the overall six-dimensional problem environment. When the time comes to compute the negative volume of the second box, the three-dimensional problem of computing the negative volume of the second box is similarly abstracted from the overall problem environment.

As previously mentioned, the hierarchical three-step problem-solving process can also be described in a bottom-up way. First, one seeks to discover useful regularities and patterns at the lowest level of the problem environment. Second, one changes the representation of the problem so that the problem becomes restated in terms of the regularities of the problem environment. This change of representation creates a new problem. Third, one tries to discover a solution to the presumably-simpler new problem (Rendell and Seshu 1990; Ioerger, Rendell, and Subramaniam 1993; Ragavan and Rendell 1993).

In this run of the two-boxes problem, the concept of negative volume is a regularity in the problem environment. Once one recognizes negative volume as a useful regularity for this problem, one changes the representation of the problem so as to create a new problem. The bottom-up interpretation of this run is that genetic programming discovered the regularity in the low level representation of the problem (i.e., that a negative volume appeared twice). Genetic programming then recoded (in ADF0) the problem in terms of the discovered regularity into a new problem at a higher level (namely, a problem involving negative volumes). That is, the representation was changed from a problem involving six linear dimensions into a problem involving two negative volumetric quantities. Third, genetic programming solved (in

Table 4.4 A change of representation recodes the length, width, and height of each box into its negative volume.

Fitness case	Negative volume of first box	Negative volume of second box	D
1	−84	−30	54
2	−630	−30	600
3	−360	−48	312
4	−135	−24	111
5	−24	−42	−18
6	−9	−180	−171
7	−405	−42	363
8	−18	−54	−36
9	−96	−120	−24
10	−80	−35	45

the result-producing branch) the problem when restated in the terms of the new representation (i.e., it discovered a subtraction in reverse order).

Table 4.4 is a 10-by-4 table obtained from the original 10-by-8 table 4.1. The 10 combinations of the original six independent variables (L_0, W_0, H_0, L_1, W_1, and H_1) have been recoded using ADF0 so that the second column of this table now contains the negative volume of the first box and the third column contains the negative volume of the second box. Specifically, the three independent variables associated with the first box ($L_0 = 3$, $W_0 = 4$, and $H_0 = 7$) have been restated as the negative volume of the first box (i.e., −84). Similarly, the change of representation has recoded the three independent variables associated with the second box ($L_1 = 2$, $W_1 = 5$, and $H_1 = 3$) as −30. The fourth column contains the value of the dependent variable, D, associated with each row of the table. These values are unchanged from the original table 4.1. For example, 54 is the value of the dependent variable, D, associated with the values (−84 and −30) of the two new independent variables in the first row of this table. The result of this change of representation is a new problem, namely a problem of symbolic regression involving eight (not six) independent variables and one dependent variable. The original six independent variables of the problem shown in Table 4.1 are, for simplicity, not shown in Table 4.4. The new problem still has 10 fitness cases.

In practice, it may be easier to solve a problem of symbolic regression involving eight independent variables than the original one with six independent variables. As it happens in this particular case, unbeknownst to genetic programming, this change of representation converts a six-dimensional nonlinear problem to a problem of conventional linear regression (a mere subtraction).

Of course, not all changes of representations are useful. A recoding based on the products of the three factors is useful for the two-boxes problem, but a recoding based on the raising one number to a power equal to the product of two other numbers would not be beneficial in facilitating the solution of this problem. Such a recoding would hopelessly encrypt the relatively simple relationship existing among the variables of this problem. The problem would be much more difficult to solve after such a change of representation.

Although we can interpret what genetic programming does as a realization of the three-step hierarchical problem-solving process, none of the three steps (either in the top-down or bottom-up form) appear as steps of genetic programming. There is no explicit decomposition of the original problem into subproblems; there is no separate and explicit solution of subproblems; and there is no explicit assembly of solutions to subproblems into a solution of the overall problem. Similarly, there is no explicit search or discovery of regularities or patterns; there is no separate and explicit recoding or changing of the representation; and there is no separate and explicit solution of any new problem in the terms of any new, higher level representation.

This example of the successful operation of genetic programming with automatically defined functions is the first of numerous successful examples in this book that provide evidence supporting main point 1:

Main point 1: Automatically defined functions enable genetic programming to solve a variety of problems in a way that can be interpreted as a decomposition of a problem into subproblems, a solving of the subproblems, and an assembly of the solutions to the subproblems into a solution to the overall problem (or which can alternatively be interpreted as a search for regularities in the problem environment, a change of representation, and a solving of a higher level problem).

Of course, it is unlikely that a human programmer would ever write a subroutine for negative volume and a main program that performed the subtraction in what most human programmers would regard as "reverse" order. However, it is important to remember that genetic programming does not produce computer programs in the style of a human programmer. Genetic programming is driven by its fitness measure, and not by the *post hoc* considerations that humans think of after they see the solution produced by genetic programming. The calculation of negative volume and the reverse subtraction are every bit as fit as a calculation of positive volume and subtraction in the more familiar order.

Since genetic programming is a probabilistic process, the result (i.e., the best-of-run program) produced by genetic programming is almost always different from one run to the next (although each result may be equally good in terms of solving the problem).

The following additional four runs of this problem illustrate the above points.

In a second run with automatically defined functions, the following 100%-correct program emerged in generation 13 of that run:

```
(progn (defun ADF0 (ARG0 ARG1 ARG2)
            (values (- (- (% ARG0 ARG0) (* ARG1 ARG0))
                    (+ (% (* ARG2 ARG1) (+ ARG1 ARG0))
                        (- (% ARG1 ARG2) (- ARG0 ARG0)))))))
```

```
(values (+ (* W1 (- (* W0 H0) (* L1 H1)))
          (ADF0 (- W1 L0) (* H0 W0) (- W0 W0)))))).
```

Here the defined function is equivalent to

$$\frac{Arg_0}{Arg_0} - Arg_1 Arg_0 - \frac{Arg_2 Arg_1}{Arg_1 + Arg_0} - \frac{Arg_1}{Arg_2} + Arg_0 - Arg_0$$

$$= 1 - Arg_1 Arg_0 - \frac{Arg_2 Arg_1}{Arg_1 + Arg_0} - \frac{Arg_1}{Arg_2}.$$

If the reader thought that the computation of negative volume was odd, the defined function found in this 100%-correct solution to the problem is positively bizarre.

The result-producing branch then calls this defined function with arguments of (- W1 L0), (* H0 W0), and (- W0 W0). Since the third argument (- W0 W0) is equivalent to zero and division by zero (using the protected division function %) equals 1, the result-producing branch is equivalent to

$$W_1(W_0 H_0 - L_1 H_1) + 1 - H_0 W_0 (W_1 - L_0) - 1$$

$$= W_1 W_0 H_0 - H_1 W_1 L_1 + 1 - W_1 W_0 H_0 - H_0 W_0 L_0 - 1$$

$$= -H_1 W_1 L_1 + 1 - H_0 W_0 L_0 - 1$$

$$= H_0 W_0 L_0 - H_1 W_1 L_1.$$

Genetic programming decomposed the original problem (which can be solved, as already shown, by a relatively simple difference between two products) into the unexpected subproblem of computing

$$1 - Arg_1 Arg_0 - \frac{Arg_2 Arg_1}{Arg_1 + Arg_0} - \frac{Arg_1}{Arg_2}.$$

It then assembled the solution to this subproblem into a 100% correct solution to the overall problem. Although this decomposition seems bizarre, it is just as good as the somewhat more straightforward solution involving negative volume, when measured in terms of the fitness measure governing this problem (i.e., finding a good fit to the data in table 4.1).

In viewing this 100%-correct solution to the problem, one is reminded of John Kendrew's reaction (1958) as the first human to see the three-dimensional structure of a protein:

"Perhaps the most remarkable features of the molecule are its complexity and lack of symmetry. The arrangement seems to be almost totally lacking in the kind of regularities which one instinctively anticipates, and it is more complicated than has been predicted by any theory of protein structure."

This example, along with numerous examples that will appear later in this book, provide evidence to support main point 2:

Main point 2: Automatically defined functions discover and exploit the regularities, symmetries, homogeneities, similarities, patterns, and modularities of the problem environment in ways that are very different from the style employed by human programmers.

In a third run with automatically defined functions, the following 100%-correct program emerged in generation 14:

```
(progn (defun ADF0 (ARG0 ARG1 ARG2)
           (values (+ (- (+ ARG1 ARG0) (+ ARG1 ARG0))
                      (* ARG0 ARG2))))
       (values (- (ADF0 L0 L1 (* W0 H0))
                  (ADF0 H1 H1 (ADF0 L1 W0 W1))))))).
```

Although ADF0's second (middle) argument, ARG1, appears twice in ADF0, it plays no role in the value returned by ADF0. Instead, ADF0 is equivalent to the positive area of the rectangle whose sides are ARG0 and ARG2, namely

$Arg_0 Arg_2$.

One invocation of ADF0 is equivalent to the product `(* L0 (* W0 H0))`. Another invocation of ADF0 produces the product `(* H1 (ADF0 L1 W0 W1))`, which is equivalent to `(* H1 L1 W1)`. The 100%-correct solution is obtained in the result-producing branch by using the calculation for area in the following way:

$$L_0(W_0 H_0) - H_1(L_1 W_1) = L_0 W_0 H_0 - H_1 L_1 W_1.$$

It would be unlikely to occur to a human programmer to solve this problem in this indirect way. Indeed, this approach is especially unlikely since the calculation of the area of a rectangle is merely ordinary two-argument multiplication, which is already available as one of the primitive functions in the result-producing branch. Human programmers do not usually write subroutines that duplicate the functionality of already-available primitive operations. However, genetic programming sometimes uses automatically defined functions to recreate already-available primitive functions.

In a fourth run, the three-argument automatically defined function of the 100%-correct program that emerged in generation 22 merely returns its second argument, ARG1, to the result-producing branch (i.e., ADF0 is a projection). The result-producing branch then uses this ADF0 to yield one of the terminals, W0, already available in the terminal set of the problem.

```
(progn (defun ADF0 (ARG0 ARG1 ARG2)
           (values ARG1)
       (values (+ (- W0 (ADF0 (% H1 H1) W0 (* L1 H1)))
                  (- (* L0 (* W0 H0)) (* W1 (* L1 H1)))))))).
```

Although human programmers do not usually call a subroutine from a main program for the sole purpose of returning a variable that is already available in the main program, this solution is just as fit as its predecessor.

In a fifth run, the 100%-correct program shown below emerged in generation 23. In this program the result-producing branch ignores the elaborate function defined in its function-defining branch and simply solves the problem at hand without using its automatically defined function.

```
(progn (defun ADF0 (ARG0 ARG1 ARG2)
          (values (* (- ARG1 ARG2) (+ (% ARG2 ARG0) (* (+ (% (*
            ARG1 ARG1) (+ (+ ARG2 ARG1) ARG1)) (- (- (% ARG2
            ARG2) (% (* ARG2 ARG0) (+ ARG2 ARG1))) (* ARG2
            ARG1))) (+ (- ARG1 ARG0) (% (+ ARG2 ARG1) ARG1))))))))
      (values (+ (+ (* (- (% H0 (% L1 L0)) W1) (* H1 L1))
                 (- L0 L0)) (* (- W0 H1) (* L0 H0)))))).
```

The availability of an automatically defined function imposes no obligation on the result-producing branch to call it.

Other genetically evolved programs solved this problem using negative area and some even solved this problem by using the available subroutine to define ordinary positive volume.

In summary, the automatically defined function ADF0 created by genetic programming can be volume, negative volume, area, negative area, or an entirely obscure function that has no simple explanation in terms of the problem domain. We did not predetermine which of these concepts would be used for the purpose of decomposing and solving the problem. Similarly, we did not predetermine whether the automatically defined function would be referenced once, twice, many times, or not at all. The functionality of the automatically defined function as well as the role, if any, assigned to it by the result-producing branch are both subject to the evolutionary process. Neither the function-defining branch nor the result-producing branch is necessarily elegant, orderly, parsimonious, predictable, or susceptible to any simple interpretation.

4.10 COMPARISON OF THE STRUCTURAL COMPLEXITY OF THE SOLUTIONS

In the foregoing sections, we looked at only selected illustrative runs of genetic programming with and without automatically defined functions. In the next two sections, we study a series of runs in order to obtain statistics for comparing results with and without automatically defined functions. We first consider the structural complexity (size) of the best-of-run programs from the successful runs within a series of runs.

We made a series of 33 runs of the two-boxes problem without automatically defined functions and 93 runs with them.

A run is considered to be a *successful run* if at least one program in the population satisfies the success predicate of the problem by generation G. If a best-of-run program satisfying the success predicate is 100%-correct, we call it a *solution*; otherwise, we refer to a best-of-run program satisfying the success predicate as a *satisfactory result*.

Nine of the 33 runs (27%) without automatically defined functions and 15 of the 93 runs (16%) with automatically defined functions were successful runs by generation 50.

The *average structural complexity*, $\bar{S}$, of a specified set of programs is the average of the values of structural complexity for each program in the set.

When the specified set is the population as a whole, $\overline{S}$ is the average of the values of structural complexity for all the programs in the population. However, $\overline{S}$ most frequently appears in this book for the small set of best-of-run programs that actually satisfy the success predicate of the problem over a series of runs. Specifically, $\overline{S}_{without}$ is the average structural complexity of the best-of-run programs that satisfy the success predicate of the problem from a series of a runs without automatically defined functions. $\overline{S}_{with}$ is similarly defined for runs with automatically defined functions. Note that $\overline{S}_{without}$ and $\overline{S}_{with}$ are each based on at most one program from each run.

The average structural complexity, $\overline{S}_{without}$, of the best-of-run programs from the nine successful runs without automatically defined functions is 17.8 points. The average structural complexity, $\overline{S}_{with}$, of the best-of-run programs from the 15 successful runs with automatically defined functions is 33.5 points.

The *structural complexity ratio*, R_S, of a problem is the ratio of $\overline{S}_{without}$ to $\overline{S}_{with}$. For this problem,

$$R_s = \frac{\text{Structural complexity without ADFs}}{\text{Structural complexity with ADFs}} = \frac{\overline{S}_{without}}{\overline{S}_{with}} = \frac{17.8}{33.5} = 0.53.$$

Since the structural complexity ratio, R_S, is less than 1 for the two-boxes problem, the best-of-run programs from the successful runs with automatically defined functions are bigger (less parsimonious) than the best-of-run programs from the successful runs without automatically defined function. That is, for this particular problem, automatically defined functions are not advantageous in terms of average structural complexity.

4.11   COMPARISON OF COMPUTATIONAL EFFORT

This section describes one way of measuring the computational effort, E, required to yield a solution (or satisfactory result) to a problem with a satisfactorily high probability.

We obtain E empirically from a series of runs. Each run is made using a particular fixed population size, M, and a particular fixed maximum number of generations, G.

The number of fitness evaluations that must be executed to yield a solution (or satisfactory result) to a problem is a reasonable measure of computational burden in an adaptive algorithm. Every adaptive algorithm starts with one or more points in the search space of the problem and then iteratively performs the following two steps: measuring the fitness of the current point(s) and using the information about fitness to create new point(s) in the search space. Fitness evaluations are common to all adaptive algorithms (probabilistic or deterministic alike), including genetic algorithms, hillclimbing, neural nets, simulated annealing, genetic classifier systems, and genetic programming. This is the case regardless of what algorithm-specific or problem-specific name may be used for fitness (e.g., payoff, goodness, benefit, score, profit, cost, utility, and error). Fitness evaluations consume a significant fraction (often an overwhelming fraction) of the computer resources required for nontrivial problems. Even if the creating of new points is also computationally intensive for a particular algorithm, there is one fitness evaluation associated with each such step of creation, so the number of fitness evaluations is still a reasonable common measure.

If every run of genetic programming were successful in yielding a solution (or satisfactory result), the number of fitness evaluations required to yield a solution (or satisfactory result) would be easy to measure. If success occurs on the same generation of every run, the number of fitness evaluations would merely be the product of the population size, M, and the number of generations that are run (assuming that exactly M operations are executed on each generation). If success occurs on different generations in different runs (but is guaranteed to occur), the number of fitness evaluations would be the product of the population size, M, and the average number of generations that are run.

Since genetic programming is a probabilistic algorithm, not all runs are successful at yielding a solution to the problem by generation G.

When a particular run of genetic programming is not successful after running the prespecified maximum number of generations, G, there is no way to know whether or when the run would ever be successful. When a successful outcome cannot be guaranteed for every run, there is no knowable value for the number of generations that will yield a solution (or satisfactory result) and the simple calculation described above cannot be used. Consequently, a probabilistic calculation is required in order to compute the number of fitness evaluations required to yield a solution (or satisfactory result) to a problem.

We can empirically observe the probability, $Y(M,i)$, that a run yields, for the first time, at least one program in the population satisfying the success predicate of the problem *on* generation i.

Once we have obtained this estimate of the *instantaneous probability of success* $Y(M,i)$ for each generation i, we can compute an estimate of the *cumulative probability of success*, $P(M,i)$, that a particular run with a population size, M, yields a solution *by* generation i. The cumulative probability, $P(M,i)$, is, of course, a monotonically increasing function of the generation i. If every run in the series yields a program satisfying the success predicate by generation G, $P(M,G)$, will be 1.0. In practice, $P(M,G)$ will often fall short of 1.00.

The probability of satisfying the success predicate by generation i at least once in R independent runs is $1-[1-P(M,i)]^R$. If we want to satisfy the success predicate with a certain specified probability z, then it must be that

$$z = 1-[1-P(M,i)]^R.$$

Throughout this book, $z = 99\%$. As can be seen, the number of independent runs, R, required to satisfy the success predicate by generation i with a satisfactorily high probability of $z = 99\%$, depends on both z and $P(M,i)$. After taking logarithms, we find

$$R = R(M,i,z) = \left\lceil \frac{\log(1-z)}{\log(1-P(M,i))} \right\rceil,$$

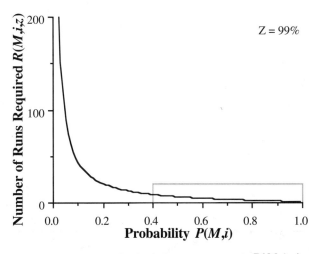

Figure 4.16 Number of independent runs required, $R(M, i, z)$, as a function of the cumulative probability of success $P(M, i)$ for $z = 99\%$.

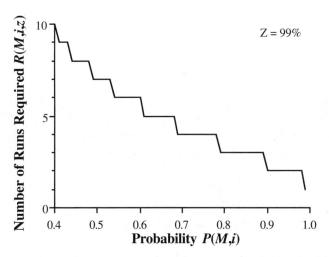

Figure 4.17 The portion of the $R(M, i, z)$ curve for which $P(M, i) > 0.4$ shows the granular nature of the function.

Without Defined Functions

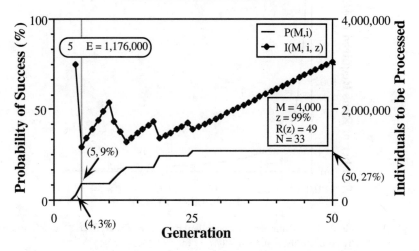

Figure 4.18 Performance curves for the two-boxes problem showing that it is sufficient to process 1,176,000 individuals to yield a satisfactory result for this problem with 99% probability and that $E_{without} = 1,176,000$ without ADFs.

where the brackets indicate the *ceiling function* for rounding up to the next highest integer.

Figure 4.16 shows a graph of the number of independent runs, $R(M,i,z)$, required to yield at least one successful run with probability $z = 99\%$ as a function of the cumulative probability of success, $P(M,i)$. The higher the probability of success, the fewer independent runs are required to yield at least one successful run. For example, if the cumulative probability of success, $P(M,i)$, is a mere 0.09, then 48 independent runs are required to yield a successful run with a 99% probability.

The $R(M,i,z)$ function has a step-like nature that is caused by the ceiling function.

Figure 4.17 spotlights the step-like nature of the $R(M,i,z)$ function by showing only the boxed portion of figure 4.16 where $P(M,i) > 0.4$. If $P(M,i)$ is 0.68, only four independent runs are required; if $P(M,i)$ is 0.78, then only three runs are required; and if $P(M,i)$ is 0.90, only two runs are required. Of course, if $P(M,i)$ is 0.99, only one run is required. Because the values of $P(M,i)$ are estimates obtained from empirically observed values of $Y(M,i)$, the value $R(M,i,z)$ is also an estimate.

Figure 4.18 presents two related curves, called the *performance curves*, for the two-boxes problem without automatically defined functions. The curves are based on 33 independent runs, each with a population size, M, of 4,000 and a maximum number of generations to be run, G, of 51 (i.e., generation 0 through generation 50). A total of 79 performance curves will appear in this book, so we now explain in detail the standard form of these curves.

The rising curve in figure 4.18 shows, by generation, the experimentally observed cumulative probability of success, $P(M,i)$, of solving the problem by generation i. This curve shows that the cumulative probability of success is 0.0% for generation 0 over these 33 runs. That is, this blind random search of 132,000 points (4,000 × 33 runs) of program space did not unearth a satisfactory result for the problem. The rising curve also shows that the cumulative probability of success stays at 0.0% for generations 1 through 3, and then rises to 3% for generation 4, 9% for generations 5 through 10, 12% for generation 11, 15% for generation 12, 18% for generations 13 through 18, 24% for generations 19 through 24, and reaches 27% for generations 25 through 50.

The second curve (made with lozenges) in figure 4.18 shows, by generation, the total number of *individuals that must be processed*, $I(M,i,z)$, in order to yield a solution (or satisfactory result) for the problem with $z = 99\%$ probability for a population size, M, by generation i. Specifically,

$$I(M,i,z) = M(i+1)R(z).$$

The *computational effort*, E, required to yield a solution (or satisfactory result) for the problem with a stated probability z is the minimal value of $I(M,i,z)$, over all the generations i between 0 and G. The first generation at which $I(M,i,z)$, attains this minimum value is called the *best generation*, $i*$. Thus, the computational effort is

$$E = I(M,i^*,z) = M(i^* + 1)R(z).$$

Note that this retrospective and empirical method of measuring computational effort, E, depends on the particular choices of values for M and G and all the other quantitative and qualitative parameters that control a run of genetic programming. The value of E thus obtained is not necessarily the minimum computational effort possible effort *for the problem*.

The second curve in figure 4.18 shows, for example, that $I(M,i,z)$ is undefined for generations 0 through 3 because the observed probability of success, $P(M,i)$, is zero for these early generations and hence the required number of runs, $R(M,i,z)$, is infinite. Of course, if we did an extremely large number of independent runs, we would find that the probability of success at generation 0 is, in fact, some small nonzero value. This nonzero probability is the probability of solving the problem by means of blind random search in program space. $I(M,0,z)$ could then be computed from this probability and would, of course, be colossal for any nontrivial problem.

For generation 4 the probability of success, $P(M,i)$, has the nonzero value of 3%. Consequently, $R(M,i,z)$ is 150. If this problem is run through to generation 4 and then abandoned (i.e., a total of 5 generations from generation 0 through to generation 4), processing a total of 3,000,000 individuals (i.e., 4,000 × 5 generations × 150 runs) is sufficient to yield a solution (or satisfactory result) for this problem with 99% probability. That is, $I(M,4,z)$ is 3,000,000.

For generation 5 where the probability of success is 9%, $R(M,i,z)$ is 49. If this problem is run through to generation 5 and then abandoned, processing a total of 1,176,000 individuals (i.e., 4,000 × 6 generations × 49 runs) is sufficient to yield a solution (or satisfactory result) for this problem with 99% probability. In other words, $I(M,5,z)$ is 1,176,000.

With Defined Functions

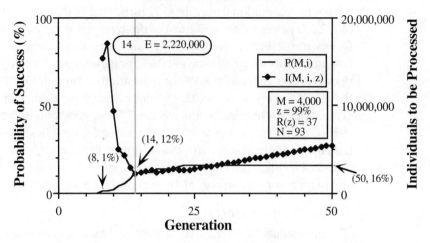

Figure 4.19 Performance curves for the two-boxes problem showing that E_{with} = 2,220,000 with ADFs.

For generations 6 through 10 the observed probability of success, $P(M,i)$, remains constant at 9% for this particular series of observations. As a result, $R(M,i,z)$ remains constant at 49 for generations 6 through 10. Therefore, more than $I(M,5,z)$ = 1,176,000 individuals must be processed to yield a solution (or satisfactory result) for this problem with 99% probability for generations 6, 7, 8, 9, and 10 because the product of 4,000 and 49 is being multiplied by the progressively larger values 7, 8, 9, 10, and 11, respectively. For generation 6, $I(M,6,z)$ is 1,372,000 (i.e., 4,000 × 7 generations × 49 runs). By generation 10, $I(M,10,z)$ reaches a value of 2,156,000 (i.e., 4,000 × 11 generations × 49 runs). When the observed $P(M,i)$, and consequently $R(M,i,z)$, remains constant over several generations, the plot of $I(M,i,z)$ resembles the rising edge of a sawtooth for those generations. As a result, the value of $I(M,5,z)$ = 1,176,000 attained at generation 5 continues to maintain its position as the current global minimum for $I(M,i,z)$ up to generation 10. The sawtooth is, of course, an artifact of the empirically observed values of $Y(M,i)$.

For generation 11 the observed probability of success, $P(M,i)$, rises 12% and $R(M,i,z)$ drops to 36. If this problem is run through to generation 11 and then abandoned, processing a total of 1,728,000 individuals (i.e., 4,000 × 12 generations × 36 runs) is sufficient to yield a solution (or satisfactory result) for this problem with 99% probability. This value of $I(M,11,z)$ of 1,728,000 for generation 11 is less than the value of $I(M,10,z)$ of 2,156,000 for generation 10, so we see a falling edge to the sawtooth that started to rise at generation 5. However, 1,728,000 is more than 1,176,000, so the value of 1,176,000 for $I(M,i,z)$ attained at generation 5 maintains its position as the global minimum for $I(M,i,z)$ up to generation 11.

As can be seen in figure 4.18, the value of 1,176,000 for $I(M,i,z)$ attained at generation 5 continues to maintain its position as the global minimum for $I(M,i,z)$ up to generation 50. Because each successive tooth of the sawtooth starts at a higher point, generation 5 is almost certainly the global minimum for $I(M,i,z)$ for all i. Consequently, the best generation, $i*$, is 5 and the computational effort without automatically defined functions, $E_{without}$, is 1,176,000 for this problem. The numbers 5 and 1,176,000 are placed in the oval in the figure to indicate this fact. A thin gray vertical line is used in the figure to highlight the fact that generation 5 is the best generation. The value of $R(M,i,z)$ for the best generation $i*$ is called $R(z)$.

This minimal value of $I(M,i,z)$ of 1,176,000 is a measure of the computational effort without automatically defined functions, $E_{without}$, necessary to yield a solution (or satisfactory result) for this problem with 99% probability. If we were required to solve this problem, were committed to a population size, M, of 4,000, and knew in advance that the global minimum of $I(M,i,z)$ occurs at generation 5, then the least expected number of fitness evaluations would be expended in solving this problem by making a series of independent runs and abandoning each such run at generation 5.

Three points on each rising cumulative probability curve are highlighted in figure 4.18. First, the value of cumulative probability is noted at the first generation for which the cumulative probability first becomes nonzero. For this figure, this occurs at generation 4, where the probability is 3%. Second, the cumulative probability is noted at generation $i*$ (the generation number highlighted in the oval). The cumulative probability is 9% for generation 5 for figure 4.18. Third, the value of the cumulative probability is noted at the final generation (generation 50). The cumulative probability is 27% for generation 50 for this figure.

The rectangular legend in figure 4.18 containing four items recites the fact that the population size, M, is 4,000, that the probability z is 99%, that the number of runs, $R(z)$, required to yield a solution (or satisfactory result) for this problem at 99% probability is 49, for the best generation $i*$ and that the curves in this figure are based on $N = 33$ independent runs.

Figure 4.19 shows the performance curves for the two-boxes problem with automatically defined functions. The population size, M, of 4,000 is the same as for the previous figure and $z = 99\%$. This figure is based on $N = 93$ runs. The cumulative probability of success is 16% at generation 50 (thus yielding 15 satisfactory results out of the 93 runs). The cumulative probability of success is 12% at generation 14, so $R(z) = 37$. The numbers 14 and 2,220,000 in the oval indicate that, if this problem is run through to generation 14, processing a total of $E_{with} = 2,220,000$ individuals (i.e., $4,000 \times 15$ generations $\times 37$ runs) is sufficient to yield a satisfactory result for this problem with 99% probability.

The *efficiency ratio*, R_E, is the ratio of the computational effort, $E_{without}$, without automatically defined functions to the computational effort, E_{with}, with automatically defined functions. For this problem,

$$R_E = \frac{\text{Effort without ADFs}}{\text{Effort with ADFs}} = \frac{E_{without}}{E_{with}} = \frac{1,176,000}{2,220,000} = 0.53.$$

Since the efficiency ratio is less than 1 for this problem, the runs using automatically defined functions require more computational effort than the runs

Table 4.5 Comparison table for the two-boxes problem.

	Without Automatically defined functions	With Automatically defined functions
Average structural complexity $\overline{S}$	17.8	33.5
Computational effort E	1,176,000	2,220,000

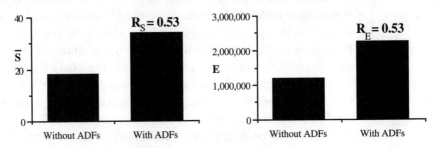

Figure 4.20 Summary graphs for the two-boxes problem.

without automatically defined functions. That is, automatically defined functions are not advantageous in terms of the computational effort required to solve this particular problem.

The advantages and disadvantages of the method described above for measuring computational effort, E, and the characteristics of an alternative measure based on wallclock time are discussed in sections 8.16, 9.14, and 10.2.

4.12 SUMMARY

Table 4.5 compares the average structural complexities, $\overline{S}_{without}$ and $\overline{S}_{with}$, and the computational efforts, $E_{without}$ and E_{with}, for the two-boxes problem with and without automatically defined functions. This table is called the *comparison table* for the problem. A total of 27 comparison tables similar to this table will appear throughout this book.

The information in the comparison table can be summarized in terms of the structural complexity ratio, R_S, and the efficiency ratio, R_E, for the problem. As it happens, both ratios are 0.53 for the two-boxes problem.

Figure 4.20 shows this information and these two ratios as a pair of bar graphs. A total of 26 *summary graphs* similar to this figure will appear throughout this book.

As can be seen from the summary graphs, automatically defined functions yielded neither a more parsimonious result nor a reduction in the computational effort required for the two-boxes problem.

One might not expect that it would be possible to simultaneously breed both a function definition and a calling program dynamically during a run in order to solve a problem. However, genetic programming with automatically defined functions is capable of solving the two-boxes problem. Nonetheless, it is disappointing that the two comparative ratios of average structural complexity and computational effort indicate that there is no advantage to automatically defined functions for this particular problem. This disappointing conclusion apparently results from the fact that the underlying regularity in the two-boxes problem consists of only two invocations of a common calculation consisting of only two multiplications. The benefits of exploiting the regularity inherent in this problem environment do not outweigh the overhead associated with automatically defined functions. The tide will turn in the next chapter.

5   Problems that Straddle the Breakeven Point for Computational Effort

The previous chapter explained the technique of automatically defined functions and illustrated it with the two-boxes problem. This simple problem provided the opportunity to define a useful function (whether it be volume, area, negative volume, or negative area) dynamically during the run and then use it in solving the problem. Unfortunately, when we compared genetic programming with and without automatically defined functions, we were disappointed to find that genetic programming with automatically defined functions did not exhibit any advantage in the two-boxes problem in terms of the average size of the evolved solutions (or satisfactory results) or the number of fitness evaluations required to yield a solution (or satisfactory result) with 99% probability. This chapter will reach the opposite conclusion as to the number of fitness evaluations and demonstrate that automatically defined functions can reduce the computational effort required to solve a problem.

In this chapter genetic programming will be used to solve both a simpler and a scaled-up version of four problems, both with and without automatically defined functions. For each of these 16 combinations, multiple runs will be made. Sixteen performance curves will be created. When these 16 performance curves are analyzed as to the number of fitness evaluations required to yield a solution (or satisfactory result) to the problem with 99% probability, automatically defined functions will prove to be non-beneficial for the simpler versions of the four problems, but beneficial for the scaled-up versions. In other words, each of the four problems straddles an apparent *breakeven point for computational effort*. The simpler versions of the four problems do not have enough regularity, symmetry, homogeneity, and modularity in their problem environments to overcome the overhead apparently associated with automatically defined functions. Like the two-boxes problem, they are *too simple* to make automatically defined functions beneficial. In contrast, the scaled-up versions of the four problems are sufficiently difficult to benefit from automatically defined functions.

The scaling is done in four domains: the order of a polynomial, the *arity* (i.e., number of arguments) of a Boolean function, the number of harmonics of a sinusoidal function, and the frequency of reuse of the constant π in a multi-term algebraic expression.

Problem 1: The simpler version of the first problem is a symbolic regression (system identification) of a quintic polynomial $x^5 - 2x^3 + x$ involving one independent variable, x; the scaled-up version is a symbolic regression of the sextic polynomial $x^6 - 2x^4 + x^2$.

Problem 2: The simpler version is a symbolic regression of the Boolean 5-symmetry function; the scaled-up version involves the 6-symmetry function.

Problem 3: The simpler version is a symbolic regression of $\sin x + \sin 2x + \sin 3x$. One additional harmonic, $\sin 4x$, is added to this expression so that the target for the scaled-up version of this problem becomes $\sin x + \sin 2x + \sin 3x + \sin 4x$.

Problem 4: The simpler version is a symbolic regression of the two-term expression $x / \pi + x^2 / \pi^2$ in which the constant value π is used three times. One additional term, $2\pi x$, is added to this expression so that the target for the scaled-up version of this problem becomes the three-term expression $x / \pi + x^2 / \pi^2 + 2\pi x$. The modularity in this problem environment is that π is used three or four times in the two different target expressions. This problem can be efficiently solved by finding the constant value π (or some constant value related to π) that can be repeatedly invoked in the solution.

The breakeven point straddled by the four problems in this chapter is the *breakeven point for computational effort*. There appears to be another breakeven point for parsimony (inverse average structural complexity) and yet another for wallclock time. The scaled-up versions of two of the four problems in this chapter appear to be on the beneficial side of the breakeven point for average structural complexity. Starting with the next chapter, almost all of the problems in this book will be on the beneficial side of the breakeven point for average structural complexity.

5.1 SEXTIC VERSUS QUINTIC POLYNOMIAL

This section considers the problem of symbolic regression of the quintic (order 5) polynomial

$$x^5 - 2x^3 + x = x(x-1)^2(x+1)^2$$

and the scaled-up version of this problem involving the sextic (order 6) polynomial

$$x^6 - 2x^4 + x^2 = x^2(x-1)^2(x+1)^2.$$

These two target functions for symbolic regression are scaled in terms of the order of the polynomials. As can be seen from the above factorization of these two polynomials, they also differ in that the squaring function is invoked twice for the quintic polynomial and three times for the sextic. They also differ in that there are only two repeated roots for the quintic polynomial, but three for the sextic. Consequently, the sextic polynomial has a

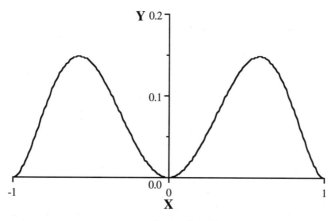

Figure 5.1 Sextic polynomial $x^6 - 2x^4 + x^2$ in the interval $[-1.0,+1.0]$.

slightly greater amount of potentially exploitable regularity and modularity than the quintic.

We consider the scaled-up version of each of the four problems first.

5.1.1 Sextic Polynomial $x^6 - 2x^4 + x^2$

Figure 5.1 graphs the values of the sextic polynomial $x^6 - 2x^4 + x^2$ in the interval $[-1, +1]$.

5.1.1.1 Preparatory Steps without ADFs

Genetic programming is capable of solving this problem of symbolic regression.

The preparatory steps for this problem are straightforward and similar to the two-boxes problem.

There is only one independent variable, x, in this problem. In addition, certain ephemeral random constants are included in the terminal set of this problem. During the creation of the individual programs in the initial random population (generation 0), whenever the *ephemeral random constant*, $\Re$, is chosen as the terminal to be located at a point of a program, a constant from a designated range is independently, separately, and randomly generated and inserted into the program at that point. The six different kinds of random constants used in this book ($\Re_{reals}$, $\Re_{bigger-reals}$, $\Re_{real-vector}$, $\Re_{v8}$, $\Re_{Boolean}$, and $\Re_{ternary}$) are defined when they are first encountered and listed in appendix A. For this problem, random floating-point constants, $\Re_{reals}$, are used. Whenever a *floating-point random constant*, $\Re_{reals}$, is chosen as the terminal to be located at a point of a program, a floating-point number between -1.000 and $+1.000$ is independently, separately, and randomly generated and inserted into the program at that point. Floating-point random constants are generated with a *granularity* of 0.001 in the sense that each of the 2,001 floating-point constants between -1.000 and $+1.000$ is equally likely to be generated.

Problems that Straddle the Break-even Point for Computational Effort

Table 5.1 Tableau without ADFs for the sextic polynomial $x^6 - 2x^4 + x^2$.

Objective:	Find a program that produces the given value of the sextic polynomial $x^6 - 2x^4 + x^2$ as its output when given the value of the one independent variable, x, as input.
Terminal set without ADFs:	X and the floating-point random constants, $\Re_{reals}$.
Function set without ADFs:	+, -, * and %.
Fitness cases:	50 random values of X from the interval [–1.0,+1.0].
Raw fitness:	The sum, over the 50 fitness cases, of the absolute value of the error between the value returned by the program and the given value of the dependent variable.
Standardized fitness:	Same as raw fitness.
Hits:	The number of fitness cases (between 0 and 50) for which the raw fitness is less than 0.01 (the hits criterion).
Wrapper:	None.
Parameters:	$M = 4,000$. $G = 51$.
Success predicate:	A program scores the maximum number of hits (i.e., 50).

Table 5.1 summarizes the key features of the problem of symbolic regression for $x^6 - 2x^4 + x^2$ without automatically defined functions.

5.1.1.2 Results without ADFs

We first consider the problem of the sextic polynomial $x^6 - 2x^4 + x^2$ using genetic programming without automatically defined functions.

Occasionally genetic programming produces an algebraically correct solution to a problem. For example, in one run, the following 100%-correct solution emerged in generation 5:

```
(* (- X (* (* X X) X)) (- X (* (* X X) X))).
```

More typically, genetic programming produces a good approximation to the target curve. The following best-of-run individual satisfying the success predicate of this problem (i.e., scoring 50 hits out of 50) from generation 37 is an example of such an approximation:

```
(% (% (* (* X 0.571) (* (- (* (+ (% 0.634094 0.68469) (+ (+ X X)
-0.5992)) (* (* (+ (% 0.634094 0.68469) (+ X -0.5992)) (* (%
0.354904 -0.7549) (* X 0.571))) (- X 0.395493))) -0.4665)
0.150497)) (+ (% 0.0211945 X) (+ X (% 0.0211945 X)))) (+ (-
0.172394 0.036392) (- (* (% -0.116905 X) (+ (% -0.116905 X) (*
(* -0.7549 0.141205) (% (% 0.354904 -0.7549) (- (* -0.5297 X) (*
```

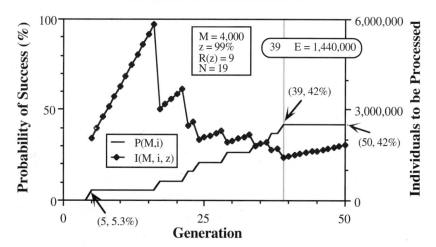

Figure 5.2 Performance curves for the symbolic regression of the sextic polynomial $x^6 - 2x^4 + x^2$ showing that $E_{without} = 1,440,000$ without ADFs.

```
(+ (% 0.354904 -0.7549) (* (+ (% 0.634094 0.68469) (+ X
-0.5992)) (* (% 0.354904 -0.7549) (- X 0.395493)))) (* 0.6823 (*
-0.5297 X))))))))) (* (+ (% 0.634094 0.68469) (+ X -0.5992)) (*
(* (+ (% 0.634094 0.68469) (+ X -0.5992)) (* (% 0.354904
-0.7549) (- X 0.395493))) (- X 0.395493)))))))).
```

The average structural complexity, $\overline{S}_{without}$, of best-of-run programs from the eight successful runs (out of the 19 runs made) for the problem of symbolic regression for $x^6 - 2x^4 + x^2$ is 79.8 points without automatically defined functions.

Figure 5.2 presents the performance curves based on these 19 runs of the problem of symbolic regression for $x^6 - 2x^4 + x^2$ without automatically defined functions. The cumulative probability of success, $P(M,i)$, is 42% by generation 39 and is still 42% by generation 50 (thus yielding eight satisfactory results from the 19 runs). The two numbers in the oval indicate that if this problem is run through to generation 39, processing a total of $E_{without}$ = 1,440,000 individuals (i.e., 4,000 × 40 generations × 9 runs) is sufficient to yield a satisfactory result for this problem with 99% probability.

5.1.1.3 Preparatory Steps with ADFs

We now consider the problem of the symbolic regression of the sextic polynomial $x^6 - 2x^4 + x^2$ using automatically defined functions.

The simplest architecture for an overall program employing automatically defined functions consists of one result-producing branch and one function-defining branch, so we adopt this architecture for this problem. Since there is only one independent variable, x, associated with this problem, it is appropriate that the automatically defined function take one argument.

Table 5.2 Tableau with ADFs for the sextic polynomial $x^6 - 2x^4 + x^2$.

Objective:	Find a program that produces the given value of the sextic polynomial $x^6 - 2x^4 + x^2$ as its output when given the value of the one independent variable, x, as input.
Architecture of the overall program with ADFs:	One result-producing branch and one one-argument function-defining branch.
Parameters:	Branch typing.
Terminal set for the result-producing branch:	X and the floating-point random constants, $\Re_{reals}$.
Function set for the result-producing branch:	+, -, * and % and the one-argument defined function ADF0.
Terminal set for the function-defining branch ADF0:	The dummy variable ARG0 and the floating-point random constants, $\Re_{reals}$.
Function set for the function-defining branch ADF0:	+, -, * and %.

This problem can appropriately employ the same straightforward approach to choosing the terminal set and function set for the two branches as the two-boxes problem. First, the terminal set, $\mathcal{T}_{rpb}$, of the result-producing branch is the same as the terminal set, $\mathcal{T}$, of the problem when automatically defined functions were not being used (i.e., the actual variable of the problem, x, plus the random constants). Second, the function set, $\mathcal{F}_{rpb}$, of the result-producing branch is the union of the available automatically defined functions (just ADF0 here) and the function set, $\mathcal{F}$, that was used when automatically defined functions were not being used. Third, the terminal set, $\mathcal{T}_{adf}$, of the function-defining branch consists of as many dummy variables as the chosen arity of the automatically defined function (plus any random constants). Since the automatically defined function has just one argument here, $\mathcal{T}_{adf}$, consists of just ARG0 (plus the random constants). Fourth, the function set, $\mathcal{F}_{adf}$, of the function-defining branch is the same as the function set, $\mathcal{F}$, of the problem when automatically defined functions were not being used.

Table 5.2 summarizes the key features of the problem of symbolic regression for $x^6 - 2x^4 + x^2$ with automatically defined functions.

5.1.1.4 Results with ADFs
A human programmer writing a program whose output is to be the value of the sextic polynomial $x^6 - 2x^4 + x^2$ might notice that $x^6 - 2x^4 + x^2$ is equal to

$$x^2(x-1)^2(x+1)^2,$$

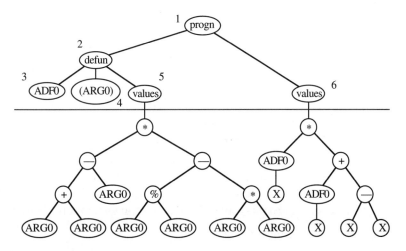

Figure 5.3 100%-correct best-of-run program from generation 10 for the symbolic regression of the sextic polynomial $x^6 - 2x^4 + x^2$ with ADFs.

and that the square is taken on three occasions in this expression. The programmer might then write the following:

```
1    ;;;- definition of the one-argument function "square"-
2    (progn (defun square (arg0)
3            (values (* arg0 arg0)))
4    ;;;- main program for computing the value of sextic
5    ;;;  polynomial-
6            (values (* (square x) (square (- x 1))
7                       (square (+ x 1))))).
```

As previously mentioned, occasionally genetic programming produces an algebraically correct solution to a problem. For example, in one run, an algebraically correct solution to this problem emerged in generation 10:

```
(progn (defun ADF0 (ARG0)
         (values (* (- (+ ARG0 ARG0) ARG0)
                    (- (% ARG0 ARG0) (* ARG0 ARG0))))))
       (values (* (ADF0 X) (+ (ADF0 X) (- X X)))))).
```

This genetically evolved solution is not equivalent to the seven-line program that the human programmer might have written; however, it exploits the same regularity in the problem environment in a somewhat different way. This particular genetically evolved solution reverses the presumed roles of the function-defining branch and the result-producing branch. The genetically evolved ADF0 is equivalent to $x - x^3$. The result-producing branch calls on ADF0 twice with the same argument, x, and then multiplies the results together to produce $x^6 - 2x^4 + x^2$.

Figure 5.3 shows this 100%-correct best-of-run individual with automatically defined functions from generation 10 as a rooted, point-labeled tree with ordered branches. The function-defining branch is on the left of this figure and the result-producing branch is on the right.

This solution is a hierarchical decomposition of the problem. First, genetic programming discovered a decomposition of the overall problem into a sub-problem of finding the algebraic square root of the target sextic polynomial (i.e., $x - x^3$). Then, genetic programming solved the subproblem. Third, genetic programming assembled the results of solving the subproblem into a solution to the overall problem by multiplying together the results of two calls to the defined function ADF0.

A second example illustrates the fact that genetic programming usually produces a good approximation to the target curve, rather than an algebraically correct solution. The following good approximation to the target sextic curve scoring 50 hits (out of 50) emerged in generation 19 of one run:

```
(progn (defun adf0 (arg0)
          (values (% (* (* -0.3842 ARG0) (- (% ARG0 ARG0) ARG0))
          (% (- (+ 0.60989 -0.1008) (% ARG0 ARG0)) (- (- ARG0
          -0.0236053) (* (* -0.3842 ARG0) (+ (% (* (* -0.3842
          ARG0) (% 0.50209 (+ (* (- ARG0 ARG0) (* 0.132095
          ARG0)) (% -0.496803 -0.183601)))) (% (- (+ 0.3786
          -0.2695) (* (* -0.3842 ARG0) (- (% ARG0 ARG0) ARG0)))
          (+ 0.60989 -0.1008))) ARG0))))))
       (values (ADF0 (- (% X X) (* X X)))))).
```

Here ADF0 simplifies (if we may use that term) to

$$-0.78264 Arg0^3 + 0.76417 Arg0^2 + 0.0184743 Arg0$$

$$+0.30069 Arg0^3 (1 - Arg0) \frac{0.072806 + 0.3842 Arg0 (1 - Arg0)}{0.1091 + 0.3842 Arg0 (1 - Arg0)}$$

The result-producing branch invokes ADF0 with an argument of $1 - x^2$.

A third example shows that when automatically defined functions are used, calls to defined functions often contain arguments that themselves consist of calls to defined functions. The following individual scoring 50 hits emerged in generation 16 of one run:

```
(progn (defun ADF0 (ARG0)
          (values (* (+ (* ARG0 0.6694) ARG0) (* (+ (+ (* (- ARG0
          ARG0) (- (% (+ -0.8264 ARG0) ARG0) (+ ARG0 (% (% ARG0
          ARG0) (+ ARG0 0.45529))))) ARG0) (% (% ARG0 ARG0) (-
          -0.7206 ARG0))) (- ARG0 0.67169)))))
       (values (ADF0 (* (+ X (* (* X 0.617294) (ADF0 (ADF0 (* (*
          X 0.617294) (* 0.7637 X)))))) (* X 0.617294)))))).
```

The average structural complexity, $\overline{S}_{with}$, of the best-of-run programs from seven successful runs (out of 13 runs) of the problem of symbolic regression for $x^6 - 2x^4 + x^2$ is 81.1 points with automatically defined functions.

Figure 5.4 presents the performance curves based on these 13 runs of the problem of symbolic regression for $x^6 - 2x^4 + x^2$ with automatically defined functions. The cumulative probability of success, $P(M, i)$, is 54% by generation

With Defined Functions

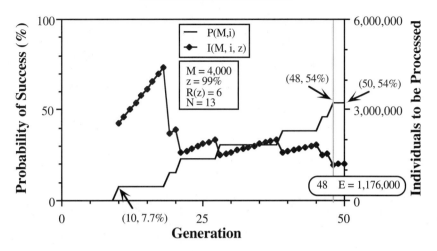

Figure 5.4 Performance curves for the symbolic regression of the sextic polynomial $x^6 - 2x^4 + x^2$ showing that E_{with} = 1,176,000 with ADFs.

Table 5.3 Comparison table for the sextic polynomial $x^6 - 2x^4 + x^2$.

	Without Automatically defined functions	With Automatically defined functions
Average structural complexity $\overline{S}$	79.8	81.1
Computational effort E	1,440,000	1,176,000

48 and is still 54% by generation 50 (thus yielding seven satisfactory results from the 13 runs). The two numbers in the oval indicate that if this problem is run through to generation 48, processing a total of E_{with} = 1,176,000 individuals (i.e., 4,000 × 49 generations × 6 runs) is sufficient to yield a satisfactory result for this problem with 99% probability.

5.1.1.5 Comparison with and without ADFs
Table 5.3 compares the average structural complexity, $\overline{S}_{without}$ and $\overline{S}_{with}$, and the computational effort, $E_{without}$ and E_{with}, for the problem of symbolic regression for $x^6 - 2x^4 + x^2$ with automatically defined functions and without them. As can be seen, the computational effort, E_{with}, required with automatically defined functions is less than the computational effort, $E_{without}$, without them. That is, automatically defined functions are beneficial for the scaled-up version of this problem. On the other hand, the average structural complexity is slightly less favorable with automatically defined functions than without them.

Figure 5.5 summarizes the information in this comparison table and shows a structural complexity ratio, R_S, of 0.98 and an efficiency ratio, R_E, of 1.22.

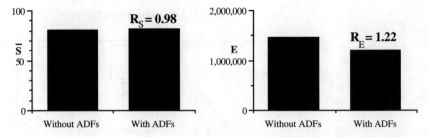

Figure 5.5 Summary graphs for the symbolic regression of the sextic polynomial $x^6 - 2x^4 + x^2$.

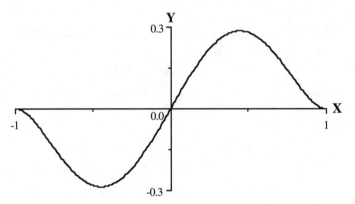

Figure 5.6 Quintic polynomial $x^5 - 2x^3 + x$ in the interval $[-1,+1]$.

The fact that the efficiency ratio is greater than 1 indicates that automatically defined functions are beneficial for the scaled-up version of this problem.

5.1.2 Quintic Polynomial $x^5 - 2x^3 + x$

When we perform symbolic regression on a similar, but simpler polynomial, we find that automatically defined functions are not beneficial as to the number of fitness evaluations.

Figure 5.6 graphs the values of the quintic polynomial $x^5 - 2x^3 + x$ in the interval $[-1, +1]$.

5.1.2.1 Preparatory Steps without ADFs

The tableau for the quintic version of this problem is identical to the tableau for the sextic version (except that the target function is the quintic polynomial $x^5 - 2x^3 + x$) and will not be shown here.

The raw fitness of an individual program in the population is the sum, over the 50 values of the independent variable, x_i, of the absolute value of the error between the value returned by the program and the target value, y_i, of the dependent variable. The only difference between a run of the symbolic regression problem for the sextic polynomial versus a run for the quintic polynomial is the fitness measure, and the only difference in the

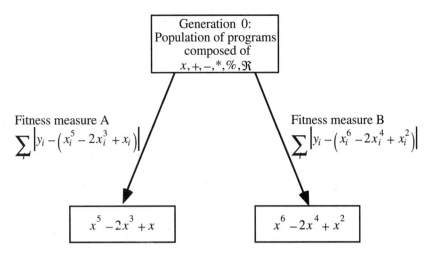

Figure 5.7 Structure arises from fitness.

fitness measure lies in the fitness cases consisting of pairs of values (x_i, y_i). All other aspects of the runs of genetic programming for the two problems are the same. In particular, the creation of the initial random generation of the population is identical. Each program in generation 0 is composed of the independent variable, X, random constants, +, −, *, and protected division %. When the problem involves the sextic polynomial, the fitness measure uses a sampling of values from the sextic curve and the result produced by genetic programming is a symbolic expression that equals (or at least approximately equals) $x^6 - 2x^4 + x^2$. When the problem involves the quintic polynomial, the fitness measure uses a sampling of values from the quintic curve and the result is a symbolic expression that mimics $x^5 - 2x^3 + x$. Thus, it is the fitness measure that determines the programmatic structure that is produced by genetic programming.

Figure 5.7 shows that, starting with the same initial population at generation 0, genetic programming gives rise to two different evolved solutions when it operates with two different fitness measures. The two different structures emerge from the same starting population as a consequence of the fitness measure.

5.1.2.2 Results without ADFs
In one run, the following algebraically correct solution emerged in generation 15:

```
(* (* (- (% X X) (* X X)) X) (- (% X X) (* X X))).
```

When automatically defined functions are not being used, the average structural complexity, $\overline{S}_{without}$, of the best-of-run programs from the 21 successful runs (out of 24 runs) of the problem of symbolic regression for the quintic polynomial $x^5 - 2x^3 + x$ runs is 69.0 points.

Figure 5.8 presents the performance curves based on these 24 runs of the problem of symbolic regression of the quintic polynomial $x^5 - 2x^3 + x$ without

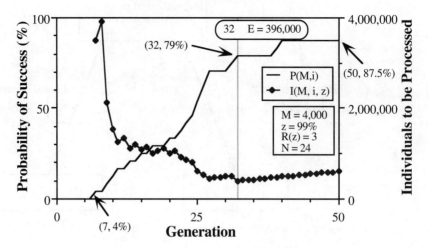

Without Defined Functions

Figure 5.8 Performance curves for the symbolic regression of the quintic polynomial $x^5 - 2x^3 + x$ showing that $E_{without}$ = 396,000 without ADFs.

automatically defined functions. The cumulative probability of success, $P(M,i)$, is 79% by generation 32 and is 87.5% by generation 50. The two numbers in the oval indicate that if this problem is run through to generation 32, processing a total of $E_{without}$ = 396,000 individuals (i.e., 4,000 × 33 generations × 3 runs) is sufficient to yield a satisfactory result for this problem with 99% probability.

5.1.2.3 Results with ADFs
We omit illustrative solutions for this simpler version of the problem and proceed directly to the comparative statistics.

When automatically defined functions are being used, the average structural complexity, $\overline{S}_{with}$, of the best-of-run programs from the 33 successful runs (out of 61 runs) of the problem of symbolic regression for the quintic polynomial $x^5 - 2x^3 + x$ is 64.0 points.

Figure 5.9 presents the performance curves based on these 61 runs of the problem of symbolic regression of the quintic polynomial $x^5 - 2x^3 + x$ with automatically defined functions. The cumulative probability of success, $P(M,i)$, is 54% by generation 49 and is 54% by generation 50. The two numbers in the oval indicate that if this problem is run through to generation 49, processing a total of E_{with} = 1,200,000 individuals (i.e., 4,000 × 50 generations × 6 runs) is sufficient to yield a satisfactory result for this problem with 99% probability.

5.1.2.4 Comparison with and without ADFs
Table 5.4 compares the average structural complexity, $\overline{S}_{without}$ and $\overline{S}_{with}$, and the computational effort, $E_{without}$ and E_{with}, for the symbolic regression of $x^5 - 2x^3 + x$ with automatically defined functions and without them. As can

With Defined Functions

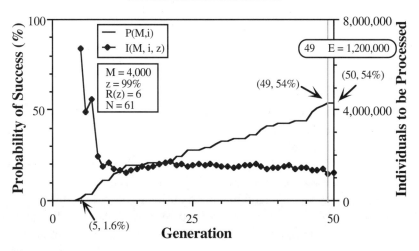

Figure 5.9 Performance curves for the symbolic regression of the quintic polynomial $x^5 - 2x^3 + x$ showing that $E_{with} = 1,200,000$ with ADFs.

Table 5.4 Comparison table for the quintic polynomial $x^5 - 2x^3 + x$.

	Without ADFs	With ADFs
Average structural complexity $\bar{S}$	69.0	64.0
Computational effort E	396,000	1,200,000

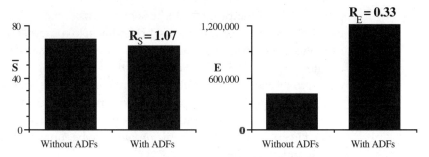

Figure 5.10 Summary graphs for the quintic polynomial $x^5 - 2x^3 + x$.

be seen, the situation for the quintic polynomial $x^5 - 2x^3 + x$ is the opposite to the sextic polynomial. The computational effort, E_{with}, required with automatically defined functions is greater than the computational effort, $E_{without}$, without them. In other words, automatically defined functions are not beneficial for the simpler version of this problem.

Figure 5.10 summarizes the information in this comparison table and shows a structural complexity ratio, R_S, of 1.07 and an efficiency ratio, R_E, of 0.33. The fact that the efficiency ratio is much less than 1 indicates that automatically defined functions are not beneficial for the simpler version of this problem.

It appears that the simpler quintic polynomial is on non-beneficial side of an apparent breakeven point for computational effort and that the higher-order sextic polynomial in on the beneficial side of this breakeven point. The sextic polynomial is not, of course, a particularly challenging target function for floating-point symbolic regression using genetic programming. The comparative simplicity of sextic polynomials in relation to the vast space of polynomials that might be a target for symbolic regression suggests that automatically defined functions may enhance the performance of symbolic regression for all but the simplest target polynomials.

5.2   THE BOOLEAN 6-SYMMETRY VERSUS 5-SYMMETRY

The Boolean symmetry function is often used as a benchmark in the fields of neural networks and machine learning. Boolean functions are attractive for experiments in genetic programming for several reasons. First, it is often possible to understand how the structure of a program contributes to the overall performance of the program for a Boolean function. Second, there are few practical obstacles (e.g., overflows, underflows) to computer implementation of evolved Boolean programs. Third, the easily quantifiable search space facilitates analysis of results. Fourth, no time-consuming simulations are required to measure fitness. Fifth, the number of possible fitness cases is finite and small enough, for many problems, to permit testing of 100% of the fitness cases. Sixth, Boolean problems are amenable to the several optimizations (described in appendix E) that enable problems to be run with a relatively modest amount of computer time.

5.2.1   The Boolean 6-Symmetry Problem

The Boolean *symmetry function* of k Boolean arguments returns T (true) if its Boolean arguments are symmetric, and otherwise returns NIL (false). Symmetry is determined by verifying that the first argument matches the last argument; the second argument matches the second-to-last argument; and so forth. If the number of arguments is odd, no comparison is made of the middle argument.

For example, if the six arguments are 1, 0, 1, 1, 0, and 1 (where we use 1 to denote T and 0 to denote NIL), then the 6-symmetry function returns T. On

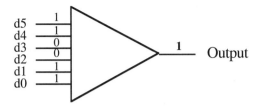

d5   1
d4   1
d3   0
d2   0
d1   1
d0   1

      1   Output

Figure 5.11   Boolean 6-symmetry function with inputs of 1, 1, 0, 0, 1, and 1 and an output of 1.

the other hand, the 6-symmetry function returns NIL if its arguments are 0, 0, 1, 1, 0, and 1. The 5-symmetry function returns T if its five arguments are 0, 0, 1, 0, and 0.

Figure 5.11 shows that the output of the 6-symmetry function is 1 for inputs of 1, 1, 0, 0, 1, and 1.

The symmetry function is suitable for our purposes here because the pairwise matching of the inputs imparts a certain amount of regularity and modularity to this problem environment. The 5-symmetry and 6-symmetry functions are scaled in terms of their number of arguments. The 6-symmetry function has a slightly greater amount of potentially exploitable regularity and modularity than the 5-symmetry function because only two matches are performed in computing the 5-symmetry function whereas three matches are performed for the 6-symmetry function.

5.2.1.1   Preparatory Steps without ADFs

In applying genetic programming to the Boolean 6-symmetry function, the terminal set, $\mathcal{T}$, consists of the six Boolean arguments, so that

$\mathcal{T}=\{$D0, D1, D2, D3, D4, D5$\}$.

The following function set consisting of four primitive Boolean functions satisfies the sufficiency requirement (because it is computationally complete) and satisfies the closure requirement:

$\mathcal{F}=\{$AND, OR, NAND, NOR$\}$

with an argument map of

$\{2, 2, 2, 2\}$.

In addition, this function set is convenient in the sense that it produces programs that are relatively easy to understand.

The set of possible fitness cases for this problem consists of the $2^6 = 64$ combinations of the six Boolean arguments.

The raw fitness of a program is the number of fitness cases for which the program returns the correct value. Raw fitness ranges between 0 and 64 and a larger value is better.

The standardized fitness of a program is the sum, over the 64 fitness cases, of the Hamming distance (error) between the value returned by the program and the correct value of the Boolean function. Standardized fitness ranges

Table 5.5   Tableau without ADFs for Boolean 6-symmetry problem.

Objective:	Find a program that produces the value of the Boolean 6-symmetry function as its output when given the value of the six independent Boolean variables as input.
Terminal set without ADFs:	D0, D1, D2, D3, D4, and D5.
Function set without ADFs:	AND, OR, NAND, and NOR.
Fitness cases:	All $2^6 = 64$ combinations of the six Boolean arguments D0, D1, D2, D3, D4, and D5.
Raw fitness:	The number of fitness cases for which the value returned by the program equals the correct value of the 6-symmetry function.
Standardized fitness:	The standardized fitness of a program is the sum, over the $2^6 = 64$ fitness cases, of the Hamming distance (error) between the value returned by the program and the correct value of the 6-symmetry function.
Hits:	Same as raw fitness.
Wrapper:	None.
Parameters:	$M = 16,000$. $G = 51$.
Success predicate:	A program scores the maximum number of hits.

between 0 and 64 and a value closer to 0 is better. Raw fitness is 64 minus standardized fitness.

We chose a population size, M, of 16,000 based on our view of the likely difficulty of this problem (and to match the population size used for Boolean problems throughout chapter 6).

Table 5.5 summarizes the key features of the problem of symbolic regression of the Boolean 6-symmetry function without automatically defined functions.

5.2.1.2   Results without ADFs

In one run of the Boolean 6-symmetry problem without automatically defined functions, the following 100%-correct best-of-run 145-point individual emerged in generation 34:

```
(NOR (NOR (AND (NOR D2 D3) (NAND (NOR (AND D5 (NAND (AND D2 D3)
(NOR (NAND (NOR (AND D3 D3) (AND D3 D3)) (AND (NAND D0 D0) (NOR
D4 D1))) (OR D0 D5)))) (NAND D0 D0)) D0)) (NOR (AND (OR (NOR (OR
(NAND D4 D4) (NAND (AND D1 D0) (NAND D1 D0))) (AND (OR D5 D2)
D4)) (NAND D3 D2)) (NAND (NOR D2 D5) (NAND D2 D0))) (OR (OR
(NAND (AND D2 D3) D2) (NOR (AND D5 (NAND (NAND (NAND (AND D5
```

Without Defined Functions

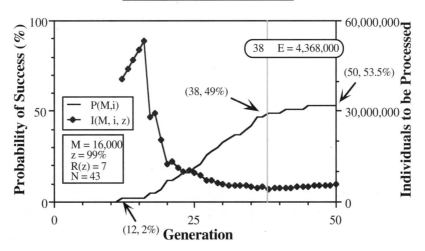

Figure 5.12 Performance curves for the Boolean 6-symmetry problem showing that $E_{without}$ = 4,368,000 without ADFs.

```
(NAND D0 D2)) (OR (NAND (AND D4 D1) (NAND D5 D2)) D1)) (OR (AND
D1 D4) (NOR D4 D1))) (NAND D3 D5))) (NAND D0 D0))) (NOR (AND D3
D3) (AND D3 D3))))) (NAND (NAND (AND D5 (NAND D0 D0)) (OR (NAND
(NOR (OR D4 D5) (NOR D2 D1)) (AND (AND (AND D2 D4) D0) D0)) D1))
(OR (AND D1 D4) (NOR D4 D1)))).
```

The average structural complexity, $\overline{S}_{without}$, of the 100%-correct solutions from the 23 successful runs (out of 43 runs) of the Boolean 6-symmetry problem is 143.0 points without automatically defined functions.

Figure 5.12 presents the performance curves based on these 43 runs for the problem of symbolic regression of the Boolean 6-symmetry function without automatically defined functions. The cumulative probability of success, $P(M,i)$, is 49% by generation 38 and is 54% by generation 50. The two numbers in the oval indicate that if this problem is run through to generation 38, processing a total of $E_{without}$ = 4,368,000 individuals (i.e., 16,000 × 39 generations × 7 runs) is sufficient to yield a solution to this problem with 99% probability.

5.2.1.3   Preparatory Steps with ADFs

We now consider the Boolean 6-symmetry problem using automatically defined functions.

A human programmer writing a program for the 6-symmetry function might conceivably employ the fact that any Boolean function can be written in disjunctive normal form and write a disjunction of clauses, each consisting of the conjunction of the six Boolean arguments or their negations, for each of the 32 combinations of the arguments that returns a value of T. However, a human programmer would almost certainly not code this problem in this tedious way. Instead, the programmer would prob-

Problems that Straddle the Break-even Point for Computational Effort

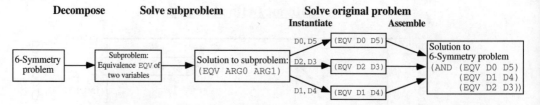

Figure 5.13 Three-step top-down hierarchical approach applied to the 6-symmetry problem.

ably write a subroutine EQV capable of testing for the equivalence (i.e., the even-2-parity) of two Boolean arguments and then call this two-argument subroutine with three different instantiations of the two dummy variables (formal parameters). The programmer might write something like the following ten-line overall program:

```
1    ;;;—definition of the two-argument equivalence function
2    ;;;  EQV (even-2-parity)—
3    (progn (defun EQV (arg0 arg1)
4            (values (OR (AND arg0 arg1)
5                        (NOR arg0 arg1))))
6    ;;;—main program for Boolean 6-symmetry of
7    ;;;  d0, d1, d2, d3, d4, and d5—
8            (values (AND (AND (EQV d0 d5)
9                              (EQV d1 d4))
10                         (EQV d2 d3))))
```

Lines 3 through 5 constitute the function-defining branch of this overall program. This code implements the EQV function by returning T if dummy variables, ARG0 and ARG1, are either both T or both NIL.

Lines 8 through 10 constitute a main program that calls the two-argument EQV function three times: first testing the equivalence of D0 and D5, then testing D1 and D4, and finally testing D2 and D3.

Figure 5.13 diagrams the way the above ten-line program applies the hierarchical three-step problem-solving process in its top-down form to the 6-symmetry problem. The original overall problem is at the left. In the step labeled "decompose" near the top left of the figure, the original problem is decomposed into one subproblem for determining the equivalence of two Boolean arguments. In the step labeled "solve subproblem" in the top middle of the figure, the subproblem is solved. Finally, in the step labeled "solve original problem" near the top right, the solution of the subproblem is instantiated with three different pairs of Boolean arguments and these three results are assembled using the AND function into a solution to the overall problem.

The ten-line program above can also be interpreted in terms of the bottom-up way of describing the hierarchical three-step problem-solving process. First, one seeks to discover useful regularities at the lowest level of the problem environment. In this problem, the useful regularities are the equivalence of the first and last arguments, the equivalence of the second and second-to-last arguments, and the equivalence of the middle two arguments. Second, one

Table 5.6 The new problem created by a change of representation using the new independent variables R0, R1, and R2 for the 6-symmetry problem.

Fitness case	R0	R1	R2	6-symmetry
0	NIL	NIL	NIL	NIL
1	NIL	NIL	T	NIL
2	NIL	T	NIL	NIL
3	NIL	T	T	NIL
4	T	NIL	NIL	NIL
5	T	NIL	T	NIL
6	T	T	NIL	NIL
7	T	T	T	T

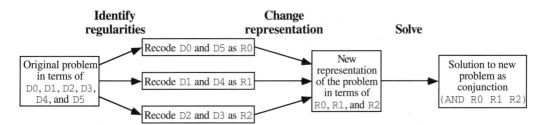

Figure 5.14 Three-step bottom-up hierarchical approach applied to the 6-symmetry problem.

changes the representation of the problem so that the problem becomes restated in terms of the regularities. In the recoding, each of the three designated pairs of the original independent variables is replaced by one new independent variable. Specifically, D0 and D5 are replaced by the single bit R0 indicating whether D0 and D5 are equivalent; D1 and D4 are replaced by the single bit R1 indicating whether they are equivalent; and D2 and D3 are replaced by the single bit R2 indicating whether they are equivalent. The 6-symmetry problem has six independent variables (and $2^6 = 64$ fitness cases).

If we focus only on the new variables, table 5.6 shows the new problem created by a change of representation that recodes the three designated pairs of the original independent variables into the new independent variables R0, R1, and R2 for the 6-symmetry problem. There are eight different combinations of the new independent variables, R0, R1, and R2. There is one value of the dependent variable associated with each. The problem still has 64 fitness cases.

After the change of representation, the problem is much simpler even though the full problem now actually has nine independent variables (three of which are related to the original six). It is solved when the result-producing branch uses the simple conjunction (AND) of the three new independent variables, R0, R1, and R2.

Figure 5.14 shows the application of the three-step bottom-up hierarchical approach applied to the 6-symmetry problem. The first step is to "identify

Table 5.7 Tableau with ADFs for Boolean 6-symmetry problem.

Objective:	Find a program that produces the value of the Boolean 6-symmetry function as its output when given the value of the six independent Boolean variables as input.
Architecture of the overall program with ADFs:	One result-producing branch and one two-argument function-defining branch defining ADF0.
Parameters:	Branch typing.
Terminal set for the result-producing branch:	D0, D1, D2, D3, D4, and D5.
Function set for the result-producing branch:	ADF0, AND, OR, NAND, and NOR.
Terminal set for the function-defining branch ADF0:	The two dummy variables ARG0 and ARG1.
Function set for the function-defining branch ADF0:	AND, OR, NAND, and NOR.

regularities." The three recoding rules are the regularities. The second step is to "change representation." This step changes the representation of the original problem stated in terms of the six independent variables D0, D1, D2, D3, D4, and D5 into a new problem stated in terms of the three new independent variables, R0, R1, and R2. The third step is to "solve" the problem now that it has been restated in terms of the new representation. The problem is solved by taking the conjunction (AND R0 R1 R2).

This problem can appropriately employ the same straightforward approach to choosing the terminal set and function set for the two branches as the sextic-polynomial problem and the two-boxes problem. First, the terminal set, $\mathcal{T}_{rpb}$, of the result-producing branch is the same as the terminal set, $\mathcal{T}$, of the problem when automatically defined functions were not being used (i.e., the actual variables of the problem, D0, D1, D2, D3, D4, and D5). Second, the function set, $\mathcal{F}_{rpb}$, of the result-producing branch is the union of the available automatically defined functions (just ADF0 here) and the function set, $\mathcal{F}$, when automatically defined functions were not being used. Third, the terminal set, $\mathcal{T}_{adf}$, of the function-defining branch consists of as many dummy variables as the chosen arity of the automatically defined function involved. Since the automatically defined function has two arguments here, $\mathcal{T}_{adf}$ consists of ARG0 and ARG1. Fourth, the function set, $\mathcal{F}_{adf}$, of the function-defining branch is the same as the terminal set, $\mathcal{F}$, of the problem when automatically defined functions were not being used.

Table 5.7 summarizes the key features of the problem of symbolic regression of the Boolean 6-symmetry function using automatically defined functions.

5.2.1.4 Results with ADFs

In one run, the following 100%-correct 78-point program emerged on generation 16:

```
(progn (defun ADF0 (ARG0 ARG1)
            (values (NAND (NOR (NOR (AND ARG0 ARG1) (OR ARG0 ARG1))
               (NOR (AND ARG0 ARG0) (NOR ARG0 ARG0))) (OR (NOR (AND
               ARG1 ARG1) (NOR ARG0 ARG0)) (NOR (NOR ARG1 ARG0) (OR
               ARG0 ARG0))))))
        (values (NOR (ADF0 (AND (AND D1 D5) (NAND (NOR (NAND D4
            D1) (NOR (ADF0 D1 D4) (AND D1 D5))) (AND (OR D4 D3) (OR
            D3 D4)))) (AND (ADF0 D2 D3) (NAND (NOR (NAND D4 D1)
            (ADF0 D2 D3)) (OR D5 D1)))) (NAND (ADF0 D1 D4) (ADF0 D5
            D0))))).
```

The average structural complexity, $\overline{S}_{with}$, of the 100%-correct solutions from the 18 successful runs (out of 28 runs) of the 6-symmetry problem is 78.8 points with automatically defined functions. The program above is typical as to the size of the solutions produced by genetic programming with automatically defined functions.

In another run, the following 100%-correct program of below-average size (66 points) emerged on generation 13:

```
(progn (defun adf0 (ARG0 ARG1)
            (values (NAND (OR (NAND (OR ARG1 ARG0) (AND ARG0 ARG1))
               (NOR ARG1 ARG1)) (NAND (NAND (OR ARG0 ARG0) (NAND
               (AND ARG1 ARG0) (NAND ARG0 (OR (NOR (AND ARG1 ARG1)
               (NOR ARG1 ARG1)) (NAND (NOR (NOR ARG0 ARG1) (OR ARG1
               ARG0)) (AND ARG1 ARG1)))))) (NOR (OR ARG0 ARG1) (AND
               ARG1 ARG0))))))
        (values (AND (ADF0 D5 D0) (AND (ADF0 D1 D4) (ADF0 (ADF0
            (AND D2 D2) D3) (ADF0 D0 D0)))))).
```

In this program the 49-point `ADF0` computes the equivalence of its two Boolean arguments. Then the 17-point result-producing branch computes the three-way conjunction of the equivalence of `D5` and `D0`, the equivalence of `D1` and `D4`, and the value returned by the last nine points of this result-producing branch. This three-way conjunction is computed by the first two `AND`s appearing in the result-producing branch. The last nine points of the result-producing branch,

```
(ADF0 (ADF0 (AND D2 D2) D3) (ADF0 D0 D0)),
```

compute the equivalence of `D2` and `D3` in a rather complicated way. Since `(ADF0 D0 D0)` is always true and `(ADF0 <<X>> T)` is always `<<X>>`, for all `<<X>>`, the outer `ADF0` of this nine-point subexpression returns the value of `(ADF0 (AND D2 D2) D3)` which, in turn, simplifies to `(ADF0 D2 D3)`.

We can interpret this 66-point solution in terms of the top-down way of describing the hierarchical three-step problem-solving process described in chapter 1. First, the overall problem of computing the 6-symmetry function is decomposed into the subproblem of finding the equivalence (EQV) of two Boolean arguments. Second, ADF0 expresses the solution to this subproblem. Third, the solution to the overall problem is assembled in the result-producing branch using the primitive AND function twice (the first two occurrences of AND in the result-producing branch) and five different instantiations of the solution to the subproblem of finding the two-argument equivalence (ADF0). Although a human programmer would undoubtedly be more efficient and invoke ADF0 only three times in solving this problem, the genetically evolved program is 100%-correct.

The above solution to the 6-symmetry problem illustrates three of the five ways itemized in chapter 3 by which the hierarchical problem-solving approach can be beneficial: hierarchical decomposition, parametrized reuse, and abstraction.

First, the hierarchical decomposition is manifested by the fact that the overall program for solving the problem consists of the 49-point automatically defined function ADF0 and the 17-point result-producing branch.

Second, the five times that the result-producing branch is used to compute the equivalence of its two dummy variables illustrate parametrized reuse of the solution to the ADF0 subproblem. Generalization comes from such parametrized reuse. ADF0 is a general way of determining equivalence and may be reused on any combination of Boolean values or expressions. ADF0 is invoked five times by the result-producing branch with the following different combinations of values for its two dummy variables:

- (ADF0 D5 D0),
- (ADF0 D1 D4),
- (ADF0 (AND D2 D2) D3),
- (ADF0 D0 D0), and
- (ADF0 (ADF0 (AND D2 D2) D3) (ADF0 D0 D0)).

Third, each time ADF0 is invoked by the result-producing branch with two particular combinations of values, abstraction is occurring. All actual variables of the problem that are not involved with that particular invocation of ADF0 are momentarily irrelevant. For example, when (ADF0 D5 D0) is being evaluated, D1, D2, and D3 are all irrelevant.

Figure 5.15 presents the performance curves based on the 28 runs of the problem of symbolic regression for 6-symmetry with automatically defined functions. The cumulative probability of success, $P(M,i)$, is 61% by generation 29 and is 64% by generation 50. The two numbers in the oval indicate that if this problem is run through to generation 29, processing a total of $E_{without} = 2,400,000$ individuals (i.e., $16,000 \times 30$ generations $\times 5$ runs) is sufficient to yield a solution to this problem with 99% probability.

With Defined Functions

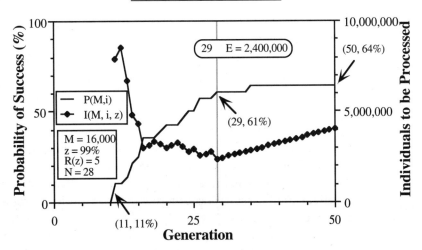

Figure 5.15 Performance curves for the 6-symmetry problem showing that $E_{with} = 2,400,000$ with ADFs.

Table 5.8 Comparison table for Boolean 6-symmetry problem.

	Without ADFs	With ADFs
Average structural complexity $\bar{S}$	143.0	78.8
Computational effort E	4,368,000	2,400,000

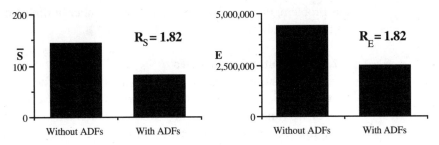

Figure 5.16 Summary graphs for the 6-symmetry problem.

5.2.1.5 Comparison with and without ADFs

Table 5.8 compares the average structural complexity, $\bar{S}_{without}$ and $\bar{S}_{with}$, and the computational effort, $E_{without}$ and E_{with}, for the Boolean 6-symmetry problem with automatically defined functions and without them. As can be seen, the computational effort, E_{with}, required with automatically defined functions is less than the computational effort, $E_{without}$, without them. That is, automatically defined functions are beneficial for the scaled-up version of this problem. In addition, the average structural complexity is considerably less with automatically defined functions than without them, so automatically defined functions are also beneficial as to the parsimony. However, as previously mentioned, we do not start seeing a reasonably consistent advantage in program size with automatically defined functions until we start encountering the more difficult problems in chapter 6 and beyond.

Figure 5.16 summarizes the information in this comparison table and shows a structural complexity ratio, R_S, of 1.82 and an efficiency ratio, R_E, of, by coincidence, 1.82. The fact that the efficiency ratio is greater than 1 indicates that automatically defined functions are beneficial for the scaled-up version of this problem.

5.2.2 The Boolean 5-Symmetry Problem

In this subsection we state the comparable statistics for the symbolic regression of the simpler five-argument version of the Boolean symmetry problem.

The tableau for the 5-symmetry problem is identical to the tableau for the 6-symmetry problem (except for the target function, the actual variables of the problem, the population size, and the number of fitness cases) and will not be shown here.

5.2.2.1 Results without ADFs

When automatically defined functions are not used, the average structural complexity, $\bar{S}_{without}$, of the best-of-run programs from the 374 successful runs (out of 375 runs) of the Boolean 5-symmetry problem is 57.4 points.

Figure 5.17 presents the performance curves based on these 375 runs for the Boolean 5-symmetry problem without automatically defined functions. The cumulative probability of success, $P(M,i)$, is 91% by generation 14 and is 99.7% by generation 50. The two numbers in the oval indicate that if this problem is run through to generation 14, processing a total of $E_{without}$ = 120,000 individuals (i.e., $4{,}000 \times 15$ generations $\times 2$ runs) is sufficient to yield a solution to this problem with 99% probability.

5.2.2.2 Results with ADFs

When automatically defined functions are used, the average structural complexity, $\bar{S}_{with}$, of the best-of-run programs from the 60 successful runs (out of 62 runs) of the Boolean 5-symmetry problem is 72.1 points.

Without Defined Functions

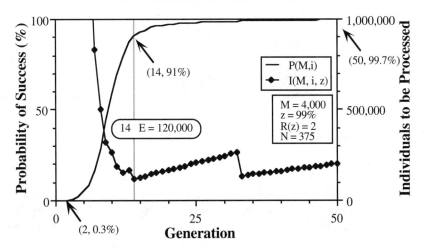

Figure 5.17 Performance curves for the Boolean 5-symmetry problem showing that $E_{without} = 120,000$ without ADFs.

With Defined Functions

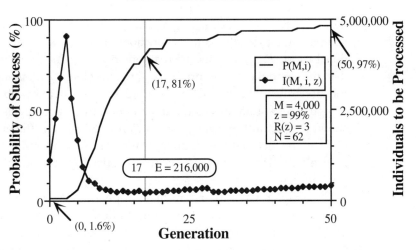

Figure 5.18 Performance curves for the 5-symmetry problem showing that $E_{with} = 216,000$ with ADFs.

Table 5.9 Comparison table for the Boolean 5-symmetry problem.

	Without ADFs	With ADFs
Average structural complexity $\bar{S}$	57.4	72.1
Computational effort E	120,000	216,000

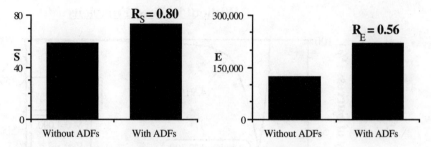

Figure 5.19 Summary graphs for the Boolean 5-symmetry problem.

Figure 5.18 presents the performance curves based on these 62 runs of the Boolean 5-symmetry problem with automatically defined functions. The cumulative probability of success, $P(M,i)$, is 81% by generation 17 and is 97% by generation 50. The two numbers in the oval indicate that if this problem is run through to generation 17, processing a total of $E_{with} = 216,000$ individuals (i.e., $4,000 \times 18$ generations $\times 3$ runs) is sufficient to yield a solution to this problem with 99% probability.

5.2.2.3   Comparison with and without ADFs

Table 5.9 compares the average structural complexity, $\overline{S}_{without}$ and $\overline{S}_{with}$, and the computational effort, $E_{without}$ and E_{with}, for the Boolean 5-symmetry problem with automatically defined functions and without them. The computational effort, E_{with}, required with automatically defined functions is greater than the computational effort, $E_{without}$, without them. Automatically defined functions are not beneficial for the simpler version of this problem.

Figure 5.19 summarizes the information in this comparison table and shows a structural complexity ratio, R_S, of 0.80 and an efficiency ratio, R_E, of 0.56. The fact that the efficiency ratio is less than 1 indicates that automatically defined functions are not beneficial for the simpler version of this problem.

The simpler 5-symmetry problem appears to be on the non-beneficial side of the breakeven point for computational effort and the 6-symmetry problem in on the beneficial side of this breakeven point. The 6-symmetry problem is not, of course, a particularly challenging target function for Boolean symbolic regression using genetic programming. Thus, this apparent breakeven point is located in a rather unchallenging area of the space of all possible Boolean functions. If this is true, then symbolic regression of all but the simplest Boolean functions may benefit from automatically defined functions.

5.3   THE FOUR-SINE VERSUS THREE-SINE PROBLEMS

This section considers the problem of symbolic regression of the three-term expression

$$\sin x + \sin 2x + \sin 3x$$

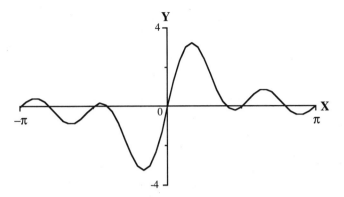

Figure 5.20 Graph of $\sin x + \sin 2x + \sin 3x + \sin 4x$ in the interval $[-\pi, +\pi]$.

and the scaled-up version of this problem involving the four-term expression $\sin x + \sin 2x + \sin 3x + \sin 4x$.

These two target functions for symbolic regression are scaled in terms of the number of harmonics of a sinusoidal function. The additional harmonic appearing in the four-term expression gives the four-term expression a slightly greater amount of potentially exploitable regularity than the three-term expression.

5.3.1 The Four-Sine Problem – $\sin x + \sin 2x + \sin 3x + \sin 4x$

Figure 5.20 graphs $\sin x + \sin 2x + \sin 3x + \sin 4x$ in the interval $[-\pi, +\pi]$.

5.3.1.1 Preparatory Steps without ADFs

The preparatory steps for this problem are similar to the problems of floating-point symbolic regression of the sextic and quintic polynomials. However, the target function here is more difficult to learn than the sextic polynomial. Experience indicates that we can expect to evolve only an approximate solution to this target with our chosen population size of 4,000. We therefore stated the success predicate in terms of a cumulative error of 13.000 over the 50 fitness cases. Given the range over which the target function varies, this success predicate corresponds to an average error of about 3% per fitness case.

Table 5.10 summarizes the key features of the problem of symbolic regression for $\sin x + \sin 2x + \sin 3x + \sin 4x$ without automatically defined functions.

5.3.1.2 Results without ADFs

In one run without automatically defined functions, the following individual satisfying the success predicate of this problem emerged in generation 43:

```
(% (% (% (% (* -0.210999 -0.6071) (- (% 0.153397 X) (* X
0.25949))) (- (* X X) (* X 0.25949))) (- X X)) (- (% 0.108994 X)
(* (- (* X X) (- X X)) (- (* X (* (* (* -0.210999 -0.6071)
```

Table 5.10 Tableau without ADFs for $\sin x + \sin 2x + \sin 3x + \sin 4x$.

Objective:	Find a program that produces the given value of $\sin x + \sin 2x + \sin 3x + \sin 4x$ as its output when given the value of the one independent variable, x, as input.
Terminal set without ADFs:	X and the random constants $\Re_{reals}$.
Function set without ADFs:	+, -, * and %.
Fitness cases:	50 evenly spaced values of X between $-\pi$ and π.
Raw fitness:	The sum, over the fitness cases, of the absolute value of the error between the value returned by the program and the given value of the dependent variable.
Standardized fitness:	Same as raw fitness.
Hits:	The number of fitness cases for which the absolute value of the error is less than 0.05 (the hits criterion).
Wrapper:	None.
Parameters:	$M = 4,000$. $G = 51$.
Success predicate:	A program has standardized fitness below 13.000.

Without Defined Functions

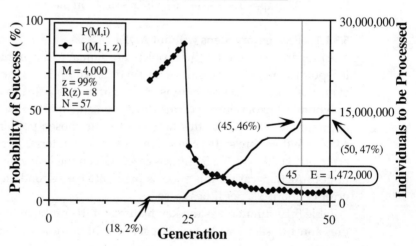

Figure 5.21 Performance curves for $\sin x + \sin 2x + \sin 3x + \sin 4x$ showing that $E_{without} = 1,472,000$ without ADFs.

Table 5.11 Tableau with ADFs for $\sin x + \sin 2x + \sin 3x + \sin 4x$.

Objective:	Find a program that produces the given value of $\sin x + \sin 2x + \sin 3x + \sin 4x$ as its output when given the value of the one independent variable, x, as input.
Architecture of the overall program with ADFs:	One result-producing branch and one one-argument function-defining branch.
Parameters:	Branch typing.
Terminal set for the result-producing branch:	X and the random constants $\Re_{reals}$.
Function set for the result-producing branch:	+, -, * and % and the one-argument defined function ADF0.
Terminal set for the function-defining branch ADF0:	The dummy variable ARG0 and the random constants $\Re_{reals}$.
Function set for the function-defining branch ADF0:	+, -, * and %.

```
-0.5213) (- (* (- (- (* 0.010498 0.7955) (+ X (* 0.010498
0.7955))) X) (* (- (* X X) (* X 0.25949)) (* (- (* X X) (* X
0.25949)) (* X 0.25949)))) (+ (+ X 0.301804) (+ X 0.25949)))))
(+ (- (% 0.153397 X) (* (- (* X X) (* X 0.25949)) (- (* X
0.25949) (+ (+ X 0.301804) (* 0.010498 0.7955))))) (* 0.010498
0.7955)))))).
```

The average structural complexity, $\bar{S}_{without}$, of the best-of-run programs from the 27 successful runs (out of 57 runs) of the problem of symbolic regression for $\sin x + \sin 2x + \sin 3x + \sin 4x$ is 111.7 points without automatically defined functions.

Figure 5.21 presents the performance curves based on these 57 runs of the problem of symbolic regression for $\sin x + \sin 2x + \sin 3x + \sin 4x$ without automatically defined functions. The cumulative probability of success, $P(M,i)$, is 46% by generation 45 and is 47% by generation 50. The two numbers in the oval indicate that if this problem is run through to generation 45, processing a total of $E_{without} = 1,472,000$ individuals (i.e., $4,000 \times 46$ generations $\times 8$ runs) is sufficient to yield a satisfactory result for this problem with 99% probability.

5.3.1.3 Preparatory Steps with ADFs

We now consider the problem of symbolic regression of $\sin x + \sin 2x + \sin 3x + \sin 4x$ using automatically defined functions.

Table 5.12 Number of invocations of ADF0 for $\sin x + \sin 2x + \sin 3x + \sin 4x$.

Run	Generation at which satisfactory result emerged	Number of invocations of ADF0
1	50	2
2	34	7
3	30	0
4	38	1
5	24	1
6	30	6
7	21	1
8	22	1
9	40	3
10	39	1
11	18	3
12	14	2
13	22	1
14	24	2
15	23	1
16	28	3
17	33	2
18	40	8
19	26	1

The preparatory steps for this problem are similar to those of the problem of symbolic regression of the sextic polynomial.

Table 5.11 summarizes the key features of the problem of symbolic regression for $\sin x + \sin 2x + \sin 3x + \sin 4x$ using automatically defined functions.

5.3.1.4 Results with ADFs

We made 37 runs of the problem of symbolic regression for $\sin x + \sin 2x + \sin 3x + \sin 4x$, of which 19 were successful.

Table 5.12 shows the number of invocations of ADF0 for these 19 successful runs. The number of invocations ranges from zero to eight, the average being 2.42. The result-producing branch ignores ADF0 only in one of these 19 runs (run 3) indicating that there is a strong competitive advantage associated with automatically defined functions. Curiously, none of the 19 runs employ exactly four automatically defined functions.

In run 1, the following 104-point program emerges on generation 50. It invokes ADF0 twice, scores 22 (out of 50) hits, and has a standardized fitness of 11.11.

```
(progn (defun ADF0 (ARG0)
          (values (- (- (% (% -0.4954 0.6199) (% 0.6342 0.40779))
            (* (* (* ARG0 ARG0) (% (- (- (- -0.3338 ARG0) (% ARG0
```

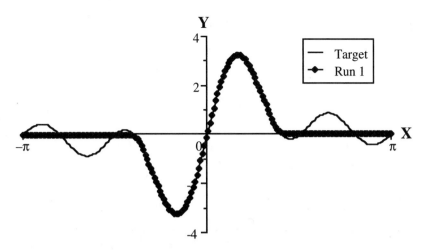

Figure 5.22 Comparison of target curve and best-of-run program of run 1 for $\sin x + \sin 2x + \sin 3x + \sin 4x$.

```
          0.7341)) (* ARG0 -0.315002)) (* ARG0 ARG0))) (* (- (-
          (% (% -0.4954 0.586) (+ ARG0 (+ ARG0 0.6199))) (* (-
          0.82939 ARG0) (* (- (* (* (- 0.82939 ARG0) ARG0) (*
          (% -0.4954 0.586) ARG0)) 0.071304) (% (- (- (% (%
          -0.4954 0.586) (+ ARG0 ARG0)) (% -0.4954 0.586)) (*
          ARG0 ARG0)) (+ (- 0.071304 0.332504) (+ 0.76689
          -0.332)))))) (+ ARG0 0.078995)) (* ARG0 ARG0)))) (+
          ARG0 0.078995))))
   (values (% (% (+ (+ X X) X) (ADF0 (* X X))) (ADF0
          -0.0867)))).
```

Since this program's standardized fitness satisfies the success predicate of this problem (requiring a standardized fitness of 13.000 or better) and is better than any other program in this series of 37 runs, this program is the best-of-all program for these runs.

Figure 5.22 compares the target curve with this best-of-all program over the interval $[-\pi, \pi]$. As can be seen, this program tracks the target curve very well for many parts of the interval, but deviates in the areas where the target curve oscillates near the x-axis.

In run 2, the following program from generation 17 invokes ADF0 seven times, has a standardized fitness of 12.88, scores 16 hits, and satisfies the success predicate of the problem:

```
(progn (defun ADF0 (ARG0)
          (values (- (* ARG0 ARG0) (- 0.08439636 0.3044014))))
       (values (+ (% X (ADF0 (ADF0 (* X X)))) (% (ADF0 (ADF0
          -0.05509901)) (% (% (ADF0 X) (+ -0.24420166 (+
          0.9324951 0.5493927))) (- (+ (% X (ADF0 (* X (* X (ADF0
          (* X (+ 0.33459473 0.19510078))))))) (% (* (- X X) X)
          (% X (+ 0.9324951 0.5493927)))) (* X
          0.19510078))))))))).
```

With Defined Functions

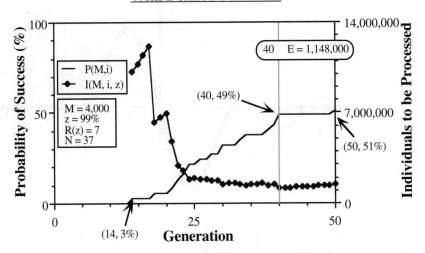

Figure 5.23 Performance curves for $\sin x + \sin 2x + \sin 3x + \sin 4x$ showing that $E_{with} = 1{,}148{,}000$ with ADFs.

When ADF0 is invoked only once, the problem environment is being decomposed, but it is not being decomposed in a way that results in any reuse. Run 4 illustrates this. The program below from generation 38 invokes ADF0 once, has a standardized fitness of 12.68, and satisfies the success predicate of the problem:

```
(progn (defun ADF0 (ARG0)
          (values (- (% (* (+ 0.37609863 (* (* (+ 0.37609863 (*
             (* (+ 0.37609863 (* (+ (* ARG0 ARG0) (% 0.05239868
             ARG0)) ARG0)) ARG0) ARG0)) ARG0) ARG0)) ARG0) (% (%
             (- -0.10990143 ARG0) (+ 0.4028015 0.9240036)) ARG0))
             (% 0.05239868 (+ ARG0 (+ 0.37609863 (* (+ (* ARG0
             ARG0) (% 0.05239868 ARG0)) ARG0)))))))))
          (values (% (- (* (- X -0.06840515) (* (* (- (% -0.2975006
             X) X) (- 0.7836914 (- 0.7836914 -0.041404724))) X)) X)
             (ADF0 (* (* X X) (- 0.7836914 (- X X))))))))).
```

The average structural complexity, $\overline{S}_{with}$, of the best-of-run programs from the 19 successful runs (out of 37 runs) of the problem of symbolic regression of $\sin x + \sin 2x + \sin 3x + \sin 4x$ is 85.7 points with automatically defined functions.

Figure 5.23 presents the performance curves based on these 37 runs of the problem of symbolic regression for $\sin x + \sin 2x + \sin 3x + \sin 4x$ with automatically defined functions. The cumulative probability of success, $P(M,i)$, is 49% by generation 40 and is 51% by generation 50. The two numbers in the oval indicate that if this problem is run through to generation 40, processing a total of $E_{with} = 1{,}148{,}000$ individuals (i.e., 4,000 × 41 generations × 7 runs) is sufficient to yield a satisfactory result for this problem with 99% probability.

Table 5.13 Comparison table for $\sin x + \sin 2x + \sin 3x + \sin 4x$.

	Without ADFs	With ADFs
Average structural complexity $\bar{S}$	111.7	85.7
Computational effort E	1,472,000	1,148,000

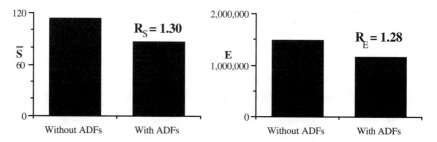

Figure 5.24 Summary graphs for $\sin x + \sin 2x + \sin 3x + \sin 4x$.

5.3.1.5 Comparison with and without ADFs

Genetic programming sometimes produces algebraically correct solutions to the problems of the quintic and sextic polynomials. However, the results produced by genetic programming for this problem are more typical of more complex problems in that the results are good approximations to the target curves, but not algebraically correct solutions. For example, the two results exhibited above from generations 50 and 17 do not resemble a sum of four harmonics. They are, however, reasonably good approximations to the target curve.

After seeing the above results from generations 50 and 17, the reader may be straining to see any evidence of any regularity or modularity when automatically defined functions are used. The result from generation 50 does exhibit some reuse (two invocations of ADF0) and the result from generation 17 does exhibit some modularity (i.e., the problem is broken into two parts). However, the amount of reuse is minimal and the modularity is completely mystifying. Moreover, the meager regularity and the mystifying modularity are not grounded on the fact that the problem actually involves four harmonics.

The reader may consequently be wondering whether there is any evidence that such meager regularity and modularity is beneficial. The answer is that evidence comes in the form of the performance statistics with and without automatically defined functions.

Table 5.13 compares the average structural complexity, $\bar{S}_{without}$ and $\bar{S}_{with}$, and the computational effort, $E_{without}$ and E_{with}, for the problem of symbolic regression for $\sin x + \sin 2x + \sin 3x + \sin 4x$ with automatically defined functions and without them. As can be seen, automatically defined functions are beneficial for the scaled-up version of this problem.

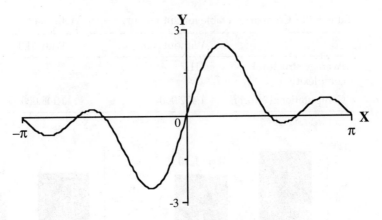

Figure 5.25 Graph of $\sin x + \sin 2x + \sin 3x$ in the interval $[-\pi, +\pi]$.

Figure 5.24 summarizes the information in this comparison table and shows a structural complexity ratio, R_S, of 1.30 and an efficiency ratio, R_E, of 1.28. The fact that the efficiency ratio is greater than 1 indicates that automatically defined functions are beneficial for the scaled-up version of this problem.

Indeed, this problem makes the important point that genetic programming does not produce results in the style of a human programmer. However meager the regularity and however mystifying the modularity, automatically defined functions have demonstrably extracted something beneficial from this problem environment as evidenced by the fact that they reduced the number of fitness evaluations required to yield a satisfactory result for this problem with 99% probability.

5.3.2 The Three-Sine Problem – $\sin x + \sin 2x + \sin 3x$

In this subsection we state the comparable statistics for the symbolic regression of the simpler three-expression target function $\sin x + \sin 2x + \sin 3x$.

Figure 5.25 graphs $\sin x + \sin 2x + \sin 3x$ in the interval $[-\pi, +\pi]$.

The tableau for the three-sine version of this problem is identical to the tableau for the four-sine version (except that the target function is $\sin x + \sin 2x + \sin 3x$) and will not be shown here.

5.3.2.1 Results without ADFs
When automatically defined functions are not being used, the average structural complexity, $\bar{S}_{without}$, of the best-of-run programs from the 46 successful runs (out of 48 runs) of the problem of symbolic regression for $\sin x + \sin 2x + \sin 3x$ is 86.0 points.

Figure 5.26 presents the performance curves based on these 48 runs of the problem of symbolic regression for $\sin x + \sin 2x + \sin 3x$ without automatically defined functions. The cumulative probability of success, $P(M,i)$, is 92% by generation 35 and is 96% by generation 50. The two numbers in the oval indicate that if this problem is run through to generation 35, processing a total

Without Defined Functions

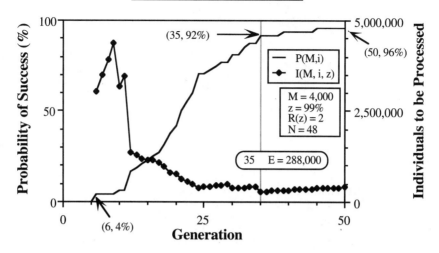

Figure 5.26   Performance curves for $\sin x + \sin 2x + \sin 3x$ showing that $E_{without} = 288,000$ without ADFs.

With Defined Functions

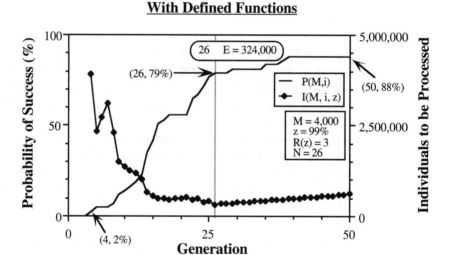

Figure 5.27   Performance curves for $\sin x + \sin 2x + \sin 3x$ showing that $E_{with} = 324,000$ with ADFs.

Table 5.14   Comparison table for $\sin x + \sin 2x + \sin 3x$.

	Without ADFs	With ADFs
Average structural complexity $\overline{S}$	86.0	78.7
Computational effort E	288,000	324,000

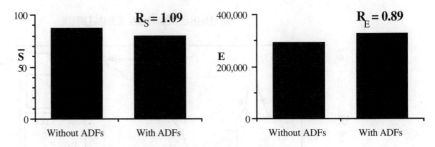

Figure 5.28 Summary graphs for $\sin x + \sin 2x + \sin 3x$.

of $E_{without} = 288{,}000$ individuals (i.e., $4{,}000 \times 36$ generations $\times 2$ runs) is sufficient to yield a satisfactory result for this problem with 99% probability.

5.3.2.2 Results with ADFs

When automatically defined functions are being used, the average structural complexity $\bar{S}_{with}$, of the best-of-run programs from the 23 successful runs (out of 26 runs) of the problem of symbolic regression for $\sin x + \sin 2x + \sin 3x$ is 78.7 points.

Figure 5.27 presents the performance curves based on these 26 runs of the problem of symbolic regression for $\sin x + \sin 2x + \sin 3x$ with automatically defined functions. The cumulative probability of success, $P(M,i)$, is 79% by generation 26 and is 88% by generation 50. The two numbers in the oval indicate that if this problem is run through to generation 26, processing a total of $E_{with} = 324{,}000$ individuals (i.e., $4{,}000 \times 27$ generations $\times 3$ runs) is sufficient to yield a satisfactory result for this problem with 99% probability.

5.3.2.3 Comparison with and without ADFs

Table 5.14 compares the average structural complexity, $\bar{S}_{without}$ and $\bar{S}_{with}$, and the computational effort, $E_{without}$ and E_{with}, for the problem of symbolic regression for $\sin x + \sin 2x + \sin 3x$ with automatically defined functions and without them. As can be seen, automatically defined functions are not beneficial for the simpler version of this problem.

Figure 5.28 summarizes the information in this comparison table and shows a structural complexity ratio, R_S, of 1.09 and an efficiency ratio, R_E, of 0.89. The fact that the efficiency ratio is less than 1 indicates that automatically defined functions are not beneficial for the simpler version of this problem.

The performance statistics again indicate that the simpler version of this problem is on the non-beneficial side of an apparent breakeven point for computational effort whereas the scaled-up version is on the beneficial side.

5.4 FOUR OCCURRENCES VERSUS THREE OCCURRENCES OF A REUSABLE CONSTANT

When a particular constant value is needed in more than one place in a computer program, human programmers typically `let` some variable be the value

Table 5.15 Tableau without ADFs for $x / \pi + x^2 / \pi^2 + 2\pi x$.

Objective:	Find a program that produces $x / \pi + x^2 / \pi^2 + 2\pi x$ as its output when given the value of the one independent variable, x, as input.
Terminal set without ADFs:	X and the random constants $\Re_{reals}$.
Function set without ADFs:	+, -, * and %.
Fitness cases:	10 random values of X between 0.5 and 10.0.
Raw fitness:	The sum, over the fitness cases, of the absolute value of the error between the value returned by the program and the given value of the dependent variable.
Standardized fitness:	Same as raw fitness.
Hits:	The number of fitness cases for which the absolute value of the error is less than 0.05 (the hits criterion).
Wrapper:	None.
Parameters:	$M = 4,000$. $G = 51$. Different fitness cases are chosen for each run.
Success predicate:	A program scores the maximum number of hits.

of some expression. A `let` can be viewed as an automatically defined function that takes no explicit arguments.

This section considers the problem of symbolic regression for the two-term target expression $x / \pi + x^2 / \pi^2$ and the scaled-up version of this problem involving the three-term expression $x / \pi + x^2 / \pi^2 + 2\pi x$ for values of the independent variable x in the interval [0.5, 10.0].

These two target functions for symbolic regression are scaled in terms of the frequency of use of the constant π in the two expressions. There is a slightly greater amount of regularity in the three-term expression because π appears four times in the three-term expression, but only three times in the two-term expression.

We have seen (*Genetic Programming*, sections 10.2 and 10.11) how symbolic regression can be used to evolve a constant value. The goal in this section is to evolve a zero-argument automatically defined function (a `let`) that returns a constant value that can be used in multiple places in a main program.

5.4.1 Three-Term Expression $x / \pi + x^2 / \pi^2 + 2\pi x$

We first consider the problem of evolving a program for the three-term expression, $x / \pi + x^2 / \pi^2 + 2\pi x$, in which π appears four times.

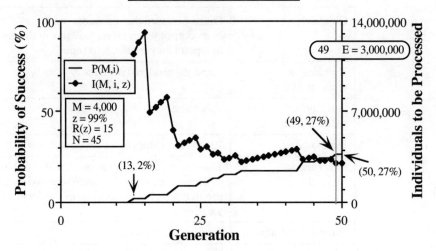

Without Defined Functions

Figure 5.29 Performance curves for $x / \pi + x^2 / \pi^2 + 2\pi x$ showing that $E_{without} =$ 3,000,000 without ADFs.

5.4.1.1 Preparatory Steps without ADFs

The preparatory steps for this problem without automatically defined functions are similar to the previous problems of floating-point symbolic regression.

Table 5.15 summarizes the key features of the problem of symbolic regression of $x / \pi + x^2 / \pi^2 + 2\pi x$ without automatically defined functions.

5.4.1.2 Results without ADFs

In one run without automatically defined functions, the following 95-point best-of-generation program scoring 10 hits (out of 10) emerged in generation 39:

```
(+ (- (- (- (% X X) (* 0.062698 (% (+ -0.140305 (% (+ (- X X) (%
X X)) X)) 0.8454))) (* X -0.8292)) (- (* (- -0.754196 -0.6319)
(* X X)) (% (+ X -0.135101) (* -0.5475 -0.3238)))) (* (% (+
-0.140305 0.4821) (- (% (- (% X X) (* 0.062698 (% (- X X)
0.8454))) (+ -0.322502 X)) (% (% (% (+ (- -0.3107 0.8454) (*
-0.926 -0.7599)) (% (- -0.754196 -0.6319) (+ X X))) (* X X)) (*
-0.5475 -0.3238)))) (- (* -0.163101 0.9323) (* (- -0.754196
-0.6319) (* X X)))))).
```

Of course, the random constants are intermixed throughout this expression in this program.

The average structural complexity, $\bar{S}_{without}$, of the best-of-run programs from the 12 successful runs (out of 45 runs) of the problem of symbolic regression for $x / \pi + x^2 / \pi^2 + 2\pi x$ is 86.6 points without automatically defined functions.

Figure 5.29 presents the performance curves based on these 45 runs of the problem of symbolic regression for $x / \pi + x^2 / \pi^2 + 2\pi x$ without

Table 5.16 Tableau with ADFs for $x / \pi + x^2 / \pi^2 + 2\pi x$.

Objective:	Find a program that produces $x / \pi + x^2 / \pi^2 + 2\pi x$ as its output when given the value of the one independent variable, x, as input.
Architecture of the overall program with ADFs:	One result-producing branch and one zero-argument function-defining branch.
Parameters:	Branch typing.
Terminal set for the result-producing branch:	X and the random constants $\Re_{reals}$.
Function set for the result-producing branch:	+, −, * and % and the zero-argument defined function ADF0.
Terminal set for the function-defining branch ADF0:	Random constants $\Re_{reals}$. (There are no dummy variables in ADF0 for this problem.)
Function set for the function-defining branch ADF0:	+, −, * and %.

automatically defined functions. The cumulative probability of success, $P(M,i)$, is still 27% at generation 49 and is 27% by generation 50. The two numbers in the oval indicate that if this problem is run through to generation 49, processing a total of $E_{without} = 3{,}000{,}000$ individuals (i.e., $4{,}000 \times 50$ generations $\times$ 15 runs) is sufficient to yield a satisfactory result for this problem with 99% probability.

5.4.1.3 Preparatory Steps with ADFs

The principle being illustrated by this problem is to evolve an automatically defined function that returns a constant value that can be used in more than one place in a main program. Consequently, given our intent for this problem, the terminals in the terminal set of ADF0 are restricted to random constants. ADF0 takes no arguments and has no access to X, the actual variable of the problem. Only the result-producing branch has access to X. If the constant that evolves in ADF0 is useful, it will be invoked repeatedly by the result-producing branch. This repeated use of ADF0 should result in some observable increase in efficiency in solving the problem.

Table 5.16 summarizes the key features of the problem of symbolic regression for $x / \pi + x^2 / \pi^2 + 2\pi x$ with automatically defined functions.

Since ADF0 contains no variables and therefore always evaluates to the same constant for every fitness case, a considerable amount of computer time can be saved in this problem by evaluating the program tree in ADF0 once and caching the value obtained.

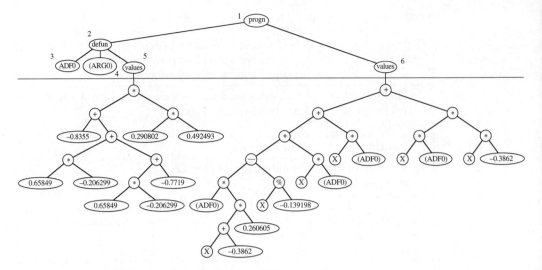

Figure 5.30 Best-of-run program scoring 10 hits from generation 44 for the symbolic regression of $x / \pi + x^2 / \pi^2 + 2\pi x$ with ADFs.

5.4.1.4 Results with ADFs

When automatically defined functions are used, genetic programming found the following 42-point program scoring 10 hits (out of 10) in generation 44 of one run:

```
(progn (defun ADF0 ()
            (values (* (+ -0.8355 (+ (* 0.65849 -0.206299) (+ (*
            0.65849 -0.206299) -0.7719))) (* 0.290802
            0.492493)))))
        (values (+ (+ (+ (- (* (ADF0) (* (+ X -0.3862) 0.260605))
            (% X -0.139198)) (* X (ADF0))) (* X (ADF0))) (* (* X
            (ADF0)) (* X -0.3862)))))).
```

Figure 5.30 shows this best-of-run program as a rooted, point-labeled tree with ordered branches.

ADF0 is invoked four times in this evolved solution. The target expression $x / \pi + x^2 / \pi^2 + 2\pi x$ contains four occurrences of the constant π. The result-producing branch of this evolved program closely matches the target expression. However, ADF0 evaluates to –0.269115.

What happened to π? As is usually the case, the style of the program evolved by genetic programming is nothing like the style of a program written by a human programmer. A human programmer would, of course, notice the four appearances of the common constant π in the three-term expression $x / \pi + x^2 / \pi^2 + 2\pi x$ and would probably write a `let` that bound the constant value 3.14159 to some named variable (perhaps called PI). The program with the `let` is simpler, more understandable, and more efficient because the common constant can be computed once and then reused in several different places in the program. Genetic programming also uncovers a regularity consisting of a constant in this problem environment; however, the regularity that it discovers and reuses is –0.269115, not 3.14159.

Table 5.17 Constant values evolved in ADF0 in 10 runs of the symbolic regression of $x / \pi + x^2 / \pi^2 + 2\pi x$.

Run	Constant value evolved in ADF0	Number of invocations of ADF0
1	−0.2691	4
2	−0.1066	3
3	−0.2117	9
4	74.5470	9
5	−4.5752	6
6	−3.7371	5
7	7.7536	25
8	0.2238	6
9	−0.8334	14
10	−99.8550	7

With Defined Functions

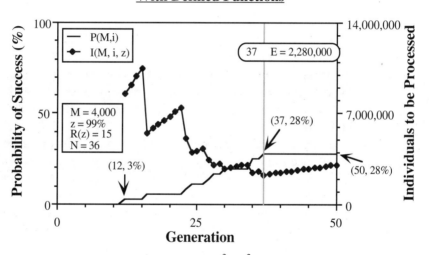

Figure 5.31 Performance curves for $x / \pi + x^2 / \pi^2 + 2\pi x$ showing that $E_{with} = 2{,}280{,}000$ with ADFs.

Table 5.18 Comparison table for $x / \pi + x^2 / \pi^2 + 2\pi x$.

	Without ADFs	With ADFs
Average structural complexity $\overline{S}$	86.6	94.3
Computational effort E	3,000,000	2,280,000

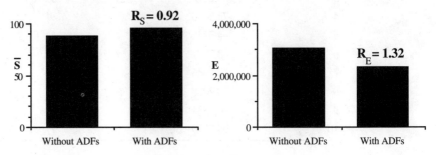

Figure 5.32 Summary graphs for $x / \pi + x^2 / \pi^2 + 2\pi x$.

Table 5.17 shows the constant value evolved for the 10 successful runs of the problem of symbolic regression for $x / \pi + x^2 / \pi^2 + 2\pi x$ and the number of invocations of ADF0 for each run. In each instance, the evolved constant is called repeatedly (with the number of invocations of the constant value ranging between 3 and 25). However, the evolved constant is not 3.14159 in any instance. Moreover, there are precisely four invocations of ADF0 in only one of the 10 runs.

The average structural complexity, $\overline{S}_{with}$, of the best-of-run programs form the 10 successful runs (out of 36 runs) of the problem of symbolic regression for $x / \pi + x^2 / \pi^2 + 2\pi x$ is 94.3 points with automatically defined functions.

Figure 5.31 presents the performance curves based on these 36 runs of the problem of symbolic regression for $x / \pi + x^2 / \pi^2 + 2\pi x$ with automatically defined functions. The cumulative probability of success, $P(M, i)$, is 28% by generation 37 and is 28% by generation 50. The two numbers in the oval indicate that if this problem is run through to generation 37, processing a total of $E_{with} = 2,280,000$ individuals (i.e., $4,000 \times 38$ generations $\times 15$ runs) is sufficient to yield a satisfactory result for this problem with 99% probability.

5.4.1.5 Comparison with and without ADFs

Table 5.18 compares the average structural complexity, $\overline{S}_{without}$ and $\overline{S}_{with}$, and the computational effort, $E_{without}$ and E_{with}, for the problem of symbolic regression for $x / \pi + x^2 / \pi^2 + 2\pi x$ both with automatically defined functions and without them. As can be seen, automatically defined functions are beneficial for the scaled-up version of this problem.

Figure 5.32 summarizes the information in this comparison table and shows a structural complexity ratio, R_S, of 0.92 and an efficiency ratio,

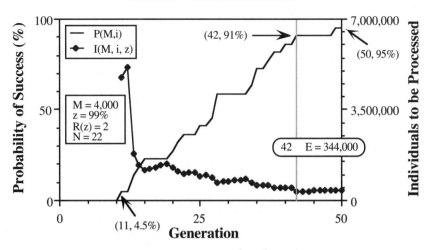

Figure 5.33 Performance curves for $x / \pi + x^2 / \pi^2$ showing that $E_{without} = 344,000$ without ADFs.

R_E, of 1.32. The fact that the efficiency ratio is greater than 1 indicates that automatically defined functions are beneficial for the scaled-up version of this problem.

5.4.2 The Two-Term Expression $x / \pi + x^2 / \pi^2$

In the simpler version of this problem, the target invokes π only three times. The tableau for this version of this problem is identical to the tableau for the previous version (except that the target function is $x / \pi + x^2 / \pi^2$) and will not be shown here.

5.4.2.1 Results without ADFs
In one run without automatically defined functions, the following 41-point satisfactory result scoring 10 hits (out of 10) emerged in generation 14:

```
(* (+ 0.311905 X) (* 0.126205 (+ (- (- (+ (+ 0.311905 X)
0.633194) (* 0.106995 (* (+ (- (- (+ 0.311905 (- X 0.091904)) (*
0.126205 (+ (- X 0.091904) 0.633194))) 0.091904) 0.633194) (*
0.126205 (- X 0.00639343))))) 0.091904) 0.633194))).
```

As before, the random constants are intermixed throughout this expression in this best-of-run program.

The average structural complexity, $\overline{S}_{without}$, of the best-of-run programs from the 21 successful runs (out of 22 runs) to the problem of symbolic regression for $x / \pi + x^2 / \pi^2$ is 60.6 points without automatically defined functions.

Figure 5.33 presents the performance curves based on these 22 runs of the problem of symbolic regression for $x / \pi + x^2 / \pi^2$ without automatically defined functions. The cumulative probability of success, $P(M,i)$, is

With Defined Functions

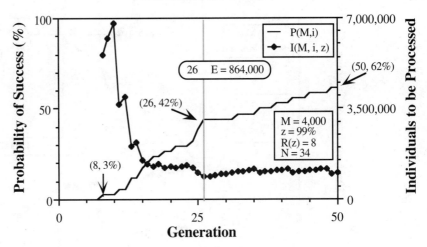

Figure 5.34 Performance curves for $x / \pi + x^2 / \pi^2$ showing that $E_{with} = 864,000$ with ADFs.

91% by generation 42 and is 95% by generation 50. The two numbers in the oval indicate that if this problem is run through to generation 42, processing a total of $E_{without} = 344,000$ individuals (i.e., $4,000 \times 43$ generations $\times$ 2 runs) is sufficient to yield a satisfactory result for this problem with 99% probability.

5.4.2.2 Results with ADFs

In one run with automatically defined functions the following 76-point program scoring 10 hits (out of 10) emerged in generation 8:

```
(progn (defun ADF0 ()
          (values (- (+ (* (- -0.5931 0.916) (+ -0.9225
           -0.0545044)) (+ (* 0.170105 -0.1652) (* 0.7473
           0.358994))) (* (* (% -0.9369 0.134201) (- 0.442
           0.8804)) (- (* (+ -0.223602 0.9648) (+ -0.00400543
           0.6232)) (+ 0.2592 0.708496))))))
       (values (% (- (* (+ X (ADF0)) (% X (ADF0))) (% (- (- (* X
           0.843) (* X -0.3687)) (% X X)) (+ (+ (ADF0) (ADF0))
           (ADF0)))) (- (+ (- X X) (+ (ADF0) X)) (- (- (ADF0)
           (ADF0)) (- -0.3031 X)))))).
```

In this best-of-run program ADF0 evaluates to 3.2717. ADF0 is called six times to provide this constant value for use in the calculation and two more times to produce a zero.

The average structural complexity, $\bar{S}_{with}$, of the best-of-run programs from the 21 successful runs (out of 34 runs) to the problem of symbolic regression for $x / \pi + x^2 / \pi^2$ is 73.4 points with automatically defined functions.

Figure 5.34 presents the performance curves based on these 34 runs of the problem of symbolic regression for $x / \pi + x^2 / \pi^2$ with automatically defined functions. The cumulative probability of success, $P(M,i)$, is 42%

Table 5.19 Comparison table for $x / \pi + x^2 / \pi^2$.

	Without ADFs	With ADFs
Average structural complexity $\bar{S}$	60.6	73.4
Computational effort E	344,000	864,000

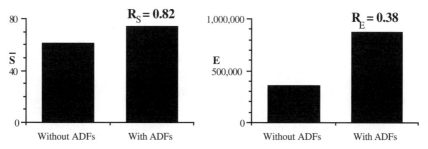

Figure 5.35 Summary graphs for $x / \pi + x^2 / \pi^2$.

by generation 26 and is 62% by generation 50. The two numbers in the oval indicate that if this problem is run through to generation 26, processing a total of E_{with} = 864,000 individuals (i.e., 4,000 × 27 generations × 8 runs) is sufficient to yield a satisfactory result for this problem with 99% probability.

5.4.2.3 Comparison with and without ADFs

Table 5.19 compares the average structural complexity, $\bar{S}_{without}$ and $\bar{S}_{with}$, and the computational effort, $E_{without}$ and E_{with}, for the problem of symbolic regression for $x / \pi + x^2 / \pi^2$, with automatically defined functions and without them. As can be seen, automatically defined functions are not beneficial for the simpler version of this problem.

Figure 5.35 summarizes the information in this comparison table and shows a structural complexity ratio, R_S, of 0.82 and an efficiency ratio, R_E, of 0.38. The fact that the efficiency ratio is less than 1 indicates that automatically defined functions are not beneficial for the simpler version of this problem.

Again we see that the simpler version of this problem is on the non-beneficial side of an apparent breakeven point for computational effort; however, the scaled-up version is on the beneficial side.

5.5 SUMMARY

Table 5.20 compiles the observations from the 16 experiments in this chapter into one table. The first four rows apply to the simpler version of each problem and the last four rows apply to the scaled-up version of each problem. As can be seen, for the simpler versions of each of the problems,

Table 5.20 Summary table of the structural complexity ratio, R_S, and the efficiency ratio, R_E, for the simpler version and the scaled-up version of the four problems in this chapter.

Problem	Structural complexity ratio R_S	Efficiency ratio R_E
Quintic polynomial $x^5 - 2x^3 + x$	1.07	0.33
Boolean 5-symmetry	0.80	0.56
Three-sines $\sin x + \sin 2x + \sin 3x$	1.09	0.89
Two-term $x / \pi + x^2 / \pi^2$	0.82	0.38
Sextic polynomial $x^6 - 2x^4 + x^2$	0.98	1.22
Boolean 6-symmetry	1.82	1.82
Four-sines $\sin x + \sin 2x + \sin 3x + \sin 4x$	1.30	1.28
Three-term $x / \pi + x^2 / \pi^2 + 2\pi x$	0.92	1.32

the efficiency ratio is less than 1 (indicating that fewer fitness evaluations are required to yield a satisfactory result for the problem with a 99% probability without automatically defined functions than with them). As in the simple two-boxes problem, automatically defined functions are not beneficial for these simpler versions. However, for the scaled-up versions of the four problems, the efficiency ratio is greater than 1 (indicating more computational effort is required without automatically defined functions than with them). That is, automatically defined functions are beneficial for these problems. These four groups of problems straddle a breakeven point for computational effort.

Figure 5.36 is a bar chart summarizing the values of the efficiency ratio, R_E, for the simpler version (gray bars) and the scaled-up version (black bars) of the four problems shown in table 5.20. The black bars representing the scaled-up versions of the problems are on the beneficial side of the breakeven point for computational effort for all four problems.

Automatically defined functions exhibit no consistent effect on the average structural complexity of the evolved programs for the four problems in this chapter; however, they do exhibit a reasonably consistent advantage as to parsimony for the more difficult problems encountered in later chapters.

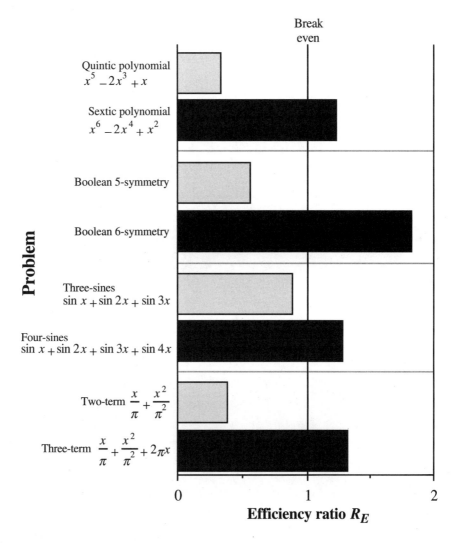

Figure 5.36 The efficiency ratio, R_E, of the scaled-up versions of all four problems in this chapter are greater than 1.

6 Boolean Parity Functions

Genetic programming with automatically defined functions did not exhibit any advantage in the two-boxes problem (chapter 4) in terms of the average size of the evolved solutions or the computational effort when compared to genetic programming without automatically defined functions. For the simpler versions of the four problems presented in chapter 5, automatically defined functions demonstrated no advantage in terms of fitness evaluations; however, automatically defined functions were advantageous for the scaled-up versions of each of the four problems. Thus, there appears to be a breakeven point for computational effort for these four problems; automatically defined functions facilitate problem-solving on the beneficial side of that breakeven point.

The problem of symbolic regression of the Boolean even-parity function considered in this chapter is distinctly on the beneficial side of the breakeven point for computational effort.

Parity problems are scaled in terms of the number of their arguments (arity, order). The chapter begins by stating the problem of learning the parity function. Multiple function-defining branches and hierarchical automatically defined functions are introduced.

We then establish a baseline for the computational effort, $E_{without}$, without automatically defined functions and the average structural complexity, $\overline{S}_{without}$, without automatically defined functions for the even-3-, 4-, 5-, and 6-parity problems using a population size of 16,000. Then, values of E_{with} and $\overline{S}_{with}$ are obtained with automatically defined functions for the same progression of parity problems with the same population size. The efficiency ratio, R_E, and the structural complexity ratio, R_S, are then computed for the parity problems in this progression.

The advantages of automatically defined functions are further demonstrated by solving the even-parity problems of order 7, 8, 9, 10, and 11 with a population size of only 4,000.

6.1 THE EVEN-PARITY PROBLEM

The Boolean *even-k-parity function* of k Boolean arguments returns T if an even number of its Boolean arguments are T, and otherwise returns NIL.

Table 6.1 Truth table for Boolean even-3-parity function.

Fitness case	D2	D1	D0	Even-3-parity
0	NIL	NIL	NIL	T
1	NIL	NIL	T	NIL
2	NIL	T	NIL	NIL
3	NIL	T	T	T
4	T	NIL	NIL	NIL
5	T	NIL	T	T
6	T	T	NIL	T
7	T	T	T	NIL

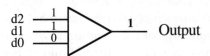

Figure 6.1   Boolean even-3-parity function with inputs of 1, 1, and 0 an output of 1.

Figure 6.1 shows that the output of the even-3-parity function is 1 for inputs of 1 (representing T), 1, and 0 (representing NIL).

A Boolean function can be represented and fully defined by its *truth table*. Table 6.1 shows the truth table for the even-3-parity function. Each row of the truth table corresponds to one of the eight fitness cases for this problem.

Parity functions are often used to check the accuracy of stored or transmitted binary data in computers because a change in the value of any one of its arguments toggles the value of the function. Because of this sensitivity to its inputs, the parity function is difficult to learn and is often used as a benchmark in the fields of machine learning and neural networks.

Throughout this book, we use the widely-used numbering scheme for identifying Boolean functions wherein the values of the function for the 2^k combinations of its k Boolean arguments are concatenated into a 2^k-bit binary number and then converted to the equivalent decimal number. For example, the values of the even-3-parity function for the $2^3 = 8$ combinations of its three inputs are 0, 1, 1, 0, 1, 0, 0, and 1 (reading table 6.1 up from the fitness case consisting of three T values to the fitness case consisting of three NIL values). Since $01101001_2 = 105_{10}$, the even-3-parity function is referred to as three-argument Boolean rule 105. Similarly, the even-4-parity function is four-argument Boolean rule 38,505; the even-5-parity function is five-argument rule 1,771,476,585; and the 6-symmetry function (subsection 5.2.1) is six-argument Boolean rule 9,225,659,030,704,492,545.

6.2   PREPARATORY STEPS WITHOUT ADFs

To establish a baseline for measuring the effectiveness of automatically defined functions, we first measure the performance of genetic programming in solving the even-3-, 4-, 5-, and 6-parity problems without automatically defined functions.

In applying genetic programming to the even-parity problem of k arguments, the terminal set, $\mathcal{T}$, consists of the k Boolean arguments D0, D1, D2, ... involved in the problem, so that

$\mathcal{T} = \{$D0, D1, D2, ...$\}$.

The function set, $\mathcal{F}$, consists of the following computationally complete set of four primitive Boolean functions:

$\mathcal{F} = \{$AND, OR, NAND, NOR$\}$

with an argument map for the function set, $\mathcal{F}$, of

$\{2, 2, 2, 2\}$.

The Boolean even-parity functions appear to be the most difficult Boolean functions to find with a blind random search of a space of programs composed of functions from the function set, $\mathcal{F}$, and terminals from the terminal set, $\mathcal{T}$. Even though there are only 256 different Boolean functions with three arguments and one output, the Boolean even-3-parity function is so difficult to find by a blind random search of program space (over $\mathcal{T}$ and $\mathcal{F}$) that we did not encounter a random program with this behavior after 10,000,000 trials (*Genetic Programming*, table 9.3). In addition, the even-3-parity function appears to be the most difficult to learn using genetic programming with the function set, $\mathcal{F}$, and terminal set, $\mathcal{T}$ (*Genetic Programming*, table 9.4). The even-parity problem is much more difficult to learn than the symmetry problem of the same order.

The set of possible fitness cases for this problem consists of the 2^k combinations of the k Boolean arguments. Since this number of fitness cases is finite and relatively small (for small values of k), we use all 2^k combinations as the fitness cases for learning this function.

The raw fitness of a program is the number of fitness cases (out of 2^k) for which the program returns the correct value. Raw fitness ranges between 0 and 2^k, and a larger value is better.

The standardized fitness of a program is the sum, over the 2^k fitness cases, of the Hamming distance (error) between the value returned by the program and the correct value of the Boolean function. Standardized fitness ranges between 0 and 2^k, and a value closer to 0 is better. Raw fitness is 2^k minus standardized fitness.

Our goal here is to make performance curves based on a series of runs, with a constant population size, of the even 3-, 4-, 5-, and 6-parity problems, with and without automatically defined functions. Of these eight versions, the even-6-parity problem without automatically defined functions will prove to be the most difficult to solve. The largest population that our existing computing equipment can handle is 16,000. In fact, a population of size 16,000 can be handled only if the individual programs in the population are represented as arrays (described in appendix D), rather than as LISP S-expressions. As

Table 6.2 Tableau without ADFs for the even-3-parity problem.

Objective:	Find a program that produces the value of the Boolean even-3-parity function as its output when given the values of the three independent Boolean variables as its input.
Terminal set without ADFs:	D0, D1, and D2.
Function set without ADFs:	AND, OR, NAND, and NOR.
Fitness cases:	All $2^3 = 8$ combinations of the three Boolean arguments D0, D1, and D2.
Raw fitness:	The number of fitness cases for which the value returned by the program equals the correct value of the even-3-parity function.
Standardized fitness:	The standardized fitness of a program is the sum, over the $2^3 = 8$ fitness cases, of the Hamming distance (error) between the value returned by the program and the correct value of the Boolean even-3-parity function.
Hits:	Same as raw fitness.
Wrapper:	None.
Parameters:	$M = 16,000$. $G = 51$.
Success predicate:	A program scores the maximum number of hits.

will shortly be seen, a population size, M, of 16,000 is barely satisfactory. It is sufficiently large to yield solutions without automatically defined functions on 100% of the runs of the even-3- and 4-parity problems and on 44% of the runs of the even-5-parity problem.

The computational effort, E, required to yield a solution to this problem, of course, depends on the choice of the major parameter of population size, M, as well as the choices for the minor quantitative and qualitative control parameters of the run. We have no reason to believe that the population size, M, of 16,000 and the maximum number of generations to be run, G, of 51, is optimal for any particular size of parity problem. In any event, no one pair of choices for M and G can be optimal over a range of problem sizes. Constant values of M, G, and the minor parameters are used here to minimize the variation in parameters while we do our comparative analysis of performance.

Table 6.2 summarizes the key features of the problem of symbolic regression for the even-3-parity function without automatically defined functions. This table can be applied to the 4-, 5-, and 6-parity problems merely by appropriately enlarging the terminal set; expanding the set of fitness cases; and increasing the numerical range of values for raw fitness, standardized fitness, and hits.

Without Defined Functions

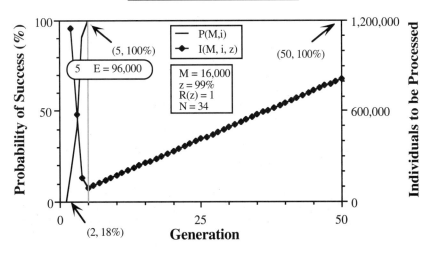

Figure 6.2 Performance curves for the even-3-parity problem showing that $E_{without}$ = 96,000 without ADFs.

6.3 EVEN-3-PARITY WITHOUT ADFs

Genetic programming is capable of solving the even-3-parity problem without automatically defined functions.

In one run (out of 34 runs) of the even-3-parity problem without automatically defined functions, genetic programming discovered the following 35-point program with a perfect value of raw fitness of 8 (out of a possible value of 2^3 = 8) in generation 4:

```
(NAND (OR (AND D1 D2) (NAND (AND (NAND D0 D0) (NOR D1 D2)) (NAND
(NAND D1 D1) (AND D2 D0)))) (OR (OR (AND (AND D0 D2) D1) (NOR
(AND D2 D0) D1)) (NOR D2 D0))).
```

The average structural complexity, $\overline{S}_{without}$, of the 100%-correct solutions from the 34 successful runs (out of 34 runs) of the even-3-parity problem without automatically defined functions is 44.6 points.

Figure 6.2 presents the performance curves based on the 34 runs for the even-3-parity problem without automatically defined functions. The cumulative probability of success, $P(M,i)$, is 100% by generation 5. Note that since $P(M,i)$ is computed from empirical data, this probability of 100% is not a guarantee of a solution for this problem by generation 5. If a much larger number of runs were made, some runs would not produce a solution by generation 5. The two numbers in the oval indicate that if this problem is run through to generation 5, processing a total of $E_{without}$ = 96,000 individuals (i.e., 16,000 × 6 generations × 1 run) is sufficient to yield a solution to this problem with 99% probability. Only one run is required to solve this problem with 99% probability with this large population size because $P(M,i)$ exceeds 99% at generation 5. $P(M,i)$ is only 91% at generation 4, thus making $R(M,i,z)$ = 2. The number of individuals to be processed is therefore 160,000 (i.e., $16,000 \times 5$ generations $\times 2$ runs) for generation 4. This is higher than for generation 5 (where $R(M, i, z)$ is 1). For generations 6 through 50, $I(M, i, z)$ is necessarily higher than it is for generation 5 because M and $R(M, i, z)$ are constant and i is greater than 5. Consequently, $I(M, i, z)$ for generations 5 through 50 (and beyond) ramps up as the rising edge of a sawtooth. The fact that $P(M, i)$ is 0% for generation 0 indicates that a blind random search of 544,000 programs (i.e., $34 \times 16,000$) in the space of possible programs (over $\mathcal{F}$ and $\mathcal{T}$) did not yield even one solution to this problem.

6.4 EVEN-4-PARITY WITHOUT ADFs

Genetic programming discovered the following 127-point program with a perfect value of raw fitness of 16 (out of 16) in generation 13 of one run of the even-4-parity problem without automatically defined functions:

```
(NAND (NOR (NAND (NOR (AND (NOR D3 D1) (AND D2 D0)) (NAND (OR
(NAND (NOR D2 D0) (AND D1 D3)) (OR (AND D1 D0) (NOR D2 (OR (OR
D3 D2) (OR D3 D3))))) (NAND (AND (OR D2 D1) (AND D0 D1)) (OR
(AND D3 D2) (NOR D2 D3))))) (OR (AND (OR D0 D2) (NAND (AND D0
D3) (AND D2 D1))) (NAND (NOR D2 D1) (NOR D3 D0)))) (NOR (NAND
(AND (NOR (AND D1 D0) (NOR D2 D3)) (OR (AND D2 D0) (OR D3 D1))) (NOR
(AND D3 D2) (NOR D0 D1))) (AND (NOR (AND D3 D3) (NAND (NOR
D2 (AND (NOR D1 D0) (NAND D3 D2))) (AND D1 D3))) (NOR (OR D0 D3)
(AND D3 D0))))) (OR (OR D1 D0) (AND (NAND D3 D2) (NAND D1
D2)))).
```

The average structural complexity, $\overline{S}_{without}$, of the 100%-correct solutions from the 18 successful runs (out of 18 runs) to the even-4-parity problem without automatically defined functions is 112.6 points.

Figure 6.3 presents the performance curves for the even-4-parity problem without automatically defined functions over the series of 18 runs. The cumulative probability of success, $P(M, i)$, is 100% by generation 23. The numbers in the oval indicate that, if this problem is run through to generation 23, processing a total of $E_{without} = 384,000$ individuals (i.e., $16,000 \times 24$ generations $\times 1$ run) is sufficient to yield a solution to this problem with 99% probability.

6.5 EVEN-5-PARITY WITHOUT ADFs

The following 321-point program with a perfect value of raw fitness of 32 (out of 32) was discovered in generation 38 in one run of the even-5-parity problem without automatically defined functions:

```
(NAND (NAND (NOR (NOR (NOR (NAND D1 D2) (AND D1 D3)) (NOR (NOR (NOR
(NAND D1 D2) (AND D1 D3)) (AND (NAND (OR (OR D3 D1) (NOR D1
D4)) (NOR (OR D0 D0) (NOR D2 D1))) (OR (AND (OR D4 D1) (AND D2
D0)) (NAND (NAND D2 D2) (NOR D1 (NOR D2 D0)))))) (NAND (NAND
(AND D2 (NAND (AND (AND (NAND D3 (NAND D2 D0)) (OR (OR D1 D1)
(AND D3 D2))) D0) D0)) (AND D1 D4)) (NAND (AND D2 D0) (NOR (NAND D4
D0) D3))))) (NAND (NAND (AND D2 (NAND (AND (AND (NAND D3 D2)
```

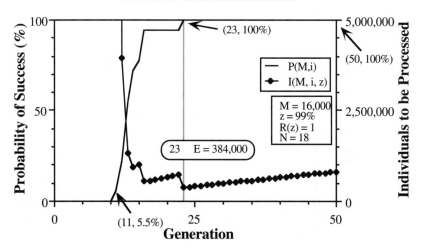

Figure 6.3 Performance curves for the even-4-parity problem showing that $E_{without} = 384,000$ without ADFs.

```
(OR (OR D1 D1) (AND D3 D2))) D0) D0)) (AND D1 D4)) (NAND (AND D2 D0)
(NOR (NOR (OR D0 D2) (AND (NOR D4 (AND (NAND D4 D3) (OR D0 D2)))
(NAND (NAND D0 D4) (OR D0 D1)))) (AND D2 (NAND (AND (AND
(NOR (NOR (AND D1 D3) (NOR D3 D4)) (AND D1 D3)) (OR (OR D1 D1)
(AND D3 D2))) D0) D0)))))) (OR (NAND (NAND D3 D4) (NAND D1 D2))
(NOR D3 D4))) (NAND (NAND (NAND (NOR D4 D3) (OR D0 D4)) (NOR (NOR
(OR (NAND (NAND (NAND D1 (NOR D3 D4)) (NOR D2 D1)) (OR (OR
D3 D4) (NOR (NOR (OR D0 D0) (NOR D2 D1)) D1))) (OR (AND D4 D3)
(NOR D3 D4))) (AND (OR (NAND (NOR (NOR D4 D0) (OR (NOR (NAND D1
D2) (NOR D3 D4)) D1)) (AND (AND D2 (NAND (AND D2 D0) (NAND D3
D3))) (AND D1 D1))) (OR D2 D2)) (AND (OR D0 D2) (OR D1 D0))))
(NAND (NAND (AND (NAND D3 D4) (NOR (AND (NOR D0 D3) (NAND D2
D0)) (OR (NOR D3 D4) (OR D2 D1)))) (NOR (NOR D4 D0) (NOR (OR
(NOR D2 D1) D0) (AND (NOR D4 (AND (NAND D4 D0) (NOR D1 D4)))
(NAND (NAND D0 D4) (OR D0 D1)))))) (NAND (AND D1 D3) (AND (AND
D2 (OR D3 D0)) (AND D2 (AND D1 D4))))))) (NOR (AND D0 D2)
(NOR D3 D4)))).
```

Notice the unwieldy size of this 321-point solution. Indeed, the average structural complexity, $\overline{S}_{without}$, of the 100%-correct solutions from the 11 successful runs (out of 25 runs) of the even-5-parity problem without automatically defined functions is 299.9 points.

Figure 6.4 presents the performance curves for the even-5-parity problem without automatically defined functions over the series of 25 runs. The cumulative probability of success, $P(M, i)$, is 4% by generation 34 and 44% by generation 50. The numbers in the oval indicate that, if this problem is run through to generation 50, processing a total of $E_{without} = 6,528,000$ individuals (i.e., $16,000 \times 51$ generations $\times 8$ runs) is sufficient to yield a solution to this problem with 99% probability.

Without Defined Functions

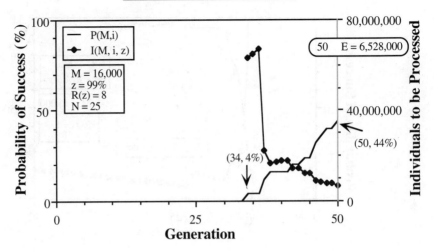

Figure 6.4 Performance curves for the even-5-parity problem showing that $E_{without} = 6{,}528{,}000$ without ADFs.

Recall that the computational effort, $E_{without}$, was 96,000 for the 3-parity problem and was 384,000 for the 4-parity problem. Now it is 6,528,000 for the 5-parity problem. In other words, as the order of this problem increases, the computational effort without automatically defined functions grows rapidly and nonlinearly.

6.6 EVEN-6-PARITY WITHOUT ADFs

We are unable to continue the progressive comparison of the computational effort, $E_{without}$, necessary to solve the even-parity problem with increasing numbers of arguments without automatically defined functions with our chosen population size, M, of 16,000 and our chosen maximum number of generations to be run, G, of 51.

We made 19 runs of the even-6-parity problem without automatically defined functions with a population size of 16,000 and with each run being abandoned, as usual, after generation 50. Every run made progress toward solving the problem; however, none found a 100%-correct solution.

Figure 6.5 shows, by generation, the progress made by the 19 unsuccessful runs of the even-6-parity problem without automatically defined functions. The curve on the bottom is the standardized fitness, by generation, of the best of the 19 best-of-generation programs. For example, the best of the 19 best-of-generation programs for generation 0 has a standardized fitness of 29 (i.e., it scores 35 hits out of 64); the best of the 19 best-of-generation programs for generation 50 has a standardized fitness of 6 (i.e., it scores 58 hits out of 64). The curve in the middle is the average, by generation, of the standardized fitness of the 19 best-of-generation programs. It reaches 9.1 (54.9 hits) by

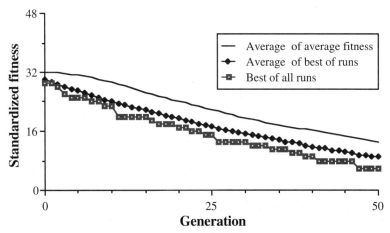

Figure 6.5 Three measures showing the progressive improvement in fitness of the 19 unsuccessful runs of the even-6-parity problem without ADFs.

generation 50. The curve on the top is the average, by generation, of the 19 values of the average standardized fitness of the population of 16,000 as a whole. It reaches 13.1 by generation 50. All three curves indicate that genetic programming is making progress in solving this problem.

Genetic programming is presumably capable of solving the even-6-parity problem without automatically defined functions. This problem is surely solvable with a larger population size; however, 16,000 is the largest population our existing computing equipment can handle. This problem is probably also solvable by continuing the runs for additional generations.

Although we did not get one solution, much less the multiple solutions necessary for construction of a meaningful performance curve, we can make a rough estimate of the computational effort, $E_{without}$, for this problem. Suppose that the number of hits leaps to 64 on generation 50 of the 19th run so that the final run of this series becomes successful. The probability of success, $P(16,000, 50, 0.99)$, then becomes 0.053, instead of 0.0. If we then compute $R(z)$ and $E_{without}$ in the usual way based on this hypothetical success and this admittedly inadequate number of successes, we find that $R(z)$ would be 86 and that $E_{without}$ would be 70,176,000 (i.e., 16,000 × 51 generations × 86 runs). This rough estimate probably understates the true value of $E_{without}$. Based on this rough estimate, the progression of values of $E_{without}$ for the even-3-, 4-, 5-, and 6-parity problems without automatically defined functions then becomes 96,000, 384,000, 6,528,000, and 70,176,000. That is, there is an explosive growth in $E_{without}$ as the problem is scaled up along the dimension of the number of arguments.

Even though none of 19 runs actually produced a solution to the problem, the average structural complexity, $\overline{S}_{without}$, of the solutions can also be roughly estimated.

Figure 6.6 shows, by generation, the average of the structural complexity of the 19 best-of-generation programs (called the *average of the best*) and the average, over the 19 runs, of the average value of the structural complexity of the 16,000 programs in the population as a whole (called the *average of the average*).

On generation 50, the 19 best-of-generation programs score between 52 and 58 hits. The average of the structural complexity values for these 19 programs is 328.0. Based on the upward trend of this curve, the true value of the average structural complexity, $\overline{S}_{without}$, of a set of actual 100%-correct solutions is likely to be somewhat above 328.0. Thus, we adopt 328.0 as a rough (probably understated) estimate for $\overline{S}_{without}$ for solutions to the even-6-parity problem without automatically defined functions.

6.7 MULTIPLE FUNCTION-DEFINING BRANCHES

In all the problems in chapters 4 and 5, there was only one function-defining branch in the overall computer program when automatically defined functions were being used. The parity problem will illustrate the more general situation where there are multiple function-defining branches.

A human programmer writing code for the even-3-parity or even-4-parity functions would probably choose to call upon either the odd-2-parity function (also known as the *exclusive-or* function XOR, the inequality function, and two-argument Boolean rule 6) or the even-2-parity function (also known as the equivalence function EQV, and two-argument Boolean rule 9).

For example, given the function set available here, the human programmer writing code for the even-3-parity of D0, D1, and D2 might write something like the following:

```
1    ;;;- definition of the two-argument exclusive-or function
2    ;;;  ODD-2-PARITY (XOR)-
3    (progn (defun ODD-2-PARITY (arg0 arg1)
4           (values (NOR (AND arg0 arg1)
5                   (NOR arg0 arg1))))
6    ;;;- main program for the even-3-parity of D0, D1, and D2-
7           (values (ODD-2-PARITY D0
8                   (nand (ODD-2-PARITY D1 D2)
9                   (ODD-2-PARITY D1 D2))))
```

Lines 3 through 5 constitute the function definition for the two-argument ODD-2-PARITY.

Lines 7 through 9, the main program, calls the two-argument ODD-2-PARITY function three times in order to compute the even-3-parity of D0, D1, and D2.

A human programmer writing code for the even-5-parity function and parity functions of higher order would probably also want to call upon either the even-3-parity (three-argument Boolean rule 105) or the odd-3-parity (three-argument Boolean rule 150) as building blocks. Parity functions of order three

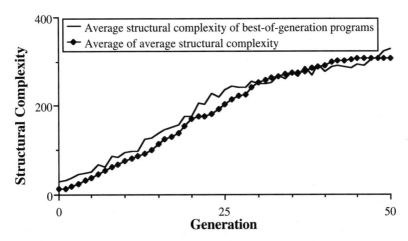

Figure 6.6 Two structural complexity measures of the 19 unsuccessful runs of the even-6-parity problem without ADFs.

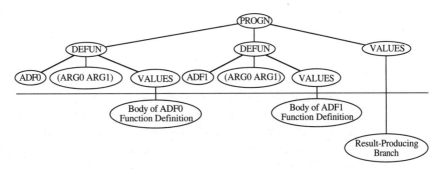

Figure 6.7 Overall structure of a program with two function-defining branches and one result-producing branch.

greatly facilitate writing code for the higher-order parity functions. Neither of these functions is, of course, in the original set, $\mathcal{F}$, of available primitive functions. The fact that the programmer might want to use both a 2-parity function and a 3-parity function suggests that more than one function-defining branch might be desirable for higher-order parity problems. Multiple function-defining branches can be implemented merely by adding additional defuns to the progn of the overall program.

Figure 6.7 shows an abstraction of the overall structure of a program with two function-defining branches (each taking two dummy variables ARG0 and ARG1) and the one result-producing branch.

6.8 HIERARCHICAL AUTOMATICALLY DEFINED FUNCTIONS

It is common in ordinary programming to define one function in terms of other already-defined functions. For example, a human programmer needing the sine and cosine functions in several places in a main program would write subroutines for them and then repeatedly call the subroutines from the main program. Then, if the tangent function were needed, the programmer might write a subroutine for the tangent in terms of the already-available sine and cosine functions. Defining one subroutine in terms of other, already-defined subroutines creates a hierarchy of function definitions. Such hierarchies leverage the value of previously written code. The sine function can be called directly when it is needed and it will be invoked indirectly whenever the tangent is needed.

Once there is more than one function-defining branch, the question arises as to the nature of the relationship among the function-defining branches. There are several possibilities.

First, there might be no references among the function-defining branches. That is, ADF0, ADF1, etc. might appear in the function set of the result-producing branch, but never in the function set of any automatically defined function. In the context of a graph in which the points represent automatically defined functions and a directed line represents a direct reference by one automatically defined function to another, this possibility corresponds to a graph consisting of isolated points.

Second, there might be no restriction on the nature of the references among the function-defining branches. This possibility permits an automatically defined function to refer recursively to itself (directly or indirectly). When an automatically defined function refers to itself, its name can appear in its own function set or in the function set of a another automatically defined function to which the first automatically defined function refers (directly or indirectly). This possibility corresponds to a directed cyclic graph of references among the function-defining branches.

Third, there might be a hierarchy of references among the function-defining branches in which the name of any automatically defined function that has already been defined (i.e., has already been evaluated sequentially by the progn) may appear in the function set of any subsequent function definition. For example, if there are three function-defining branches, ADF0 can appear in the function set of ADF1 and ADF2, but not vice versa. ADF1 can appear in the function set of ADF2, but not vice versa. This possibility corresponds to a directed acyclic graph of references among the function-defining branches.

The second and third possibilities are called *hierarchical automatically defined functions*.

The first approach (used in chapters 15 to 20 herein) is especially appropriate when the function-defining branches serve as pattern detectors that fire when certain unrelated conditions are satisfied. The second approach involving recursion will not be used at all in this book. The third approach will be used most frequently herein.

Figure 6.8 shows an abstraction of an overall program with hierarchical automatically defined functions. The first function-defining branch, ADF0, consists of invariant points of type 2, 3, 4, and 5 above the dotted line and a body of type 7. The second function-defining branch, ADF1, also consists of invariant points of type 2, 3, 4, and 5 above the dotted line and a body

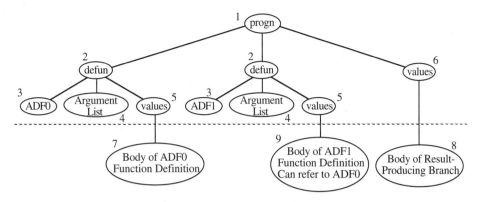

Figure 6.8 Program with hierarchical ADFs.

composed of points of a new type 9. Points of type 9 may contain references to the already-defined function ADF0. In contrast, points of type 7 do not contain references to ADF1. The result-producing branch consists of one invariant point of type 6 and a body consisting of points of type 8. The result-producing branch can refer to both ADF0 and ADF1.

The idea of hierarchical automatically defined functions can be illustrated with the following overall program for solving the even-5-parity problem:

```
1   ;;;- definition of ADF0 for even-2-parity function-
2   (progn (defun ADF0 (arg0 arg1)
3              (values (OR (AND arg0 arg1)
4                          (NOR arg0 arg1))))
5   ;;;- definition of ADF1 for odd-3-parity function-
6          (defun ADF1 (arg0 arg1 arg2)
7              (values (adf0 arg0 (adf0 arg1 arg2))))
8   ;;;-main program for even-5-parity of D0, D1, D2, D3, D4-
9          (values (adf0 (adf0 (nand d3 d3) d4)
10                        (adf1 d0 d1 d2))))
```

Lines 2–4 define the even-2-parity function ADF0 of two dummy variables, ARG0 and ARG1.

Lines 6–7 define the odd-3-parity function ADF1 of three dummy variables, ARG0, ARG1, and ARG2. ADF1 is a hierarchical automatically defined function because it references the already-defined ADF0.

Lines 9–10 are the result-producing main program. The result-producing branch calls both ADF0 and ADF1 in solving the overall problem.

The above 10-line program for the even-5-parity problem illustrates four of the five ways itemized in chapter 3 in which the hierarchical problem-solving approach can be beneficial: hierarchical decomposition, recursive application of hierarchical decomposition, parameterized reuse, and abstraction.

First, the hierarchical decomposition is illustrated by the fact that the overall program for solving the problem consists of the two automatically defined functions, ADF0, ADF1, as well as a result-producing branch.

Second, the two times that the result-producing branch invokes ADF0 and the two times that ADF1 invokes ADF0 illustrate parameterized reuse of the solution to a subproblem. ADF0 is a general way of computing the even-2-parity function. Generalization comes from such parameterized reuse.

Third, the recursive application of the entire three-step hierarchical decomposition process is illustrated by the fact that ADF1 invokes ADF0. The solution to the subproblem represented by ADF1 (i.e., the odd-3-parity function) is solved by the same three-step hierarchical problem-solving process as is used to solve the overall problem. The subproblem represented by ADF1 is solved by decomposing the odd-3-parity subproblem into the sub-subproblem represented by ADF0 (i.e., the even-2-parity function). Then the sub-subproblem ADF0 is solved. Finally, the solution to the odd-3-parity subproblem is obtained by assembling solutions to the even-2-parity sub-subproblem. Note that the term "recursive application" from chapter 3 does not involve recursion (in the sense of an ADF calling itself).

Fourth, each time ADF0 or ADF1 are invoked with a particular combination of their two or three arguments, abstraction is occurring. All the other variables of this problem are momentarily irrelevant.

6.9   PREPARATORY STEPS WITH ADFs

The explosive growth in the number of fitness evaluations and the average structural complexity for solving progressively more difficult parity problems can be controlled if we exploit the underlying regularities and symmetries of these problems and hierarchically decompose the problem into more tractable subproblems. This can be accomplished by discovering one or more reusable functions parameterized by dummy variables.

In applying genetic programming with automatically defined functions to the even-3-parity problem, we first decide on the architecture for the overall program.

The Boolean parity function returns only a single Boolean value. This single value will be the value returned by the result-producing branch of the yet-to-be-evolved overall program.

We now consider the number of arguments to be possessed by the automatically defined functions.

There is usually no advantage to enabling automatically defined functions to take more arguments than there are actual variables of the problem. This suggests an upper bound on the number of arguments for the automatically defined functions that is equal to the arity of the problem (i.e., 3 for the 3-parity problem).

A zero-argument automatically defined function merely provides a way to evolve a constant (in a problem where there are no side effects on the system and no global variables). In the case of the Boolean domain, there are only two Boolean constants, T and NIL. These two constants are not particularly useful and, in any event, can, if needed, be easily evolved without recourse to an automatically defined function.

There are only four rather uninteresting one-argument Boolean functions. Two are constant functions; one is the identity function; and the fourth is the negation function. Since we already have both NAND and NOR in the function set, the one-argument negation function does not seem to be particularly useful.

Thus, two appears to be the practical lower bound on the number of arguments for interesting automatically defined functions in the Boolean domain.

Three competing considerations affect our choice between two and three as the number of arguments for the automatically defined functions for the even-3-parity problem.

First, as a general principle, we want to impose as few *a priori* constraints as practical in order to give the evolutionary process the opportunity to define whatever functional subunits that it might find useful. The availability of a dummy variable to an automatically defined function does not create any requirement that the function actually refer to that argument or actually use it in any meaningful way. Thus, this first consideration suggests a choice of three, rather than two (for this problem of arity 3).

Second, being always mindful of the practical consideration of computer time and our need to achieve multiple successful runs in order to produce performance curves, we must consider the fact that each additional available dummy variable in a function-defining branch slows genetic programming. Our overarching purpose is, of course, to evolve the contents of the functional subunits and the result-producing branch. The architectural choices merely establish a loose framework in which the actual work-performing code can evolve. Although we generally favor as few constraints of any kind as possible on the evolutionary process, this second consideration suggests a choice of two, rather than three, arguments.

Third, since we intend to do a comparative analysis of the even-3-, 4-, 5-, and 6-parity problems, we prefer to have a formula that applies to all four situations, rather than a series of unrelated decisions. If the even-3-parity problem were the only problem under consideration, the first consideration (flexibility) would clearly outweigh the second (practicality) because the amount of computer time involved in the even-3-parity problem is insignificant. Programs tend to be larger as the number of arguments increase. Moreover, the number of fitness cases is 2^k, where k is the arity of the problem. Thus, six-argument automatically defined functions are very time-consuming in the context of the 6-parity problem. Thus, we decided against a formula calling for automatically defined functions of arity k for the even-k-parity problem since that formula would mandate using six-argument automatically defined functions for the even-6-parity problem. Given the alternatives and constraints, the exclusion of that formula resulted in our adoption of a formula calling for automatically defined functions of arity $k–1$ for the even-3-, 4-, 5-, and 6-parity problems.

Because we are interested in evolving hierarchical automatically defined functions, we decided that each program in the population should have more than one function-defining branch. Since we envisaged (incorrectly, as it turned out) that a solution of the even-5-parity problem would usually involve lower-order parity functions, two function-defining branches appeared to be sufficient for the even-6-parity problem (and presumably also for the even-3-, 4-, and 5-parity problems). Of course, three function-defining branches might also have been a good choice. The availability of an additional function-defining branch does not create any requirement that it actually be used. However, each additional function-defining branch slows genetic programming. Therefore, we decided that each individual overall program in the population will consist of two function-defining branches. Since we are interested in evolving hierarchical solutions, we also decided that defined function ADF1 can refer hierarchically to ADF0.

The first major step in preparing to use genetic programming is to identify the set of terminals and the second major step is to identify the function set. When automatically defined functions are involved, these two steps must be performed separately for each branch of the overall problem. For this problem, each of the three branches is composed of different ingredients.

We first consider the first function-defining branch for the even-3-parity problem.

The function set, $\mathcal{F}_{adf0}$, for ADF0 consists only of the set, $\mathcal{F}$, of primitive functions for the parity problem, namely

$\mathcal{F}_{adf0} = \{$AND, OR, NAND, NOR$\}$

with an argument map of

$\{2, 2, 2, 2\}$.

The terminal set, $\mathcal{T}_{adf0}$, for ADF0 consists of two dummy variables and is

$\mathcal{T}_{adf0} = \{$ARG0, ARG1$\}$.

The function-defining branch ADF0 is a composition of primitive functions from the function set, $\mathcal{F}_{adf0}$, and terminals from the terminal set, $\mathcal{T}_{adf0}$.

We next consider the second function-defining branch.

The function set, $\mathcal{F}_{adf1}$, for ADF1 consists of the union of the set, $\mathcal{F}$, of primitive functions for the parity problem and the now-defined function ADF0 thereby enabling the function-defining branch for ADF1 to refer hierarchically to the now-defined function ADF0. That is,

$\mathcal{F}_{adf1} = \{$ADF0, AND, OR, NAND, NOR$\}$

with an argument map of

$\{2, 2, 2, 2, 2\}$.

The terminal set, $\mathcal{T}_{adf1}$, for ADF1 consists of two dummy variables.

$\mathcal{T}_{adf1} = \{$ARG0, ARG1$\}$.

Note that although we use the same names, ARG0 and ARG1, for the dummy variables of both ADF0 and ADF1, these dummy variables are only defined locally within a particular automatically defined function.

The function-defining branch ADF1 is a composition of functions from the function set, $\mathcal{F}_{adf1}$, and terminals from the terminal set, $\mathcal{T}_{adf1}$.

Note that the actual variables of the problem (i.e., D0, D1, and D2) do not appear in either function-defining branch.

We now consider the result-producing branch.

The function set, $\mathcal{F}_{rpb}$, of the result-producing branch contains the four primitive Boolean functions from $\mathcal{F}$ and the two automatically defined functions ADF0 and ADF1.

$\mathcal{F}_{rpb} = \{$ADF0, ADF1, AND, OR, NAND, NOR$\}$

with an argument map of

$\{2, 2, 2, 2, 2, 2\}$.

The terminal set, $\mathcal{T}_{rpb}$, for the result-producing branch consists of the three actual variables of the even-3-parity problem, so

$\mathcal{T}_{rpb} = \{$D0, D1, D2$\}$.

Note that the result-producing branch does not contain any dummy variables, such as ARG0 or ARG1.

The result-producing branch is a composition of functions from the function set, $\mathcal{F}_{rpb}$, and terminals from the terminal set, $\mathcal{T}_{rpb}$.

When the overall program is evaluated, the progn evaluates each branch in sequence. The function definition for ADF0 is evaluated first. Then, the function definition for ADF1 is evaluated. ADF1 may contain a reference to ADF0, which, by this time, has already been defined. Finally, the result-producing branch is evaluated. This branch may contain references to both ADF0 and ADF1, which have both, by this time, been defined. The value returned by the overall program consists only of the value returned by the last argument of the progn (i.e., the result of evaluating the result-producing branch).

One might include the actual variables of the problem (i.e., the terminals from the terminal set, $\mathcal{T}$) in the terminal sets of the function-defining branches. Although there are specific problems for which it may be desirable to give the function-defining branches direct access to some or all of the actual variables, we generally view such inclusion as inconsistent with the goal of encouraging generality in the function-defining branches. Accordingly, our convention in this book is not to include the actual variables of the problem in the function-defining branches.

Table 6.3 summarizes the key features of the problem of symbolic regression of the even-3-parity function with automatically defined functions.

In what follows, genetic programming will be allowed to evolve a function definition in each of the two function-defining branches of each program and then, at its discretion, to call one, two, or neither of these automatically defined functions. We do not specify what program tree will be evolved in the function-defining branches. We do not specify whether the defined functions will actually be used (it being possible, as we have already seen, to solve this

Table 6.3 Tableau with ADFs for the even-3-parity problem.

Objective:	Find a program that produces the value of the Boolean even-3-parity function as its output when given the values of the three independent variables as its input.
Architecture of the overall program with ADFs:	One result-producing branch and two two-argument function-defining branches, with ADF1 hierarchically referring to ADF0.
Parameters:	Branch typing.
Terminal set for the result-producing branch:	D0, D1, and D2.
Function set for the result-producing branch:	ADF0, ADF1, AND, OR, NAND, and NOR.
Terminal set for the function-defining branch ADF0:	ARG0 and ARG1.
Function set for the function-defining branch ADF0:	AND, OR, NAND, and NOR.
Terminal set for the function-defining branch ADF1:	ARG0 and ARG1.
Function set for the function-defining branch ADF1:	AND, OR, NAND, NOR, and ADF0 (hierarchical reference to ADF0 by ADF1).

problem without automatically defined functions by evolving the entire program in the result-producing branch). We do not require that a function-defining branch refer to or use all of its available dummy variables. We do not require that the second automatically defined function actually refer to the first automatically defined function. We do not require that either automatically defined function be useful; an automatically defined function may, for example, duplicate a primitive function that is already available as a primitive function in the function set of the result-producing branch. We do not require that the automatically defined functions be different from one another. Instead, the structure of all three branches is determined by the combined effect, over many generations, of the selective pressure exerted by the fitness measure and by the effects of the operations of Darwinian reproduction and crossover.

An enormous amount of computer time can be saved on Boolean problems with various optimization techniques. One technique involves identifying the particular Boolean function performed by the bodies of ADF0 and ADF1 (using the numbering scheme previously described for Boolean functions); creating a lookup table for automatically defined functions; and then

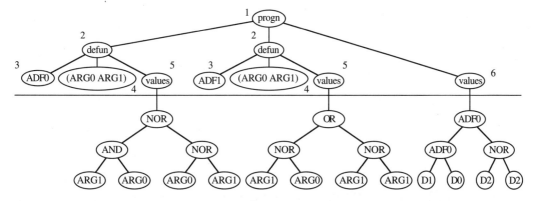

Figure 6.9 100%-correct best-of-run program from generation 2 of a run of the even-3-parity problem with ADFs.

using the lookup tables in lieu of evaluating the entire body of the ADF for each fitness case. This technique is used on the even-6-parity problem.

A second optimization technique is to identify the Boolean function using the numbering scheme described in section 6.1, convert the bodies of ADF0 and ADF1 into disjunctive normal form (DNF), and then compile and cache each different function. The number of different cached functions grows with problem size and there is a corresponding dropoff in the number of references to each such cached function. Consequently, this technique is used only on the 3-, 4-, and 5-parity problems.

These optimizations accelerate runs of the parity problem in this chapter by between one and two orders of magnitude.

6.10   EVEN-3-PARITY WITH ADFs

In one run (out of 33 runs) of the even-3-parity problem with automatically defined functions, genetic programming discovered the following 21-point program in generation 2 with a perfect value of raw fitness of 8:

```
(progn (defun ADF0 (ARG0 ARG1)
           (values (NOR (AND ARG1 ARG0) (NOR ARG0 ARG1))))
       (defun ADF1 (ARG0 ARG1)
           (values (OR (NOR ARG1 ARG0) (NOR ARG1 ARG1))))
       (values (ADF0 (ADF0 D1 D0) (NOR D2 D2)))) .
```

Figure 6.9 shows this 100%-correct best-of-run individual with automatically defined functions from generation 2 as a rooted, point-labeled tree with ordered branches. The function-defining branches are on the left and in the middle of this figure and the result-producing branch is on the right.

The first branch of this best-of-run program is a function definition for the two-argument ADF0, which, when simplified, is equivalent to the ODD-2-PARITY function (XOR).

The second branch defines the two-argument `ADF1`. Although `ADF1` potentially may refer hierarchically to `ADF0`, this particular `ADF1` does not refer to `ADF0`. However, `ADF1`'s lack of references to `ADF0` hardly matters since `ADF1` is not called by the result-producing branch.

The result-producing branch of this best-of-run individual contains two references to `ADF0` in nested form. Upon substitution of `ODD-2-PARITY` for `ADF0`, it becomes

```
(ODD-2-PARITY (ODD-2-PARITY D1 D0) (NOR D2 D2)).
```

When simplified, this is equivalent to

```
(ODD-2-PARITY (ODD-2-PARITY D1 D0) (NOT D2)),
```

which is a correct solution to the even-3-parity problem.

This solution evolved by genetic programming can be interpreted as a hierarchical decomposition of the problem. Genetic programming discovered a decomposition of the overall problem involving the `ODD-2-PARITY` subproblem. Then, genetic programming solved the subproblem by evolving a 100%-correct Boolean expression for the `ODD-2-PARITY` function in the body of `ADF0`. Third, genetic programming assembled the results of solving the `ODD-2-PARITY` subproblems into a solution of the overall even-3-parity problem by invoking `ADF0` twice in a nested way in the result-producing branch.

Note that we did not specify in advance that `ADF0` would be used to define the `ODD-2-PARITY` function, as opposed to, say, the if-then function, the even-2-parity function, or some other Boolean function. We did not specify that the `ODD-2-PARITY` function would be defined in the first branch as opposed to the second branch. We did not specify that the second branch would be ignored by the result-producing branch.

The average structural complexity, $\overline{S}_{with}$, of the 100%-correct programs from the 33 successful runs of the even-3-parity problem is 48.2 points with automatically defined functions (versus a value of $\overline{S}_{without}$ of 44.6 without automatically defined functions). That is, the even-3-parity problem is on the non-beneficial side of the breakeven point for average structural complexity.

Figure 6.10 presents the performance curves based on the 33 runs for the even-3-parity problem with automatically defined functions. The cumulative probability of success, $P(M,i)$, is 94% by generation 2 and is 100% by generation 3. The two numbers in the oval indicate that if this problem is run through to generation 3, processing a total of $E_{with} = 64{,}000$ individuals (i.e., $16{,}000 \times 4$ generations $\times 1$ run) is sufficient to yield a solution to this problem with 99% probability. The fact that $P(M,i)$ is 39% for generation 0 is discussed in chapter 26.

The 96,000 individuals that must be processed for the even-3-parity problem without automatically defined functions (as shown in figure 6.2) is 1.5 times the 64,000 individuals needed with automatically defined functions. That is, the even-3-parity problem is on the beneficial side of the breakeven point for computational effort.

With Defined Functions

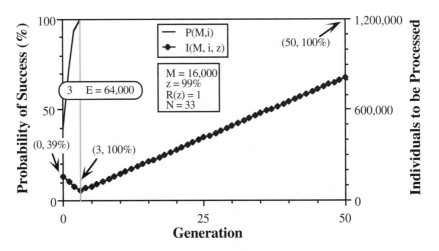

Figure 6.10   Performance curves for the even-3-parity problem showing that E_{with} = 64,000 with ADFs.

Table 6.4   Comparison table for the even-3-parity problem.

	Without ADFs	With ADFs
Average structural complexity $\bar{S}$	44.6	48.2
Computational effort E	96,000	64,000

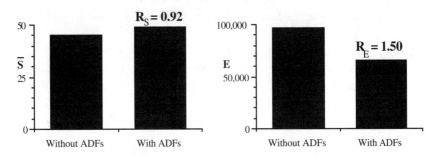

Figure 6.11   Summary graphs for the even-3-parity problem.

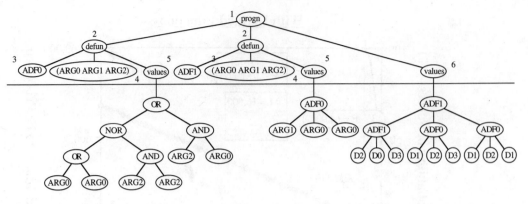

Figure 6.12 100%-correct best-of-run program from generation 4 of a run of the even-4-parity problem with ADFs.

Table 6.4 compares the average structural complexity, $\bar{S}_{without}$ and $\bar{S}_{with}$, and the computational effort, $E_{without}$ and E_{with}, for this problem with automatically defined functions and without them.

Figure 6.11 summarizes the information in this comparison table and shows a structural complexity ratio, R_S, of 0.92 and an efficiency ratio, R_E, of 1.50.

6.11 EVEN-4-PARITY WITH ADFs

Since the even-4-parity function takes four arguments, our formula for making the architectural choices specifies that both automatically defined functions take three dummy variables. Note that the mere availability of a dummy variable to an automatically defined function does not create any requirement that the function either refer to that argument or use it in any meaningful way.

In one run (out of 18 runs) of the even-4-parity problem with automatically defined functions, genetic programming discovered the following program containing 28 points with a perfect value of raw fitness of 16 in generation 4:

```
(progn (defun ADF0 (ARG0 ARG1 ARG2)
          (values (OR (NOR (OR ARG0 ARG0) (AND ARG2 ARG2)) (AND
            ARG2 ARG0)))))
       (defun ADF1 (ARG0 ARG1 ARG2)
         (values (ADF0 ARG1 ARG0 ARG0)))
       (values (ADF1 (ADF1 D2 D0 D3) (ADF0 D1 D2 D3) (ADF0 D1 D2
         D1))))).
```

Figure 6.12 depicts this 100%-correct best-of-run program as a rooted, point-labeled tree with ordered branches.

The function definition for ADF0 is equivalent to the three-argument Boolean rule 165 which, when simplified, is (EVEN-2-PARITY ARG0 ARG2). That is, ADF0 ignores its second dummy variable (ARG1) and then performs the even-2-parity function on its first and third dummy variables, ARG0 and ARG2.

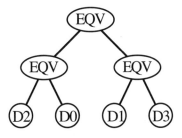

Figure 6.13 Simplified form of the result-producing branch of one solution to the even-4-parity problem with ADFs.

A function is considered to be a *parity rule* if its overall behavior exactly matches that of the even or odd parity function on any subset of two or more of its arguments (or their negations). For example, `ADF0` above is a parity rule as would be a four-argument automatically defined function that has the behavior of `(ODD-2-PARITY (NOT ARG2) ARG3)`.

The function definition for `ADF1` ignores its third dummy variable (`ARG2`) and is equivalent to `(EVEN-2-PARITY ARG1 ARG0)`.

Thus, the result-producing branch can be simplified to

```
(EVEN-2-PARITY (EVEN-2-PARITY D2 D0) (EVEN-2-PARITY D1 D3)),
```

which is a solution to the even-4-parity problem.

Figure 6.13 depicts this simplified form of the result-producing branch of the above best-of-run program from generation 4 as a rooted, point-labeled tree with ordered branches. `EQV` denotes the even-2-parity (equivalence) function.

The solutions from two other runs are noteworthy.

First, the following best-of-run individual from generation 5 containing 53 points is interesting in that `ADF1` merely permuted the order of the three arguments of `ADF0`:

```
(progn (defun ADF0 (ARG0 ARG1 ARG2)
         (values (OR (OR (NOR ARG1 ARG0) (AND ARG0 ARG1)) (NOR
           (NAND ARG0 ARG2) (NAND (NAND (OR ARG0 ARG0) (OR ARG1
           ARG0)) (NAND (AND ARG0 ARG2) (NAND ARG0 ARG1))))))))
       (defun ADF1 (ARG0 ARG1 ARG2)
         (values (ADF0 ARG1 ARG2 ARG0)))
       (values (OR (ADF0 (ADF1 D0 D2 D0) (ADF1 D2 D3 D1) (ADF1 D0
         D3 D0)) (NOR (OR D2 D0) (ADF1 D3 D1 D1)))))).
```

Although all three of `ADF0`'s dummy variables appear in the body `ADF0`, only two of them (`ARG0` and `ARG1`) actually affect the value returned by `ADF0`. `ADF0` is equivalent to three-argument Boolean rule 153, which is `(EVEN-2-PARITY ARG0 ARG1)`. `ADF1` is, in turn, equivalent to `(EVEN-2-PARITY ARG1 ARG2)`.

In a different run, `ADF1` in the following best-of-run 123-point program from generation 9 always returns the constant `NIL`:

```
(progn (defun ADF0 (ARG0 ARG1 ARG2)
          (values (OR (NAND (OR (OR ARG1 ARG1) (OR ARG0 ARG1))
            (NAND (AND ARG0 ARG1) (OR (AND (NAND ARG0 ARG1) (NOR
            ARG0 ARG1)) ARG0))) (NOR (NAND (OR ARG1 ARG2) (NOR
            ARG2 ARG0)) (NOR (AND ARG2 ARG0) (AND ARG0 ARG0))))))
       (defun ADF1 (ARG0 ARG1 ARG2)
          (values (NOR (OR (NAND (OR ARG0 ARG2) (AND ARG2 ARG0))
            (NAND (NOR (NAND ARG1 ARG0) ARG0) (ADF0 (AND (NOR
            ARG0 ARG2) ARG2) ARG0 (NAND ARG2 ARG0)))) (OR (NOR
            ARG2 ARG1) (NAND (NOR ARG0 ARG1) (NAND ARG0
            ARG2))))))
       (values (NOR (AND (ADF1 (ADF0 D3 D1 D0) (OR D1 D3) (ADF1
          D1 D2 D0)) (OR (OR D1 D2) (ADF0 D1 D2 D3))) (ADF0 (ADF0
          (NAND D2 D2) (NOR D0 D0) (AND D0 D0)) (NAND (ADF0 D1 D3
          D0) (ADF0 D3 D1 D2)) (NOR (AND D2 D1) (ADF0 D2 D2
          D2)))))).
```

The average structural complexity, $\overline{S}_{with}$, of the 100%-correct programs from the 18 successful runs (out of 18 runs) of the even-4-parity problem is 60.1 points with automatically defined functions (versus a value of $\overline{S}_{without}$ of 112.6 without automatically defined functions).

Recall that the average structural complexity, $\overline{S}_{with}$, of solutions to the even-3-parity problem was 48.2 points with automatically defined functions (versus 44.6 without them). Automatically defined functions are not beneficial as to average structural complexity for the even-parity problem of order 3, but they are beneficial for the even-parity problem of order 4. Thus, for the even-parity problem, the breakeven point for average structural complexity appears to be between three and four.

Figure 6.14 presents the performance curves based on these 18 runs for the even-4-parity problem with automatically defined functions. The cumulative probability of success, $P(M, i)$, is 56% by generation 5 and is 100% by generation 10. The two numbers in the oval indicate that if this problem is run through to generation 10, processing a total of E_{with} = 176,000 individuals (i.e., 16,000 × 11 generations × 1 run) is sufficient to yield a solution to this problem with 99% probability.

The 384,000 individuals that must be processed for the even-4-parity problem without automatically defined functions (as shown in figure 6.3) is 2.18 times the 176,000 individuals needed with automatically defined functions.

Table 6.5 compares the average structural complexity, $\overline{S}_{without}$ and $\overline{S}_{with}$, and the computational effort, $E_{without}$ and E_{with}, for the even-4-parity problem with automatically defined functions and without them.

Figure 6.15 summarizes the information in this comparison table and shows a structural complexity ratio, R_S, of 1.87 and an efficiency ratio, R_E, of 2.18.

6.12 EVEN-5-PARITY WITH ADFs

Four dummy variables are available to both ADF0 and ADF1 for the even-5-parity problem.

With Defined Functions

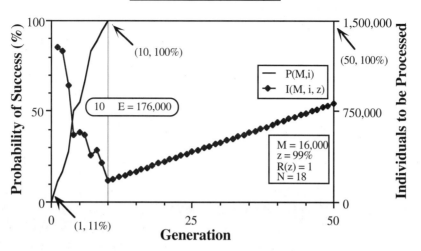

Figure 6.14 Performance curves for the even-4-parity problem showing that $E_{with} = 176,000$ with ADFs.

Table 6.5 Comparison table for the even-4-parity problem.

	Without ADFs	With ADFs
Average structural complexity $\bar{S}$	112.6	60.1
Computational effort E	384,000	176,000

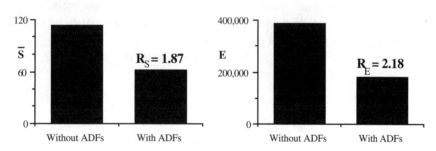

Figure 6.15 Summary graphs for the even-4-parity problem.

All 19 runs that we made of the even-5-parity problem using automatically defined functions produced 100%-correct solutions.

In one run, genetic programming discovered the following 51-point program with a perfect value of raw fitness of 32 in generation 9:

```
(progn (defun ADF0 (ARG0 ARG1 ARG2 ARG3)
              (values (AND (NAND ARG2 ARG0)
                      (AND (NAND ARG2 ARG0)
                          (OR ARG2 ARG0))))))
       (defun ADF1 (ARG0 ARG1 ARG2 ARG3)
          (values (ADF0 (NOR ARG2 ARG2)
                        (NAND (OR ARG2 ARG0) (NOR ARG1 ARG0))
                        (ADF0 ARG1 ARG3 ARG3 ARG3)
                        (ADF0 ARG1 ARG1 ARG3 ARG3))))
          (values (ADF1 (ADF0 D1 D1 D0 D4) (ADF0 D3 D4 D2 D2)
                        (ADF0 D0 D2 D4 D1) (OR D1 D1))))).
```

The result-producing branch of this program calls on ADF0 and ADF1 to produce the even-5-parity function.

ADF0 is equivalent to the four-argument Boolean rule 23,130 which, in turn, is equivalent to (ODD-2-PARITY ARG0 ARG2).

ADF1 hierarchically invokes ADF0 and is equivalent to the four-argument Boolean rule 15,555. When simplified, ADF1 is equivalent to the following three-argument combination of the even-2-parity function and the odd-2-parity function:

```
(EVEN-2-PARITY ARG1 (ODD-2-PARITY ARG2 ARG3)).
```

In other words, both of the function-defining branches in this particular 100% correct solution define two lower-order parity functions, one with two arguments and one with three.

If we substitute these definitions into the result-producing branch, we find that it simplifies to:

```
(EVEN-3-PARITY (ODD-2-PARITY D3 D2) (ODD-2-PARITY D0 D4) D1),
```

which mimics the target even-5-parity function.

Whenever automatically defined functions are used to solve a problem, we can view the problem as having been decomposed into subproblems. In this decomposition, the result-producing branch solves the overall problem and the function-defining branches solve the subproblems. The subproblems in this particular run involve Boolean rules 23,130 and 15,555. Genetic programming creates one computer program for rule 23,130 and a second program for rule 15,555 in the bodies of the two function-defining branches. Genetic programming also creates a solution to the overall even-5-parity problem in the body of the result-producing branch. The solution to the second subproblem (rule 15,555) hierarchically invokes the solution to the already-solved first subproblem (rule 23,130) on three occasions.

Figure 6.16 shows the directed acyclic graph of references in which ADF0 is used to define ADF1 and in which ADF0 and ADF1 are used together to define the even-5-parity function.

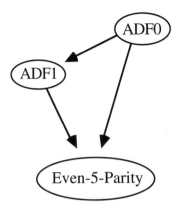

Figure 6.16 Hierarchical arrangement of function definitions for ADF0 and ADF1 employed by the best-of-run program from generation 9 for the even-5-parity problem with ADFs.

A human programmer would probably decompose a high-order parity problem into lower-order parity problems. However, we were surprised to find that genetic programming does not usually solve parity problems by means of lower-order parity functions. The single 100%-correct solution above (and the solutions to the even-3-parity and even-4-parity problems cited in the previous sections) should not lead the reader into thinking that genetic programming with automatically defined functions mimics the style of human programmers. In fact, the run described above is not typical at all; it is the *only run* of 19 runs in which genetic programming solved the even-5-parity problem using a hierarchical composition of two lower-order parity functions. In seven of the other runs, one of the automatically defined functions is a lower-order parity function, but the other is not. In a *majority* of the 19 runs, neither of the automatically defined functions is a lower-order parity function.

The following 233-point program is an example of one of the 11 solutions from the 19 runs that does not use any lower-order parity functions:

```
(progn (defun ADF0 (ARG0 ARG1 ARG2 ARG3)
          (values (AND (OR (NOR (NAND ARG1 ARG3) (AND (OR (AND
             ARG3 ARG3) (AND (OR (AND ARG3 ARG2) (NAND ARG2 ARG3))
             ARG2)) (OR (NOR ARG3 ARG1) (NOR ARG0 ARG3))))) (NAND
             (AND ARG0 ARG3) (OR ARG2 ARG1))) (AND (NAND (NOR ARG1
             ARG2) (NAND ARG1 ARG2)) (OR (NAND ARG2 ARG1) (NAND
             ARG1 ARG3))))))
       (defun ADF1 (ARG0 ARG1 ARG2 ARG3)
          (values (ADF0 (OR (NOR ARG1 ARG1) (ADF0 (NOR ARG2 ARG2)
             (AND ARG2 ARG0) (NOR ARG2 ARG2) (NAND ARG3 ARG1)))
             (AND (NAND (AND ARG0 ARG1) (OR ARG1 ARG1)) (ADF0 (ADF0
             ARG1 ARG0 ARG0 ARG1) (ADF0 ARG1 ARG1 ARG0 ARG3)
             (NOR ARG3 ARG0) (NAND ARG1 ARG0))) (AND (ADF0 (NOR
             ARG2 ARG1) (NOR ARG2 ARG2) (NAND ARG0 ARG0) (ADF0
             ARG3 ARG0 ARG0 ARG2)) (AND (NOR ARG0 ARG0) (NOR ARG3
             ARG0))) (ADF0 (ADF0 (NOR ARG1 ARG1) (OR ARG1 ARG1)
```

```
                (AND ARG0 ARG1) (NAND ARG3 ARG1)) (NOR (ADF0 ARG1
                ARG2 ARG1 ARG0) (AND ARG0 ARG3)) (OR (NAND ARG3 ARG2)
                (AND ARG1 ARG1)) (NOR (NAND ARG3 ARG0) (OR ARG0
                ARG0))))))
        (values (NAND (ADF1 (ADF0 (NOR D1 D3) (OR D0 D0) (ADF1 D1
           D3 D3 D2) (OR (AND (AND D0 D0) (NAND D1 D4)) (NAND
           (ADF0 D3 D0 D4 D0) (NOR (ADF0 D3 D2 D2 D3) (NOR D1
           D0))))) (OR (ADF1 D4 D2 D4 D3) (ADF1 D0 D0 D1 D3)) (AND
           (ADF1 D1 D3 D3 D2) (OR D4 D1)) (NOR (NOR D3 D4) (OR D0
           D4))) (OR (NAND D3 D2) (NAND (ADF0 D3 D0 D4 D0) (NOR
           (AND D0 D0) (NOR D1 D0))))))))
```

In this program ADF0 is the four-argument Boolean rule 7,420 and ADF1 is the rule 13,159. Neither are parity rules.

In another of the 19 runs, ADF0 defines Boolean rule 13,260 which is equivalent to (EVEN-2-PARITY ARG1 ARG3) but ADF1 defines rule 65,535 (the four-argument function returning the constant T). The latter is, of course, not a parity rule.

```
(progn (defun ADF0 (ARG0 ARG1 ARG2 ARG3)
           (values (AND (AND (OR ARG1 ARG3) (OR (NAND ARG1 ARG1)
              (NAND ARG3 ARG3))) (OR (NAND ARG1 ARG1) (NAND ARG3
              ARG3)))))
       (defun ADF1 (ARG0 ARG1 ARG2 ARG3)
          (values (OR (OR (NAND ARG0 ARG0) (AND ARG2 ARG0)) (ADF0
             (NAND ARG2 ARG3) (ADF0 ARG0 ARG0 ARG0 ARG3) (NOR ARG2
             ARG0) (NAND ARG0 ARG2)))))
       (values (ADF0 (OR (ADF0 D4 D0 D3 D1) (AND D3 D2)) (ADF0
          (OR D3 D2) (ADF0 D0 D3 D3 D1) (ADF1 D1 D2 D1 D2) (ADF0
          D2 D4 D0 D0)) (ADF1 (NOR D1 D0) (NAND D0 D0) (AND D4
          D1) (OR D2 D4)) (NOR D2 D2)))).
```

In another of the 19 runs, ADF0 defines rule 61,455 which is equivalent to (EVEN-2-PARITY ARG2 ARG3). ADF1 defines rule 21,845 that is equivalent to (NOT ARG0) and is not, of course, a parity rule.

In another run, the solution shown below emerged on generation 16:

```
(progn (defun ADF0 (ARG0 ARG1 ARG2 ARG3)
           (values (NAND (OR (OR (NOR ARG3 ARG0) (OR ARG1 ARG3))
              (NAND (AND ARG2 ARG1) (NOR ARG3 ARG2))) (NOR (AND (OR
              ARG3 ARG0) (AND ARG2 ARG0)) (AND (NAND (AND ARG2
              ARG1) (NOR ARG3 ARG2)) (OR ARG2 ARG2))))))
       (defun adf1 (ARG0 ARG1 ARG2 ARG3)
          (values (NOR (AND (ADF0 (ADF0 ARG0 ARG2 ARG2 ARG0) (OR
             (NOR ARG1 (NAND ARG3 ARG1)) ARG2) (ADF0 ARG0 ARG0
             ARG0 ARG2) (ADF0 ARG2 ARG3 ARG1 ARG1)) (OR (NOR ARG1
             (NOR ARG1 (NAND ARG0 ARG0))) ARG2)) (AND (NAND ARG0
             ARG0) (NAND ARG2 ARG2)))))
       (values (ADF1 (NAND (ADF0 (NAND D1 D1) (OR D2 D2) (ADF0
          D4 D1 D1 D1) (ADF1 D3 D2 D4 D2)) (NOR (NOR (OR D1 D0)
          (NAND D1 D1)) (NOR D1 D1))) (ADF1 (NAND (NOR (NOR (OR
```

```
            D1 D0) (NAND D1 D1)) (NOR D1 D1)) (NAND D1 D4)) (NOR D0
            D4) (NAND (OR D1 D4) (NOR D1 D3)) (AND (AND D2 D1) (OR
            D4 D0))) (ADF1 (NOR (ADF1 D3 D0 D3 D3) (ADF1 D0 D2 D3
            D4)) (AND (NAND D4 D2) (OR D2 D3)) (NOR (ADF1 D3 D0 D3
            D3) (ADF1 D2 D0 D4 D4)) (OR (AND D0 D0) (ADF1 D3 D2 D4
            D4))) (ADF1 (NAND (ADF1 D0 D2 D1 D2) (AND D4 D1)) (NAND
            (OR D3 D0) (ADF0 D4 D2 D0 D2)) (NOR (ADF1 D0 D0 D0 D3)
            (ADF0 D2 D2 D4 D0)) (AND D1 D4))))).
```

In this program, the four-argument ADF0 is merely a projection that returns the value of dummy variable ARG2.

In the solution shown below from yet another of the 19 runs, ADF1 defines Boolean rule 15,420, which is equivalent to (ODD-2-PARITY ARG1 ARG2), but ADF0 is a function that merely recreates the NOR function (Boolean rule 1,285) that is already available in the set of primitive functions. NOR is not, of course, a parity rule.

```
(progn (defun ADF0 (ARG0 ARG1 ARG2 ARG3)
            (values (NOR ARG2 ARG0)))
        (defun ADF1 (ARG0 ARG1 ARG2 ARG3)
            (values (AND (OR (NAND ARG2 ARG2) (NAND ARG2 ARG1)) (OR
              ARG2 ARG1))))
        (values (ADF1 (NOR (NOR D1 D4) (NAND D1 D3)) (ADF1 (ADF1
            D2 D3 D0 D3) (ADF0 D3 D2 D3 D4) (ADF1 D4 D2 D1 D1) (NOR
            D4 D0)) (ADF1 (ADF1 D3 D3 D3 D3) D4 D0 D2) (AND (ADF0
            D0 D3 D3 D2) (NOR D1 D0))))).
```

In summary, this sampling from the 19 runs illustrates how an automatically defined function may

- ignore some of its dummy variables,
- recreate a primitive function that is already in the function set of the problem,
- be entirely ignored,
- define a constant value, or
- return a value identical to one of the dummy variables.

Table 6.6 shows the characteristics of the 19 solutions to the even-5-parity problem. Column 2 shows the rule number for the Boolean function defined by ADF0. Column 3 indicates whether ADF0 is a parity rule. Column 4 shows the rule number for the Boolean function defined by ADF1. Column 5 indicates whether ADF1 is a parity rule. As can be seen, only one of the 19 runs (5%) shown in the table employs two lower-order parity functions. Seven of the 19 runs (37%) employ a lower-order parity function in exactly one of the two function-defining branches. The even-5-parity problem is solved in 11 (58%) of the 19 runs without using any lower-order parity function whatsoever.

While it would be virtually inconceivable for a human programmer to write subroutine implementing Boolean rules such as 7,420 and 13,159 to

Table 6.6 Characteristics of 19 solutions to the even-5-parity problem.

Run	ADF0	Is ADF a parity rule?	ADF1	Is ADF a parity rule?
1	23130	(ODD-2-PARITY ARG0 ARG2)	15555	(EVEN-3-PARITY ARG1 ARG2 ARG3)
2	01285	No	15420	(ODD-2-PARITY ARG1 ARG2)
3	03920	No	13260	(ODD-2-PARITY ARG1 ARG3)
4	61455	(EVEN-2-PARITY ARG2 ARG3)	21845	No
5	13260	(ODD-2-PARITY ARG1 ARG3)	65535	No
6	04010	No	21930	(ODD-2-PARITY ARG0 ARG3)
7	50115	(EVEN-2-PARITY ARG1 ARG2)	13226	No
8	07420	No	13159	No
9	42469	No	19568	No
10	43600	No	52392	No
11	61680	No	43690	No
12	25198	No	59135	No
13	29199	No	02176	No
14	14192	No	65535	No
15	64201	No	58431	No
16	45067	No	63487	No
17	40960	No	53232	No
18	50115	(EVEN-2-PARITY ARG1 ARG2)	13226	No
19	00596	No	27560	No

solve the even-5-parity problem, this approach is typical of the majority of runs of genetic programming with automatically defined functions. From the point of view of the fitness measure that drives the evolutionary process, rules 7,420 and 13,159 are just as good as the even-3-parity and even-2-parity in solving the problem at hand.

Of course, genetic programming has no particular attachment to rules 7,420 and 13,159. A glance at table 6.6 indicates that 30 different rules appear in its 19 rows.

Table 6.7 summarizes the percentages of occurrence of the three different programming motifs that genetic programming evolved for the 19 runs shown in table 6.6. As can be seen, in a majority of the runs, both of the function-defining branches are not parity rules.

The following final point should not be overlooked concerning the character of the solutions produced by these 19 runs: All 19 runs used their automatically defined functions. As already demonstrated, the even-5-parity problem can be solved without automatically defined functions using the four primitive functions and actual variables of the problem contained in the result-producing branch. Automatically defined functions are available, but there is no requirement that genetic programming actually use them. For simpler problems, the result-producing branch may solve the problem on an occasional one or two runs out of a series of runs without actually invoking the available automatically defined functions (e.g., one of 19 solutions to the four-sine problem in table 5.12 did not use the available automatically defined function). We rarely see this on more difficult problems. In other words, the

Table 6.7   Motifs of the 19 solutions for the even-5-parity problem.

Motif	Percentage of runs
Lower-order parity functions in both `ADF0` and `ADF1`	5%
A lower-order parity function in either	37%
No lower-order parity function in either `ADF0` or `ADF1`	58%

With Defined Functions

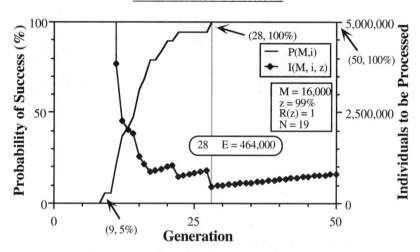

Figure 6.17   Performance curves for the even-5-parity problem showing that E_{with} = 464,000 with ADFs.

individuals in the population that do not actively employ their available automatically defined functions usually lose the race within the population to those individuals that actually use their automatically defined functions.

The average structural complexity, $\overline{S}_{with}$, of the 100%-correct programs from the 19 successful runs (out of 19 runs) for the even-5-parity problem is 156.8 points with automatically defined functions (versus a value of $\overline{S}_{without}$ of 299.9). There is a considerable reduction in the overall size of the programs that solve this problem with automatically defined functions.

Figure 6.17 presents the performance curves based on the 19 runs for the even-5-parity problem with automatically defined functions. The cumulative probability of success, $P(M, i)$, is 63% by generation 15 and 100% by generation 28. The two numbers in the oval indicate that if this problem is run through to generation 28, processing a total of E_{with} = 464,000 individuals (i.e., 16,000 × 29 generations × 1 run) is sufficient to yield a solution to this problem with 99% probability.

Table 6.8 compares the average structural complexity, $\overline{S}_{without}$ and $\overline{S}_{with}$, and the computational effort, $E_{without}$ and E_{with}, for the even-5-parity problem with automatically defined functions and without them. The 6,528,000 individuals that must be processed for the even-5-parity problem without

Table 6.8 Comparison table for the even-5-parity problem.

	Without ADFs	With ADFs
Average structural complexity $\overline{S}$	299.9	156.8
Computational effort E	6,528,000	464,000

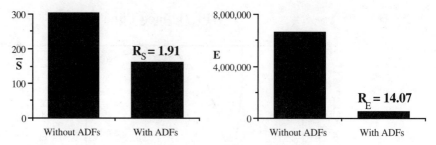

Figure 6.18 Summary graphs for the even-5-parity problem.

automatically defined functions (as shown in figure 6.4) is 14.07 times the 464,000 individuals needed with automatically defined functions.

Figure 6.18 summarizes the information in this comparison table and shows a structural complexity ratio, R_S, of 1.91 and an efficiency ratio, R_E, of 14.07 for the even-5-parity problem.

6.13 EVEN-6-PARITY PROBLEM WITH ADFs

When automatically defined functions are being used, programs for the even-6-parity problem contain two five-argument functions.

The reader will recall that we were unable to solve the even-6-parity problem with a population size of 16,000 without automatically defined functions (section 6.6). However, 90% of the runs with automatically defined functions solve the problem by generation 50.

The average structural complexity, $\overline{S}_{with}$, of the 100%-correct programs from the 19 successful runs (out of 21 runs) of the even-6-parity problem is 184.8 points with automatically defined functions.

Figure 6.19 presents the performance curves based on 21 runs with automatically defined functions for the even-6-parity problem with automatically defined functions with a population size of 16,000. The cumulative probability of success, $P(M,i)$, is 90% by generation 41 and is still 90% by generation 50. The two numbers in the oval indicate that if this problem is run through to generation 41, processing a total of $E_{with} = 1,344,000$ (i.e., $16,000 \times 42$ generations $\times 2$ runs) individuals is sufficient to yield a solution to this problem with 99% probability.

Table 6.9 compares the average structural complexity, $\overline{S}_{without}$ and $\overline{S}_{with}$, and the computational effort, $E_{without}$ and E_{with}, for the even-6-parity problem with automatically defined functions and without them. This table

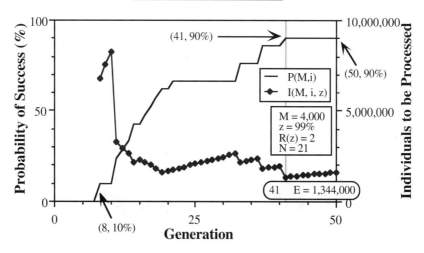

With Defined Functions

Figure 6.19 Performance curves for the even-6-parity problem showing that $E_{with} = 1,344,000$ with ADFs.

Table 6.9 Comparison table for the even-6-parity problem.

	Without ADFs	With ADFs
Average structural complexity $\overline{S}$	328.0	184.8
Computational effort E	70,176,000	1,344,000

includes the rough estimates (section 6.6) of 70,176,000 for $E_{without}$ and 328.0 for $\overline{S}_{without}$ for the even-6-parity problem without automatically defined functions.

Figure 6.20 summarizes the information in this comparison table and shows a structural complexity ratio, R_S, of 1.77 and an efficiency ratio, R_E, of 52.2 for the even-6-parity problem.

6.14 SUMMARY FOR THE EVEN-3-, 4-, 5-, AND 6-PARITY PROBLEMS

Table 6.10 compiles the observations from the above runs of the even 3-, 4-, 5-, and 6-parity problems into a single table. As can be seen, for the even 3-, 4-, 5-, and 6-parity problems, the efficiency ratio, R_E, is greater than 1 (indicating that fewer fitness evaluations are required to yield a solution to the problem with 99% probability with automatically defined functions than without them). The even 3-, 4-, 5-, and 6-parity problems are all beyond the breakeven point for computational effort.

The structural complexity ratio, R_S, is less than 1 for the even-3-parity problem, but greater than 1 for the even-4-, 5-, and 6-parity problems. The

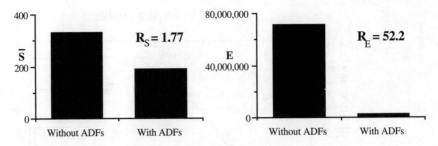

Figure 6.20 Summary graphs for the even-6-parity problem.

Table 6.10 Summary table of the structural complexity ratio, R_S, and the efficiency ratio, R_E, for the even-3-, 4-, 5-, and 6-parity problems.

Problem	Structural complexity ratio R_S	Efficiency ratio R_E
Even-3-parity	0.92	1.50
Even-4-parity	1.87	2.18
Even-5-parity	1.91	14.07
Even-6-parity	1.77	52.2

breakeven point for average structural complexity for the even-parity problem appears to be between three and four.

6.15 SCALING FOR THE EVEN-3-, 4-, 5-, AND 6-PARITY PROBLEMS

This section considers the question of how the average structural complexity and the computational effort change as a function of problem size for the even-parity problem.

We first consider the average structural complexity, $\bar{S}_{without}$ and $\bar{S}_{with}$, of the genetically evolved solutions to the even-parity problem, with and without automatically defined functions.

Table 6.11 consolidates the values of the average structural complexity, $\bar{S}_{without}$ and $\bar{S}_{with}$, of 100% correct solutions of the even-3-, 4-, 5-, and 6-parity problems, with and without automatically defined functions, for a population size of 16,000. The value of 328.0 for $\bar{S}_{without}$ shown in this table for the even-6-parity problem without automatically defined functions is the rough estimate from section 6.6.

Figure 6.21 shows the average structural complexity, $\bar{S}_{without}$ and $\bar{S}_{with}$, for the solutions produced on the successful runs of the even-3-, 4-, 5-, and 6-parity problems. The horizontal axis reflects the arity k (the order, number of arguments, number of input bits) of the problem.

When we perform a linear least-squares regression on the four points for the runs without automatically defined functions, we find that the structural complexity, $\bar{S}_{without}$, can be expressed in terms of the number of arguments, A, as

Table 6.11 Comparison of the average structural complexity of solutions to the even-3-, 4-, 5-, and 6-parity problems, with and without ADFs.

	3	4	5	6
$\bar{S}_{without}$	44.6	112.6	299.9	328.0
$\bar{S}_{with}$	48.2	60.1	156.8	184.8

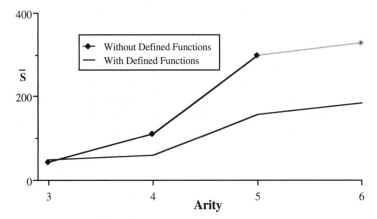

Figure 6.21 Comparison of average structural complexity of solutions to the even-3-, 4-, 5-, and 6-parity problems, with and without ADFs.

$$\bar{S}_{without} = -270.6 + 103.8A,$$

with a correlation of 0.96. The slope indicates that it takes about a hundred additional points in the program tree to handle each additional argument to the parity function.

In contrast, when we perform the linear regression for the runs with automatically defined functions, we find that the structural complexity, $\bar{S}_{with}$, can be expressed in terms of the number of arguments, A, as

$$\bar{S}_{with} = -115.5 + 50.6A,$$

with a correlation of 0.95. The slope indicates that it takes only about an additional fifty points in the program tree to handle each additional argument to the parity function. The slope with automatically defined functions is only about a half of the slope without them. Thus, as the size of the problem is scaled up, the average size of the solutions with automatically defined functions grows at less than half the rate than without them.

This conclusion stands even though the value of 328.0 for $\bar{S}_{without}$ for the even-6-parity problem is only a rough estimate and not actual data. Figure 6.6 indicates that the general direction in $\bar{S}_{without}$ averaged over the 19 runs is toward the mid 300s thereby making the value of $\bar{S}_{without}$ for the even-6-parity problem greater than the actual values of 44.6, 112.6, and 299.9 for the even-3-, 4-, and 5-parity problems, respectively. Any actual value of $\bar{S}_{without}$ for the even-6-parity problem in the mid 300s or higher

Table 6.12 Comparison of the computational effort for the even-3-, 4-, 5-, and 6-parity problems, with and without ADFs.

	3	4	5	6
$E_{without}$	96,000	384,000	6,528,000	70,176,000
E_{with}	64,000	176,000	464,000	1,344,000

will support the conclusion that the average size of the solutions produced by genetic programming increases as a function of problem size at a lower rate with automatically defined functions than without them.

We now turn our attention to the computational effort required for the even-parity problem, with and without automatically defined functions.

Table 6.12 consolidates the values of the computational effort with and without automatically defined functions, for the even-3-, 4-, 5-, and 6-parity problems with a population size of 16,000. Since we were unable to solve the even-6-parity problem without automatically defined functions after 19 runs, the value of 70,176,000 for $E_{without}$ shown in this table for the even-6-parity problem without automatically defined functions is the rough estimate computed in section 6.6.

Figure 6.22 shows the computational effort for the even-3-, 4-, 5-, and 6-parity problems with and without automatically defined functions. When automatically defined functions are not used, there is an explosive growth in $E_{without}$ (spanning about three orders of magnitude) as a function of problem size. The curve applicable to automatically defined functions closely hugs the horizontal axis and is barely visible on this figure.

Figure 6.23 shows the same data as figure 6.22 using a logarithmic scale on the vertical axis, thereby making the graph applicable to automatically defined functions visible. The computational effort is dramatically less with automatically defined functions than without them.

When we perform a linear regression on the progression of values of computational effort, $E_{without}$ (96,000, 384,000, 6,528,000, and 70,176,000), we find that $E_{without}$ can be expressed in terms of the number of arguments, A, as

$$E_{without} = -78,100,000 + 21,640,000A,$$

with a correlation of 0.82.

A glance at figure 6.23 suggests trying an *exponential regression* (i.e., a linear regression on the logarithm of the dependent variable). When we perform an exponential regression on the four-point curve without automatically defined functions, we find that the computational effort, $E_{without}$, can be stated in terms of the number of arguments, A, as

$$E_{without} = 77.1 \times 10^{0.982A},$$

with a correlation of 0.99. The exponential regression produces a better fit to this data than the linear regression; however, all conclusions must be tempered by the considerable uncertainty introduced by the rough estimate we used for the value of $E_{without}$ for the even-6-parity problem and by the small

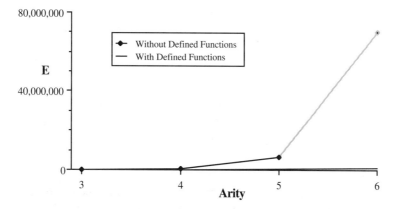

Figure 6.22   Comparison of computational effort for the even-3-, 4-, 5-, and 6-parity problems, with and without ADFs.

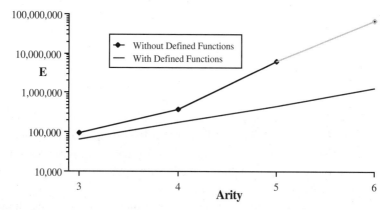

Figure 6.23   Comparison of computational effort for the even-3-, 4-, 5-, and 6-parity problems, with and without ADFs, with logarithmic scale.

number of data points involved. In addition, the fact that a curve can be fit to empirical data does not, of course, establish the existence of any causal relationship between the variables involved.

When we perform a linear regression on the progression of values of E_{with} (64,000, 176,000, 464,000, and 1,344,000), we find that the computational effort, E_{with}, can be stated in terms of the number of arguments, A, as

$$E_{with} = -1,350,000 + 413,000A,$$

with a correlation of 0.92. It takes about 22 million additional fitness evaluations to handle each additional argument to the parity function without automatically defined functions as compared to about four hundred thousand with them. This is a ratio of about 52:1.

When we perform an exponential regression on the four-point curve with automatically defined functions, we find that the computational effort, E_{with}, can be stated in terms of the number of arguments, A, as

$$E_{with} = 3070 \times 10^{0.439A},$$

with a correlation of 0.99. This exponential function is a better fit to this data than the straight line. The exponent is only 0.439 with automatically defined functions as compared to 0.982 without them.

The conclusion (main point 6) that will prove to be common to the three problems in this book for which a progression of scaled-up versions is studied (the parity problem, the lawnmower problem of chapter 8, and the bumblebee problem of chapter 9) is that the computational effort increases as a function of problem size at a lower rate with automatically defined functions than without them. Both the linear regression and the exponential regression support this conclusion for this problem. Note that the lower rate (not the functional form) is the conclusion that will prove to be consistent with the data from all three problems. This discussion of scaling will continue in sections 8.15 and 9.13 and in chapter 10.

6.16 HIGHER-ORDER EVEN-PARITY PROBLEMS

As previously mentioned, after 19 runs with a population size of 16,000, we were unable to evolve any solutions to the even-6-parity problem without automatically defined functions. Nonetheless, we can solve the even-parity problem for orders 7, 8, 9, 10, and 11 with hierarchical automatically defined functions. In fact, we can do so with a population size of only 4,000 because we will not be making any runs without automatically defined functions in this section. We stopped this demonstration at the even-11-parity because the even-11-parity problem is extremely time-consuming (given our practice of using 100% of the 2^k possible fitness cases in our runs of Boolean problems).

We decided to use two four-argument automatically defined functions throughout this section. This choice was not made on the basis of any analysis of the nature of the Boolean parity problem, but instead was made on the basis of available computer time. For historical reasons, the runs in this section involving a population of size 4,000 are the only runs in this book employing fitness proportionate selection and greedy over-selection (rather than tournament selection).

6.16.1 Even-7-Parity Problem

In one run of the even-7-parity problem, the following 102-point best-of-run program from generation 10 achieved a perfect value of raw fitness of 128 (out of 128):

```
(progn (defun ADF0 (ARG0 ARG1 ARG2 ARG3)
         (values (AND (OR (OR ARG0 ARG3) (NOR ARG3 ARG3)) (NOR
           (NOR ARG0 ARG1) (AND ARG1 ARG0)))))
       (defun ADF1 (ARG0 ARG1 ARG2 ARG3)
         (values (NOR (ADF0 (ADF0 ARG3 ARG0 ARG0 ARG2) (OR ARG1
           ARG1) (OR ARG1 ARG1) (OR ARG0 ARG1)) (AND (NOR ARG1
           ARG3) (ADF0 ARG3 ARG0 ARG0 ARG2))))
```

```
(values (ADF1 (OR (ADF0 D4 D5 D4 D5) (AND D7 D2)) (ADF1
    (ADF0 (AND D2 D8) (ADF1 D0 D2 D9 D3) (ADF0 D4 D3 D4 D0)
    (NAND D0 D3)) (NAND D0 D8) (AND D7 D6) (OR D7 D1))
    (ADF1 (OR D7 D8) (ADF0 D9 D2 D9 D9) (AND D7 D3) (NOR D4
    D7)) (OR (NOR D6 D7) (ADF0 D2 D2 D3 D4)))))).
```

The first branch of this program defines a four-argument `ADF0` (rule 26,214) which ignores two of its four arguments and is equivalent to

```
(ODD-2-PARITY ARG0 ARG1).
```

The second branch defines a four-argument `ADF1` (rule 26,265) in terms of `ADF0` and is equivalent to

```
(EVEN-3-PARITY ARG0 ARG1 ARG3).
```

Substituting the definitions of `ADF0` and `ADF1`, the result-producing branch becomes

```
(EVEN-2-PARITY (EVEN-2-PARITY (NAND D0 D2) (ODD-2-PARITY D3 D1))
        (ODD-2-PARITY (EVEN-2-PARITY (NOT D5) D4)
            (OR D2 D0))),
```

which is equivalent to the target even-7-parity function. Thus, in this particular run, two lower-order parity functions were used as the basis for solving the problem.

In another run of the even-7-parity problem, a 100%-correct 92-point best-of-run program appears in generation 14. The first branch of this program defines a four-argument `ADF0` (rule 42,245). The second branch of this program defines a four-argument `ADF1` (rule 49,980) which ignores one of its four arguments. `ADF1` is equivalent to

```
(ODD-3-PARITY D3 D2 D1).
```

Figure 6.24 presents the performance curves based on 29 runs for the even-7-parity problem with automatically defined functions. The cumulative probability of success, $P(M,i)$, is 20.7% by generation 17, and 34.5% by generation 50. The two numbers in the oval indicate that if this problem is run through to generation 17, processing a total of $E_{with} = 1,440,000$ (i.e., $4,000 \times 18$ generations $\times$ 20 runs) individuals is sufficient to yield a solution to this problem with 99% probability.

The search space of 7-argument Boolean functions returning one value is of size $2^{2^7} = 2^{128} \approx 10^{38}$.

6.16.2 Even-8-Parity Problem

The 8-, 9-, 10-, and 11-parity problems can be similarly solved using hierarchical automatically defined functions. While runs of the even-7-parity function (which has $2^7 = 128$ fitness cases) are time-consuming, they are still sufficiently fast to enable us to accumulate enough successful runs after expending a reasonable amount of computer time to allow us to make

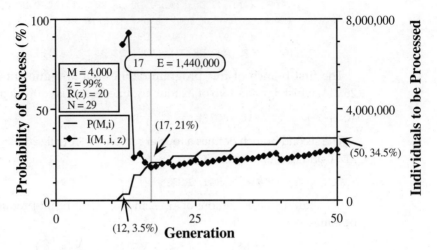

Figure 6.24 Performance curves for the even-7-parity problem showing that $E_{with} = 1,440,000$ with ADFs.

a meaningful performance curve. This is not the case for runs of the even-8-parity problem and higher-order parity problems. Consequently, for each of the 8-, 9-, 10-, and 11-parity problems, we made one set of four simultaneous runs on our four-processor parallel LISP machine. The 8-, 9-, 10-, and 11-parity problems were each solved at least once within our first (and only) set of four runs for these problems.

In one run of the even-8-parity problem, the best of generation 24 contains 186 points and attains a perfect value of raw fitness of 256. The first branch of this program defines a four-argument ADF0 (rule 10,280). The second branch of this program defined a four-argument ADF1 (rule 26,214). This branch then ignores two of its four arguments and is equivalent to

```
(ODD-2-PARITY ARG0 ARG1).
```

ADF0 is not a parity rule.

6.16.3   Even-9-Parity Problem

The best of generation 40 of one run of the even-9-parity problem evolved a parity function of order four as one of its automatically defined functions. This program contains 224 points and attains a perfect value of raw fitness of 512. The first branch defines a four-argument ADF0 (rule 1,872). The second branch of this program defines a four-argument ADF1 (rule 27,030) which is equivalent to the odd-4-parity function. Thus, the even-9-parity problem employs a parity function of order four as one of the two available automatically defined functions. This solution to the 9-parity problem is the first time we have seen the emergence of a 4-parity function.

6.16.4 Even-10-Parity Problem

In a run of the even-10-parity problem, the best of generation 40 contains 200 points and attains a perfect value of raw fitness of 1,024. The first branch of this program defines a four-argument ADF0 (rule 38,791). The second branch of this program defines a four-argument ADF1 (rule 23,205). This branch then ignores one of its four arguments and is equivalent to

```
(EVEN-3-PARITY D3 D2 D0).
```

Notice that 186, 224, and 200 are the number of points in the above solutions with automatically defined functions for the even-8-, 9-, and 10-parity problems, respectively. In comparison, solutions to the far simpler even-5-parity problem average 299.9 points without automatically defined functions.

6.16.5 Even-11-Parity Problem

Finally, in one run of the even-11-parity problem, the best of generation 21 contains 220 points and attains a perfect value of raw fitness of 2,048. It is shown below:

```
(progn (defun ADF0 (ARG0 ARG1 ARG2 ARG3)
           (values (NAND (NOR (NAND (OR ARG2 ARG1) (NAND ARG1
             ARG2)) (NOR (OR ARG1 ARG0) (NAND ARG3 ARG1))) (NAND
             (NAND (NAND (NAND ARG1 ARG2) ARG1) (OR ARG3 ARG2))
             (NOR (NAND ARG2 ARG3) (OR ARG1 ARG3))))))
         (defun ADF1 (ARG0 ARG1 ARG2 ARG3)
           (values (ADF0 (NAND (OR ARG3 (OR ARG0 ARG0)) (AND (NOR
             ARG1 ARG1) (ADF0 ARG1 ARG1 ARG3 ARG3))) (NAND (NAND
             (ADF0 ARG2 ARG1 ARG0 ARG3) (ADF0 ARG2 ARG3 ARG3
             ARG2)) (ADF0 (NAND ARG3 ARG0) (NOR ARG0 ARG1) (AND
             ARG3 ARG3) (NAND ARG3 ARG0))) (ADF0 (NAND (OR ARG0
             ARG0) (ADF0 ARG3 ARG1 ARG2 ARG0)) (ADF0 (NOR ARG0
             ARG0) (NAND ARG0 ARG3) (OR ARG3 ARG2) (ADF0 ARG1 ARG3
             ARG0 ARG0)) (NOR (ADF0 ARG2 ARG1 ARG2 ARG0) (NAND
             ARG3 ARG3)) (AND (AND ARG2 ARG1) (NOR ARG1 ARG2)))
             (AND (NAND (OR ARG3 ARG2) (NAND ARG3 ARG3)) (OR (NAND
             ARG3 ARG3) (AND ARG0 ARG0))))))
         (values (OR (ADF1 D1 D0 (ADF0 (ADF1 (OR (NAND D1 D7) D1)
           (ADF0 D1 D6 D2 D6) (ADF1 D6 D6 D4 D7) (NAND D6 D4)) (ADF1
           (ADF0 D9 D3 D2 D6) (OR D10 D1) (ADF1 D3 D4 D6 D7) (ADF0
           D10 D8 D9 D5)) (ADF0 (NOR D6 D9) (NAND D1 D10) (ADF0 D10
           D5 D3 D5) (NOR D8 D2)) (OR D6 (NOR D1 D6))) D1) (NOR
           (NAND D1 D10) (ADF0 (OR (ADF0 D6 D2 D8 D4) (OR D4 D7))
           (NOR D10 D6) (NOR D1 D2) (ADF1 D3 D7 D7 D6)))))).
```

The first branch of this program defines the four-argument ADF0 (rule 50,115). This branch is equivalent to

```
(EVEN-2-PARITY ARG1 ARG2).
```

The second branch defines a four-argument `ADF1` which is equivalent to the even-4-parity function.

Substituting the definitions of the defined functions `ADF0` and `ADF1`, the result-producing branch simplifies to

```
(OR (EVEN-4-PARITY
        D1
        D0
        (EVEN-2-PARITY (EVEN-2-PARITY
                        (NAND D1 D10)
                        (EVEN-2-PARITY D5 D3)))
                    (EVEN-4-PARITY
                        (EVEN-2-PARITY D3 D2)
                        (OR D10 D1)
                        (EVEN-4-PARITY D3 D4 D6 D7)
                        (EVEN-2-PARITY D8 D9))
        D1)
    (NOR (NAND D1 D10)
        (EVEN-2-PARITY (NOR D10 D6) (NOR D1 D2))))).
```

The even-2-parity function (`ADF0`) appears six times and the even-4-parity function (`ADF1`) appears three times in this simplified version of the 100%-correct solution to the even-11-parity problem. In other words, genetic programming solved the even-11-parity problem by automatically decomposing it into parity functions of lower orders.

The unsimplified version of the 100%-correct solution to the even-11-parity problem employing automatically defined functions contains only 220 points. This size is smaller than the solutions without automatically defined functions to the far simpler even-5-parity problem (which average 299.9 points).

Figure 6.25 shows the simplified version of the result-producing branch of this best-of-run individual from generation 21 for the even-11-parity problem.

The above solution to the even-11-parity problem emerged on generation 21 of one of our four runs. Because the other three runs had each only reached

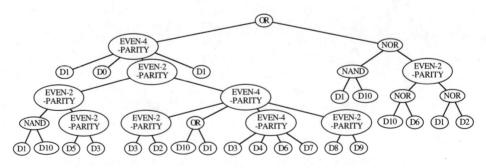

Figure 6.25 The result-producing branch of the best-of-run program from generation 21 for the even-11-parity problem is assembled from even-2-parity and even-4-parity functions.

the neighborhood of 21 generations and because of the time-consuming nature of this problem, the other three runs were abandoned.

The search space of 11-argument Boolean functions returning one value is of size $2^{2^{11}} = 2^{2,048} \approx 10^{616}$.

A videotape visualization of the solution to the even-11-parity problem (and 21 problems from *Genetic Programming*) can be found in Koza and Rice 1992a. See also Koza 1992b.

7 Determining the Architecture of the Program

In applying genetic programming with automatically defined functions to a problem, it is first necessary to make a group of choices concerning the architecture of the yet-to-be-evolved overall programs in the population. We have called this group of architectural choices the sixth major step in preparing to use genetic programming.

The sixth major step involves determining

(a) the number of function-defining branches,

(b) the number of arguments possessed by each function-defining branch, and

(c) if there is more than one function-defining branch, the nature of the hierarchical references (if any) allowed between the function-defining branches.

After this sixth major step has been performed, the first and second major steps in preparing to use genetic programming must be performed for each branch of the overall program. That is, it is necessary to specify the terminal set and function set for the result-producing branch as well as the terminal set and function set for each function-defining branch in the overall program.

Once all of the preparatory steps have been performed, a run of genetic programming may be made.

Sometimes these architectural choices flow so directly from the nature of the problem that they are virtually mandated. However, in general, we have no way of knowing *a priori* the optimal number of automatically defined functions or the optimal number of arguments for each such defined function that will be useful for a given problem.

How should these architectural choices be made? How important are these choices in determining whether genetic programming can solve a problem? How influential are these choices in determining the amount of computational effort required to solve a problem?

Five different methods for making these architectural choices are discussed in this book:

• prospective analysis of the nature of the problem,

• seemingly sufficient capacity,

- affordable capacity,
- retrospective analysis of the results of actual runs, and
- evolutionary selection of the architecture.

We start by reviewing the three of these five methods that we have used so far in this book.

Then we will discuss the method of retrospective analysis. The retrospective analysis for the even-5-parity problem indicate that it can be solved with any of 15 different architectures that might reasonably have been chosen for it.

We defer discussion of the method of evolutionary determination of the architecture until chapters 21 through 25 in which it will become clear that we need not make any architectural choice at all.

7.1 METHOD OF PROSPECTIVE ANALYSIS

When we were preparing to solve the two-boxes problem (chapter 4), we used the method of prospective analysis of the nature of the problem. We chose three as the number of arguments for the automatically defined function because we knew that boxes have dimensionality 3 and could therefore reasonably anticipate a useful decomposition involving a subproblem of dimensionality 3. Also, because we knew the problem involved only boxes (and not, say, a mixture of circles and pyramids), we could reasonably anticipate that the result-producing branch could assemble a solution through multiple uses of just one automatically defined function.

If we had not known that this problem involved boxes (i.e., if the problem had been presented as an unidentified problem of symbolic regression over six independent variables), we would have had no reason either to choose three as the number of arguments for the automatically defined function or to choose one as the number of automatically defined functions. In that event, we probably would have chosen five (i.e., one less than the number of independent variables) or perhaps six as the number of arguments for the automatically defined functions. In addition, we probably would have made more than one automatically defined function available to each overall program because we would not have known how many exploitable regularities might be present in the problem environment.

Of course, if the problem had a natural decomposition involving a subproblem of dimensionality 4, our choice of five or six as the number of arguments for the automatically defined function would almost certainly not have precluded a solution. Indeed, we have repeatedly seen that genetic programming often ignores available dummy variables in the body of an automatically defined function. Similarly, a solution to the problem would almost certainly not have been foreclosed if the number of available automatically defined functions that we chose had been less than the number of exploitable regularities of the problem environment. More likely, some of the potential gain in performance from exploiting some of the regularities would have been lost.

Similarly, in the Boolean 6-symmetry problem (subsection 5.2.1), we used our knowledge that the symmetry function involves a process of pairwise matching in choosing two as the number of arguments and one as the number of automatically defined functions. If we had not known that matching was involved in the symmetry problem, we probably would have made the same choices we did for the Boolean 6-parity problem (chapter 6).

The amount of prospective analysis that is appropriate based on foreknowledge of the nature of the problem depends on the user's goals. At one extreme, if the user's goal is to solve a practical problem, then it is appropriate to use all available analytic techniques, all available foreknowledge about the underlying regularities, symmetries, and homogeneities of the problem, and all available information about the problem environment in choosing the architecture. At the other extreme, if the user is studying the nature of automated problem solving, the focus will be using the minimum amount of human analysis and knowledge.

7.2 METHOD OF PROVIDING SEEMINGLY SUFFICIENT CAPACITY

For many problems, the architectural choices can be made on the basis of trying to provide seemingly sufficient capacity. Our approach to making the architectural choices for the Boolean even-parity problems in chapter 6 illustrated this approach. We envisaged that solutions to the even-3-, 4-, 5-, and 6-parity problems would involve lower-order parity functions. We therefore made a seemingly sufficient number of automatically defined functions (each with a seemingly sufficient number of arguments) available to the yet-to-be-evolved overall programs.

As previously mentioned, we were wrong in anticipating that genetic programming would usually decompose these parity problems into lower-order parity functions (table 6.6). Nonetheless, we provided seemingly sufficient capacity to enable genetic programming to make such a decomposition. In fact, genetic programming did make a decomposition into lower-order functions; it just turned out that the lower-order functions usually were not parity rules.

The sextic-polynomial problem (subsection 5.1.1) also illustrates this approach of providing seemingly sufficient capacity. We envisaged a solution based on the repeated roots of the polynomial. In actual practice, genetic programming never produced a solution based on the repeated roots; instead, it frequently used the available automatically defined function as a squaring function and used the result-producing branch to identify the square root of the polynomial. Nonetheless, we attempted to provide seemingly sufficient capacity and, in fact, provided sufficient capacity to solve the problem.

The four-sines problem (subsection 5.3.1) also illustrates the method of providing seemingly sufficient capacity.

7.3   METHOD OF USING AFFORDABLE CAPACITY

Considerable additional computer resources (time and virtual memory) are required by each additional function-defining branch, especially if they are permitted to call one another hierarchically. Additional computer resources are also consumed by additional arguments for each automatically defined function. Thus, in practice, the amount of computer resources that one can afford to devote to a particular problem will strongly influence or dictate the architectural choice. Although we would like to have had the luxury of analyzing the problems in this book using the first two methods described above, computer time was, in fact, the controlling factor in most of the architectural choices actually made.

We used a four-processor parallel Texas Instruments Explorer II$^+$ computer (a LISP machine) of late 1980s vintage for all the runs of problems reported in this book. Except for a few simple problems in the early chapters, a single run of most problems in this book consumed between about a half day to several days of computer time on one processor. Single runs of some problems required up to 10 days. Moreover, memory fragmentation due to garbage collection over the duration of a run and other behaviors peculiar to LISP machines are an additional practical factor limiting the length of runs. As already discussed in section 6.16, our architectural choices for the even-6-, 7-, 8-, 9-, 10-, and -11-parity problems were dictated almost entirely by considerations of available computer resources, not by clever considerations of how to decompose Boolean problems. It would have been interesting to see how genetic programming solved the 11-parity problem if the overall program consisted of a half dozen 11-argument automatically defined functions. Indeed, an accurate way of stating our actual methodology is as follows: In making these choices, we hoped that the capacity that we could afford to devote to the problem would prove to be sufficient to solve the problem.

7.4   METHOD OF RETROSPECTIVE ANALYSIS

A retrospective analysis can be used to determine the optimal number of automatically defined functions and number of arguments that they each possess for a given problem. If one is dealing with a number of related problems, a retrospective analysis of one problem may provide guidance for making the required architectural choice for a similar problem.

A retrospective analysis may also indicate whether, and to what extent, architectural choices matter in runs of genetic programming with automatically defined functions.

The idea is to make a number of runs of the problem with different combinations of the number of automatically defined functions and the number of arguments that they each possess, to compute the computational effort required to solve the problem with each such architecture, and to identify the optimal architecture.

Boolean functions are often good candidates for conducting comparative experiments. The Boolean even-5-parity problem is the smallest problem that has interesting decompositions. A population size of 4,000 is used in this section. Fifteen different architectures will be tested with the number of automatically defined functions ranging between one and five and with their number of arguments ranging between two and four. A single run of the even-5-parity problem requires about 6 to 18 hours with this population size depending on the architecture.

Except for the choice of 4,000 as the population size, our approach to the problem is the same as described in tables 6.2 and 6.3. When there are two or more function-defining branches, each automatically defined function can refer hierarchically to every other already-defined (lower-numbered) function.

7.4.1 Baseline for the Even-5-Parity Problem without ADFs

We first solve the even-5-parity problem *without* automatically defined functions with a population size of 4,000.

The average structural complexity, $\bar{S}_{without}$, of the 100%-correct programs from the 11 successful runs (out of 25 runs) of the even-5-parity problem without automatically defined functions is 299.89 points.

Figure 7.1 presents the performance curves based on the 25 runs of the even-5-parity problem without automatically defined functions. The cumulative probability of success, $P(M,i)$, is 44% by generation 50. The two numbers in the oval indicate that if this problem is run through to generation 50, processing a total of $E_{without}$ = 1,632,000 individuals (i.e., 4,000 × 51 generations × 8 runs) is sufficient to yield a solution to this problem with 99% probability.

With Defined Functions

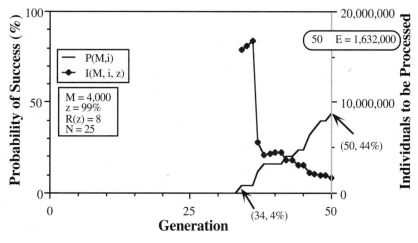

Figure 7.1   Performance curves for the even-5-parity problem showing that $E_{without}$ = 1,632,000 without ADFs.

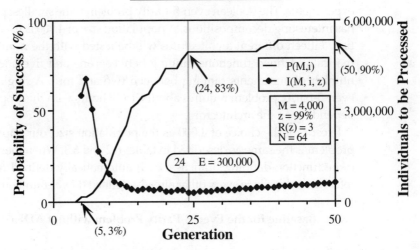

Figure 7.2 Performance curves for the even-5-parity problem showing that E_{with} = 300,000 with ADFs having an argument map of {2}.

We now proceed to solve this problem with 15 different architectures using automatically defined functions. Each group of runs is identified by the argument map associated with the set of their automatically defined functions.

7.4.2   One Two-Argument ADF

Figure 7.2 presents the performance curves based on 64 runs of the even-5-parity problem with one two-argument automatically defined function showing that it is sufficient to process 300,000 individuals to yield a solution with 99% probability.

7.4.3   One Three-Argument ADF

Figure 7.3 presents the performance curves based on 35 runs of the even-5-parity problem with one three-argument automatically defined function showing that it is sufficient to process 384,000 individuals to yield a solution with 99% probability.

7.4.4   One Four-Argument ADF

Figure 7.4 presents the performance curves based on 75 runs of the even-5-parity problem with one four-argument automatically defined function, showing that it is sufficient to process 592,000 individuals to yield a solution with 99% probability.

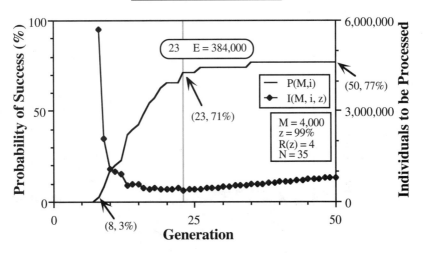

Figure 7.3 Performance curves for the even-5-parity problem showing that E_{with} = 384,000 with ADFs having an argument map of {3}.

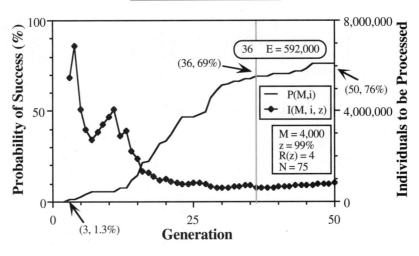

Figure 7.4 Performance curves for the even-5-parity problem showing that E_{with} = 592,000 with ADFs having an argument map of {4}.

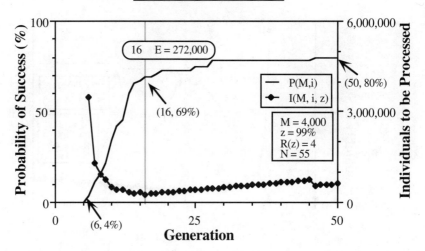

With Defined Functions

Figure 7.5 Performance curves for the even-5-parity problem showing that E_{with} = 272,000 with ADFs having an argument map of {2, 2}.

7.4.5 Two Two-Argument ADFs

Figure 7.5 presents the performance curves based on 55 runs of the even-5-parity problem with two two-argument automatically defined functions, showing that it is sufficient to process 272,000 individuals to yield a solution with 99% probability.

7.4.6 Two Three-Argument ADFs

Figure 7.6 presents the performance curves based on 93 runs of the even-5-parity problem with two three-argument automatically defined functions, showing that it is sufficient to process E_{with} = 400,000 individuals to yield a solution with 99% probability. Figure E.1 reports on an additional 32 runs made for this problem with the computer code shown in that appendix; the computational effort, E_{with}, measured by means of those 32 runs is also 400,000.

7.4.7 Two Four-Argument ADFs

Figure 7.7 presents the performance curves based on 43 runs of the even-5-parity problem with two four-argument automatically defined functions, showing that it is sufficient to process 656,000 individuals to yield a solution with 99% probability.

7.4.8 Three Two-Argument ADFs

Figure 7.8 presents the performance curves based on 117 runs of the even-5-parity problem with three two-argument automatically defined functions,

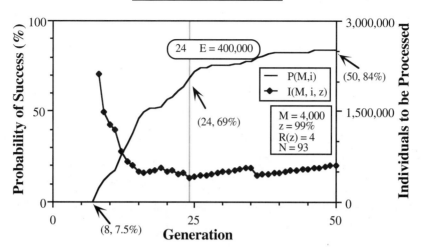

Figure 7.6   Performance curves for the even-5-parity problem showing that E_{with} = 400,000 with ADFs having an argument map of {3, 3}.

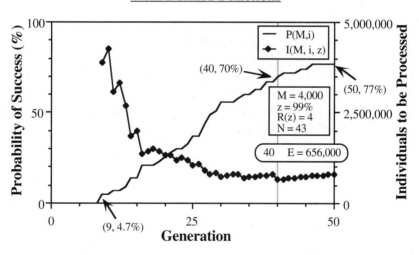

Figure 7.7   Performance curves for the even-5-parity problem showing that E_{with} = 656,000 with ADFs having an argument map of {4, 4}.

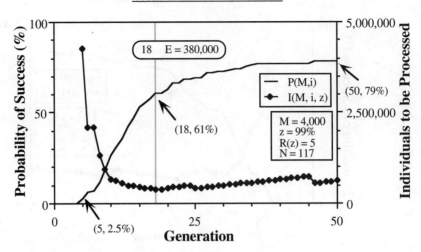

With Defined Functions

Figure 7.8 Performance curves for the even-5-parity problem showing that $E_{with} = 380,000$ with ADFs having an argument map of {2, 2, 2}.

showing that it is sufficient to process 380,000 individuals to yield a solution with 99% probability.

7.4.9 Three Three-Argument ADFs

Figure 7.9 presents the performance curves based on 36 runs of the even-5-parity problem with three three-argument automatically defined functions, showing that it is sufficient to process 272,000 individuals to yield a solution with 99% probability.

7.4.10 Three Four-Argument ADFs

Figure 7.10 presents the performance curves based on 37 runs of the even-5-parity problem with three four-argument automatically defined functions, showing that it is sufficient to process 672,000 individuals to yield a solution with 99% probability.

7.4.11 Four Two-Argument ADFs

Figure 7.11 presents the performance curves based on 58 runs of the even-5-parity problem with four two-argument automatically defined functions, showing that it is sufficient to process 360,000 individuals to yield a solution with 99% probability.

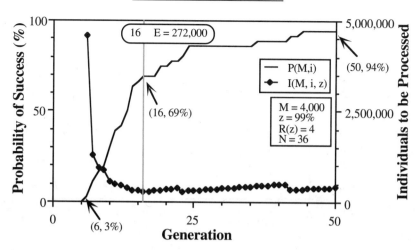

Figure 7.9 Performance curves for the even-5-parity problem showing that $E_{with} = 272,000$ with ADFs having an argument map of {3, 3, 3}.

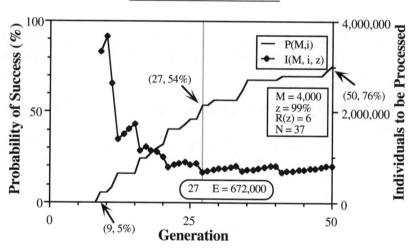

Figure 7.10 Performance curves for the even-5-parity problem showing that $E_{with} = 672,000$ with ADFs having an argument map of {4, 4, 4}.

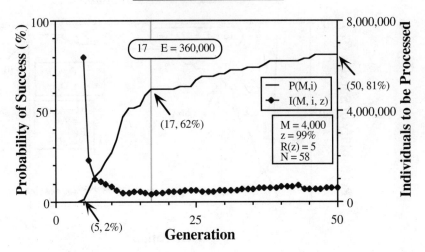

With Defined Functions

Figure 7.11 Performance curves for the even-5-parity problem showing that $E_{with} = 360{,}000$ with ADFs having an argument map of {2, 2, 2, 2}.

7.4.12 Four Three-Argument ADFs

Figure 7.12 presents the performance curves based on 40 runs of the even-5-parity problem with four three-argument automatically defined functions, showing that it is sufficient to process 420,000 individuals to yield a solution with 99% probability.

7.4.13 Four Four-Argument ADFs

Figure 7.13 presents the performance curves based on 44 runs of the even-5-parity problem with four four-argument automatically defined functions, showing that it is sufficient to process 912,000 individuals to yield a solution with 99% probability.

7.4.14 Five Two-Argument ADFs

Figure 7.14 presents the performance curves based on 67 runs of the even-5-parity problem with five two-argument automatically defined functions, showing that it is sufficient to process 360,000 individuals to yield a solution with 99% probability.

7.4.15 Five Three-Argument ADFs

Figure 7.15 presents the performance curves based on 63 runs of the even-5-parity problem with five three-argument automatically defined functions, showing that it is sufficient to process 512,000 individuals to yield a solution with 99% probability.

With Defined Functions

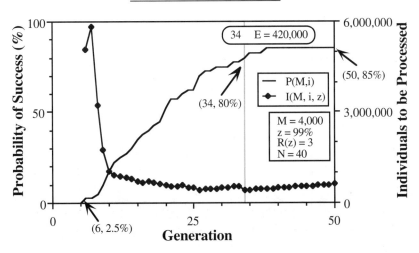

Figure 7.12 Performance curves for the even-5-parity problem showing that $E_{with} = 420{,}000$ with ADFs having an argument map of {3, 3, 3, 3}.

With Defined Functions

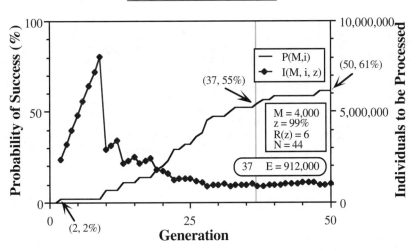

Figure 7.13 Performance curves for the even-5-parity problem showing that $E_{with} = 912{,}000$ with ADFs having an argument map of {4, 4, 4, 4}.

With Defined Functions

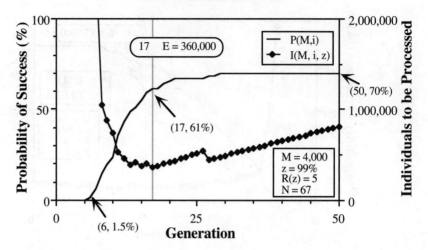

Figure 7.14 Performance curves for the even-5-parity problem showing that E_{with} = 360,000 with ADFs having an argument map of {2, 2, 2, 2, 2}.

With Defined Functions

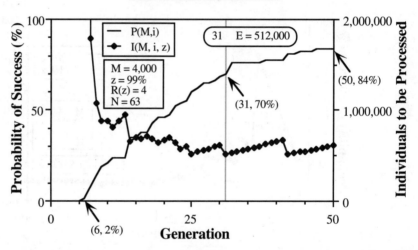

Figure 7.15 Performance curves for the even-5-parity problem showing that E_{with} = 512,000 with ADFs having an argument map of {3, 3, 3, 3, 3}.

With Defined Functions

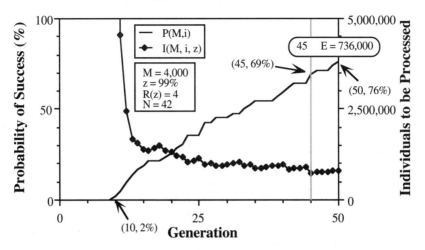

Figure 7.16 Performance curves for the even-5-parity problem showing that $E_{with} = 736,000$ with ADFs having an argument map of {4, 4, 4, 4, 4}.

7.4.16 Five Four-Argument ADFs

Figure 7.16 presents the performance curves based on 42 runs of the even-5-parity problem with five four-argument automatically defined functions, showing that it is sufficient to process 736,000 individuals to yield a solution with 99% probability.

7.5 SUMMARY OF RETROSPECTIVE ANALYSIS

The results in the previous 15 sub-subsections show that genetic programming is capable of solving the even-5-parity problem with all 15 combinations of architectures with a population size of 4,000.

Table 7.1 consolidates the results of the runs with these 15 combinations of choices of different numbers of defined functions (the first column) and different numbers of arguments that they each possess (the second column). The third column shows the computational effort, E_{with}, required. E_{with} is the minimal value of $I(M, i, z)$ and is realized at generation $i*$ (shown in the fourth column). The probability of success at generation $i*$ is $P(M, i^*)$ (shown in the fifth column). The number of independent runs required is $R(z)$ (shown in the sixth column). The probability of success at generation 50, $P(M, 50)$, is shown in the seventh column.

As previously mentioned in subsection 7.4.1, the baseline value for computational effort, $E_{without}$, required for the even-5-parity problem without automatically defined functions and with a population size of 4,000 is 1,632,000.

When automatically defined functions are used with *any of the 15* architectures, E_{with} always proves to be considerably less than this value of

Table 7.1 Consolidated table of the computational effort, E_{with}, and other statistics for 15 different architectures for the even-5-parity problem.

Number of ADFs	Number of arguments	E_{with}	i^*	$P(M, i^*)$	$R(z)$	$P(M, 50)$
1	2	300,000	24	83%	3	90%
1	3	384,000	23	71%	4	77%
1	4	592,000	36	69%	4	76%
2	2	272,000	16	69%	4	80%
2	3	400,000	24	69%	4	84%
2	4	656,000	40	70%	4	77%
3	2	380,000	18	61%	5	79%
3	3	272,000	16	69%	4	94%
3	4	672,000	27	54%	6	76%
4	2	360,000	34	62%	5	81%
4	3	420,000	34	80%	3	85%
4	4	912,000	37	55%	6	61%
5	2	360,000	17	61%	5	70%
5	3	512,000	31	70%	4	84%
5	4	736,000	45	69%	4	76%

1,632,000 for $E_{without}$. Specifically, E_{with} varies from a low of 272,000 (17% of 1,632,000) to a high of 912,000 (56% of 1,632,000).

The conclusion is that *the decision to use automatically defined functions* is far more important than the decision to use a particular architecture for the automatically defined functions.

Table 7.2 presents the values of computational effort, E_{with}, from table 7.1 as a two-dimensional table. E_{with} attains its minimum value of 272,000 for the 15 architectural choices when there are two two-argument defined functions and three three-argument defined functions.

Figure 7.17 presents the computational effort, E_{with}, from table 7.2 for each of the 15 combinations of choices of the number of automatically defined functions and the number of arguments that they each possess. The global minimum value of E_{with} in this table is 272,000; it is realized for both two two-argument automatically defined functions and three three-argument automatically defined functions.

The last row of table 7.2 shows that the computational effort is distinctly higher for this problem when the defined functions have four arguments. The last column of the table shows that the most computational effort is required for five automatically defined functions when they each possess three or four arguments. This problem is most readily solved when both the number of automatically defined functions and the number of arguments is three or less. Additional arguments and additional automatically defined functions are excessive, in retrospect, for this problem.

Table 7.2 Computational effort, E_{with}, for 15 different architectures for the even-5-parity problem with ADFs.

# Arguments \ # ADFs	1	2	3	4	5
2	300,000	272,000	380,000	360,000	360,000
3	384,000	400,000	272,000	420,000	512,000
4	592,000	656,000	672,000	912,000	736,000

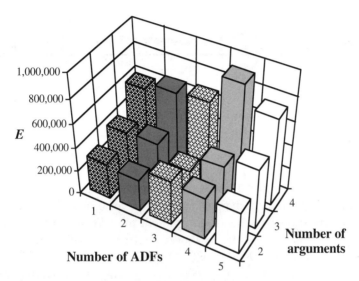

Figure 7.17 Computational effort, E_{with}, for 15 different architectures for the even-5-parity problem with ADFs.

However, the key result of these experiments is that this problem is solved for *all 15* architectural choices with automatically defined functions. Moreover, *all 15* architectural choices are superior to the case when automatically defined functions are not used. The architectural choice can merely affect the the number of fitness evaluations by a factor of up to 3.4:1.

The 15 architectures that we have just examined are uniform in the sense that they do not include architectures in which the automatically defined functions within a program possess different number of arguments. There are 3^k different ways of assigning a number of arguments (between two and four) to k hierarchical automatically defined functions. Thus, there are 360 different architectures when the number of arguments is between two and four and when k is between 2 and 5. The 345 nonuniform architectures are arguably subsumed, in one sense, by one of the 15 uniform architectures examined above because automatically defined functions are capable of selectively ignoring their dummy variables. However, they do present genetic programming with a different working environment.

Determining the Architecture of the Program

With Defined Functions

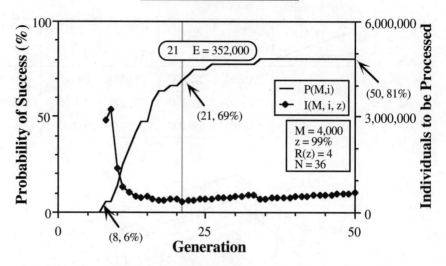

Figure 7.18 Performance curves for the even-5-parity problem showing that E_{with} = 352,000 with ADFs having an argument map of {2, 3}.

It is obviously impractical to test all 345 of these additional architectures; however, we tested a few such architectures out of curiosity. For example, figure 7.18 presents the performance curves based on 36 runs of the even-5-parity problem when the argument map for the automatically defined functions is {2,3}. This figure shows that it is sufficient to process 352,000 individuals to yield a solution with 99% probability.

The value of E_{with} of 352,000 is intermediate between the 272,000 fitness evaluations required for two two-argument automatically defined functions and the 400,000 fitness evaluations required for two three-argument automatically defined functions.

Table 7.3 shows the efficiency ratio, R_E, for the 15 combinations of the number of automatically defined functions and the number of arguments for the even-5-parity problem. Each entry in this table is obtained by dividing the corresponding entry from table 7.2 by 1,632,000, the baseline computational effort, $E_{without}$, without automatically defined functions (subsection 7.4.1). All 15 efficiency ratios are above 1, indicating that automatically defined functions are beneficial. The largest efficiency ratio of 6.00 is achieved for the two architectures for which E_{with} is 272,000. The lowest two efficiency ratios (the 2.22 in the lower right corner and the 1.79 near that corner) are obtained when an apparently excessive number (4) of arguments is used in conjunction with an apparently excessive number (4 or 5) of automatically defined functions. The additional overhead associated with these two excessive architectures apparently counterbalances the advantages of using automatically defined functions on this problem.

The data in table 7.3 for the 15 different architectures for the even-5-parity problem, the data in table 6.10 concerning the even-3-, 4-, 5-, and 6-parity

Table 7.3 Efficiency ratios, R_E, for 15 different architectures for the even-5-parity problem.

# ADFs # Arguments	1	2	3	4	5
2	5.44	6.00	4.29	4.53	4.53
3	4.25	4.08	6.00	3.88	3.18
4	2.76	2.49	2.43	1.79	2.22

problems, the data in table 5.20 for the scaled-up versions of the four problems from chapter 5, the fact that it is possible to solve the even-parity problems of orders 6, 7, 8, 9, 10, and 11 with automatically defined functions (section 6.16), and the data in numerous additional tables that will appear later in this book all provide evidence to support main point 3 of this book:

Main point 3: For a variety of problems, genetic programming requires less computational effort to solve a problem with automatically defined functions than without them, provided the difficulty of the problem is above a certain relatively low problem-specific breakeven point for computational effort.

This conclusion accurately reflects the cumulative evidence in this book over a range of problems from different fields. Like the other main points of this book, it is not stated as a theorem; no mathematical proof is offered.

There are no exceptions to this conclusion anywhere in this book or in any runs of any other problems of which I am aware. Exceptions to this conclusion will almost certainly be uncovered as automatically defined functions are studied further. These probable future exceptions should then lead, over time, to refinement, modification, and qualification of this conclusion concerning the effect on automated problem-solving of regularities, symmetries, and homogeneities in problem environments.

The above conclusion is, of course, already qualified in the sense that it incorporates the imprecisely defined concept of breakeven point. The simple and scaled-up versions of the four problems from chapter 5 strongly suggest that there are problems with with sufficient modularity to benefit from hierarchical decomposition and that there are problems whose modularity is so meagre that they do not so benefit. However, I do not claim to define precisely the nature of this separation or its exact location in the space of problems.

Nonetheless, the validity of experimentally obtained evidence is not negated by the absence of mathematical proofs or complete explanations of observed phenomena. Indeed, most science (unlike almost all "computer science") proceeds without airtight proofs. First, questions are raised. Then, experiments are conducted to accumulate evidence. Next, explanations that encapsulate the observed evidence are formalized. Additional experiments are then conducted, usually with the result that the current hypothesis must be refined, modified, or qualified. Finally, at some point, a unifying theory emerges.

We now consider the average structural complexity of the solutions evolved by genetic programming with automatically defined functions.

Table 7.4 Average structural complexity, $\bar{S}_{with}$, of the solutions to the even-5-parity problem for 15 different architectures with ADFs.

# Arguments \ # ADFs	1	2	3	4	5
2	82.5	99.5	119.3	131.0	149.5
3	119.4	152.6	176.0	217.1	248.5
4	166.0	225.8	271.0	391.5	436.6

Table 7.4 presents the average structural complexity, $\bar{S}_{with}$, for each of the 15 combinations of choices of different numbers of automatically defined functions with different numbers of arguments of solutions to the even-5-parity problem with automatically defined functions.

Table 7.5 presents the structural complexity ratio, R_S, for each of the 15 architectures. Each entry in this table is obtained by dividing the corresponding entry from table 7.4 by 299.89, the average structural complexity, $\bar{S}_{without}$, of solutions to the even-5-parity problem without automatically defined functions (subsection 7.4.1). Except for two of these 15 architectures, these ratios are greater than 1 (indicating that the average structural complexity, $\bar{S}_{with}$, of the solutions is less when automatically defined functions are being used). The two exceptions occur when there are four or five four-argument automatically defined functions. One explanation for the two exceptions is that they employ an excessive number (four or five) of automatically defined functions and an excessive number (four) of arguments (for a problem with only five independent variables).

The following 11 exceptions prevent making an unqualified statement that automatically defined functions improve the parsimony of the solutions evolved by genetic programming:

(1) the two-boxes problem (figure 4.20),

(2) the simpler versions of the four problems in chapter 5 (the first four rows of table 5.20),

(3) the scaled-up versions of two of the four problems in chapter 5 (specifically, the sextic polynomial $x^6 - 2x^4 + x^2$ and the three-term expression $x / \pi + x^2 / \pi^2 + 2\pi x$, as shown in the fifth and eighth rows of table 5.20),

(4) the even-3-parity problem (figure 6.11),

(5) the two architectural choices (out of 15) for the even-5-parity problem (table 7.5), and

(6) the subset-creating version of the transmembrane problem (table 18.13).

Eleven exceptions may seem so excessive as to bring the entire proposition into question. However, a closer examination indicates that eight of these 11 exceptions relate to very simple problems. The first of the eight exceptions relates to the two-boxes problem. Four relate to the simpler versions of the four problems in chapter 5. Two additional exceptions (the sextic polynomial

Table 7.5 Structural complexity ratios, R_S, for 15 different architectures for the even-5-parity problem.

# ADFs # Arguments	1	2	3	4	5
2	3.64	3.01	2.51	2.29	2.01
3	2.51	1.97	1.70	1.38	1.21
4	1.81	1.32	1.11	0.77	0.69

and the three-term expression) are both "scaled-up" versions of their respective pair of problems from chapter 5; however, both of these "scaled-up" versions are, in fact, still relatively simple problems. The even-3-parity problem is also the simplest problem in the progression of parity problems. Moreover, the offending ratios for these three last problems (0.98, 0.92, and 0.92, respectively) are all close to 1.

The simplicity of these first eight exceptions suggests the existence of a breakeven point for average structural complexity. That is, eight of the 11 exceptions can reasonably be explained because the problems lie on the wrong side of a breakeven point for average structural complexity.

The three other exceptions involve the subset-creating version of the transmembrane problem (where the "average" structural complexity in table 18.13 comes from only one successful run) and the two extreme architectures for the even-5-parity problem. The first of these three exceptions may, of course, be a matter of inadequate measurement. There is not sufficient evidence to support any particular explanation for exceptions relating to the two extreme architectural choices (out of 15) for the even-5-parity problem. It may be that an architecture can be so excessive and mismatched to the problem at hand as to outweigh the potential advantages of automatically defined functions. This possible explanation suggests future experimentation over a additional types of problems.

In spite of the absence of sufficient evidence to adopt any particular explanation for the two exceptions, the evidence does support a conclusion that is true most of the time: Automatically defined functions do improve the parsimony of the solutions evolved by genetic programming provided the difficulty of the problem is above a breakeven point for average structural complexity. That is, genetic programming usually (but not always) yields solutions that have smaller average overall size with automatically defined functions than without them. This qualified conclusion is stated as main point 4:

Main point 4: For a variety of problems, genetic programming usually yields solutions with smaller overall size (lower average structural complexity) with automatically defined functions than without them, provided the difficulty of the problem is above a certain problem-specific breakeven point for average structural complexity.

Main point 4 was an unanticipated product of our experiments on automatically defined functions. Before starting these experiments, I expected automatically defined functions to reduce computational effort in some way; however, I did not expect any improvement in parsimony. In retrospect, an improvement in parsimony from automatically defined functions seems very reasonable since decomposing problems into subproblems and reusing the solutions to subproblems should reduce the total size of the program.

Whenever I give a talk on genetic programming, someone always asks how the genetically evolved programs can be made smaller and simpler. Holding aside my general concern that forcing programs to be parsimonious may be counterproductive in the overall effort to get computers to program themselves without being explicitly programmed, I have previously given the following three answers:

First, the population of programs can be simplified during a run by means of the editing operation (*Genetic Programming*, subsection 6.5.3).

Second, the genetically evolved best-of-run program can be simplified after it is produced by genetic programming in a post-run process (by means of the editing techniques described in *Genetic Programming*, appendix F).

Third, parsimony can be made part of the fitness measure (see the block-stacking problem in *Genetic Programming*, subsection 18.1.3). However, the overt incorporation of parsimony into the fitness measure raises significant practical and theoretical issues. The practical issue concerns finding a principled way to choose the relative shares for these two competing factors in the fitness calculation and the gradient to be used in allocating these shares. A blended fitness measure trades off a certain amount of correctness for a certain amount of parsimony (Koza 1972). Should the relative share of the blended measure be based on a percentage, an additive formula, or some other formula? If, say, a percentage is chosen, should one allocate 5%, 10%, 25%, 33%, or some other percentage to parsimony as opposed to correctness? Even more vexing, how does one apportion the allocated percentages over imperfect programs with lesser or greater degrees of parsimony or correctness. It is not at all clear how to do this in a principled way over a wide range of problems.

For the particular (and important) case of symbolic regression (system-identification) problems, the minimum description length (MDL) principle has been suggested as a way to make this tradeoff in a principled way with a minimum of *ad hoc* choices (Iba, Kurita, de Garis, and Sato 1993; Iba, de Garis, and Sato 1993, 1994). However, unparsimonious structures play a unique and important role in genetic programming. Many of the seemingly extraneous parts of genetically evolved programs apparently serve as reservoirs of genetic material; premature efforts to simplify programs may deny the population the needed diversity of genetic material with which to fashion the ultimate solution to the problem. This concern can be partially addressed by deferring the blending of parsimony into the fitness measure until relatively late in the run (e.g., after attainment of some reasonably high level of fitness using the original fitness measure) or until at least one or a certain number of solutions (or satisfactory results) is found using the original fitness measure.

The results of the experimental research reported herein, as reflected in main point 4, indicate that there is a fourth way to achieve parsimony in genetic programming: automatically defined functions. Parsimony appears to be an emergent property of most runs of genetic programming with automatically defined functions. The advantage of achieving parsimony by means of automatically defined functions is that this approach does not require any predefined arbitrary tradeoff between the competing elements of the fitness measure and does not appear to be limited to one particular class of problems (e.g., symbolic regression problems).

8 The Lawnmower Problem

The progression of parity problems in chapters 6 and 7 provide evidence in favor of the proposition that automatically defined functions are beneficial in terms of both computational effort and parsimony; however, they are constraining because they are so time-consuming. The lawnmower problem discussed in this chapter is an especially-constructed, fast-running problem designed to provide a flexible testbed for studying automatically defined functions. The lawnmower problem was specifically designed with the expectation that it would

- be much faster to run than the parity problem (it yields solutions with a population size of 1,000, rather than 16,000 or 4,000),
- be hard enough that its problem environment has exploitable regularities,
- be hard enough to have interesting hierarchical decompositions,
- have a sufficiently rich and varied function set to enable the problem to be solved in many distinctly different ways,
- be on the beneficial side of the breakeven point for computational effort,
- be on the beneficial side of the breakeven point for average structural complexity,
- be scalable with a much finer granularity than merely the number of arguments (3, 4, 5, and 6) to the parity function, and
- be so much faster to solve that we can say, in spite of all of the difficulties and uncertainties inherent in measuring wallclock time, that this problem is clearly on the beneficial side of the breakeven point for wallclock time when automatically defined functions are used.

In addition to the above characteristics, the lawnmower problem illustrates another interesting aspect of hierarchical computer programming. In the foregoing chapters, information was transmitted to the genetically evolved reusable subprograms solely by means of explicit arguments. The automatically defined functions were usually repeatedly used with different instantiations of these explicit arguments. When the transmitted values are received by the automatically defined function, they are bound to dummy variables (formal parameters) that appear locally inside the function. An alternative to the explicit transmission of information to a subprogram is the implicit transmission of information by means of side effects on the state of the system. In the lawnmower problem considered in this chapter, one of the two automatically defined functions takes no explicit arguments at all.

8.1 THE PROBLEM

In the lawnmower problem, the goal is to find a program for controlling the movement of a lawnmower so that the lawnmower cuts all the grass in the yard. The desired program is to be executed exactly once, so the program must contain within itself all the operations needed to solve the problem. The lawnmower problem is scaled in terms of the size of the lawn.

We first consider a version of this problem in which the lawnmower operates in a discrete 8-by-8 toroidal square area of lawn that initially has grass in all 64 squares. Later we will scale the lawn down to 48 and 32 squares and scale it up to 80 and 96 squares and compare the results to the results obtained for the 64-square lawn.

Each square of the lawn is uniquely identified by a vector of integers modulo 8 of the form (i,j), where $0 \le i, j \le 7$. The lawnmower starts at location (4,4) facing north. Note that we use the usual mathematical notation, (4,4), to denote a vector of numbers (rather than the style of LISP). The state of the lawnmower consists of its location on one of the 64 squares of the lawn and the direction in which it is facing. The lawn is toroidal in all four directions, so that whenever the lawnmower moves off the edge of the lawn, it reappears on the opposite side.

The lawnmower is capable of turning left. It can also move forward one square in the direction in which it is currently facing. Being a somewhat magical lawnmower, it can jump by a specified displacement in the vertical and horizontal directions in the plane. Whenever the lawnmower moves onto a new square (either by means of a single move or a jump), it mows all the grass, if any, remaining in the single square on which it arrives. The lawnmower has no sensors.

Figure 8.1 shows the 64 squares of the lawn. The origin (0,0) is in the upper left corner. The numbering of the squares increases going down and going to the right. There are no obstacles in the yard.

A human programmer writing a program to solve this problem would almost certainly not solve it by tediously writing a sequence of 64 separate mowing operations (and appropriate turning actions). Instead, a human programmer would exploit the considerable homogeneity and symmetry of this problem environment by writing a program that mows a certain small area of the lawn in a particular way, then repositions the lawnmower in some regular way, and then repeats the particular mowing action on the new area of the lawn. That is, the human programmer would decompose the overall problem into a subproblem (i.e., mowing a small area), solve the subproblem, and then repeatedly use the subproblem solution at different places on the lawn in order to solve the overall problem.

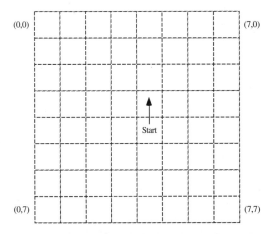

Figure 8.1 Starting location and orientation of the lawnmower in a lawn with 64 squares.

8.2 PREPARATORY STEPS WITHOUT ADFs

The operations of turning left and mowing one square take no arguments. Each of these operations changes the state of the lawnmower. It is largely a matter of convention as to whether such zero-argument side-effecting functions are treated as members of the function set or as members of the terminal set. For purposes of exposition, we adopt the convention throughout this book of treating zero-argument side-effecting functions as terminals, but treating zero-argument ADFs as functions. For purposes of programming, we treat all zero-argument functions as terminals (appendix E).

Since it may be desirable to be able to manipulate the numerical location of the lawnmower using arithmetic operations, random constants should be available as ingredients of programs for solving this problem. The random constants, $\Re_{v8}$, appropriate for this problem are vectors (i,j) composed of two integers modulo 8. These vector random constants range over the 64 possibilities between (0,0) and (7,7).

Thus, the terminal set for this problem consists of two zero-argument side-effecting operators and random vector constants.

$\mathcal{T} = \{$ (LEFT), (MOW), $\Re_{v8}\}$.

The operator LEFT takes no arguments and turns the orientation of the lawnmower counterclockwise by 90° (without moving the lawnmower). Since the programs will be performing arithmetic operations, it is necessary that all terminals and functions return a value that can serve as a legitimate argument to the arithmetic operations. Thus, to ensure closure, LEFT returns the vector value (0,0).

The operator MOW takes no arguments and moves the lawnmower in the direction it is currently facing and mows the grass, if any, in the square to which it is moving (thereby removing all the grass, if any, from that square). MOW does not change the orientation of the lawnmower. For example, if the lawnmower is at location (1,3) and facing east, MOW increments the first component (i.e., the x location) of the state vector of the lawnmower thus moving the lawnmower to location (2,3) with the lawnmower still facing east. As a further example, if the lawnmower is at location (7,3) and facing east, MOW moves the lawnmower to location (0,3) because of the toroidal geometry. To ensure closure, MOW also returns the vector value (0,0).

The function set consists of

$\mathcal{F} = \{$V8A, FROG, PROGN$\}$

with an argument map of

$\{2, 2, 1\}$.

V8A is two-argument vector addition function modulo 8. For example, (V8A (1,2) (3,7)) returns the value (4,1).

FROG is a one-argument operator that causes the lawnmower to move relative to the direction it is currently facing by an amount specified by its vector argument and to mow the grass, if any, in the square on which the lawnmower arrives (thereby removing all the grass, if any, from that square). FROG does not change the orientation of the lawnmower. For example, if the lawnmower is at location (1,2) and is facing east, (FROG (5,3)) causes the lawnmower to end up at location (6,5) with the lawnmower still facing east. The grass, if any, at the location (6,5) is mowed. FROG acts as the identity operator on its argument so, for example, (FROG (5,3)) returns the value (5,3).

The solution to this problem does not, of course, require both the MOW and FROG operators. The function set was intentionally enriched by the inclusion of both operators so there would be many alternative approaches to solving the problem and to permit solutions combining local activity (using MOW) with nonlocal activity (using FROG).

The goal is to mow all 64 squares of grass with a single execution of the program. The movement of the lawnmower is terminated when either the lawnmower has executed a total of 100 LEFT turns or a total of 100 movement-causing operations (i.e., MOWs or FROGs). The raw fitness of a particular program is the amount of grass (from 0 to 64) mowed within this allowed amount of time. Since the yard contains no obstacles and the toroidal topology of the yard is perfectly homogeneous and symmetrical, it is only necessary to measure fitness over one fitness case for this problem.

A population size of only 1,000 appears to be satisfactory for this problem.

Table 8.1 summarizes the key features of the 64-square lawnmower problem in an unobstructed yard without automatically defined functions.

8.3 LAWN SIZE OF 64 WITHOUT ADFs

The only way to write a computer program to mow all 64 squares of the lawn with the available movement-causing and turning operators involves tediously writing a program consisting of at least 64 MOWs or FROGs so that all 64 squares of the lawn are mowed. One possible orderly way of writing this tedious

Table 8.1 Tableau without ADFs for the 64-square lawnmower problem.

Objective:	Find a program to control a lawnmower so that it mows the grass on all 64 squares of lawn in an unobstructed toroidal yard.
Terminal set without ADFs:	(LEFT), (MOW), and the random constants $\mathfrak{R}_{v8}$.
Function set without ADFs:	V8A, FROG, and PROGN.
Fitness cases:	One fitness case consisting of a toroidal lawn with 64 squares, each initially containing grass.
Raw fitness:	Raw fitness is the amount of grass (from 0 to 64) mowed within the maximum allowed number of state-changing operations.
Standardized fitness:	Standardized fitness is the total number of squares (i.e., 64) minus raw fitness.
Hits:	Same as raw fitness.
Wrapper:	None.
Parameters:	$M = 1,000$. $G = 51$.
Success predicate:	A program scores the maximum number of hits.

program involves mowing all eight squares of lawn in the vertical column beginning at the starting location (4,4), turning left upon returning to (4,4), moving one square to the west, turning left three times so as to face north again, and then mowing the remaining seven squares of lawn in the new vertical column. This process can then be continued for the remaining columns.

The following handwritten 100%-correct 100-point program implements the above approach using the ordinary PROGN LISP connective that is capable of taking an indefinite number of arguments:

```
(PROGN (MOW) (MOW) (MOW) (MOW) (MOW) (MOW) (MOW) (MOW)
        (LEFT) (MOW) (LEFT) (LEFT) (LEFT)
        (MOW) (MOW) (MOW) (MOW) (MOW) (MOW) (MOW) (MOW)
        (LEFT) (MOW) (LEFT) (LEFT) (LEFT)
        (MOW) (MOW) (MOW) (MOW) (MOW) (MOW) (MOW) (MOW)
        (LEFT) (MOW) (LEFT) (LEFT) (LEFT)
        (MOW) (MOW) (MOW) (MOW) (MOW) (MOW) (MOW) (MOW)
        (LEFT) (MOW) (LEFT) (LEFT) (LEFT)
        (MOW) (MOW) (MOW) (MOW) (MOW) (MOW) (MOW) (MOW)
        (LEFT) (MOW) (LEFT) (LEFT) (LEFT)
        (MOW) (MOW) (MOW) (MOW) (MOW) (MOW) (MOW) (MOW)
        (LEFT) (MOW) (LEFT) (LEFT) (LEFT)
        (MOW) (MOW) (MOW) (MOW) (MOW) (MOW) (MOW) (MOW)
        (LEFT) (MOW) (LEFT) (LEFT) (LEFT)
        (MOW) (MOW) (MOW) (MOW) (MOW) (MOW) (MOW) (MOW)).
```

If one uses only the two-argument PROGN that is actually available in the function set specified above, the 197-point program below is an equivalent implementation of the above. This program requires an average of 3.08 points for each of the 64 squares of lawn.

```
((PROGN (PROGN (PROGN (PROGN (PROGN (PROGN (PROGN (MOW) (MOW))
                                          (PROGN (MOW) (MOW)))
                                   (PROGN (PROGN (MOW) (MOW))
                                          (PROGN (MOW) (MOW))))
                            (PROGN (PROGN (LEFT) (PROGN (MOW) (LEFT)))
                                   (PROGN (LEFT) (LEFT))))
                     (PROGN (PROGN (PROGN (PROGN (MOW) (MOW))
                                          (PROGN (MOW) (MOW)))
                                   (PROGN (PROGN (MOW) (MOW))
                                          (PROGN (MOW) (MOW))))
                            (PROGN (PROGN (LEFT) (PROGN (MOW) (LEFT)))
                                   (PROGN (LEFT) (LEFT)))))
              (PROGN (PROGN (PROGN (PROGN (PROGN (MOW) (MOW))
                                          (PROGN (MOW) (MOW)))
                                   (PROGN (PROGN (MOW) (MOW))
                                          (PROGN (MOW) (MOW))))
                            (PROGN (PROGN (LEFT) (PROGN (MOW) (LEFT)))
                                   (PROGN (LEFT) (LEFT))))
                     (PROGN (PROGN (PROGN (PROGN (MOW) (MOW))
                                          (PROGN (MOW) (MOW)))
                                   (PROGN (PROGN (MOW) (MOW))
                                          (PROGN (MOW) (MOW))))
                            (PROGN (PROGN (LEFT) (PROGN (MOW) (LEFT)))
                                   (PROGN (LEFT) (LEFT))))))
       (PROGN (PROGN (PROGN (PROGN (PROGN (PROGN (MOW) (MOW))
                                          (PROGN (MOW) (MOW)))
                                   (PROGN (PROGN (MOW) (MOW))
                                          (PROGN (MOW) (MOW))))
                            (PROGN (PROGN (LEFT) (PROGN (MOW) (LEFT)))
                                   (PROGN (LEFT) (LEFT))))
                     (PROGN (PROGN (PROGN (PROGN (MOW) (MOW))
                                          (PROGN (MOW) (MOW)))
                                   (PROGN (PROGN (MOW) (MOW))
                                          (PROGN (MOW) (MOW))))
                            (PROGN (PROGN (LEFT) (PROGN (MOW) (LEFT)))
                                   (PROGN (LEFT) (LEFT)))))
              (PROGN (PROGN (PROGN (PROGN (PROGN (MOW) (MOW))
                                          (PROGN (MOW) (MOW)))
                                   (PROGN (PROGN (MOW) (MOW))
                                          (PROGN (MOW) (MOW))))
                            (PROGN (PROGN (LEFT) (PROGN (MOW) (LEFT)))
                                   (PROGN (LEFT) (LEFT))))
                     (PROGN (PROGN (PROGN (MOW) (MOW))
                                   (PROGN (MOW) (MOW)))
                            (PROGN (PROGN (MOW) (MOW))
                                   (PROGN (MOW) (MOW))))))))).
```

As one would expect, genetic programming is capable of solving this problem without automatically defined functions.

As usual, the randomly created programs of generation 0 are not very effective at mowing much of the lawn. For example, the best of generation 0 mows only eight squares of the lawn.

```
(PROGN (PROGN (FROG (V8A (MOW) (1,7))) (FROG (FROG (7,4))))
(PROGN (V8A (PROGN (LEFT) (MOW)) (FROG (MOW))) (PROGN (FROG
(MOW)) (V8A (4,0) (MOW))))).
```

Figure 8.2 shows the trajectory of this 22-point best-of-generation program. As can be seen, the lawnmower MOWs and FROGs around the lawn in its

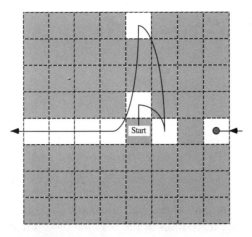

Figure 8.2 8-scoring trajectory of the best of generation 0 of one run of the 64-square lawnmower problem without ADFs.

not-too-successful effort to mow all 64 squares before the allowed amount of time or the program is exhausted. In practice, this program exhausts itself before it runs out of time. The eight mowed squares are unshaded and the 56 unmowed squares are shaded in gray.

Subtrees of somewhat effective programs in this problem typically mow small portions of the lawn. If two programs are selected from the population based on their fitness (i.e., such that more fit programs are more likely to be selected than less fit programs), both of the selected programs will usually mow more lawn than a randomly selected program of their generation. Moreover, a randomly selected subtree from either of these selected individuals will, on average, mow more lawn than a randomly selected subtree from a randomly selected program for its generation. Thus, the effect of the crossover operation in this problem is to create new programs which will, on average, mow an increasing and above-average amount of lawn.

A genealogical audit trail can provide further insight into how genetic programming works. An audit trail consists of a record of the ancestors of a given individual and of each genetic operation that was performed on the ancestors in order to produce the individual. For the crossover operation, the audit trail includes the particular crossover points chosen within each parent. When automatically defined functions are involved, the crossover point can be in either the body of the result-producing branch or in one of the function-defining branches.

The way that the crossover operation creates offspring programs that mow an increasing and above-average amount of lawn is illustrated by an examination of the genealogical audit trail for the best-of-generation program of the next generation (i.e., generation 1) of this run.

Parent A of the best of generation 1 is the 8th best program in the population for generation 0. This parent from generation 0 consists of the following 23-point program mowing seven squares of lawn:

```
1    (PROGN (PROGN (7,6)
2                       (PROGN (V8A (MOW) (MOW)) (V8A (LEFT) (MOW))))
3              (V8A (PROGN (MOW) (V8A (MOW) (LEFT)))
4                  (PROGN (PROGN (7,5) (3,1))
5                          (V8A (MOW) (MOW))))))).
```

This program contains seven MOW operations and achieves a raw fitness of 7.

Figure 8.3 shows the U-shaped 7-scoring trajectory of parent A from generation 0. The seven mowed squares are unshaded and the 57 unmowed squares are shaded in gray. The lawnmower starts at the starting location (4,4), mows north two squares, turns left, mows west three squares to the square marked by the arrow labeled "1," and turns left (south). This activity corresponds to the first three lines of the five-line program above. The fifth line of the program then causes the lawnmower to mow two additional squares to the south.

Parent B of the best of generation 1 is the 31st best program of generation 0 and consists of the following 14-point program mowing five squares of lawn from generation 0:

```
(FROG (V8A (V8A (FROG (0,4)) (FROG (4,2)))
           (PROGN (PROGN (3,2) (MOW))
                   (V8A (MOW) (1,4))))).
```

This program contains two MOW and three FROG operations and scores a raw fitness of 5.

Figure 8.4 shows the gyrating 5-scoring trajectory of parent B from generation 0. The five mowed squares are unshaded and the 59 unmowed squares are shaded in gray.

Note that neither parent A nor parent B is as good as the best of generation 0 (which mowed eight squares of lawn). However, both parents mow an above-average amount of lawn as is usually the case when parents are selected from the population on the basis of their fitness.

The best of generation 1 of this run mows 11 squares of lawn. This 33-point program is

```
1    (PROGN (PROGN (7,6)
2                       (PROGN (V8A (MOW) (MOW)) (V8A (LEFT) (MOW))))
3              (V8A (PROGN (MOW) (V8A (MOW) (LEFT)))
4                  (PROGN (V8A (V8A (FROG (0,4))
5                                    (FROG (4,2)))
6                          (PROGN (PROGN (3,2) (MOW))
7                                  (V8A (MOW) (1,4))))
8                          (V8A (MOW) (MOW))))))).
```

This eight-line offspring program contains nine MOW and two FROG operations and scores a raw fitness of 11 because the lawnmower reaches 11 different squares with those 11 operations. The crossover fragment contributed by parent B is in boldface above. It is inserted into parent A in lieu of line 4 (the underlined portion) of parent A shown earlier.

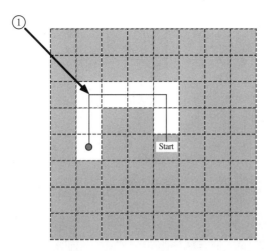

Figure 8.3 U-shaped 7-scoring trajectory of parent A from generation 0 of one run of the 64-square lawnmower problem without ADFs.

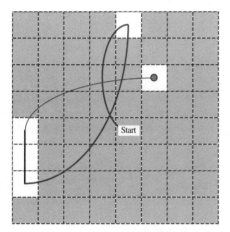

Figure 8.4 Gyrating 5-scoring trajectory of parent B from generation 0 of one run of the 64-square lawnmower problem without ADFs.

Figure 8.5 shows the 11-scoring trajectory of the best of generation 1. The 11 mowed squares are unshaded and the 53 unmowed squares are shaded in gray. The first three lines of this eight-line offspring program are identical to the first three lines of the five-line program for parent A. These three lines cause the lawnmower, starting at (4,4), to mow north two squares, turn left, mow west three squares to the square marked by the arrow labeled "1," and turn left (south). The lawnmower is thus at the square marked by the arrow labeled "1." The crossover operation inserts the boldface code constituting almost all of lines 4 through 7 of the eight-line offspring. This code comes from parent B. The lawnmower's action between arrow 1 and the arrow 2 comes from the crossover fragment contributed by parent B. The final two MOWs (southward) correspond to line five of parent A and line eight of the offspring.

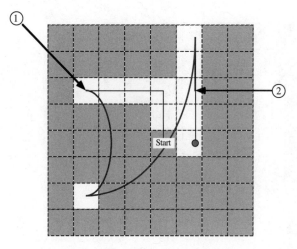

Figure 8.5 11-scoring trajectory of the best of generation 1 of one run of the 64-square problem without ADFs.

Without Defined Functions

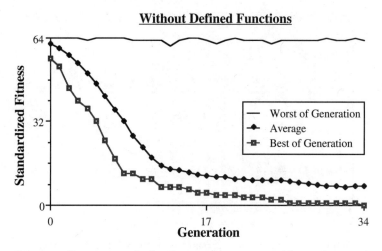

Figure 8.6 Fitness curves for the 64-square lawnmower problem without ADFs.

No program from generation 0 mows as many as 11 squares of lawn. Indeed, the best from generation 0 mows only eight squares. Parents 1 and 2 mow only seven and five squares, respectively. They are above average, but not the best, of their generation. This particular offspring in generation 1 mows 11 squares because the creative effect of the crossover operation directed the search of program space into a new and promising region. In this instance, the new area of the search space contains an offspring that achieves the new higher level of fitness of 11. The 11-scoring best of generation 1 follows an irregular trajectory in its attempt to solve the problem.

This run is a typical run of genetic programming in that as one proceeds from generation to generation, the fitness of the best-of-generation program and the average fitness of the population as a whole generally improve. For example, for generation 5, the best-of-generation program consists of 119 points and mows 32 of the 64 squares of lawn, as shown below:

```
(V8A (PROGN (PROGN (PROGN (PROGN (MOW) (MOW)) (V8A (MOW) (MOW)))
(PROGN (PROGN (MOW) (0,5)) (V8A (FROG (PROGN (PROGN (V8A (V8A
(LEFT) (MOW)) (PROGN (3,7) (MOW))) (V8A (PROGN (MOW) (LEFT))
(V8A (V8A (FROG (0,4)) (FROG (4,2))) (PROGN (PROGN (3,2) (MOW))
(V8A (MOW) (1,4)))))) (PROGN (FROG (PROGN (PROGN (PROGN (PROGN
(MOW) (MOW)) (FROG (LEFT))) (PROGN (MOW) (V8A (MOW) (MOW))))
(PROGN (V8A (PROGN (0,3) (7,2)) (V8A (MOW) (MOW))) (PROGN (V8A
(MOW) (MOW)) (PROGN (LEFT) (MOW)))))) (V8A (FROG (7,2)) (V8A
(7,3) (5,5))))) (V8A (V8A (V8A (3,7) (LEFT)) (PROGN (6,7)
(LEFT))) (PROGN (V8A (5,6) (LEFT)) (PROGN (MOW) (MOW))))))) (V8A
(PROGN (MOW) (V8A (MOW) (LEFT))) (PROGN (PROGN (7,5) (3,1)) (V8A
(MOW) (MOW))))) (V8A (PROGN (FROG (MOW)) (FROG (6,0))) (PROGN
(PROGN (MOW) (MOW)) (V8A (MOW) (MOW))))).
```

This considerably more successful program is much larger than its predecessors. Indeed, increasing size is necessary for improved performance in this problem.

Figure 8.6 presents the fitness curves for this run showing, by generation, the standardized fitness of the best-of-generation program, the standardized fitness of the worst-of-generation program, and the average of the standardized fitness for the population as a whole. The figure starts at generation 0 and ends at generation 34 when a 100% effective lawnmower (i.e., one with a standardized fitness of 0) is evolved on this particular run.

As one progresses from generation to generation in a typical run of genetic programming, the fitness of the population as a whole generally improves. The hits histogram is a useful monitoring tool for visualizing the progressive learning of the population as a whole during a particular run. The horizontal axis of the *hits histogram* represents the number of hits (0 to 64) while the vertical axis represents the number of individuals in the population (0 to 1,000) scoring that number of hits.

Figure 8.7 shows the hits histograms for generations 0, 5, 20, and 34 of this run. Note the left-to-right undulating movement of both the high point and the center of mass of these three histograms over the generations. This "slinky" movement reflects the improvement of the population as a whole.

Figure 8.8 shows the structural complexity of the best-of-generation program and the average of the values of structural complexity of the programs in the population as a whole for this run of the 64-square lawnmower problem without automatically defined functions. The structural complexity of the best of generation 0 is 23 and the average of the structural complexity of all the programs in the population for generation 0 is 9.7.

The following 296-point individual achieving a raw fitness of 64 emerged on generation 34 of this run without automatically defined functions:

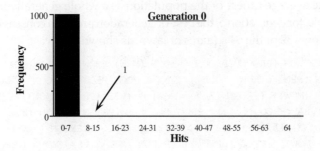

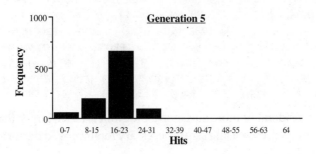

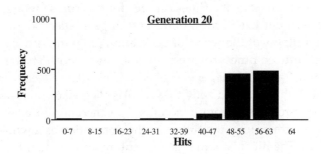

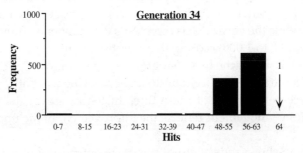

Figure 8.7 Hits histograms for generations 0, 5, 20, and 34 of the 64-square lawnmower problem without ADFs.

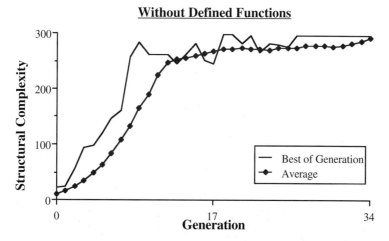

Figure 8.8 Structural complexity curves of a run of the 64-square lawnmower problem without ADFs.

```
(V8A (V8A (V8A (FROG (PROGN (PROGN (V8A (MOW) (MOW)) (FROG
(3,2))) (PROGN (V8A (PROGN (V8A (PROGN (PROGN (MOW) (2,4)) (FROG
(5,6))) (PROGN (V8A (MOW) (6,0)) (FROG (2,2)))) (V8A (MOW)
(MOW))) (PROGN (V8A (PROGN (PROGN (0,3) (7,2)) (FROG (5,6)))
(PROGN (V8A (MOW) (6,0)) (FROG (2,2)))) (V8A (MOW) (MOW))))
(PROGN (FROG (MOW)) (PROGN (PROGN (PROGN (V8A (MOW) (MOW)) (FROG
(LEFT))) (PROGN (MOW) (V8A (MOW) (MOW))))) (PROGN (V8A (PROGN
(0,3) (7,2)) (V8A (MOW) (MOW))) (PROGN (V8A (MOW) (MOW)) (PROGN
(LEFT) (MOW))))))))) (V8A (PROGN (V8A (PROGN (PROGN (MOW) (2,4))
(FROG (5,6))) (PROGN (V8A (MOW) (6,0)) (FROG (2,2)))) (V8A (MOW)
(MOW))) (V8A (FROG (LEFT)) (FROG (MOW))))) (V8A (FROG (V8A
(PROGN (V8A (PROGN (V8A (MOW) (MOW)) (FROG (3,7))) (V8A (PROGN
(MOW) (LEFT)) (V8A (MOW) (5,3)))) (PROGN (PROGN (V8A (PROGN (LEFT)
(MOW)) (V8A (1,4) (LEFT))) (PROGN (FROG (MOW)) (V8A (MOW)
(3,7)))) (V8A (PROGN (FROG (MOW)) (V8A (LEFT) (MOW))) (V8A (FROG
(1,2)) (V8A (MOW) (LEFT)))))) (PROGN (V8A (FROG (3,1)) (V8A
(FROG (PROGN (PROGN (V8A (MOW) (MOW)) (FROG (3,2))) (FROG (FROG
(5,0))))) (V8A (PROGN (FROG (MOW)) (V8A (MOW) (MOW))) (V8A (FROG
(LEFT)) (FROG (MOW)))))) (PROGN (PROGN (PROGN (PROGN (LEFT)
(MOW)) (V8A (MOW) (3,7))) (V8A (V8A (MOW) (MOW)) (PROGN (LEFT)
(LEFT)))) (V8A (FROG (PROGN (3,0) (LEFT))) (V8A (PROGN (MOW)
(LEFT)) (FROG (5,4)))))))) (PROGN (FROG (V8A (PROGN (V8A (PROGN
(PROGN (V8A (PROGN (PROGN (MOW) (2,4)) (FROG (5,6))) (PROGN (V8A
(MOW) (1,2)) (FROG (2,2)))) (V8A (MOW) (MOW))) (FROG (3,7)))
(V8A (PROGN (PROGN (MOW) (2,4)) (FROG (5,6))) (PROGN (V8A (MOW)
(6,0)) (FROG (2,2))))) (PROGN (PROGN (V8A (FROG (MOW)) (V8A
(1,4) (LEFT))) (PROGN (FROG (MOW)) (V8A (MOW) (3,7)))) (V8A
(PROGN (FROG (MOW)) (V8A (LEFT) (MOW))) (V8A (FROG (1,2)) (V8A
(MOW) (LEFT)))))) (PROGN (V8A (PROGN (FROG (2,4)) (V8A (MOW)
(MOW))) (V8A (FROG (MOW)) (LEFT))) (PROGN (3,0) (LEFT))))) (FROG
(V8A (7,4) (MOW)))))) (V8A (V8A (PROGN (MOW) (4,3)) (V8A (LEFT)
(6,1))) (MOW))).
```

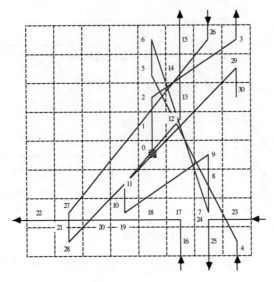

Figure 8.9 First partial trajectory of 296-point program for operations 0 through 30 without ADFs.

This 296-point program solves the problem by agglomerating enough erratic movements so as to cover the entire area of the lawn within the allowed maximum number of operations. In fact, the way that this program solves the problem is so tedious and convoluted that it can be easily visualized only after dividing the trajectory of the lawnmower into three epochs.

Figure 8.9 shows a partial trajectory of this best-of-run 296-point individual for the first epoch consisting of mowing operations 0 through 30; figure 8.10 shows a partial trajectory for the second epoch involving mowing operations 31 through 60; and figure 8.11 shows the third epoch involving mowing operations 61 through 85. Since all 64 squares are mowed in these figures, they are all unshaded.

As can be seen, even though the problem environment contains considerable regularity in that it requires mowing all 64 squares of the lawn in an unobstructed toroidal yard, this solution involves a tangled agglomeration of irregular movements. For example, between mowing operations 2 and 3, the lawnmower FROGs up two rows and three columns to the right; between operations 4 and 5, the mower FROGs up six rows and three columns to the left; and between operations 6 and 7, the mower FROGs up two (i.e., down six) and two columns to the right.

There is a close relationship between the size of a program and its fitness. Since raw fitness is higher for better individuals for this problem, this relationship can be seen by comparing structural complexity to raw fitness (rather than standardized fitness).

Figure 8.12 shows, by generation, the raw fitness and the structural complexity of the best-of-generation program for this run without automatically defined functions. The vertical axis on the left of the figure runs between 0 and the number of squares of lawn (64). The vertical axis on the right runs

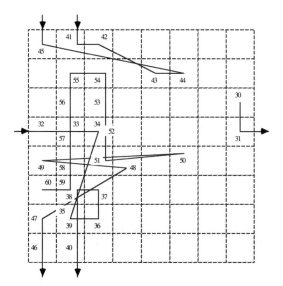

Figure 8.10 Second partial trajectory of 296-point program for operations 31 through 60 without ADFs.

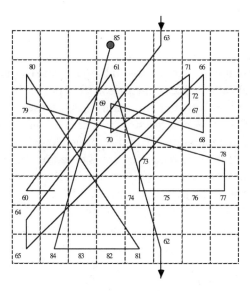

Figure 8.11 Third partial trajectory of 296-point program for operations 61 through 85 without ADFs.

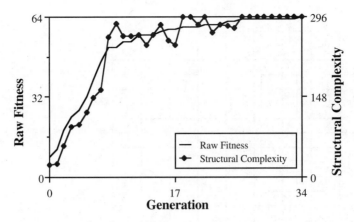

Figure 8.12 Superimposition of the raw fitness and structural complexity of the best-of-generation programs for the 64-square lawnmower problem without ADFs.

between 0 and 296 (so that the graph of structural complexity and the graph of raw fitness intersect at generation 34 for the known 100%-correct 296-point program for this run). The superimposition of these two graphs in this way shows the close relationship between structural complexity and fitness for this particular problem when it is run without automatically defined functions.

The average structural complexity, $\overline{S}_{without}$, of the 100%-correct programs from the 35 successful runs (out of 38 runs) of the 64-square lawnmower problem without automatically defined functions is 280.8 points. It takes an average of about four and a half functions and terminals in these program trees to mow one square of lawn. The successful programs are large because they make no use of the inherent regularity of the problem environment.

Figure 8.13 presents the performance curves based on the 38 runs of the 64-square lawnmower problem without automatically defined functions. Only 3% of the runs are successful by generation 17. The cumulative probability of success, $P(M,i)$, is 92% by generation 49 and 92% by generation 50. The two numbers in the oval indicate that if this problem is run through to generation 49, processing a total of $E_{without}$ = 100,000 individuals (i.e., $1,000 \times 50$ generations $\times 2$ runs) is sufficient to yield a solution to this problem with 99% probability.

See also Koza 1993c, 1994a.

8.4 LAWN SIZE OF 32 WITHOUT ADFs

When the size of the problem is scaled down by 50% from 64 to 32 squares of lawn (an 8-by-4 configuration), the average structural complexity, $\overline{S}_{without}$, of the 100%-correct programs from the 64 successful runs (out of 64 runs) without automatically defined functions is 145.0. This is a drop from the value of 280.8 for the 64-square lawn; however, it still takes an average of about four and a half functions and terminals in the program trees to mow one square of lawn.

Without Defined Functions

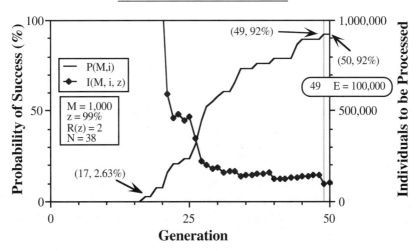

Figure 8.13 Performance curves for the 64-square lawnmower problem showing that $E_{without} = 100{,}000$ without ADFs.

Without Defined Functions

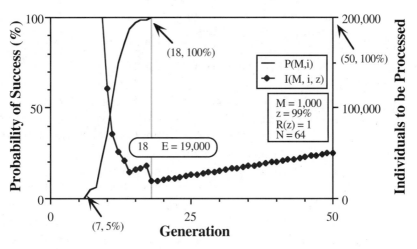

Figure 8.14 Performance curves for the 32-square lawnmower problem showing that $E_{without} = 19{,}000$ without ADFs.

As one would expect, the computational effort decreases substantially.

Figure 8.14 presents the performance curves based on the 64 runs of the 32-square lawnmower problem without automatically defined functions. The cumulative probability of success, $P(M,i)$, is 100% by generation 18. The two numbers in the oval indicate that if this problem is run through to generation 18, processing a total of $E_{without}$ = 19,000 individuals (i.e., 1,000 × 19 generations × 1 run) is sufficient to yield a solution to this problem with 99% probability.

8.5   LAWN SIZE OF 48 WITHOUT ADFs

When the lawn size is 48 (an 8-by-6 configuration), the average structural complexity, $\overline{S}_{without}$, of the 100%-correct programs from the 39 successful runs (out of 43 runs) without automatically defined functions is 217.6 (i.e., about 4.5 times the lawn size).

Figure 8.15 presents the performance curves based on the 43 runs of the 48-square lawnmower problem without automatically defined functions. The cumulative probability of success, $P(M,i)$, is 91% by generation 27 and 98% by generation 50. The two numbers in the oval indicate that if this problem is run through to generation 27, processing a total of $E_{without}$ = 56,000 individuals (i.e., 1,000 × 28 generations × 2 runs) is sufficient to yield a solution to this problem with 99% probability.

8.6   LAWN SIZE OF 80 WITHOUT ADFs

When the lawn size is 80 (an 8-by-10 configuration), the average structural complexity, $\overline{S}_{without}$, of the 100%-correct programs from the 32 successful runs (out of 90 runs) without automatically defined functions is 366.1 (i.e., about 4.6 times the lawn size).

Figure 8.16 presents the performance curves based on the 90 runs of the 80-square lawnmower problem without automatically defined functions. The cumulative probability of success, $P(M,i)$, is 35.6% by generation 50. The two numbers in the oval indicate that if this problem is run through to generation 50, processing a total of $E_{without}$ = 561,000 individuals (i.e., 1,000 × 51 generations × 11 runs) is sufficient to yield a solution to this problem with 99% probability.

8.7   LAWN SIZE OF 96 WITHOUT ADFs

When the lawn size is 96 (an 8-by-12 configuration), the average structural complexity, $\overline{S}_{without}$, of the 100%-correct programs from the 14 successful runs (out of 284 runs) without automatically defined functions is 408.8 (i.e., about 4.3 times the lawn size). The progression in values of average structural complexity, $\overline{S}_{without}$, of the solutions to the lawnmower problem with lawn sizes of 32, 48, 64, 80, and 96 is 145.0, 217.6, 280.8, 336.1, and 408.8, respectively.

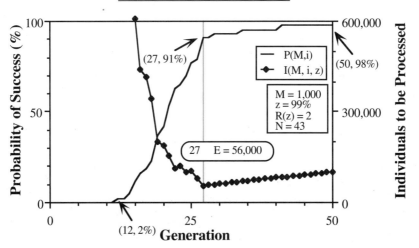

Figure 8.15 Performance curves for the 48-square lawnmower problem showing that $E_{without}$ = 56,000 without ADFs.

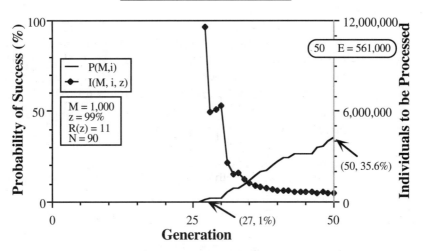

Figure 8.16 Performance curves for the 80-square lawnmower problem showing that $E_{without}$ = 561,000 without ADFs.

Without Defined Functions

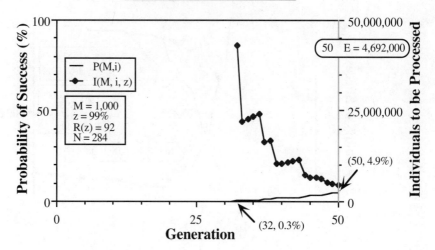

Figure 8.17 Performance curves for the 96-square lawnmower problem showing that $E_{without} = 4{,}692{,}000$ without ADFs.

Thus, as the size of the lawn increases in equal increments of 16 squares, the size of the solutions becomes more and more unwieldy.

Figure 8.17 presents the performance curves based on the 284 runs of the 96-square lawnmower problem without automatically defined functions. The cumulative probability of success, $P(M,i)$, is 4.9% by generation 50. The two numbers in the oval indicate that if this problem is run through to generation 50, processing a total of $E_{without} = 4{,}692{,}000$ individuals (i.e., $1{,}000 \times 51$ generations $\times 92$ runs) is sufficient to yield a solution to this problem with 99% probability.

The progression in values of computational effort, $E_{without}$, for the lawnmower problem with lawn sizes of 32, 48, 64, 80, and 96 is 19,000, 56,000, 100,000, 561,000, and 4,692,000, respectively. Thus, as the size of the lawn increases, dramatically more computational effort is required to yield a solution to the problem without automatically defined functions.

8.8 PREPARATORY STEPS WITH ADFs

Each of the solutions presented in the previous section for solving the lawnmower problem without automatically defined functions contained at least 64 MOWs or FROGs when the lawn size is 64. However, a human programmer would never consider solving this problem in this tedious way. Instead, a human programmer would write a program that first mows a certain small subarea of the lawn in some orderly way; the lawnmower would then be repositioned to a new subarea of the lawn in some orderly (probably tessellating) way; and the mowing action would be repeated on the new subarea of the lawn. The program would contain enough invocations of the orderly method for mowing subareas so as to completely mow the entire lawn. That is, a human programmer would exploit the considerable regularity and symmetry inherent in the problem environment by decomposing the problem into subproblems and would then repeatedly use the solution to the subproblem in order to solve the overall problem.

In applying genetic programming with automatically defined functions to the lawnmower problem, we decided that each individual overall program in the population will consist of two function-defining branches (defining a zero-argument function called ADF0 and a one-argument function ADF1) and a final (rightmost) result-producing branch. The second defined function ADF1 can hierarchically refer to the first defined function ADF0. We envisaged that the first automatically defined function, ADF0, should be capable of limited, local motion and that the second automatically defined function, ADF1, should be capable of motion over larger distances.

We first consider the two function-defining branches.

The terminal set, $\mathcal{T}_{adf0}$, for the zero-argument defined function ADF0 consists of

$\mathcal{T}_{adf0} = \{$ (LEFT), (MOW), $\mathfrak{R}_{v8}\}$.

The function set, $\mathcal{F}_{adf0}$, for the zero-argument defined function ADF0 is

$\mathcal{F}_{adf0} = \{$V8A, PROGN$\}$

with an argument map of

$\{2, 2\}$.

The body of ADF0 is a composition of primitive functions from the function set, $\mathcal{F}_{adf0}$, and terminals from the terminal set, $\mathcal{T}_{adf0}$.

The terminal set, $\mathcal{T}_{adf1}$, for the one-argument defined function ADF1 taking dummy variable ARG0 consists of

$\mathcal{T}_{adf1} = \{$ARG0, (LEFT), (MOW), $\mathfrak{R}_{v8}\}$.

The function set, $\mathcal{F}_{adf1}$, for the one-argument defined function ADF1 is

$\mathcal{F}_{adf1} = \{$ADF0, V8A, FROG, PROGN$\}$,

with an argument map of

$\{0, 2, 1, 2\}$.

The body of ADF1 is a composition of primitive functions from the function set, $\mathcal{F}_{adf1}$, and terminals from the terminal set, $\mathcal{T}_{adf1}$.

We now consider the result-producing branch.

The terminal set, $\mathcal{T}_{rpb}$, for the result-producing branch is

$\mathcal{T}_{rpb} = \{$ (LEFT), (MOW), $\mathfrak{R}_{v8}\}$.

The function set, $\mathcal{F}_{rpb}$, for the result-producing branch is

$\mathcal{F}_{rpb} = \{$ADF0, ADF1, V8A, FROG, PROGN$\}$,

Table 8.2 Tableau with ADFs for the 64-square lawnmower problem.

Objective:	Find a program to control a lawnmower so that it mows the grass on all 64 squares of lawn in an unobstructed yard.
Architecture of the overall program with ADFs:	One result-producing branch and two function-defining branches, with ADF0 taking no arguments and ADF1 taking one argument, and with ADF1 hierarchically referring to ADF0.
Parameters:	Branch typing.
Terminal set for the result-producing branch:	(LEFT), (MOW), and the random constants $\Re_{v8}$.
Function set for the result-producing branch:	ADF0, ADF1, V8A, FROG, and PROGN.
Terminal set for the function-defining branch ADF0:	(LEFT), (MOW), and the random constants $\Re_{v8}$.
Function set for the function-defining branch ADF0:	V8A and PROGN.
Terminal set for the function-defining branch ADF1:	ARG0, (LEFT), (MOW), and the random constants $\Re_{v8}$.
Function set for the function-defining branch ADF1:	V8A, PROGN, and FROG, and ADF0 (hierarchical reference of ADF0 by ADF1).

with an argument map of

$\{0, 1, 2, 1, 2\}$.

The result-producing branch is a composition of the functions from the function set, $\mathcal{F}_{rpb}$, and terminals from the terminal set, $\mathcal{T}_{rpb}$.

Table 8.2 summarizes the key features of the lawnmower problem in an unobstructed yard with 64 squares with automatically defined functions.

8.9 Lawn Size of 64 with ADFs

When genetic programming with automatically defined functions is applied to this problem, the results are very different from the haphazard solutions obtained without automatically defined functions.

We illustrate this by examining five particular runs (out of 76) of this problem.

In the first illustrative run of this problem with automatically defined functions, the following 100%-correct 78-point program scoring 64 (out of 64) emerged in generation 2 (a very early generation):

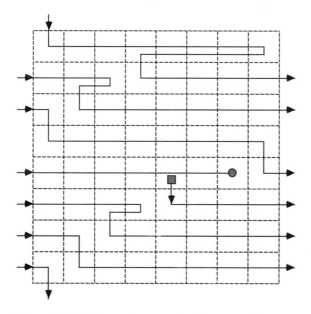

Figure 8.18   Trajectory of row-mowing lawnmower from run 1 with ADFs.

```
(progn (defun ADF0 ()
           (values (V8A (PROGN (V8A (V8A (LEFT) (6,5)) (PROGN
               (MOW) (LEFT)))) (V8A (PROGN (MOW) (MOW)) (V8A (MOW)
               (MOW)))) (V8A (PROGN (V8A (1,4) (MOW)) (PROGN (3,1)
               (MOW))) (PROGN (PROGN (3,1) (MOW)) (PROGN (LEFT)
               (LEFT)))))))
       (defun ADF1 (ARG0)
          (values (V8A (PROGN (FROG (PROGN ARG0 (ADF0))) (V8A
              (PROGN (MOW) (ADF0)) (V8A (V8A (ADF0) (3,4)) (V8A
              (ADF0) ARG0)))) (V8A (FROG (FROG (MOW))) (PROGN (PROGN
              (MOW) (3,5)) (PROGN (MOW) (MOW)))))))
       (values (V8A (ADF1 (ADF1 (V8A (7,1) (LEFT)))) (V8A (V8A
           (PROGN (LEFT) (LEFT)) (V8A (7,0) (LEFT))) (FROG (V8A
           (ADF0) (MOW))))))))).
```

The result-producing branch of this 78-point program contains two invocations of ADF1, one invocation of ADF0, four LEFTs, and one MOW. ADF1 contains four invocations of ADF0, no turns, and five MOWs. ADF0 contains eight MOWs and four LEFTs.

Figure 8.18 shows the trajectory of the row-mowing lawnmower for this 78-point program from run 1 with automatically defined functions. The lawnmower here takes advantage of the inherent regularity of the problem environment. It mows an entire row consisting of eight consecutive squares in an easterly direction and then proceeds to the next row to the south and does the same. The fact that the entire trajectory can be conveniently presented in only one figure testifies to this solution's predominantly regular behavior.

This solution is a hierarchical decomposition of the problem. First, genetic programming discovered a decomposition of the overall problem into eight subproblems each consisting of mowing a single row of eight consecutive squares. Then, genetic programming discovered a sequence of turns and moves to implement the mowing of an entire row of eight squares. Third, genetic programming assembled the results of the row mowing subproblem by repositioning the lawnmower to the adjacent row.

In run 2, the best of generation 0 is the following 54-point program scoring 56 (out of 64):

```
(progn (defun ADF0 ()
          (values (PROGN (PROGN (V8A (V8A (MOW) (LEFT)) (PROGN
             (6,4) (MOW))) (V8A (V8A (4,3) (3,3)) (V8A (LEFT)
             (LEFT)))) (PROGN (V8A (PROGN (3,7) (5,3)) (V8A (MOW)
             (MOW))) (PROGN (V8A (MOW) (LEFT)) (PROGN (MOW)
             (MOW))))))))
        (defun ADF1 (ARG0)
          (values (FROG (PROGN (V8A (FROG (ADF0)) (PROGN (ADF0)
             (ADF0))) (V8A (V8A (LEFT) (1,5)) (PROGN (ADF0)
             (LEFT))))))))
        (values (ADF1 (ADF1 (PROGN (ADF1 (LEFT)) (PROGN (LEFT)
             (ADF0))))))))).
```

The raw fitness of 56 achieved by the best of generation 0 with automatically defined functions is considerably better than the raw fitness (i.e., eight) of the previously cited best of generation 0 without automatically defined functions.

Figure 8.19 shows the improvement in fitness from generation to generation for this run with automatically defined functions.

Figure 8.20 shows the hits histograms for generations 0, 1, 2, 3, 4, and 5 of the same run of this problem with automatically defined functions. The first

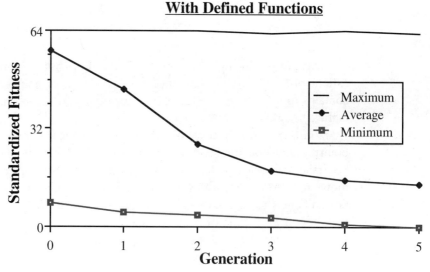

Figure 8.19   Fitness curves of run 2 for the 64-square lawnmower problem with ADFs.

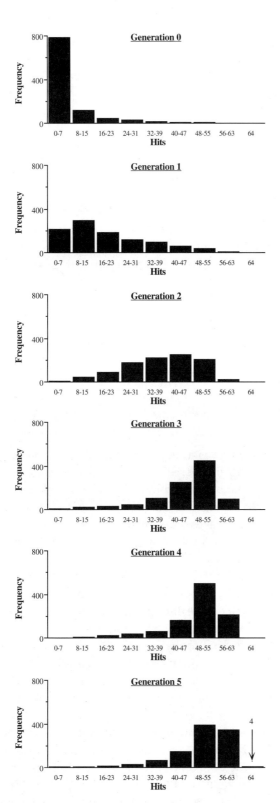

Figure 8.20 Hits histograms for run 2 of the 64-square lawnmower problem for generations 0 through 5 with ADFs.

The Lawnmower Problem

eight buckets each represent a range of eight values of hits; the ninth bucket contains only programs whose raw fitness (i.e., hits) is precisely 64 (i.e., a 100%-correct solution). Note the arrow on the histogram for generation 5 pointing to the simultaneous emergence of four 100%-correct individuals in the population on that generation.

Figure 8.21 shows the structural complexity curves for run 2 of the 64-square lawnmower problem with automatically defined functions. The figure shows, by generation, the structural complexity in the best-of-generation program and the average of the structural complexity of the programs in the population as a whole. The structural complexity of the best of generation 0 is 63 and the average of the structural complexity of the programs in the population as a whole for generation 0 is 28.7 with automatically defined functions.

The following 100%-correct 42-point program scoring 64 (out of 64) emerged in generation 5:

```
(progn (defun ADF0 ()
            (values (PROGN (V8A (0,1) (2,0)) (V8A (V8A (PROGN (MOW)
              (LEFT)) (V8A (MOW) (LEFT))) (PROGN (V8A (LEFT) (LEFT))
              (PROGN (MOW) (MOW))))))))
        (defun ADF1 (ARG0)
          (values (V8A (FROG (FROG (ADF0))) (PROGN (PROGN (V8A
            (MOW) (ADF0)) (V8A (ADF0) (MOW))) (V8A (FROG (ADF0))
            (V8A ARG0 ARG0))))))
        (values (ADF1 (ADF1 (ADF1 (ADF1 (ADF0))))))).
```

This 42-point solution is a hierarchical decomposition of the problem. Genetic programming discovered the decomposition of the overall problem, discovered the content of each subroutine, and assembled the results of the multiple calls to the subroutines into a solution of the overall problem. The result-producing branch does not contain any LEFT, MOW, or FROG operations at all. ADF1 contains four invocations of ADF0, two MOWs, and no LEFT or FROG operations. ADF0 contains four MOWs and four LEFTs.

Figure 8.22 shows the column-mowing trajectory of the lawnmower for this 42-point solution. Note the difference between this regular trajectory and the haphazard character of the three partial trajectories shown in figures 8.10, 8.11, and 8.12. The lawnmower here takes advantage of the regularity of the problem environment. It performs a tessellating activity that covers the entire lawn. Specifically, it mows four consecutive squares in a column in a northerly direction, shifts one column to the west, and then does the same thing in the next column. This solution involves only eight multiple visits to the same square.

When this 42-point program is evaluated, ADF0 is executed first by the result-producing branch. ADF0 begins with a PROGN whose first argument is (V8A (0,1) (2,0)). Since vector addition V8A has no side effects and since the return value of PROGN is the value returned by its last (second) argument, this first argument to the PROGN can be ignored. Since the

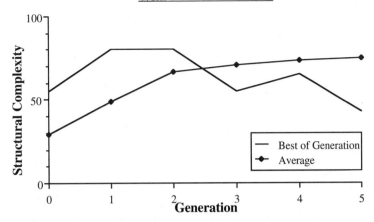

With Defined Functions

Figure 8.21 Structural complexity curves of run 2 of the 64-square lawnmower problem with ADFs.

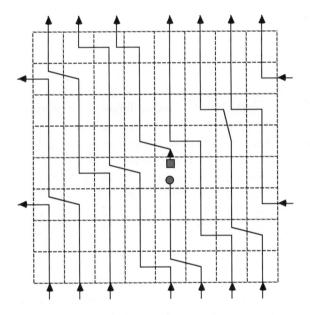

Figure 8.22 Trajectory of column-mowing lawnmower from run 2 with ADFs.

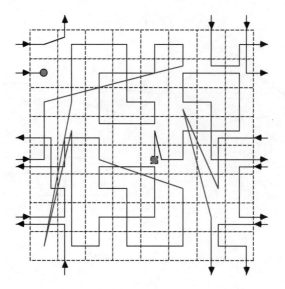

Figure 8.23 Trajectory of swirler from run 3 of lawnmower problem with ADFs.

remainder of ADF0 contains only MOW and LEFT operations, ADF0 returns (0,0). As it turns out, ADF1 never uses its dummy variable.

The basic activity of ADF0 is to mow four squares of lawn in a northwest-erly zigzag pattern. This zigzag action is illustrated at the starting point (4,4) in the middle of the figure. ADF0 moves forward (i.e., north) one square and mows that square; it then turns left (i.e., west) and moves forward and mows that square; it then turns left three times (so that it is again oriented north); and it then moves and mows two squares.

The northwesterly zigzag mowing activity of ADF0 is then repeatedly invoked. The result-producing branch invokes ADF1 a total of four times. Each time ADF1 is invoked, ADF0 is invoked four times. This hierarchy of invocations produces a total of 16 calls for the zigzag activity of ADF0. Be-cause of the initial direct call of ADF0 at the beginning of the evaluation of the result-producing branch, the last of the 16 hierarchical invocations of ADF0 is not needed since the program is terminated by virtue of the comple-tion of the overall task.

This zigzagging solution is a hierarchical decomposition and solution of the problem involving three simultaneous, automatic discoveries. Genetic programming discovered a decomposition of the overall problem into 16 subproblems each consisting of the northwesterly zigzag mowing pattern. Genetic programming also discovered the sequence of turns and moves to implement the northwesterly zigzag mowing action. In addi-tion, genetic programming assembled the results of the mowing motion into a solution of the overall problem by appropriately repositioning the lawnmower.

In run 3, the following 107-point "swirler" emerged in generation 5 as a 100%-correct solution to the problem:

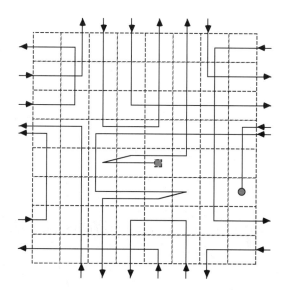

Figure 8.24 Trajectory of crisscrosser of run 4 of lawnmower problem with ADFs.

```
(progn (defun ADF0 ()
          (values (V8A (V8A (V8A (PROGN (7,0) (2,5)) (V8A (6,4)
            (MOW))) (PROGN (V8A (LEFT) (MOW)) (V8A (5,1)
            (LEFT)))) (V8A (V8A (V8A (MOW) (0,1)) (PROGN (PROGN
            (PROGN (LEFT) (LEFT)) (V8A (LEFT) (MOW))) (PROGN (V8A
            (0,1) (MOW)) (V8A (LEFT) (0,6)))))) (PROGN (PROGN
            (MOW) (MOW)) (PROGN (LEFT) (MOW))))))))
       (defun ADF1 (ARG0)
          (values (PROGN (FROG (V8A (V8A (V8A (V8A (PROGN (3,2)
            (ADF0)) (V8A (ADF0) (MOW))) (FROG (5,1))) (V8A (PROGN
            (3,2) (ADF0)) (V8A (ADF0) (MOW)))) (V8A ARG0 ARG0)))
            (FROG (PROGN (FROG (7,4)) (V8A (MOW) (MOW))))))))
       (values (ADF1 (V8A (PROGN (PROGN (MOW) (3,6)) (ADF1 (V8A
         (LEFT) (LEFT)))) (PROGN (PROGN (PROGN (V8A (ADF1 (MOW))
         (PROGN (ADF0) (2,0))) (PROGN (ADF1 (MOW)) (ADF1
         (ADF0)))) (PROGN (ADF1 (1,5)) (V8A (2,6) (LEFT))))
         (ADF1 (ADF0))))))))).
```

Figure 8.23 shows that the trajectory of this 107-point program consists of a counterclockwise swirling motion which very efficiently covers 100% of the lawn.

In run 4, the following 95-point crisscrosser emerged in generation 4 as a 100%-correct solution:

```
(progn (defun ADF0 ()
          (values (V8A (PROGN (V8A (V8A (V8A (6,6) (MOW)) (PROGN
            (1,6) (V8A (MOW) (LEFT)))) (V8A (MOW) (0,1))) (V8A
            (V8A (MOW) (MOW)) (PROGN (MOW) (MOW)))) (PROGN (PROGN
            (V8A (6,7) (MOW)) (V8A (LEFT) (MOW))) (PROGN (V8A
            (MOW) (LEFT)) (PROGN (0,6) (MOW)))))))
```

```
(defun ADF1 (ARG0)
    (values (V8A (PROGN (V8A (PROGN (MOW) (MOW)) (V8A (5,1)
        (LEFT))) (PROGN (FROG (LEFT)) (V8A ARG0 ARG0))) (V8A
        (PROGN (PROGN (MOW) (6,2)) (V8A (ADF0) (MOW))) (PROGN
        (V8A ARG0 (ADF0)) (FROG (ADF0))))))))
    (values (FROG (PROGN (ADF1 (PROGN (LEFT) (5,1))) (PROGN
        (FROG (ADF0)) (PROGN (V8A (PROGN (ADF1 (3,7)) (FROG
        (MOW))) (ADF1 (ADF1 (MOW)))) (PROGN (FROG (FROG
        (LEFT))) (V8A (FROG (2,0)) (PROGN (5,0) (ADF0)))))))))))).
```

Figure 8.24 shows that the trajectory of this best-of-run individual criss-crosses the lawn with both vertical and horizontal motions in such as way as to mow the entire lawn.

In run 5, the following 56-point jumping column mower emerged in generation 5 as a 100%-correct solution:

```
(progn (defun ADF0 ()
        (values (PROGN (PROGN (2,4) (MOW)) (V8A (PROGN (V8A
            (PROGN (MOW) (5,0)) (PROGN (MOW) (MOW))) (V8A (MOW)
            (MOW))) (V8A (PROGN (MOW) (MOW)) (V8A (5,6)
            (6,6)))))))
    (defun ADF1 (ARG0)
        (values (PROGN (PROGN (PROGN (FROG (ADF0)) (PROGN (4,5)
            (MOW))) (V8A (V8A (1,6) ARG0) (FROG (ADF0)))) (V8A
            (FROG (ADF0)) (PROGN (FROG (MOW)) (FROG (ADF0)))))))
    (values (ADF1 (V8A (V8A (ADF1 (ADF0)) (PROGN (6,2)
        (3,7))) (ADF1 (FROG (MOW))))))).
```

The column mowing behavior of this 56-point program can be seen when it is simplified to the following equivalent 29-point program:

```
(progn (defun ADF0 ()
        (values (PROGN (MOW) (MOW) (MOW) (MOW) (MOW) (MOW)
                        (MOW) (MOW) (3,4))))
    (defun ADF1 (ARG0)
        (values (PROGN (FROG (ADF0)) (MOW) (FROG (ADF0)) (V8A
            (FROG (ADF0)) (PROGN (MOW) (FROG (ADF0)))))))
    (values (ADF1 (progn (ADF1 (ADF0)) (ADF1 (MOW)))))).
```

Figure 8.25 shows that the trajectory of this jumping column mower mows an entire vertical column of the lawn and then jumps to another column and repeats this behavior.

The 76 100%-correct solutions obtained in 76 runs of the lawnmower problem with automatically defined functions can be classified, as shown in table 8.3, into five motifs based on the general nature of their trajectories. A human programmer would probably write a program using a motif involving row or column mowing; however, as can be seen, only about half of the 76 runs employed this motif. This table is reminiscent of table 6.7 which demonstrated that genetic programming employed parity functions only 42% of the time in solving the Boolean 5-parity problem.

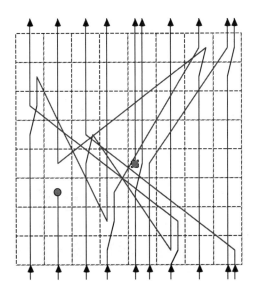

Figure 8.25 Trajectory of jumping column mower of run 5 of lawnmower problem with ADFs.

Table 8.3 Motifs of the trajectories of 76 solutions to the lawnmower problem with ADFs.

Motif	Percentage of 76 runs
Row or column mowing	49%
Zigzagging	20%
Large swirls	17%
Crisscrossing	10%
Tight swirls	4%

A videotape visualization of these trajectories can be found in *Genetic Programming II Videotape: The Next Generation* (Koza and Rice 1994).

The average structural complexity, $\bar{S}_{with}$, of the 100%-correct programs from the 76 successful runs of the 64-square lawnmower problem with automatically defined functions is 76.9 points.

Figure 8.26 presents the performance curves based on the 76 runs (out of 76 runs) of the 64-square lawnmower problem with automatically defined functions. The cumulative probability of success, $P(M, i)$, is 100% by generation 10. The two numbers in the oval indicate that if this problem is run through to generation 10, processing a total of $E_{with} = 11,000$ individuals (i.e., 1,000 × 11 generations × 1 run) is sufficient to yield a solution to this problem with 99% probability.

Table 8.4 compares the average structural complexity, $\bar{S}_{without}$ and $\bar{S}_{with}$, and the computational effort, $E_{without}$ and E_{with}, for the lawnmower problem with automatically defined functions and without them.

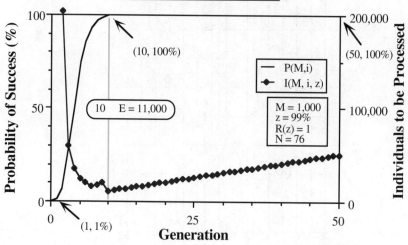

Figure 8.26 Performance curves for the 64-square lawnmower problem showing that $E_{with} = 11,000$ with ADFs.

Table 8.4 Comparison table for the 64-square lawnmower problem.

	Without ADFs	With ADFs
Average structural complexity $\overline{S}$	280.8	76.9
Computational effort E	100,000	11,000

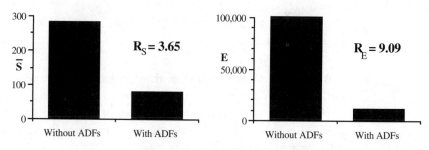

Figure 8.27 Summary graphs for the 64-square lawnmower problem.

With Defined Functions

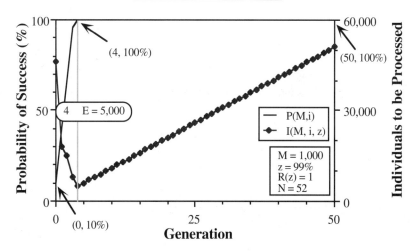

Figure 8.28 Performance curves for the 32-square lawnmower problem showing that E_{with} = 5,000 with ADFs.

Table 8.5 Comparison table for the 32-square lawnmower problem.

	Without ADFs	With ADFs
Average structural complexity $\bar{S}$	145.0	66.3
Computational effort E	19,000	5,000

Figure 8.27 summarizes the information in this comparison table and shows a structural complexity ratio, R_S, of 3.65 and an efficiency ratio, R_E, of 9.09.

8.10 LAWN SIZE OF 32 WITH ADFs

When the size of the problem is scaled down from 64 to 32 squares, the average structural complexity, $\bar{S}_{with}$, of the 100%-correct programs from the 52 successful runs (out of 52 runs) of the 32-square lawnmower problem with automatically defined functions is 66.3 points. This value is only slightly smaller than the average structural complexity of 76.9 when the lawn had 64 squares.

Figure 8.28 presents the performance curves based on the 52 runs of the 32-square lawnmower problem with automatically defined functions. The cumulative probability of success, $P(M,i)$, is 100% by generation 4. The two numbers in the oval indicate that if this problem is run through to generation 4, processing a total of E_{with} = 5,000 individuals (i.e., 1,000 × 5 generations × 1 run) is sufficient to yield a solution to this problem with 99% probability.

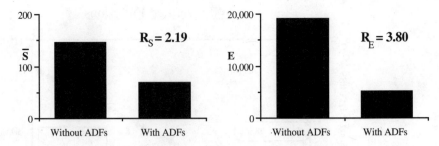

Figure 8.29 Summary graphs for the 32-square lawnmower problem.

With Defined Functions

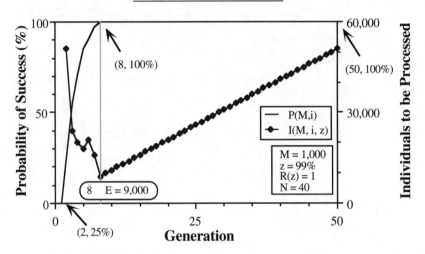

Figure 8.30 Performance curves for the 48-square lawnmower problem showing that E_{with} = 9,000 with ADFs.

Table 8.6 Comparison table for the 48-square lawnmower problem.

	Without ADFs	With ADFs
Average structural complexity $\overline{S}$	217.6	69.0
Computational effort E	56,000	9,000

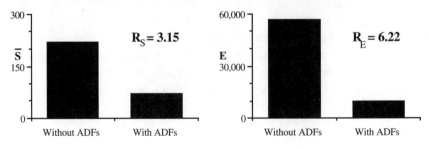

Figure 8.31 Summary graphs for the 48-square lawnmower problem.

With Defined Functions

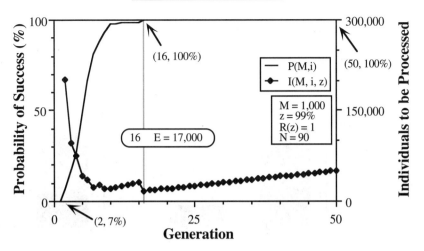

Figure 8.32 Performance curves for the 80-square lawnmower problem showing that E_{with} = 17,000 with ADFs.

Table 8.5 compares the average structural complexity, $\overline{S}_{without}$ and $\overline{S}_{with}$, and the computational effort, $E_{without}$ and E_{with}, for the 32-square lawnmower problem with automatically defined functions and without them.

Figure 8.29 summarizes the information in this comparison table and shows a structural complexity ratio, R_S, of 2.19 and an efficiency ratio, R_E, of 3.80.

8.11 LAWN SIZE OF 48 WITH ADFs

When the size of the lawn is 48 squares, the average structural complexity, $\overline{S}_{with}$, of the 100%-correct programs from the 40 successful runs (out of 40) of the lawnmower problem with automatically defined functions is 69.0 points.

Figure 8.30 presents the performance curves based on the 40 runs of the 48-square lawnmower problem with automatically defined functions. The cumulative probability of success, $P(M,i)$, is 100% by generation 8. The two numbers in the oval indicate that if this problem is run through to generation 8, processing a total of E_{with} = 9,000 individuals (i.e., 1,000 × 9 generations × 1 run) is sufficient to yield a solution to this problem with 99% probability.

Table 8.6 compares the average structural complexity, $\overline{S}_{without}$ and $\overline{S}_{with}$, and the computational effort, $E_{without}$ and E_{with}, for the 48-square lawnmower problem with automatically defined functions and without them.

Figure 8.31 summarizes the information in this comparison table and shows a structural complexity ratio, R_S, of 3.15 and an efficiency ratio, R_E, of 6.22.

Table 8.7 Comparison table for the 80-square lawnmower problem.

	Without ADFs	With ADFs
Average structural complexity $\overline{S}$	366.1	78.8
Computational effort E	561,000	17,000

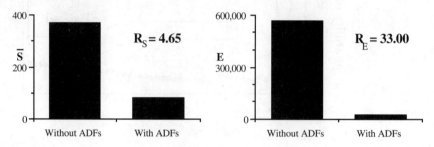

Figure 8.33 Summary graphs for the 80-square lawnmower problem.

8.12 LAWN SIZE OF 80 WITH ADFs

When the lawn size is 80, the average structural complexity, $\overline{S}_{with}$, of the 100%-correct programs from the 90 successful runs (out of 90) of the lawnmower problem with automatically defined functions is 78.8 points.

Figure 8.32 presents the performance curves based on the 90 runs of the 80-square lawnmower problem with automatically defined functions. The cumulative probability of success, $P(M,i)$, is 100% by generation 16. The two numbers in the oval indicate that if this problem is run through to generation 16, processing a total of E_{with} = 17,000 individuals (i.e., 1,000 × 17 generations × 1 run) is sufficient to yield a solution to this problem with 99% probability.

Table 8.7 compares the average structural complexity, $\overline{S}_{without}$ and $\overline{S}_{with}$, and the computational effort, $E_{without}$ and E_{with}, for the 80-square lawnmower problem with automatically defined functions and without them.

Figure 8.33 summarizes the information in this comparison table and shows a structural complexity ratio, R_S, of 4.65 and an efficiency ratio, R_E, of 33.00.

8.13 LAWN SIZE OF 96 WITH ADFs

When the lawn size is 96, the average structural complexity $\overline{S}_{with}$, of the 100%-correct programs from the 137 successful runs (out of 137) of the lawnmower problem with automatically defined functions is 84.9 points. The reader may recall that only 14 of 284 runs were successful for the 96-square lawnmower problem without automatically defined functions.

Figure 8.34 presents the performance curves based on the 137 runs of the 96-square lawnmower problem with automatically defined functions. The

With Defined Functions

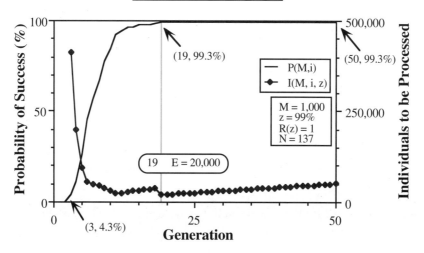

Figure 8.34 Performance curves for the 96-square lawnmower problem showing that E_{with} = 20,000 with ADFs.

Table 8.8 Comparison table for the 96-square lawnmower problem.

	Without ADFs	With ADFs
Average structural complexity $\overline{S}$	408.8	84.9
Computational effort E	4,692,000	20,000

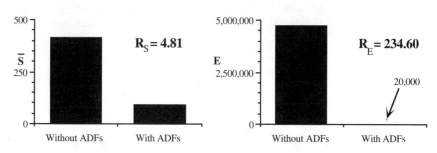

Figure 8.35 Summary graphs for the 96-square lawnmower problem.

Table 8.9 Summary table of the structural complexity ratio, R_S, and the efficiency ratio, R_E, for the lawnmower problem with lawn sizes of 32, 48, 64, 80, and 96 squares.

Problem	Structural complexity ratio R_S	Efficiency ratio R_E
Lawnmower – lawn size 32	2.19	3.80
Lawnmower – lawn size 48	3.15	6.22
Lawnmower – lawn size 64	3.65	9.09
Lawnmower – lawn size 80	4.65	33.00
Lawnmower – lawn size 96	5.06	234.60

Table 8.10 Comparison of the average structural complexity of solutions to the lawnmower problem, with and without ADFs.

	32	48	64	80	96
$\overline{S}_{without}$	145.0	217.6	280.8	366.1	408.8
$\overline{S}_{with}$	66.3	69.0	76.9	78.8	84.9

cumulative probability of success, $P(M,i)$, is 100% by generation 19. The two numbers in the oval indicate that if this problem is run through to generation 19, processing a total of $E_{with} = 20{,}000$ individuals (i.e., $1{,}000 \times 20$ generations $\times 1$ run) is sufficient to yield a solution to this problem with 99% probability.

Table 8.8 compares the average structural complexity, $\overline{S}_{without}$ and $\overline{S}_{with}$, and the computational effort, $E_{without}$ and E_{with}, for the 96-square lawnmower problem with automatically defined functions and without them.

Figure 8.35 summarizes the information in this comparison table and shows a structural complexity ratio, R_S, of 4.81 and an efficiency ratio, R_E, of 234.6.

8.14   SUMMARY FOR LAWN SIZES OF 32, 48, 64, 80, AND 96

This chapter considered a problem with substantial symmetry and regularity in its problem environment. Five differently sized versions of the problem were solved, both with and without automatically defined functions.

For a fixed lawn size of 64, substantially fewer fitness evaluations are required to yield a solution to the problem with 99% probability with automatically defined functions than without them. Moreover, the average size of the programs that successfully solved the problem is considerably smaller with automatically defined functions than without them.

Table 8.9 compiles the observations from the experiments in this chapter into one table. As can be seen, for the lawnmower problem with lawn sizes of 32, 48, 64, 80, and 96 squares, the efficiency ratio is greater than 1 (indicating that fewer fitness evaluations are required to yield a solution

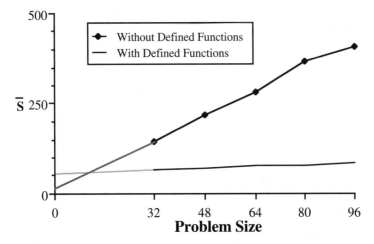

Figure 8.36 Comparison of average structural complexity of solutions to the lawnmower problem for lawn sizes of 32, 48, 64, 80, and 96, with and without ADFs.

to the problem with 99% probability with automatically defined functions than without them).

In other words, for the lawnmower problem with lawn sizes of 32, 48, 64, 80, and 96, genetic programming with automatically defined functions yields a solution after fewer fitness evaluations than the solutions that are produced without automatically defined functions. What is more, genetic programming with automatically defined functions yields a solution that is smaller in overall size than the solutions that are produced without automatically defined functions. Moreover, automatically defined functions produce their greatest benefit in terms of reducing the number of fitness evaluations for the largest version of the problem.

8.15 SCALING FOR LAWN SIZES OF 32, 48, 64, 80, AND 96

The question arises as to how the average structural complexity, $\bar{S}$, and the computational effort, E, changes as a function of problem size for the lawnmower problem.

We first consider the average structural complexity, $\bar{S}$, of the genetically evolved solutions.

Table 8.10 consolidates the previously reported values of average structural complexity for lawns of sizes 32, 48, 64, 80, and 96, with and without automatically defined functions for the lawnmower problem.

Figure 8.36 shows the relationship between the average structural complexity, $\bar{S}_{without}$ and $\bar{S}_{with}$, of solutions for lawn sizes of 32, 48, 64, 80, and 96, with and without automatically defined functions. As can be seen, the graphs are approximately straight lines, with and without automatically defined functions. However, these two lines are different.

As previously observed, the average structural complexity, $\bar{S}_{without}$, of a solution to the lawnmower problem without automatically defined functions ranges between 145.0 and 408.8 for lawns of sizes 32, 48, 64, 80, and 96; it is about four and a half times the size of the lawn. However, with automatically defined functions, the structural complexity, $\overline{S}_{with}$, of the successful solutions lies in the narrow range between 66.3 and 84.9. When the size of the problem is scaled up from 64 to 80 to 96 squares of lawn, the average size of a successful solution increases from 76.9 to only 78.8 and to 84.9. Conversely, when the size of the problem is scaled down from 64 to 48 to 32 squares of lawn, the average size of a successful solution decreases from 76.9 to 69.0 and to 66.3, respectively.

When we perform a linear least-squares regression on the five points relating to the runs without automatically defined functions, we find that the structural complexity, $\overline{S}_{without}$, can be expressed in terms of the lawn size, L, as

$$\overline{S}_{without} = 13.2 + 4.2L,$$

with a correlation of 1.00. The slope of 4.2 indicates that it takes approximately an additional 4.2 points in the program tree to mow each additional square of lawn. The vertical intercept of 13.2 (shown by the point where the dotted line intercepts the vertical axis in figure 8.36) suggests the program size associated with a hypothetical lawn size of zero.

In contrast, when we perform a linear regression on the five points relating to the runs with automatically defined functions, we find that the structural complexity, $\overline{S}_{with}$, can be stated in terms of lawn size, L, as

$$\overline{S}_{with} = 56.39 + 0.29L,$$

with a correlation of 0.98. The slope indicates that it takes only about an additional 0.29 points in the program tree to mow each additional square of lawn. This slope with automatically defined functions is only about a fourteenth of the slope (4.2) without automatically defined functions. On the other hand, the vertical intercept of 56.39 (associated with a solution for a hypothetical lawn size of zero) is much larger with automatically defined functions than without them. We interpret this to mean that there is a substantial fixed overhead associated with automatically defined functions, but relatively little additional cost associated with growth in the size of this problem. Conversely, there is much less fixed overhead involved without automatically defined functions, but a substantial additional cost associated with growth in the size of the problem.

The scaling of the average structural complexity of solutions to this problem (and for the parity problem in section 6.15, and the bumblebee problem in section 9.13) provides evidence in support of main point 5:

Main point 5: For the three problems herein for which a progression of several scaled-up versions is studied, the average size of the solutions produced by genetic programming increases as a function of problem size at a lower rate with automatically defined functions than without them.

This result is especially striking because our implementation of genetic programming is (for most problems herein) strongly predisposed to create larger programs when automatically defined functions are being used.

Table 8.11 Comparison of computational effort for lawns of sizes 32, 48, 64, 80, and 96 for the lawnmower problem, with and without ADFs.

	32	48	64	80	96
$E_{without}$	19,000	56,000	100,000	561,000	4,692,000
E_{with}	5,000	9,000	11,000	17,000	20,000

During the creation of the initial random population and when new programs are created by crossover, we impose limitations on the size of the programs thus created. The limitations differ depending on whether programs in the population are represented using our usual LISP S-expressions or using the array method. (The only time that the array method, described in appendix D, is used herein is with the 3-, 4-, 5-, and 6-parity problems in chapter 6 and with the comparative study of the 15 architectures of the even-5-parity problem in chapter 7).

When programs are represented using the usual LISP S-expressions, these limitations are imposed by the choices of two minor control parameters called $D_{initial}$ and $D_{created}$ (appendix D). The default value for the maximum size (measured by depth), $D_{initial}$, is 6 for the random individuals generated for the initial population. The default value for the maximum size (measured by depth), $D_{created}$, is 17 for programs created by the crossover operation. These default values of $D_{initial}$ and $D_{created}$ apply to the lawnmower problem.

The important point is that the limitations imposed by $D_{initial}$ and $D_{created}$ are applied *separately* to *each branch* of an overall program. Thus, the average size of programs in generation 0 with automatically defined functions are much larger (by a multiple approximately equal to the total number of branches in the overall program) than the average size without automatically defined functions. For example, since there are two automatically defined functions in the lawnmower problem, the multiple is about 3. This multiple is only approximate because the function sets of the various branches are typically different (e.g., because of the inclusion of the automatically defined functions in the function set of the result-producing branch and possibly in the function sets of one or more function-defining branches).

Remarkably, the observed improvement in parsimony with automatically defined functions for this problem occurs after the population overcomes the substantial (3-to-1) predisposition in favor of larger programs. This predisposition is apparent in figure 8.8 which shows that the structural complexity without automatically defined functions of the best of generation 0 is 23 and the average of the values of structural complexity for the population as a whole for generation 0 is 9.7. In contrast, figure 8.21 shows that the structural complexity with automatically defined functions of the best of generation 0 is 63 (i.e., about three times larger) and the average structural complexity of the entire population for generation 0 is 28.7 (i.e., also about three times larger).

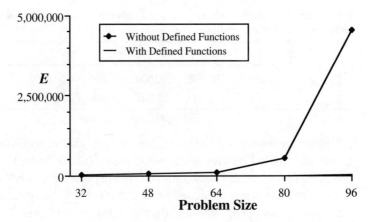

Figure 8.37 Comparison of computational effort for lawn sizes of 32, 48, 64, 80, and 96, with and without ADFs.

Problems run with the array method (e.g., the even-3-, 4-, 5-, and 6-parity problems in chapter 6 and the comparative study of the 15 architectures of the even-5-parity problem of chapter 7) are not biased in this way. There is a size neutrality when the array method is being used.

We now consider the computational effort required for the lawnmower problem, with and without automatically defined functions.

Table 8.11 consolidates the values of computational effort for lawn sizes 32, 48, 64, 80, and 96, with and without automatically defined functions.

Figure 8.37 shows the computational effort, $E_{without}$ and E_{with}, for lawn sizes of 32, 48, 64, 80, and 96, both with and without automatically defined functions. As can be seen, the relationship between the values of the computational effort, $E_{without}$ (i.e., 19,000, 56,000, 100,000, 561,000, and 4,692,000) and the lawn size is steep and nonlinear. The explosive growth of $E_{without}$ (spanning more than two orders of magnitude) as a function of problem size is evident from the figure when automatically defined functions are not involved. The graph applicable to automatically defined functions is visible on this figure only as a thickening of the horizontal axis. The rate of increase of E_{with} is dramatically less.

Figure 8.38 shows the same data as figure 8.37 using a logarithmic scale on the vertical axis, thereby making the graph of E_{with} visible.

When we perform a linear regression on the five-point curve without automatically defined functions, we get a correlation of only 0.77 because of the nonlinearity of this set of data. In particular, the computational effort, $E_{without}$, can be stated in terms of the lawn size, L, as

$$E_{without} = -2,855,000 + 61,570L.$$

Figure 8.39 shows the poor fit between the actual data for $E_{without}$ and the straight line produced by the linear regression (dotted line) for the lawnmower problem.

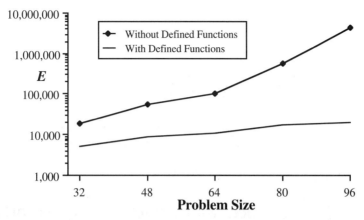

Figure 8.38 Comparison of computational effort for lawn sizes of 32, 48, 64, 80, and 96, with and without ADFs, with logarithmic scale.

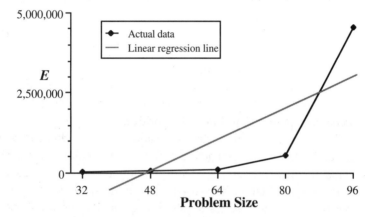

Figure 8.39 Comparison of actual data for $E_{without}$ and linear regression line for the lawnmower problem without ADFs.

When we perform an exponential regression on the five-point curve without automatically defined functions, we find that the computational effort, $E_{without}$, can be stated in terms of the lawn size, L, as

$$E_{without} = 944.2 \times 10^{0.0362L},$$

with a correlation of 0.98. That is, an exponential is a better fit to the observed data. The computational effort, $E_{without}$, without automatically defined functions grows approximately exponentially with problem size for this problem.

In contrast, the progression of values of computational effort, E_{with}, with automatically defined functions (5,000, 9,000, 11,000 and 17,000 and 20,000) is a nearly linear sequence for the problem sizes of 32, 48, 64, 80, and 96. In fact, when we perform a linear regression on the five-point curve with automatically defined functions, we find that the computational effort, E_{with}, can be expressed in terms of the lawn size, L, as

$$E_{with} = -2,800 + 237.5L,$$

with a correlation of 0.99. The slope indicates that it takes about an additional 237.5 fitness evaluations for each additional square of lawn.

The scaling of $E_{without}$ and E_{with} for this problem (and for the parity problem in section 6.15 and the bumblebee problem in section 9.13) provide evidence in support of main point 6:

Main point 6: For the three problems herein for which a progression of several scaled-up versions is studied, computational effort increases as a function of problem size at a lower rate with automatically defined functions than without them.

8.16   WALLCLOCK TIME FOR THE LAWNMOWER PROBLEM

The question arises as to whether automatically defined functions are beneficial in terms of the amount of elapsed time required to yield a solution (or satisfactory result) to a problem.

Every adaptive algorithm starts with one or more points in the search space of the problem and then iteratively performs the following two steps: measuring the fitness of the current point(s) and using the information about fitness to create new point(s) in the search space. The trajectory through the search space, starting at the initial point(s) and ending at the final point(s), is generally different for different algorithms.

The computational burden of an adaptive algorithm can be measured in several different ways. Each measure has particular advantages and disadvantages. The measure, E, of computational effort (described in section 4.11) is the method that we have used so far in this book. E is the minimum number of fitness evaluations required to get a solution (or satisfactory result) with a specified, satisfactorily high probability (say 99%).

For genetic programming, we have demonstrated, for several problems, that less computational effort, E, is required to solve the problem with automatically defined functions than without them, provided the difficulty of the problem is above a certain breakeven point for computational effort (main point 3). However, as previously mentioned, this measure treats all fitness evaluations as if they were equally burdensome. It is conceivable, therefore, that automatically defined functions might be beneficial in terms of E, but not beneficial in terms of elapsed time (wallclock time).

We deferred the discussion of wallclock time to this chapter because we are unable to compute wallclock time for the Boolean problems in this book in a meaningful manner. The reason is that our implementation of the Boolean problems is extensively optimized (as described in section 6.9) with the specific objective of converting programs of vastly different sizes and shapes into programs that consume almost equal (and much less) wallclock time. These optimizations produce a speedup of between one and two orders of magnitude (e.g., 17:1 for the even-5-parity problem with {4, 4} as the argument map for the automatically defined functions). The progression of even-parity

Table 8.12 Analysis of wallclock time for the 64-square lawnmower problem with ADFs.

Generation	Duration of generation	Cumulative elapsed time	$P(M,i)$	$R(M,i,z)$	$W(M,i,z)$
0	30.25	30.25	0.00%	—	—
1	15.49	45.74	5.07%	89	4,070.86
2	16.98	62.72	12.08%	36	2,257.92
3	18.50	81.22	28.74%	14	1,137.08
4	17.94	99.16	50.48%	7	694.12
5	16.15	115.31	71.50%	4	461.24
6	12.54	127.85	83.57%	3	383.55
7	10.88	138.73	90.82%	2	277.46
8	8.00	146.73	100.00%	1	146.73

problems in chapter 6 and the comparison of the 15 architectures in chapter 7 simply could not have been run in any reasonable amount of time without these optimizations, so we did not have the luxury to forgo these optimizations.

The lawnmower problem in this chapter and the bumblebee problem in the next chapter were specifically designed to run fast enough, without any distorting optimizations, to permit a comparative study of wallclock time.

Measurement of wallclock time is performed by collecting timestamps at the beginning of each run and at the end of each generation within the run.

If every run of genetic programming were successful in yielding a solution (or satisfactory result), the wallclock time required to yield a solution (or satisfactory result) would be easy to measure. If success is guaranteed to occur, the observed average wallclock time is simply the sum of the elapsed times for all the runs in a series of runs divided by the number of runs. When a particular run of genetic programming is not successful after running the prespecified maximum number of generations, G, there is no way to know whether or when the run would ever be successful. There is no knowable value for the elapsed time required that will yield a solution (or satisfactory result) and this simple averaging calculation cannot be used. Measuring the computational burden in terms of wallclock time is similar to measuring the computational burden in terms of E in that, in general, it requires a probabilistic calculation that accounts for the fact that not all of the runs in a series are successful.

Table 8.12 shows an analysis of the wallclock time for a series of runs of the 64-square lawnmower problem with automatically defined functions. A new series of 414 runs was made because the previous series of 76 runs (used to make figure 8.26) did not contain timestamps for each individual generation.

Column 2 shows the average duration, in seconds, for each generation.

Column 3 shows the cumulative elapsed time for the generations.

Column 4 states, as a percentage, the value of the observed cumulative probability of success, $P(M,i)$, for the 64-square lawnmower problem with automatically defined functions for this series of 414 runs. The values of $P(M, i)$ in this table of observed values are similar to (but, of course, slightly different than) the values of $P(M, i)$ obtained in the previous series (of 76 runs) used to make the performance curves in figure 8.26. For example, $P(M, i)$ reached a value of 85.53% for generation 6 for the previous series of 76 runs and 83.57% for the series of 414 runs. $P(M, i)$ reached a value of 97.37% for generation 8, 98.68% for generation 9, and 100% for generation 10 in the previous series of 76 runs, whereas it reached 100% for generation 8 in the series of 414 runs.

Column 5 shows the number of independent runs, $R(M, i, z)$, required to yield a solution to the problem with a satisfactorily high probability of $z = 99\%$ associated with the value of $P(M, i)$ in column 4.

Column 6 of table 8.12 shows $W(M, i, z)$, the amount of *wallclock time that must be expended* in order to yield a solution (or satisfactory result) for a problem with a probability of z, for a population size M, by generation i. $W(M, i, z)$ is measured in seconds.

Note that the time required to create the initial random population in generation 0 is included for generation 0 in the table. Because of this, the average duration shown for generation 0 is about twice the duration for other early generations for this particular problem.

In generation 1, table 8.12 shows that the observed cumulative probability of success, $P(M, i)$, is a mere 5.07%. With this low observed cumulative probability of success, a total of $R(M, i, z) = 89$ independent runs are required to solve this problem with a probability of 99%. The average cumulative elapsed time for a run to generation 1 is 45.74 seconds. Thus, the amount of computer time, $W(M, i, z)$, required to yield a solution with 99% probability is 4,070.86 seconds (about 1.1 hours) if this problem is run to generation 1 and abandoned.

For generation 6, the observed cumulative probability of success, $P(M, i)$, is 83.57%. Consequently, $R(M, i, z)$ is now only 3. The average cumulative elapsed time for a run to generation 6 is 127.85 seconds. Thus, the amount of computer time, $W(M, i, z)$, necessary to yield a solution is 383.55 seconds (about 6.4 minutes) if this problem is run to generation 6 and abandoned.

On generation 8, the observed cumulative probability of success, $P(M, i)$, reaches 100%, so $R(M, i, z) = 1$. The average elapsed time for one run to generation 8 is 146.73 seconds, so the amount of computer time, $W(M, i, z)$, necessary to yield a solution is 146.73 seconds (about 2.4 minutes) if this problem is run to generation 8 and abandoned. Generation 8 is the best generation and $R(z)$ is 1 for generation 8.

We define the *wallclock time with automatically defined functions*, W_{with}, as the minimum value, over the generations, of $W(M, i, z)$ with ADFs. For the 64-square lawnmower problem with ADFs, W_{with} is 146.73 seconds.

Figure 8.40 contains the wallclock performance curves for the 64-square lawnmower problem with automatically defined functions. This figure is constructed in the same general way as all the other performance curves in this book. The rising curve is the cumulative probability of success, $P(M, i)$.

Table 8.13 Analysis of wallclock time for the 64-square lawnmower problem without ADFs.

Generation	Duration of generation	Cumulative elapsed time	$P(M,i)$	$R(M,i,z)$	$W(M,i,z)$
0	20.44	20.44	0.00	—	—
1	7.70	28.15	0.00	—	—
2	9.56	37.70	0.00	—	—
3	13.26	50.96	0.00	—	—
4	17.44	68.41	0.00	—	—
5	19.63	88.04	0.00	—	—
6	20.33	108.37	0.00	—	—
7	27.93	136.30	0.00	—	—
8	34.96	171.26	0.00	—	—
9	36.37	207.63	0.00	—	—
10	41.26	248.89	0.00	—	—
11	44.56	293.44	0.00	—	—
12	42.19	335.63	0.00	—	—
13	47.22	382.85	0.00	—	—
14	57.37	440.22	0.00	—	—
15	63.78	504.00	0.00	—	—
16	50.04	554.04	0.00	—	—
17	45.04	599.07	0.00	—	—
18	38.70	637.78	0.00	—	—
19	37.63	675.41	0.00	—	—
20	41.63	717.04	0.00	—	—
21	52.19	769.22	0.61	749	576,147
22	53.89	823.11	3.68	123	101,243
23	47.77	870.88	19.63	22	19,159
24	46.60	917.48	25.15	16	14,680
25	54.48	971.96	33.74	12	11,664
26	48.05	1,020.01	35.58	11	11,220
27	69.41	1,089.42	35.58	11	11,984
28	59.38	1,148.80	39.88	10	11,488
29	43.06	1,191.86	46.01	8	9,535
30	58.33	1,250.19	51.53	7	8,751
31	54.14	1,304.33	51.53	7	9,130
32	51.85	1,356.18	51.53	7	9,493
33	57.08	1,413.26	52.15	7	9,893
34	75.08	1,488.33	52.15	7	10,418
35	51.17	1,539.50	54.60	6	9,237
36	36.67	1,576.17	55.83	6	9,457
37	32.91	1,609.08	55.83	6	9,654
38	37.10	1,646.18	55.83	6	9,877
39	40.50	1,686.68	67.48	5	8,433
40	36.50	1,723.18	85.89	3	5,170
41	22.88	1,746.05	90.18	2	3,492
42	29.60	1,775.65	92.64	2	3,551
43	24.75	1,800.40	92.64	2	3,601
44	64.67	1,865.07	92.64	2	3,730
45	73.00	1,938.07	92.64	2	3,876
46	72.00	2,010.07	92.64	2	4,020
47	43.33	2,053.40	92.64	2	4,107
48	34.00	2,087.40	92.64	2	4,175
49	32.67	2,120.07	92.64	2	**4,240**

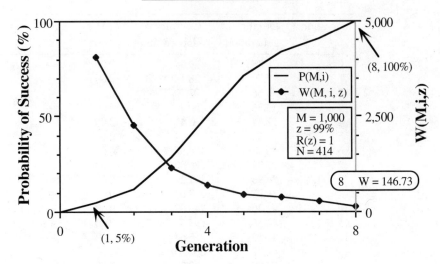

Figure 8.40 Wallclock-performance curves for the 64-square lawnmower problem with ADFs.

The second curve is *W(M, i, z)* from table 8.12. The minimum value, W_{with}, of 146.73 for *W(M, i, z)* attained at generation 8 is shown in the oval along with the number of the generation (8) on which it is attained.

We now determine the wallclock time, $W_{without}$, without automatically defined functions.

Table 8.13 shows an analysis of the wallclock time for a series of run of the 64-square lawnmower problem without automatically defined functions.

Column 4 presents the value of the observed cumulative probability of success, $P(M,i)$, for the 64-square lawnmower problem without automatically defined functions. These values are based on a separate series of 163 runs; these values are very similar to the values in figure 8.13. As can be seen, the average duration of a generation without automatically defined functions is about the same for the first few generations of this table as in table 8.12 with automatically defined functions; however, the durations grow considerably for later generations of this table. Significantly, the observed cumulative probability of success, $P(M,i)$, is only 92.64% by generation 49 without automatically defined functions as compared to 90.82% for generation 7 with automatically defined functions (table 8.12).

For generation 49, $R(M,i,z)$ is only 2 for table 8.13 (without automatically defined functions). The average elapsed time for one run to generation 49 is 2,120 seconds (about 35 minutes), so the amount of computer time, $W(M, i, z)$, necessary to yield a solution is 4,240 seconds (about 71 minutes) if this problem is run to generation 49 and abandoned.

Based on table 8.13, the wallclock time, $W_{without}$, without automatically defined functions for the 64-square version of this problem is 4,240 seconds. This is 28.9 times longer than the wallclock time, W_{with}, with automatically defined functions for this version.

Table 8.14   Wallclock ratios, R_W, for the lawnmower problem.

Problem size	Wallclock ratio R_W
32	6.13
48	10.4
64	28.9
80	68.5
96	1049.0

The *wallclock ratio*, R_W, is the ratio of the average wallclock time, $W_{without}$, without automatically defined functions to the average wallclock time, W_{with}, with automatically defined functions.

$$R_W = \frac{W \text{ without ADFs}}{W \text{ with ADFs}} = \frac{W_{without}}{W_{with}}.$$

For the 64-square lawnmower problem, the wallclock ratio, R_W, is 28.9.

Table 8.14 shows the wallclock ratio, R_W, for the lawnmower problem with lawn sizes of 32, 48, 64, 80, and 96. As can be seen, all five wallclock ratios are considerably greater than 1, indicating that runs with automatically defined functions require less wallclock time than the runs without automatically defined functions for this problem.

In other words, automatically defined functions are beneficial both in terms of computational effort, E, and wallclock time, W, for this problem.

A similar table appears in section 9.14 and shows that less wallclock time is required with automatically defined functions than without them for all four sizes of the bumblebee problem. Wallclock time is revisited in section 10.2.

9 The Bumblebee Problem

This chapter examines a problem in the domain of floating-point numbers that was especially constructed to permit the study of scaling. The goal is to find a program for controlling the movement of a bumblebee so that it visits all the locations in the plane containing flowers. The bumblebee problem is scaled in terms of the number of flowers to be visited. Four progressively more difficult versions of this problem will be run, each with and without automatically defined functions.

The bumblebee problem provides another example of a problem in the domain of floating-point numbers.

9.1 THE PROBLEM

The location of each flower is specified by a two-dimensional vector of floating-point coordinates. The bee starts at the origin (0.00,0.00). The x-location of a flower is a randomly chosen floating-point number between –5.00 and +5.00; the y-location is also a randomly chosen floating-point number between –5.00 and +5.00. No flower can be within the square of side 0.02 centered on any other flower or within the square of side 0.02 centered at the origin. The number of flowers is 25, 20, 15, and 10 in the four versions of the problem.

9.2 PREPARATORY STEPS WITHOUT ADFs

The terminal set for this problem consists of vectors with floating-point components. Specifically,

$T=$ {BEE, NEXT-FLOWER, $\Re_{\text{real-vector}}$}.

BEE is the current location of the bumblebee in the plane expressed as a two-dimensional vector of floating-point values.

NEXT-FLOWER is a terminal that is set to the position of a randomly chosen unvisited flower belonging to the current fitness case.

Each random constant $\Re_{\text{real-vector}}$ consists of a vector (x,y), each component of which is a floating-point value between –5.0000 and +5.0000.

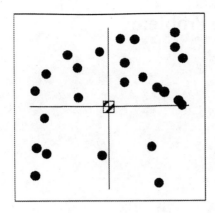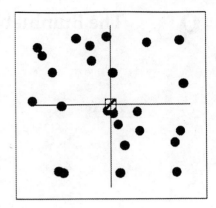

Figure 9.1 Two fitness cases for the bumblebee problem with 25 flowers.

The function set consists of

$\mathcal{F} = \{\text{V+}, \text{V-}, \text{GO-X}, \text{GO-Y}, \text{PROGN}\}$

with an argument map of

$\{2, 2, 1, 1, 2\}.$

V+ and V- are two-argument functions for floating-point vector addition and subtraction.

GO-X takes a single vector as its argument and moves the bee the distance in the x-direction specified by the x-component of its vector argument. GO-X always returns (0.0, 0.0).

GO-Y operates in a similar way in the y-direction.

Because this problem is time-consuming and because we need multiple, successful runs for all eight versions of this problem to do the desired analysis, we compromised on the number of fitness cases by allocating only enough computer time to this problem to support two fitness cases for each run.

Figure 9.1 shows the two fitness cases for this problem for a run with 25 flowers.

Each program is evaluated once for each fitness case. The raw fitness of a particular program is the sum, over the two fitness cases, of the number of flowers visited by the bumblebee. If there are 25 flowers, raw fitness varies between 0 and 50. The bee is deemed to have reached a flower when it enters the square of side 0.02 centered on the flower. We use a square rather than a circle because less computer time is required to compute the bee's arrival within the square. If the bee reaches a flower, the bee is credited with visiting it regardless of whether the flower is the one designated by NEXT-FLOWER. The bumblebee is limited to 100 movements per fitness case and it receives credit for all flowers visited in the current fitness case when this limit is reached.

Table 9.1 summarizes the key features of the bumblebee problem with 25 flowers without automatically defined functions.

Table 9.1 Tableau without ADFs for the bumblebee problem with 25 flowers.

Objective:	Find a program to control a bumblebee so that it visits all 25 flowers in the plane.
Terminal set without ADFs:	BEE, NEXT-FLOWER, and the random constants $\Re_{\text{real-vector}}$.
Function set without ADFs:	V+, V-, GO-X, GO-Y, and PROGN.
Fitness cases:	Two fitness cases, each consisting of 25 randomly chosen vector locations in the plane.
Raw fitness:	Raw fitness is the sum, over the two fitness cases, of the number of flowers (from 0 to 50) visited before the maximum number of movements per fitness case is exceeded.
Standardized fitness:	Standardized fitness is twice the number of flowers (i.e., 50) minus raw fitness.
Hits:	Same as raw fitness.
Wrapper:	None.
Parameters:	$M = 4{,}000$. $G = 51$.
Success predicate:	A program scores the maximum number of hits.

9.3 RESULTS WITH 25 FLOWERS WITHOUT ADFs

The following 525-point program visiting all 25 flowers in both fitness cases emerged on generation 37 of one run:

```
(V+ (PROGN (V+ (PROGN (V- (GO-X (GO-X NEXT-FLOWER))) (V- (PROGN
(GO-Y (PROGN (V- (GO-Y NEXT-FLOWER) (GO-X NEXT-FLOWER)) (PROGN
(GO-X (V- NEXT-FLOWER BEE)) (V- NEXT-FLOWER BEE)))) (V- (V- (GO-Y
(V- NEXT-FLOWER BEE)) (V+ BEE (-3.4751,4.0123))) (PROGN (PROGN
(GO-X (V- NEXT-FLOWER BEE)) (V- BEE NEXT-FLOWER)) NEXT-FLOWER)))
(GO-X (GO-Y (V- NEXT-FLOWER BEE)))))) (V- (PROGN (V+ (PROGN (V+
(GO-X NEXT-FLOWER) NEXT-FLOWER) (V- (PROGN (PROGN (V- (GO-Y NEXT-
FLOWER) (V+ BEE (-3.4751,4.0123))) BEE) (GO-X (GO-Y (V- NEXT-
FLOWER BEE)))) (PROGN (PROGN (GO-X (V- NEXT-FLOWER BEE)) (V- BEE
NEXT-FLOWER)) NEXT-FLOWER))) (PROGN (V- (GO-Y (PROGN (GO-X (V-
NEXT-FLOWER BEE)) (V- NEXT-FLOWER BEE))) (GO-Y NEXT-FLOWER)) (GO-
X NEXT-FLOWER))) (V- (PROGN (PROGN (V+ BEE (GO-Y (V- NEXT-FLOWER
BEE))) BEE) (GO-X NEXT-FLOWER)) (PROGN (PROGN (GO-X (V- NEXT-
FLOWER BEE)) (V- BEE NEXT-FLOWER)) NEXT-FLOWER))) (GO-X (GO-Y (V-
NEXT-FLOWER BEE))))) (PROGN (V- (GO-X (PROGN (PROGN (GO-X (V-
NEXT-FLOWER BEE)) (GO-Y (V- NEXT-FLOWER BEE))) NEXT-FLOWER))
(PROGN (V- NEXT-FLOWER BEE) (PROGN BEE NEXT-FLOWER))) (GO-Y (PROGN
(GO-X (V- NEXT-FLOWER BEE)) (V- NEXT-FLOWER BEE))))) (PROGN (V-
(PROGN (V+ (GO-X NEXT-FLOWER) (V+ (GO-X (GO-Y (V- NEXT-FLOWER
BEE))) (V+ (PROGN (GO-X NEXT-FLOWER) (V+ (0.55423,4.9729) (GO-X
```

```
BEE))) (V+ (GO-Y (GO-X (V- NEXT-FLOWER BEE))) (GO-X (GO-X (V-
NEXT-FLOWER BEE))))))) (V- (V- (GO-Y NEXT-FLOWER) (GO-X NEXT-
FLOWER)) (PROGN (PROGN (GO-X (V- NEXT-FLOWER BEE)) (V- BEE NEXT-
FLOWER)) NEXT-FLOWER))) (GO-X (GO-Y (V- NEXT-FLOWER BEE))))
(PROGN (GO-X (PROGN (V+ (GO-X NEXT-FLOWER) (V- NEXT-FLOWER BEE))
(V- (PROGN (GO-Y (PROGN (V- (GO-Y NEXT-FLOWER) (GO-X NEXT-FLOWER))
(PROGN (GO-X (V- NEXT-FLOWER BEE)) (V- NEXT-FLOWER BEE)))) (V-
(GO-X (GO-Y (V- NEXT-FLOWER BEE))) (PROGN (PROGN (GO-X (V- NEXT-
FLOWER BEE)) (V- BEE NEXT-FLOWER)) NEXT-FLOWER))) (GO-X (GO-Y (V-
NEXT-FLOWER BEE)))))) (GO-X BEE)))) (PROGN (V+ (PROGN NEXT-FLOWER
NEXT-FLOWER) (PROGN (V- (PROGN (GO-Y (PROGN (PROGN (PROGN (GO-X
(V- NEXT-FLOWER BEE)) (V- BEE NEXT-FLOWER)) NEXT-FLOWER) (PROGN
(GO-X (V- NEXT-FLOWER BEE)) (V- NEXT-FLOWER BEE)))) (V- (V- (GO-Y
NEXT-FLOWER) (V+ BEE (-3.4751,4.0123))) (PROGN (PROGN (V+ BEE (GO-
Y (V- NEXT-FLOWER BEE))) BEE) NEXT-FLOWER))) (PROGN (PROGN (GO-Y
(PROGN (PROGN (PROGN (GO-X (V- NEXT-FLOWER BEE)) (V- BEE NEXT-
FLOWER)) NEXT-FLOWER) (PROGN (GO-X (V- NEXT-FLOWER BEE)) (V- NEXT-
FLOWER BEE)))) (V- (V- (GO-Y NEXT-FLOWER) (V+ BEE
(-3.4751,4.0123))) (PROGN (PROGN (V+ BEE (GO-Y (V- NEXT-FLOWER
BEE))) BEE) NEXT-FLOWER))) (PROGN BEE NEXT-FLOWER))) (V- (V- (GO-X
NEXT-FLOWER) (V+ (PROGN (GO-Y NEXT-FLOWER) (PROGN (V+ (V+ (GO-X
(GO-X BEE)) (V- BEE NEXT-FLOWER)) (GO-Y (GO-X (V- NEXT-FLOWER
BEE)))) (V- NEXT-FLOWER BEE))) (V+ BEE (GO-Y (V- NEXT-FLOWER
BEE))))) (PROGN (PROGN (V- NEXT-FLOWER BEE) (V- (PROGN (PROGN (V+
BEE (GO-Y (V- NEXT-FLOWER BEE))) BEE) (GO-X NEXT-FLOWER)) (PROGN
(PROGN (GO-X (V- NEXT-FLOWER BEE)) (V- BEE NEXT-FLOWER)) NEXT-
FLOWER))) (GO-Y (PROGN (GO-Y NEXT-FLOWER) (PROGN (V+ (V+ (GO-X
(GO-X BEE)) (GO-X NEXT-FLOWER)) (GO-Y (GO-X (V- NEXT-FLOWER
BEE)))) (V- NEXT-FLOWER BEE))))))) (PROGN (V- (PROGN (V+ (GO-X
NEXT-FLOWER) (V+ (PROGN (PROGN (1.51137,1.48552) NEXT-FLOWER)
(GO-Y NEXT-FLOWER)) (V+ (PROGN (GO-X NEXT-FLOWER) (V+
(0.55423,4.9729) (GO-X BEE))) (V+ (GO-Y (GO-X (GO-Y (V- NEXT-
FLOWER BEE)))) (GO-X (GO-X (V- NEXT-FLOWER BEE))))))) (V- (V- (GO-
Y NEXT-FLOWER) (V+ NEXT-FLOWER (-3.4751,4.0123))) (PROGN (PROGN
(GO-X (V- NEXT-FLOWER BEE)) (V- BEE NEXT-FLOWER)) NEXT-FLOWER)))
(GO-X (GO-Y (V- NEXT-FLOWER BEE)))) (PROGN (GO-X (PROGN (V+ (GO-X
NEXT-FLOWER) (V- NEXT-FLOWER BEE)) (V- (PROGN (GO-Y (PROGN (V-
(GO-Y NEXT-FLOWER) (GO-X NEXT-FLOWER)) (PROGN (GO-X (V- NEXT-
FLOWER BEE)) (V- NEXT-FLOWER BEE)))) (V- (V- (GO-X NEXT-FLOWER)
(V+ BEE (-3.4751,4.0123))) (PROGN (PROGN (GO-X (V- NEXT-FLOWER
BEE)) (V- BEE NEXT-FLOWER)) NEXT-FLOWER))) (GO-X (GO-Y (V- NEXT-
FLOWER BEE)))))) (GO-X BEE)))))
```

Figure 9.2 shows, for one of the two fitness cases, the trajectory of the bumble-bee as it visits all 25 flowers under the control of the above best-of-run program from generation 37 without automatically defined functions.

The average structural complexity, $\overline{S}_{without}$, of the best-of-run programs from the 27 successful runs (out of 34 runs) of the bumblebee problem with 25 flowers is 452.0 points without automatically defined functions.

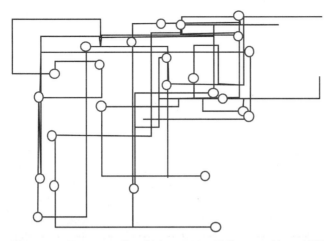

Figure 9.2 Trajectory of bumblebee visiting 25 flowers without ADFs.

For the bumblebee problem with 25 flowers, figure 9.3 presents the performance curves based on the 34 runs of this problem without automatically defined functions. The cumulative probability of success, $P(M,i)$, is 6% by generation 23 and is 79% by generation 50. The two numbers in the oval indicate that if this problem is run through to generation 50, processing a total of $E_{without} = 612,000$ individuals (i.e., $4,000 \times 51$ generations $\times 3$ runs) is sufficient to yield a satisfactory result for this problem with 99% probability.

9.4 PREPARATORY STEPS WITH ADFs

In applying genetic programming with automatically defined functions to the bumblebee problem, we decided that each overall program in the population would consist of one one-argument automatically defined function and one result-producing branch.

The terminal set, $\mathcal{T}_{adf}$, for ADF0 is

$$\mathcal{T}_{adf} = \{\text{ARG0}, \text{BEE}, \Re_{\text{real-vector}}\}.$$

The function set, $\mathcal{F}_{adf}$, for ADF0 is

$$\mathcal{F}_{adf} = \{\text{V+}, \text{V-}, \text{GO-X}, \text{GO-Y}, \text{PROGN}\}$$

with an argument map of

$$\{2, 2, 1, 1, 2\}.$$

The body of ADF0 is a composition of primitive functions from the function set, $\mathcal{F}_{adf}$, and terminals from the terminal set, $\mathcal{T}_{adf}$.

The terminal set, $\mathcal{T}_{rpb}$, for the result-producing branch is

$$\mathcal{T}_{rpb} = \{\text{BEE}, \text{NEXT-FLOWER}, \Re_{\text{real-vector}}\}.$$

The function set, $\mathcal{F}_{rpb}$, for the result-producing branch is

$$\mathcal{F}_{rpb} = \{\text{ADF0}, \text{V+}, \text{V-}, \text{GO-X}, \text{GO-Y}, \text{PROGN}\}$$

Without Defined Functions

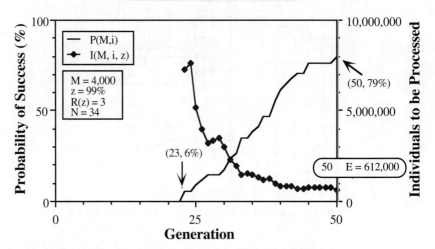

Figure 9.3 Performance curves for the bumblebee problem with 25 flowers showing that $E_{without} = 612{,}000$ without ADFs.

with an argument map of

$\{1, 2, 2, 1, 1, 2\}$.

The result-producing branch is a composition of the functions from the function set, $\mathcal{F}_{rpb}$, and terminals from the terminal set, $\mathcal{T}_{rpb}$.

Table 9.2 summarizes the key features of the bumblebee problem with 25 flowers with automatically defined functions.

9.5 RESULTS WITH 25 FLOWERS WITH ADFs

In one run of the bumblebee problem with 25 flowers with automatically defined functions, the following 100%-correct 219-point program scoring 50 (out of 50) emerged in generation 18:

```
(progn (defun ADF0 (ARG0)
          (values (GO-X (V+ (GO-Y (V- ARG0 BEE)) (V- ARG0 BEE)))))
       (values (V- (PROGN (V- (PROGN (V- (V- (PROGN (V- (GO-X
          NEXT-FLOWER) (GO-Y NEXT-FLOWER)) NEXT-FLOWER) (V- NEXT-
          FLOWER (ADF0 NEXT-FLOWER))) (V- NEXT-FLOWER (V+ (ADF0
          (PROGN (V- (GO-X NEXT-FLOWER) (GO-Y NEXT-FLOWER)) NEXT-
          FLOWER)) (V- (V+ (V+ (GO-Y NEXT-FLOWER) (PROGN (GO-Y
          NEXT-FLOWER) (ADF0 NEXT-FLOWER))) (ADF0 (V+ (GO-Y NEXT-
          FLOWER) (V- NEXT-FLOWER BEE)))) (V- NEXT-FLOWER (ADF0
          NEXT-FLOWER)))))) (V- (PROGN (V- (GO-X NEXT-FLOWER)
          (GO-Y NEXT-FLOWER)) (V- NEXT-FLOWER (V- NEXT-FLOWER
          (ADF0 (V+ (ADF0 NEXT-FLOWER) (V- NEXT-FLOWER (ADF0 NEXT-
          FLOWER))))))) (V- (V- (PROGN (V- (V- (PROGN (V- (GO-X
          NEXT-FLOWER) (GO-Y NEXT-FLOWER)) NEXT-FLOWER) (V- NEXT-
          FLOWER (ADF0 NEXT-FLOWER))) (GO-Y NEXT-FLOWER)) NEXT-
```

Table 9.2 Tableau with ADFs for the bumblebee problem with 25 flowers.

Objective:	Find a program to control a bumblebee so that it visits all 25 randomly located flowers.
Architecture of the overall program with ADFs:	One result-producing branch and one one-argument function-defining branch.
Parameters:	Branch typing.
Terminal set for the result-producing branch:	BEE, NEXT-FLOWER, and the random constants $\Re_{\text{real-vector}}$.
Function set for the result-producing branch:	ADF0, V+, V-, GO-X, GO-Y, and PROGN.
Terminal set for the function-defining branch ADF0:	ARG0, BEE, and the random constants $\Re_{\text{real-vector}}$.
Function set for the function-defining branch ADF0:	V+, V-, GO-X, GO-Y, and PROGN.

```
FLOWER) (V- (V+ (V- (V- (GO-X NEXT-FLOWER) (GO-Y NEXT-
FLOWER)) (ADF0 NEXT-FLOWER)) (V+ NEXT-FLOWER (PROGN
NEXT-FLOWER BEE))) (V- NEXT-FLOWER (ADF0 NEXT-
FLOWER)))) (V- NEXT-FLOWER (ADF0 NEXT-FLOWER))))) (V-
NEXT-FLOWER (V+ (ADF0 NEXT-FLOWER) (V- (V+ (V+ (GO-Y
NEXT-FLOWER) (PROGN (GO-Y (GO-Y (GO-X BEE))) (ADF0 NEXT-
FLOWER))) (ADF0 (V+ (GO-Y NEXT-FLOWER) (V- NEXT-FLOWER
BEE)))) (V- NEXT-FLOWER (ADF0 NEXT-FLOWER)))))) (GO-X
(V+ (ADF0 (PROGN (V- (GO-X NEXT-FLOWER) (V- NEXT-FLOWER
(V+ (PROGN (PROGN NEXT-FLOWER BEE) (ADF0 NEXT-FLOWER))
(V- (ADF0 NEXT-FLOWER) (V- (ADF0 NEXT-FLOWER) (GO-Y
NEXT-FLOWER)))))) NEXT-FLOWER)) (V- (ADF0 (V+ (ADF0
NEXT-FLOWER) (V- NEXT-FLOWER (ADF0 (V+ (ADF0 NEXT-
FLOWER) NEXT-FLOWER))))) (ADF0 NEXT-FLOWER))))) (V-
NEXT-FLOWER (V- (PROGN (V- (GO-X (ADF0 (V- NEXT-FLOWER
BEE))) (GO-Y NEXT-FLOWER)) (ADF0 (V+ (ADF0 NEXT-FLOWER)
(V- NEXT-FLOWER (ADF0 (V+ (ADF0 NEXT-FLOWER) NEXT-
FLOWER)))))) (V- (ADF0 NEXT-FLOWER) (V+ (V- NEXT-FLOWER
(ADF0 NEXT-FLOWER)) (GO-X NEXT-FLOWER)))))))))) .
```

In this program, ADF0 moves the bee in the *x*-direction by the difference of ARG0 and BEE and then moves the bee in the *y*-direction by the difference of ARG0 and BEE.

Figure 9.4 shows, for one of the two fitness cases, the trajectory of the bee visiting the 25 flowers for this 219-point program with automatically defined functions.

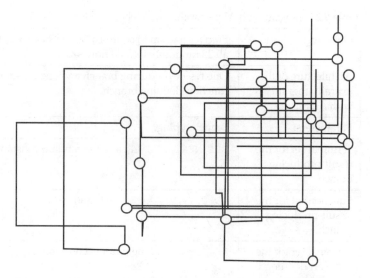

Figure 9.4 Trajectory of bumblebee visiting 25 flowers with ADFs.

The average structural complexity, $\overline{S}_{with}$, of best-of-run programs from the 31 successful runs (out of 31 runs) of the bumblebee problem with 25 flowers with automatically defined functions is 245.9 points.

In comparing the solutions obtained with and without automatically defined functions, it is obvious that the 525-point solution without automatically defined functions shown in section 9.3 (which is reasonably close to the average size of 452.0 points) is much larger than the 219-point solution with automatically defined functions (which is reasonably close to the average size of 245.9 points).

For the bumblebee problem with 25 flowers, figure 9.5 presents the performance curves based on the 31 runs of this problem with automatically defined functions. The cumulative probability of success, $P(M,i)$, is 100% by generation 47. The two numbers in the oval indicate that if this problem is run through to generation 47, processing a total of $E_{with} = 192,000$ individuals (i.e., $4,000 \times 48$ generations $\times 1$ run) is sufficient to yield a satisfactory result for this problem with 99% probability.

Since the bee ought to be able to perform some kind of generalized calculation in deciding how to navigate toward the next flower, there is considerable regularity and symmetry in this problem environment.

It is certainly not obvious from examining the bumblebee's trajectory in figure 9.4 that automatically defined functions have successfully exploited the considerable regularity of this problem environment. In fact, the overall impression created by figure 9.4 for the case with automatically defined functions does not appear to be fundamentally different from the tangled and disorderly appearance of figure 9.2 for the case without automatically defined functions. However, even though it is not visually obvious from the trajectory that automatically defined functions have successfully exploited the considerable regularity of this problem environment, there is evidence

With Defined Functions

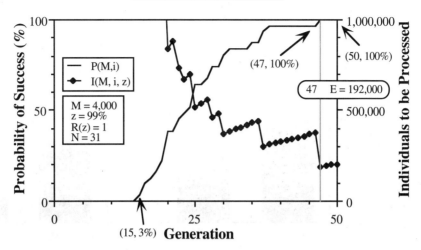

Figure 9.5 Performance curves for the bumblebee problem with 25 flowers showing that E_{with} = 192,000 with ADFs.

that they have done so in the form of the two performance curves. When one sees the difference in computational effort of 612,000 versus 192,000, the advantageous effect of automatically defined functions is unmistakable. For this problem, the statistics provide the means for seeing that the evolved programs employing automatically defined functions succeed in exploiting the problem environment in a different and better way than the evolved programs not employing automatically defined functions. The human observer is often not able to understand or visualize how automatically defined functions exploit the problem environment.

Table 9.3 compares the average structural complexity, $\overline{S}_{without}$ and $\overline{S}_{with}$, and the computational effort, $E_{without}$ and E_{with}, with automatically defined functions and without them for the bumblebee problem with 25 flowers.

Figure 9.6 summarizes the information in the table for the bumblebee problem with 25 flowers and shows a structural complexity ratio, R_S, of 1.84 and an efficiency ratio, R_E, of 3.20.

9.6 RESULTS WITH 20 FLOWERS WITHOUT ADFs

We then scaled this problem down so that only 20 flowers are visited for each fitness case.

The average structural complexity, $\overline{S}$, of the best-of-run programs from the 35 successful runs (out of 36 runs) without automatically defined functions is 386.9 points for the bumblebee problem with 20 flowers.

For the bumblebee problem with 20 flowers, figure 9.7 presents the performance curves based on the 36 runs of this problem without automatically defined functions. The cumulative probability of success, $P(M,i)$, is

Table 9.3 Comparison table for the bumblebee problem with 25 flowers.

	Without ADFs	With ADFs
Average structural complexity $\bar{S}$	452.0	245.9
Computational effort E	612,000	192,000

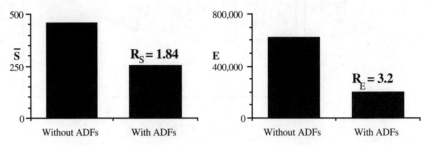

Figure 9.6 Summary graphs for the bumblebee problem with 25 flowers.

92% by generation 40 and 97% by generation 50. The two numbers in the oval indicate that if this problem is run through to generation 40, processing a total of $E_{without}$ = 328,000 individuals (i.e., 4,000 × 41 generations × 2 runs) is sufficient to yield a satisfactory result for this problem with 99% probability.

9.7   RESULTS WITH 20 FLOWERS WITH ADFs

For the bumblebee problem with 20 flowers, the average structural complexity, $\bar{S}$, of the best-of-run programs from the 37 successful runs (out of 38) with automatically defined functions is 225.0 points.

For the bumblebee problem with 20 flowers, figure 9.8 presents the performance curves based on the 38 runs of this problem with automatically defined functions. The cumulative probability of success, $P(M, i)$, is 92% by generation 32 and 97% by generation 50. The two numbers in the oval indicate that if this problem is run through to generation 32, processing a total of E_{with} = 264,000 individuals (i.e., 4,000 × 33 generations × 2 runs) is sufficient to yield a satisfactory result for this problem with 99% probability.

For the bumblebee problem with 20 flowers, table 9.4 compares the average structural complexity, $\bar{S}_{without}$ and $\bar{S}_{with}$, and the computational effort, $E_{without}$ and E_{with}, with automatically defined functions and without them.

Figure 9.9, which summarizes the information in the table for the bumblebee problem with 20 flowers, shows a structural complexity ratio, R_S, of 1.72 and an efficiency ratio, R_E, of 1.24.

9.8   RESULTS WITH 15 FLOWERS WITHOUT ADFs

We then further scaled this problem down to only 15 flowers.

Without Defined Functions

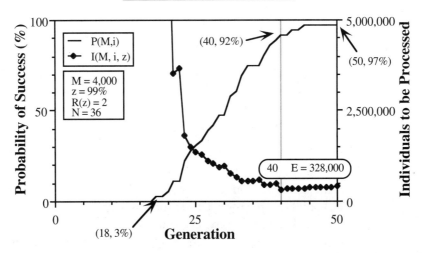

Figure 9.7 Performance curves for the bumblebee problem with 20 flowers showing that $E_{without} = 328,000$ without ADFs.

With Defined Functions

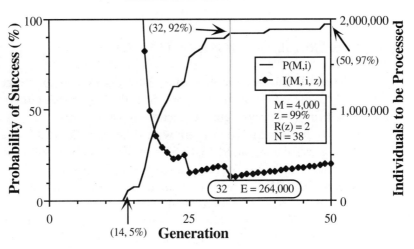

Figure 9.8 Performance curves for the bumblebee problem with 20 flowers showing that $E_{with} = 264,000$ with ADFs.

Table 9.4 Comparison table for the bumblebee problem with 20 flowers.

	Without ADFs	With ADFs
Average structural complexity $\overline{S}$	386.9	225.0
Computational effort E	328,000	264,000

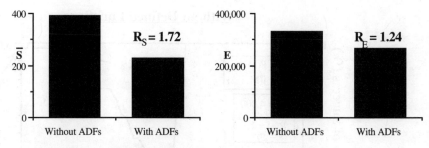

Figure 9.9 Summary graphs for the bumblebee problem with 20 flowers.

The average structural complexity, $\bar{S}$, of the best-of-run programs from the 35 successful runs (out of 35 runs) without automatically defined functions is 328.4 points for the bumblebee problem with 15 flowers.

For the bumblebee problem with 15 flowers, figure 9.10 presents the performance curves based on the 35 runs of this problem without automatically defined functions. The cumulative probability of success, $P(M,i)$, is 100% by generation 39. The two numbers in the oval indicate that if this problem is run through to generation 39, processing a total of $E_{without} = 160{,}000$ individuals (i.e., $4{,}000 \times 40$ generations $\times 1$ run) is sufficient to yield a satisfactory result for this problem with 99% probability.

9.9   RESULTS WITH 15 FLOWERS WITH ADFs

For the bumblebee problem with 15 flowers, the average structural complexity, $\bar{S}$, of the best-of-run programs from the 50 successful runs (out of 50 runs) with automatically defined functions is 190.8 points.

For the bumblebee problem with 15 flowers, figure 9.11 presents the performance curves based on the 50 runs of this problem without automatically defined functions. The cumulative probability of success, $P(M,i)$, is 100% by generation 32. The two numbers in the oval indicate that if this problem is run through to generation 32, processing a total of $E_{with} = 132{,}000$ individuals (i.e., $4{,}000 \times 33$ generations $\times 1$ run) is sufficient to yield a satisfactory result for this problem with 99% probability.

For the bumblebee problem with 15 flowers, table 9.5 compares the average structural complexity, $\bar{S}_{without}$ and $\bar{S}_{with}$, and the computational effort, $E_{without}$ and E_{with}, with automatically defined functions and without them.

Figure 9.12, which summarizes the information in the table for the bumblebee problem with 15 flowers, shows a structural complexity ratio, R_S, of 1.72 and an efficiency ratio, R_E, of 1.21.

9.10   RESULTS WITH 10 FLOWERS WITHOUT ADFs

Finally, we scaled this problem down to only 10 flowers.

Without Defined Functions

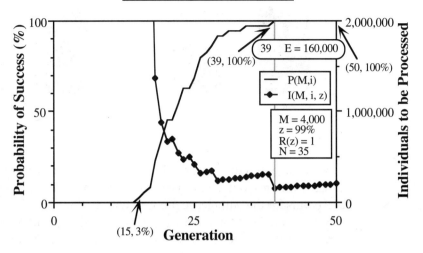

Figure 9.10 Performance curves for the bumblebee problem with 15 flowers showing that $E_{without}$ = 160,000 without ADFs.

With Defined Functions

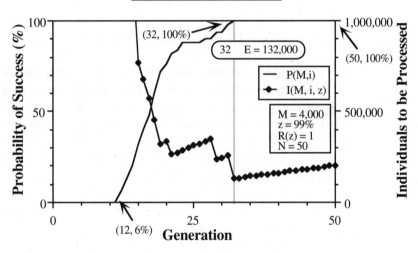

Figure 9.11 Performance curves for the bumblebee problem with 15 flowers showing that E_{with} = 132,000 with ADFs.

Table 9.5 Comparison table for the bumblebee problem with 15 flowers.

	Without ADFs	With ADFs
Average structural complexity $\bar{S}$	328.4	190.8
Computational effort E	160,000	132,000

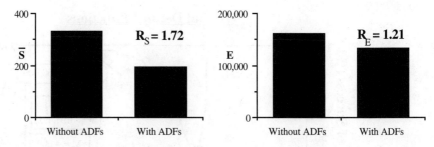

Figure 9.12 Summary graphs for the bumblebee problem with 15 flowers.

The average structural complexity, $\overline{S}$, of the best-of-run programs from the 35 successful runs (out of 35 runs) without automatically defined functions is 224.2 points for the bumblebee problem with 10 flowers.

For the bumblebee problem with 10 flowers, figure 9.13 presents the performance curves based on the 35 runs of this problem without automatically defined functions. The cumulative probability of success, $P(M,i)$, is 100% by generation 28. The two numbers in the oval indicate that if this problem is run through to generation 28, processing a total of $E_{without} = 116{,}000$ individuals (i.e., $4{,}000 \times 29$ generations $\times 1$ run) is sufficient to yield a satisfactory result for this problem with 99% probability.

9.11 RESULTS WITH 10 FLOWERS WITH ADFs

For the bumblebee problem with 10 flowers, the average structural complexity, $\overline{S}$, of the best-of-run programs from the 33 successful runs (out of 33 runs) with automatically defined functions is 150.9 points.

For the bumblebee problem with 10 flowers, figure 9.14 presents the performance curves based on the 33 runs of this problem with automatically defined functions. The cumulative probability of success, $P(M,i)$, is 100% by generation 23. The two numbers in the oval indicate that if this problem is run through to generation 23, processing a total of $E_{with} = 96{,}000$ individuals (i.e., $4{,}000 \times 24$ generations $\times 1$ run) is sufficient to yield a satisfactory result for this problem with 99% probability.

For the bumblebee problem with 10 flowers, table 9.6 compares the average structural complexity, $\overline{S}_{without}$ and $\overline{S}_{with}$, and the computational effort, $E_{without}$ and E_{with}, with automatically defined functions and without them.

Figure 9.15, which summarizes the information in the table for the bumblebee problem with 10 flowers, shows a structural complexity ratio, R_S, of 1.49 and an efficiency ratio, R_E, of 1.20.

9.12 SUMMARY FOR 10, 15, 20, AND 25 FLOWERS

Table 9.7 compiles the observations from the above experiments into one table. As can be seen, for the bumblebee problem, the efficiency ratio, R_E, is always greater than 1 (indicating that fewer fitness evaluations are required to yield a satisfactory result for the problem with 99% probability

Without Defined Functions

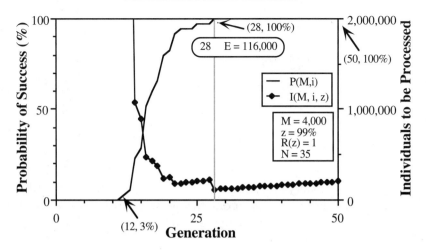

Figure 9.13 Performance curves for the bumblebee problem with 10 flowers showing that $E_{without}$ = 116,000 without ADFs.

With Defined Functions

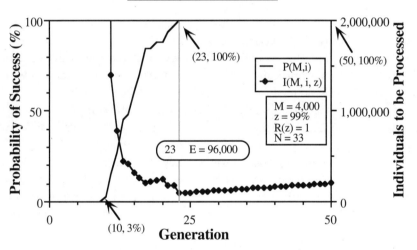

Figure 9.14 Performance curves for the bumblebee problem with 10 flowers showing that E_{with} = 96,000 with ADFs.

Table 9.6 Comparison table for the bumblebee problem with 10 flowers.

	Without ADFs	With ADFs
Average structural complexity $\overline{S}$	224.2	150.9
Computational effort E	116,000	96,000

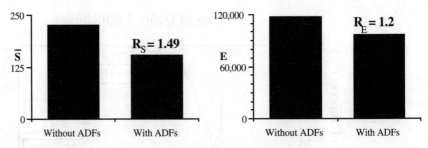

Figure 9.15 Summary graphs for the bumblebee problem with 10 flowers.

with automatically defined functions than without them). The structural complexity ratio, R_S, is also always greater than 1 (indicating that the overall size of the solutions to the problem is smaller with automatically defined functions than without them).

9.13 SCALING WITH 10, 15, 20, AND 25 FLOWERS

This section examines the average structural complexity, $\overline{S}$, and the computational effort, E, as a function of problem size for the bumblebee problem.

We first consider the average structural complexity, $\overline{S}$, of the genetically evolved solutions to the bumblebee problem, with and without automatically defined functions.

Table 9.8 consolidates the previously reported values of the average structural complexity for 10, 15, 20, and 25 flowers, with and without automatically defined functions for the bumblebee problem.

Figure 9.16 shows the average structural complexity, $\overline{S}$, of solutions for 10, 15, 20, and 25 flowers, with and without automatically defined functions. The graphs are approximately linear, both with and without automatically defined functions; however, they are different.

When we perform a linear least-squares regression on the four points relating to the runs without automatically defined functions, we find that the structural complexity, $\overline{S}_{without}$, can be stated in terms of the number of flowers, F, as

$$\overline{S}_{without} = 88.21 + 14.84F,$$

with a correlation of 0.99. The slope is 14.84, so it takes an average of 14.84 points in the program tree to handle each additional flower.

In contrast, when we perform a linear regression on the runs with automatically defined functions, we find that structural complexity, $\overline{S}_{with}$, can be stated in terms of the number of flowers, F, as

$$\overline{S}_{with} = 90.26 + 6.44F,$$

with a correlation of 0.99. The vertical intercept of 90.26 here is only slightly larger than the intercept (88.21) without automatically defined functions. However, the slope of 6.44 here is only 43% of the slope (14.84) without

Table 9.7 Summary table of the structural complexity ratio, R_S, and the efficiency ratio, R_E, for the bumblebee problem with 10, 15, 20, and 25 flowers.

Problem	Structural complexity ratio R_S	Efficiency ratio R_E
Bumblebee – 10 flowers	1.49	1.20
Bumblebee – 15 flowers	1.72	1.21
Bumblebee – 20 flowers	1.72	1.24
Bumblebee – 25 flowers	1.84	3.20

Table 9.8 Comparison of the average structural complexity of solutions of the bumblebee problem.

	10	15	20	25
$\overline{S}_{without}$	224.2	328.4	386.9	452.0
$\overline{S}_{with}$	150.9	190.8	225.0	245.9

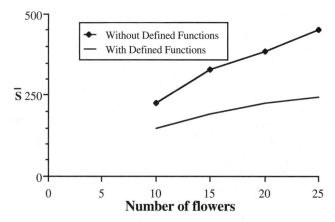

Figure 9.16 Comparison of average structural complexity, $\overline{S}$, of solutions to the bumblebee problem with 10, 15, 20, and 25 flowers, with and without ADFs.

automatically defined functions. That is, it takes an average of only 6.44 points in the program tree to handle each additional flower with automatically defined functions. That is, as the size of the problem is scaled up, the size of the solutions seems to grow at less than half the rate with automatically defined functions than without them.

We now consider the computational effort required for the bumblebee problem, with and without automatically defined functions.

Table 9.9 consolidates the values of computational effort for 10, 15, 20, and 25 flowers, with and without automatically defined functions for the bumblebee problem.

Figure 9.17 shows the computational effort for 10, 15, 20, and 25 flowers, both with and without automatically defined functions. As can be seen, the values of the computational effort, $E_{without}$, without automatically defined functions (116,000, 160,000, 328,000, and 612,000) grow very rapidly with problem size.

When we perform a linear regression on the progression of values of computational effort, $E_{without}$, without automatically defined functions (116,000, 160,000, 328,000, and 612,000), we find that the computational effort, $E_{without}$, can be stated in terms of the number of flowers, F, as

$$E_{without} = -275,600 + 33,120F,$$

with a correlation of 0.95. It takes about 33,120 additional fitness evaluations to handle each additional flower without automatically defined functions.

When we perform a linear regression on the nonmonotonic progression of values of E_{with} obtained from the empirical data with automatically defined functions (96,000, 132,000, 264,000 and 192,000), we find that the computational effort, E_{with}, can be stated in terms of the number of flowers, F, as

$$E_{with} = 24,000 + 8,400F,$$

with a correlation of 0.74. This correlation of 0.74 is much smaller than we have seen in previous comparisons because of the nonmonotonicity of this particular set of observed data, the sparsity of data for doing the regression, the possible inappropriateness of the model, or a combination

Table 9.9 Comparison of computational effort for 10, 15, 20, and 25 flowers for the bumblebee problem.

	10	15	20	25
$E_{without}$	116,000	160,000	328,000	612,000
E_{with}	96,000	132,000	264,000	192,000

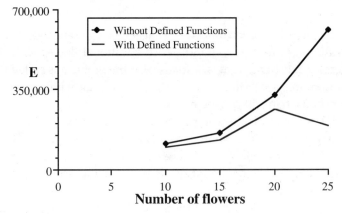

Figure 9.17 Comparison of computational effort for 10, 15, 20, and 25 flowers, with and without ADFs.

of these factors. Nonetheless, it takes only about 8,400 additional fitness evaluations to handle each additional flower with automatically defined functions. The slope of 8,400 with automatically defined functions is only about 25% of the slope (33,120) without automatically defined functions. That is, as the size of the problem is scaled up, the computational effort grows at less than a quarter of the rate with automatically defined functions than without them.

9.14   WALLCLOCK TIME FOR THE BUMBLEBEE PROBLEM

Table 9.10 shows the wallclock ratio, R_W, for the bumblebee problem with 10, 15, 20, and 25 flowers. As can be seen, the four wallclock ratios are each greater than 1, indicating that the runs with automatically defined functions require less wallclock time than the runs without automatically defined functions.

Thus, automatically defined functions are beneficial both in terms of computational effort and wallclock time for this problem.

There are various advantages, disadvantages, and common attributes to measuring computational burden by means of $E_{without}$, E_{with}, and R_E as opposed to measuring it by means of $W_{without}$, W_{with}, and R_W.

The major advantages of the computational effort, E, as a measure of computational burden are that it provides a hardware-independent, software-independent, and algorithm-independent way of comparing the performance of adaptive algorithms. These advantages derive from the fact that E treats all fitness evaluations equally. These advantages go hand in hand with the major disadvantage of E: it ignores differences in elapsed wallclock time.

The major advantage of wallclock time as a measure of computational burden is that it speaks directly to the management of computer resources. It directly reflects the different sizes, shapes, and contents of the program trees evolved by genetic programming. Wallclock time has the disadvantage of being algorithm-dependent, hardware-dependent, and software-dependent.

Both groups of measures have the desirable attribute of explicitly incorporating unsuccessful runs in the measurement of the performance of the algorithm.

Both groups of measures share several undesirable attributes. They are time-consuming to compute; they are retrospective in nature; they are sometimes

Table 9.10   Wallclock ratios, R_W, for the bumblebee problem.

Problem size	Wallclock ratio R_W
10	1.008
15	1.522
20	1.820
25	3.576

very sensitive to small variations in the observed data (especially when the probability of success is high); and they are sensitive to the choice of G (especially when the probability of success is low).

The algorithm-independence of E arises from the fact that fitness evaluations lie at the heart of every adaptive algorithm. Fitness evaluations are common to all adaptive algorithms (probabilistic and deterministic). Every adaptive algorithm starts with at least one point in the search space of the problem. For example, simple hillclimbing algorithms and simulated annealing typically start with a single point in the multidimensional search space of the problem; neural net paradigms typically start with a single vector in the search space of weight vectors; genetic methods typically start with a population of chromosome strings or other structures from the search space of the problem. Adaptive algorithms then iteratively evaluate the fitness of the current point(s) and use that information to create new point(s). Not every new point created by an adaptive algorithm is necessarily better (except in hill climbing algorithms). Nonetheless, the goal of an adaptive algorithm is to travel through the search space of the problem so as eventually to find better points in the search space. Focusing on fitness evaluations is usually informative because fitness evaluations are almost always computationally burdensome for interesting problems. Moreover, fitness evaluations come from the nature of the problem, not the nature of the particular adaptive algorithm being used. The algorithm-independence of fitness evaluations is desirable because it offers the possibility of comparing different adaptive algorithms.

The hardware-independence and software-independence of E arises from the fact that the computation of E is not specific to any particular piece of computing machinery or any particular programming language or operating system. We have used LISP machines (whose machine code is especially designed for LISP) for genetic programming whereas most other users have used general purpose workstations. The use of a LISP machine undoubtedly facilitates execution of genetic programming when implemented in a manner based on the representation of a program as a parse tree. (It certainly also facilitates development of software for genetic programming). A measure such as E permits direct comparison of our results with the results obtained by others using different platforms. (Our own runs of genetic programming have been made using four different configurations of LISP machines, so comparing wallclock time would be difficult even among our own runs.) There is no need to pay any attention to differences between the particular hardware or operating systems of the particular platforms when a measure such as E is used.

The most important disadvantage of E is that it treats all fitness evaluations and all individuals equally. The computational burden associated with the evaluation of fitness of different points in the search space can be different for several reasons. The computational burden, of course, depends on the specific content of the programs (e.g., a call to the cosine function is more time-consuming than a simple addition). In the case of genetic programming, the computational burden also depends, in part, on the size of the programs. It is comforting that the solutions produced by genetic programming with automatically defined functions tend to be smaller than the solutions produced without automatically defined functions. However, the solutions are unusual points in the search space and the computational burden of a run of genetic programming depends on the cumulative size, over all individuals in the population and over all generations, not on the size of the one solution (or the handful of solutions) that ultimately emerge on the final successful generation of the run. More important, E does not reflect the substantial extra cost associated with handling automatically defined functions. Another reason why counting the number of fitness evaluations might be misleading is that wallclock time reflects the actual time required to evaluate the fitness of the particular points in the search space of the problem that are actually visited by the adaptive algorithm. The trajectory of one adaptive algorithm may conceivably create a disproportionately large number of intermediate points whose fitness evaluations are extraordinarily burdensome whereas the trajectory of another algorithm may create candidates that may be evaluated more easily. For example, some trajectories for some problems may contain many infeasible points that might cause the simulation involved in the fitness evaluation of the problem to time out.

Wallclock time is, of course, an appropriate measure of computational burden for any adaptive algorithm. For a given problem, different adaptive algorithms trace different trajectories through the search space of the problem. These trajectories may differ as to both their generational length (i.e., number of iterations or cycles of the algorithms required to yield a solution) and the computational burden associated with the particular points along the trajectory actually traced by a particular algorithm through the search space. In many problems, certain points in the search may take more time to process than others. For example, in many control problems, a trajectory containing many poor points may require more processing time than other trajectories. For certain algorithms, the step of creating new points is computationally intensive. For example, back propagation requires a large number of calculations to convert the current single point in the search space into the next. In contrast, the computational burden associated with the step of creating a new point in the search space is extremely low with the conventional genetic algorithm operating on fixed-length strings (because crossover, mutation, and reproduction of strings are extremely fast and simple operations). This burden is somewhat greater for genetic programming than the conventional genetic algorithm (but still low in comparison to the burden of the fitness evaluations for a nontrivial problem). Of course, genetic methods use a population of points, whereas most adaptive algorithms operate on just a single point at a time. For certain algorithms, there are certain fixed front-end or back-end costs.

Studying wallclock time is especially pertinent in connection with genetic programming because genetic programming differs from most other adaptive algorithms in that the individual points along the trajectory traced through program space have different sizes and shapes. If all other things are equal, a larger program will usually take more wallclock time to evaluate than a smaller program. In contrast, for most adaptive algorithms, the structure undergoing adaptation is fixed throughout the run. For example, in the conventional genetic algorithm, the structure undergoing adaptation is typically a fixed-length character string. In neural networks being trained using back-propagation, the structure undergoing adaptation is a fixed-size vector containing the weights for the fixed number of connections in the neural network.

$E_{without}$, E_{with}, R_E, $W_{without}$, W_{with}, and R_W all share the advantage of explicitly recognizing the reality that every run of the algorithm does not necessarily yield a solution (or a satisfactory result). Many adaptive algorithms (e.g., simulated annealing, back propagation) have explicit probabilistic steps that determine whether or when a particular run actually yields a solution. Other seemingly nonprobabilistic learning algorithms are so dependent on artifacts (e.g., the order of presentation of data) that their overall performance in solving problems must be regarded as effectively probabilistic. Many reports of the performance of these algorithms ignore or underplay this probabilistic nature by neglecting or dismissing the failed runs in discussions of the performance of the algorithm. The effectively probabilistic nature of many adaptive algorithms is also often masked by the presentation of problems that are so simple that the algorithms always seem to work.

One disadvantage of both groups of measures is that they are particularly sensitive to the vagaries of empirical data when the probability of success approaches 100%. We use E to illustrate this point. When $P(M,i)$ is between 0.78 and 0.89, only three independent runs, $R(z)$, are required $P(M,i)$; when $P(M,i)$ is between 0.90 and 0.98, only two independent runs are required; and when $P(M,i)$ is 0.99 or more, only one run is required. The effect of an observed value of 0.99 versus 0.98 for $P(M,i)$ is that E decreases by a factor of 2. We sometimes see this abrupt drop in E when a problem that genetic programming seems to solve on every run encounters its first unsuccessful run (thus changing $P(M,i)$ from 100% to some value below 0.99).

Both groups of measures are also particularly sensitive when $P(M,i)$ is small. When $P(M,i)$ is small, $R(M,i,z)$ is large. In that regime, a small change in $P(M,i)$ causes a large change in $R(M,i,z)$.

In addition, both groups of measures depend on a reasonable choice of G. If G is too small for a given problem, the best generation i^* may appear to be generation G (i.e., the last generation of the run). When this happens (especially when $P(M,i)$ is small and $R(M,i,z)$ is large), there is a question as to whether the true global minimum for $I(M,i,z)$ or $W(M,i,z)$ has been achieved (i.e., whether the apparent best generation is merely an artifact of an insufficiently large choice for G).

Both groups of measures share the disadvantage that they are ultimately based on a count of the number of occurrences of an all-or-nothing event (i.e., getting a result that satisfies the success predicate of the problem). The fact that no credit is given for progress toward a solution may be a very reasonable and realistic characteristic for a performance measure for an adaptive algorithm whose goal is to solve a problem. However, this fact makes such a performance measure very time-consuming to compute because it requires multiple successful runs. If $P(M,i)$ is low, a large number of unsuccessful runs will continue through generation G for each successful run. Because the method is time-consuming, less data may be available than we might like for computing this measure (for a given amount of available computational resources).

A minor disadvantage of E is that it is not a complete measure of the computational burden. The computational burden of an adaptive algorithm depends on the effort required to initialize the algorithm, the number of new points created during a run, the effort required to create new points, the number of fitness evaluations made during the run, and the effort required to do those fitness evaluations. E does not specifically measure the computational burden of initialization. However, the computational burden required to initialize an adaptive algorithm is usually very small in relation to its other steps.

In addition, adaptive algorithms vary in the way that the overall computational burden is divided between the step of creating new points and the step of evaluating the fitness of the created points. For example, the number of new points created during a run varies significantly from algorithm to algorithm. Some adaptive algorithms (e.g., simulated annealing and many neural network paradigms) create only one new point for each generation (cycle) of the algorithm. On the other hand, hillclimbing algorithms typically create multiple tentative new points on each generation, evaluate them all, and then select the best alternative as the new point in the search space. Parallel search algorithms and genetic algorithms create a large number of new points at each generation. In addition, the computational burden required to create the new points varies significantly from algorithm to algorithm. The creation of a new point is relatively burdensome for some adaptive algorithms (e.g., back propagation) but it is relatively easy and simple with others (e.g., genetic algorithms). However, the importance of these differences should not be exaggerated because the number of new points that are created by an adaptive algorithm on each generation is usually equal to (or at least proportional to) the number of fitness evaluations (because a fitness evaluation is associated with each new point). Thus, except for the initialization step, the computational burden associated with an adaptive algorithm ends up depending more or less directly on the number of fitness evaluations.

There are some uncertainties involved in measuring wallclock time on a LISP machine. Many of the key activities of the LISP machine on which we did the work reported in this book involve the creation of elaborate linked structures that represent LISP S-expressions, which causes CONSing. Our implementation of genetic programming relies heavily on dynamic memory allocation and memory reclamation. In LISP machines, memory cells that are no longer in use are reclaimed by means of periodic garbage collection. The time required for a run varies in part due to memory fragmentation that inevitably occurs as the amount of time since the machine was booted increases. In practice, many runs are necessarily made before the machine is rebooted. A consequence of these activities that are peculiar to LISP machines and our implementation of genetic programming is that the wallclock times for a given set of identical runs of genetic programming may vary substantially and unpredictably depending on several interrelated factors (e.g., the amount of time since rebooting, etc.) even if they all perform exactly the same computation. These uncertainties are themselves significantly related to the cumulative structural complexity of the programs in the population as a whole (the biomass).

One could circumvent these difficulties by inserting a counter inside the interpreter function in the kernel of the code for genetic programming. Since different operations take different amounts of time, the increments to this counter would be a function of the particular operation being performed. This approach would result in a reliable and repeatable machine-specific measure of wallclock time. This measure could even be considered machine-independent if there were agreement on a particular table of times for each of the primitive operations. However, maintaining this count would require that it be retrieved from memory, incremented, and stored for each terminal that is actually evaluated and each primitive function that is actually executed. This counter would slow down the run since retrieving the counter, adding the operation-specified increment, and storing the result must all be performed in the innermost loop.

Another important factor in the amount of wallclock time required to measure fitness is the number of functions and terminals that are actually evaluated in the entire population of programs. The wallclock time is not directly proportional to the number of functions and terminals that are actually evaluated in a given program because different amounts of time may be required to evaluate the different functions and terminals. The number of functions and terminals that are actually evaluated in a given program is not always the same as the number of functions and terminals in the program (i.e., its structural complexity) because only part of a program may actually be executed and because multiple calls to automatically defined functions result in repeated references to all of the points represented in the bodies of those automatically defined functions. Partial execution may occur because of explicit conditional branching operations in the program, because many functions (e.g., the non-strict AND and OR functions) are defined so as to short-circuit the evaluation of some of their arguments when the outcome becomes established, and because programs are often terminated by the time-out limits imposed in fitness calculations involving simulations. The impact of branching operations and non-strict operators cannot necessarily be estimated by relying on averages since we frequently see the formation of large intron-like (i.e., ignored) structures in the program trees produced by genetic programming (section 25.13 of *Genetic Programming*). More important, when automatically defined functions are being used, the number of functions and terminals that are actually evaluated in a given program depends on the extent to which the result-producing branch calls other branches and the extent to which the function-defining branches hierarchically invoke other function-defining branches.

10 The Increasing Benefits of ADFs as Problems are Scaled Up

Chapters 6, 8 and 9 focused on problems for which a progression of several scaled-up versions were considered.

Table 6.10 showed that both the efficiency ratio, R_E, and the structural complexity ratio, R_S, are greater than 1 for the even-4-, 5-, and 6-parity problems. Table 8.9 showed the same for the lawnmower problem with lawn sizes of 32, 48, 64, 80, and 96. Table 9.7 showed the same for the bumblebee problem with 10, 15, 20, and 25 flowers. Accordingly, main points 3 and 4 stated that automatically defined functions reduce the computational effort required to solve these problems and usually improve the parsimony of the solutions produced by genetic programming.

The regression analyses (both linear and exponential) concerning the parity problem (section 6.15), the lawnmower problem (section 8.15), and the bumblebee problem (section 9.13) indicated that the average structural complexity increases as a function of problem size at a lower rate with automatically defined functions than without them (main point 5) and that the computational effort increases as a function of problem size at a lower rate with automatically defined functions than without them (main point 6).

The focus in this chapter changes from the values of $\overline{S}$ and E to the values of the two ratios, R_S and R_E. Specifically, this chapter explores the question of how the efficiency ratio, R_E, and the structural complexity ratio, R_S, in tables 6.10, 8.11, and 9.10 change as a function of problem size.

10.1 THE BENEFITS OF ADFs AS A FUNCTION OF PROBLEM SIZE

We first examine the efficiency ratios contained in the three tables.

Figure 10.1 plots the efficiency ratios, R_E, from table 6.10 as a function of the arity of the parity problem (excluding the ratio for the 6-parity problem in table 6.10 of 52.2 based on the rough estimate of section 6.6).

Figure 10.2 plots the efficiency ratios, R_E, from table 8.9 as a function of the size of the lawn in the lawnmower problem.

Figure 10.3 plots the efficiency ratios, R_E, from table 9.7 as a function of the number of flowers in the bumblebee problem.

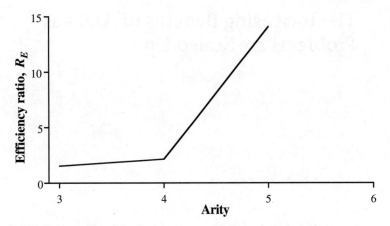

Figure 10.1 Graph of efficiency-ratio, R_E, for the even-parity problems.

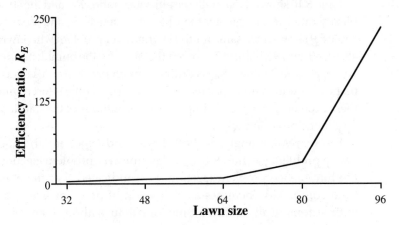

Figure 10.2 Graph of efficiency-ratio, R_E, for the lawnmower problem with lawn sizes of 32, 48, 64, 80, and 96.

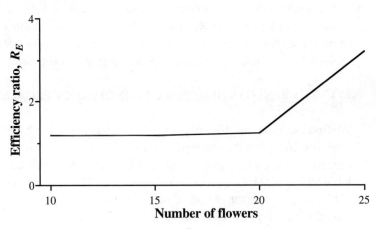

Figure 10.3 Graph of efficiency-ratio, R_E, for the bumblebee problem with 10, 15, 20, and 25 flowers.

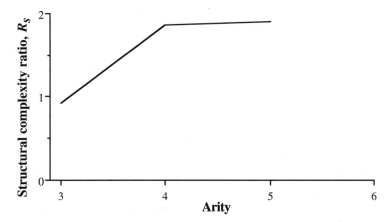

Figure 10.4 Graph of structural-complexity-ratio, R_S, for the even-parity problems.

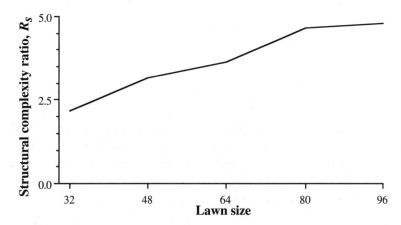

Figure 10.5 Graph of structural-complexity-ratio, R_S, for the lawnmower problem with lawn sizes of 32, 48, 64, 80, and 96.

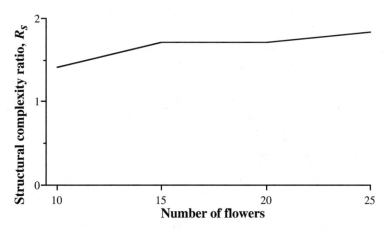

Figure 10.6 Graph of structural-complexity-ratio, R_S, for the bumblebee problem with 10, 15, 20, and 25 flowers.

The Increasing Benefits of ADFs as Problems are Scaled Up

The efficiency ratios, R_E, increase strictly monotonically as the problem size increases. That is, the benefit conferred by automatically defined functions as to computational effort increases as problems are scaled up. This point is closely related to, but slightly different from, the subject of main points 3 and 6.

We now reexamine the structural complexity ratios contained in the same three tables.

Figure 10.4 plots the structural complexity ratios, R_S, from table 6.10 as a function of the arity of the parity problem (excluding the ratio for the even-6-parity problem of 1.77 based on the rough estimate of section 6.6).

Figure 10.5 plots the structural complexity ratios, R_S, from table 8.9 as a function of the size of the lawn in the lawnmower problem.

Figure 10.6 plots the structural complexity ratios, R_S, from table 9.7 as a function of the number of flowers in the bumblebee problem.

The structural complexity ratios, R_S, increase monotonically (i.e., do not decrease) as the problem size increases. That is, benefits as to parsimony conferred by automatically defined functions increases as problems are scaled up. This point is closely related to the subject of main points 4 and 5.

This evidence supports main point 7 of this book:

Main point 7: For the three problems herein for which a progression of several scaled-up versions is studied, the benefits in terms of computational effort and average structural complexity conferred by automatically defined functions increase as the problem size is scaled up.

This main point is important because it suggests that the advantages of exploiting modularities by means of hierarchies becomes greater as problems become larger and more realistically sized.

10.2   WALLCLOCK TIME

The evidence from the two problems for which wallclock time is computed for a progression of scaled-up versions (i.e., the lawnmower problem in section 8.16 and the bumblebee problem in section 9.14) also supports the conclusion that the advantages conferred by automatically defined functions increase as the problem size is scaled up. For both problems, the wallclock ratios, R_W, increase monotonically as the problem size increases.

Figure 10.7 plots the wallclock ratios, R_W, as a function of the lawn size in the lawnmower problem.

Figure 10.8 plots the wallclock ratios, R_W, as a function of the number of flowers in the bumblebee problem.

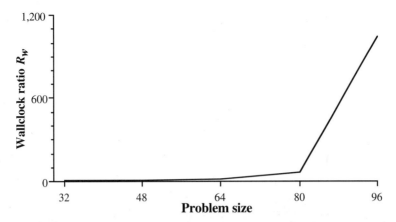

Figure 10.7 Graph of wallclock-ratio, R_S, for the lawnmower problem with lawn sizes of 32, 48, 64, 80, and 96.

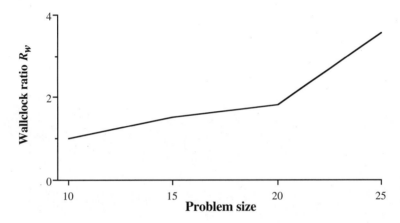

Figure 10.8 Graph of wallclock-ratio, R_W, for the bumblebee problem with 10, 15, 20, and 25 flowers.

The Increasing Benefits of ADFs as Problems are Scaled Up

11 Finding an Impulse Response Function

In the foregoing chapters, information was explicitly transmitted to the genetically evolved reusable subprograms by explicit arguments or was implicitly transmitted to the subprograms by means of the state of the system. Information can be implicitly transmitted in another way: by global variables. This chapter presents a problem in which information is transmitted to the evolved subprograms in two ways: by a global variable and by an explicit argument.

The problem in this chapter is to find the impulse response function for a linear time-invariant system. Martin A. Keane conceived the impulse response problem (Keane, Koza, and Rice 1993) and we subsequently applied automatically defined functions to this problem (Koza, Keane, and Rice 1993).

The fact that the automatically defined functions in this problem are real-valued functions of a single variable permits the automatically defined functions to be visualized graphically. This, in turn, enables us to visualize, in some instances, the often-illusive connection between program structure and program performance in the problem domain. It also enables us to visualize the effect of crossover on program performance. Section 11.7 traces the genealogical audit trail of illustrative offspring produced by crossover in both the function-defining branch and the result-producing branch.

11.1 THE PROBLEM

For many problems in control engineering, it is desirable to find a function, such as the impulse response function or transfer function, for a system for which one does not have an analytical model.

In this chapter genetic programming is used to find a good approximation, in symbolic form, to the impulse response function for a linear time-invariant system using only the observed discrete-time response of the system to a particular known forcing function.

The reader unfamiliar with control engineering should focus on the fact that we are searching the space of possible functions for a real-valued

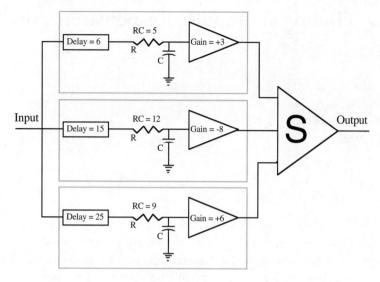

Figure 11.1 A linear time-invariant system.

function that satisfies certain requirements, rather than on the engineering interpretation of the impulse response function.

Figure 11.1 shows a linear time-invariant system (i.e., a *plant*) that sums the outputs of three major components. Each component consists of a pure time-delay element, a lag circuit containing a resistor and a capacitor, and a gain element. The first component of this system, for example, has a time delay of 6, a gain of +3, and a time constant, RC, of 5. For computational simplicity and without loss of generality, we use the discrete-time version of this system in this chapter.

In the problem of system identification, one is given the observed response of the unknown system to a particular known input. Figure 11.2 shows a particular square input, $i(t)$, that rises from an amplitude of 0 to 1 at time 3 and falls back to an amplitude of 0 at time 23. It also shows the response, $o(t)$, of the system when this square input is used as a forcing function.

The output of a linear continuous-time time-invariant system is given by the continuous-time convolution of the input, $i(t)$, and the impulse response function, $H(t)$. That is,

$$o(t) = \int_{-\infty}^{t} i(t - \tau)H(\tau)d\tau.$$

The output of a linear discrete-time time-invariant system is given by the discrete-time convolution

$$o(t) = \sum_{\tau=-\infty}^{t} i(t - \tau)H(\tau).$$

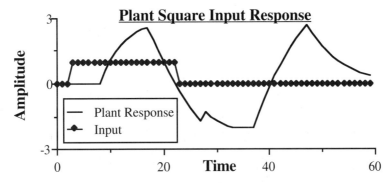

Figure 11.2 Plant response when a square input is the forcing function.

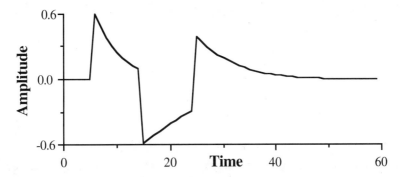

Figure 11.3 Impulse response function, $H(t)$.

The impulse response function, $H(t)$, for the system above is known to be

$$\begin{cases} 0 & \text{if } t < 6 \\ \dfrac{3\left(1-\frac{1}{5}\right)^{t-6}}{5} & \text{otherwise} \end{cases} + \begin{cases} 0 & \text{if } t < 15 \\ \dfrac{-8\left(1-\frac{1}{12}\right)^{t-15}}{12} & \text{otherwise} \end{cases} + \begin{cases} 0 & \text{if } t < 25 \\ \dfrac{6\left(1-\frac{1}{9}\right)^{t-25}}{9} & \text{otherwise} \end{cases}$$

Figure 11.3 shows the impulse response function, $H(t)$, for the system. We now show how an approximation to this impulse response can be discovered by genetic programming using just the observed discrete-time time-domain response to the square forcing function. The discrete-time version of the square input and the system's discrete-time time-domain response to the square input shown in figure 11.2 are the givens in this problem; the goal is to find a good approximation to the impulse response of figure 11.3.

11.2 PREPARATORY STEPS WITHOUT ADFs

The candidate impulse response functions are compositions of the primitive functions and terminals of the problem. The single independent variable in the impulse response function is the time, T. In addition, the impulse response function may contain numerical constants. Thus, the terminal set, T, for this problem consists of

$T = \{ \text{T}, \Re_{\text{bigger-reals}} \}$,

where the floating-point random constant, $\Re_{\text{bigger-reals}}$, ranges between −10.000 and +10.000 (with a granularity of 0.001).

For this problem, knowledge of control engineering suggests that the function set might consist of some kind of decision-making operator, the four arithmetic operations, and the exponential function. Thus, the function set, F, for this problem is

$F = \{ +, -, *, \%, \text{EXPP}, \text{IFLTE} \}$

with an argument map of

$\{2, 2, 2, 2, 1, 4\}$.

The protected division function $\%$ (section 4.2) protects against the possibility of division by zero. However, the potential of an overflow or underflow arising from the creation of extremely large or small floating point values always exists whenever arithmetic operations are performed on a computer. The presence of the exponential function in the function set of this particular problem guarantees the creation of extreme values. Extreme values may be created by the exponential function alone, by one of the four ordinary arithmetic functions operating on values returned by the exponential function, or even by the arithmetic functions alone. Thus, it is necessary to protect all four arithmetic functions so that if the absolute value of the result is greater than some very large value or less than some very small value, then some nominal value (with the appropriate sign) is instead returned. This protection can be provided either by writing magnitude-protected versions of all four arithmetic operations or by trapping the overflow or underflow errors in a manner appropriate to the computer being used. Ordinarily, the one-argument protected exponential function EXPP returns the numerical result obtained by raising e to the power indicated by its one argument and the two-argument arithmetic operations of $+$, $-$, $*$, and $\%$ return the numerical result obtained by performing these operations. However, whenever the absolute value of the result of evaluating any of these five functions exceeds the limits of the machine (i.e., about 10^{-38} or 10^{38} when floating-point numbers are used for our Texas Instruments Explorer II$^+$ computer), then some nominal value (10^{10} or 10^{-10}, respectively, with the appropriate sign) is instead returned.

The four-argument conditional branching function IFLTE ("If Less Than or Equal") evaluates and returns its third argument if its first argument is less than or equal to its second argument and otherwise evaluates and returns its fourth argument. For example, (IFLTE 2.0 3.5 A B) evaluates to the value of A.

Each computer program in the population is a composition of primitive functions from the function set, F, and terminals from the terminal set, T.

Of course, if we had some knowledge about the specific plant being analyzed that suggested the utility of certain other functions (e.g., sine), we could also have included those functions in, $\mathcal{F}$, as well.

For this problem, the fitness of an individual impulse response function in the population is measured in terms of the difference between the known observed discrete-time time-domain response of the system to a particular forcing function and the response computed by convolving the individual impulse response function and the forcing function. The smaller the difference, the better. The exact impulse response of the system would yield a difference of zero.

Specifically, each individual in the population is tested against a simulated environment consisting of $N_{fc} = 60$ fitness cases, each representing the output, $o(t)$, of the given system for various times between 0 and 59 when the square input, $i(t)$, is used as the forcing function for the system. The fitness of any given impulse response function, $G(t)$, in the population is the sum, over the 60 fitness cases, of the squares of the differences between the observed response, $o(t)$, of the system to the forcing function, $i(t)$, (i.e., the square input) and the response computed by convolving the forcing function, $i(t)$, and the given genetically evolved impulse response, $G(t)$. That is, the fitness is

$$ f(G) = \sum_{i=1}^{N_{fc}} \left[o(t_i) - \sum_{\tau=-\infty}^{t} i(t_i - \tau) G(\tau) \right]^2 . $$

Our choice of 4,000 as the population size and our choice of 51 as the maximum number of generations to be run reflect an estimate on our part of the likely complexity of this problem and the limitations of available computer time and memory.

Table 11.1 summarizes the key features of the impulse-response problem without automatically defined functions.

11.3   RESULTS OF ONE RUN WITHOUT ADFs

A review of one particular run will serve to illustrate how genetic programming progressively approximates the desired impulse response function.

One would not expect any individual from the randomly generated initial population to be very good. In generation 0, the fitness of the worst impulse response function in the population is very poor; its fitness is the enormous value of 4.7×10^{77}. This worst-of-generation individual consisted of seven points and is

```
(- T (* (EXPP T) (EXPP T))),
```

which is equivalent to

$$ t - e^{2t} . $$

Table 11.1 Tableau without ADFs for the impulse-response problem.

Objective:	Find a program that approximates the impulse response function of a three-component time-invariant linear system.
Terminal set without ADFs:	The time T and the random constants $\Re_{\text{bigger-reals}}$.
Function set without ADFs:	+, -, *, %, EXPP, and IFLTE.
Fitness cases:	60 consecutive integral values of time T between 0 and 59.
Raw fitness:	The squares of the differences between the observed response, $o(t)$, of the system to the forcing function, $i(t)$ (i.e., the square input) and the response computed by convolving the forcing function, $i(t)$, and the genetically produced impulse response, $G(t)$.
Standardized fitness:	Same as raw fitness.
Hits:	The number of fitness cases for which the response to the square input of the genetically produced individual comes within 0.5 of the plant response.
Wrapper:	None.
Parameters:	$M = 4{,}000$. $G = 51$.
Success predicate:	A program has a value of fitness of 20.00 or less over the 60 fitness cases.

The fitness of the worst 40% of the population for generation 0 is 10^{10} (or worse).

The median individual for generation 0 is, when simplified, equivalent to

$$-9.667 - 2.407t$$

and has a fitness of 10,260,473.

The fitness of the best impulse response function of generation 0 is 93.7 (i.e., an average squared error of about 1.56 for each of the 60 fitness cases). This program has seven points and is

```
(% (% -2.46 T) (+ T -9.636)),
```

which is equivalent to

$$\frac{\dfrac{-2.46}{t}}{t - 9.636} = \frac{-2.46}{t^2 - 9.636t}.$$

Figure 11.4 compares the best-of-generation impulse response function from generation 0 and the correct impulse response, $H(t)$, for the system. As can be seen, there is little resemblance between this best of generation 0 and the correct impulse response. Indeed, the signs of the values returned by the best of generation 0 are incorrect for almost every value of time.

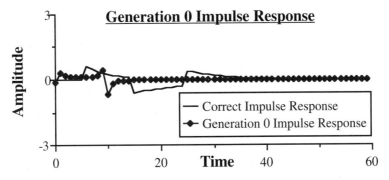

Figure 11.4 Comparison of the best of generation 0 without ADFs (whose fitness is 93.7) with the correct impulse response function.

In successive generations, the fitness of the worst-of-generation individual in the population, the median individual, and the best-of-generation program all tend to progressively improve (i.e., drop). In addition, the average fitness of the population as a whole tends to improve. The fitness of the best-of-generation program drops to 81.88 for generation 3, 76.09 for generation 5, 70.65 for generation 7, and 48.26 for generations 8 and 9. Of course, the vast majority of individual computer programs in the population are still very poor.

By generation 10, the fitness of the best-of-generation program improves to 40.02. This individual has 111 points and is shown below:

```
(IFLTE (EXPP (IFLTE T T T 2.482)) (EXPP (+ (% 9.39 T) (IFLTE (IFLTE
T 9.573 T -6.085) (% T 0.217001) (EXPP -6.925) (% T T)))) (EXPP (*
(- (+ T -4.679) (EXPP T)) (IFLTE (% -5.631 T) (% -1.675 -1.485) (+
T 2.623) (EXPP T)))) (% (EXPP (- T T)) (- (+ (* -1.15399 -5.332) (%
(% (* (IFLTE -8.019 T 0.338 T) (% T 8.571)) (- (* (- 1.213 T) (+
(EXPP T) (+ 7.605 6.873))) (IFLTE (+ T T) (* -5.749 T) (+ T T) (- T
T)))) (* T 6.193))) (IFLTE (% (EXPP T) (EXPP (* -3.817 T))) (* T
6.193) (- -8.022 7.743) (+ T -9.464)))))).
```

Note the subexpression (- -8.022 7.743) in the last line which evaluates to –15.765. The value –15.765 was evolved from the floating-point random constants –8.022 and 7.743 originally created in generation 0.

Figure 11.5 compares the genetically evolved best-of-generation impulse response function from generation 10 and the correct impulse response. As can be seen, this individual bears some resemblance to the correct impulse response for the system.

As one proceeds from generation 20 to 30 and to 40, the fitness of the best program in the population improves from 19.85 to 12.37 and to 6.97.

By generation 50, the best-of-generation program shown below has 286 points and a fitness value of 5.22 (i.e., a mean squared error of only about 0.87 for each of the 60 fitness cases):

```
(IFLTE (EXPP (IFLTE T T T 2.482)) (EXPP (- -8.022 7.743)) (EXPP (*
(- (% (% (* (IFLTE -8.019 T 0.338 T) (- -5.392 T)) T) (% (* (EXPP
```

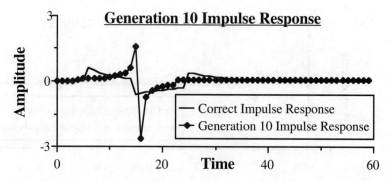

Figure 11.5 Comparison of the best of generation 10 without ADFs (whose fitness is 40.02) with the correct impulse response function.

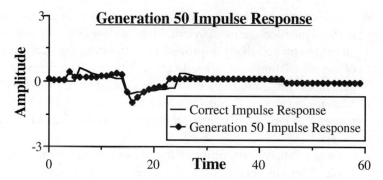

Figure 11.6 Comparison of the best of generation 50 (whose fitness is 5.22) without ADFs with the correct impulse response function.

```
(EXPP -5.221)) (IFLTE (* T T) (IFLTE (% -5.631 T) (% -1.675 -1.485)
(+ T 2.623) (EXPP T)) (- 9.957 -4.115) (% -8.978 T))) (- (IFLTE
(EXPP T) T 1.1 (EXPP 2.731)) (% (* (* -3.817 T) (% T 8.571)) (IFLTE
-8.019 T 0.338 T))))) (EXPP (IFLTE T 9.573 T -6.085))) (IFLTE (% -
5.631 T) (% -1.675 -1.485) (+ T 2.623) (EXPP T)))) (% (EXPP (IFLTE
-8.019 T 0.338 T)) (- (+ (* -1.15399 -5.332) (% (% (* (IFLTE -8.019
T 0.338 T) 8.571) (% T 8.571)) (- (+ (* -1.15399 -5.332) (% (% (*
(IFLTE -8.019 T 0.338 T) (% T 8.571)) T) (% (* (EXPP (EXPP -5.221))
(IFLTE (* T T) (IFLTE (EXPP (- -8.022 7.743)) (% -1.675 -1.485) (+
T 2.623) (EXPP T)) (- 9.957 -4.115) (% -8.978 T))) (- (IFLTE (EXPP
T) T 1.1 (EXPP 2.731)) (% (- -8.022 7.743) (EXPP 2.731))))))))
(IFLTE (% (EXPP T) (- 9.957 -4.115)) (* T 6.193) (IFLTE (% -5.631
T) (% -1.675 -1.485) (+ T 2.623) (EXPP T)) (+ T -9.464))))) (IFLTE
(% (EXPP T) (- -8.022 7.743)) (* T 6.193) (IFLTE (% (EXPP T) (EXPP
(* -3.817 T))) (- (IFLTE (+ T -4.679) (- -5.392 T) 1.1 (EXPP
2.731)) (% (+ T T) (* -1.15399 -5.332))) (- -8.022 (% -8.022 (- (*
(- (* (- 1.213 T) 0.217001) (% -5.631 T)) (+ (EXPP T) (- (IFLTE (+
T -4.679) (- -5.392 T) 1.1 (EXPP 2.731)) (EXPP (% T 0.217001)))))))
(IFLTE (+ T T) T (* T 6.193) (- T T))))) (+ T -9.464)) (+ T -
9.464))))).
```

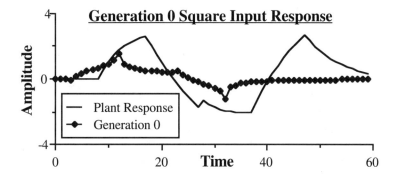

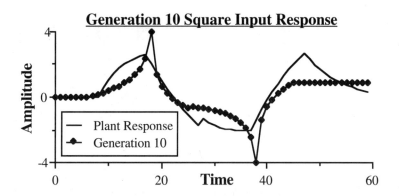

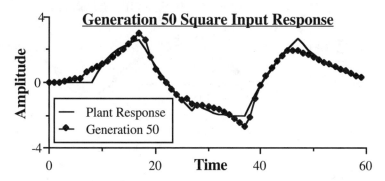

Figure 11.7 Response of best-of-generation programs from generations 0, 10, and 50 to the square input.

Figure 11.6 compares the genetically produced best-of-generation impulse response function from generation 50 and the correct impulse response.

The above impulse response function is not by any means the exact impulse response function, $H(t)$, for the system. However, this genetically created impulse response function is very good (although it may not appear so at first glance).

Since the fitness measure is actually based on the time-domain response of the system to the square input, the performance of the genetically produced

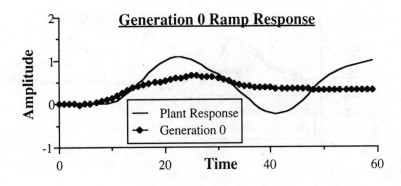

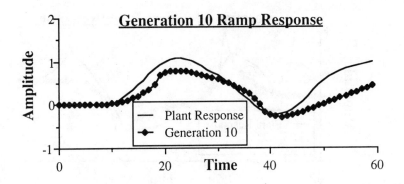

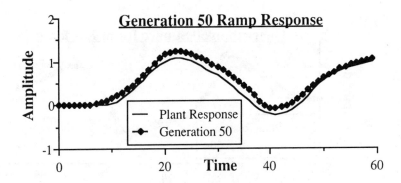

Figure 11.8 Response of the best-of-generation programs from generations 0, 10, and 50 to the ramp input.

best-of-generation impulse response functions from generations 0, 10, and 50 can be better appreciated by examining the computed time domain responses of the system to the square input for these individuals.

Figure 11.7 compares the plant response (which is the same in all three panels of this figure) to the square input and the response to the square input using the best-of-generation impulse response functions from generations 0, 10, and 50. As can be seen in the first and second panels of this figure, the best-of-generation programs from generations 0 and 10 do not perform very well, although generation 10 is considerably better than generation 0. However, as can be seen in the third panel of this figure, the performance of the best of generation 50 is close to the plant response (the total squared error being only 5.22 over the 60 fitness cases).

If we define a hit to be any fitness case (out of the 60) for which the time-domain response to the square input of the genetically produced individual comes within 0.5 of the plant response, then the number of hits improves from 17 for the best of generation 0, to 29 for the best of generation 10, and to 54 for the best of generation 50.

Control system performance is often characterized in terms of response to certain forcing functions (input signals) such as ramps and steps. Accordingly, the performance of the genetically evolved impulse response function can be further demonstrated by considering four additional forcing functions: a ramp input, a unit-step input, a shorter unit-square input, and a noise signal.

Figure 11.8 shows the plant response to a particular unit ramp input (whose amplitude is 0 between times 0 and 3, whose amplitude linearly ramps up from 0 to 1 between times 3 and 23, and whose amplitude is 1 between times 23 and 59). It also shows the response to this ramp input using the best-of-generation programs from generations 0, 10, and 50. As can be seen, the performance of the best of generation 50 is close to the plant response for the ramp input (the total squared error being only 7.2 over the 60 fitness cases).

Figure 11.9 compares the plant response to a particular unit-step input (where the amplitude of the input steps up from 0 to 1 at time 3) and the response to the step input using the best-of-generation programs from generations 0, 10, and 50. The performance of the best of generation 50 is also close to the plant response for the unit-step input (the total squared error being only 12.9 over the 60 fitness cases).

Figure 11.10 compares the plant response to a particular short unit-square input (whose amplitude steps up from 0 to 1 at time 15 and steps down at time 23) and the response to this short unit-square input using the best-of-generation programs from generations 0, 10, and 50. As can be seen, the performance of the best of generation 50 is also close to the plant response for this short unit-square input (the total squared error being only 17.1 over the 60 fitness cases).

Figure 11.11 shows a noise signal which we will use as the forcing function for our fourth and final test. The random values in the range [0,1] are

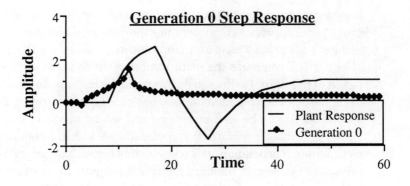

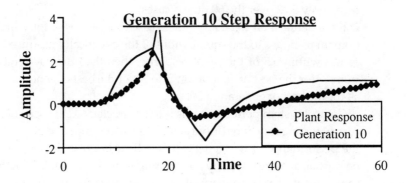

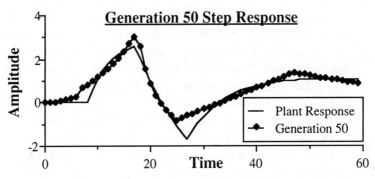

Figure 11.9 Response of the best-of-generation programs from generations 0, 10 and 50 to the unit-step input

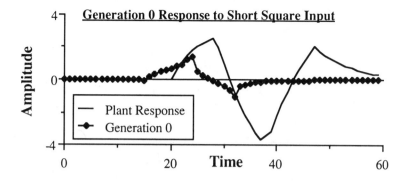

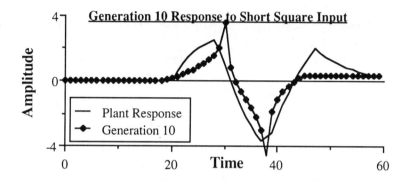

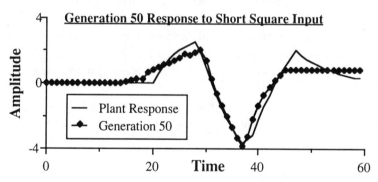

Figure 11.10 Response of the best-of-generation programs from generations 0, 10 and 50 to the short unit-square input.

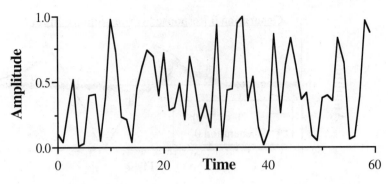

Figure 11.11 Noise signal.

obtained for each time step by a separate call to the Park-Miller randomizer (Park and Miller 1988).

Figure 11.12 compares the plant response to this noise signal and the response to the noise signal using the best-of-generation programs from generations 0, 10, and 50. The performance of the best of generation 50 is also close to the plant response for the noise signal (the total squared error being only 18.3 over the 60 fitness cases).

Genetic programming is well suited to control problems where the exact solution is not known and where engineers do not expect, as a practical matter, to achieve the actual optimal solution. The solution to a problem produced by genetic programming is not just a numerical solution applicable to a single specific combination of numerical input(s), but, instead, comes in the form of a function in symbolic form (i.e., a computer program). As can be seen, we have evolved an impulse response function which closely models the output behavior of the unknown system when the system is presented with a variety of inputs.

Note that we did not pre-specify the size and shape of the result. We did not specify that the result obtained in generation 50 would have 286 points. As we proceed from generation to generation, the size and shape of the best-of-generation programs changes as a result of the selective pressure exerted by Darwinian natural selection and crossover.

11.4 RESULTS OF SERIES OF RUNS WITHOUT ADFs

Over a series of 28 runs, the average structural complexity, $\bar{S}_{without}$, of the best-of-run programs from the 16 successful runs (out of 28 runs) of the impulse-response problem is 285.9 points without automatically defined functions.

Figure 11.13 presents the performance curves based on the 28 runs of the impulse-response problem without automatically defined functions. The cumulative probability of success, $P(M,i)$, is 50% by generation 39 and 57% by generation 50. The two numbers in the oval indicate that if this problem is run through to generation 39, processing a total of $E_{without} = 1,120,000$

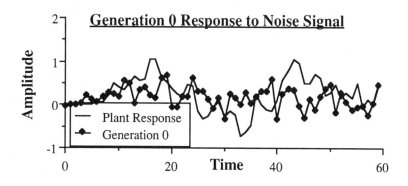

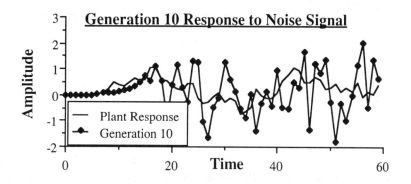

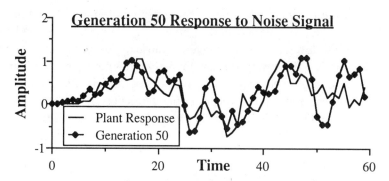

Figure 11.12 Response of the best-of-generation programs from generations 0, 10 and 50 to the noise signal.

Without Defined Functions

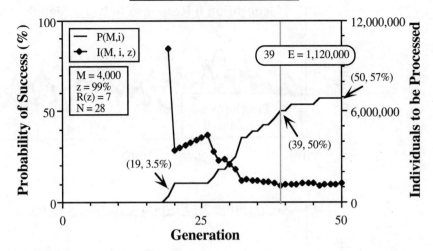

Figure 11.13 Performance curves for the impulse-response problem showing that $E_{without}$ = 1,120,000 without ADFs.

individuals (i.e., 4,000 × 40 generations × 7 runs) is sufficient to yield a satisfactory result for this problem with 99% probability.

11.5 PREPARATORY STEPS WITH ADFs

In applying genetic programming using automatically defined functions to this problem, we wanted to have an automatically defined function with multiple arguments. However, because of the many time steps and the convolution, this problem is already very time-intensive. Therefore, we compromised and decided that each overall program in the population will have one one-argument automatically defined function and that the independent variable of the problem, T, will be available to the automatically defined function as a global variable.

The terminal set, $\mathcal{T}_{adf}$, for the automatically defined function ADF0 is

$$\mathcal{T}_{adf} = \{\text{T}, \text{ARG0}, \mathfrak{R}_{\text{bigger-reals}}\}.$$

The function set, $\mathcal{F}_{adf}$, for the function-defining branch is the same as before, namely

$$\mathcal{F}_{adf} = \{+, -, *, \%, \text{EXPP}, \text{IFLTE}\}$$

with the same argument map, namely

$$\{2, 2, 2, 2, 1, 4\}.$$

The terminal set, $\mathcal{T}_{rpb}$, for the body of the result-producing branch does not contain the dummy variable ARG0 and is simply

$$\mathcal{T}_{rpb} = \{\text{T}, \mathfrak{R}_{\text{bigger-reals}}\}.$$

Table 11.2 Tableau with ADFs for the impulse-response problem.

Objective:	Find a program that approximates the impulse response function of a three-component time-invariant linear system.
Architecture of the overall program with ADFs:	One result-producing branch and one one-argument function-defining branch.
Parameters:	Branch typing.
Terminal set for the result-producing branch:	The time T and the random constants $\mathfrak{R}_{\text{bigger-reals}}$.
Function set for the result-producing branch:	+, -, *, %, EXPP, IFLTE, and the one-argument defined function ADF0.
Terminal set for the function-defining branch ADF0:	The time T, the dummy variable ARG0, and the random constants $\mathfrak{R}_{\text{bigger-reals}}$.
Function set for the function-defining branch ADF0:	+, -, *, %, EXPP, and IFLTE.

However, the function set, $\mathcal{F}_{rpb}$, for the result-producing branch contains the automatically defined function ADF0, so that

$$\mathcal{F}_{rpb} = \{\text{ADF0}, +, -, *, \%, \text{EXPP}, \text{IFLTE}\}$$

with an argument map of

$$\{1, 2, 2, 2, 2, 1, 4\}.$$

Table 11.2 summarizes the key features of the impulse-response problem with automatically defined functions.

11.6 RESULTS OF ONE RUN WITH ADFs

In generation 0 of one run of this problem using automatically defined functions, the worst impulse response function in the population is

```
(progn (defun ADF0 (ARG0)
        (values (EXPP (+ ARG0 T)))
       (values (* T (ADF0 (+ T T)))))).
```

In this program, ADF0 returns the exponential of its argument, ARG0, plus T, so that when the result-producing branch calls its ADF0 with the numerical argument (+ T T), ADF0 returns e^{3t}.

The result-producing branch then multiplies the returned value by T so that this individual program as a whole is equivalent to te^{3t}.

This sharply monotonically increasing function of T bears no resemblance to the correct impulse function of the system. Its fitness has the enormous value of 1.6×10^{77}.

The median individual of the population is

```
(progn (defun ADF0 (ARG0)
          (- ARG0 -8.354))
       (values (ADF0 T))).
```

This program is equivalent to the following simple linear function of T:

$t + 8.354$.

The fitness of this monotonically increasing function of T is 2,249,945.

The fitness of the best-of-generation impulse response function for generation 0 is 101.03 (i.e., an average squared error of about 1.68 per fitness case). This best-of-generation program has 35 points, has only one call to ADF0, and is

```
(progn (defun ADF0 (ARG0)
          (values (* (+ (IFLTE T T ARG0 ARG0) (* T ARG0))
                     (* (EXPP 4.152) (EXPP 9.587)))))
       (values (% (IFLTE (% T 1.364) (EXPP -2.113)
                         (ADF0 T) (% -2.421 T))
                  (% (- T 6.653) (% T T)))))).
```

When the defined function ADF0 is called with the argument T, it simplifies to

$926370(t + t^2)$.

ADF0 is called by the result-producing branch only when $t=0$, so the result-producing branch is equivalent to

$$\begin{cases} 1.0 & \text{if } t = 0 \\ \dfrac{-2.421}{t - 6.653t} & \text{otherwise} \end{cases}$$

Figure 11.14 compares the best-of-generation impulse response function from generation 0 and the correct impulse response, $H(t)$. As can be seen, there is little resemblance between this best of generation 0 and the correct impulse response for the problem. Indeed, the two rarely even have the same sign.

By generation 5, the fitness of the best-of-generation program improves slightly to 98.42. This individual has 60 points and is shown below:

```
(progn (defun ADF0 (ARG0)
          (values (* (+ (IFLTE T T ARG0 ARG0) (- (IFLTE (EXPP
                     -4.936) (% T ARG0) (- T T) T) (EXPP (* T T)))) (*
                     (EXPP 4.152) (EXPP -3.399)))))
       (values (% (IFLTE (% T (EXPP (ADF0 (+ (ADF0 -5.769) (-
                  (% T T) (IFLTE 6.518 T 3.851 -0.087)))))) (EXPP -2.113)
                  (ADF0 T) (% -2.421 T)) (% (- T 6.653) (% T T)))))).
```

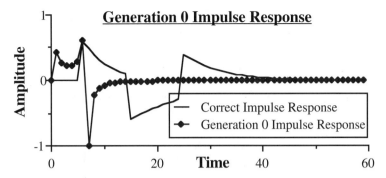

Figure 11.14 Comparison of best of generation 0 with ADFs (whose fitness is 101.03) with the correct impulse response function.

The result-producing branch of this individual calls its ADF0 three times. In one instance, ADF0 is called with the expression shown above in boldface, namely

```
(ADF0 -5.769)
```

as its argument. Second, ADF0 is called with the underlined expression

<u>(ADF0 (+ **(ADF0 -5.769)** (- (% T T) (IFLTE 6.518 T 3.851 -0.087))))</u>

as its argument. The first call to ADF0 is embedded inside this second call. Third, ADF0 is called with just T as its argument (via the underlined expression near the end of the result-producing branch).

The defined function ADF0 can be simplified to

$$
\begin{cases}
2.12338(\arg 0 - e^t) & \text{if } \dfrac{t}{\arg 0} \geq 0.00718 \\[2em]
2.12338(\arg 0 + t - e^t) & \text{otherwise}
\end{cases}
$$

By generation 15, the fitness of the best-of-generation program improves to 43.47. This individual has 36 points, calls its particular ADF0 twice, and is shown below:

```
(progn (defun ADF0 (ARG0)
          (values (% (- 7.732 ARG0)
                     (* (IFLTE -5.295 -3.354 T 1.567)
                        (EXPP (* T -5.788))))))
       (values (% (IFLTE (% T 1.364) (% (- T 6.653) (% T T))
                     (ADF0 T) (% -2.421 (ADF0 T)))
                  (% T 1.364)))).
```

The result-producing branch of this program is equivalent to

$$
\begin{cases}
\dfrac{-3.0222}{adf(t)t} & \text{if } t < 25 \\[2em]
\dfrac{1.364 \; adf(t)}{t} & \text{otherwise.}
\end{cases}
$$

Since the defined function ADF0 is called with the argument T in both instances, it simplifies to

$$\frac{7.732 - t}{te^{-5.788t}}$$

thereby making the result-producing branch equivalent to

$$\begin{cases} \dfrac{-3.0222e^{-5.788t}}{7.732 - t} & \text{if } t < 25 \\[3ex] \dfrac{7.732 - t}{0.733te^{-5.788t}} & \text{otherwise.} \end{cases}$$

Figure 11.15 compares the genetically produced best-of-generation impulse response function from generation 15 and the correct impulse response. As can be seen, this individual has a small negative hump approximately where the correct impulse response has a large negative hump, but otherwise bears little resemblance to the correct impulse response function.

Figure 11.16 shows that, as we proceed from generation to generation, the standardized fitness of the best-of-generation program tends to improve progressively.

By generation 50, the best-of-generation program shown below has 81 points, calls its ADF0 twice, and has a fitness value of 11.38 (i.e., an average squared error of only about 0.19 per fitness case) :

```
(progn (defun ADF0 (ARG0)
          (values (% (- 6.511 T) (* (% (% (% (+ T ARG0) (- 5.141
             -3.671)) (- 6.511 0.421)) (* (IFLTE -5.295 -3.354 T
             1.567) (EXPP (* T -5.788)))) (EXPP (* T -5.788)))))))
       (values (% (IFLTE (% (- T 6.653) (% T (- T 6.653))) (% T
          1.364) (IFLTE (% T 1.364) (% (- T 6.653) (% T T)) 1.364
          (% -2.421 (ADF0 T))) (% -2.421 (ADF0 T))) (% (- T
          6.653) (% T (% (% T 1.364) (% T (% T 1.364))))))))).
```

Since both calls to the defined function ADF0 are with the argument T, ADF0 simplifies to

$$\begin{cases} 1.0 & \text{if } t \geq 15 \\ 6.511 & \text{if } t = 0 \\ 174.707 - 26.8328t & \text{otherwise.} \end{cases}$$

The result-producing branch is equivalent to

$$\begin{cases} \dfrac{2.5377}{t - 6.653} & \text{if } 25 < t < 47 \\[3ex] \dfrac{-4.5042}{adf(t)[t - 6.653]} & \text{otherwise.} \end{cases}$$

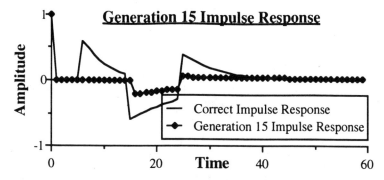

Figure 11.15 Comparison of the best of generation 15 with ADFs (whose fitness is 98.42) with the correct impulse response function.

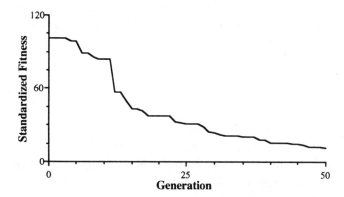

Figure 11.16 Fitness of best-of-generation program with ADFs.

Figure 11.17 compares the genetically produced best-of-generation impulse response function from generation 50 and the correct impulse response. As can be seen, the two curves are substantially similar.

The performance of the genetically produced best-of-generation impulse response functions from generations 0, 15, and 50 can be appreciated by examining the response of the system to the square input.

Figure 11.18 compares the plant response (which is the same in all three panels of the figure) to the square input and the response to the square input using the best-of-generation impulse response functions from generations 0, 15, and 50. As can be seen in the first and second panels of this figure, the performance of the best-of-generation programs from generations 0 and 15 is not very good, although generation 15 is considerably better than generation 0. However, as can be seen in the third panel of this figure, the performance of the best of generation 50 is close to the plant response (the total squared error being only 11.38 over the 60 fitness cases).

The number of hits improves from 14 for the best-of-generation program of generation 0, to 26 for generation 15, and to 41 for generation 50.

The ability of the genetically evolved impulse response function to generalize can be demonstrated by considering the same four additional forcing

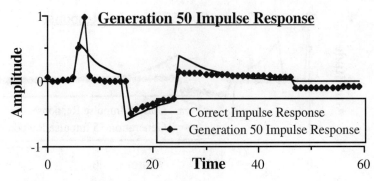

Figure 11.17 Comparison of the best of generation 50 with ADFs (whose fitness is 11.38) with the correct impulse response function.

functions to the system – the ramp input, the unit-step input, the shorter unit-square input, and the noise signal. Note that since we are operating in discrete time, there is no generalization of the system in the time domain. That is, there is no need to simulate the system with a finer temporal granularity.

Figure 11.19 shows the plant response to the ramp input and the response to the ramp input using the best-of-generation programs from generations 0, 15, and 50. As can be seen, the performance of the best of generation 50 is close to the plant response for the ramp input (the total squared error being only 6.38 over the 60 fitness cases).

Figure 11.20 compares the plant response to the step input and the response to the step input using the best-of-generation programs from generations 0, 15, and 50. As can be seen, the performance of the best of generation 50 is also close to the plant response for the unit-step input (the total squared error being only 19.86 over the 60 fitness cases).

Figure 11.21 compares the plant response to the short unit-square input and the response to the short unit-square input using the best-of-generation programs from generations 0, 15, and 50. The performance of the best of generation 50 is also close to the plant response for the short unit-square (the total squared error being only 12.59 over the 60 fitness cases).

Figure 11.22 compares the plant response to the noise signal (figure 11.11) and the response to this noise signal using the best-of-generation programs from generations 0, 15, and 50. As can be seen, the performance of the best of generation 50 is also close to the plant response for the noise signal (the total squared error being only 6.40 over the 60 fitness cases). The total square error is 17.17 for generation 0 and 10.56 for generation 15.

The hits histogram is a useful monitoring tool for visualizing the progressive learning of the population as a whole during a particular run. The horizontal axis of the hits histogram represents the number of hits (0 to 60) while the vertical axis represents the number of individuals in the population (0 to 4,000) scoring that number of hits.

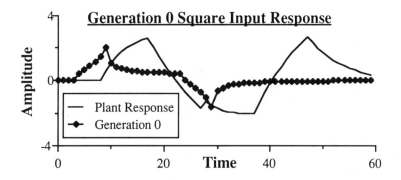

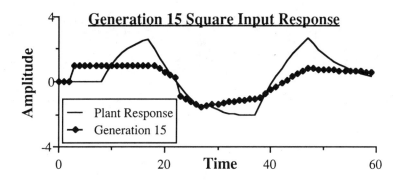

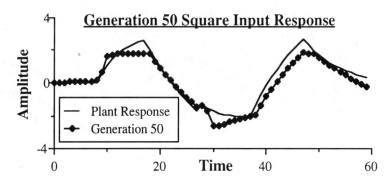

Figure 11.18 Response of the best-of-generation programs from generations 0, 15, and 50 to the square input with ADFs.

Finding an Impulse Response Function

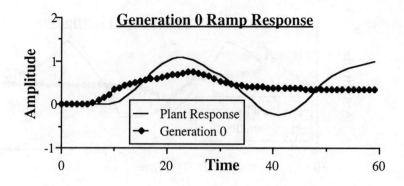

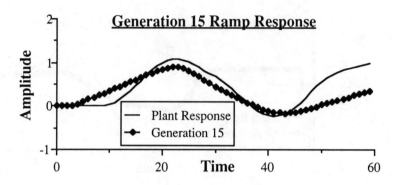

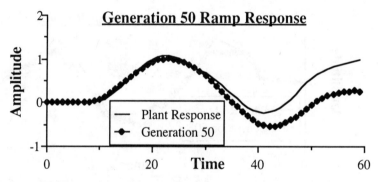

Figure 11.19 Response of the best-of-generation programs from generations 0, 15, and 50 to the ramp input with ADFs.

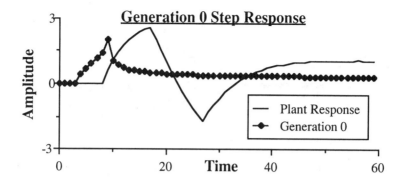

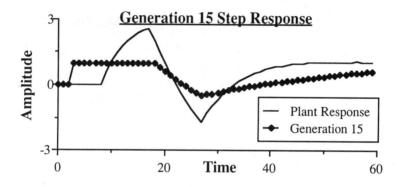

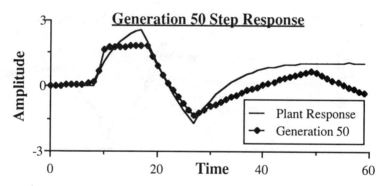

Figure 11.20   Response of the best-of-generation programs from generations 0, 15, and 50 to the unit-step input with ADFs.

Finding an Impulse Response Function

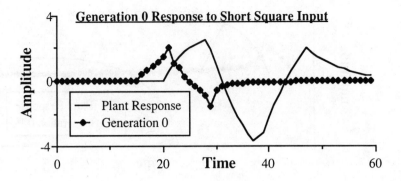

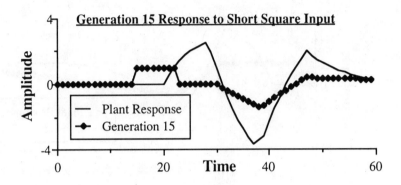

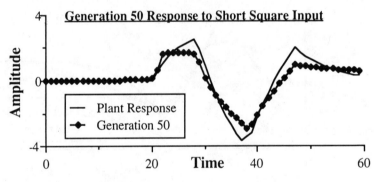

Figure 11.21 Response of the best-of-generation programs from generations 0, 15, and 50 to the short unit-square input with ADFs.

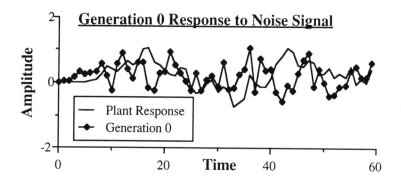

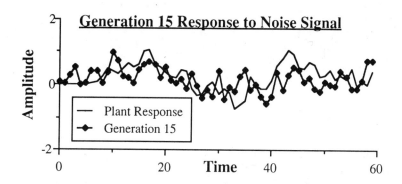

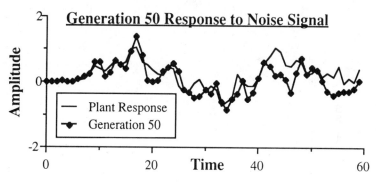

Figure 11.22 Response of the best-of-generation programs from generations 0, 15, and 50 to the noise signal with ADFs.

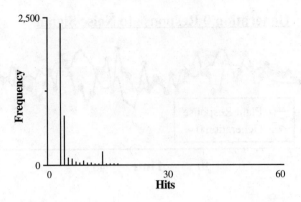

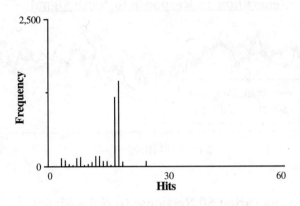

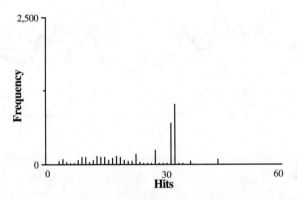

Figure 11.23 Hits histograms for generations 0, 15, and 50 of the impulse-response problem with ADFs.

Figure 11.23 shows the hits histograms for generations 0, 15, and 50 of this run.

11.7 GENEALOGICAL AUDIT TRAIL WITH ADFs

The creative role of crossover is illustrated by an examination of the genealogical audit trail for the best-of-generation program for generations 15 and 50 of this run. As it happens, the fitness of the best-of-generation program improves sharply between generations 14 and 15 and between generations 49 and 50. Specifically, the fitness of the best-of-generation program is 49.96 for generation 14 and 43.47 for generation 15 and it is 12.09 for generation 49 and 11.38 for generation 50. The crossover producing the best-of-generation program for generation 15 (involving two parents from generation 14) occurs in the result-producing branch. Moreover, the crossover producing the best-of-generation program for generation 50 (involving two parents from generation 49) occurs in the function-defining branch.

11.7.1 Crossover in the Result-producing Branch

As previously mentioned, the best of generation 15 has a fitness of 43.47, calls its ADF0 twice, and is shown below:

```
(progn (defun ADF0 (ARG0)
           (% (- 7.732 ARG0)
             (* (IFLTE -5.295 -3.354 T 1.567)
                (EXPP (* T -5.788)))))
         (values (% (IFLTE (% T 1.364) (% (- T 6.653) (% T T))
                   (ADF0 T) (% -2.421 (ADF0 T)))
                 (% T 1.364)))).
```

The best of generation 15 is one of the offspring resulting from a crossover involving the result-producing branch of the seventh best individual from generation 14 (which we will call "parent A" for the duration of this discussion of generation 14) and 297th-best individual from generation 14 (which we will call "parent B").

Parent A from generation 14 has 40 points, has a fitness value of 57.20 (i.e., not the best of its generation), scores 25 hits, has two calls to its ADF0, and is shown below:

```
(progn (defun ADF0 (ARG0)
           (values (% (- 7.732 ARG0)
                     (* (IFLTE -5.295 -3.354 T 1.567)
                        (EXPP (* T -5.788))))))
         (values (% (IFLTE (% T 1.364) (% (- T 6.653) (% T T))
                   (ADF T) (% -2.421 (ADF T)))
                 (% (- T 6.653) (% T T))))).
```

Parent B from generation 14 has 37 points, has a fitness value of 83.74, scores 18 hits, calls its ADF0 twice, and is shown below:

```
(progn (defun ADF0 (ARG0)
          (values (EXPP (- T ARG0))))
        (values (% (IFLTE (% T 1.364) (% (- T 6.653) (% T T))
                   (% T T)
                   (IFLTE (% T 1.364) (EXPP -2.113)
                      -2.421 (% -2.421 T)))
                (% (- T 6.653) (% T T)))))).
```

As previously mentioned, the name ADF0 refers to the automatically defined function defined within the particular individual program involved (i.e., parent A, parent B, and the offspring in generation 15).

Figure 11.24 compares parents 1 and 2 with the correct impulse response for the system as a function of t. As can be seen, parent A differs significantly from the correct impulse response between time steps 6 and 16. However, parent A resembles the correct impulse response in that it is zero between times 1 and 6, has a negative hump (albeit smaller) between times 17 and 24, has a positive hump (albeit very much smaller) between times 25 and 40, and is near zero after time 40.

The crossover points within parents 1 and 2 from generation 14 are both in the result-producing branches. The best of generation 15 consists of all of parent A from generation 14 except for its underlined portion. The crossover operation inserts the underlined portion of parent B into parent A (at the underlined location within parent A) in order to create the best of generation 15. Specifically, parent A from generation 14 contains the expression

```
(% (- T 6.653) (% T T))
```

in its result-producing branch. This expression is equivalent to

$t - 6.653$.

However, the best of generation 15 contains the expression

```
(% T 1.364)
```

which is equivalent to

$$\frac{t}{1.364}.$$

Both of these expressions represent straight lines. Moreover, the two expressions have somewhat similar slopes (1.00 and 0.73, respectively) and somewhat similar y-intercepts (– 6.653 and zero, respectively). When these expressions appear in a denominator, they are very similar for large values of t. The expression from parent B ends up in the denominator of the offspring best-of-generation program of generation 15 and it replaces the expression from parent A (which is in the denominator of parent A).

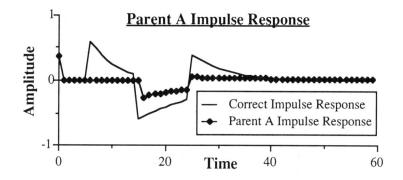

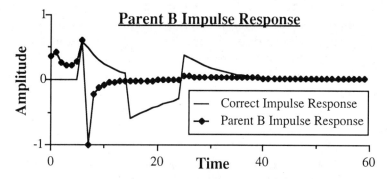

Figure 11.24 Correct impulse response function compared to the impulse response functions for parents A and B from generation 14 with ADFs.

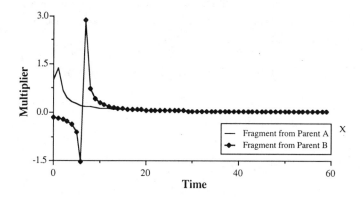

Figure 11.25 Comparison of expressions from parents A and B from generation 14 with ADFs.

Finding an Impulse Response Function

Figure 11.25 shows the reciprocals of both of these linear expressions as a function of *t*. The curves represent the expressions from parents A and B from generation 14. As can be seen, for larger values of *t*, these two curves are virtually identical, whereas, for small values of *t*, they differ substantially. Note that the value of the curve for parent A at time 0 is the consequence of our definition of the protected division function %.

The first two panels of figure 11.26 show the square input responses as a function of *t* for parents A and B from generation 14. As can be seen, both parents A and B are reasonably similar to the plant's response (representing the actual impulse response of the system) after about time 20. However, parent A from generation 14 differs considerably from the plant response between about time 10 and time 20, while parent B from generation 14 is much more similar to the plant response during the same period of time. The third panel of this figure shows that, after the crossover which created the best-of-generation program for generation 15, the square input response for those early times is much closer to the plant response than in generation 14.

In other words, the effect of the crossover that created the best of generation 15 from the two parents from generation 14 is to improve performance for a portion of the time domain. The difference between these two parents is sufficient to cause their offspring in generation 15 to have a fitness of 43.47 whereas parent A has a fitness of 57.20 and parent B has a fitness of 83.74. We have observed similar "case handling" behavior by the crossover operation in many other problems, including the Boolean 11-multiplexer problem in *Genetic Programming* (subsection 7.4.1) and in the videotape (Koza and Rice 1992a). That is, crossover recombines parts of the structures of the parents so as to improve fitness.

11.7.2 Crossover in the Function-Defining Branch

As previously mentioned, the best of generation 50 calls its ADF0 twice, has a fitness value of 11.38, and is

```
(progn (defun ADF0 (ARG0)
          (values (% (- 6.511 T) (* (% (% (% (+ T ARG0) (- 5.141
            -3.671)) (- 6.511 0.421)) (* (IFLTE -5.295 -3.354 T
            1.567) (EXPP (* T -5.788))))) (EXPP (* T -5.788))))))
       (values (% (IFLTE (% (- T 6.653) (% T (- T 6.653))) (% T
          1.364) (IFLTE (% T 1.364) (% (- T 6.653) (% T T)) 1.364
          (% -2.421 (ADF0 T))) (% -2.421 (ADF0 T))) (% (- T
          6.653) (% T (% (% T 1.364) (% T (% T 1.364))))))))).
```

This individual is one of the offspring resulting from a crossover involving the function-defining branches of the best of generation 49 (which we will call "parent C" for the duration of this discussion of generation 49) and 85th-best individual from generation 49 (which we will call "parent D").

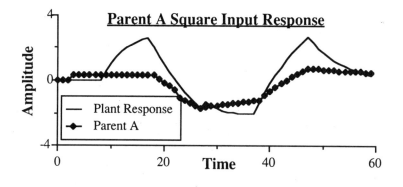

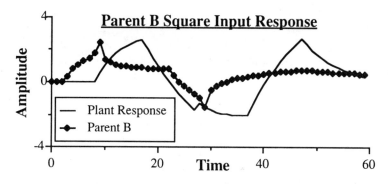

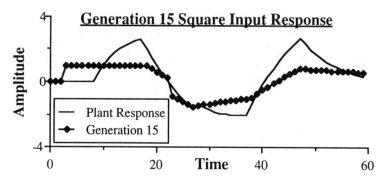

Figure 11.26 Correct square input response function compared to the square input response functions for parents A and B from generation 14 and for the best of generation 15 with ADFs.

Parent C from generation 49 has 107 points and a fitness value of 12.09 (which happens to be tied with the fitness of the best of generation 49). It scores 37 hits, calls its ADF0 twice, and is shown below:

```
(progn (defun ADF0 (ARG0)
          (values (% (- 6.511 T) (* (% (% (% (+ T ARG0) (- 5.141
              -3.671)) (IFLTE (- 6.511 (IFLTE T T T ARG0))
              (IFLTE (% T T) (* T ARG0) ARG0 (* T ARG0))
              (IFLTE T T  ARG0 ARG0) (IFLTE -5.295 -3.354 T
              1.567))) (* (IFLTE -5.295 -3.354 T 1.567) (EXPP (*
              T -5.788)))) (EXPP (* T -5.788))))))
          (values (% (IFLTE (% (- T 6.653) (% T (- T 6.653))) (% T
              1.364) (IFLTE (% T 1.364) (% (- T 6.653) (% T T)) 1.364
              (% -2.421 (ADF0 T))) (% -2.421 (ADF0 T))) (% (- T 6.653)
              (% T (% (% T 1.364) (% T (% T 1.364)))))))))).
```

Parent D from generation 49 has 168 points, has a fitness value of 14.47, scores 28 hits, calls its ADF0 once, and is shown below:

```
(progn (defun ADF0 (ARG0)
          (values (% (- 6.511 T) (* (% (% (% (+ T ARG0) (- 5.141
              -3.671)) (IFLTE (- 6.511 (IFLTE T T T ARG0)) (IFLTE
              (- 6.511 0.421) (* T ARG0) ARG0 (* T -5.788))
              (IFLTE T T ARG0 ARG0) (- ARG0 T))) (* (IFLTE -5.295
              (% (% -9.522 0.421) (IFLTE (IFLTE T T T ARG0) (IFLTE
              (IFLTE T ARG0 T ARG0) (* T ARG0) (IFLTE (IFLTE T T
              -3.671 ARG0) (+ (IFLTE T T ARG0 ARG0) (* T ARG0))
              (IFLTE T T ARG0 ARG0) (- 6.511 T)) (* (- T ARG0)
              (IFLTE T T ARG0 ARG0))) (IFLTE T T ARG0 ARG0) (-
              6.511 T))) T 1.567) (EXPP (* T -5.788)))) (EXPP (* T
              -5.788))))))
          (values (% (IFLTE (% T 1.364) (% (- T 6.653) (% T T))
              (IFLTE (% T 1.364) (% (- T 6.653) (% T T)) (% T (% (%
              (- T 6.653) (% T T)) (% T (% T 1.364)))) (- T 6.653))
              (% -2.421 (ADF0 T))) (% (- T 6.653) (% T (% T
              1.364)))))).
```

The first two panels of figure 11.27 compare parents C and D from generation 49 with the correct impulse response for this system as a function of *t*. Since both parents C and D are high ranking individuals from an advanced generation of a successful run, these two individuals are reasonably similar to the correct impulse response of the system. Nonetheless, both parents C and D from generation 49 differ from each other and from the correct impulse response. The third panel of this figure shows that, after the crossover that created the best-of-generation program for generation 50, the square input response for those early times is substantially closer to the plant response than in generation 49.

The crossover points within parents C and D from generation 49 are both in the function-defining branches. As it happens, both of the two calls to ADF0 in the result-producing branch of the best of generation 50,

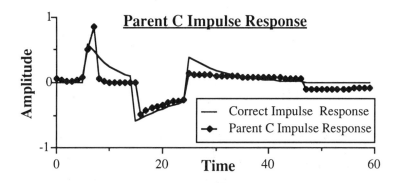

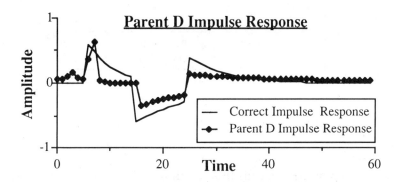

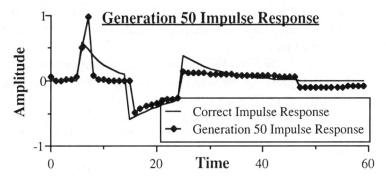

Figure 11.27 Correct impulse response function compared to the impulse response functions for parents C and D from generation 49 and for the best of generation 50 with ADFs.

Finding an Impulse Response Function

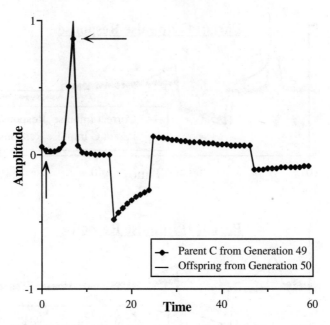

Figure 11.28 Superimposition of the impulse reponse of parent C from generation 49 onto the best-of-generation impulse response of generation 50.

both of the two calls to ADF0 in the result-producing branch of parent C from generation 49, and the one call to ADF0 in the result-producing branch of parent D from generation 49 all use just T as their arguments. Because of this, we are able to visualize the behavior of all three of the function-defining branches.

Figure 11.28 provides another visualization of the effect of crossover by superimposing the impulse response of parent C from generation 49 onto the impulse response of the best of generation 50. The horizontal arrow near the top of the figure and the vertical arrow near the negative vertical axis of the figure highlight the slight differences between the two curves.

Figure 11.29 shows the difference between the two curves. As can be seen, there is a noticeable difference at $t = 1$ and $t = 7$. Between $t = 16$ and $t = 60$, the difference is 0.

Figure 11.30 shows the behavior of the function-defining branches of both parents C and D of generation 49 as a function of t (ADF0 being called with an argument of T for these two parents).

The best of generation 50 consists of all of parent C from generation 49 except for its underlined portion. The crossover operation inserts the underlined portion of parent D into parent C, instead of the underlined portion of parent C, in order to create the best of generation 50. The underlined portion of parent D is the small subexpression

```
(- 6.511 0.421)
```

which is equivalent to the numerical constant value 6.090.

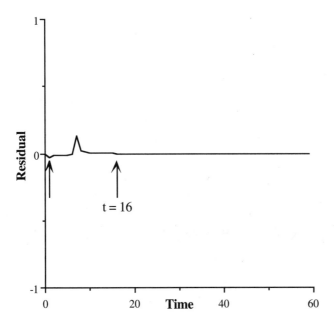

Figure 11.29 Difference between parent C of generation 49 and the best of generation 50.

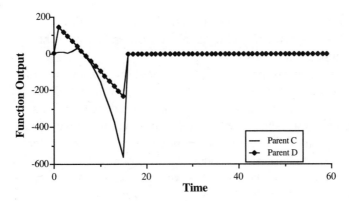

Figure 11.30 Behavior of the function-defining branches of parents C and D from generation 49 when the argument to ADF0 is T.

The underlined portion of parent C (which is replaced to create the best-of-generation program for generation 50) consists of

```
(IFLTE (- 6.511 (IFLTE T T T ARG0))
       (IFLTE (% T T) (* T ARG0) ARG0 (* T ARG0))
       (IFLTE T T ARG0 ARG0)
       (IFLTE -5.295 -3.354 T 1.567))).
```

When ARG0 is T, this entire expressions reduces to merely T.

Thus, the effect of the crossover in the function-defining branches of these two parents is to exchange a numerical constant for the variable T in parent C. The function-defining branch of the best of generation 50 then reduces to just

Finding an Impulse Response Function

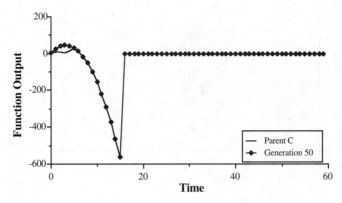

Figure 11.31 Behavior of the function-defining branches of parent C from generation 49 and the best of generation 50 when the argument to ADF0 is T.

```
(% (- 6.511 T)
   (* (% (% (% (+ T ARG0) (- 5.141 -3.671))
          6.090)
      (* (IFLTE -5.295 -3.354 T 1.567) (EXPP (* T -5.788))))
   (EXPP (* T -5.788))))).
```

Figure 11.31 shows the behavior of the function-defining branch of parent C from generation 49 and the function-defining branch of the best of generation 50 as a function of t. As can be seen, the effect of this change is a small change for the early time steps.

The first two panels of figure 11.32 show the square input responses as a function of t for parents C and D from generation 49. Parents C and D differ from each other and from the plant's square input response. The third panel of this figure shows that, after the crossover that created the best-of-generation program for generation 50, the square input response for those early times is closer to the plant response than in generation 49.

The difference between these two parents was sufficient to cause their offspring in generation 50 to have a fitness of 11.38 while parent C has a fitness of 12.09 and parent D has a fitness of 14.47.

11.8 RESULTS OF SERIES OF RUNS WITH ADFs

The average structural complexity, $\overline{S}_{with}$, of the best-of-run programs from 13 successful runs (out of 18 runs) of the impulse-response problem is 157.7 points with automatically defined functions.

Automatically defined functions facilitate the discovery of an impulse response function by reducing the amount of computational effort required to solve the problem.

Figure 11.33 presents the performance curves based on the 18 runs of the impulse-response problem with automatically defined functions. The cumulative probability of success, $P(M,i)$, is 72% by generations 47 and 50. The two numbers in the oval indicate that if this problem is run through to

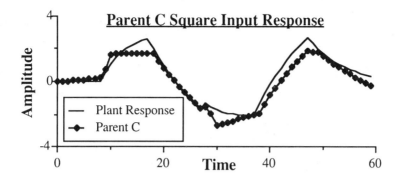

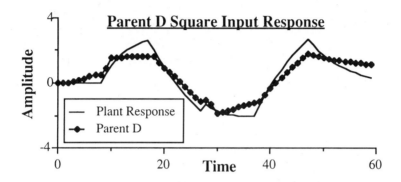

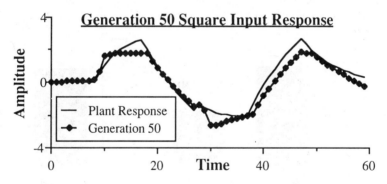

Figure 11.32 Correct square input response function compared with the square input response functions for parents C and D from generation 49 and for the best of generation 50 with ADFs.

With Defined Functions

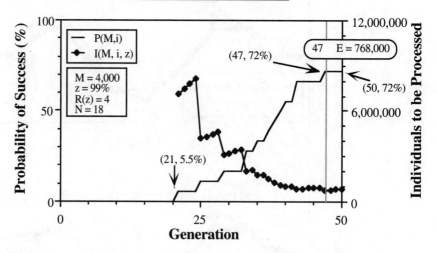

Figure 11.33 Performance curves for the impulse-response problem showing that E_{with} = 768,000 with ADFs.

Table 11.3 Comparison table for the impulse-response problem.

	Without ADFs	With ADFs
Average structural complexity $\bar{S}$	285.9	157.7
Computional effort E	1,120,000	768,000

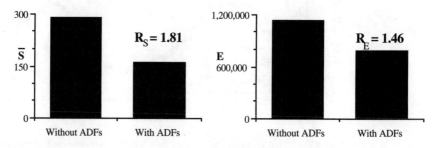

Figure 11.34 Summary graphs for the impulse-response problem.

generation 47, processing a total of $E_{with} = 768{,}000$ individuals (i.e., $4{,}000 \times 48$ generations $\times 4$ runs) is sufficient to yield a satisfactory result for this problem with 99% probability.

11.9   SUMMARY

We have demonstrated the use of genetic programming, both with and without automatically defined functions, to evolve a good approximation, in symbolic form, to an impulse response function for an unknown time-invariant linear system using only the observed discrete-time response of the unknown system to a unit-square input.

Table 11.3 compares the average structural complexity, $\overline{S}_{without}$ and $\overline{S}_{with}$, and the computational effort, $E_{without}$ and E_{with}, for the impulse-response problem.

Figure 11.34 summarizes the information in this comparison table and shows a structural complexity ratio, R_S, of 1.81 and an efficiency ratio, R_E, of 1.46.

12 Artificial Ant on the San Mateo Trail

The artificial ant problem in this chapter shows that automatically defined functions can be beneficial when the problem environment contains only a modest amount of regularity. The amount of regularity present in this problem environment is not as great as that of the Boolean even-parity problem (chapter 6), the lawnmower problem (chapter 8), or the bumblebee problem (chapter 9). The regularity that is potentially exploitable by a reusable subprogram in this problem consists of a common inspecting motion that can be undertaken in only a few directions.

In addition, in this problem all the information that is transmitted to the subprograms is by means of side effects on the state of a system.

12.1 THE PROBLEM

In this problem, the goal is to find a program for controlling the movement of an artificial ant so as to find all of the food lying along a series of irregular trails on a two-dimensional toroidal grid.

The ant's sensory ability is limited to sensing the presence or absence of food in the single square of the grid that the ant is currently facing. The ant's potential actions are limited to turning right, turning left, and moving forward one square.

The *San Mateo trail* consists of nine parts, each made up of a square 13-by-13 grid containing different discontinuities in the sequence of food. The discontinuities include single and double gaps, corners where a single piece of food is missing, corners where there are two pieces of food that are missing in the trail's current direction, and corners where there are two pieces of food that are missing to the left or to the right of the current direction of the trail.

The original version of this problem was developed and solved by Jefferson et al. 1991 and Collins and Jefferson 1991 using both a finite-state automaton and a neural network for the John Muir trail (*Genetic Programming*, subsection 3.3.2). A solution to this original version of the problem using genetic programming for the Santa Fe trail is described in *Genetic Programming* (section 7.2). In addition, this original version of the problem was solved using genetic programming on the more difficult Los Altos Hills trail as described in *Genetic Programming* (section 7.2). This more difficult trail has some discontinuities in which the food is displaced by two squares to the left or to the right of the trail's current direction.

The San Mateo trail presented here is more difficult than the Los Altos Hills trail in that it has discontinuities in which the food is displaced by two squares to the left or right of the trail's current direction and then further displaced by one square forward. In the Santa Fe trail and the Los Altos Hills trail, all the different types of discontinuities appeared in a single trail, so the problem had only one fitness case. We precluded trivial tessellating trajectories from achieving high scores on the Los Altos Hills trail by embedding the food in a large array of 10,000 squares. Unfortunately, this large array necessitated running each simulation for a large number of time steps (3,000). This, in turn, consumed a large amount of computer time. In order to solve this more difficult version of the problem within the available amount of computer time, we divided the trail into parts (fitness cases) and distributed the different types of discontinuities among the parts. Trivial tessellating trajectories could then be precluded with disproportionately fewer empty squares. To further save computer time, we did not make the 13-by-13 grid toroidal. Instead, the border of each 13-by-13 part of the trail is electrified so as to immediately terminate the current fitness case should ant ever wander into the electric fence.

Figure 12.1 shows the nine parts of the San Mateo trail. Food is represented by solid black squares. The starting point of the ant within each part is in the middle of the top row (denoted by a small circle). The ant faces south at the start of each fitness case. There are 96 pieces of food in the trail as a whole. For convenience of illustration, gaps in the trail are indicated by gray squares; however, the ant cannot distinguish between gray squares and white squares. In the first of the nine parts of the trail, the only discontinuities in the trail are one single gap and one double gap. In the second part, there are two single gaps at corners, one double gap at a corner, and two additional single gaps. The third part contains an instance of the most difficult discontinuity, namely where food is missing in the current direction of the trail, where there is no food to the left (or right) of the current direction of the trail, and where the trail resumes two squares to the left (or right). Although this figure gives us global knowledge of the trail, the ant's sensors give it only a very narrow local view of its world. Since there is no food on the gray squares, the ant need not actually visit them.

12.2 PREPARATORY STEPS WITHOUT ADFs

RIGHT, LEFT, and MOVE are operators that take no explicit arguments but have side effects on the state of the system.

RIGHT changes the orientation of the ant by turning the ant to the right (clockwise) by 90° (without moving the ant).

LEFT similarly changes the orientation of the ant to the left (counter-clockwise).

MOVE moves the ant forward in the direction it is currently facing. When an ant moves into a square, it eats the food, if any, in that square (thereby removing that piece of food from that square). If there is no food, execution of the program continues; however, if there is food, the eating of the food throws the execution of the program back to its beginning. Thus, MOVE has side effects on both the state of the ant and the state of the trail.

In accordance with our usual convention in this book, zero-argument side-effecting functions are treated as terminals. Thus, the terminal set, T, for this problem consists of

$T = \{$ (RIGHT), (LEFT), (MOVE) $\}$.

The function set, F, consists of

$F = \{$ IF-FOOD-AHEAD, PROGN $\}$

with an argument map of

$\{2, 2\}$.

IF-FOOD-AHEAD permits the ant to sense the single adjacent square in the direction the ant is currently facing. This conditional branching operator takes two arguments and executes the first argument if (and only if) there is currently food in the single adjacent square in the direction the ant is currently facing, and executes the second argument if (and only if) there is currently no food in that square. This conditional branching operator is implemented in LISP as a macro as follows:

```
1 #+TI (setf sys:inhibit-displacing-flag t)
2 (defmacro if-food-ahead (then-argument else-argument)
3  '(if *food-directly-in-front-of-ant-p*
4      (eval ',then-argument)
5      (eval ',else-argument))).
```

As can be seen on line 2 of this macro definition, two arguments are supplied to the macro: the then-argument and the else-argument. On line 3 the first argument of the if operator is the predicate *food-directly-in-front-of-ant-p*, which evaluates to T if uneaten food is present directly in front of the ant, but which otherwise evaluates to NIL. This predicate acquires its value after a calculation involving the ant's current facing-direction and the current food status of the two-dimensional grid. If food is present, the if operator causes the evaluation of the then-argument on line 4, using the LISP evaluation function eval. If food is not present, the if operator causes the evaluation of the else-argument on line 5 using eval. Additional details are in *Genetic Programming* (subsection 6.1.1). Macros are similarly used to implement the IF-OBSTACLE in section 13.2, the IF-MINE operator in section 14.2, the IF operator in section 15.2, the IFLTE operator in section 18.5.1, and the IFLTZ operator in section 18.10.

The ant's goal is to eat as much food as possible from the nine parts of the San Mateo trail.

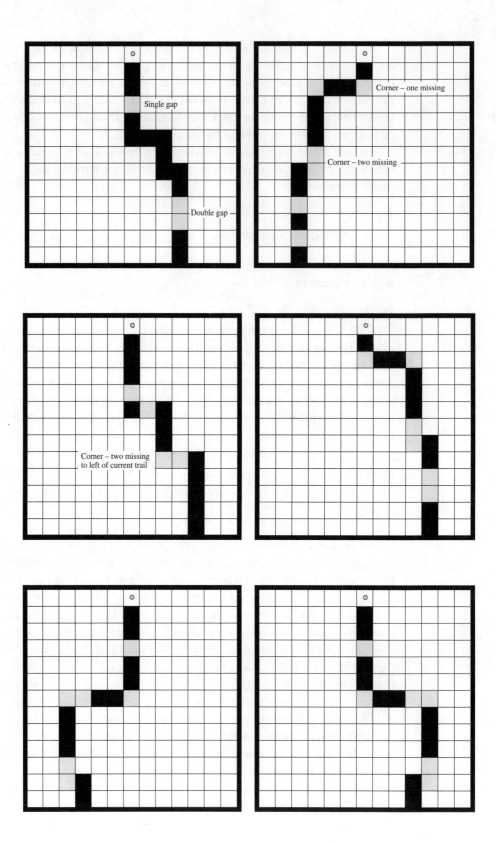

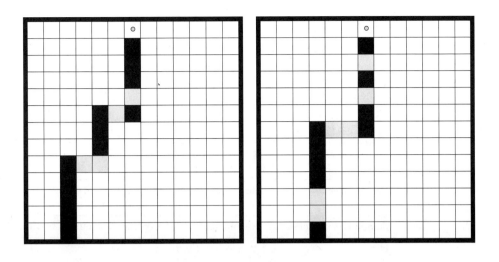

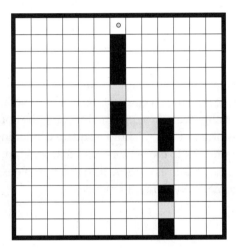

Figure 12.1 The nine parts of the San Mateo trail for the artificial ant problem.

The raw fitness of a particular program is the number of pieces of food (from 0 to 96) eaten over the nine parts of the trail. Only the total number of pieces of food accumulated over all nine fitness cases is available to genetic programming.

A loop causes repeated invocation of a program until either time runs out or the ant succeeds in eating all of the food in the current part of the trail. The movement of the ant is terminated on any particular part of the trail when the ant touches the electrified outer boundary of the 13-by-13 grid or when it has executed a total of 120 RIGHT or LEFT turns or 80 MOVEs for the current part of the trail. The amount of food eaten up to the time of termination on each part of the trail is accumulated over the nine parts of the trail.

Standardized fitness is the total amount of available food (i.e., 96) minus the raw fitness.

Table 12.1 Tableau without ADFs for the artificial ant problem.

Objective:	Find a program to control an artificial ant so that it can find all 96 pieces of food located on the San Mateo trail.
Terminal set without ADFs:	`(RIGHT)`, `(LEFT)`, and `(MOVE)`.
Function set without ADFs:	`IF-FOOD-AHEAD` and `PROGN`.
Fitness cases:	9 fitness cases, each consisting of a 13-by-13 grid with food in some squares.
Raw fitness:	The sum, over the nine fitness cases, of the food eaten within the allowed amount of time for each fitness case.
Standardized fitness:	The total amount of food (i.e., 96) minus raw fitness.
Hits:	Same as raw fitness.
Wrapper:	None.
Parameters:	$M = 4{,}000$. $G = 51$.
Success predicate:	A program scores the maximum number of hits.

The version of the problem presented here differs from the earlier versions of this problem in that there are nine fitness cases (instead of one overall trail); in that the grid is bounded (rather than toroidal) and touching the boundary is lethal; and in that the execution of a MOVE onto a square containing food throws execution of a program back to the beginning of that program.

Table 12.1 summarizes the key features of the artificial ant problem for the San Mateo trail without automatically defined functions.

12.3 RESULTS WITHOUT ADFs

The following 95-point individual collecting 96 (out of 96) pieces of food emerged on generation 13 of one run:

```
(PROGN (IF-FOOD-AHEAD (PROGN (IF-FOOD-AHEAD (MOVE) (RIGHT))
(RIGHT)) (LEFT)) (IF-FOOD-AHEAD (IF-FOOD-AHEAD (IF-FOOD-AHEAD
(MOVE) (RIGHT)) (MOVE)) (PROGN (PROGN (MOVE) (RIGHT)) (PROGN
(IF-FOOD-AHEAD (IF-FOOD-AHEAD (PROGN (MOVE) (RIGHT)) (PROGN
(PROGN (IF-FOOD-AHEAD (IF-FOOD-AHEAD (LEFT) (LEFT)) (PROGN
(LEFT) (MOVE))) (PROGN (IF-FOOD-AHEAD (MOVE) (RIGHT)) (PROGN
(RIGHT) (LEFT)))) (PROGN (PROGN (PROGN (PROGN (LEFT) (MOVE))
(IF-FOOD-AHEAD (RIGHT) (LEFT))) (PROGN (IF-FOOD-AHEAD (LEFT)
(RIGHT)) (PROGN (LEFT) (LEFT)))) (IF-FOOD-AHEAD (PROGN (PROGN
(MOVE) (MOVE)) (IF-FOOD-AHEAD (MOVE) (MOVE))) (IF-FOOD-AHEAD
(MOVE) (MOVE)))))) (PROGN (PROGN (PROGN (PROGN (LEFT) (MOVE))
(IF-FOOD-AHEAD (RIGHT) (LEFT))) (PROGN (IF-FOOD-AHEAD (LEFT)
(RIGHT)) (PROGN (LEFT) (LEFT)))) (IF-FOOD-AHEAD (MOVE) (LEFT))))
(IF-FOOD-AHEAD (PROGN (MOVE) (MOVE)) (PROGN (PROGN (RIGHT)
(MOVE)) (MOVE)))))))).
```

Without Defined Functions

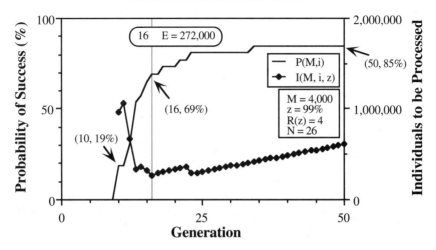

Figure 12.2 Performance curves for the artificial ant showing that $E_{without} = 272,000$ without ADFs.

The average structural complexity, $\bar{S}_{without}$, of solutions to the artificial ant problem over 22 successful runs (out of 26) is 90.9 points without automatically defined functions.

Figure 12.2 presents the performance curves based on the 26 runs of this problem without automatically defined functions. The cumulative probability of success, $P(M,i)$, is 69% by generation 16 and is 85% by generation 50. The two numbers in the oval indicate that if this problem is run through to generation 16, processing a total of $E_{without} = 272,000$ individuals (i.e., $4,000 \times 17$ generations $\times 4$ runs) is sufficient to yield a solution to this problem with 99% probability.

See also Koza 1993b.

12.4 PREPARATORY STEPS WITH ADFs

In applying genetic programming with automatically defined functions to the artificial ant problem, we decided that each individual overall program in the population would consist of one function-defining branch defining a zero-argument function called `ADF0` and one result-producing branch.

We first consider the function-defining branch.

The terminal set, $\mathcal{T}_{adf}$, for the zero-argument defined function `ADF0` consists of

$$\mathcal{T}_{adf} = \{ (\text{RIGHT}), (\text{LEFT}), (\text{MOVE}) \}.$$

The function set, $\mathcal{F}_{adf}$, for the zero-argument defined function `ADF0` is

$$\mathcal{F}_{adf} = \{ \text{IF-FOOD-AHEAD}, \text{PROGN} \}$$

with an argument map of

$$\{2, 2\}.$$

Table 12.2 Tableau with ADFs for the artificial ant problem.

Objective:	Find a program to control an artificial ant so that it can find all 96 pieces of food located on the San Mateo trail.
Architecture of the overall program with ADFs:	One result-producing branch and one zero-argument function-defining branch.
Parameters:	Branch typing.
Terminal set for the result-producing branch:	(RIGHT), (LEFT), and (MOVE).
Function set for the result-producing branch:	ADF0, IF-FOOD-AHEAD, and PROGN.
Terminal set for the function-defining branch ADF0:	(RIGHT), (LEFT), and (MOVE).
Function set for the function-defining branch ADF0:	IF-FOOD-AHEAD, and PROGN.

The body of ADF0 is a composition of primitive functions from the function set, $\mathcal{F}_{adf}$, and terminals from the terminal set, $\mathcal{T}_{adf}$.

We now consider the result-producing branch.

The terminal set, $\mathcal{T}_{rpb}$, for the result-producing branch is

$$\mathcal{T}_{rpb} = \{\,(\text{RIGHT}), (\text{LEFT}), (\text{MOVE})\,\}.$$

The function set, $\mathcal{F}_{rpb}$, for the result-producing branch is

$$\mathcal{F}_{rpb} = \{\text{ADF0}, \text{IF-FOOD-AHEAD}, \text{PROGN}\}$$

with an argument map of

$$\{0, 2, 2\}.$$

The result-producing branch is a composition of the functions from the function set, $\mathcal{F}_{rpb}$, and terminals from the terminal set, $\mathcal{T}_{rpb}$.

Table 12.2 summarizes the key features of the artificial ant problem for the San Mateo trail with automatically defined functions.

12.5 RESULTS WITH ADFs

In one run, about half (2,044 of the 4,000) of the individuals in generation 0 score 0 in their search for food over the nine parts of the San Mateo trail. Many of these individuals turn and look, but are immobile; others turn away from the trail and run into the electric fence without encountering any food. Another 20% (868) score 18 out of 96 because there are, over the nine parts of the trail, 18 pieces of food available to a program that merely moves south

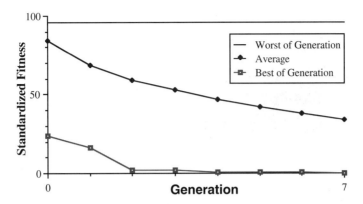

Figure 12.3 Fitness curves for the artificial ant problem with ADFs.

whenever food is present to the south. About 1% of the 4,000 individuals score between 54 and 72.

Figure 12.3 shows, by generation, the fitness of the best-of-generation program. As can be seen, the fitness of the best-of-generation program and the average fitness of the population as a whole both tend to improve (i.e., drop) from generation to generation.

Figure 12.4 shows the hits histograms for generations 0, 2, 5, and 7 of this run. The "slinky" left-to-right undulating movement of both the high point and the center of mass of these histograms reflects the improvement of the population as a whole.

Figure 12.5 shows the structural complexity curves for this run of the artificial ant problem with automatically defined functions. The figure shows, by generation, the structural complexity in the best-of-generation program and the average of the values of structural complexity for all the programs in the population.

In generation 7 of this run, the following 100%-correct solution to the artificial ant problem emerged:

```
(progn  (defun ADF0 ()
            (values (PROGN (IF-FOOD-AHEAD (IF-FOOD-AHEAD (MOVE)
            (RIGHT)) (PROGN (LEFT) (MOVE))) (PROGN (IF-FOOD-AHEAD
            (IF-FOOD-AHEAD (MOVE) (LEFT)) (PROGN (PROGN (RIGHT)
            (LEFT)) (PROGN (LEFT) (MOVE)))) (IF-FOOD-AHEAD (LEFT)
            (RIGHT))))
        (values (PROGN (PROGN (MOVE) (ADF0)) (PROGN (IF-FOOD-AHEAD
        (MOVE) (MOVE)) (PROGN (ADF0) (ADF0)))))).
```

In this program, ADF0 is invoked three times from the result-producing branch. The result-producing branch serves to reposition the ant just before the first and second invocations of ADF0.

Figure 12.6 shows the trajectory for the ninth fitness case of the ant for this run. In this figure (and the following figures in this section), the light lines represent movements initiated by the result-producing branch of the program; the heavy lines indicate movements initiated by the automatically

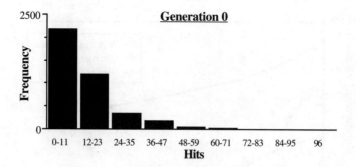

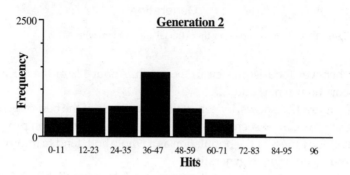

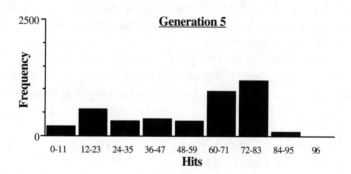

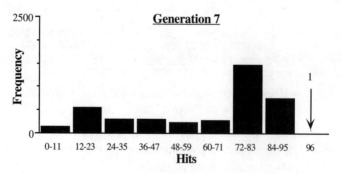

Figure 12.4 Hits histogram for the artificial ant problem with ADFs.

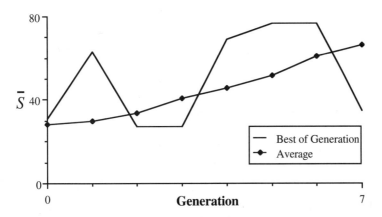

Figure 12.5 Structural complexity curves for the artificial ant problem with ADFs.

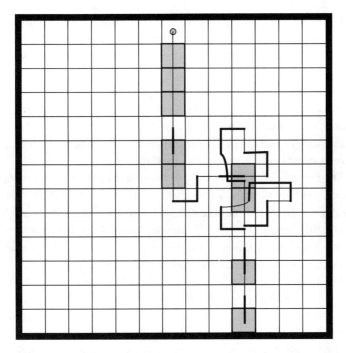

Figure 12.6 Trajectory of the artificial ant for the ninth fitness case of the best-of-run program from generation 7 with ADFs.

Artificial Ant on the San Mateo Trail

defined function ADF0. The figure is suggestive of the reuse of a semicircular counterclockwise inspecting motion.

The best-of-run individual from generation 7 of run 1 can be simplified to the following:

```
(progn (defun ADF0 ()
          (values (IF-FOOD-AHEAD
                     (MOVE)                                        ;a
                     (PROGN (LEFT) (MOVE)                          ;b
                        (IF-FOOD-AHEAD
                           (MOVE)                                  ;c
                           (PROGN (LEFT) (MOVE)                    ;d
                              (IF-FOOD-AHEAD (LEFT)
                                 (RIGHT))))))))))
       (values (PROGN (MOVE) (ADF0) (MOVE) (ADF0) (ADF0))))
    ;                   1      P      2      Q      R
```

Figure 12.7 shows the trajectory of the artificial ant executing this semicircular counterclockwise inspecting motion specified by the best-of-run individual from generation 7 of run 1. For simplicity, this figure shows only part of the 13-by-13 grid and contains food in only four squares. As usual, the ant starts at the circle in the top row.

Since the ant encounters food on each of its first four downward movements, evaluation of the program terminates upon execution of the first MOVE operation (labeled 1) in the result-producing branch. The four places on the trajectory where this occurs are also labeled 1.

The remainder of the trajectory shown in figure 12.7 represents three evaluations of the program. These three executions occur in the absence of any food. Each circle denotes the ant's exit from one invocation of ADF0. The two small, filled circles (labeled E) denote the ant's exit from the first and second of the three evaluations of the program. The large filled circle denotes the ant's exit from the third evaluation of the program.

The lines labeled 2 in figure 12.7 denote movements caused by the second MOVE operation of the result-producing branch.

Points in the figure labeled with capital letters (P, Q, or R) denote invocations of ADF0 by the result-producing branch.

All the bold lines in the figure denote movements caused by the MOVE operations on lines b and d of ADF0.

This solution is a hierarchical decomposition of the problem. Genetic programming discovered a decomposition of the overall problem into a reusable subroutine for performing an inspecting motion. Genetic programming simultaneously evolved the sequence of sensor tests, turns, and moves to implement this inspecting motion. Finally, genetic programming simultaneously evolved stage-setting sensor tests, turns, and moves and assembled the inspecting motions into a solution of the overall problem.

The above program for the artificial-ant problem illustrates two of the five ways itemized in chapter 3 in which the hierarchical problem-

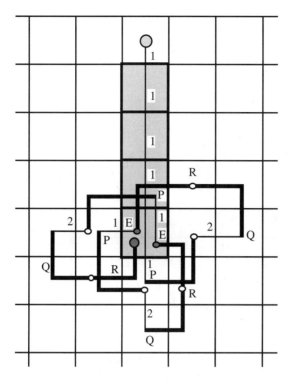

Figure 12.7 Trajectory of the artificial ant for the ninth fitness case of run 1, showing its semi-circular counterclockwise inspecting motion with ADFs.

solving approach can be beneficial: hierarchical decomposition and identical reuse.

Hierarchical decomposition is evident because the overall program for solving the problem consists of an automatically defined function, ADF0, as well as a result-producing branch.

In addition, the three times that the result-producing branch invokes ADF0 illustrate the identical reuse of the solution to a subproblem.

Of course, genetic programming produces a variety of different programs in different runs. For example, in a second successful run of this problem, all of the ant's actual movements are controlled by ADF0, as opposed to the result-producing branch. An examination shows that there are no MOVE operations in the result-producing branch of the 44-point program scoring 96 (out of 96) from generation 5 of run 2:

```
(progn (defun ADF0 ()
            (values (PROGN (PROGN (PROGN (PROGN (PROGN (MOVE)
            (MOVE)) (IF-FOOD-AHEAD (MOVE) (LEFT))) (PROGN (PROGN
            (IF-FOOD-AHEAD (IF-FOOD-AHEAD (MOVE) (RIGHT)) (IF-
            FOOD-AHEAD (MOVE) (LEFT))) (IF-FOOD-AHEAD (RIGHT)
            (PROGN (LEFT) (LEFT)))) (IF-FOOD-AHEAD (MOVE)
            (RIGHT)))) (PROGN (MOVE) (RIGHT))) (IF-FOOD-AHEAD
            (MOVE) (PROGN (RIGHT) (MOVE))))))))
```

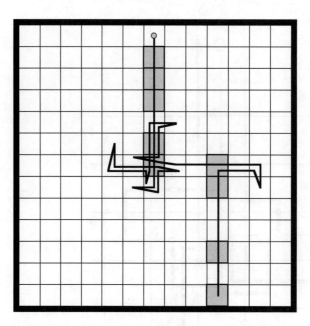

Figure 12.8 Trajectory of the artificial ant for the ninth fitness case of run 2, where all movements are controlled by ADF0.

```
(values (PROGN (PROGN (PROGN (ADF0) (LEFT)) (ADF0))
  (PROGN (RIGHT) (LEFT))))).
```

Figure 12.8 shows the trajectory for the ninth fitness case of the ant where all movements are controlled by `ADF0`. This entire trajectory is shown with a line.

In a third successful run, the following 34-point program scoring 96 (out of 96) emerged in generation 8:

```
(progn  (defun ADF0 ()
          (values (PROGN (PROGN (PROGN (IF-FOOD-AHEAD (MOVE)
            (LEFT)) (PROGN (MOVE) (IF-FOOD-AHEAD (MOVE) (LEFT))))
            (IF-FOOD-AHEAD (MOVE) (RIGHT))) (PROGN (IF-FOOD-AHEAD
            (MOVE) (RIGHT)) (RIGHT)))))
        (values (PROGN (IF-FOOD-AHEAD (MOVE) (LEFT)) (PROGN
          (PROGN (MOVE) (PROGN (ADF0) (MOVE))) (PROGN (PROGN
          (ADF0) (MOVE)) (MOVE)))))).
```

Figure 12.9 shows the trajectory for the ninth fitness case of the ant while it is under the control of this 34-point program from run 3. In this solution, the food is primarily eaten under the control of the result-producing branch (although the ant spends about half of its time under the control of the function-defining branch).

The average structural complexity, $\bar{S}_{with}$, of solutions to the artificial ant problem over 19 successful runs (out of 19 runs) is 71.7 points with automatically defined functions.

Figure 12.10 presents the performance curves based on the 19 runs of the artificial ant problem with automatically defined functions. The cumulative

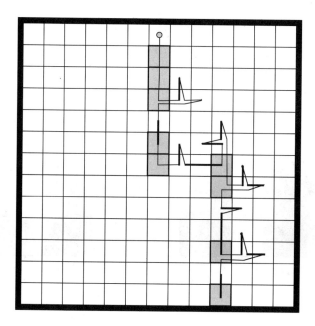

Figure 12.9 Trajectory of the artificial ant for the ninth fitness case of run 3, where movements are primarily controlled by the result-producing branch.

With Defined Functions

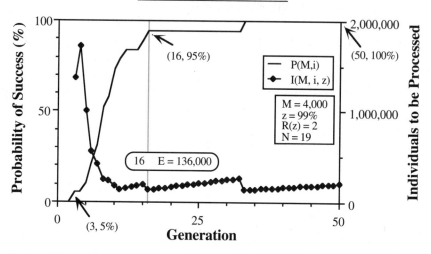

Figure 12.10 Performance curves for the artificial ant showing that $E_{with} = 136,000$ with ADFs.

Artificial Ant on the San Mateo Trail

Table 12.3 Comparison table for the artificial ant problem.

	Without ADFs	With ADFs
Average structural complexity $\bar{S}$	90.9	71.7
Computional effort E	272,000	136,000

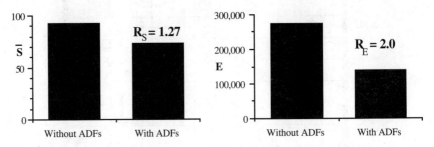

Figure 12.11 Summary graphs for the artificial ant problem.

probability of success, $P(M,i)$, is 95% by generation 16 and is 100% by generation 33. The two numbers in the oval indicate that if this problem is run through to generation 16, processing a total of $E_{with} = 136,000$ individuals (i.e., 4,000 × 17 generations × 2 runs) is sufficient to yield a solution to this problem with 99% probability.

12.6 SUMMARY

Table 12.3 compares the average structural complexity, $\bar{S}_{without}$ and $\bar{S}_{with}$, and the computational effort, $E_{without}$ and E_{with}, for the artificial ant problem with automatically defined functions and without them.

Figure 12.11 summarizes the information in this comparison table and shows a structural complexity ratio, R_S, of 1.27 and an efficiency ratio, R_E, of 2.00.

13 Obstacle-Avoiding Robot

As previously mentioned, one of our design considerations in creating the lawnmower problem was that it be amenable to scaling both in terms of the size of the grid and the complexity of the problem itself. Chapter 8 has already explored the scaling of the lawnmower problem along the axis representing lawn size. The obstacle-avoiding-robot problem considered in this chapter scales the lawnmower problem along the axis of problem complexity. The environment of this problem is more complicated in that obstacles disrupt the homogeneity of the grid and prevent the straightforward exploitation of the environment.

13.1 THE PROBLEM

In this problem, an autonomous mobile robot attempts to mop the floor in a room containing harmless but time-wasting obstacles (posts). The obstacles do not harm the robot, but every failed move or jump counts toward the overall limitation on the number of operations available for the task.

As was the case in the lawnmower problem, the state of the robot consists of its location in the room and the direction in which it is facing. Each square in the room is uniquely identified by a vector of integers modulo 8 of the form (i,j), where $0 \le i, j \le 7$. The robot starts at location $(4,4)$, facing north. The room is toroidal, so that whenever the robot moves off the edge of the room it reappears on the opposite side.

Six non-touching obstacles are randomly positioned in a room laid out on an 8-by-8 grid. Figure 13.1 shows two typical rooms. The origin $(0,0)$ is in the upper left corner. The numbering of the squares increases going down and going to the right.

The robot is capable of turning left, of moving forward one square in the direction in which it is currently facing, and of jumping by a specified displacement in the vertical and horizontal directions. Whenever the robot succeeds in moving onto a new square (by means of either a single move or a jump), it mops the location of the floor onto which it moves.

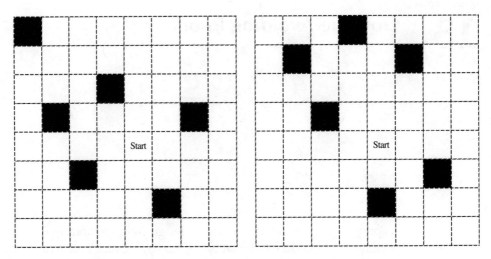

Figure 13.1 Two rooms, each with six posts, with the obstacle-avoiding robot in its starting location.

13.2 PREPARATORY STEPS WITHOUT ADFs

The operators for this problem are similar, but not identical, to the operators in the lawnmower problem.

The operator MOP takes no arguments and moves the robot in the direction it is currently facing and mops the location of the floor onto which it is moving. MOP does not change the orientation of the lawnmower. To ensure closure, MOP returns the vector value (0,0). When the MOP operator attempts to move the robot to a location occupied by an obstacle, the robot does not move; however, the attempted MOP counts toward the overall limit on the number of operations that may be executed in just the same way as a successful MOP does.

FROG is a one-argument operator that causes the robot to move relative to the direction it is currently facing by an amount specified by its vector argument. FROG does not change the orientation of the lawnmower. To ensure closure, FROG acts as the identity operator on its argument. If the FROG operator attempts to move the robot to a location occupied by an obstacle, the FROG fails in the same way as the MOP operator.

The operator LEFT takes no arguments and is identical to the LEFT operator of the lawnmower problem. It changes the orientation of the robot by turning the robot to the left by 90° (without moving it). To ensure closure, LEFT returns the vector value (0,0).

The two-argument IF-OBSTACLE conditional branching operator executes its first argument if an obstacle is immediately in front of the robot in the direction the robot is currently facing, but otherwise executes its second argument. This operator enables the robot to avoid time-wasting attempts to move to a location occupied by an obstacle. Since there are side-effecting functions in this problem, IF-OBSTACLE must be implemented as a macro as described in section 12.2.

V8A is the two-argument addition function for vectors of integers modulo 8 and is identical to the V8A function of the lawnmower problem.

The terminal set for this problem consists of the two side-effecting zero-argument operators and random vector constants modulo 8, $\mathfrak{R}_{v8}$.

$\mathcal{T} = \{ (\text{LEFT}), (\text{MOP}), \mathfrak{R}_{v8} \}.$

The function set consists of

$\mathcal{F} = \{ \text{IF-OBSTACLE}, \text{V8A}, \text{FROG}, \text{PROGN} \}$

with an argument map of

$\{2, 2, 1, 2\}.$

Two fitness cases are used for this problem. With six obstacles (and 58 unobstructed squares) in the room for each of the two fitness cases, raw fitness ranges between 0 and 116. A program in the population is executed once for each fitness case. The movement of the robot is terminated when the robot has executed either 100 LEFT turns or 100 movement-causing operations (i.e., a MOP or FROG) for a particular fitness case. Execution of IF-OBSTACLE, (LEFT), PROGN, and V8A do not count toward this limit.

The contribution to raw fitness of a program by a particular fitness case is the number of squares (from 0 to 58) mopped within the allowed time. The raw fitness of a program is the sum, over the two fitness cases, of the number of squares mopped. Only the total number of squares mopped over both fitness cases is available to genetic programming.

The use of numerous fitness cases is desirable for this problem in order to avoid overspecialization of the evolved programs to a particular arrangement of obstacles. Each run of this problem is fairly time-consuming. As usual, many runs of a problem must be made, both with and without automatically defined functions, in order to compute the structural complexity ratio for the problem and to make the performance curves that yield the efficiency ratio for the problem. The goal of exploring whether automatically defined functions facilitate automated problem-solving is more important to us in this book than the goal of finding the very best solution or most general solution to a particular problem. These competing goals dictate that a compromise be made for this problem. We decided to allocate only enough computer time to this problem to support two fitness cases.

This problem requires that the robot test for the presence of an obstacle prior to most (but not necessarily all) of its contemplated moving or jumping operations. Execution of a test does not count toward the 100 state-changing operations.

This problem is similar to, but considerably harder than, the lawnmower problem (where a population of only 1,000 was used). Consequently, a population size of 4,000 is used here.

Because this problem is harder than the lawnmower problem, we defined mopping 112 of the 116 squares to be a satisfactory result for this problem. This change increases the percentage of successful runs and shortens the

Table 13.1 Tableau without ADFs for the obstacle-avoiding-robot problem.

Objective:	Find a program to control an autonomous mobile robot so that the robot mops all 58 free squares of the floor in a room.
Terminal set without ADFs:	(LEFT), (MOP), and the random constants $\Re_{v8}$.
Function set without ADFs:	IF-OBSTACLE, V8A, FROG, and PROGN.
Fitness cases:	Two fitness cases, each with obstacles in 6 of the 64 squares of the room.
Raw fitness:	Raw fitness (from 0 to 116) is the sum, over the two fitness cases, of the number of squares in the room mopped by the robot within the allowed amount of time.
Standardized fitness:	Standardized fitness is the total number of squares to be mopped (i.e., 116) minus raw fitness.
Hits:	Same as raw fitness.
Wrapper:	None.
Parameters:	$M = 4{,}000$. $G = 51$.
Success predicate:	A program scores 112 (out of 116) hits.

average length of the successful runs (in generations); however, it prevents direct comparison of the results of this problem and the results of the lawnmower problem.

Table 13.1 summarizes the key features of the obstacle-avoiding-robot problem without automatically defined functions.

D'haeseleer (1994) uses the obstacle-avoiding robot problem as one of four problems for testing his new context-preserving crossover operation. See subsection F.13.1 in appendix F.

13.3 RESULTS WITHOUT ADFs

In one run without automatically defined functions, the following 330-point program scoring 112 (out of 116) emerged on generation 33:

```
(V8A (PROGN (PROGN (FROG (V8A (FROG (V8A (V8A (PROGN (FROG
(4,5)) (IF-OBSTACLE (V8A (PROGN (MOP) (MOP)) (LEFT)) (PROGN
(MOP) (MOP)))) (PROGN (V8A (LEFT) (MOP)) (PROGN (LEFT) (MOP))))
(PROGN (V8A (PROGN (MOP) (LEFT)) (PROGN (LEFT) (LEFT))) (PROGN
(PROGN (MOP) (LEFT)) (V8A (MOP) (5,5)))))) (MOP))) (IF-OBSTACLE
(2,2) (MOP))) (PROGN (FROG (V8A (PROGN (FROG (V8A (V8A (PROGN
(MOP) (MOP)) (FROG (3,0)))) (PROGN (PROGN (V8A (MOP) (MOP))
(PROGN (4,7) (PROGN (MOP) (MOP))))) (PROGN (LEFT) (LEFT))))) (V8A
(PROGN (PROGN (MOP) (LEFT)) (V8A (MOP) (MOP))) (PROGN (V8A
```

```
(LEFT) (MOP)) (IF-OBSTACLE (MOP) (3,6))))) (MOP))) (V8A (PROGN (MOP)
(MOP)) (FROG (MOP))))) (V8A (V8A (PROGN (V8A (MOP) (MOP)) (PROGN (PROGN
(V8A (PROGN (4,2) (MOP)) (PROGN (2,6) (MOP))) (V8A (V8A (PROGN (FROG
(4,5)) (PROGN (V8A (PROGN (MOP) (LEFT)) (PROGN (LEFT) (LEFT))) (PROGN
(PROGN (MOP) (LEFT)) (PROGN (MOP) (FROG (5,0))))))) (PROGN (FROG (PROGN
(PROGN (MOP) (MOP)) (PROGN (6,5) (MOP)))) (PROGN (LEFT) (MOP)))) (PROGN
(V8A (V8A (PROGN (MOP) (MOP)) (LEFT)) (PROGN (LEFT) (LEFT))) (PROGN
(PROGN (MOP) ·
(LEFT)) (V8A (FROG (V8A (MOP) (1,1))) (MOP)))))) (PROGN (V8A
(PROGN (MOP) (MOP)) (FROG (MOP))) (PROGN (PROGN (IF-OBSTACLE
(IF-OBSTACLE (MOP) (LEFT)) (V8A (MOP) (MOP))) (PROGN (V8A (MOP)
(3,0)) (V8A (PROGN (MOP) (MOP)) (PROGN (MOP) (0,7))))) (FROG
(FROG (V8A (V8A (FROG (V8A (4,1) (MOP))) (MOP)) (MOP))))))))
(V8A (V8A (PROGN (V8A (MOP) (1,1)) (IF-OBSTACLE (5,0) (PROGN
(MOP) (MOP)))) (PROGN (PROGN (V8A (LEFT) (3,0)) (V8A (FROG
(IF-OBSTACLE (2,3) (MOP))) (FROG (V8A (FROG (PROGN (PROGN (MOP)
(LEFT)) (V8A (MOP) (5,5)))) (MOP))))) (FROG (FROG (3,2)))))
(PROGN (MOP) (2,3)))) (PROGN (V8A (V8A (MOP) (MOP)) (MOP))
(PROGN (V8A (V8A (V8A (IF-OBSTACLE (MOP) (MOP)) (FROG (MOP)))
(V8A (FROG (V8A (MOP) (1,1))) (MOP))) (V8A (PROGN (V8A (PROGN
(PROGN (MOP) (MOP)) (IF-OBSTACLE (IF-OBSTACLE (V8A (LEFT) (6,4))
(PROGN (2,4) (LEFT))) (PROGN (IF-OBSTACLE (0,5) (MOP)) (PROGN
(MOP) (MOP))))) (V8A (6,4) (LEFT))) (FROG (6,0))) (PROGN (PROGN
(V8A (PROGN (MOP) (LEFT)) (PROGN (LEFT) (LEFT))) (V8A (MOP) (V8A
(PROGN (MOP) (LEFT)) (V8A (MOP) (1,1))))) (PROGN (PROGN (MOP)
(MOP)) (PROGN (6,5) (MOP)))))) (V8A (FROG (FROG (V8A (MOP)
(1,1)))) (V8A (V8A (PROGN (MOP) (MOP)) (IF-OBSTACLE (1,5)
(LEFT))) (IF-OBSTACLE (IF-OBSTACLE (MOP) (LEFT)) (V8A (MOP)
(MOP))))))))).
```

As one would expect, this best-of-run program consists of a tedious sequence of irregular movements, jumps, and turns that eventually mops 112 of the 116 squares of the room. It also contains a sufficient number of tests for obstacles to permit the attainment of this score of 112 within the constraints on the number of operations.

Figure 13.2 shows, for the first fitness case, the partial trajectory traced by the robot while it is under the control of this 330-point best-of-run program for operations 0 through 30; figure 13.3 shows the partial trajectory for operations 30 through 60; and figure 13.4 shows the partial trajectory for operations 60 through 91.

Even though the problem environment contains considerable regularity, this 330-point program without automatically defined functions necessarily operates in a irregular and haphazard fashion, with no common approach visible among the various parts of the overall 91-operation trajectory.

The average structural complexity, $\bar{S}_{without}$, of the best-of-run programs from the seven successful runs (out of 10 runs) of the obstacle-avoiding robot without automatically defined functions is 336.1 points.

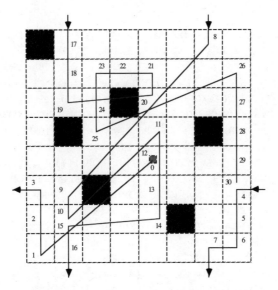

Figure 13.2 Partial trajectory of the obstacle-avoiding robot executing the 330-point program for operations 0 through 30 without ADFs.

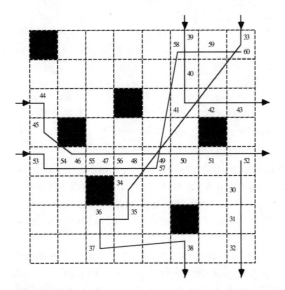

Figure 13.3 Partial trajectory of the obstacle-avoiding robot executing the 330-point program for operations 31 through 60 without ADFs.

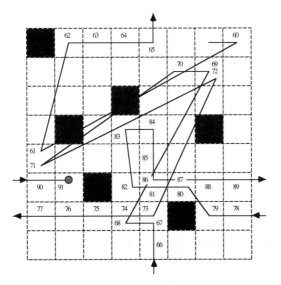

Figure 13.4 Partial trajectory of the obstacle-avoiding robot executing the 330-point program for operations 61 through 91 without ADFs.

Without Defined Functions

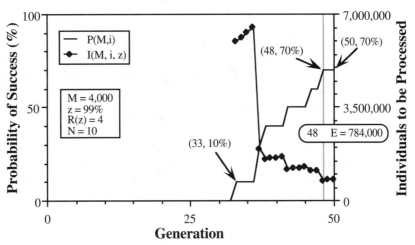

Figure 13.5 Performance curves for the obstacle-avoiding-robot problem showing that $E_{without} = 784,000$ without ADFs.

Figure 13.5 presents the performance curves based on the 10 runs of the obstacle-avoiding-robot problem without automatically defined functions. The cumulative probability of success, $P(M,i)$, is 70% by generations 48 and 50. The two numbers in the oval indicate that if this problem is run through to generation 48, processing a total of $E_{without} = 784{,}000$ individuals (i.e., $4{,}000 \times$ 49 generations $\times$ 4 runs) is sufficient to yield a satisfactory result for this problem with 99% probability.

13.4 PREPARATORY STEPS WITH ADFs

A human programmer would never consider solving this problem using the tedious style employed by the genetically evolved program without automatically defined functions in the previous section. Instead, a human programmer would write a program that first tests a certain small subarea of the room for time-consuming obstacles in some orderly way and then mops that small subarea in some orderly way. The human programmer would then reposition the robot to a new subarea of the room in some orderly (probably tessellating) way, and then repeat the testing and mopping actions in the new subarea of the room. The program would contain enough invocations of the orderly method for dealing with subareas of the room so as to mop at least the requisite 112 squares within the allowed number of operations. That is, a human programmer would exploit the considerable regularity of the problem environment by decomposing the problem into subproblems and would then repeatedly invoke the solution to the subproblem in order to solve the overall problem.

In applying genetic programming with automatically defined functions to this problem, we used the same arrangement of ADFs used in the lawnmower problem. Specifically, we decided that each individual in the population would consist of one result-producing branch and two function definitions in which ADF0 takes no arguments and ADF1 takes one argument. The second defined function ADF1 can hierarchically refer to the first defined function ADF0.

Table 13.2 summarizes the key features of the obstacle-avoiding-robot problem with automatically defined functions.

13.5 RESULTS WITH ADFs

In one run of this problem with automatically defined functions, the following 101-point program achieving a perfect raw fitness of 116 emerged on generation 27:

```
(progn (defun ADF0 ()
            (values (PROGN (PROGN (V8A (PROGN (MOP) (MOP)) (V8A
              (PROGN (IF-OBSTACLE (5,3) (MOP)) (MOP)) (V8A (LEFT)
              (MOP)))) (V8A (V8A (LEFT) (LEFT)) (V8A (LEFT) (1,0))))
              (V8A (PROGN (MOP) (MOP)) (IF-OBSTACLE (LEFT)
              (MOP))))))
```

Table 13.2 Tableau with ADFs for the obstacle-avoiding-robot problem.

Objective:	Find a program to control an autonomous mobile robot so that the robot mops all 58 free squares of the floor in a room.
Architecture of the overall program with ADFs:	One result-producing branch and two function-defining branches, with ADF0 taking no arguments and ADF1 taking one argument, and with ADF1 hierarchically referring to ADF0.
Parameters:	Branch typing.
Terminal set for the result-producing branch:	(LEFT), (MOP), and the random constants $\Re_{v8}$.
Function set for the result-producing branch:	ADF0, ADF1, IF-OBSTACLE, V8A, FROG, and PROGN.
Terminal set for the function-defining branch ADF0:	(LEFT), (MOP), and the random constants $\Re_{v8}$.
Function set for the function-defining branch ADF0:	IF-OBSTACLE, V8A, and PROGN.
Terminal set for the function-defining branch ADF1:	ARG0, (LEFT), (MOP), and the random constants $\Re_{v8}$.
Function set for the function-defining branch ADF1:	IF-OBSTACLE, V8A, FROG, PROGN, and ADF0 (hierarchical reference to ADF0 by ADF1).

```
(defun ADF1 (ARG0)
    (values (PROGN (PROGN (PROGN (PROGN (V8A (FROG ARG0)
     (PROGN (ADF0) (3,1))) (PROGN (PROGN (IF-OBSTACLE (MOP)
     (ADF0)) (V8A (ADF0) (ADF0))) (IF-OBSTACLE (PROGN (0,4)
     (ADF0)) (PROGN (PROGN (ADF0) ARG0) (V8A (ADF0) (V8A
     (PROGN (PROGN (ADF0) (V8A (ADF0)) (ADF0))) (PROGN (V8A
     (V8A (ADF0) (MOP)) (V8A (ADF0) (7,7))) (PROGN (ADF0)
     (6,4)))) (FROG ARG0))))))) (PROGN (ADF0) (V8A (ADF0)
     (ADF0)))) (V8A (ADF0) (ADF0))) (PROGN (V8A (ADF0)
     (ADF0)) (V8A (ADF0) (ADF0))))))
   (values (V8A (V8A (ADF1 (7,0)) (ADF1 (ADF1 (7,0)))) (ADF1
    (ADF0)))))).
```

The success predicate for this problem treats a score of 112 as a success for purpose of making the performance curves, but runs with automatically defined functions were permitted to run on in order to achieve a perfect score of 116.

This 101-point program can be simplified to the following equivalent 57-point program:

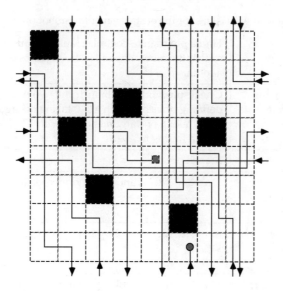

Figure 13.6 Trajectory of the robot using the 101-point program for the obstacle-avoiding-robot problem with ADFs

```
(progn (defun ADF0 ()
          (values (PROGN (MOP) (MOP) (IF-OBSTACLE (5,3) (MOP))
                         (MOP) (LEFT) (MOP) (LEFT)
                         (LEFT) (LEFT) (MOP) (MOP) (IF-OBSTACLE
           (LEFT) (MOP)))))
        (defun ADF1 (ARG0)
          (values (PROGN (FROG ARG0) (ADF0)
                         (IF-OBSTACLE (MOP) (ADF0)) (ADF0) (ADF0)
                         (IF-OBSTACLE (ADF0)
                            (PROGN (ADF0) (ADF0) (ADF0) (ADF0)
                                   (ADF0) (ADF0) (MOP) (ADF0)
                                   (ADF0) (FROG ARG0)))
                  (ADF0) (ADF0) (ADF0) (ADF0) (ADF0)
                  (ADF0) (ADF0) (ADF0) (ADF0))))
        (values (progn (ADF1 (7,0)) (ADF1 (ADF1 (7,0))) (ADF1
           (ADF0)))))).
```

Figure 13.6 shows the trajectory of the robot for this 101-point best-of-run program with automatically defined functions. In contrast to the three partial trajectories shown in figures 13.2, 13.3, and 13.4, this best-of-run program takes advantage of the regularity of the problem environment by mopping down each column and then shifting to the left. This orderly action is interrupted from time to time by the obstacles; however, after making a slight deviation to avoid the obstacle, the orderly mopping action immediately resumes.

This 101-point program may be exploiting the fact that no two obstacles happen to be in the same column. If this were so, this behavior would be the consequence of the very small number of fitness cases. Genetic programming adapts only to the instances of the environment to which it is exposed. If the

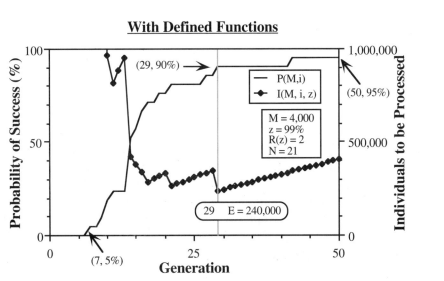

With Defined Functions

Figure 13.7 Performance curves for the obstacle-avoiding-robot problem showing that E_{with} = 240,000 with ADFs.

Table 13.3 Comparison table for the obstacle-avoiding-robot problem.

	Without ADFs	With ADFs
Average structural complexity $\overline{S}$	336.1	123.9
Computional effort E	784,000	240,000

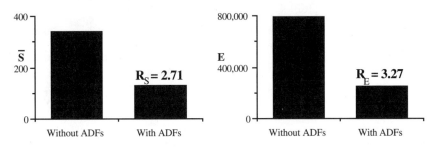

Figure 13.8 Summary graphs for the obstacle-avoiding-robot problem.

set of fitness cases is sufficiently representative of some more general problem that the human user has in mind, genetic programming may evolve a program that is also applicable to that more general problem.

The average structural complexity, $\overline{S}_{with}$, of the best-of-run programs of the 20 successful runs (out of 21 runs) of the problem of the obstacle-avoiding robot with automatically defined functions is 123.9 points.

Figure 13.7 presents the performance curves based on the 21 runs of the obstacle-avoiding-robot problem with automatically defined functions. The cumulative probability of success, $P(M,i)$, is 90% by generation 29 and 95%

by generation 50. The two numbers in the oval indicate that if this problem is run through to generation 29, processing a total of $E_{with} = 240,000$ individuals (i.e., $4,000 \times 30$ generations $\times 2$ runs) is sufficient to yield a satisfactory result for this problem with 99% probability.

13.6 SUMMARY

Table 13.3 compares the average structural complexity, $\overline{S}_{without}$ and $\overline{S}_{with}$, and the computational effort, $E_{without}$ and E_{with}, for the problem of the obstacle-avoiding robot with automatically defined functions and without them.

Figure 13.8 summarizes the information in this comparison table and shows a structural complexity ratio, R_S, of 2.71 and an efficiency ratio, R_E, of 3.27.

14 The Minesweeper Problem

The minesweeper problem considered in this chapter is similar to the lawnmower problem (chapter 8) and the problem of the obstacle-avoiding robot (chapter 13); however, in this third problem of the progression, the obstacles are lethal.

14.1 THE PROBLEM

In this problem, a minesweeper attempts to traverse a mine-infested area of toroidal ocean. If the crew operating the scanning equipment does not constantly check for the presence of the mines before virtually every contemplated forward movement of the ship, the ship will quickly fall victim to a mine. When the ship hits a mine, it is destroyed and loses the opportunity to continue its voyage and accumulate additional credit.

14.2 PREPARATORY STEPS WITHOUT ADFs

This problem is similar to the problem of the obstacle-avoiding robot, except for the lethality of the mines. Thus, we adopt the terminal set and the function set from that problem (merely changing the name of the IF-OBSTACLE conditional testing operation to IF-MINE and the name of the MOP operator to SWEEP).

Since there are side effecting functions in this problem, IF-MINE must be implemented as a macro as described in section 12.2.

Because the conditional branching operator IF-MINE should be invoked before every contemplated move, this problem is considerably harder to solve than the problem of the obstacle-avoiding robot. In a small preliminary set of test runs without automatically defined functions, genetic programming did not evolve any program that scored 112 (the threshold used in the success predicate in the previous problem involving the obstacle-avoiding robot). Genetic programming did, however, find programs scoring the full 116 with automatically defined functions. In order to avoid expending excessive computer time on this problem in order to obtain multiple successful runs without automatically defined functions, we lowered the number of squares in the definition of the success predicate (both with and without automatically defined functions) to 109. This change increases the percentage of successful runs and shortens the average length of the successful runs (in generations); however, it prevents direct comparison of the results of this problem and the results of the lawnmower and obstacle-avoiding robot.

The use of numerous fitness cases is desirable for this problem in order to avoid memorization by the evolved programs of the particular arrangements of mines in the environments that it sees. However, because each run of this problem is time-consuming, we compromised on the number of fitness cases and allocated only enough computer time to this problem to support two fitness cases. The mines are located in the same places as the obstacles in the problem of the obstacle-avoiding robot.

With the differences noted above, the tableaux from the obstacle-avoiding-robot problem (tables 13.1 and 13.2) apply to this problem.

14.3 RESULTS WITHOUT ADFs

In one run without automatically defined functions, the following 340-point program scoring 109 (out of 116) emerged on generation 50:

```
(V8A (V8A (V8A (PROGN (V8A (FROG (FROG (V8A (FROG (PROGN (IF-
MINE (SWEEP) (SWEEP)) (PROGN (PROGN (SWEEP) (SWEEP)) (PROGN
(LEFT) (SWEEP))))) (V8A (5,3) (FROG (5,2))))))) (PROGN (V8A
(PROGN (V8A (FROG (SWEEP)) (V8A (4,6) (SWEEP))) (V8A (V8A (3,7)
(4,7)) (PROGN (FROG (V8A (FROG (3,5)) (FROG (LEFT)))) (V8A (FROG
(PROGN (SWEEP) (SWEEP))) (V8A (IF-MINE (SWEEP) (SWEEP)) (FROG
(0,2))))))) (PROGN (LEFT) (SWEEP))) (V8A (SWEEP) (FROG (V8A
(PROGN (PROGN (SWEEP) (SWEEP)) (IF-MINE (SWEEP) (LEFT))) (V8A
(PROGN (SWEEP) (LEFT)) (IF-MINE (LEFT) (SWEEP)))))))))) (FROG
(2,1))) (FROG (V8A (IF-MINE (V8A (SWEEP) (SWEEP)) (V8A (FROG
(SWEEP)) (PROGN (5,4) (SWEEP)))) (V8A (FROG (V8A (PROGN (FROG
(V8A (PROGN (PROGN (SWEEP) (SWEEP)) (V8A (2,6) (SWEEP))) (V8A
(PROGN (SWEEP) (LEFT)) (IF-MINE (LEFT) (SWEEP))))) (V8A (SWEEP)
(3,3))) (FROG (SWEEP)))) (PROGN (V8A (V8A (SWEEP) (SWEEP))
(PROGN (LEFT) (SWEEP))) (V8A (FROG (SWEEP)) (V8A (PROGN (PROGN
(5,4) (SWEEP)) (V8A (FROG (FROG (6,2))) (PROGN (PROGN (LEFT)
(SWEEP)) (PROGN (SWEEP) (SWEEP))))) (IF-MINE (0,7)
(SWEEP)))))))))) (SWEEP)) (PROGN (V8A (PROGN (PROGN (FROG (V8A
(FROG (3,5)) (FROG (LEFT)))) (V8A (FROG (PROGN (V8A (IF-MINE
(SWEEP) (LEFT)) (PROGN (SWEEP) (SWEEP))) (IF-MINE (SWEEP)
(SWEEP)))) (PROGN (V8A (SWEEP) (0,5)) (IF-MINE (SWEEP)
(SWEEP))))) (PROGN (5,6) (3,0))) (FROG (FROG (3,5)))) (FROG
(PROGN (V8A (IF-MINE (IF-MINE (IF-MINE (1,6) (5,5)) (PROGN (IF-
MINE (SWEEP) (SWEEP)) (V8A (IF-MINE (SWEEP) (FROG (V8A (V8A
(0,6) (3,7)) (FROG (SWEEP))))) (V8A (V8A (SWEEP) (SWEEP)) (PROGN
(LEFT) (SWEEP)))))) (V8A (FROG (5,2)) (PROGN (5,4) (SWEEP))))
(V8A (FROG (V8A (PROGN (PROGN (SWEEP) (SWEEP)) (V8A (2,6)
(SWEEP))) (V8A (PROGN (SWEEP) (LEFT)) (IF-MINE (LEFT)
(SWEEP))))) (PROGN (V8A (FROG (SWEEP)) (FROG (V8A (PROGN (PROGN
```

```
(5,4) (SWEEP)) (IF-MINE (SWEEP) (LEFT))) (V8A (PROGN (SWEEP) (LEFT))
(IF-MINE (LEFT) (SWEEP)))))) (V8A (FROG (V8A (PROGN
(PROGN (SWEEP) (SWEEP)) (V8A (2,6) (SWEEP))) (V8A (PROGN (SWEEP)
(LEFT)) (IF-MINE (LEFT) (SWEEP))))) (FROG (3,5)))))) (V8A (V8A
(PROGN (SWEEP) (LEFT)) (PROGN (SWEEP) (LEFT))) (PROGN (FROG
(SWEEP)) (IF-MINE (V8A (V8A (FROG (FROG (3,5))) (PROGN (PROGN
(LEFT) (SWEEP)) (PROGN (SWEEP) (SWEEP))))) (PROGN (SWEEP)
(LEFT))) (V8A (PROGN (PROGN (FROG (V8A (FROG (3,5)) (FROG
(LEFT)))) (V8A (IF-MINE (LEFT) (SWEEP)) (V8A (IF-MINE (SWEEP)
(SWEEP)) (FROG (0,2))))) (PROGN (PROGN (PROGN (SWEEP) (LEFT))
(FROG (SWEEP))) (V8A (PROGN (SWEEP) (LEFT)) (PROGN (SWEEP)
(LEFT))))) (V8A (PROGN (SWEEP) (LEFT)) (PROGN (SWEEP)
(LEFT))))))))))) .
```

Figure 14.1 shows a partial trajectory of this best-of-run 340-point individual for operations 0 through 30; figure 14.2 shows the continuation of the trajectory for operations 30 through 60 of the first fitness case; figure 14.3 shows the remainder of the trajectory for operations 60 through 84.

As can be seen from these three figures, the whole 84-operation trajectory traced out by this 340-point program operates in a seemingly arbitrary fashion even though the problem environment contains considerable regularity.

The average structural complexity, $\bar{S}_{without}$, of the best-of-run programs from the 11 successful runs (out of 22 runs) of the minesweeper problem without automatically defined functions is 342.4 points.

Figure 14.4 presents the performance curves based on the 22 runs of the minesweeper problem without automatically defined functions. The cumulative probability of success, $P(M,i)$, is 50% by generation 50. The two numbers in the oval indicate that if this problem is run through to generation 50, processing a total of $E_{without} = 1,428,000$ individuals (i.e., $4,000 \times 51$ genera-

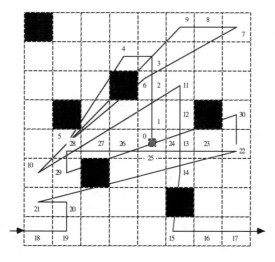

Figure 14.1 Partial trajectory of the minesweeper executing the 340-point program for operations 0 through 30 without ADFs.

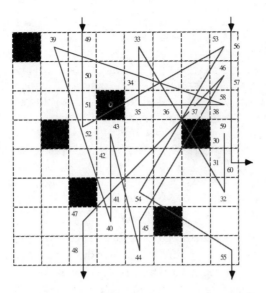

Figure 14.2 Partial trajectory of the minesweeper for operations 30 through 60 without ADFs.

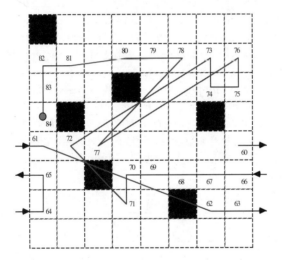

Figure 14.3 Partial trajectory of the minesweeper for operations 60 through 84 without ADFs.

tions × 7 runs) is sufficient to yield a satisfactory result for this problem with 99% probability.

14.4 PREPARATORY STEPS WITH ADFs

In applying genetic programming with automatically defined functions to this problem, we used the same arrangement of ADFs used for the lawnmower and the obstacle-avoiding robot. Specifically, we decided that each individual in the population would consist of one result-producing branch and two function-defining branches. ADF0 takes no arguments and ADF1 takes one argument. The second defined function ADF1 can hierarchically refer to ADF0.

Without Defined Functions

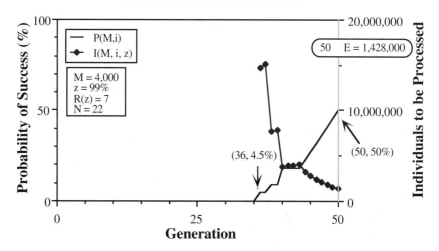

Figure 14.4 Performance curves for the minesweeper problem showing that $E_{without} = 1,428,000$ without ADFs.

14.5 RESULTS WITH ADFs

In one run of this problem with automatically defined functions, the following 104-point program emerged on generation 36 with a perfect raw fitness of 116:

```
(progn (defun ADF0 ()
          (values (IF-MINE (V8A (IF-MINE (PROGN (LEFT) (SWEEP))
            (IF-MINE (LEFT) (SWEEP))) (IF-MINE (PROGN (LEFT)
            (5,7)) (IF-MINE (V8A (LEFT) (3,0)) (V8A (SWEEP)
            (1,2))))) (PROGN (V8A (V8A (SWEEP) (LEFT)) (IF-MINE
            (LEFT) (SWEEP))) (IF-MINE (V8A (LEFT) (3,0)) (V8A
            (SWEEP) (1,2)))))))
        (defun ADF1 (ARG0)
          (values (FROG (V8A (V8A (PROGN (LEFT) (ADF0)) (V8A ARG0
            ARG0)) (IF-MINE (PROGN ARG0 ARG0) (V8A (ADF0)
            (ADF0))))))
        (values (V8A (PROGN (PROGN (PROGN (V8A (V8A (V8A (ADF0)
          (ADF0)) (ADF1 (SWEEP))) (ADF1 (ADF1 (LEFT)))) (PROGN
          (ADF1 (7,7)) (PROGN (PROGN (ADF1 (ADF1 (LEFT))) (PROGN
          (IF-MINE (V8A (ADF0) (ADF0)) (V8A (FROG (SWEEP)) (V8A
          (ADF0) (ADF0)))) (FROG (ADF1 (ADF1 (ADF0))))))) (PROGN
          (PROGN (LEFT) (7,5)) (ADF1 (LEFT)))))) (V8A (ADF0)
          (SWEEP))) (ADF1 (ADF1 (ADF0)))) (V8A (ADF1 (ADF0))
          (SWEEP))))).
```

The success predicate for this problem treats a score of 109 as a success for purpose of making the performance curves, but runs with automatically defined functions were permitted to run on in order to achieve a perfect score of 116.

In run 2 with automatically defined functions, an 84-point program with a perfect score of 116 emerged on generation 36:

```
(progn (defun ADF0 ()
         (values (IF-MINE (V8A (IF-MINE
                               (PROGN (LEFT) (SWEEP))
                               (IF-MINE (LEFT) (SWEEP)))
                         (IF-MINE
                           (PROGN (LEFT) (5,7))
                           (IF-MINE
                             (PROGN (LEFT) (3,0))
                             (PROGN (SWEEP) (1,2)))))
                  (PROGN (SWEEP) (LEFT)
                         (IF-MINE (LEFT) (SWEEP))
                         (IF-MINE (PROGN (LEFT) (3,0))
                         (PROGN (SWEEP) (1,2)))))))
       (defun ADF1 (ARG0)
         (values (FROG (V8A (V8A (PROGN (LEFT) (ADF0))
                           (V8A ARG0 ARG0))
                     (IF-MINE ARG0
                   (V8A (ADF0) (ADF0)))))))
       (values (PROGN (ADF0) (ADF0) (ADF1 (SWEEP))
                 (ADF1 (ADF1 (LEFT)))
                 (ADF1 (7,7)) (ADF1 (ADF1 (LEFT)))
                 (IF-MINE (PROGN (ADF0) (ADF0))
                         (PROGN (FROG (SWEEP)) (ADF0)
                                 (ADF0)))
                  (FROG (ADF1 (ADF1 (ADF0))))
                  (LEFT) (ADF1 (LEFT))
                  (ADF0) (SWEEP) (ADF1 (ADF1 (ADF0)))
                  (ADF1 (ADF0)) (SWEEP)))).
```

The behavior of ADF0 in this program from run 2 can be analyzed by considering five cases.

Figure 14.5 shows case 1 wherein no mine is detected ahead of the minesweeper, the minesweeper moves north, turns left, and heads west for two squares since no mines are ahead of the minesweeper at that point.

Figure 14.6 shows case 2 in which a mine is detected ahead of the minesweeper, the minesweeper immediately turns left to avoid it, and then finds no other mines and keeps moving.

Figure 14.7 shows case 3 wherein no mine is detected ahead, the minesweeper moves north, turns left, finds a mine, and turns left again to avoid the mine (thus heading south).

Figure 14.8 shows case 4 wherein no mine is detected ahead, the minesweeper moves north, and turns left. Seeing no mine, it moves forward (west), finds a mine, and turns left (thus facing south).

Figure 14.9 shows case 5 wherein a mine is detected ahead of the minesweeper, the minesweeper turns left to avoid it, detects another mine, and turns left again (thus facing south).

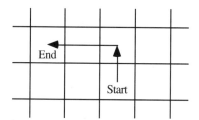

Figure 14.5 Case 1 of ADF0 from run 2 for the minesweeper problem.

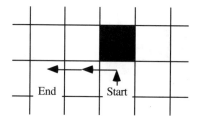

Figure 14.6 Case 2 of ADF0 from run 2 for the minesweeper problem.

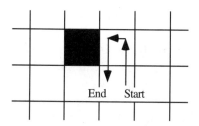

Figure 14.7 Case 3 ADF0 from run 2 for of the minesweeper problem.

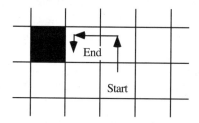

Figure 14.8 Case 4 of ADF0 from run 2 for the minesweeper problem.

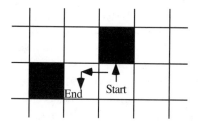

Figure 14.9 Case 5 of ADF0 from run 2 for the minesweeper problem.

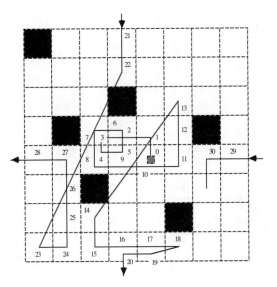

Figure 14.10 Partial trajectory of 84-point program for run 2 of the minesweeper problem for operations 0 through 30 with ADFs.

Figure 14.10 shows the trajectory of the minesweeper for this 84-point program with automatically defined functions for operations 0 through 30 for run 2 of the minesweeper problem; figure 14.11 shows the continuation of this trajectory for operations 30 through 60; figure 14.12 shows the final part of this trajectory for operations 60 through 98.

Here, in contrast to the lawnmower problem, the regularity being exploited by the automatically defined functions is not immediately obvious from inspection of the trajectory. No obvious qualitative difference is evident between the trajectory with automatically defined functions (figures 14.10, 14.11, and 14.12) and the trajectory without them (figures 14.1, 14.2, 14.3). Nonetheless, the beneficial effect of automatically defined functions becomes apparent when one sees the statistics, over a series of runs, of the average structural complexity and the computational effort.

The average structural complexity, $\overline{S}_{with}$, of the 49 successful runs (out of 50 runs) of the minesweeper problem with automatically defined functions is 119.9 points.

Figure 14.13 presents the performance curves based on the 50 runs of the minesweeper problem with automatically defined functions. The cumulative probability of success, $P(M,i)$, is 94% by generation 25 and 98% by generation 50. The two numbers in the oval indicate that if this problem is run through to generation 50, processing a total of $E_{with} = 208,000$ individuals (i.e., 4,000 × 26 generations × 2 runs) is sufficient to yield a satisfactory result for this problem with 99% probability.

As previously mentioned, the use of only two fitness cases for this problem and the obstacle-avoiding robot problem was a compromise made to save computer time. In making this compromise we placed greater weight on demonstrating certain points about automatically defined functions

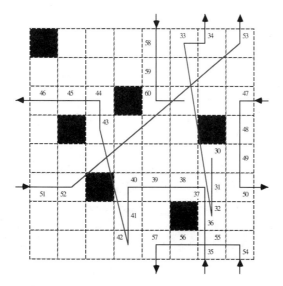

Figure 14.11 Partial trajectory of the minesweeper for run 2 of operations 30 through 60 with ADFs.

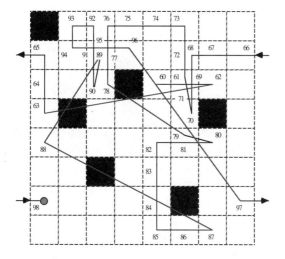

Figure 14.12 Partial trajectory of the minesweeper for run 2 of operations 60 through 98 with ADFs.

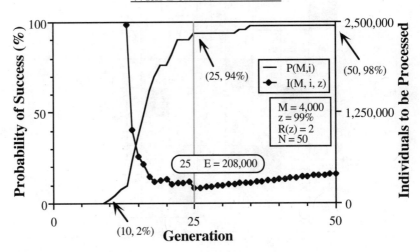

With Defined Functions

Figure 14.13 Performance curves for the minesweeper problem showing that $E_{with} = 208,000$ with ADFs.

Table 14.1 Comparison table for the minesweeper problem.

	Without ADFs	With ADFs
Average structural complexity $\bar{S}$	342.4	119.9
Computional effort E	1,428,000	208,000

than in finding robust and complete solutions to the problems. The price for this compromise was that the evolved programs for both problems are overfitted to the minuscule number of fitness cases. For example, when one of the best-of-run results from the obstacle-avoiding robot problem was retested on 1,000 fitness cases (instead of just two), it scored only 45,278 hits (78%) out of a possible 58,000 with automatically defined functions and 25,625 without them. When one of the best-of-run results from the minesweeper problem was retested, it scored only 32,945 hits with automatically defined functions and a mere 8,372 without them.

The two problems, of course, differ as to the importance of looking before moving. When one of the best-of-run results from the obstacle-avoiding robot problem was retested on 1,000 fitness cases, 73% of its moves (measured by a counter inserted into the programs) were unprotected blind moves with automatically defined functions as compared to 92% without them. When one of the best-of-run results from the minesweeper problem was retested, 10% of its moves were unprotected blind moves with automatically defined functions as compared to 87% without them. Thus, the successful programs without automatically defined functions were memorizing the environment more than the programs with them. The fact that so few (10%) of the moves

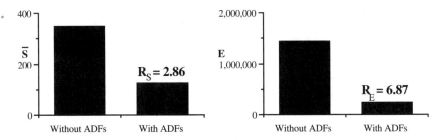

Figure 14.14 Summary graphs for the minesweeper problem.

Table 14.2 Summary table of the structural complexity ratio, R_S, and the efficiency ratio, R_E, for the lawnmower, obstacle-avoiding-robot, and minesweeper problems.

Problem	Structural complexity ratio R_S	Efficiency ratio R_E
Lawnmower – lawn size 64	3.65	9.09
Obstacle-avoiding robot	2.71	3.27
Minesweeper	2.86	6.87

with automatically defined functions are unprotected probably indicates that the behaviors in the ADFs are reused in different situations and therefore must be more general.

14.6 SUMMARY

Table 14.1 compares the average structural complexity, $\overline{S}_{without}$ and $\overline{S}_{with}$, and the computational effort, $E_{without}$ and E_{with}, for the minesweeper problem with automatically defined functions and without them.

Figure 14.14 summarizes the information in this comparison table and shows a structural complexity ratio, R_S, of 2.86 and an efficiency ratio, R_E, of 6.87.

We are unable to identify, either by analysis of the evolved programs or by visualization of the trajectories of the minesweeper, the exact mechanism by which the successful programs with automatically defined functions lower the computational effort and their average size. Nonetheless, the structural complexity ratio, R_S, of 2.86 and the efficiency ratio, R_E, of 6.87 is evidence that the automatically defined functions have discovered and exploited some regularity in this problem environment.

Both the problem of the obstacle-avoiding robot and the minesweeper problem demonstrate the benefits of automatically defined functions in an environment that is more complicated than the lawnmower problem.

Table 14.2 summarizes the structural complexity ratio, R_S, and the efficiency ratio, R_E, for the lawnmower, obstacle-avoiding-robot, and minesweeper problems.

15 Automatic Discovery of Detectors for Letter Recognition

This chapter (and chapters 16 through 20) present problems which, when solved using automatically defined functions, illustrate the simultaneous discovery of initially-unknown detectors and a way of combining the just-discovered detectors. The detectors that are dynamically discovered during the run of genetic programming are then repeatedly used in solving the problem.

The goal of dynamically discovering feature detectors, rather than prespecifying them, has been a theme in the field of automated pattern recognition from its earliest days (Uhr and Vossler 1966). Indeed, for many problems, finding the detectors (i.e., identifying the regularities and patterns of the problem environment), doing the recoding (i.e., changing the representation), and finding a way of solving the recoded problem really is *the problem*.

In fact, the broad goal of dynamically discovering detectors has been a common thread running through the field of machine learning since its earliest days. Arthur Samuel's 1959 pioneering work involving learning to play the game of checkers raised this issue. The pattern being recognized in Samuel's system was not a pattern of pixels in an array, but rather an arrangement of checker pieces on a playing board. The problem in Samuel's checker player was not to classify patterns, but rather to play checkers. In spite of these differences, Samuel recognized the importance of getting learning to occur without predetermining the size and shape of the solution and of "[getting] the program to generate its own parameters [detectors] for the evaluation polynomial" (Samuel 1959).

In Samuel's system, machine learning consisted of progressively adjusting numerical coefficients in an algebraic expression of a predetermined functional form (specifically, a polynomial of a specified order). Each component term of the polynomial represented a handcrafted detector (parameter) reflecting some aspect of the current state of the board (e.g., number of pieces, center control, etc.). The polynomial calculated the value of a board to the player by weighting each handcrafted detector with a numerical coefficient. Thus, the polynomial could be used to compare the boards that would arise if the player were to make various alternative moves. The best move could then be selected from among the alternatives on the basis of the polynomial. If a particular polynomial was good at assigning values to boards, good moves would result. In Samuel's system, the numerical coefficients of the polynomial were adjusted with experience, so that the predictive quality of the polynomial progressively improved. In addition to hand-crafting the detectors, Samuel predetermined the way the detectors would be combined to solve the problem by selecting the particular functional form of the polynomial. Samuel's 1959 checker player can be viewed in terms of the bottom-up formulation of the hierarchical problem-solving process.

15.1 THE PROBLEM

Figure 15.1 shows the letters I and L, each presented in a 6-by-4 pixel grid of binary (ON or OFF) values.

The goal in this letter-recognition problem is to discover a computer program that can take any of the 2^{24} possible patterns of bits as its input and produce a correct identification I, L, or NIL (i.e., not the letter I or L) for the pattern as its output.

Note that the correct identification of a pattern of pixels requires not only establishing that all the specific pixels that must be ON are indeed ON, but also inspecting other pixels on the grid to exclude the possibility of an imperfect letter or another letter.

15.2 PREPARATORY STEPS WITHOUT ADFs

There are, of course, many different ways to structure a computer program to perform the task of letter recognition. The programs that are to be evolved in this chapter consist of hierarchical combinations of local detectors.

If one were trying to describe the letter L to someone unfamiliar with the Roman alphabet, one might give a dynamic description involving progressively drawing a vertical line of, say, five pixels downward from some specified starting location and then progressively drawing a horizontal line of, say, two pixels to the right. This dynamic description of the pattern contains both local and hierarchical aspects. The progressive pixel-by-pixel drawing of the vertical and horizontal segments is a local activity; the assembly of the two segments into the whole letter L occurs at a higher level of the hierarchy.

The local aspects of this dynamic approach to constructing a letter can be implemented using a slow-moving *turtle* with limited vision. The turtle's vision is limited to its immediate neighborhood of the nine pixels centered at its current location. The pixel where the turtle is currently located is called "X" (center) and the eight neighboring pixels are called N, NE, E, SE, S, SW, W, and NW.

The hierarchical aspects of constructing a letter can be implemented by a mechanism for moving the turtle. The turtle starts at a designated location on the grid and can move one step at a time to the north (up), south (down), east (right), west (left), northeast, southeast, southwest, and northeast. The sequence of movements of the turtle can be varied according to what the turtle sees at its current local position.

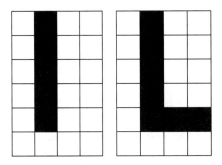

Figure 15.1 The letters I and L.

If there were only two categories to be recognized (say just the letter I and the negative category NIL), a Boolean expression might be convenient both for implementing the computation required to do the required classification and for controlling the sensing and moving activities of the turtle. However, when there are more than two possible outcomes, a decision tree is more suitable for a multi-way classification of patterns (Quinlan 1986).

The terminal set, T, without automatically defined functions is

$T = \{$ I, L, NIL, X, N, NE, E, SE, S, SW, W, NW, (GO-N), (GO-NE), (GO-E),
(GO-SE), (GO-S), (GO-SW), (GO-W), (GO-NE) $\}$.

The first three terminals in T (i.e., I, L, and NIL) are the three categories into which a given pattern may be classified.

The next nine terminals in T (i.e., X, N, NE, E, SE, S, SW, W, and NW) are the turtle's sensors of its nine-pixel local neighborhood.

The last eight terminals in T (i.e., (GO-N), (GO-NE), (GO-E), (GO-SE), (GO-S), (GO-SW), (GO-W), (GO-NE)) are zero-argument side-effecting operators that can move the turtle one step in any one of the eight possible directions from its current location. For example, the side-effecting operator (GO-N) moves the turtle north (up) one step in the 6-by-4 grid. For simplicity, the grid is toroidal. As the turtle moves, the values of the nine sensors (X, N, NE, E, SE, S, SW, W, and NW) are dynamically redefined to reflect the turtle's new location. Each operator returns the value (T or NIL) of the pixel to which the turtle moves (i.e., it returns the new X).

The function set, F, without automatically defined functions is

$F_{rpb} = \{$ IF, AND, OR, NOT, HOMING $\}$

with an argument map of

$\{3, 2, 2, 1, 1\}$.

Since the overall program is to be a decision tree, the function set includes the three-argument decision-making if-then-else operator. The conditional IF operator first evaluates its first argument. The IF operator executes its second (then) argument if (and only if) its first argument evaluates to something other than NIL; the IF operator executes its third (else) argument if (and only if) its first argument evaluates to NIL. This IF operator is implemented as a macro in the same manner as the `IF-FOOD-AHEAD` operator for the artificial ant problem (section 12.2). The fact that this `IF` operator always evaluates its first argument and then only evaluates exactly one of its two remaining arguments is significant when these arguments themselves contain side-effecting operations.

The `AND`, `OR`, and `NOT` are included in the function set to enable the program to create logical predicates.

The values returned by the Common LISP functions `AND` and `OR` are the usual Boolean values; however, these functions have a behavior that becomes significant when their arguments contain side-effecting operations. Specifically, if the first argument to a two-argument `AND` evaluates to `NIL`, the second argument of the `AND` is not evaluated at all and the `AND` returns `NIL`. Similarly, if the first argument to a two-argument `OR` evaluates to something other than `NIL`, the second argument of the `OR` is similarly short-circuited and the `OR` returns that non-`NIL` value. Consequently, any side-effecting operator contained in a short-circuited second argument is never executed.

The one-argument `HOMING` operator first remembers the current location of the turtle and then evaluates its argument. `HOMING` has the additional effect of rubber-banding the turtle back to its previously remembered position after completion of the evaluation of its argument. For example, suppose the turtle starts at a certain position on the grid having an ON to its east and an ON to its northeast. Then,

```
(HOMING (AND (GO-E) (GO-N)))
```

would first move the turtle east; because the turtle sees an ON in that location, the second argument of the `AND` would then be evaluated, moving the turtle to the north. Because the turtle would also see an ON in the new location (to the northeast of its initial position), the call to `(GO-N)` would return `T`, as would the `AND`. The value returned by the `HOMING` is the value returned by its one argument, so the `HOMING` returns `T`. The `HOMING` also returns the turtle to the remembered position that it was in before beginning the `HOMING`. `HOMING` is equivalent to the brackets in a Lindenmayer system (Prusinkiewicz and Lindenmayer 1990).

Because of the complexity of the programs evolved by genetic programming for this problem, our ability to analyze and understand the evolved programs for this problem can be greatly enhanced by imposing a constrained syntactic structure that separates the different kinds of activity within the decision tree. Specifically, the first (antecedent) argument of each `IF` operator is constrained to be a composition of the three Boolean functions (`AND`, `OR`, `NOT`), the `HOMING` function, and the eight turtle-moving operators, namely `(GO-N)`, `(GO-NE)`, `(GO-E)`, `(GO-SE)`, `(GO-S)`, `(GO-SW)`, `(GO-W)`, and `(GO-NE)`. In addition, the second (then) and third (else) arguments of each `IF` operator are constrained to be compositions of the `IF` operator and the category-specifying terminals (`I`, `L`, and `NIL`). The initial random population is randomly generated in conformity with these constraints; structure-preserving crossover is used to preserve this constrained syntactic structure.

The fitness cases for genetic programming must be chosen to represent a sufficient variety of situations that the program is likely to generalize to handle all possible combinations of inputs. In this regard, the fitness cases are similar to the small set of combinations of inputs that are used to test and debug computer programs written by human programmers.

Each individual in the population is tested against an environment consisting of 78 fitness cases, each consisting of a 6-by-4 pixel pattern and the correct identification (I, L, or NIL) for that pattern. The set of fitness cases is constructed to include the two positive fitness cases (the two letters) and 76 different negative fitness cases. The negative cases include every version of the letters I and L with one ON pixel deleted; every version of the letters I and L with one extraneous ON pixel added adjacent to the correct pixels; checkerboard patterns; the all-ON and all-OFF pattern; various patterns bearing some resemblance to I, L, or other letters; and various random patterns bearing no resemblance to I, L, or other letters.

Figure 15.2 shows seven negative fitness cases in which one pixel of the letter L is missing.

Figure 15.3 shows 14 negative fitness cases in which one pixel is added to the letter L.

Figure 15.4 shows ten negative fitness cases that are somewhat like the letter L.

Figure 15.5 shows five negative fitness cases in which one pixel of the letter I is missing.

Figure 15.6 shows 12 of the 13 negative fitness cases in which the letter I is augmented by one pixel. The 13th such fitness case happens to be identical to

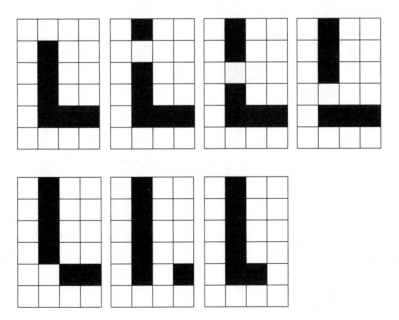

Figure 15.2 Letter L with one pixel missing.

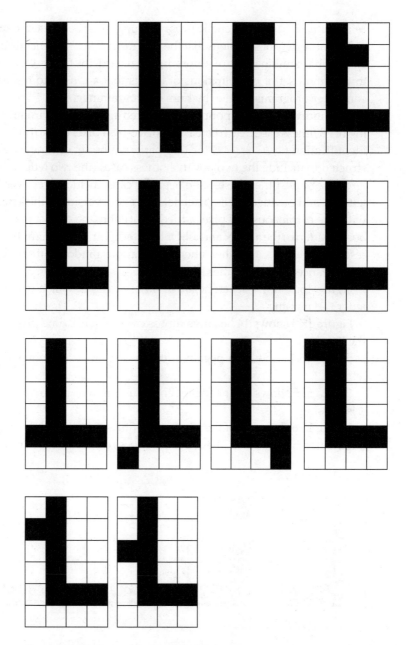

Figure 15.3 Letter L with one pixel added.

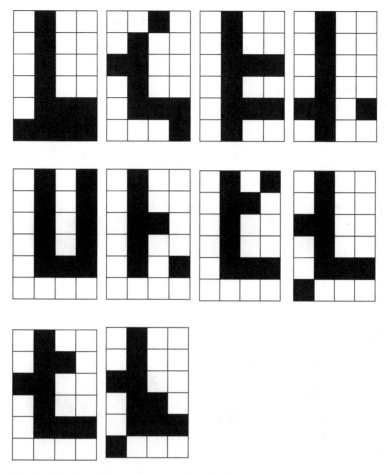

Figure 15.4 Extra fitness cases resembling the letter L.

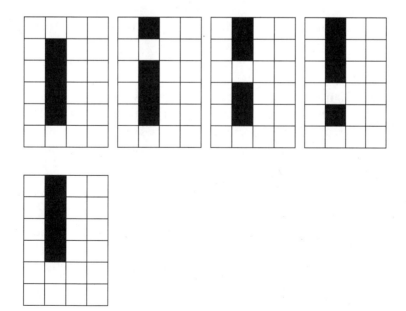

Figure 15.5 Letter I with one pixel missing.

Automatic Discovery of Detectors for Letter Recognition

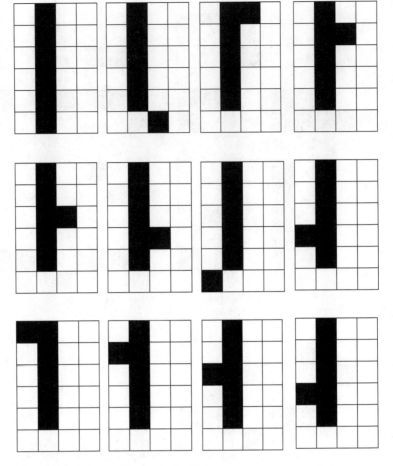

Figure 15.6 Letter I with one pixel added.

one of the fitness cases where one pixel is deleted from the L (i.e., the last fitness case shown in figure 15.2).

Figure 15.7 shows ten negative fitness cases with little similarity to the letters I or L.

Figure 15.8 shows 18 additional negative fitness cases.

When a genetically evolved program in the population is tested against a particular fitness case, the outcome can be

- a *true-positive* (i.e., the program correctly identifies an I as an I or an L as an L),

- a *true-negative* (i.e., the program correctly identifies a pattern that is not an I or L as NIL),

- a *false-positive* (i.e., the program incorrectly identifies a non-letter as either an I or an L),

- a *false-negative* (i.e., the program incorrectly identifies an I as an NIL or an L as NIL), or

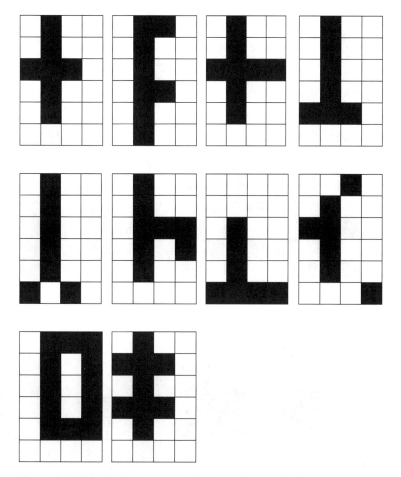

Figure 15.7 Ten extra fitness cases with little similarity to the letters I or L.

- a *wrong-positive* (i.e., the program incorrectly identifies an I as an L or an L as I).

For this problem, fitness is the sum, over the fitness cases, of the weighted errors produced by the program. The smaller the sum of the weighted errors, the better. A 100%-correct pattern-recognizer would have a fitness of 0. True-positives and true-negatives contribute 0 to the sum. False-positives and wrong-positives contribute 1. False-negatives contribute 23 (i.e., the number of pixels minus 1). This choice of 23 maintains consistency with work (done earlier) reported in section 15.8 involving translation-invariant letter recognition.

Our choice of 8,000 as the population size reflects our estimate as to the likely difficulty of this problem and the practical limitations on available computer time and memory.

Table 15.1 summarizes the key features of the letter-recognition problem involving the letters I and L without automatically defined functions.

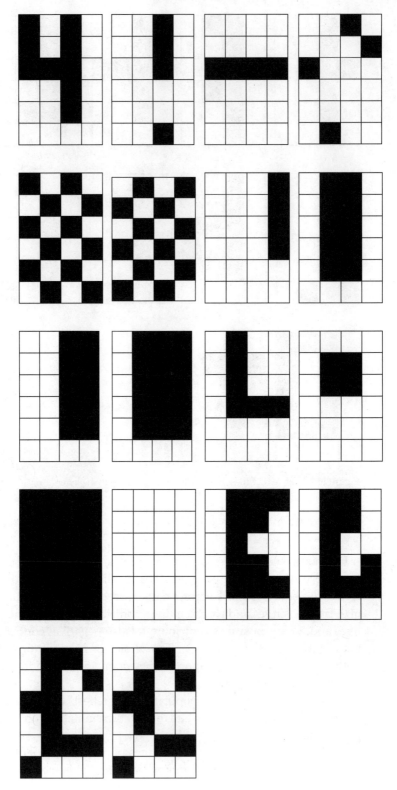

Figure 15.8 18 additional negative fitness cases.

Table 15.1 Tableau without ADFs for the letter-recognition problem.

Objective:	Find a program that identifies a given 6-by-4 pixel pattern as being an I, L, or neither (NIL).
Terminal set without ADFs:	I, L, NIL, X, N, NE, E, SE, S, SW, W, NW, (GO-N), (GO-NE), (GO-E), (GO-SE), (GO-S), (GO-SW), (GO-W), and (GO-NE).
Function set without ADFs:	IF, AND, OR, NOT, and HOMING.
Fitness cases:	78 fitness cases, each consisting of a 6-by-4 pixel pattern and the associated correct identification (I, L, or NIL) for that pattern.
Raw fitness:	The sum, over the 78 fitness cases, of the weighted errors produced by program.
Standardized fitness:	Same as raw fitness.
Hits:	The number (unweighted) of fitness cases for which the identification produced by the program is correct.
Wrapper:	None.
Parameters:	$M = 8{,}000$. $G = 51$.
Success predicate:	A program scores the maximum number of hits.

15.3 RESULTS WITHOUT ADFs

This problem is very time-consuming. We made several runs without automatically defined functions. Each run exhibited progressively better fitness, eventually coming close to a perfect score (i.e., a standardized fitness of 2); however, no run without automatically defined functions produced a solution to this problem. Because of the progressive improvement within these runs, we believe that this problem can be solved without automatically defined functions if given a larger population or if permitted to run for more generations. There was, however, no prospect of getting multiple successful runs of this problem without automatically defined functions with any reasonable amount of computer time.

15.4 PREPARATORY STEPS WITH ADFs

In applying genetic programming with automatically defined functions to the problem of letter recognition, we want the result-producing branch to return the identification of the pattern. The desired biases toward both local inspection and overall hierarchical structure can be attained by specifying that the result-producing branch is capable of sensing only the single pixel where the turtle is currently located, and does not have direct access to any other pixels. The result-producing branch can expand its view somewhat by calling on detectors (ADFs) that are capable of sensing the nine-pixel local neighborhood of the turtle. In addition, the result-producing branch can globally expand its view by moving the turtle. The result-producing branch will consist of compositions of the operations for moving the turtle and Boolean conjunctions, disjunctions, and negations operating on the values returned by the detectors.

The function-defining branches define detectors that examine the entire nine-pixel local neighborhood of the turtle and evaluate compositions of Boolean functions involving what the turtle sees. That is, the function definitions will be compositions of the Boolean conjunctions, disjunctions, and negations and the nine pixel sensors (X, N, NE, E, SE, S, SW, W, and NW).

In applying genetic programming with automatically defined functions to this problem, we decided that each individual overall program in the population will consist of five function-defining branches (defining detectors called ADF0 through ADF4) and a final result-producing branch. Since the automatically defined functions are designed merely for detecting small local 3-by-3 patterns, they have no need to refer hierarchically to one another.

We first consider the five function-defining branches (i.e., the detectors).

Since the five function-defining branches are to define detectors that are capable of analyzing what the turtle sees at its current location on the grid, the terminal set for ADF0, ADF1, ADF2, ADF3, and ADF4 consists of the nine pixel sensors, so that

$\mathcal{T}_{adf}$ = {X, N, NE, E, SE, S, SW, W, NW}.

The function set, $\mathcal{F}_{adf}$, for the five function-defining branches is

$\mathcal{F}_{adf}$ = {AND, OR, NOT}

with an argument map of

{2, 2, 1}.

Notice that there are no side-effecting functions in the function-defining branches. They are designed solely for detecting small local patterns, not for moving the turtle.

Each of the five function-defining branches is a composition of functions from the function set, $\mathcal{F}_{adf}$, and terminals from the terminal set, $\mathcal{T}_{adf}$.

This is the first problem in this book in which there are multiple function-defining branches and yet the function-defining branches do not refer hierarchically to one another. Moreover, this is the first problem where all the automatically defined functions have identical terminal sets, function sets, and argument maps. In implementing structure-preserving crossover in this situation, one might assign one common type to all five like branches (called *like-branch typing*) or one might assign five separate types to the five branches (i.e., our default approach of branch typing). An experiment involving branch typing and like-branch typing is found in *Genetic Programming* (section 25.11). We have chosen to continue to use our usual branch-typing for this problem even though like-branch typing would have been a reasonable choice.

We now consider the result-producing branch.

We envisage that the result-producing branch of each program will be a decision tree consisting of compositions of decision-making functions that return the identification I, L, or NIL.

Thus, the terminal set, $\mathcal{T}_{rpb}$, for the result-producing branch is

$$\mathcal{T}_{rpb} = \{\texttt{I, L, NIL, (GO-N),(GO-NE),(GO-E),(GO-SE),(GO-S),}$$
$$\texttt{(GO-SW),(GO-W),(GO-NE)}\}.$$

The five automatically defined functions (ADF0 through ADF4) that constitute the detectors are included in the function set of the result-producing branch.

Thus, the function set, $\mathcal{F}_{rpb}$, for the result-producing branch is

$$\mathcal{F}_{rpb} = \{\texttt{ADF0, ADF1, ADF2, ADF3, ADF4, IF, AND, OR, NOT, HOMING}\}$$

with an argument map of

$$\{0, 0, 0, 0, 0, 3, 2, 2, 1, 1\}.$$

The result-producing branch is a composition of the functions from the function set, $\mathcal{F}_{rpb}$, and terminals from the terminal set, $\mathcal{T}_{rpb}$.

Our ability to analyze and understand the evolved programs for this problem can be greatly enhanced by imposing a constrained syntactic structure. Specifically, the first (antecedent) argument of each IF operator is constrained to be a composition of the three Boolean functions (AND, OR, NOT), the five automatically defined functions (ADF0, ADF1, ADF2, ADF3, and ADF4), the HOMING function, and the eight turtle-moving operators, namely (GO-N), (GO-NE),(GO-E),(GO-SE),(GO-S),(GO-SW),(GO-W), and (GO-NE). In addition, the second (then) and third (else) arguments of each IF operator are constrained to be either calls to the IF operator or the category-specifying terminals (I, L, and NIL).

Table 15.2 summarizes the key features of the letter-recognition problem involving the letters I and L with automatically defined functions.

15.5 RESULTS WITH ADFs

A review of one particular successful run will illustrate how genetic programming simultaneously evolves the detectors and evolves a way of combining the detectors for the problem of letter recognition.

The 8,000 randomly generated individuals found in the initial generation of the population (generation 0) are, as one would expect, not very good. The worst individual pattern-recognizer in the population for generation 0 has 44 points and has the highly unfavorable fitness (weighted error) of 3,535. This worst-of-generation program is

```
(progn (defun ADF0 ()
          (values (AND (NOT S) (NOT SW))))
       (defun ADF1 ()
          (values (AND (OR S W) (AND N N))))
```

Table 15.2 Tableau with ADFs for the letter-recognition problem.

Objective:	Find a program that identifies a given 6-by-4 pixel pattern as being an I, L, or NIL (neither).
Architecture of the overall program with ADFs:	One result-producing branch and five zero-argument function-defining branches. No hierarchical references between function-defining branches.
Parameters:	Branch typing among the five automatically defined functions (detectors).
Terminal set for the result-producing branch:	I, L, NIL, (GO-N), (GO-NE), (GO-E), (GO-SE), (GO-S), (GO-SW), (GO-W), and (GO-NE).
Function set for the result-producing branch:	IF, AND, OR, NOT, HOMING, ADF0, ADF1, ADF2, ADF3, and ADF4.
Terminal set for the function-defining branches ADF0, ADF1, ADF2, ADF3, and ADF4:	X, N, NE, E, SE, S, SW, W, and NW.
Function set for the function-defining branches ADF0, ADF1, ADF2, ADF3, and ADF4:	AND, OR, and NOT.
Types of points for result-producing branch:	The result-producing branch is to be a decision tree. • The IF operator (which is always at the root). • Point in first argument (condition part) of an IF. • Point in second (then) or third (else) argument of an IF.
Rules of construction for result-producing branch:	• The root node must be an IF. • The first argument (condition part) of an IF may contain any composition of the three Boolean operators (AND, OR, NOT), the five automatically defined functions (ADF0, ADF1, ADF2, ADF3, and ADF4), HOMING, and the eight turtle-moving operators (GO-N), (GO-NE), (GO-E), (GO-SE), (GO-S), (GO-SW), (GO-W), and (GO-NE). • The second (then) and third (else) argument of an IF contain only other IFs or category-specifying terminals (I, L, or NIL).

```
(defun ADF2 ()
  (values (AND (OR W E) (OR X W))))
(defun ADF3 ()
  (values (AND (OR N E) (AND X NE))))
(defun ADF4 ()
  (values (OR (NOT N) (OR NE SW))))
(values (IF (OR (ADF3) (GO-N)) (IF (ADF4) I NIL)
                              (IF (GO-N) I L)))).
```

However, even in a randomly created population of programs, some individuals are better than others. For example, an individual at the 33rd percentile of generation 0 has fitness of 1,771.

The median program (i.e., the 50th percentile) from generation 0 has 18 points and a fitness of 152.

```
(progn (defun ADF0 ()
         (values (NOT NE)))
       (defun ADF1 ()
         (values (AND N X)))
       (defun ADF2 ()
         (values (OR N NW)))
       (defun ADF3 ()
         (values (AND W NE)))
       (defun ADF4 ()
         (values (AND W W)))
       (values (IF (GO-E) L I))).
```

The best of generation 0 has 186 points and a fitness of 53.

Figure 15.9 shows, by generation, the fitness of the best-of-generation program. As can be seen, it tends to improve (i.e., drop) from generation to generation.

Figure 15.10 shows the hits histograms for generations 15, 30, and 50 of this run. The horizontal axis of the hits histogram represents the number of hits (0 to 78); the vertical axis represents the number of individuals in the population (0 to 8,000) scoring that number of hits. Four solutions to the problem emerge at generation 50.

By generation 50, the best-of-generation program has 312 points (of which 149 are in the result-producing branch) and has the perfect fitness value of 0. This best-of-run individual is shown below:

```
(progn (defun ADF0 ()
         (values (OR (OR (AND W SE) (OR (AND (NOT (OR SW SW))
           (NOT (AND X SW))) (NOT (OR (NOT S) (AND X NW)))))
           (AND (OR (NOT S) (AND W SE)) (OR (OR S X)
           (NOT N))))))
       (defun ADF1 ()
         (values (AND (AND (NOT (NOT X)) (NOT (OR S X)))
                      (NOT (OR S X)))))
       (defun ADF2 ()
         (values (OR (AND (NOT (AND W E)) (OR (AND NW W) (NOT
           NW))) (OR (OR (AND N E) (AND S SE)) (OR (AND W (NOT
```

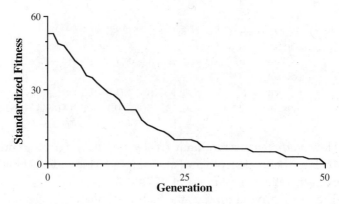

Figure 15.9 Standardized fitness of the best-of-generation programs of the letter-recognition problem with ADFs.

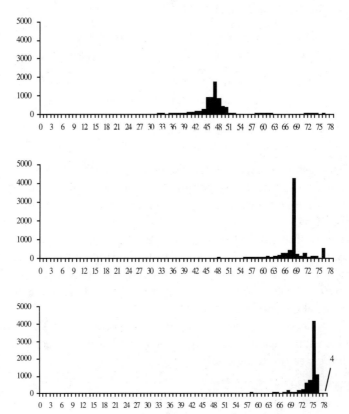

Figure 15.10 Hits histograms for generations 15, 30, and 50 of the letter-recognition problem with ADFs.

```
            NW)) (OR SE NE))))))
(defun ADF3 ()
  (values (AND (NOT (AND (NOT SE) (OR W SW))) (OR (NOT
    (OR NW (NOT NW))) (AND (NOT S) (AND (NOT (AND (NOT
    SE) (OR W SW))) (OR (NOT (OR NW (NOT (AND (NOT SE)
    (OR W SW))))) (AND (NOT S) (OR (NOT (NOT NW)) (NOT
    SE))))))))))
(defun ADF4 ()
  (values (AND (NOT (OR (OR W SW) (OR NW NW))) (AND (AND
    (AND X N) (NOT NE)) (AND (NOT (OR (OR E SW) (OR NW
    NW))) (AND (AND (AND (AND X N) (NOT NE)) (NOT NE))
    (OR (OR N SE) (OR X E))))))))
(values (IF (OR (NOT (ADF4)) (AND (OR (NOT (AND (GO-S)
  (GO-S))) (AND (OR (NOT (AND (GO-S) (GO-S))) (AND (NOT
  (AND (ADF3) (ADF3))) (HOMING (GO-S)))) (OR (NOT (AND
  (GO-S) (GO-S))) (AND (HOMING (GO-N)) (HOMING (GO-
  N)))))) (OR (NOT (ADF4)) (AND (OR (NOT (AND (GO-S)
  (GO-S))) (AND (OR (NOT (AND (GO-S) (GO-S))) (AND (NOT
  (AND (ADF3) (ADF3))) (HOMING (GO-N)))) (OR (NOT (AND
  (GO-S) (GO-S))) (AND (HOMING (GO-N)) (HOMING (GO-
  N)))))) (OR (NOT (AND (GO-S) (GO-S))) (AND (NOT (AND
  (GO-S)
  (ADF3))) (HOMING (GO-N))))))))))) ;;; antecedent of outermost IF
(IF (HOMING (AND (GO-S) (ADF0))) (IF (GO-S) NIL L) (IF
(HOMING (GO-S)) (IF (ADF1) L I) (IF (ADF1) L NIL)));
;; then-part of outermost IF
(IF (OR (OR (GO-E) (ADF3)) (AND (OR (NOT (ADF4)) (AND
(NOT (ADF3)) (OR (NOT (AND (GO-S) (GO-S))) (AND (NOT
(GO-S)) (AND (ADF3) (ADF3)))))) (HOMING (GO-N)))) (IF
(ADF2) (IF (GO-S) L NIL) (IF (GO-S) (IF (ADF3) L NIL)
(IF (GO-S) NIL L))) (IF (NOT (ADF1)) (IF (GO-E) NIL I)
(IF (ADF1) L L))) ;;; else-part of outermost IF
))) .
```

The performance of the 100%-correct best-of-run individual from generation 50 from the run described above can be understood by first considering how this program successfully recognizes the pixel pattern for the letter L. To aid in this process, figure 15.11 identifies the seven pixels that must be ON for the pattern to be the letter L with the Roman numerals I through VII and identifies the 14 adjacent pixels that must be OFF for the letter L with the lower-case letters a through n. The turtle always starts at pixel III for any pattern.

When the best-of-run individual from generation 50 encounters an L, it moves the turtle 25 times. Figure 15.12 shows the 25 steps in this trajectory, with the turtle starting at pixel III and ending at pixel n. The figure omits certain numbers where the turtle repetitively moves back and forth over the same two adjacent pixels.

Since the result-producing branch begins with (IF (OR (NOT (ADF4)) ..., the defined function ADF4 is evaluated with the turtle at its starting location

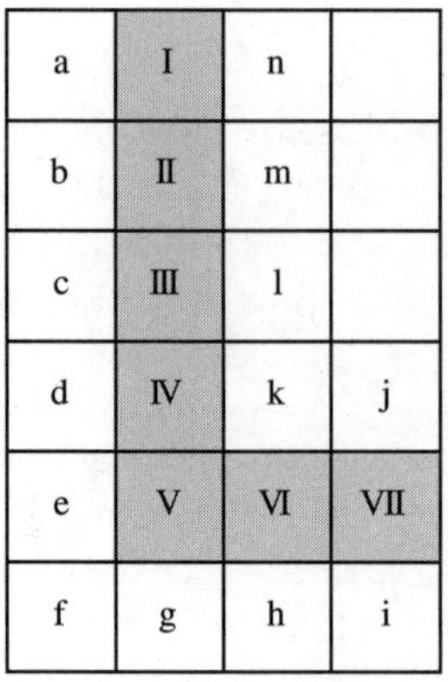

a
I
n
b
II
m
c
III
l
d
IV
k
j
e
V
VI
VII
f
g
h
i

Figure 15.11 The seven ON and 14 OFF pixels constituting the letter L.

4
6
14
18
25
5
9
17
0
10
20
1
11
21
2
12
22
23
3
13
24

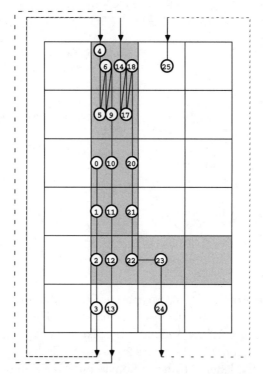

Figure 15.12 Trajectory of the turtle for identifying an L for best-of-run program from generation 50.

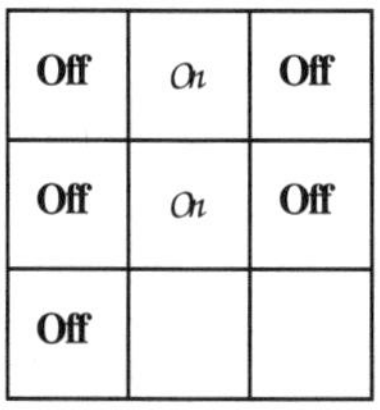

Off	O_n	Off
Off	O_n	Off
Off		

Figure 15.13 Arrangement of pixels required to cause ADF4 to return T.

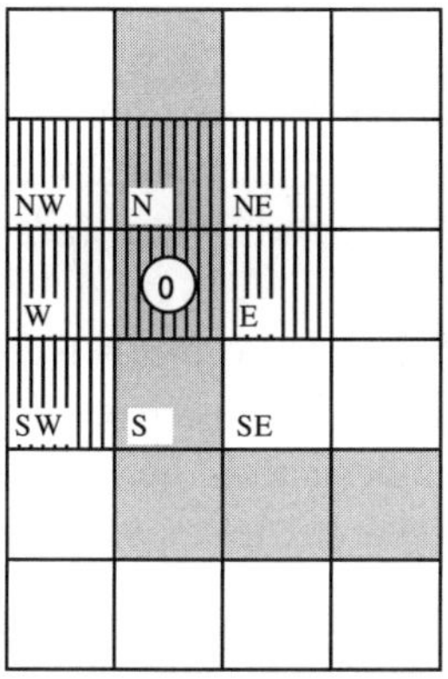

Figure 15.14 Detector ADF4 applied at pixel III at turtle step 0.

(pixel III) at turtle step 0. Detector ADF4 examines seven of the nine pixels within view.

Figure 15.13 shows the seven pixel values required to cause the function definition for ADF4 to return a value of T. ADF4 depends on seven pixels, lacks any reference to pixel S, and effectively ignores pixel SE.

When the turtle is located at pixel III (as shown in figure 15.14), pixels II and III are ON, and pixels b, c, d, m, and l are OFF, ADF4 returns T. These latter five pixels all lie adjacent to the vertical segment of the L. As a result, when the turtle is at pixel III, ADF4 acts as a detector for two of the three vertically stacked pixels of a potential L being ON and as a detector for five of the six pixels adjacent to the potential L being OFF. ADF4 is an incomplete detector for a vertical line segment.

Since ADF4 returns T when the turtle is located at pixel III, (NOT (ADF4)) is NIL, so the second clause of the first OR must be evaluated. This second clause begins with (AND (OR (NOT (AND (GO-S) (GO-S)))).... When the first argument of the inner AND, namely (GO-S), is evaluated, the turtle moves south (down the vertical segment of the L) from pixel III to pixel IV. Since pixel IV is ON after this turtle step 1, the (GO-S) operator returns T, thus necessitating evaluation of the second argument of this inner AND. This second argument, which consists of another (GO-S) operator, moves the turtle south again from pixel IV to pixel V. Since pixel V is also ON after turtle step 2, the inner AND returns T. However, the NOT necessitates evaluation of the second argument of the OR, namely

Automatic Discovery of Detectors for Letter Recognition

```
(AND (OR (NOT (AND (GO-S) ... )) ... )).
```

The (GO-S) operator (the first argument to the inner AND above) now moves the turtle south to pixel g. Pixel g is OFF at turtle step 3, since it is below the vertical segment of the L. When we evaluate the two-argument Boolean AND function, it skips evaluation of the second argument whenever the first argument evaluates to NIL. (Similarly, evaluation of the second argument of the OR function is skipped whenever the first argument evaluates to T.) The second (GO-S) argument to the AND is replaced with an ellipsis, since it will not be evaluated. This illustrates the fact that when side-effecting operators are contained in arguments to Boolean functions, the operators are conditionally executed depending on the context. Since the NOT negates the NIL returned by the AND, the second argument to the OR containing seven points is also skipped. We replace it with a second ellipsis.

Now, two (GO-S) operators move the turtle to pixels I and II (since the grid is toroidal) at turtle steps 4 and 5. The (GO-N) moves the turtle back to pixel I at turtle step 6, but the HOMING rubber-bands the turtle back to pixel II at turtle step 7. This sequence is repeated at turtle steps 8 and 9, leaving the turtle at pixel II.

Detector ADF4 is now applied at pixel II. Figure 15.15 shows that when the turtle is located at pixel II, ADF4 returns T when pixels I and II are ON and when pixels a, b, c, m, and n are OFF.

Detector ADF4 returns T and thereby provides the new information that pixels a and n are OFF. As a result, by turtle step 9, seven pixels (a, b, c, d, l, m, and n) have been verified as being OFF by two different applications of detector ADF4 and one additional pixel (g) has been verified as being OFF by the (GO-S) operator. In addition, five pixels (I, II, III, IV, and V) have been verified (often repetitively) as being ON. Several pixels have been verified by more than one action by turtle step 9.

Between turtle steps 10 and 21, the turtle repetitively moves up and down (because of several HOMINGs) along the vertical segment of the L, but provides no new information.

The turtle arrives at pixel IV at turtle step 21 and begins evaluation of the last six points of the antecedent clause of the outermost IF of the result-producing branch, namely

```
(AND (NOT (AND (GO-S) (ADF3)))
     (HOMING (GO-N))))))))).
```

The (GO-S) operator moves the turtle to pixel V (the junction of the L, which is ON) and executes detector ADF3.

Figure 15.16 shows the pixel values required to cause ADF3 to return a value of T. As can be seen, ADF3 examines five pixels (NW, W, SW, S, and SE) to see if they are all OFF.

Figure 15.17 shows that when the turtle is located at pixel V (the corner of the L), ADF3 returns T when pixels d, e, f, g, and h are OFF. These five pixels

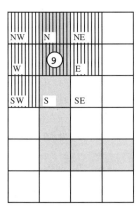

Figure 15.15 Detector `ADF4` applied at pixel II at turtle step 9.

Off		
Off		
Off	Off	Off

Figure 15.16 Arrangement of pixels required to cause `(ADF3)` to return a value of `T`.

all lie adjacent to the corner of the `L`, so `ADF3` acts as a detector for emptiness adjacent to the corner of an `L`.

Since the `NOT` negates the return value of the `AND`, the `(HOMING (GO-N))` is not executed.

For the letter `L`, the antecedent part of the outermost `IF` of the result-producing branch evaluates to `NIL`, so that the second (then) argument of the `IF` is skipped and the third (else) argument is executed. The `(GO-E)` operator moves the turtle east to pixel VI (which is ON) and causes detector `ADF2` to be evaluated for turtle step 23.

Figure 15.18 shows that `ADF2` examines six pixels. `ADF2` returns a value of `NIL` when `NW`, `W`, and `E` are ON and when `N`, `NE`, and `SE` are OFF.

Figure 15.19 shows that when the turtle is located at pixel VI at turtle step 23, `ADF2` returns a value of `NIL` when pixels IV, V, and VII are ON and when pixels i, j, and k are OFF.

The result now depends on the following expression involving detector `ADF2`:

```
1 (IF (ADF2)
2     (IF (GO-S) L NIL)
3     (IF (GO-S)
4         (IF (ADF3) L NIL)
5         (IF (GO-S) NIL L)) … ).
```

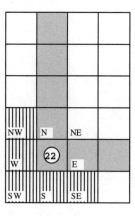

Figure 15.17   Detector ADF3 applied at pixel V at turtle step 22.

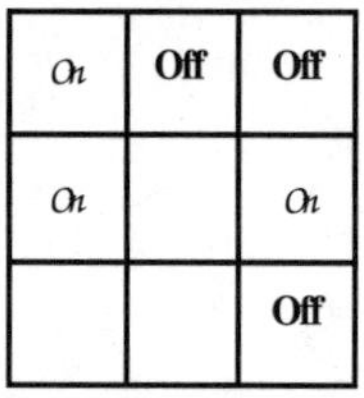

On	Off	Off
On		On
		Off

Figure 15.18   Arrangement of pixels required to cause ADF2 to return a value of NIL.

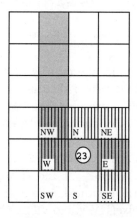

Figure 15.19   Detector ADF2 applied at pixel VI at turtle step 23.

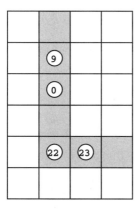

Figure 15.20 Turtle steps 0, 9, 22, and 23, where detectors ADF4, ADF4, ADF3, and ADF2, respectively, are applied.

For the letter L, ADF2 evaluates to NIL on line 1. As a result, line 2 is skipped and the (GO-S) operator on line 3 moves the turtle south to pixel h at turtle step 24. Since pixel h is OFF, line 4 is skipped and the (GO-S) operator on line 5 moves the turtle toroidally to pixel n for turtle step 25. Since pixel n is OFF for the L, the result-producing branch returns L, which is indeed the correct identification of the pattern.

If detector ADF2 were to return T on line 1 above, this indicates either that pixel i, j or k is ON or that pixel VII is OFF (since pixels IV and V were previously established as being ON). Any of these four possibilities would mean that the pattern is a flawed pattern for which NIL (rather than L or I) should be returned. For example, if pixel VII were OFF and pixel i were ON or if pixel VII were ON and pixel i were ON, the pattern would be a flawed L. In these situations, the (GO-S) operator on line 2 would be executed, thereby moving the turtle to pixel h. Since pixel h is already known to be OFF, the result-producing branch would return NIL, which under the circumstances would be a correct identification of the pattern. Similarly, the result-producing branch returns the value NIL for the 14 fitness cases for which there is an extraneous ON pixel adjacent to an L (in locations a through n) and the seven fitness cases for which there is a missing pixel within an L (in locations I through VII).

In summary, the best-of-run individual from generation 50 applies detectors at turtle steps 0, 9, 22, and 23 and considers direct input from the turtle over 25 steps in order to determine that all seven pixels (I through IV) that should be ON for an L are indeed ON and that all 14 pixels that should be OFF for an L are indeed OFF, as shown in figure 15.20.

In identifying the letter I, the turtle moves up and down the vertical column consisting of pixels I through V and pixel g for the first 22 turtle steps much as in the identification of the L. However, when the turtle moves east on turtle step 23, pixel VI is OFF for the I.

The detector ADF0 is used to determine that certain patterns should be classified as NIL, although it is not used in classifying the positive cases.

Although `ADF1` is merely the constant function `NIL`, it appears, and is used, in the result-producing branch.

Even when automatically defined functions are used, this problem is so time-consuming that we have only made two successful runs. We do not contemplate making a performance curve for this problem.

15.6   GENEALOGICAL AUDIT TRAILS WITH ADFs

A genealogical audit trail shows the way that the crossover operation creates offspring programs that are progressively more fit at classifying patterns.

For example, most of the genetic material for the best of generation 15 comes from the 180th best program in the population from generation 14. In fact, the best of generation 15 differs from this first parent only by the six-point subtree of `ADF1`, shown below in boldface. Parent A from generation 14 scores 47 hits and is shown below:

```
(progn (defun ADF0 ()
         (values (OR (OR (AND (OR S X) (OR N SW)) (OR (AND (NOT
           (OR SW SW)) (NOT (AND X SW))) (OR (OR (AND X NW) (AND
           SE NE)) (AND (OR NE E) (OR X SW))))) (AND (OR (NOT S)
           (NOT (OR S SW))) (OR (AND W SE) (NOT N)))))))
       (defun ADF1 ()
         (values (AND (AND (NOT (NOT X)) (NOT (OR S X)))    (OR W
           (NOT (AND N SW)))))))
       (defun ADF2 ()
         (values (OR (AND (NOT (AND W E)) (OR (AND NW W) (NOT
           NW))) (OR (OR (AND N E) (AND S SE)) (OR (AND W (NOT
           NW)) (OR SE NE))))))
       (defun ADF3 ()
         (values (AND (NOT (AND (NOT SE) (OR W SW))) (OR (NOT
           (OR NW (NOT NW))) (AND (NOT S) (OR (NOT (NOT NW))
           (NOT SE)))))))
       (defun ADF4 ()
         (values (AND (NOT (OR (OR W SW) (OR NW NW))) (AND (AND
           (AND X N) (NOT NE)) (OR (OR N SE) (OR X E))))))
       (values (IF (OR (NOT (ADF4)) (AND (NOT (ADF3)) (OR (NOT
         (AND (GO-S) (GO-S))) (AND (NOT (AND (ADF3) (ADF3)))
         (HOMING (GO-N)))))) (IF (HOMING (AND (GO-S) (ADF0)))
         (IF (GO-S) NIL L) (IF (HOMING (GO-S)) (IF (ADF1) L I)
         (IF (GO-W) L NIL))) (IF (OR (OR (GO-E) (ADF3)) (AND
         (ADF3) (ADF3))) (IF (HOMING (GO-N)) (IF (ADF1) L NIL)
         (IF (ADF3) NIL L)) (IF (NOT (ADF1)) (IF (GO-E) NIL I)
         (IF (ADF1) L L)))))).
```

Parent B from generation 14 scores 48 hits and contributes only the four-point subtree from its `ADF1`, shown in boldface below.

```
(progn (defun ADF0 ()
         (values (OR (OR (AND (OR S X) (OR N SW)) (OR (OR (AND X
           SW) E) (AND S NW))) (AND (OR (NOT S) (AND S SE)) (AND
```

```
                (AND W SW) (OR NW W))))))
      (defun ADF1 ()
         (values (AND (AND (NOT (NOT X)) (NOT (OR S X))) (OR
            (AND (AND SW NW) (NOT SW)) (NOT (AND N SW))))))
      (defun ADF2 ()
         (values (OR (AND (NOT (AND W E)) (OR (AND NW W) (NOT
            NW))) (OR (OR (AND N E) (AND S SE)) (OR (AND W SE)
            (OR SE NE))))))
      (defun ADF3 ()
         (values (AND (NOT (AND (OR SW N) (OR W SW))) (OR (NOT
            (OR NW NE)) (NOT (OR NW NE))))))
      (defun ADF4 ()
         (values (AND (NOT (OR (OR W SW) (OR NW NW))) (AND (AND
            (AND X N) (NOT NE)) (AND X N)))))
      (values (IF (OR (NOT (AND (GO-S) (GO-S))) (AND (NOT
         (ADF3)) (HOMING (GO-N)))) (IF (HOMING (AND (GO-S)
         (ADF0))) (IF (ADF3) L NIL) (IF (HOMING (GO-S)) (IF
         (ADF1) L I) (IF (GO-W) L NIL))) (IF (OR (OR (GO-E)
         (HOMING (AND (GO-S) (ADF0)))) (AND (ADF3) (ADF3)))
         (IF (HOMING (ADF2)) (IF (ADF3) L NIL) (IF (GO-S) NIL
         L)) (IF (NOT (ADF1)) (IF (ADF0) NIL I) (IF (ADF1) L
         L)))))).
```

The best of generation 15 scores 56 hits and consists of parent A of generation 14 with the insertion of the highlighted four-point subtree from parent B of generation 14. This offspring is shown below with the inserted crossover fragment shown in boldface

```
(progn (defun ADF0 ()
            (values (OR (OR (AND (OR S X) (OR N SW)) (OR (AND (NOT
               (OR SW SW)) (NOT (AND X SW))) (OR (OR (AND X NW) (AND
               SE NE)) (AND (OR NE E) (OR X SW))))) (AND (OR (NOT S)
               (NOT (OR S SW))) (OR (AND W SE) (NOT N))))))
         (defun ADF1 ()
            (values (AND (AND (NOT (NOT X)) (NOT (OR S X))) (NOT
            (OR S X)))))
         (defun ADF2 ()
            (values (OR (AND (NOT (AND W E)) (OR (AND NW W) (NOT
               NW))) (OR (OR (AND N E) (AND S SE)) (OR (AND W (NOT
               NW)) (OR SE NE))))))
         (defun ADF3 ()
            (values (AND (NOT (AND (NOT SE) (OR W SW))) (OR (NOT
               (OR NW (NOT NW))) (AND (NOT S) (OR (NOT (NOT NW))
               (NOT SE)))))))
         (defun ADF4 ()
            (values (AND (NOT (OR (OR W SW) (OR NW NW))) (AND (AND
               (AND X N) (NOT NE)) (OR (OR N SE) (OR X E))))))
         (values (IF (OR (NOT (ADF4)) (AND (NOT (ADF3)) (OR (NOT
            (AND (GO-S) (GO-S))) (AND (NOT (AND (ADF3) (ADF3)))
            (HOMING (GO-N)))))) (IF (HOMING (AND (GO-S) (ADF0)))
            (IF (GO-S) NIL L) (IF (HOMING (GO-S)) (IF (ADF1) L I)
```

```
(IF (GO-W) L NIL))) (IF (OR (OR (GO-E) (ADF3)) (AND (ADF3)
(ADF3))) (IF (HOMING (GO-N)) (IF (ADF1) L NIL) (IF (ADF3)
NIL L)) (IF (NOT (ADF1)) (IF (GO-E) NIL I)
(IF (ADF1) L L))))))) .
```

The result of the crossover is that ADF1 in the above offspring program
from generation 15 is always NIL. This has the effect of making it impossible
for the first two IFs that test ADF1 to return a classification of L. The third
occurrence of ADF1 has the effect of preventing access to the fourth occurrence of ADF1.

15.7 DETECTORS OF DIFFERENT SIZES AND SHAPES

Before solving the letter-recognition problem described above, we decided
that there would be five detectors, each capable of examining a 3-by-3 pixel
subarea of the overall 6-by-4 pixel grid.

Solving this problem does not depend on using square subareas. One might
have decided to include detectors capable of examining subareas of different
sizes and shapes. For example, one might have decided to have three 3-by-3
detectors, one 1-by-3 detector capable of examining a horizontal row of width
3, and one 3-by-1 detector capable of examining a vertical column of height 3.

For example, if ADF0 is the 1-by-3 detector capable of examining a horizontal row of width 3, the terminal set for ADF0 consists only of the three sensors
X, E, and W. Similarly, if ADF1 is the 3-by-1 detector capable of examining a
vertical column of height 3, the terminal set for ADF1 consists only of the
three sensors X, N, and S.

The following 100%-correct 244-point program emerged in generation 22
of a run:

```
(progn (defun ADF0 ()
         (values (AND (AND X (AND (AND X (OR W E)) (AND X (OR W
           E)))) (AND (OR W E) (NOT E)))))
       (defun ADF1 ()
         (values (OR N (OR N N))))
       (defun ADF2 ()
         (values (NOT (OR (NOT SE) NE))))
       (defun ADF3 ()
         (values (OR (AND X E) (OR (OR W NE) (NOT (AND (OR E N)
           (NOT SW))))))
       (defun ADF4 ()
         (values (OR (NOT (NOT SW)) (NOT SW))))
       (values (IF (OR (OR (OR (ADF3) (OR (GO-W) (HOMING (OR
         (HOMING (HOMING (OR (GO-W) (AND (OR (GO-S) (OR (GO-S)
         (GO-W))) (OR (GO-S) (ADF3))))))) (AND (NOT (AND (OR
         (GO-S) (GO-S)) (OR (GO-S) (GO-W)))) (OR (GO-S) (OR
         (GO-S) (OR (OR (ADF3) (ADF3)) (OR (GO-S) (GO-
         S)))))))))) (GO-S)) (OR (GO-E) (GO-W))) (IF (OR
         (ADF3) (OR (GO-W) (GO-S))) (IF (ADF3) NIL I) (IF (AND
         (GO-E) (NOT (HOMING (OR (HOMING (OR (HOMING (HOMING
```

```
(ADF2))) (AND (NOT (AND (OR (GO-S) (GO-E)) (OR (ADF0)
(ADF3)))) (OR (GO-S) (GO-E))))) (OR (GO-E) (GO-
E)))))) (IF (OR (GO-S) (ADF3)) L I) (IF (OR (OR (ADF3)
(OR (GO-S) (GO-W))) (OR (GO-W) (ADF3))) (IF (AND (GO-
E) (NOT (GO-S))) (IF (AND (ADF1) (AND (NOT (AND (OR
(GO-S) (GO-S)) (OR (OR (ADF3)
(ADF3)) (OR (ADF3) (OR (GO-S) (GO-S)))))) (OR (GO-S)
(OR (GO-S) (OR (OR (ADF3) (ADF3)) (OR (GO-S) (GO-
S))))))) L I) (IF (OR (GO-W) (AND (NOT (AND (OR (GO-E)
(GO-W)) (OR (GO-S) (GO-S)))) (OR (GO-S) (AND (OR (GO-
E) (GO-S)) (HOMING (ADF2)))))) NIL NIL)) (IF (AND (GO-
S) (NOT (HOMING (OR (HOMING (HOMING (ADF2))) (GO-W)))))
(IF (OR (OR (GO-W) (GO-S)) (AND (NOT (AND (OR (GO-S) (GO-
S)) (OR (GO-S) (GO-S)))) (OR (GO-S) (GO-S)))) L
NIL) (IF (ADF0) L NIL))))) (IF (ADF0) L NIL)))).
```

In this program ADF0 examines only X, E, and W, and ADF1 examines only
N (although it is capable of also examining S and X).

15.8 TRANSLATION-INVARIANT LETTER RECOGNITION

In the letter-recognition problem described above, the letters were situated at
a particular location within the 6-by-4 pixel grid. Genetic programming is
also capable of solving translation-invariant letter-recognition problems.

We introduced a wrapper that caused the execution of the overall program
from each of the 24 possible starting locations in the 6-by-4 grid area. Equiva-
lently, one can view the 6-by-4 grid area as a cellular space in which the same
overall program is embedded at each location (i.e., a *cellular automaton*). As
one would expect, this version of the problem is far more time-consuming
than the original highly time-consuming version. To reduce the amount of
computer time required, we simplified the problem to one of identifying only
the letter I (and the negative category NIL). If any of the 24 executions programs identified a pattern as the letter I, the pattern is classified as an
I. Otherwise, the pattern is classified as a NIL. Sixty fitness cases were used
(all but the 18 patterns of figure 15.8).

In one run, the following 100%-correct program capable of translation-invariant recognition of the letter I emerged in generation 32:

```
(progn (defun ADF0 ()
        (values (OR (AND (NOT (NOT SW)) (OR (NOT E) (OR S E)))
          (NOT (AND (AND (NOT SE) (OR S S)) (NOT E))))))
      (defun ADF1 ()
        (values (NOT (OR E SW))))
      (defun ADF2 ()
        (values (OR (OR (OR (AND S X) (NOT NE)) (OR (NOT N) (OR
          (OR (OR (OR (AND S X) (NOT NE)) (NOT N)) (NOT NE))
          (OR (OR (OR (OR X NW) (NOT NE)) (OR (NOT N) (AND S
          S))) (NOT (NOT (AND S S)))))))) (NOT (NOT (NOT (AND S
```

```
                  X)))))))
     (defun ADF3 ()
       (values (OR (NOT (OR (NOT NW) (AND SE SW))) (OR (AND
         (AND SE SW) (NOT W)) (AND E W)))))
     (defun ADF4 ()
       (values (AND (AND (NOT (OR X W)) (OR (NOT S) (OR N X)))
         (NOT (NOT (OR SE X))))))
     (values (IF (AND (NOT (AND (ADF1) (ADF0))) (AND (AND
       (ADF1) (AND (GO-N) (NOT (ADF0)))) (OR (ADF3) (AND
       (ADF1) (AND (GO-N) (NOT (ADF0))))))) (IF (OR (GO-N)
       (OR (ADF0) (GO-W))) (IF (GO-N) NIL NIL) (IF (OR (OR
       (GO-N) (AND (ADF1) (ADF0))) (GO-W)) (IF (GO-N) NIL
       NIL) (IF (GO-W) NIL I))) (IF (ADF0) NIL NIL)))).
```

The result-producing branch of this program returns either I or NIL.

15.9   SUMMARY

This chapter has described an approach for simultaneously discovering detectors and a way of combining the detectors to solve a problem. The approach was illustrated using a problem of letter recognition. The genetically evolved detectors were repeatedly invoked to produce a solution to the overall problem.

See also Koza 1993a.

16 Flushes and Four-of-a-Kinds in a Pinochle Deck

The problem of recognizing a flush or four-of-a-kind in a five-card hand from a pinochle deck is another example of a problem whose solution can be facilitated by the automatic discovery of reusable, initially-unknown detectors.

16.1 THE FLUSH PROBLEM

In this problem, five cards are drawn (without replacement) from a 24-card pinochle deck. The *denomination* of a card can be ace, king, queen, jack, ten, or nine; the *suit* of a card can be club, diamond, heart, or spade. A five-card hand is a *flush* if all five cards are of the same suit. A hand contains a *four-of-a-kind* if four of the five cards share the same denomination.

We first consider the flush problem where the goal is to discover a computer program that determines whether a given hand dealt from a 24-card pinochle deck is a flush.

16.2 PREPARATORY STEPS WITHOUT ADFs

We envisage that the input to each program for the flush problem will be the five cards of the hand and that each program will be a decision tree consisting of a composition of decision-making functions that return the identification FLUSH or NIL.

The terminal set, T, for the flush problem consists of the five cards in the hand and the constants FLUSH and NIL for naming the category into which the hand is classified.

$T = \{$CARD0, CARD1, CARD2, CARD3, CARD4, NIL, FLUSH$\}$.

The function set, F, consists of

$F = \{$SUIT, DENOM, IF, AND, OR, NOT, EQ$\}$

with an argument map of

$\{1, 1, 3, 2, 2, 1, 2\}$.

SUIT returns the suit of a card; DENOM returns the denomination of a card. Both SUIT and DENOM return NIL if the argument is anything other than a card. For example, if CARD0 is the ace of hearts, (SUIT CARD0) returns HEART; (DENOM CARD0) returns ACE; and (DENOM FLUSH) returns NIL.

In addition, IF, AND, OR, NOT, and EQ (equal) are the usual LISP functions.

Each program in the population could reasonably be an unconstrained composition of functions from the function set, $\mathcal{F}$, and terminals from the terminal set, $\mathcal{T}$; however, experience indicates that the programs produced by genetic programming composed of functions playing distinctly different roles can be very difficult to analyze, understand, and verify. In this problem, the role of two of the functions (SUIT and DENOM) is to detect the characteristics of a card. The EQ function tests for equality. The role of three of the functions (AND, OR, and NOT) is to perform logical analysis. Finally, the role of the conditional decision-making operator IF is to perform the classification of the hand into the two categories. Experience also indicates that we can greatly enhance our ability to analyze, understand, and verify such genetically evolved programs if we impose a constrained syntactic structure on the programs.

Specifically, we structure each program as a decision tree whose root node must always be an IF. Programs typically contain many additional IFs. The first (condition) argument of every IF must be a composition only of EQ, AND, OR, and NOT; the five cards (CARD0, CARD1, CARD2, CARD3, and CARD4); and the detecting functions (SUIT and DENOM). In particular, the first argument of an IF does not contain another IF. The second (then) and third (else) argument of each IF contains only other IF operators or categories (FLUSH or NIL). The effect of these constraints is that the condition part of each IF is truly a condition and the action part of each IF is truly a consequence (i.e., another IF or a category).

It is not clear whether the constrained syntactic structure hinders or improves the performance of genetic programming in discovering a suitable program; however, it is clear that it substantially increases our ability to understand the genetically evolved programs. The use of the constrained syntactic structure does not, however, entirely eliminate the problem of opacity; the analysis of genetically evolved programs often still requires considerable effort.

We do not have sufficient computer time to measure the fitness of each individual in the population of each generation of a run against all 42,504 possible five-card pinochle hands. Consequently, we construct a sampling of fitness cases for the purpose of evolving a solution to the problem. For reasons that will soon become clear, we call this sampling the *in-sample fitness cases* for the problem. The in-sample fitness cases for this problem consist of 1,000 random hands, of which half are random flushes and half are random hands that are not flushes. To be useful, a randomized set of fitness cases such as this must be sufficiently large that it is representative of the problem environment as a whole.

When a genetically evolved program in the population is tested against a particular fitness case, the outcome can be

- a true-positive (i.e., the program correctly predicts that the given hand is a flush when the hand is, in fact, a flush),

- a true-negative (i.e., the program correctly predicts that the given hand is not a flush when the hand is, in fact, not a flush),

- a false-positive (i.e., the program "overpredicts" that the given hand is a flush when the hand is, in fact, not a flush), or

- a false-negative (i.e., the program "underpredicts" that the given hand is not a flush when the hand is, in fact, a flush).

Fitness will measure how well a genetically evolved program predicts whether a given five-card hand is a flush. Consider a first vector of $N_{fc} = 1,000$ correct answers (with the integer 1 representing FLUSH and the integer 0 representing NIL) for the set of 1,000 in-sample fitness cases in a space of dimensionality N_{fc}. Now consider a second vector of N_{fc} of 1,000 predictions (1 or 0) produced by a particular genetically evolved program for the set of 1,000 in-sample fitness cases. Suppose each vector is transformed into a zero-mean vector by subtracting the average value of all its components from each component. Fitness can be measured by the correlation coefficient C. Specifically, the *in-sample correlation, C,* is the cosine of the angle in this space of dimensionality N_{fc} between the zero-mean vector of correct answers and the zero-mean vector of predictions. A correlation C of –1.0 indicates that the pair of vectors point in opposite directions in N_{fc}-space (i.e., greatest negative correlation); a correlation of +1.0 indicates coincident vectors (i.e., greatest positive correlation); a correlation C of 0.0 indicates orthogonality (i.e., no correlation). Additional discussion of correlation and other measures of agreement between observed data and predicting programs is contained in subsection 18.5.2.

The in-sample correlation, C, lends itself immediately to being the measure of raw fitness for a genetically evolved computer program. Since raw fitness ranges between –1.0 and +1.0 (higher values being better), standardized fitness can then be defined as

$$\frac{1-C}{2}.$$

Standardized fitness ranges between 0.0 and +1.0, lower values being better and a value of 0 being best. Specifically, a standardized fitness of 0 indicates perfect agreement between the predicting program and the observed reality; a standardized fitness of +1.0 indicates perfect disagreement; a standardized fitness of 0.50 indicates that the predictor is no better than random.

Table 16.1 summarizes the key features of the flush problem without automatically defined functions.

16.3   RESULTS WITHOUT ADFs

The following 54-point program from generation 20 of one run of the flush problem achieved 500 true positives and 500 true negatives, with no false positives or false negatives. Consequently, it achieved a correlation of 1.00 and a standardized fitness of 0.0.

```
(IF (EQ (SUIT CARD2) (SUIT CARD4)) (IF (EQ (SUIT CARD1) (SUIT
CARD3)) (IF (EQ (SUIT CARD0) (SUIT CARD3)) (IF (EQ (SUIT CARD2)
(SUIT CARD3)) (IF (EQ (SUIT CARD0) (SUIT CARD3)) (IF CARD1 FLUSH
FLUSH) (IF CARD2 NIL NIL)) (IF CARD1 NIL FLUSH)) (IF CARD0 NIL
FLUSH)) (IF CARD1 NIL FLUSH)) (IF CARD1 NIL FLUSH)).
```

This best-of-run program from generation 20 can be rewritten as

```
1    (IF (EQ (SUIT CARD2) (SUIT CARD4))
2        (IF (EQ (SUIT CARD1) (SUIT CARD3))
3            (IF (EQ (SUIT CARD0) (SUIT CARD3))
4                (IF (EQ (SUIT CARD2) (SUIT CARD3))
5                    (IF (EQ (SUIT CARD0) (SUIT CARD3)) FLUSH NIL)
6                    NIL)
7                NIL)
8            NIL)
9        NIL).
```

When so simplified, it can be seen that the suit of CARD3 is compared to the suits of CARD1, CARD0, and CARD2 on lines 2, 3, and 4 and then recompared to the suit of CARD0 on line 5. The suit of CARD2 is compared to the suit of CARD4 on the first line. If all of these comparisons indicate equality, the hand is correctly classified as a flush. If any comparison fails, the hand is classified as not being a flush.

The true measure of performance for a predicting program is how well it generalizes to different cases from its problem environment. We are able to say that the above best-of-run program from generation 20 successfully generalizes perfectly to the entire problem environment for this particular problem because we fully understand the nature of the problem environment and because we are able to analyze the actual operation of the program in order to verify that it does indeed solve the problem. In general, it is not possible to verify a genetically evolved program in this way for more complicated classification problems.

As an alternative to verifying a genetically evolved program by analytic means, we can *cross-validate* the performance of such a program by testing it against unseen additional fitness cases (called the *out-of-sample* fitness cases). For this problem, there are 42,504 possible five-card hands from a pinochle deck. Although it would be prohibitively time-consuming to measure the fitness of all 4,000 individual programs in all 51 generations of every run of genetic programming against this entire universe of 42,504 fitness cases, we can readily measure the fitness for the one best-of-run program from generation 20 against these 42,504 fitness cases. When we test the generality of the best-of-run program by testing it against all possible 42,504 hands, we find that the two vectors in 42,504-space agree exactly. The value of *out-of-sample correlation* for the best-of-run program over the entire set of 42,504 five-card pinochle hands is therefore also 1.00.

Table 16.1 Tableau without ADFs for the flush problem.

Objective:	Find a program that identifies whether a given five-card hand from a pinochle deck is a flush.
Terminal set without ADFs:	CARD0, CARD1, CARD2, CARD3, CARD4, NIL, and FLUSH.
Function set without ADFs:	SUIT, DENOM, IF, AND, OR, NOT, and EQ.
Fitness cases:	1,000 in-sample fitness cases, of which a half are random flushes and half are random hands that are not flushes.
Raw fitness:	Correlation C (ranging from -1.0 to $+1.0$).
Standardized fitness:	Standardized fitness is $$\frac{1-C}{2}.$$
Hits:	Not used for this problem.
Wrapper:	None.
Parameters:	$M = 4,000.$ $G = 51.$
Success predicate:	A program scores the maximum number of hits.
Types of points:	• The IF operator (which is always at the root). • Point in first argument (condition part) of IF. • Point in second (then) or third (else) argument of IF.
Rules of construction:	• The root node must be an IF. • The condition (first) argument of an IF may contain any composition of the Boolean operators (EQ, AND, OR, and NOT), the five cards (CARD0, CARD1, CARD2, CARD3, and CARD4), and the detecting functions (SUIT and DENOM without automatically defined functions but ADF0 and ADF1 with automatically defined functions). • The second (then) and third (else) argument of an IF contains only other IFs or references to the terminals for the two categories (FLUSH or NIL).

Since this out-of-sample set of 42,504 fitness cases happens to be an exhaustive set of the entire problem environment, we can say that this best-of-run program from generation 10 is a 100% correct solution to the overall problem of identifying flushes from a pinochle deck. Thus, for this particular problem, we have both analytically verified and empirically verified that the genetically evolved program is a perfect solution to the problem.

Note that for more complicated problems, cross validation does not usually involve testing a predicting program against all possible unseen fitness cases; it merely involves testing against different set(s) of previously unseen fitness cases. We were able to do an exhaustive cross-validation here only because the number of possible five-card hands is only 42,504.

It is interesting to note that we first tried this problem with only 250 randomly chosen in-sample fitness cases. In those preliminary runs, we learned that a set of fitness cases of such a small size is not sufficiently representative of the overall problem environment to permit evolution of a 100%-correct predicting programs for this problem (except perhaps by coincidence). Genetic programming routinely evolved programs that were capable of perfectly classifying the sets of 250 in-sample fitness cases (i.e., these evolved programs scored only true positives and true negatives on the 250 in-sample fitness cases). However, these programs were overly specialized to the particular fitness cases used in the evolutionary process; they did not contain a complete chain of equality comparisons necessary to correctly handle all possible five-card hands; and they did not generalize. For example, one of these evolved programs verified the equality of the suits of CARD0 and CARD1 and then verified the equality of the suits of CARD2, CARD3, and CARD4, but did not verify that the suit common to the CARD0 and CARD1 was the same as the suit common to CARD2, CARD3, and CARD4. As it happened, none of the 250 in-sample hands was a non-flush in which the suit common to CARD0 and CARD1 was not the same suit that was in common with CARD2, CARD3, and CARD4. Of course, when tested against previously unseen hands, this program did not correctly classify all the new hands. That is, this predicting program did not generalize well and failed to score 100% in the cross-validation test. Genetic programming did not make a mistake in evolving this program. Quite to the contrary, genetic programming did precisely what it was told to do: it evolved a highly fit program that successfully grappled with the given problem environement.

This result is another example of the principle that you get what you pay for with genetic programming. Genetic programming breeds highly fit programs based on the available fitness measure operating on available fitness cases. If the fitness cases are not sufficiently representative of the entire problem environment, the genetically evolved solution will not solve the more general problem represented by the full problem environment (i.e., will not generalize). The full problem environment resides in the mind of the user of genetic programming. If a learning paradigm is to successfully generalize to the full problem, the full problem must be communicated by the user to a learning paradigm in some way. Genetic programming is not clairvoyant; it relies on the user to provide a sufficiently representative set of fitness cases to enable genetic programming to solve the problem residing in the mind of the user.

16.4   PREPARATORY STEPS WITH ADFs

In applying genetic programming with automatically defined functions to the problem of identifying flushes, we envisage that automatically defined functions will be used to define detectors that will examine the given five-card hand and that the result-producing branch will perform some kind of logical analysis on the results produced by the detectors in order to classify the hand. We decided that each overall program in the population will consist of a result-producing branch and two three-argument function-defining branches.

The terminal set, T_{adf}, for each of the three-argument defined functions ADF0 and ADF1 is

$T_{adf} = \{$ARG0, ARG1, ARG2$\}$.

The function set, F_{adf0}, for ADF0 is

$F_{adf0} = \{$SUIT, DENOM, AND, OR, NOT, EQ$\}$

with an argument map of

$\{1, 1, 2, 2, 1, 2\}$.

Because ADF1 may not hierarchically refer to ADF0, the function set, F_{adf1}, for ADF1 is

$F_{adf1} = \{$SUIT, DENOM, AND, OR, NOT, EQ$\}$

with an argument map of

$\{1, 1, 2, 2, 1, 2\}$.

The body of ADF0 is a composition of the primitive functions from its function set, F_{adf0}, and the terminals from the terminal set, T_{adf}. Similarly, ADF1 is a composition of elements of F_{adf1}, and T_{adf}.

The terminal set, T_{rpb}, for the result-producing branch is

$T_{rpb} = \{$CARD0, CARD1, CARD2, CARD3, CARD4, NIL, FLUSH$\}$.

The function set, F_{rpb}, for the result-producing branch is

$F_{rpb} = \{$ADF0, ADF1, IF, AND, OR, NOT$\}$

with an argument map of

$\{3, 3, 3, 2, 2, 1\}$.

The result-producing branch is a composition of the functions from the function set, F_{rpb}, and terminals from the terminal sets T_{rpb}. The constrained syntactic structure created by the rules of construction described in table 16.1

Table 16.2 Tableau with ADFs for the flush problem.

Objective:	Find a program that identifies whether a given five-card hand from a pinochle deck is a flush.
Architecture of the overall program with ADFs:	One result-producing branch and two three-argument function-defining branches, with no hierarchical references.
Parameters:	Branch typing.
Terminal set for the result-producing branch:	CARD0, CARD1, CARD2, CARD3, CARD4, NIL, and FLUSH.
Function set for the result-producing branch:	ADF0, ADF1, IF, EQ, AND, OR, and NOT.
Terminal set for the two function-defining branches ADF0 and ADF1.	ARG0, ARG1, and ARG2.
Function set for the two function-defining branches ADF0 and ADF1.	EQ, SUIT, DENOM, AND, OR, and NOT.

apply with the exception that when automatically defined functions are being used, the two defined functions (ADF0 and ADF1) are the detecting functions (rather than DENOM and SUIT).

Table 16.2 summarizes the key features of the flush problem with automatically defined functions.

16.5   RESULTS WITH ADFs

In generation 13 of one run, the following 63-point program achieved 500 true positive and 500 true negatives, with no false positives or false negatives. The correlation of this program is 1.00.

```
(progn (defun ADF0 (ARG0 ARG1 ARG2)
         (values (EQ ARG2 ARG0)))
       (defun ADF1 (ARG0 ARG1 ARG2)
         (values (NOT (EQ (SUIT ARG2) (OR (SUIT ARG1) ARG1)))))
       (values (IF (ADF1 CARD0 CARD2 CARD4) (IF (ADF0 CARD2
         CARD0 CARD4) FLUSH NIL) (IF (ADF1 CARD2 CARD1 CARD2)
         (IF CARD3 NIL NIL) (IF (ADF1 CARD1 CARD3 CARD4) (IF
         CARD2 NIL NIL) (IF (ADF1 CARD2 CARD1 CARD2) (IF CARD3
         NIL NIL) (IF (ADF1 CARD3 CARD0 CARD3) (IF CARD3 NIL
         NIL) (IF CARD3 FLUSH NIL)))))))).
```

We can greatly simplify the above program by noting that ADF1 tests for the inequality of the suits of its second and third arguments (ignoring ARG0).

Moreover, as it happens, the one occurrence of ADF0 is irrelevant, since it merely provides an indirect way for NIL to be returned for a particular situation where NIL should be returned. If we define a new function S= for two-way suit equality (and delete each unreferenced argument), the above program can be rewritten and simplified to

```
(IF (s= CARD2 CARD4)
    (IF (s= CARD1 CARD2)
        (IF (s= CARD3 CARD4)
            (IF (s= CARD1 CARD2)
                (IF (s= CARD0 CARD3) FLUSH NIL)
                NIL)
            NIL)
        NIL)
    NIL).
```

It is now clear that this program correctly performs the desired classification.

When cross-validated against the exhaustive set of 42,504 fitness cases, this program achieves a correlation of 1.00 with no false positives and no false negatives. Thus, we have both analytically verified and empirically verified (cross-validated) that the genetically evolved program is a perfect solution to the problem.

16.6 FLUSHES AND FOUR-OF-A-KINDS

In this section, the problem is changed to require identification of both flushes and an additional type of hand, the four-of-a-kind. The 1,000 fitness cases are modified for this new three-way classification problem so that a third are flushes, a third are four-of-a-kinds, and a third are neither. If these three symbolic categories are represented by the numerical values –1, 0, and +1, respectively, raw fitness (correlation) can again be computed as the cosine of the angle in N_{fc}-space between the zero-mean vector of correct answers and the zero-mean vector of predictions.

This very time-consuming three-way problem is considerably more difficult to solve than the flush problem described earlier in this chapter. Each of several runs without automatically defined functions exhibited progressively better fitness, coming close to a perfect score; however, none of our runs without automatically defined functions ever produced a solution to this problem.

Genetic programming did produce solutions to this new problem when automatically defined functions were used; however, this new problem is so time-consuming that it is not feasible to make enough runs to obtain enough solutions for the construction of a meaningful performance curve. Nonetheless, it is instructive to look at the following especially interesting 294-point program, which appeared in generation 43 with a correlation of 1.00 of one particular run with automatically defined functions. This program correctly classified every flush in the set of fitness cases as a flush, every four-of-a-kind as a four-of-a-kind, and every other hand as NIL.

```
(progn (defun ADF0 (ARG0 ARG1 ARG2)
          (values (AND (EQ (SUIT ARG2) (AND (EQ (OR (NOT (SUIT
             ARG2)) (SUIT ARG1)) (SUIT ARG0)) (OR (NOT ARG0) (SUIT
             ARG1)))) (OR (NOT ARG0) (SUIT ARG0))))))
       (defun ADF1 (ARG0 ARG1 ARG2)
          (values (EQ (DENOM ARG2) (DENOM ARG1))))
       (values (IF (ADF0 CARD1 (OR (ADF1 (ADF1 (ADF0 CARD4 CARD1
          CARD1) CARD3 (NOT CARD1)) (AND CARD2 CARD1) (AND CARD2
          CARD2)) (AND CARD2 CARD2)) CARD0) (IF (ADF0 CARD3 CARD1
          CARD4) (IF CARD4 FLUSH FLUSH) (IF CARD3 NIL FLUSH)) (IF
          (ADF1 (ADF0 CARD4 CARD4 CARD2) (AND CARD2 CARD1) (OR
          CARD3 CARD3)) (IF (ADF1 (OR CARD3 CARD3) (AND CARD2
          CARD4) (AND CARD2 CARD1)) (IF (ADF1 (OR CARD3 CARD3)
          (AND CARD2 CARD1) (AND CARD2 CARD2)) (IF CARD2 FOUR-OF-
          A-KIND FOUR-OF-A-KIND) (IF (ADF1 (ADF0 CARD4 CARD4
          CARD2) (OR CARD4 CARD3) (OR CARD0 CARD3)) (IF CARD2
          FOUR-OF-A-KIND NIL) (IF CARD4 NIL NIL))) (IF (ADF1
          (ADF0 CARD4 CARD4 CARD2) (AND CARD2 CARD1) (OR CARD0
          CARD3)) (IF (ADF1 (ADF0 CARD4 CARD4 CARD2) (AND CARD2
          CARD2) (OR CARD0 CARD3)) (IF CARD2 FOUR-OF-A-KIND FOUR-
          OF-A-KIND) (IF CARD4 NIL NIL)) (IF CARD4 NIL NIL))) (IF
          (ADF1 (ADF0 CARD4 CARD4 CARD2) (OR CARD4 CARD3) (OR
          CARD0 CARD3)) (IF (ADF1 (ADF1 (ADF1 CARD3 CARD2 CARD1)
          (AND CARD3 CARD4) (OR CARD3 CARD3)) (AND CARD2 CARD2)
          (OR CARD0 CARD3)) (IF (ADF1 (ADF0 CARD4 CARD4 CARD2)
          (AND CARD2 CARD2) (OR CARD0 CARD0)) (IF (ADF1 (ADF0
          CARD2 CARD1 CARD1) (AND CARD2 CARD1) (OR CARD3 CARD3))
          (IF CARD2 FOUR-OF-A-KIND FOUR-OF-A-KIND) (IF (OR (ADF1
          CARD3 CARD2 CARD1) (OR CARD0 CARD3)) (IF (ADF1 (OR
          CARD3 CARD3) (AND CARD2 CARD4) (OR CARD3 CARD3)) (IF
          CARD2 FOUR-OF-A-KIND FOUR-OF-A-KIND) (IF (ADF1 (ADF0
          CARD4 CARD4 CARD2) (AND CARD2 CARD1) (OR CARD0 CARD2))
          (IF (ADF1 (ADF0 CARD4 CARD4 CARD2) (OR CARD4 CARD3) (OR
          CARD0 CARD3)) (IF CARD2 FOUR-OF-A-KIND NIL) (IF CARD4
          NIL NIL)) (IF CARD4 NIL NIL)))) (IF CARD4 NIL NIL))) (IF
          CARD4 NIL NIL)) (IF CARD4 NIL NIL)) (IF CARD4 NIL
          NIL)))))).
```

When analyzed, this program proves to generalize successfully over the
entire problem environment. In the above program, ADF0 tests for the equality of the suits of its three arguments and ADF1 tests for the equality of the
denomination of its second and third arguments (ignoring its ARG0). If, for
the purposes of explanation, we define a new function S3= for three-way
suit-equality and a new function D2= as two-way denomination-equality (and
delete each unreferenced argument), the above program can be simplified to

```
(IF (S3= CARD1 CARD2 CARD0)
    (IF (S3= CARD3 CARD1 CARD4) FLUSH NIL)
        (IF (D2= CARD1 CARD3)
            (IF (D2= CARD4 CARD1)
```

```
(IF (D2= CARD1 CARD2)
    FOUR-OF-A-KIND
    (IF (D2= CARD4 CARD0) FOUR-OF-A-KIND NIL))
  (IF (D2= CARD1 CARD0)
      (IF (D2= CARD2 CARD0) FOUR-OF-A-KIND NIL)
      NIL))
  (IF (D2= CARD4 CARD0)
      (IF (D2= CARD2 CARD0)
          (IF (D2= CARD4 CARD3)
              FOUR-OF-A-KIND
              (IF (D2= CARD1 CARD0) FOUR-OF-A-KIND NIL))
          NIL)
      NIL))).
```

We can now see that this program correctly performs the desired three-way classification of a five-card hand from a pinochle deck.

This program achieves a correlation of 1.00 with no false positives and no false negatives when cross-validated against the exhuastive set of 42,504 fitness cases. Again, we have both analytically verified and empirically verified (cross-validated) that the genetically evolved program is a perfect solution to the problem at hand.

17 Introduction to Biochemistry and Molecular Biology

This chapter provides an introduction to certain computational aspects of biochemistry and molecular biology that are relevant to the problems considered in subsequent chapters.

17.1 CHROMOSOMES AND DNA

The structure of all living things on earth is specified by the information contained in nucleic acids, largely as *chromosomes* composed of *deoxyribonucleic acid (DNA)*.

The informational content of the DNA molecule can be viewed as a character string over a four-character alphabet representing the four *nucleotide bases*, namely adenine (**A**), cytosine (**C**), guanine (**G**), and thymine (**T**).

Different fonts (tabulated in appendix C) are used in this and subsequent chapters to distinguish among the multiple single-letter codes used by biochemists and molecular biologists. For example, the single letter **C** denotes the nucleotide base cytosine mentioned above; C denotes the carbon atom; C denotes the amino acid residue cysteine (explained below); and C denotes the carboxy terminal (end) of a protein (explained below).

The DNA molecule consists of a long sequence of these four nucleotide bases. The *genome* of a biological individual is the sequence of nucleotide bases along the DNA of all of its chromosomes. The *human genome* contains about 2,870,000,000 nucleotide bases. The genome of a simple bacterium, such as *Escherischia coli,* contains about 4 million nucleotide bases.

Normally two molecules of DNA are interwound to form a double helix. Each DNA molecule redundantly stores information in complementary pairs so each nucleotide base is always paired with a particular other base in the complementary strand of DNA. Cytosine (**C**) is always paired with guanine (**G**) and vice versa; adenine (**A**) is paired with thymine (**T**) and vice versa. Thus, each strand of DNA contains the same information as the other strand.

Many higher organisms are *diploid* in the sense that they carry DNA (not necessarily exactly identical) from both parents.

17.2 ROLE OF PROTEINS

Proteins are responsible for such a wide variety of biological structures and functions that it can be said that the structure and function of living organisms are primarily determined by proteins (Stryer 1988). For example, some proteins are used to generate nerve impulses (e.g., rhodopsin is the photoreceptor protein in retinal rod cells). Proteins enable signals to be communicated through the nervous system. Other proteins transport particles such as electrons, atoms, or large macromolecules within living organisms (e.g., hemoglobin transports oxygen in blood). Some proteins store particular particles for later use (e.g., myoglobin stores oxygen in muscle). Some proteins provide physical structure (e.g., collagen gives skin and bone their high tensile strength). Other proteins create physical contractile motion (e.g., actin and myosin). Proteins are the basis of the immune system (e.g., antibodies recognize and combine in highly specific ways with foreign entities such as bacteria). Hormonal proteins transmit chemical instructions. Other proteins control the expression of the genetic information contained in the nucleic acids. Growth-factor proteins control growth and differentiation.

Perhaps the most important role of proteins is that they catalyze chemical reactions in biological systems. Nearly all chemical reactions in biological systems are catalyzed by a specific macromolecule (i.e., an enzyme) and nearly all known enzymes are proteins. The catalytic power of enzymes is enormous, often changing the rate of a reaction by so many orders of magnitude that they can effectively be viewed as determining whether or not the reaction occurs.

17.3 TRANSCRIPTION AND TRANSLATION

The informational content of DNA controls the manufacture of proteins by the processes of transcription and translation. A typical protein is manufactured using the information contained in about one thousand nucleotide bases (a *kilobase*). Proteins are manufactured by the ribosomes. A *ribosome* can be viewed as a small factory whose input consists of the available molecular raw materials and the informational content of the DNA molecule and whose output consists of a protein.

The *transcription* process maps the information contained in the DNA molecule onto a messenger RNA (mRNA) molecule. This mapping is a one-to-one mapping of one nucleotide base of DNA onto one base of mRNA. Cytosine (**C**) on DNA is mapped to guanine (**G**) of mRNA; guanine (**G**) on DNA is mapped to cytosine (**C**) of mRNA; thymine (**T**) on DNA is mapped to adenine (**A**) of mRNA. Adenine (**A**) of DNA is mapped to uracil (**U**), a substance that is closely related to thymine (**T**).

The ribosomes translate the sequential information of the messenger RNA into a protein using the genetic code. The proteins of all living things on earth are composed of linear strings of the same 20 amino acids. The *translation* process maps a consecutive sequence of three bases of mRNA (called a *codon*) into one of the 20 amino acids. Translation is performed in accordance with the *genetic code* that maps each of the 64 possible combinations of the bases found on mRNA into one of the 20 amino acids. In the genetic code, between one and six of the 64 possible combinations can be mapped to one amino acid. For example, a ribosome will translate a codon of messenger RNA consisting of the nucleiotide bases **G**, **G**, and **C** into the amino acid glycine (G).

The amino acid residue called for by the codon of messenger RNA is supplied to the ribosome by a molecule of *transfer RNA* (tRNA) from the milieu of the cell. Each molecule of tRNA carries an *anti-codon* which can bind, by means of complementary base pairing, to a particular one of the 64 codons of mRNA.

The genetic code is common to virtually all living things on earth.

Not all of the nucleotide bases of DNA are actually transcribed and translated into amino acids. The nucleotide bases that are ultimately expressed into amino acids by the processes of transcription and translation are called *exons*. The unexpressed nucleotide bases of DNA are called *introns*. The introns are edited out.

A typical protein contains around 330 amino acids (i.e., about a thousand actually transcribed and translated nucleotide bases). For humans, only about 3% of the 2,870,000,000 bases of the DNA are actually transcribed and translated into amino acids by means of the genetic code. If about 10^8 bases of human DNA are actually expressed and if the human proteins average about 10^3 bases, then there would be around 10^5 human proteins. In simpler organisms, virtually 100% of the DNA is expressed. If all the 4,000,000 bases of the DNA of the *Escherichia coli* bacterium are expressed and if *E. coli* proteins average 1,000 bases, then there would be about 4,000 genes in *E. coli*. A *gene* is the area of DNA that becomes expressed as a protein by the processes of transcription and translation.

Table 17.1 shows the standard single-letter codes for the 20 amino acids occurring in proteins in alphabetic order, along with the full name of the amino acid, the standard three-letter code for the amino acid, and the combinations of bases of mRNA that are translated into that particular amino acid. An asterisk is used to indicate that the third base does not matter. For example, row 1 of this table shows **GC*** for the amino acid alanine, indicating that alanine arises from **GCA**, **GCC**, **GCG**, and **GCU**. There are $4^3 = 64$ three-character combinations of the four bases. A particular amino acid may arise from between one and six combinations of bases. **UAU**, **UAC**, and **UGA** are stop codons that terminate the translation process and do not appear in this table. **AUG** codes for the start codon and for methionine. If it were not for the fact that the initial methionine is frequently edited out of the final protein by post-translational editing processes, the first amino acid of all proteins would be methionine. This table is the *genetic code*. With certain exceptions that may reflect evolutionary development, the genetic code is virtually universal for all life forms on earth.

Table 17.1 The 20 amino acids and the genetic code.

One-letter code	Amino acid	Three-letter code	Genetic code
A	Alanine	Ala	GC*
C	Cysteine	Cys	UGU, UGC
D	Aspartic Acid	Asp	GAU, GAC
E	Glutamic Acid	Glu	GAA, GAG
F	Phenylalanine	Phe	UUU, UUC
G	Glycine	Gly	GG*
H	Histidine	His	CAU, CAC
I	Isoleucine	Ile	AUU, AUC, AUA
K	Lysine	Lys	AAA, AAG
L	Leucine	Leu	UUA, UUG,CU*
M	Methionine	Met	AUG
N	Asparagine	Asn	AAU, AAC
P	Proline	Pro	CC*
Q	Glutamine	Gln	CAA, CAG
R	Arginine	Arg	CG*, AGA, AGG
S	Serine	Ser	UC*, AGU, AGC
T	Threonine	Thr	AC*
V	Valine	Val	GU*
W	Tryptophan	Trp	UGG
Y	Tyrosine	Tyr	UAU, UAC

17.4 AMINO ACIDS AND PROTEIN STRUCTURE

Proteins are a relatively homogeneous class of molecules in spite of their many different and wide-ranging biological functions. All proteins are composed of amino acids arranged in a linear chain. The molecular structure of the beginning and the end of every protein chain, as well as the molecular structure of the bonding of the adjacent amino acids along every chain, is identical for all proteins. Proteins differ in the particular sequence of the 20 amino acids that appear along the chain and in the three-dimensional structure that arises as a consequence of the particular sequence of amino acids.

A protein consists of a sequence of *amino acids* (also called *residues*). The *backbone* (*main chain*) of a protein starts at an N *terminal* (*amino terminal*) consisting of H_3^+N- and ends at its C *terminal* (*carboxy terminal*) consisting of $-COO-$. Between these two ends, a protein consists of repetitions of a nonvariable group of six atoms and a variable group of atoms, called the *side chain*. Three of the six nonvariable atoms appear along the backbone of the protein. The backbone contains repetitions of one nitrogen atom N, one central carbon atom (called the α-*carbon* or C_α *carbon*), and a second carbon atom

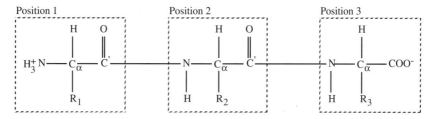

Figure 17.1 Hypothetical protein of length three with unspecified side chains: R_1, R_2, and R_3.

(called the C' carbon). The other three of the six nonvariable atoms are attached to the backbone. The attached atoms include one hydogen atom H covalently bonded to the nitrogen of the backbone, another H covalently bonded to the C_α carbon atom of the backbone, and one oxygen atom O bonded to the C' carbon of the backbone. There are as many repetitions of these six atoms as there are amino acids in the protein. The bond linking the C' carbon of each group to the nitrogen N of the next group along the chain is called a *peptide bond*. Consequently, proteins are called *polypeptides*.

The *side chain* attached to each α-carbon C_α along the backbone is the variable part of the protein. The particular side chain that is attached to each particular α-carbon is specified by the three bases of the codon of mRNA (and therefore originally by the three nucleotide bases of the DNA that were transcribed into the three bases of the codon of mRNA).

Figure 17.1 shows a hypothetical protein sequence in which three unspecified side chains R_1, R_2, and R_3, each connected to an α-carbon atom C_α. Position 1 of this figure contains the N terminal (the H_3^+N-). Side chain R_1 is connected to its α-carbon. Position 2 is the generic intermediate position of the protein; its side chain, R_2, is connected to its α-carbon. Position 3 contains the C terminal (the $-COO^-$). Side chain R_3 is connected to its α-carbon. The backbone of the protein runs horizontally through the middle of the figure connecting the N, C_α, C', N, C_α, C', N, and C_α. If the length of the protein sequence were greater than 3 (the average is about 330), there would be additional copies of the entire structure shown in position 2 of this figure – that is, the N, C_α, and C' of the backbone, the H, H, and O connected to these three backbone atoms, and one of the 20 possible side chains.

Each of the 20 possible side chains is a particular chemical composition of atoms. The side chain for the amino acid glycine (denoted Gly or G) consists of only one atom (a hydrogen H). The side chains of the other 19 amino acids each consist of several atoms. For example, the side chain of the amino acid cysteine (Cys or C) consists of one sulfur S, one carbon C, and two hydrogen atoms ($-CH_2-S$). The side chain for serine (Ser or S) consists of one carbon C, one oxygen O, and three hydrogen atoms ($-CH_2-OH$).

Figure 17.2 shows a hypothetical protein sequence of length 3; it is the same as figure 17.1, except that the side chains, R_1, R_2, and R_3, are now specified as glycine, cysteine, and serine.

Introduction to Biochemistry and Molecular Biology

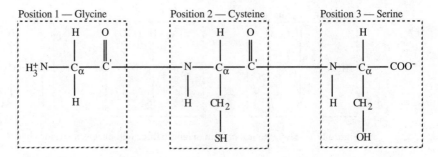

Position 1 — Glycine   Position 2 — Cysteine   Position 3 — Serine

Figure 17.2   Hypothetical protein consisting of glycine, cysteine, and serine.

```
RPDFCLEPPY TGPCKARIIR YFYNAKAGLC QTFVYGGCRA KRNNFKSAED    50

CMRTCGGA                                                 58
```

Figure 17.3   Primary structure of bovine pancreatic trypsin inhibitor (BPTI).

17.5   PRIMARY STRUCTURE OF PROTEINS

The sequence of amino acid residues along a protein chain is called the *primary structure* of a protein. For example, the primary structure of the hypothetical protein of figure 17.2 is Gly-Cys-Ser using the standard three-letter codes for amino acid residues and GCS using the standard one-letter codes. Once the primary structure is specified, all atoms of the protein are specified.

As a further illustration, bovine pancreatic trypsin inhibitor (BPTI) is an atypically small protein containing only 58 amino acid residues (about a fifth of the number in an average protein). Figure 17.3 shows the one-letter codes for the 58 amino acid residues in the primary structure of BPTI.

17.6   SECONDARY STRUCTURE OF PROTEINS

Amino acid residues along the protein chain often arrange themselves locally into certain features, α-helices and β-strands being the most common. These features constitute the *secondary structure* of the protein. The *α-helix* is a regular spiral-like structure in which the main chain spirals much like the red spiral stripe on a barber's pole. The *β-strand* is a flatter regular structure in which the main chain zigzags like a sheet of corrugated metal. Two β-strands may form a β-sheet in which alternate amino acid residues along each zigzagging β-strand are joined by hydrogen bonds.

Table 17.2 shows the secondary structure of bovine pancreatic trypsin inhibitor (BPTI). BPTI contains two α-helices and two β-strands.

The first α-helix (called H1), shown in table 17.2, encompasses six residues of BPTI beginning with the proline located at the second position along the backbone of the protein starting at the N-terminal end (referred to as "proline 2" or "Pro 2" using the three-letter code for amino acids) and ending with the glutamic acid located at the seventh position (referred to as "Glu 7"). The

Table 17.2   Features of the secondary structure and the disulfide bonds of bovine pancreatic trypsin inhibitor (BPTI).

Feature	Type of feature	Start	End
H1	α-helix	Pro 2	Glu 7
H2	α-helix	Ser 47	Gly 56
S1	β-strand	Leu 29	Tyr 35
S2	β-strand	Ile 18	Asn 24
SS1	Disulfide bond	Cys 5	Cys 55
SS2	Disulfide bond	Cys 14	Cys 38
SS3	Disulfide bond	Cys 30	Cys 51

second α-helix, H2, starts at serine 47 (Ser 47) and ends at glycine 56 (Gly 56). The average α-helix is about a dozen residues long, so helix H2 is of average size.

The first β-strand, B1, of BPTI in table 17.2 starts at leucine (Leu) 29 and ends at tyrosine (Tyr) 35. The second β-strand, B2, starts at isoleucine (Ile) 18 and ends at asparagine (Asn) 24.

About a quarter of all amino acid residues of a typical protein are organized into α-helices and approximately another quarter of all residues are organized into β-strands.

The omega loop (chapter 19) is an irregular loop structure on the surface of a protein; the omega loop is shaped somewhat like the Greek letter Ω. Ω-loops account for approximately another quarter of all residues and are considered by some to be another secondary structure of proteins. The 3_{10}-*helix* (which is tighter than the α-helix) occurs much less frequently than the α-helices and β-strands. There are no omega loops in BPTI.

In addition, the *disulfide bond* is an important stability-conferring structure that covalently links distant pairs of cysteine residues in some proteins. BPTI has three disulfide bonds: one linking Cysteine 5 with Cysteine 55; one linking Cysteine 14 and Cysteine 38; and one linking Cysteine 30 and Cysteine 51. We include the disulfide bonds along with the α-helices and β-strands as part of table 17.2 (even though these covalent disulfide bonds are properly considered part of the protein's primary structure).

Figures 17.4 through 17.7 show the general structure (after Hamaguchi 1993) of the backbone of BPTI. Circles denote the location of the α-carbons along the backbone. These two-dimensional figures give a general idea of the arrangement of the features of BPTI; however, they do not purport to be an accurate projection from any perspective of the three-dimensional structure of BPTI. A more accurate three-dimensional view of this protein appears in *Genetic Programming II Videotape: The Next Generation* (Koza and Rice 1994).

In figure 17.4 each of the 58 residues of BPTI is represented by a circle containing the residue number and the one-letter code for the residue. Residue 1

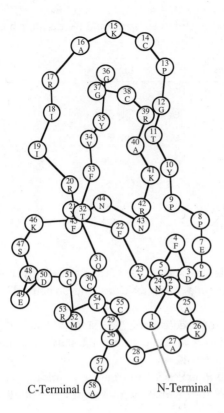

Figure 17.4 General structure of bovine pancreatic trypsin inhibitor.

at the N-terminal end of the protein is arginine (R); residue 58 at the C-terminal end is alanine (A). Both residues 1 and 58 are found near the bottom of this figure.

Figure 17.5 shows the two α-helices of BPTI, one located between residues 2 and 7 and one located between residues 47 and 56. In this figure, the 58 residues along the backbone are reduced to open circles to highlight the α-helices.

Figure 17.6 highlights the two β-strands of BPTI, one running between residues 18 and 24 and the other running between residues 29 and 35. Contrary to the impression that might be created by this two-dimensional figure, the two β-strands do not intersect in three-dimensional space.

Figure 17.7 shows the three disulfide bonds; one linking cysteines 5 and 55; one linking cysteines 14 and 38; and one linking cysteines 30 and 51.

17.7 TERTIARY STRUCTURE OF PROTEINS

As a protein is being manufactured by a ribosome, the entire protein chain spontaneously folds into a unique three-dimensional spatial arrangement, called its *native structure, conformation,* or the *tertiary structure* of the protein. The tertiary structure of a protein consists of the three-dimensional spatial arrangement of all the atoms of the protein. The behavior and function of a

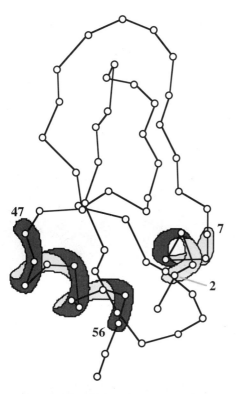

Figure 17.5 The two α-helices of bovine pancreatic trypsin inhibitor.

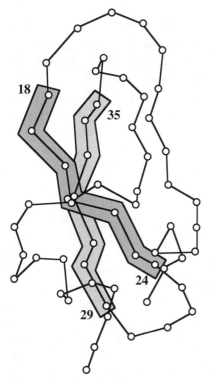

Figure 17.6 The two β-strands of bovine pancreatic trypsin inhibitor.

Introduction to Biochemistry and Molecular Biology

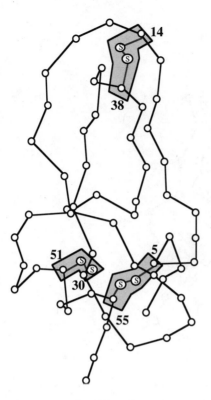

Figure 17.7 The three disulfide bonds of bovine pancreatic trypsin inhibitor.

protein in an organism is primarily dependent on the precise three-dimensional location of its individual atoms. For example, certain key areas, called *active sites*, may interact with particular other molecules in highly specific ways. Knowledge of the three-dimensional structure of a protein is usually required to fully understand how a protein performs its biological function.

The three-dimensional structure into which a protein spontaneously folds is a unique characteristic of the particular protein (under specified prevailing physiological conditions). This unique three-dimensional structure is thought by many to be a global energy minimum or near-minimum for the protein (or at least the minimum or near-minimum that is accessible to all unfolded states of the chain starting from the time of its manufacture by the ribosome).

It is broadly true that the unique three-dimensional spatial structure of a protein is determined by the primary sequence of the protein (Anfinsen 1973). In certain special cases, other molecules (e.g., chaperon molecules) may aid in the folding of some particular proteins; certain other molecules may sometimes be necessary to maintain the folded conformation of some proteins; and various post-translational modifications may occur after the protein's manufacture by the ribosome for some proteins.

Determining the relationship between the primary structure of a protein (i.e., the linear sequential arrangement of amino acids) and its three-dimensional structure (i.e., the three-dimensional coordinates of every atom of the protein) is the premiere problem of contemporary molecular biology and is called the *protein folding problem* (Schulz and Schirmer 1979; Gierasch and King 1990; Branden and Tooze 1991; Lesk 1991; Creighton 1993).

The nature of the protein folding problem can be appreciated by considering the three-dimensional coordinates of the atomic structure of one small part of one particular protein. The Protein Data Bank (PDB) maintained by the Brookhaven National Laboratory in Upton, New York (Bernstein et al. 1977) is the worldwide computerized repository of the three-dimensional coordinates of the atomic structure of proteins.

Table 17.3 shows two small portions of the tertiary structure of bovine pancreatic trypsin inhibitor (BPTI) from the PDB. Specifically, the table shows the x, y, and z three-dimensional coordinates for 20 of the 918 atoms listed in the PDB for BPTI (under the code 5PTI). The 20 atoms shown come from two groups, 10 being associated with Cysteine 5 and 10 with Cysteine 55. The first and second columns of the table identify the amino acid residues; the third and fourth columns identify the individual atoms belonging to the protein backbone and the cysteine residues. The fifth, sixth, and seventh columns show the x, y, and z coordinates of the atom.

The protein backbone consists of the six atoms common to each residue of every protein sequence. Atoms 74–77 are the nitrogen, the α-carbon, the C'-carbon, and the oxygen, respectively, belonging to the protein backbone for Cysteine 5; atoms 883–886 are the nitrogen, the α-carbon, the C'-carbon, and the oxygen, respectively, belonging to the protein backbone for Cysteine 55.

Atom 81 is the hydrogen of the backbone that is bonded to the α-carbon for Cysteine 5; atom 890 is the hydrogen of the backbone bonded to the α-carbon of Cysteine 55.

Atom 80 is the hydrogen (called the *amide hydrogen,* denoted by D-H) of the backbone bonded to the nitrogen of the main chain for Cysteine 5; atom 889 is the amide hydrogen of the backbone bonded to the nitrogen of the main chain for Cysteine 55.

Each cysteine side chain consists of one sulfur, one carbon, and three hydrogen atoms (i.e., $-CH_2-S$). Atom 78 is the carbon belonging to Cysteine 5 (called the β-carbon of the residue); atom 887 is the corresponding β-carbon of Cysteine 55. Atom 79 is the sulfur of Cysteine 5; atom 888 is the corresponding sulfur of Cysteine 55. Atoms 82–83 are the two hydrogen atoms belonging to Cysteine 5; atoms 891–892 are the corresponding two hydrogen atoms belonging to Cysteine 55.

As an illustration of the way that proteins fold in three-space as shown by the PDB, consider atoms 79 and 888 (the sulfur atoms, S, belonging to the two cysteines, Cysteine 5 and Cysteine 55). The three-dimensional coordinates of sulfur atom 79 are

[31.075, 12.797, -7.325]

and the coordinates of sulfur atom 888 are

[29.664, 13.161, -5.893].

The Euclidean distance between these two sulfur atoms is 2.043 Ås. Using the fact that one hydrogen atom is about one Å in size, these two sulfur atoms

Table 17.3 Two small portions of the tertiary structure of bovine pancreatic trypsin inhibitor (BPTI) from the Protein Data Bank.

Amino acid residue	Residue number	Atom number	Atom	x	y	z
Cys	5	74	N	32.757	10.236	-6.732
Cys	5	75	α-C	31.286	10.029	-6.794
Cys	5	76	C	30.864	8.652	-7.254
Cys	5	77	O	29.690	8.279	-7.116
Cys	5	78	β-C	30.794	11.065	-7.789
Cys	5	79	γ-S	31.075	12.797	-7.325
Cys	5	80	D-H	33.206	10.888	-7.363
Cys	5	81	α-H	30.964	10.266	-5.800
Cys	5	82	β1-H	31.501	10.869	-8.603
Cys	5	83	β2-H	29.793	10.892	-8.171
Cys	55	883	N	28.364	15.919	-6.980
Cys	55	884	α-C	28.337	14.779	-7.839
Cys	55	885	C	27.258	14.663	-8.899
Cys	55	886	O	27.484	13.831	-9.733
Cys	55	887	β-C	28.265	13.520	-5.893
Cys	55	888	γ-S	29.664	13.161	-5.893
Cys	55	889	D-H	27.614	15.974	-6.323
Cys	55	890	α-H	29.253	14.775	-8.417
Cys	55	891	β1-H	27.388	13.519	-6.349
Cys	55	892	β2-H	28.059	12.720	-7.695

are, in the context of proteins, very close to one another in three-space. In other words, although these two cysteine residues occupy very distant positions in the primary sequence (positions 5 and 55), they are physically very close in three-space after the protein spontaneously folds into its tertiary structure. In fact, after the folding, the two sulfur atoms of the cysteine residues participate in a disulfide bond. Disulfide bonds confer considerable additional stability to the three dimensional structure into which the protein has folded itself. Similarly, the sulfur atoms of Cysteine 14 and Cysteine 38 and the sulfur atoms of Cysteine 30 and Cysteine 51 are very close in the folded protein and, in fact, form a disulfide bond.

The protein folding problem can be restated in terms of figure 17.3 showing the amino acid residues of the primary structure and in terms of table 17.3 showing the tertiary structure as follows: Given the primary sequence of amino acid residues of a protein in the format of figure 17.3, predict the three-dimensional x, y, and z coordinates for 100% of the atoms of the protein in the format of table 17.3.

In the past, the primary sequences of proteins were typically determined through time-consuming chemical analysis of the proteins themselves. However, because the primary sequence of proteins is specified by the underlying chromosomal DNA sequence and because of the extensive current worldwide effort to map the entire DNA sequences of various organisms (e.g., *E. coli* bacteria, yeast, fruit fly, white mouse, and humans in the *Human Genome Project*), primary sequences are becoming available at a rapid rate. As of the end of 1993, the primary structures of approximately 33,329 proteins containing 11,484,420 amino acid residues from various organisms have been determined and deposited in various computerized databases (such as the SWISS-PROT database).

In contrast, determining the tertiary structure of proteins requires x-ray crystallography or nuclear magnetic resonance (NMR) techniques. These determinations are exceedingly time-consuming, the crystallographic method currently requiring about three years of work for each protein studied. Consequently, the number of proteins whose tertiary structures is known is a tiny fraction of the number of proteins whose primary structures is known. For example the April 1993 quarterly release of the Protein Data Bank contains 1,110 fully annotated atomic coordinate entries (of which 56 were new for that quarter). Many of the studies in the PDB are of the same protein with different levels of crystallographic resolution, of the same protein under different conditions, of mutants of the same protein (natural or engineered), and of functionally similar proteins from different species (often those thought to be evolutionarily related). Depending on the criteria for similarity, there are only about 150 to 200 "different" tertiary structures available in the PDB. This number is, of course, only a tiny fraction of the estimated 100,000 different proteins in humans and the estimated 4,000 different proteins in *E. coli*. This already considerable gap is widening.

Thus, there is a major need for automated methods of predicting tertiary structure from primary structure. Since the rules for protein folding are largely unknown, artificial intelligence, machine learning, and automatic programming may provide a way to satisfy part of this need. In some cases, approximate or likely solutions to problems involving the secondary and tertiary structure of proteins may have practical uses in increasing the understanding of proteins.

Of course, the fact that there are only 150 to 200 different tertiary structures in the PDB is a severe limitation on the operation of automated methods for prediction that rely on recognizing and generalizing patterns and relationships. All such methods, whether they be based on statistics, neural networks, genetic algorithms, decision trees, clustering, or other methods of machine learning or automatic programming, must be guided by a reasonably large number of examples of the relationship between the variables of interest. The study of protein folding is further complicated by the fact that the 150 to 200 different proteins in the PDB are atypical of proteins in general in a number of important respects. For example, the proteins contained in the PDB are those for which it is practical, economical, politically acceptable, or possible to isolate the protein in stable form and to grow crystals. In addition, because of the many practical limitations of crystallographic techniques, the PDB tends to contain atypically short proteins. The average length of proteins in the PDB is only about 175 residues, compared to an overall average length of roughly 330 for all proteins. There are, of course, many more degrees of freedom in the folding process for proteins of average and above-average size than there are for atypically small proteins.

17.8   QUARTERNARY STRUCTURE OF PROTEINS

Some proteins contain more than one *chain* (*subunit*). The three-dimensional spatial arrangement of subunits is the *quaternary structure* of a protein.

For example, hemoglobin (an oxygen-transporting protein) contains four subunits called α_1, α_2, β_1, and β_2. The two alpha subunits are identical and the two beta subunits are identical. Moreover, the alpha subunits are very similar to the beta subunits. Each of these four subunits of hemoglobin is, in turn, very similar to the myoglobin molecule. An iron-containing heme group is associated with the myoglobin molecule. Oxygen binds to the iron molecule thereby permitting oxygen to be stored by myoglobin. Oxygen similarly binds to the four iron molecules in hemoglobin thereby permitting oxygen to be transported in the bloodstream.

A single human red blood cell contains about 275,000,000 molecules of hemoglobin. These molecules are identical except for the physical location in three-space of their constituent atoms.

17.9   GENETIC ALGORITHMS AND MOLECULAR BIOLOGY

Genetic algorithms are being increasingly applied to problems of molecular biology. Lucasius and Kateman 1989 applied genetic algorithms to chemometrics. Konagaya and Kondou 1993 extracted stochastic motifs from sequences using a genetic algorithm and the minimum description length (MDL) principle. Platt and Dix 1993 constructed restriction maps using a genetic algorithm. Cedeno and Vemuri 1993 investigated DNA mapping with genetic algorithms. Fickett and Cinkosky 1993 applied the genetic algorithm to assembling chromosome physical maps. Sun 1993 used genetic algorithms with a reduced representation model of protein structure prediction. Unger and Moult (1993a, 1993b, 1993c) applied genetic algorithms to evolving self-avoiding curves resembling the way proteins fold. See also Cantor and Lim 1991 and Lim, Fickett, Cantor, and Robbins 1993.

Ishikawa et al. (1993) and Tajima (1993) applied parallel genetic algorithms to sequence alignment. Schulze-Kremer (1993) applied genetic algorithms to tertiary structure prediction for the protein crambin. See also Takagi (1993).

Jones (1993) used genetic algorithm for searching databases of chemical strcutures. Lucasius et al. (1991) used genetic algorithms for a conformational analysis of DNA. Marcel et al. (1992) used genetic algorithms for a conformational analysis of a dinucleotide photodimer. Hibbert (1993) studied the display of chemical structures in two dimensions using genetic algorithms.

Le Grand (1993) tested the genetic algorithm for performing conformational search on polypeptides and proteins on 46-residue protein crambin with the AMBER potential energy function. A knowledge-based potential energy function was developed and used to predict the structures of melittin, pancreatic polypeptide, and crambin.

18 Prediction of Transmembrane Domains in Proteins

Many problems involving the computational analysis of proteins are similar to the pattern-recognition problems in chapter 15 and 16 in that a major part of the problem is the dynamic evolution of initially-unknown reusable feature detectors.

In addition, a number of problems from computational biology are similar to the flush problem of chapter 16 in that correlation is a reasonable measure for fitness when genetic programming is applied to the problem.

However, there are four important practical differences between the flush problem and problems from the real world. First, the entire problem environment (i.e., the universe of fitness cases) was known for the flush problem, but it is not usually known for problems from the real world. Second, the entire problem environment was sufficiently small for the flush problem (i.e., 42,504 five-card hands) that it was possible to cross-validate a genetically evolved predicting program by exhaustively testing it against the entire environment; this is also generally not the case for problems from the real world. Third, a 100%-correct solution to the flush problem is attainable so there is no question as to how to define the success predicate of the problem; we usually do not have the luxury of sufficient foreknowledge to know how to do this for a problem from the real world. Fourth, the problem environment is fully understood so it is possible to verify analytically that a program is a 100%-correct solution to the problem; we rarely have the luxury of certainty for a practical problem.

This chapter and chapters 19 and 20 consider several problems of pattern recognition and classification from computational biology.

The problem of deciding whether a given protein segment is a transmembrane domain provides an opportunity to illustrate the automatic discovery of reusable feature detectors, to again employ correlation as the fitness measure, to incorporate iteration into genetically evolved computer programs, and to illustrate the use of state (memory) in genetically evolved programs.

In this chapter, genetic programming is used to create a computer program for predicting whether or not a given subsequence of amino acids in a protein is a transmembrane domain of the protein. Genetic programming will be given a set of differently-sized protein segments and the correct classification for each segment. The predicting program will consist of initially-unspecified detectors, an initially-unspecified iterative calculation incorporating the as-yet-undiscovered detectors, and an initially-unspecified final result-producing calculation incorporating the results of the as-yet-undiscovered iteration.

Although we will give a biological interpretation of the results, the automated process does not know the chemical characteristics or biological meaning of the sequence of amino acids appearing in the protein segment. Similarly, the reader may ignore the biological interpretation and view this problem as a one-dimensional pattern recognition problem. The techniques used in this chapter to do calculations on a protein sequence can be applied to any sequence or time series (e.g., economic data).

18.1 BACKGROUND ON TRANSMEMBRANE DOMAINS IN PROTEINS

Membranes play many important roles in living things. A *transmembrane protein* (Yeagle 1993) is embedded in a membrane in such a way that part of the protein is located on one side of the membrane, part is within the membrane, and part is on the opposite side of the membrane. The membrane involved may be a cellular membrane or some other type of membrane. Transmembrane proteins often cross back and forth through the membrane several times and have short loops immersed in the different milieu on each side of the membrane. Understanding the behavior of transmembrane proteins requires identification of the portion(s) of the protein that are actually embedded within the membrane, such portion(s) being called the *transmembrane domain(s)* of the protein. The lengths of the transmembrane domains of a protein are usually different from one another and the lengths of the non-transmembrane areas are also usually different from one another.

Transmembrane proteins often perform functions such as sensing the presence of certain particles or certain stimuli on one side of the membrane and transporting particles or transmitting signals to the other side of the membrane. For example, the transmembrane protein rhodopsin is the photosensitive pigment of retinal rod cells. Cystic fibrosis transmembrane conductance regulator is a transmembrane protein implicated in the genetic disease of cystic fibrosis that controls the flow of chloride in and out of lung cells. When a functionally correct copy of the gene producing this protein is not inherited from at least one parent, thick mucous builds up, causing lung damage and eventual death (often by age 20 or 30).

The goal in this section is to use genetic programming to evolve a computer program for predicting whether or not a particular protein segment (i.e., a subsequence of amino acid residues extracted from the entire sequence) is a transmembrane domain. Biological membranes are of oily *hydrophobic* (water-hating) composition. The amino acids in the transmembrane domain of a protein that are exposed to the membrane therefore have a pronounced, but not overwhelming, tendency to be hydrophobic. Many transmembrane domains are α-helices.

It should be noted that some transmembrane domains are β-sheets (Schirmer and Cowan 1993). Protein segments of this type can be identified as being transmembrane domains by the predominantly hydrophobic nature of the particular residues that the β-sheet actually exposes to the membrane. Because they are extremely difficult to analyze in the laboratory, very few transmembrane proteins of this latter type currently appear in the existing computerized databases. This bias in the computerized databases has the practical effect of excluding transmembrane proteins of the β-sheets type from our experiments here.

Figure 18.1 shows a topological model of the transmembrane protein bacteriorhodopsin from the *Halobacterium salinarium* bacterium (Teufel et al. 1993). Bacteriorhodopsin is a photosensitive protein that enables bacteria to respond to light. It acts as a light-driven proton pump. The left of the figure corresponds to the outside of the cell and the right corresponds to the intracellular region. Bacteriorhodopsin is a 248-residue protein that is folded into a bundle of seven α-helices. The N-terminal end of the protein (residue 1) is located outside the cell. The seven α-helices are embedded in the cellular membrane of the bacterium and are shown in the large rectangles. These seven transmembrane domains are then connected by relatively short extramembrane loops, three on the outside of the cell and three on the inside. The C-terminal end of the protein (residue 248) is located inside the cell. If the membrane is viewed as a mattress, the seven transmembrane domains (α-helices) are the springs.

The hydrophobicity scale of Kyte and Doolittle (1982) assigns a numerical value for hydrophobicity to each of the 20 amino acid residues.

Table 18.1 shows the 20 amino acid residues (columns 3, 4, and 5) arranged in order according to the Kyte-Doolittle hydrophobicity scale. The 20 Kyte-Doolittle hydrophobicity values in column 2 can reasonably be clustered into the three categories shown in column 1: seven of the 20 amino acid residues can be categorized as hydrophobic, six as *neutral*, and seven as *hydrophilic* (water-loving). As can be seen, isoleucine (I) has the largest positive value in the table and is therefore the most hydrophobic residue according to this scale. On the other hand, R, K, D, and E are the most hydrophilic; they are electrically charged.

Hydrophobicity is not a precisely defined characteristic. Over a dozen other different hydrophobicity scales appear in the literature. The Hopp-Woods hydrophobicity scale (Hopp and Woods 1981) is one of the many other such scales. These alternative scales differ considerably from one another as to the relative numerical value assigned to the 20 amino acids. In some instances, the differences are great enough to affect the rank order of the amino acids and the categories into which the amino acids are most naturally clustered. There is no consensus on which hydrophobicity scale, if any, is best suited for this particular problem. Nonetheless, the Kyte-Doolittle scale and the resulting three categories are suitable for the limited purpose of discussing how hydrophobicity relates to whether a protein segment is a transmembrane domain.

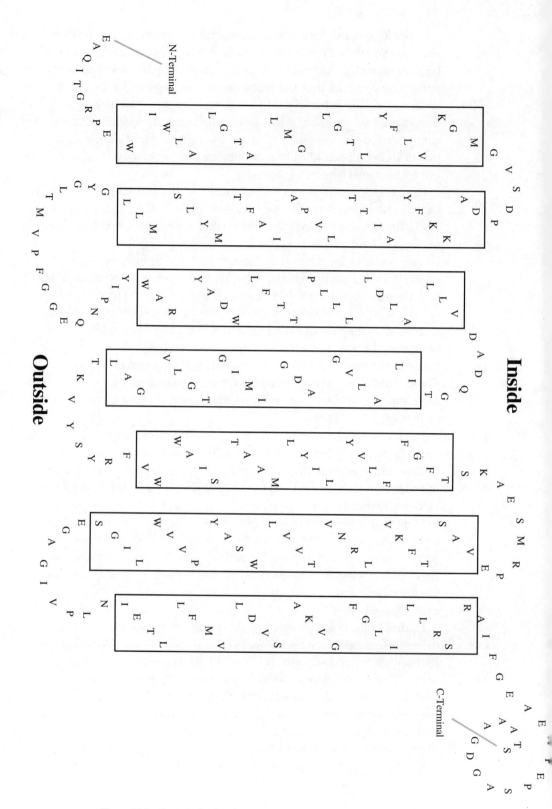

Figure 18.1 Bacteriorhodopsin protein consisting of seven transmembrane α-helices.

Table 18.1 Kyte-Doolittle hydrophobicity values for the 20 amino acid residues.

Category	Kyte-Doolittle value	One-letter code for amino acid	Amino acid	Three-letter code for amino acid
Hydrophobic	+4.5	I	Isoleucine	Ile
Hydrophobic	+4.2	V	Valine	Val
Hydrophobic	+3.8	L	Leucine	Leu
Hydrophobic	+2.8	F	Phenylalanine	Phe
Hydrophobic	+2.5	C	Cysteine	Cys
Hydrophobic	+1.9	M	Methionine	Met
Hydrophobic	+1.8	A	Alanine	Ala
Neutral	−0.4	G	Glycine	Gly
Neutral	−0.7	T	Threonine	Thr
Neutral	−0.8	S	Serine	Ser
Neutral	−0.9	W	Tryptophan	Trp
Neutral	−1.3	Y	Tyrosine	Tyr
Neutral	−1.6	P	Proline	Pro
Hydrophilic	−3.2	H	Histidine	His
Hydrophilic	−3.5	Q	Glutamine	Gln
Hydrophilic	−3.5	N	Asparagine	Asn
Hydrophilic	−3.5	E	Glutamic Acid	Glu
Hydrophilic	−3.5	D	Aspartic Acid	Asp
Hydrophilic	−3.9	K	Lysine	Lys
Hydrophilic	−4.0	R	Arginine	Arg

Figure 18.2 shows the 161 amino acid residues of mouse peripheral myelin protein 22. This protein is one of the 33,329 proteins appearing in release 27 in late 1993 of the SWISS-PROT computerized database of protein sequences (Bairoch and Boeckmann 1991) and is identified in that database by the locus name "PM22_MOUSE". The first residue (at the N-terminal end of the protein) is methionine (M); the 161st residue (at the C-terminal end) is leucine (L). This protein has transmembrane domains located at residues 2–31, 65–91, 96–119, and 134–156. These four transmembrane domains are boxed in the figure.

For example, the third transmembrane domain of mouse peripheral myelin protein 22 consists of the 24 residues (boxed in figure 18.2) between positions 96 and 119:

FYITGFFQILAGLCVMSAAAIYTV.

The 27 residues between positions 35 and 61 (underlined and in lower case in figure 18.2) are

TTDLWQNCTTSALGAVQHCYSSSVSEW,

and are an example of a randomly chosen non-transmembrane area of this protein.

```
MLLLLLGILF LHIAVLVLLF VSTIVSQWLV GNGHttdlwq ncttsalgav    50

qhcysssvse wLQSVQATMI LSVIFSVLAL FLFFCQLFTL TKGGRFYITG   100

FFQILAGLCV MSAAAIYTVR HSEWHVNTDY SYGFAYILAW VAFPLALLSG   150

IIYVILRKRE L                                            161
```

Figure 18.2 Primary sequence of mouse peripheral myelin protein 22 with four transmembrane domains (boxed) and one randomly chosen non-transmembrane area (underlined).

Columns 2 and 3 of table 18.2 show the amino acid residues 90–125 from the neighborhood containing the third transmembrane domain (located between residues 96–119) of mouse peripheral myelin protein 22. The third column shows the hydrophobicity category of the residue as presented in column 1 of table 18.1. The fourth column shows the moving sum of the Kyte-Doolittle hydrophobicity values for the 11 residues centered on each residue (i.e., the given residue itself along with the five residues on both sides). The moving sum is conventionally multiplied by 10 for convenience. Note that the moving sums shown for residues 90–94 and 121–125 are based on residues not actually shown in this table.

As can be seen from table 18.2, the moving sum is strongly positive (indicating hydrophobicity) throughout the transmembrane domain involving residues 96–119 (except for the single residue on the very boundary of the domain). Two thirds of the 24 residues are in the hydrophobic category (containing I, V, L, F, C, M, or A). Of the remaining eight of the 24 residues, seven residues (two Gs, two Ts, two Ys, and one S) are in the neutral category (containing G, T, S, W, Y, P) and one (the Q at position 103) is in the hydrophilic category (containing H, Q, N, E, D, K, R).

Table 18.3 is similar to table 18.2 and shows the amino acid residues at positions 35–61 of mouse peripheral myelin protein 22, the hydrophobicity category of the residue, and the moving sum of the Kyte-Doolittle hydrophobicity values (multiplied by 10) for the 11 residues centered on each residue. About half of the 27 residues in positions 35–61 are neutral, about a quarter are hydrophobic, and about a quarter are hydrophilic. As can be seen, the moving sums are either negative (indicating hydrophilicity) or small positive numbers. This is a very different distribution than the distribution of the 24 residues in positions 96–119 shown in table 18.2.

Figure 18.3 graphs the moving sum of the Kyte-Doolittle hydrophobicity values (multiplied by 10) for the 11 residues centered on a given residue for mouse peripheral myelin protein 22. No moving sum is computed for the first and last five residues of the protein. The four distinct peaks on this graph correspond to the four highly hydrophobic transmembrane domains of this protein. In particular, there is a peak corresponding to positions 96–119 of table 18.2. The graph also has negative or small positives values for the positions 35–61 shown in table 18.3.

Table 18.2 Moving sums of Kyte-Doolittle hydrophobicity values for residues 90–125 of mouse peripheral myelin protein 22.

Residue number	Amino acid residue	Hydrophobicity category	Kyte-Doolittle moving sum
90	L	Hydrophobic	-12
91	T	Neutral	-9
92	K	Hydrophilic	13
93	G	Neutral	20
94	G	Neutral	-15
95	R	Hydrophilic	-12
96	F	Hydrophobic	-22
97	Y	Neutral	13
98	I	Hydrophobic	17
99	T	Neutral	66
100	G	Neutral	108
101	F	Hydrophobic	171
102	F	Hydrophobic	139
103	Q	Hydrophilic	190
104	I	Hydrophobic	170
105	L	Hydrophobic	219
106	A	Hydrophobic	242
107	G	Neutral	206
108	L	Hydrophobic	196
109	C	Hydrophobic	249
110	V	Hydrophobic	222
111	M	Hydrophobic	229
112	S	Neutral	198
113	A	Hydrophobic	195
114	A	Hydrophobic	199
115	A	Hydrophobic	129
116	I	Hydrophobic	55
117	Y	Neutral	28
118	T	Neutral	1
119	V	Hydrophobic	-26
120	R	Hydrophilic	-76
121	H	Hydrophilic	-52
122	S	Neutral	-132
123	E	Hydrophilic	-126
124	W	Neutral	-154
125	H	Hydrophilic	-209

Table 18.3 Moving sums of Kyte-Doolittle hydrophobicity values for residues 35–61 of mouse peripheral myelin protein 22.

Residue number	Amino acid residue	Hydrophobicity category	Kyte-Doolittle moving sum
35	T	Neutral	-88
36	T	Neutral	-165
37	D	Hydrophilic	-135
38	L	Hydrophobic	-108
39	W	Neutral	-111
40	Q	Hydrophilic	-87
41	N	Hydrophilic	-62
42	C	Hydrophobic	-17
43	T	Neutral	14
44	T	Neutral	-6
45	S	Neutral	45
46	A	Hydrophobic	45
47	L	Hydrophobic	48
48	G	Neutral	48
49	A	Hydrophobic	42
50	V	Hydrophobic	41
51	Q	Hydrophilic	41
52	H	Hydrophilic	15
53	C	Hydrophobic	19
54	Y	Neutral	15
55	S	Neutral	-38
56	S	Neutral	-89
57	S	Neutral	-16
58	V	Hydrophobic	-19
59	S	Neutral	-52
60	E	Hydrophilic	3
61	W	Neutral	-24

18.2 THE FOUR VERSIONS OF THE TRANSMEMBRANE PROBLEM

Now suppose that we do not know about the concept of hydrophobicity or hydrophilicity or any numerical hydrophobicity scales. The question arises as to whether it is possible to examine a set of protein segments and then perform some numerical calculation in order to classify a particular segment as being a transmembrane domain or not.

We will approach this problem in this chapter in three ways. First, we will attempt to solve it without automatically defined functions. Second, we will solve it with automatically defined functions. In this second version, the automatically defined functions will be used as detectors to create categories.

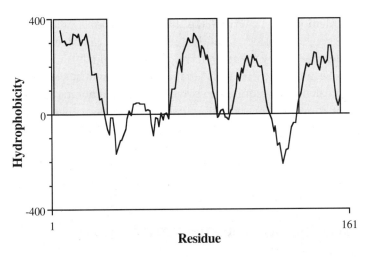

Figure 18.3 The four distinct peaks in the moving sum of the Kyte-Doolittle hydrophobicity values correspond to the four transmembrane domains of mouse peripheral myelin protein 22.

Accordingly, this version is called the *set-creating* version. Third, we will use automatically defined functions to perform ordinary arithmetic and conditional operations, rather than set-manipulating operations. This third version is called the *arithmetic-performing* version.

All three versions of the problem described in this chapter correspond to the first experiment described in Weiss, Cohen, and Indurkhya 1993. In these three versions, the inputs to the problem are entire pre-parsed protein segments; it is not necessary to parse the entire protein sequence. Chapter 20 discusses a version of the transmembrane problem, called the *lookahead* version, which involves parsing the entire protein sequence.

Before proceeding, we need to discuss two additional features of genetic programming. Section 18.3 discusses the idea of settable variables, memory, and state, and section 18.4 discusses restricted iteration.

18.3   THE IDEA OF SETTABLE VARIABLES, MEMORY AND STATE

Mathematical calculations in computer programs typically employ settable variables, memory, and state (*Genetic Programming*, sections 18.2 and 19.7).

Settable variables, such as M0, M1, M2, and M3, can provide memory (state) in a computer program. At the beginning of the execution of a program, each *settable variable* is initialized to some initial value appropriate to the problem domain (e.g., 0).

The settable variables then typically acquire other values as a result of the side-effecting action of various *setting* functions. Specifically, the one-argument setting function, SETM0, can be used to set M0 to a particular value. Similarly, the setting functions SETM1, SETM2, and SETM3 can be used to set the value of the settable variables M1, M2, and M3, respectively.

Memory can be written (i.e., the state can be set) with the setting functions SETM0, SETM1, SETM2, and SETM3. Memory can be read (i.e., the state can be interrogated) by merely referring to the terminals M0, M1, M2, and M3.

We anticipate that such settable variables will be useful in the mathematical calculation required to solve the transmembrane problem. Since we do not know how many such variables are necessary, we simply make a seemingly excessive number (e.g., four) of settable variables available and allow the evolutionary process to ignore them or to evolve a way to use them.

Teller (1993, 1994a) has extended to idea of memory to indexed memory as described in subsection F.14.1 in Appendix F. Andre (1994 b) has applied index memory to evolve a mental model (subsection F.14.2).

18.4   THE IDEA OF RESTRICTED ITERATION

Typical computer programs contain iterative operators, which perform some specified work until some condition expressed by a termination predicate is satisfied. Genetic programming is capable of evolving programs with iterative operators. For example, the iterative DU operator (Do Until) used in the block stacking problem (*Genetic Programming*, section 18.1) is a two-argument operator that iteratively performs the work specified by its first argument until the termination predicate specified by its second argument is satisfied. In the block stacking problem, the DU operator (Do Until) was permitted to appear in a program without restriction as to the number of its occurrences within the overall program and without restriction as to its locations within the program. The SIGMA operator for iterative summation was similarly unrestricted (*Genetic Programming*, section 18.2).

Of course, in a genetically evolved program both the work and the termination predicate of each occurrence of an iterative operator are initially created at random. Both are subsequently subjected to modification by the crossover operation. Consequently, iterative operators will, at best, be nested and consume enormous amounts of computer time or will, at worst, have unsatisfiable termination predicates and go into infinite loops.

One way to avoid these pitfalls is to impose time-out limits on each iterative loop individually and on all iterative loops cumulatively. These necessary limits are somewhat arbitrary. Even when such time-out limits are imposed, programs containing iterative operators are still extremely time-consuming. The worst performing and least interesting programs in the population usually consume the most computer time.

In problems where we can envisage one iterative calculation being usefully performed over a particular known, finite set, there is an attractive alternative to imposing arbitrary time-out limits. For such problems, the iteration can be restricted to exactly one iteration (or a specified number of iterations) over the finite set. In this *restricted iteration (poor man's iteration)*, the termination predicate is fixed, guaranteed to be triggered in a definite amount of time, and is not subject to evolutionary modification. No nested iterations or infinite loops are possible. The amount of computer time is capped and knowable from the usual factors (i.e., population size, number of generations, size of the programs in the population, number of fitness cases, nature of the fitness measure, and the nature of the problem).

In the case of certain problems involving the examination of the residues of a protein, iteration can reasonably be limited to the ordered set of amino acid residues of the protein sequence or protein segment involved. Thus, for this problem, there can be one iteration-performing branch, with the iteration restricted to the ordered set of amino acid residues in the protein segment. Each time iterative work is performed, the pointer identifying the current residue of the protein is advanced to the next residue of the protein segment until the end of the entire protein segment is encountered. An analogy is the repeated pressing of the space bar of a typewriter. Each time the space bar is pressed, the typing head moves one space to the right. However, repeated depressing of the space bar cannot itself move the typing head beyond the end of the typewriter carriage or cause the typing head to return to the far left. When the iteratin-terminating branch is finished, the result-producing branch produces the final output of the overall program.

Many iterative calculations work in conjunction with memory (state). Typically the work varies depending on the current value of the iteration variable (index) and the current contents of the memory. The memory transmits information from one execution of the iterative calculation to the next. In this problem the same work is executed as many times as there are residues in a protein segment, so the iteration variable here is the amino acid residue at the current position in the protein segment. Depending on the problem, the iteration variable may be explicitly available or be implicitly available through functions that permit it to be interrogated. For this problem, there will be no need for the iteration variable to be explicitly available in the terminal set.

In this problem, each settable variable is initialized to zero at the beginning of the execution of the iteration-performing branch. The settable variables then typically acquire some final value as a result of the work performed by the iteration. We make four settable variables, M0, M1, M2, and M3 available to the iterative calculation of this problem.

The following code employing the LOOP macro of Common LISP (Steele, 1990) precisely specifies the operation of restricted iteration for one protein segment (fitness case) for this problem.

```
1    (loop initially (progn (setf M0 0.0) (setf M1 0.0)
2                           (setf M2 0.0) (setf M3 0.0))
3        for residue-index from 0 below (length protein-segment)
4        for residue = (aref protein-segment residue-index)
5        do (eval IPB0)
6        finally (return (wrapper (eval RPB))))))
```

In lines 1 and 2, the settable variables, M0, M1, M2, and M3, are each set to an initial value of 0.

Line 3 specifies that the indexing variable, `residue-index`, will start at 0 and run up to one less than the `length` of the array (vector) `protein-segment`.

In line 4, the array `protein-segment` is referenced with the array-referencing function, `aref`, to extract the element (the amino acid residue) identified by the indexing variable `residue-index`. The variable `residue` is bound to the extracted value. This binding enables the yet-to-be-evolved program to detect whether the current residue is a particular amino acid.

In line 5, the iteration-performing branch, `IPB0`, is evaluated using `eval` successively for each residue in the `protein-segment`. The iteration-performing branch, `IPB0`, would typically contain references to the settable variables `M0`, `M1`, `M2`, and `M3` and the automatically defined functions `ADF0`, `ADF1`, and `ADF2` (if they are involved).

In line 6, the result-producing branch, `RPB`, is evaluated using `eval` after `IPB0` has been invoked for the last time (i.e., on the last residue of the `protein-segment`). The result-producing branch, `RPB`, typically contains references to the settable variables `M0`, `M1`, `M2`, and `M3`. The `return` in the `finally` clause causes the result of evaluating the wrapperized value of `RPB` to be returned as the overall result of the program's execution for the current fitness case. The wrapperized value of `RPB` is the classification of the `protein-segment` as a transmembrane domain or a non-transmembrane area.

In the genetically evolved programs presented later the code on lines 1–5 is called `looping-over-residues`; the result-producing branch (line 6) appears below its usual `values` function.

18.5 PREPARATORY STEPS WITHOUT ADFs

The yet-to-be-evolved program without automatically defined functions for predicting whether a given protein segment is a transmembrane domain should be capable of performing three tasks. First, it should be able to interrogate the residues and perform some calculation (e.g., grouping them into useful categories). Second, it should be able to iteratively perform some yet-to-be-determined arithmetic calculations and conditional operations involving the as-yet-undiscovered categorizations. Third, it should be able to perform some final yet-to-be-determined arithmetic calculations and conditional operations to reach a decision using the intermediate results produced by the as-yet-undiscovered iteration. A predicting program without automatically defined functions might perform the first two tasks in an iteration-performing branch and it might perform the final task in a final branch. Even though automatically defined functions are not involved in the discussion in this section, this final branch can nonetheless be aptly called a result-producing branch.

Figure 18.4 shows the structure of a two-branch predicting program without automatically defined functions consisting of an iteration-performing branch, `IPB0`, and a result-producing branch, `RPB`.

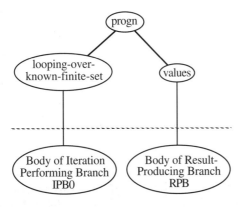

Figure 18.4 Overall two-branch program consisting of an iteration-performing branch, IPB0, and a result-producing branch, RPB, for the subset-creating version of the transmembrane problem without ADFs.

18.5.1 Terminal Set and Function Set

We now consider the terminal set and function set for each branch of the overall two-branch predicting program for the transmembrane problem without automatically defined functions.

A program for creating categories of amino acids and taking different actions based on the category to which a particular residue belongs must be able to determine what residue is at a certain position in the protein segment. In addition, such a program must be able to form categories based on the outcome of the interrogation.

Since we anticipate that numerical calculations will subsequently be performed on the presence or absence of a particular residue at a particular position in the protein segment, it seems reasonable to employ numerically-valued logic returning numerical values such as –1 and +1, rather than Boolean-valued logic returning values such as T or NIL. Numerically-valued logic permits the results of the residue-detecting operations to be freely combined with arithmetic operations and numerical constants into more complicated calculations .

One way to implement this approach is to define 20 numerically-valued zero-argument functions for determining whether the current residue in a protein segment is a particular amino acid. For example, (A?) is the zero-argument residue-detecting function returning a numerical +1 if the current residue is alanine (A) but otherwise returning a numerical –1. A similar residue-detecting function is defined for each of the 19 other amino acids. Since these 20 functions take no arguments, they are considered terminals in accordance with our usual convention in this book.

The length of the current protein segment, LEN, is a potentially useful terminal in the contemplated calculations. The settable variables, M0, M1, M2, and M3, provide memory (state) for the contemplated iterations. The random constants, $\mathfrak{R}_{\text{bigger-reals}}$, range between –10.000 and +10.000 (with a granularity of 0.001).

Thus, the terminal set, $\mathcal{T}_{ipb0}$, for the iteration-performing branch, IPB0, contains the 20 zero-argument numerically-valued residue-detecting functions, the constant terminal LEN, the settable variables M0, M1, M2, and M3, and the random constants, $\mathfrak{R}_{\text{bigger-reals}}$. That is,

$\mathcal{T}_{ipb0} = \{ (A?), (C?), \ldots, (Y?), \text{LEN}, \text{M0}, \text{M1}, \text{M2}, \text{M3}, \mathfrak{R}_{\text{bigger-reals}} \}.$

Since we envisage that sets of amino acids will be formed into categories, it seems potentially helpful to include the logical disjunctive function in the function set. Specifically, ORN is the two-argument numerically-valued disjunctive function (OR) that returns +1 if either or both of its arguments are positive, but returns –1 otherwise. For example, (ORN (A?) (C?)) returns +1 if the current residue is either alanine (A) or cysteine (C), but returns –1 if the current residue is any of the other 18 amino acids.

Since we envisage that the iteration-performing branch will perform calculations and make decisions based on these calculations, it seems reasonable to include the four arithmetic operations and a conditional operator in the function set. We have used the four arithmetic functions (+, -, *, and %) for performing arithmetic calculations and the conditional comparative operator IFLTE for making decisions on many previous problems, so we include them in the function set for the iteration-performing branch. Since there are side effecting functions in this problem (i.e., the four setting functions), IFLTE must be implemented as a macro as described in section 12.2.

The one-argument setting functions. SETM0, SETM1, SETM2, and SETM3, can be used to set the values of the settable variables, M0, M1, M2, and M3, respectively.

Thus, the function set, $\mathcal{F}_{ipb0}$, for the iteration-performing branch, IPB0, is

$\mathcal{F}_{ipb0} = \{ \text{ORN, SETM0, SETM1, SETM2, SETM3, IFLTE}, +, -, *, \% \}$

with an argument map of

$\{2, 1, 1, 1, 1, 4, 2, 2, 2, 2\}.$

Once a program has memory (state) in the form of settable variables and setting functions, the ability to do arithmetic, and the ability to conditionally perform alternative calculations based on the outcome of a conditional test, many different mathematical computations can be performed. These calculations include averages and weighted averages of the number of occurrences of amino acids belonging to a particular dynamically defined subset of amino acids.

The result-producing branch can then perform a non-iterative floating-point calculation and produce the final result of the overall program. The settable variables, M0, M1, M2, and M3, provide the way to communicate the results of the iteration-performing branch to the result-producing branch.

The terminal set, $\mathcal{T}_{rpb}$, for the result-producing branch, RPB, is

$\mathcal{T}_{rpb} = \{ \text{LEN, M0, M1, M2, M3}, \mathfrak{R}_{\text{bigger-reals}} \}.$

The function set, $\mathcal{F}_{rpb}$, for the result-producing branch, RPB, is

$\mathcal{F}_{rpb} = \{\texttt{IFLTE}, \texttt{+}, \texttt{-}, \texttt{*}, \texttt{\%}\}$

with an argument map of

$\{4, 2, 2, 2, 2\}$.

A wrapper is used to convert the floating-point value produced by the result-producing branch into a binary outcome. If the genetically evolved program returns a positive value, the segment will be classified as a transmembrane domain, but otherwise it will be classified as a non-transmembrane area.

Even though automatically defined functions are not yet involved, the overall program here contains two branches. These branches have different terminal sets and function sets. Thus, structure-preserving crossover is needed to preserve the constrained syntactic structure used in this problem. In implementing structure-preserving crossover, separate types are assigned to the two branches (i.e., branch typing is used).

In summary, when genetic programming without automatically defined functions is applied to the transmembrane problem, each individual overall two-branch program in the population consists of an iteration-performing branch, IPB0, employing four memory cells and a result-producing branch, RPB, employing the results of the iteration to produce a signed number that signifies whether the given protein segment is a transmembrane domain.

18.5.2 Correlation as the Fitness Measure

The fitness cases for this problem consist of protein segments extracted from a sample of proteins. Fitness will measure how well a genetically evolved program predicts whether the segment is a transmembrane domain.

When a genetically evolved program in the population is tested against a particular fitness case, the outcome can be

- a true-positive (i.e., the program correctly predicts that the given segment is a transmembrane domain when the segment is, in fact, transmembrane),

- a true-negative (i.e., the program correctly predicts that the given segment is not a transmembrane domain when the segment is, in fact, not transmembrane),

- a false-positive (i.e., the program *overpredicts* that the given segment is a transmembrane domain when the segment is, in fact, not transmembrane), or

- a false-negative (i.e., the program *underpredicts* that the given segment is not a transmembrane domain when the segment is, in fact, transmembrane).

The sum of the number of true positives (N_{tp}) the number of true negatives (N_{tn}), the number of false positives (N_{fp}), and the number of false negatives (N_{fn}) equals the total number of fitness cases, N_{fc}:

$$N_{fc} = N_{tp} + N_{tn} + N_{fp} + N_{fn}.$$

The performance of a predicting algorithm can be measured in several ways using N_{tp}, N_{tn}, N_{fp}, N_{fn}, and N_{fc}.

One frequently used way of measuring the performance of a predicting program is to measure its accuracy. The *accuracy* measure, Q_3, is the number of fitness cases for which the predicting program is correct divided by the total number of fitness cases. That is,

$$Q_3 = \frac{N_{tp} + N_{tn}}{N_{fc}}.$$

A value of accuracy of 1.0 is best; 0.0 is worst. The accuracy measure, Q_3, does not consider the amount of overprediction represented by N_{fp} or the amount of underprediction represented by N_{fn}. Q_3 is a somewhat specious measure because the significance of a particular reported value of Q_3 is highly dependent on the frequency of appearance of the characteristic being studied. For example, if 53% of the examples in a three-way classification problem belong to one class, then a predicting program that blindly classifies every example as belonging to that class will achieve an accuracy Q_3 of 53% (Stolorz, Lapedes, and Xia 1992). Similarly, if only 95% of the fitness cases are examples of a characteristic, then a predicting program that blindly classifies every example as positive will achieve an accuracy Q_3 of 95% (Matthews 1975).

The error rate E_3, is the number of fitness cases for which the predicting program is incorrect divided by the total number of fitness cases (Weiss, Cohen, and Indurkhya 1993). That is,

$$E_3 = \frac{N_{fp} + N_{fn}}{N_{fc}} = 1 - Q_3.$$

This frequently used measure suffers from the same deficiencies as the accuracy measure Q_3.

Another way to measure the performance of a predicting program is to measure the *percentage of agreement*, c_a, between a program's prediction and the observed reality (Matthews 1975):

$$c_a = \frac{100 N_{tp}}{N_{tp} + N_{fn}}.$$

A value of c_a of 100% is best; 0% is worst. However, c_a alone is also a somewhat specious measure, since it does not take into account the amount of overprediction (i.e., false positives). For example, a program that always makes a positive prediction would achieve a value of 100% for c_a.

The inadequacy of c_a can be counterbalanced by combining it with a measure of overprediction, c_{na}. In their early work on predicting the secondary structure of proteins, Chou and Fasman (1974b) used Q_a, a measure that combines c_a with a measure of overprediction, c_{na}. Specifically, c_{na} is the percentage of negative cases that the program correctly predicts to be negative cases:

$$c_{na} = \frac{100 N_{tn}}{N_{tn} + N_{fp}}.$$

c_a and c_{na} are then averaged to yield

$$Q_a = \frac{c_a + c_{na}}{2}.$$

The Q_a measure gives an overall estimate of the agreement between the predictions and the observed reality. If a predicting technique is accurate, c_a, c_{na}, and Q_a will be 100%. A predicting program that always makes a positive prediction would have a large amount of overprediction (i.e., a large value of N_{fp}) and would achieve a relatively low value of c_{na} and a relatively low average Q_a.

Each of the above performance measures is a potential candidate for a fitness measure for genetic programming; however, each has shortcomings. Matthews (1975) points out that the correlation between the prediction and the observed reality is a more general measure that avoids the shortcomings of each of the above measures. As it happens, the calculation of correlation is considerably simplified when the predictions and observations each take on only two possible values.

Let P_j represent the prediction for fitness case j (i.e., P_j is the output of a genetically evolved program; it is 1 if a protein segment j is predicted to be transmembrane and is 0 if the segment is predicted to be non-transmembrane). Let S_j represent the observed structure for fitness case j (i.e., S_j is 1 if protein segment j is observed to be transmembrane and is 0 if the segment is non-transmembrane).

The correlation C between the prediction P_j and the observation S_j is, in general, given by

$$C = \frac{\sum_j (S_j - \bar{S})(P_j - \bar{P})}{\sqrt{\sum_j (S_j - \bar{S})^2 \sum_j (P_j - \bar{P})^2}}$$

(Fisher 1958; Matthews 1975), where $\bar{P}$ and $\bar{S}$ are the mean values of P_j and S_j respectively, and the summations are over all N_{fc} fitness cases.

As Matthews (1975) points out, for the special case where P_n and S_n are step functions taking only the values of 0 or 1, the correlation C becomes

$$C = \frac{\dfrac{N_{tp}}{N_{fc}} - \bar{P}\bar{S}}{\sqrt{\bar{P}\bar{S}(1 - \bar{S})(1 - \bar{P})}}$$

Here $\bar{S}$ is the fraction of the fitness cases that are observed to be transmembrane; that is,

$$\bar{S} = \frac{N_{tp} + N_{fn}}{N_{fc}},$$

$\overline{P}$ is the fraction of the fitness cases that are predicted to be transmembrane,

$$\overline{P} = \frac{N_{tp} + N_{fp}}{N_{fc}}.$$

As Matthews (1975) observes, the correlation coefficient indicates how much better a particular predictor is than a random predictor. A correlation C of $+1.0$ indicates perfect agreement between a predictor and the observed reality; a correlation C of -1.0 indicates total disagreement; a correlation C of 0.0 indicates that the predictor is no better than random.

As previously mentioned in section 16.2, this formula for correlation in this problem, where the predictions and observations of a classification problem take on only two possible values, is equivalent to a calculation of the cosine of the angle in a space of dimensionality N_{fc} between the zero-mean vector of length N_{fc} of correct answers and the zero-mean vector of length N_{fc} of predictions. A correlation C of -1.0 indicates vectors pointing in opposite directions in N_{fc}-space; a correlation of $+1.0$ indicates coincident vectors; a correlation of 0.0 indicates orthogonal vectors. For a two-way classification problem, correlation can also be computed as

$$C = \frac{N_{tp} N_{tn} - N_{fn} N_{fp}}{\sqrt{\left(N_{tn} + N_{fn}\right)\left(N_{tn} + N_{fp}\right)\left(N_{tp} + N_{fn}\right)\left(N_{tp} + N_{fp}\right)}}.$$

Note that C is set to 0 when the denominator is 0.

Accordingly, C lends itself immediately to being the measure of raw fitness for a genetically evolved computer program. Since raw fitness ranges between -1.0 and $+1.0$ (higher values being better), standardized fitness can then be defined as

$$\frac{1 - C}{2}.$$

Standardized fitness ranges between 0.0 and $+1.0$, lower values being better and 0 being best. A standardized fitness of 0 indicates perfect agreement between the predicting program and the observed reality (the correct answer); $+1.0$ indicates total disagreement; and 0.50 indicates that the predictor is no better than random.

18.5.3 Fitness Cases

Release 25 of the SWISS-PROT protein data bank contains 248 mouse proteins with transmembrane domains identified in their SWISS-PROT feature tables. These proteins average 499.8 amino acid residues in length. Each such protein contains between one and 12 transmembrane domains, the average being 2.4. The transmembrane domains range in length from 15 to 101 residues, with an average of 23.0.

Of these 248 proteins, 123 are randomly chosen to create the in-sample set of fitness cases to measure fitness during the evolutionary process. One of the transmembrane domains of each of these 123 proteins is chosen at random as a positive fitness case for the in-sample set. Then, one equally long segment that is not contained in any of the protein's transmembrane domains is randomly chosen from each protein as a negative fitness case. As a result, there are 123 positive and 123 negative fitness cases in the in-sample set of fitness cases.

Table 18.4 shows the 246 in-sample fitness cases. The first column names the protein; the second column gives the length of the protein; and the third column shows the number of transmembrane domains in the protein. The fourth and fifth columns apply to the particular randomly chosen transmembrane domain (positive fitness case). The sixth and seventh columns apply to the one randomly chosen non-transmembrane area (negative fitness case) of the protein. For example, row one shows that the 19-residue transmembrane domain located at positions 287–305 (one of two transmembrane domains in the protein) and that the 19-residue non-transmembrane area located at positions 330–348 is chosen from the 3BH1_MOUSE protein.

Genetic programming is driven by fitness as measured by the set of in-sample fitness cases. However, the true measure of performance for a recognizing program is how well it generalizes to different cases from the same problem environment. 250 out-of-sample fitness cases (125 positive and 125 negative) are then created from the remaining 125 proteins in the same manner as that described above. These out-of-sample fitness cases are then used to validate the performance of the genetically evolved predicting programs.

Table 18.5 shows the 250 out-of-sample fitness cases.

An auxiliary hits measure has usually proved useful for externally monitoring runs of genetic programming. Since the hits measure is not used by genetic programming, it seemed most useful to base the definition of hits on the performance of the predicting program on the *out-of-sample* fitness cases. Therefore, hits is defined as the nearest integer to $100 \times (1.0 - \text{standardized fitness})$ for the out-of-sample set. A genetically evolved program with an out-of-sample correlation C of 1.00 will score 100 hits. Since only the best-of-generation programs (identified using in-sample fitness) are tested against the out-of-sample fitness cases, the hits measure is only computed for the best-of-generation programs.

Even with iteration restricted to a single loop in the iteration-performing branch, this problem proved extremely time-consuming. Moreover, on our first four runs of this problem we initially used an environment consisting of fewer in-sample fitness cases than described above and discovered that there was an undesirably large divergence in the values of the in-sample correlation and out-of-sample correlation. Increasing the number of in-sample fitness to the full number described above, of course, aggravated the problem of computer time. Therefore, we compromised on the maximum number of generations to be run and set G to 21.

Since we had no idea in advance what values of correlation to expect on this problem, we ran this problem with no success predicate so that all runs would continue for the full 21 generations. We then examined the values of

Table 18.4 In-sample fitness cases.

Protein	Length	Number of trans-membrane domains	Length of chosen transmem-brane domain	Location of the chosen transmem-brane domain	Length of chosen non-trans-membrane segment	Chosen non-transmem-brane area
3BH1_MOUSE	372	2	19	287–305	19	330–348
3BH3_MOUSE	372	2	19	287–305	19	330–348
5HT3_MOUSE	487	4	20	465–484	20	385–404
5HTE_MOUSE	366	7	25	24–48	25	235–259
A2AB_MOUSE	455	7	24	411–434	24	277–300
A4_MOUSE	770	1	24	700–723	24	736–759
ACE_MOUSE	1312	1	17	1265–1281	17	625–641
ACHB_MOUSE	501	4	19	277–295	22	391–412
ACHE_MOUSE	493	4	19	273–291	24	381–404
ACM1_MOUSE	460	7	23	25–47	23	277–299
AG2S_MOUSE	359	7	21	276–296	21	168–188
ANPA_MOUSE	1057	1	21	470–490	21	225–245
ATNC_MOUSE	290	1	28	40–67	28	7–34
AVRB_MOUSE	536	1	26	135–160	26	55–80
B2AR_MOUSE	418	7	23	107–129	24	363–386
B3AT_MOUSE	929	10	24	424–447	18	829–846
BASI_MOUSE	273	1	24	210–233	24	242–265
CADE_MOUSE	884	1	24	710–733	24	798–821
CADP_MOUSE	822	1	23	648–670	23	736–758
CD11_MOUSE	336	1	29	298–326	29	135–163
CD19_MOUSE	547	1	24	288–311	24	418–441
CD3D_MOUSE	173	1	27	101–127	27	138–164
CD3G_MOUSE	182	1	27	112–138	27	43–69
CD3Z_MOUSE	164	1	21	31–51	21	6–26
CD44_MOUSE	363	1	21	271–291	21	126–146
CD4L_MOUSE	260	1	24	23–46	24	142–165
CD5_MOUSE	494	1	30	372–401	30	434–463
CD8A_MOUSE	247	1	37	184–220	37	74–110
CFTR_MOUSE	1476	12	21	1009–1029	21	593–613
CIK1_MOUSE	495	6	20	290–309	21	194–214
CIKD_MOUSE	511	6	22	345–366	22	218–239
CO9_MOUSE	528	2	17	292–308	17	138–154
CR2_MOUSE	1025	1	27	964–990	27	995–1021
CX26_MOUSE	226	4	21	190–210	21	110–130
CX32_MOUSE	283	4	21	189–209	21	166–186
CX40_MOUSE	357	4	21	205–225	22	119–140
CX45_MOUSE	396	4	21	189–209	21	314–334
D3DR_MOUSE	446	7	23	33–55	25	5–29
EPOR_MOUSE	507	2	17	135–151	23	114–136
FASA_MOUSE	327	1	17	170–186	17	249–265
FCEA_MOUSE	250	1	19	205–223	19	94–112
FCEG_MOUSE	86	1	21	24–44	21	56–76
FCG2_MOUSE	329	1	26	211–236	26	271–296
FCGX_MOUSE	283	1	26	211–236	26	93–118
FLAP_MOUSE	153	3	24	5–28	31	31–61
FURI_MOUSE	793	1	21	715–735	21	348–368
GAA3_MOUSE	492	4	22	338–359	22	398–419

Protein	Length	Number of trans-membrane domains	Length of chosen transmem-brane domain	Location of the chosen transmem-brane domain	Length of chosen non-trans-membrane segment	Chosen non-transmem-brane area brane area
GAC2_MOUSE	474	4	23	299–321	24	125–148
GAD_MOUSE	449	4	23	275–297	23	114–136
GC1M_MOUSE	393	1	18	340–357	18	367–384
GCAM_MOUSE	399	1	18	346–363	18	373–390
GGNT_MOUSE	447	1	23	7–29	23	228–250
GLP_MOUSE	168	1	23	109–131	23	139–161
GLRB_MOUSE	883	4	20	546–565	19	850–868
GRPR_MOUSE	384	7	21	266–286	21	346–366
GTR2_MOUSE	523	12	21	433–453	21	260–280
HA10_MOUSE	322	1	15	308–322	15	147–161
HA12_MOUSE	365	1	23	312–334	23	145–167
HA14_MOUSE	368	1	27	304–330	27	337–363
HA17_MOUSE	334	1	22	311–332	22	145–166
HA1B_MOUSE	369	1	23	306–328	23	338–360
HA1K_MOUSE	369	1	23	306–328	23	338–360
HA1Q_MOUSE	328	1	24	266–289	24	298–321
HA1U_MOUSE	361	1	20	315–334	20	148–167
HA21_MOUSE	255	1	26	217–242	26	96–121
HA23_MOUSE	229	1	26	191–216	26	83–108
HA2D_MOUSE	256	1	26	219–244	26	97–122
HA2J_MOUSE	254	1	26	217–242	26	96–121
HA2Q_MOUSE	221	1	26	184–209	26	80–105
HA2S_MOUSE	233	1	26	196–221	26	86–111
HAM1_MOUSE	577	6	22	16–37	20	196–215
HB22_MOUSE	264	1	23	226–248	23	102–124
HB24_MOUSE	264	1	32	217–248	32	93–124
HB2D_MOUSE	265	1	21	227–247	21	104–124
HB2I_MOUSE	264	1	23	226–248	23	102–124
HB2K_MOUSE	263	1	21	225–245	21	103–123
HB2S_MOUSE	263	1	21	225–245	21	103–123
ICA1_MOUSE	537	1	24	486–509	24	232–255
IL1S_MOUSE	410	1	26	356–381	26	384–409
IL2B_MOUSE	539	1	28	241–268	28	391–418
IL5R_MOUSE	415	1	22	340–361	22	160–181
IL7R_MOUSE	459	1	25	240–264	25	350–374
INGR_MOUSE	477	1	24	254–277	24	116–139
IP3R_MOUSE	2749	8	17	2391–2407	17	2662–2678
ITA5_MOUSE	409	1	26	356–381	26	166–191
ITAM_MOUSE	1153	1	24	1106–1129	24	542–565
ITB2_MOUSE	770	1	23	702–724	23	340–362
KFMS_MOUSE	976	1	25	512–536	25	745–769
KKIT_MOUSE	975	1	23	520–542	23	249–271
KMET_MOUSE	1379	1	23	932–954	23	455–477
LEM1_MOUSE	372	1	23	333–355	23	156–178
LEM3_MOUSE	768	1	24	710–733	24	344–367
LMA_MOUSE	3084	1	17	2337–2353	17	1161–1177
LMP2_MOUSE	415	1	25	380–404	25	178–202
LSHR_MOUSE	700	7	28	363–390	24	552–575

Predicition of Transmembrane Domains in Proteins

Protein	Length	Number of trans-membrane domains	Length of chosen transmem-brane domain	Location of the chosen transmem-brane domain	Length of chosen non-trans-membrane segment	Chosen non-transmem-brane area
MAGL_MOUSE	637	1	20	517–536	20	249–268
MAN2_MOUSE	1150	1	21	6–26	21	579–599
MB1_MOUSE	220	1	23	137–159	23	179–201
MDR2_MOUSE	1276	12	42	191–232	20	518–537
MEPA_MOUSE	760	1	28	727–754	28	350–377
MPV1_MOUSE	176	2	21	94–114	21	117–137
MYP0_MOUSE	248	1	26	154–179	26	65–90
NK13_MOUSE	223	1	24	40–63	24	132–155
NK1R_MOUSE	407	7	23	32–54	25	4–28
NTTG_MOUSE	633	12	18	295–312	20	586–605
OPSD_MOUSE	348	7	25	37–61	28	5–32
PGDR_MOUSE	1098	1	25	531–555	25	254–278
PGHS_MOUSE	602	1	16	293–308	16	448–463
PLR2_MOUSE	292	1	24	230–253	24	262–285
PTPU_MOUSE	1452	1	22	743–764	22	1098–1119
RNG6_MOUSE	261	1	22	231–252	22	105–126
SYND_MOUSE	311	1	25	253–277	25	283–307
TCB1_MOUSE	173	1	35	133–167	35	50–84
TCC1_MOUSE	167	1	21	135–155	21	58–78
TCC3_MOUSE	169	1	21	137–157	21	59–79
TEA_MOUSE	453	7	25	320–344	21	246–266
THRR_MOUSE	430	7	20	274–293	23	394–416
TNR1_MOUSE	454	1	23	213–235	23	334–356
TRBM_MOUSE	577	1	24	518–541	24	248–271
TRKB_MOUSE	821	1	24	430–453	24	626–649
TYRO_MOUSE	533	1	24	474–497	24	226–249
UDP1_MOUSE	530	1	17	494–510	17	513–529
VATL_MOUSE	155	4	26	127–152	22	34–55
NK13_MOUSE	223	1	24	40–63	24	132–155
NK1R_MOUSE	407	7	23	32–54	25	4–28
NTTG_MOUSE	633	12	18	295–312	20	586–605
OPSD_MOUSE	348	7	25	37–61	28	5–32
PGDR_MOUSE	1098	1	25	531–555	25	254–278
PGHS_MOUSE	602	1	16	293–308	16	448–463
PLR2_MOUSE	292	1	24	230–253	24	262–285
PTPU_MOUSE	1452	1	22	743–764	22	1098–1119
RNG6_MOUSE	261	1	22	231–252	22	105–126
SYND_MOUSE	311	1	25	253–277	25	283–307
TCB1_MOUSE	173	1	35	133–167	35	50–84
TCC1_MOUSE	167	1	21	135–155	21	58–78
TCC3_MOUSE	169	1	21	137–157	21	59–79
TEA_MOUSE	453	7	25	320–344	21	246–266
THRR_MOUSE	430	7	20	274–293	23	394–416
TNR1_MOUSE	454	1	23	213–235	23	334–356
TRBM_MOUSE	577	1	24	518–541	24	248–271
TRKB_MOUSE	821	1	24	430–453	24	626–649
TYRO_MOUSE	533	1	24	474–497	24	226–249
UDP1_MOUSE	530	1	17	494–510	17	513–529
VATL_MOUSE	155	4	26	127–152	22	34–55

Table 18.5 Out-of-sample fitness cases.

Protein	Length	Number of trans-membrane domains	Length of chosen transmembrane domain	Chosen transmembrane domain	Length of chosen non-trans-membrane segment	Chosen non-transmembrane area
3BH2_MOUSE	265	1	19	180–198	19	223–241
4F2_MOUSE	526	1	24	76–99	24	302–325
5HTB_MOUSE	386	7	22	311–332	20	143–162
A2AA_MOUSE	450	7	25	107–131	26	5–30
A2AC_MOUSE	458	7	26	89–114	24	294–317
ACET_MOUSE	732	1	17	685–701	17	709–725
ACHA_MOUSE	457	4	20	297–316	19	107–125
ACHD_MOUSE	520	4	25	249–273	25	113–137
ACHG_MOUSE	519	4	25	241–265	22	498–519
AG2R_MOUSE	359	7	22	193–214	23	3–25
AMPE_MOUSE	945	1	23	18–40	23	482–504
ATNB_MOUSE	304	1	28	35–62	28	170–197
AVR2_MOUSE	513	1	26	136–161	26	56–81
B29_MOUSE	228	1	22	159–180	22	194–215
B3AR_MOUSE	388	7	21	324–344	23	131–153
B3LP_MOUSE	1237	10	22	822–843	23	1059–1081
C114_MOUSE	573	1	28	481–508	28	528–555
CADN_MOUSE	906	1	22	725–746	22	352–373
CAML_MOUSE	1260	1	23	1124–1146	23	1193–1215
CD12_MOUSE	336	1	29	298–326	29	135–163
CD2_MOUSE	344	1	26	204–229	26	275–300
CD3E_MOUSE	189	1	26	109–134	26	150–175
CD3H_MOUSE	206	1	21	31–51	21	119–139
CD40_MOUSE	305	1	22	194–215	22	250–271
CD45_MOUSE	1152	1	22	426–447	22	203–224
CD4_MOUSE	457	1	23	395–417	23	427–449
CD72_MOUSE	354	1	21	96–116	21	38–58
CD8B_MOUSE	213	1	31	168–198	31	69–99
CIK0_MOUSE	129	1	23	44–66	23	11–33
CIK3_MOUSE	530	6	19	316–334	22	84–105
CNCG_MOUSE	683	6	19	190–208	21	330–350
COX2_MOUSE	227	2	22	27–48	20	146–165
CTL4_MOUSE	223	1	26	162–187	26	193–218
CX31_MOUSE	270	4	21	186–206	21	108–128
CX37_MOUSE	332	4	21	78–98	21	270–290
CX43_MOUSE	381	4	21	76–96	21	181–201
CX50_MOUSE	439	4	21	161–181	21	119–139
DTCM_MOUSE	291	1	18	263–280	18	123–140
EVI2_MOUSE	223	1	26	126–151	26	175–200
FCE2_MOUSE	331	1	26	24–49	26	178–203
FCEB_MOUSE	235	4	20	90–109	20	204–223
FCG1_MOUSE	404	1	23	298–320	23	138–160
FCG3_MOUSE	261	1	20	216–235	20	99–118
FGR1_MOUSE	822	1	21	377–397	21	179–199
FLK2_MOUSE	992	1	20	545–564	20	263–282
GAA2_MOUSE	451	4	22	313–334	22	367–388
GAA6_MOUSE	443	4	22	233–254	22	352–373

Protein	Length	Number of trans-membrane domains	Length of chosen transmem-brane domain	Chosen transmem-brane domain	Length of chosen non-trans-membrane segment	Chosen non-transmem-brane area
GAC3_MOUSE	467	4	23	315–337	23	380–402
GATR_MOUSE	394	1	19	42–60	19	12–30
GC3M_MOUSE	398	1	17	346–362	17	373–389
GCBM_MOUSE	405	1	18	352–369	18	168–185
GHRH_MOUSE	650	1	24	274–297	24	126–149
GLRA_MOUSE	907	4	19	585–603	19	563–581
GP70_MOUSE	330	1	29	255–283	29	293–321
GTR1_MOUSE	492	12	21	272–292	21	229–249
GTR4_MOUSE	510	12	21	85–105	21	56–76
HA11_MOUSE	362	1	22	310–331	22	145–166
HA13_MOUSE	362	1	27	307–333	27	335–361
HA15_MOUSE	357	1	23	305–327	23	332–354
HA18_MOUSE	326	1	21	306–326	21	143–163
HA1D_MOUSE	368	1	23	306–328	23	338–360
HA1L_MOUSE	357	1	23	304–326	23	141–163
HA1T_MOUSE	372	1	20	303–322	20	142–161
HA1W_MOUSE	368	1	24	306–329	24	142–165
HA22_MOUSE	255	1	26	217–242	26	96–121
HA2B_MOUSE	248	1	26	211–236	26	93–118
HA2F_MOUSE	233	1	26	196–221	26	86–111
HA2K_MOUSE	258	1	23	221–243	23	100–122
HA2R_MOUSE	233	1	26	196–221	26	86–111
HA2U_MOUSE	227	1	26	190–215	26	83–108
HB21_MOUSE	264	1	32	217–248	32	93–124
HB23_MOUSE	232	1	23	194–216	23	86–108
HB2A_MOUSE	265	1	21	227–247	21	104–124
HB2F_MOUSE	252	1	21	214–234	21	97–117
HB2J_MOUSE	264	1	23	226–248	23	102–124
HB2Q_MOUSE	265	1	20	228–247	20	105–124
HB2U_MOUSE	263	1	21	225–245	21	103–123
IL1R_MOUSE	576	1	21	339–359	21	160–180
IL2A_MOUSE	268	1	21	237–257	21	109–129
IL4R_MOUSE	810	1	24	234–257	24	523–546
IL6R_MOUSE	460	1	28	358–385	28	410–437
IL9R_MOUSE	468	1	21	271–291	21	126–146
INSR_MOUSE	1372	1	21	947–967	21	464–484
ITA4_MOUSE	1039	1	24	984–1007	24	481–504
ITAL_MOUSE	1163	1	24	1085–1108	24	1125–1148
ITB1_MOUSE	798	1	23	729–751	23	354–376
KEK4_MOUSE	983	1	24	541–564	24	259–282
KGFR_MOUSE	707	1	21	264–284	21	122–142
KLTK_MOUSE	888	1	25	422–446	25	656–680
LECI_MOUSE	301	1	21	59–79	21	181–201
LEM2_MOUSE	612	1	22	558–579	22	269–290
LEUK_MOUSE	395	1	23	249–271	23	323–345
LMP1_MOUSE	406	1	24	371–394	24	174–197
LRPA_MOUSE	830	1	24	143–166	24	487–510

Protein	Length	Number of trans-membrane domains	Length of chosen transmem-brane domain	Chosen transmem-brane domain	Length of chosen non-trans-membrane segment	Chosen non-transmem-brane area
LY49_MOUSE	262	1	22	45–66	22	154–175
MAGS_MOUSE	582	1	20	517–536	20	550–569
MAS_MOUSE	324	7	31	104–134	29	291–319
MDR1_MOUSE	1276	12	20	831–850	18	270–287
MDR3_MOUSE	1276	12	32	704–735	21	79–99
MPRD_MOUSE	278	1	25	187–211	25	82–106
MUCM_MOUSE	476	1	18	456–473	18	220–237
NALS_MOUSE	399	1	20	25–44	20	3–22
NK12_MOUSE	223	1	24	40–63	24	132–155
NK14_MOUSE	220	1	24	39–62	24	130–153
NK2R_MOUSE	384	7	22	197–218	20	130–149
OLF3_MOUSE	312	7	20	273–292	25	1–25
PC1_MOUSE	871	1	21	25–45	21	449–469
PERF_MOUSE	554	2	17	187–203	17	86–102
PGDS_MOUSE	1089	1	24	526–549	24	252–275
PLR1_MOUSE	303	1	24	230–253	24	104–127
PM22_MOUSE	161	4	24	96–119	27	35–61
RDS_MOUSE	346	4	24	100–123	24	307–330
SCF_MOUSE	273	1	23	215–237	23	245–267
TCA_MOUSE	138	1	21	113–133	21	47–67
TCB2_MOUSE	173	1	22	147–168	22	63–84
TCC2_MOUSE	172	1	20	141–160	20	61–80
TCC4_MOUSE	190	1	21	158–178	21	69–89
TF_MOUSE	294	1	23	252–274	23	115–137
TNFA_MOUSE	235	1	21	36–56	21	8–28
TNR2_MOUSE	474	1	30	259–288	30	367–396
TRFR_MOUSE	393	7	23	29–51	22	171–192
TYR2_MOUSE	517	1	19	473–491	19	496–514
TYRR_MOUSE	537	1	24	478–501	24	508–531
UFO_MOUSE	888	1	23	444–466	23	667–689
VCA1_MOUSE	739	1	22	699–720	22	339–360

Table 18.6 Tableau without ADFs for the transmembrane problem.

Objective:	Find a program to classify whether or not a segment of a protein sequence is a transmembrane domain.
Terminal set without ADFs:	LEN, M0, M1, M2, M3, random constants $\Re_{\text{bigger-reals}}$, and 20 zero-argument functions (A?), (C?), ..., (Y?).
Function set without ADFs:	ORN, SETM0, SETM1, SETM2, SETM3, IFLTE, +, -, *, and %.
Fitness cases:	The in-sample set of fitness cases consists of 246 protein segments. The out-of-sample set of fitness cases consists of 250 protein segments.
Raw fitness:	Correlation C (ranging from -1.0 to $+1.0$).
Standardized fitness:	Standardized fitness is $$\frac{1-C}{2}.$$
Hits:	100 times the difference of 1.0 minus standardized fitness for the *out-of-sample* set (rounded to nearest integer).
Wrapper:	If the result-producing branch returns a number greater than 0, the segment is classified as a transmembrane domain; otherwise, the segment is classified as non-transmembrane.
Parameters:	$M = 4,000$. $G = 21$.
Success predicate:	A best-of-run program (as measured by in-sample correlation) scores an out-of-sample correlation of 0.94 or better.

correlation that were achieved in these runs and compared performance with and without automatically defined functions. After examining the evidence obtained from the actual runs about the distribution of values of correlation, we retrospectively established the following success predicate for the problem: a program is deemed successful if it is a best-of-run program (as measured by *in-sample* correlation) and it scores an *out-of-sample* correlation of 0.94 or better. We then made the performance curves as if this success predicate had been in place during the runs.

Note that whenever a predicting program is devised using a measure of in-sample performance and subsequently cross-validated using a measure of out-of-sample performance that only checks the out-of-sample correlation of the best-of-generation individuals, the possibility inherently exists that some other program that did not have the highest value of in-sample correlation may, in fact, have yielded a higher value of out-of-sample correlation than the first program. Such a program would not be identified here as the best-of-run program.

Table 18.7 Values of out-of-sample correlation for 11 runs of the transmembrane problem without ADFs.

Generation	Out-of-sample correlation
10	0.7124
6	0.7143
6	0.7143
12	0.8044
7	0.8044
13	0.8044
8	0.8044
3	0.8044
16	0.8054
14	0.8250
20	0.9448

Table 18.6 summarizes the key features of the transmembrane problem without automatically defined functions.

18.6 RESULTS WITHOUT ADFs FOR THE SUBSET-CREATING VERSION

In 11 runs of this problem without automatically defined functions, 10 of the 11 values of correlation are clustered in the unimpressive range between 0.7124 and 0.8250. There is one outlier with the reasonably good correlation of 0.9448.

Table 18.7 shows, in ascending order, the out-of-sample correlation attained by the best-of-run individual (as measured by in-sample correlation) during each of the 11 runs and the generation on which the best value was achieved.

The best-of-all program from the 11 runs (with an out-of-sample correlation of 0.9448 and an in-sample correlation of 0.887) has 71 points and is shown below:

```
(progn (looping-over-residues
        (SETM3 (- (+ (- (F?) (K?)) (+ (- M3 (P?))
        (+ (I?) (SETM2 (SETM3 (L?)))))) (SETM2 (SETM2 (H?)))))))
    (values (* (IFLTE (IFLTE (+ -5.606 M3) (* L M2) (% -2.786
            (IFLTE M1 M3 M2 M2)) (+ -5.606 M3)) (- (% L M3)
            (- M2 (+ M0 M1))) (* M2 M0) (* (% (+ M2 M3)
            (+ M3 L)) (% M2 L))) (* (+ (+ M2 M1) (* M2 M0))
            (% M2 M2)))).
```

If the success predicate for this problem were defined to be a value of out-of-sample correlation C of 0.94 or better, only one of these 11 runs would be deemed successful with this retrospective definition.

Although calculating computational effort based on only one successful run has virtually no statistical significance, the value of $E_{without}$ computed on the basis of this single successful run is 3,724,000.

Calculating the "average" structural complexity, $\overline{S}_{without}$, based on only one successful run is similarly suspect. This "average" of 71 is especially suspect since it is smaller than the average number of points (75.2) for the best-of-run programs from the 10 unsuccessful runs in table 18.7. Thus, there is a good chance that the true value of $\overline{S}_{without}$ is higher than 71.

Since the probability of success is only 1:11 without automatically defined functions, computation of a performance curve would entail a great many runs (perhaps a hundred or more). Even with the compromise of setting G (the maximum number of generations to be run) to only 21, a single run of this problem takes one and a half days on our computer. It is apparent that any attempt to produce a performance curve for this problem without automatically defined functions would consume a prohibitive amount of computer time. Consequently, we decided to concentrate our available resources on runs of this problem employing automatically defined functions. As will be seen below, the runs with automatically defined functions did considerably better than the runs without them.

18.7 PREPARATORY STEPS WITH ADFs FOR THE SUBSET-CREATING VERSION

The programs without automatically defined functions for the transmembrane problem were unusually opaque because they combined the residue-detecting functions, the disjunctive function, the arithmetic operations, and the conditional branching operator into one branch.

Automatically defined functions seem well suited to the task of interrogating the residues and organizing the information in some way (e.g., categorizing the residues into categories). The isolation of this task in the function-defining branches permits the iteration-performing branch to concentrate on the task of iteratively performing arithmetic calculations and conditional operations. As before, the result-producing branch performs arithmetic calculations and conditional operations to make the final decision.

Thus, we decided that the overall architecture of the predicting programs would consist of three automatically defined functions (detectors for categorization), an iteration-performing branch for performing arithmetic operations and conditional operations using the as-yet-undiscovered detectors, and a result-producing branch for performing arithmetic operations and conditional operations using the results of the as-yet-undiscovered iteration to classify the given protein segment as a transmembrane domain or a non-transmembrane area.

Figure 18.5 shows an abbreviated version of the architecture for an overall predicting program for the subset-creating version of the transmembrane problem with automatically defined functions. The overall program has five branches, three of which are ADFs; however, only one ADF is shown here to save space. In addition to the three ADFs, the overall program has an iteration-performing branch, IPB0, and a result-producing branch, RPB.

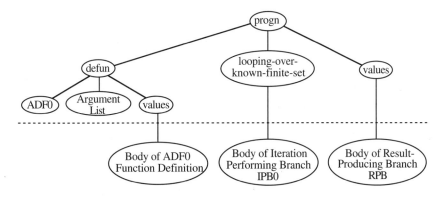

Figure 18.5 Overall program consisting of an automatically defined function, ADF0, an iteration-performing branch, IPB0, and a result-producing branch, RPB.

Having now determined the architecture for the overall program, we now consider the ingredients from which each branch of the overall program will be composed.

The terminal set, $\mathcal{T}_{adf}$, for each of the three function-defining branches ADF0, ADF1, and ADF2 contains the 20 zero-argument numerically-valued residue-detecting functions:

$\mathcal{T}_{adf} = \{ \text{(A?)}, \text{(C?)}, ..., \text{(Y?)} \}$.

The function set, $\mathcal{F}_{adf}$, for each of the three function-defining branches, ADF0, ADF1, and ADF2, contains only the two-argument numerically-valued disjunctive function:

$\mathcal{F}_{adf} = \{\text{ORN}\}$

with an argument map of

$\{2\}$.

In this problem, the function-defining branches do not refer hierarchically to one another so all three function-defining branches have identical terminal sets, function sets, and argument maps. In implementing structure-preserving crossover in this situation, one might assign one common type to all three like branches (i.e., like-branch typing) or one might assign three separate types to the three branches (i.e., branch typing). We have chosen to continue to use our usual branch-typing for this problem.

The terminal set, $\mathcal{T}_{ipb0}$, for the iteration-performing branch IPB0 is

$\mathcal{T}_{ipb0} = \{\text{M0}, \text{M1}, \text{M2}, \text{M3}, \text{LEN}, \Re_{\text{bigger-reals}}\}$,

where M0, M1, M2, and M3 are settable variables and where LEN is the length of the current protein.

Since a numerical calculation is to be performed on the results of the categorization performed by the function-defining branches, ADF0, ADF1, and ADF2 are included in the function set for the iteration-performing branch.

Predicition of Transmembrane Domains in Proteins

The function set, $\mathcal{F}_{ipb0}$, for the iteration-performing branch is

$\mathcal{F}_{ipb0} = \{\text{ADF0, ADF1, ADF2, SETM0, SETM1, SETM2, SETM3, IFLTE, +, -, *, \%}\}$

with an argument map of

$\{0, 0, 0, 1, 1, 1, 1, 4, 2, 2, 2, 2\}$.

As before, the terminal set, $\mathcal{T}_{rpb}$, for the result-producing branch, RPB, is

$\mathcal{T}_{rpb} = \{\text{LEN, M0, M1, M2, M3, } \Re_{\text{bigger-reals}}\}$.

Similarly, as before, the function set, $\mathcal{F}_{rpb}$, for the result-producing branch is

$\mathcal{F}_{rpb} = \{\text{IFLTE, +, -, *, \%}\}$

with an argument map of

$\{4, 2, 2, 2, 2\}$.

Table 18.8 summarizes the key features of the subset-creating version of the transmembrane problem with automatically defined functions.

18.8   RESULTS WITH ADFs FOR THE SUBSET-CREATING VERSION

In this section, we will see that automatically defined functions greatly facilitate solution of this problem. The correlations will prove to be higher than when automatically defined functions are not used. Moreover, these higher values of correlation will be achieved on many different runs.

We first examine run 1, the second best run with automatically defined functions.

In this run, the vast majority of the randomly generated programs in the initial random population (generation 0) have a 0.0 or near-zero correlation, C, indicating that they are no better than random in recognizing whether a protein segment is a transmembrane domain. Many of these programs achieve their poor performance because the result-producing branch returns the same value regardless of the composition of the protein segment presented. This occurs for various reasons. Sometimes the iteration-performing branch entirely ignores the three automatically defined functions (thus totally disconnecting the iteration-performing branch and the result-producing branch from the input of the problem). In other programs, the settable variables are either not set at all or effectively set to a constant value. And in other programs, the result-producing branch ignores the settable variables. The net effect is that these programs with zero correlation classify all segments the same and achieve 123 true positives and 123 false positives (or 123 true negatives and 123 false negatives) over the 246 in-sample fitness cases. For these random programs with zero correlation, the accuracy measure, Q_3, is 0.5, the error measure E_3 is 0.5, the percentage of agreement, c_a, is 100%, the measure of overprediction, c_{na}, is 0% (or vice versa), and the Q_a measure is 50%.

The best-of-generation predicting program from generation 0 of run 1 has an in-sample correlation of 0.48 and a standardized fitness of 0.26 as a result

Table 18.8 Tableau with ADFs for the subset-creating version of the transmembrane problem.

Objective:	Find a program to classify whether or not a segment of a protein sequence is a transmembrane domain.
Architecture of the overall program with ADFs:	One result-producing branch, one iteration-performing branch, and three zero-argument function-defining branches, with no ADF hierarchically referring to any other ADF.
Parameters:	Branch typing among the three automatically defined functions.
Terminal set for the iteration-performing branch:	LEN, M0, M1, M2, M3, and the random constants $\Re_{\text{bigger-reals}}$.
Function set for the iteration-performing branch:	ADF0, ADF1, ADF2, SETM0, SETM1, SETM2, SETM3, IFLTE, +, -, *, and %.
Terminal set for the result-producing branch:	LEN, M0, M1, M2, M3, and the random constants $\Re_{\text{bigger-reals}}$.
Function set for the result-producing branch:	IFLTE, +, -, *, and %.
Terminal set for the function-defining branches ADF0, ADF1, and ADF2:	Twenty zero-argument functions (A?), (C?), ..., (Y?).
Function set for the function-defining branches ADF0, ADF1, and ADF2:	Numerically valued two-argument logical disjunction function ORN.

of getting 99 true positives, 83 true negatives, 40 false positives, and 24 false negatives over the 246 in-sample fitness cases. When tested on the out-of-sample set, this 82-point program has an out-of-sample correlation of 0.43 and an out-of-sample standardized fitness of 0.28 as a result of getting 94 true positives, 85 true negatives, 40 false positives, and 31 false negatives over the 250 out-of-sample fitness cases. It scores 72 hits and is shown below:

```
(progn (defun ADF0 ()
          (values (ORN (ORN (ORN (I?) (M?)) (ORN (V?) (C?))) (ORN
            (ORN (W?) (L?)) (ORN (Y?) (A?))))))
        (defun ADF1 ()
          (values (ORN (ORN (ORN (L?) (L?)) (ORN (R?) (K?))) (ORN
            (ORN (I?) (V?)) (ORN (R?) (Q?))))))
        (defun ADF2 ()
          (values (ORN (ORN (ORN (R?) (S?)) (ORN (F?) (Q?))) (ORN
            (ORN (P?) (F?)) (ORN (Y?) (C?))))))
```

```
(progn (looping-over-residues
    (SETM0 (SETM3 (SETM0 (ADF0)))))
  (values (IFLTE (+ (- M3 M0) (+ M1 M3)) (%
    (IFLTE M0 M3 6.212 M1) (IFLTE M0 M2 M1 L)) (*
    (% M1 M2) (* M3 0.419)) (+ (% L M2) (- M0
    M2)))))))
```

In examining this program from run 1, we see that ADF0 returns 1 for any amino acid residue from the defined set {I, M, V, C, W, L, Y, A}. Six of these eight residues are hydrophobic and two (W and Y) are neutral according to the categories shown in table 18.1 (the Kyte-Doolittle hydrophobicity scale). In other words, ADF0 is an imperfect detector of hydrophobic residues in that it omits one of the hydrophobic residues (F) and includes two neutral residues (W and Y). Note that this interpretation of ADF0 is based on our knowledge of the Kyte-Doolittle hydrophobicity scale (table 18.1) and the three categories that can reasonably be induced from that table using clustering techniques; genetic programming does not have access to these Kyte-Doolittle values or the three categories.

The iteration-performing branch of the best of generation 0 refers only to ADF0. The iteration-performing branch sets the settable variable M0 to the value of ADF0 and sets the settable variable M3 to the value of M0. Since this branch only writes values into M3 and M0 (and does not ever read M3 or M0), the final values of M3 and M0 after the iteration over the entire protein segment is merely the value of ADF0 for the very last residue of the protein segment. In other words, M3 and M0 are both 1 if the last residue is in the particular subset of residues designated by ADF0. Since ADF0 is an imperfect hydrophobicity detector, the final values of M3 and M0 are usually, but not reliably, 1 if the last residue is hydrophobic. Since the settable variables M1 and M2 are not referenced by the iteration-performing branch, they both remain at their initial values of 0.

The result-producing branch can therefore be simplified to

```
(IFLTE M0 (% 6.212 (IFLTE M0 0 0 L)) (* M0 0.419) (+ 1 M0)))).
```

If M0 is 0, the best of generation 0 returns 0 (which the wrapper interprets as non-transmembrane); but if M0 is 1, then this program returns 2 (which the wrapper interprets as transmembrane). The entire protein segment is classified as being transmembrane or not on the basis of whether the last residue of the segment is in the imperfect subset defined by ADF0. For example, this program happens to correctly classify the segment consisting of residues 96–119 of mouse peripheral myelin protein 22 (table 18.2) as a transmembrane domain because residue 119 is valine (V). However, because residue 61 of the negative case shown in table 18.3 is tryptophan (W), this program incorrectly classifies the 27-residue segment from positions 35–61 of this same protein as a transmembrane domain.

This program is highly flawed, since it myopically looks at only a single residue of the protein segment in making an ill-advised decision based on a defective ADF0. However, this program is better than any of the other 3,999 programs in the population at generation 0.

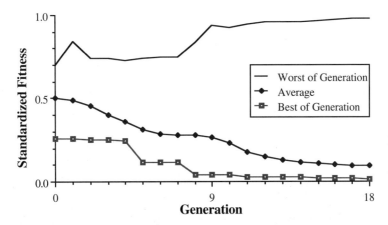

Figure 18.6 Fitness curves for run 1 of the subset-creating version of the transmembrane problem.

The worst-of-generation predicting program from generation 0 of run 1 has an in-sample correlation of –0.4. Like the best-of-generation program, it myopically looks at only one residue in the protein segment and then creates a highly imperfect hydrophobicity detector ADF1. This program achieves its negative value of correlation by then using its incomplete information in precisely the wrong way.

Figure 18.6 shows the fitness curves for this run. At generation 0, the in-sample correlation of the best-of-generation program is 0.48 and the standardized fitness is 0.26. The in-sample correlation of the worst-of-generation program is –0.40 and its standardized fitness is 0.70.

In generation 2 of run 1, the best-of-generation program achieves an incrementally better correlation (0.496 in-sample and 0.472 out-of-sample) by virtue of an incremental change consisting of just one point in the definition of ADF0.

There is a major qualitative change in the best of generation 5. The best of generation 5 is the first best-of-generation program in this run that makes its prediction based on the entire protein segment. This 62-point program has a distinctly better in-sample correlation of 0.764, an out-of-sample correlation of 0.784, a standardized fitness of 0.12, and scores 89 hits.

```
(progn (defun ADF0 ()
         (values (ORN (ORN (I?) (A?)) (ORN (ORN (L?) (G?))
         (N?)))))
       (defun ADF1 ()
         (values (ORN (ORN (ORN (ORN (G?) (D?)) (ORN (E?) (V?)))
          (ORN (ORN (R?) (E?)) (ORN (T?) (P?)))) (ORN (N?)
          (S?)))))
       (defun ADF2 ()
         (values (ORN (ORN (ORN (L?) (R?)) (ORN (V?) (P?))) (ORN
          (G?) (L?)))))
       (progn (looping-over-residues
               (SETM1 (- (+ M1 (ADF0)) (ADF1))))
```

```
(values (* (% (+ (% -9.997 M3) M1) 6.602) (+ 6.738
    (% (- M3 L) (+ M3 M2)))))))).
```

The iteration-performing branch of this program uses the settable variable M1 to create a running sum of the difference between two quantities. Specifically, as the iteration-performing branch is iteratively executed over the protein segment, M1 is set to the current value of M1 plus the difference between ADF0 and ADF1. ADF0 consists of nested ORNs involving the three hydrophobic residues (I, A, and L), one neutral residue (G), and one hydrophilic residue (N). ADF1 consists of nested ORNs involving one hydrophobic residue (V), four neutral residues (G, T, P, and S), and the four most hydrophilic residues (D, E, R, and N).

Because the neutral G residue and the hydrophilic N residue appear in both ADF0 and ADF1, there is no net effect on the running sum of the differences, M1, calculated by the iteration-performing branch when the current residue is either G or N. There is a positive contribution (from ADF0) to the running sum M1 only when the current residue is I, A, or L (all of which are hydrophobic), and there is a negative contribution (from ADF1) to the running sum M1 only when the current residue is D, E, or R (all of which are hydrophilic). The running sum M1 is a count (based on a sample of only three of the seven hydrophobic residues and only three of the seven hydrophilic residues) of the excess of hydrophobic residues over hydrophilic residues.

When simplified, the result-producing branch is equivalent to

$$1.17 \times (M_1 + 1),$$

so the protein segment is classified as a transmembrane domain whenever M1 is greater than −1. In other words, whenever the number of occurrences of the three particular hydrophobic residues (I, A, and L) equals or exceeds the number of occurrences of the three particular hydrophilic residues (D, E, and R), the segment is classified as a transmembrane domain. This relatively simple calculation is a very imperfect predictor of transmembrane domains, but it is correct more often than its ancestors.

In generation 6 of run 1, the best-of-generation program has marginally better values for correlation (0.766 in-sample and 0.834 out-of-sample) by virtue of a small evolutionary change in the definition of ADF1.

The 62-point best of generation 8 of run 1 exhibits a substantial jump in performance over all its predecessors from previous generations. The improvement arises from a small change in ADF0 and a major change in ADF1. In-sample correlation rises to 0.92; out-of-sample correlation rises to 0.89. Hits rise to 94.

```
(progn (defun ADF0 ()
         (values (ORN (ORN (ORN (I?) (M?)) (ORN (V?) (C?))) (ORN
           (ORN (L?) (G?)) (N?)))))
       (defun ADF1 ()
         (values (ORN (ORN (ORN (ORN (G?) (D?)) (ORN (E?) (V?)))
           (ORN (ORN (R?) (E?)) (ORN (T?) (P?)))) (ORN (N?)
           (S?)))))
```

```
(defun ADF2 ()
  (values (ORN (ORN (ORN (L?) (R?)) (ORN (V?) (P?))) (ORN
    (G?) (L?)))))
(progn (looping-over-residues
         (SETM1 (- (+ M1 (ADF0)) (ADF1))))
       (values (* (+ M1 M3) (+ 6.738 (% (- M3 L) (+ M3
         M2)))))))).
```

In this program, `ADF0` tests for four (I, M, C, and L) of the seven hydrophobic residues, instead of three. Moreover, isoleucine (I), the most hydrophobic residue among the seven hydrophobic residues on the Kyte-Doolittle scale, is one of the residues incorporated into `ADF0`. More important, `ADF1` tests for three neutral residues (T, P, and S) as well as three hydrophilic residues (D, E, and R). The result-producing branch calculates $7.738 M_1$.

As before, a protein segment will be classified as a transmembrane domain whenever the running sum `M1` is positive.

The three neutral residues (T, P, and S) in `ADF1` play an important role since a positive value of `M1` can be achieved only if there are enough sampled hydrophobic residues in the segment to counterbalance the sum of the number of occurrences of the four hydrophilic residues plus the number of occurrences of the three neutral residues.

In generation 11 of run 1, the 78-point best-of-generation program has an in-sample correlation of 0.94 and a standardized fitness of 0.03 as a result of getting 117 true positives, 122 true negatives, 1 false positive, and 6 false negatives over the 246 in-sample fitness cases. It has an out-of-sample correlation of 0.96 and a standardized fitness of 0.02 as a result of getting 122 true positives, 123 true negatives, 2 false positives, and 3 false negatives over the 250 out-of-sample fitness cases. This program scores 98 hits; its out-of-sample error rate is only 2.0%.

```
(progn (defun ADF0 ()
         (values (ORN (ORN (ORN (I?) (M?)) (ORN (V?) (C?))) (ORN
           (ORN (L?) (G?)) (N?)))))
       (defun ADF1 ()
         (values (ORN (ORN (ORN (ORN (G?) (D?)) (ORN (E?) (V?)))
           (ORN (ORN (R?) (E?)) (ORN (ORN (ORN (ORN (G?) (D?))
           (ORN (E?) (V?))) (ORN (ORN (R?) (K?)) (ORN (T?)
           (P?)))) (ORN (N?) (S?))))) (ORN (N?) (S?)))))
       (defun ADF2 ()
         (values (ORN (ORN (ORN (L?) (Y?)) (ORN (V?) (P?))) (ORN
           (G?) (L?)))))
       (progn (looping-over-residues
                (SETM1 (- (+ M1 (ADF0)) (ADF1))))
              (values (* (+ M1 M3) (+ 6.738 (% (- M3 L) (+ M3
                M2)))))))).
```

This program from generation 11 of run 1 is similar to, but better than, the best of generation 8. The definition of `ADF0`, the calculation of the running sum M1 in the iteration-performing branch, and the final calculation in the result-producing branch are the same. However, ADF1 differs from the best of generation 8 in that it tests for four of the seven hydrophilic residues (D, E, R, and K), not just three. Moreover, D, E, R, and K are the most hydrophilic residues from among the seven hydrophilic residues according to the Kyte-Doolittle scale. Consequently, a majority of the hydrophobic residues are effectively tested by ADF0 and a majority of the hydrophilic residues (along with three neutral residues) are tested by ADF1. This change makes the running sum M1 even better at predicting whether a protein segment is in a trans-membrane domain.

The seven sampled hydrophilic and neutral residues in ADF1 account for 40.7% of the residues in all proteins and the four sampled hydrophobic residues in ADF0 account for 18.3% (Creighton 1993). Roughly speaking, a trans-membrane prediction by the result-producing branch is triggered by a reduction in the normal ratio of better than 2:1 to a ratio of just below 1:1.

The operation of this program from generation 11 of run 1 can be summarized as follows: If the number of occurrences of I, M, C, and L in a given protein segment exceeds the number of occurrences of D, E, R, K, T, P, and S, then classify the segment as a transmembrane domain; otherwise, classify it as non-transmembrane.

As before, the residues V, G, and N play no role in the calculation of the running sum M1 since they appear in both ADF0 and ADF1.

Table 18.9 shows, by generation, on both an in-sample and an out-of-sample basis, the correlation C, the number of true positives, N_{tp}, the number of true negatives, N_{tn}, the number of false positives, N_{fp}, and the number of false negatives, N_{fn}, for the best-of-generation programs of run 1. The number of hits (out-of-sample) is also shown in the last column. As can be seen, the best value of out-of-sample correlation is first achieved on generation 11.

After generation 11, the in-sample performance of the best-of-generation program continues to improve. For example, the in-sample correlation improves from 0.94 to 0.98 between generations 11 and 18, and the number of in-sample errors (i.e., false positives plus false negatives) drops from seven to 3. Specifically, the number of false negatives drops from six to two between generations 11 and 18 while the number of false positives remains at one. The best of generation 18 differs from the best of generation 11 in that two of its function definitions are somewhat different. As a result of these changes, the best of generation 18 correctly classifies the designated segments of the proteins B2AR_MOUSE, THRR_MOUSE, GAC2_MOUSE, and GAD_MOUSE as transmembrane domains, whereas the best of generation 11 erred on these four segments.

However, this apparent improvement in run 1 after generation 11 is due to overfitting. Genetic programming is relentlessly driven to achieve better and better values of fitness. Fitness for this problem is based on the value of the correlation for the predictions made by the genetically evolved program on the *in-sample* set of fitness cases. However, the true measure of performance

Table 18.9 In-sample and out-of-sample correlation of best-of-generation programs from run 1 of the subset-creating version of the transmembrane problem.

Gener-ation	In-sample					Out-of-sample					Hits
	C	N_{tp}	N_{tn}	N_{fp}	N_{fn}	C	N_{tp}	N_{tn}	N_{fp}	N_{fn}	
0	0.48	99	83	40	24	0.43	94	85	40	31	72
1	0.48	99	83	40	24	0.43	94	85	40	31	72
2	0.50	92	92	31	31	0.47	91	93	32	34	74
3	0.50	92	92	31	31	0.47	91	93	32	34	74
4	0.50	110	72	51	13	0.54	115	74	51	10	76
5	0.76	107	110	13	16	0.78	110	113	12	15	89
6	0.77	113	104	19	10	0.83	119	110	15	6	92
7	0.77	113	104	19	10	0.83	119	110	15	6	92
8	0.92	117	119	4	6	0.89	122	114	11	3	94
9	0.92	117	119	4	6	0.89	122	114	11	3	94
10	0.92	122	114	9	1	0.83	122	106	19	3	91
11	0.94	117	122	1	6	0.96	122	123	2	3	98
12	0.94	117	122	1	6	0.96	122	123	2	3	98
13	0.95	119	121	2	4	0.94	123	119	6	2	97
14	0.95	118	122	1	5	0.93	117	124	1	8	96
15	0.96	120	121	2	3	0.92	123	117	8	2	96
16	0.96	119	122	1	4	0.93	118	123	2	7	96
17	0.96	119	122	1	4	0.93	118	123	2	7	96
18	0.98	121	122	1	2	0.94	121	122	3	4	97

for a predicting algorithm is how well it generalizes to the previously unseen out-of-sample data. In this run, the out-of-sample correlation drops from 0.96 to 0.94 between generations 11 and 18, and the number of out-of-sample errors increases from five to seven (one additional false positive and one additional false negative). The maximum value of out-of-sample correlation is attained at generation 11. After generation 11, the evolved predicting programs are being fitted more and more to the idiosyncrasies of the particular in-sample fitness cases employed in the computation of fitness. The predicting programs after generation 11 are not getting better at predicting whether protein segments are transmembrane domains. They are merely getting better at memorizing the in-sample data.

Figure 18.7 compares, for generations 8 through 18, the in-sample correlation and the out-of-sample correlation for run 1. As can be seen, the out-of-sample correlation peaks at 0.96 on generation 11, but the in-sample correlation increases over the range of this figure. Overfitting is occurring after generation 11.

Predicition of Transmembrane Domains in Proteins

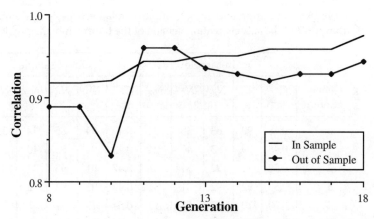

Figure 18.7 Comparison of values of in-sample and out-of-sample correlation between generations 8 and 18 for run 1 of the subset-creating version of the transmembrane problem.

The hits measure (which is based on the out-of-sample correlation) also reflects the fact that the best result is obtained at generation 11. There are 98 hits at generation 11 but only 97 at generation 18.

The continuation of run 1 out to generation 50 produces no result better than that attained at generation 11.

An examination of two other runs provides additional insights into this problem.

Run 2 is interesting because it achieves a surprisingly high out-of-sample correlation of 0.93 with its iteration-performing branch calling only one automatically defined function, ADF1. This best-of-run program emerged in generation 14 of run 2.

```
(progn (defun ADF0 ()
          (values (ORN (L?) (E?))))
       (defun ADF1 ()
          (values (ORN (ORN (E?) (K?)) (ORN (ORN (P?) (D?))
          (R?)))))
       (defun ADF2 ()
          (values (ORN (ORN (F?) (I?)) (ORN (D?) (R?)))))
       (progn (loop-over-residues
              (SETM1 (SETM2 (+ M2 (ADF1)))))
          (values (% (- (- M1 1.434) 1.434) (% (* M2 M2)
          (+ M0 -2.836)))))).
```

In this program from run 2, M1 and M2 are equal; both are the running sum of the values returned by ADF1. ADF1 returns 1 if the current residue is E, K, D, R (i.e., the four most hydrophilic residues) or P (a neutral residue). Substituting M1 for M2, and deleting M0 (which always equals 0), the result-producing branch is equivalent to

$$\frac{-2.836(M_1 - 2.868)}{M_1^2}.$$

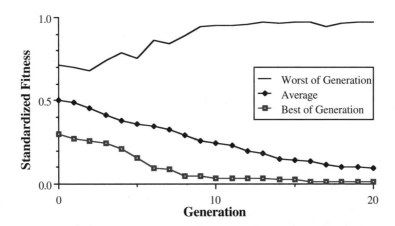

Figure 18.8 Fitness curves for run 3 of the subset-creating version of the transmembrane problem.

This expression can be positive (indicating a transmembrane domain) only if there are fewer than three residues in the segment from the set {E, K, D, R, P}. Since E, K, D, and R represent only about half of the occurrences of hydrophilic residues in a typical protein, this expression is, roughly speaking, a test that the number of hydrophilic residues in the segment is fewer than about six. This program implicitly exploits the fact that the average length of the protein segment in our set of fitness cases is 21.7 in establishing six as a threshold.

Run 3 produced the best-of-all program for any run of the subset-creating version of the transmembrane problem.

Figure 18.8 shows the fitness curves for run 3. At generation 0, the in-sample correlation of the best-of-generation program is 0.404 and the standardized fitness is 0.298. At generation 20, the in-sample correlation is 0.976 and the standardized fitness is 0.0122.

This high correlation is achieved on generation 20 of run 3 by a program with an in-sample correlation of 0.976 resulting from getting 121 true positives, 122 true negatives, 1 false positive, and 2 false negatives over the 246 in-sample fitness cases. Its out-of-sample correlation of 0.968 is the result of getting 123 true positives, 123 true negatives, 2 false positives, and 2 false negatives over the 250 out-of-sample fitness cases. It scores 98 hits. Its out-of-sample error rate is only 1.6%. This program consists of 105 points and is shown below:

```
(progn (defun ADF0 ()
         (values (ORN (ORN (ORN (I?) (H?)) (ORN (P?) (G?))) (ORN
            (ORN (ORN (Y?) (N?)) (ORN (T?) (Q?))) (ORN (A?)
            (H?))))))
       (defun ADF1 ()
         (values (ORN (ORN (ORN (A?) (I?)) (ORN (L?) (W?))) (ORN
            (ORN (T?) (L?)) (ORN (T?) (W?)))))
```

```
(defun ADF2 ()
  (values (ORN (ORN (ORN (ORN (ORN (D?) (E?)) (ORN (ORN
    (ORN (D?) (E?)) (ORN (ORN (T?) (W?)) (ORN (Q?) (D?))))
    (ORN (K?) (P?)))) (ORN (K?) (P?))) (ORN (T?) (W?)))
    (ORN (ORN (E?) (A?)) (ORN (N?) (R?))))))
  (progn (loop-over-residues
    (SETM0 (+ (- (ADF1) (ADF2)) (SETM3 M0))))
    (values (% (% M3 M0) (% (% (% (- L -0.53) (* M0
      M0)) (+ (% (% M3 M0) (% (+ M0 M3) (% M1 M2)))
      M2)) (% M3 M0))))))).
```

Ignoring the three residues common to the definition of both ADF1 and ADF2, ADF1 returns 1 if the current residue is I or L and ADF2 returns 1 if the current residue is D, E, K, R, Q, N, or P. I and L are two of the seven hydrophobic residues on the Kyte-Doolittle scale. D, E, K, R, Q, and N are six of the seven hydrophilic residues, and P is one of the neutral residues.

In the iteration-performing branch of this program from generation 20 of run 3, M0 is the running sum of the differences of the values returned by ADF1 and ADF2. M0 will be positive only if the hydrophobic residues in the protein segment are so numerous that the occurrences of I and L outnumber the occurrences of the six hydrophilic residues and one neutral residue of ADF2. M3 is the same as the accumulated value of M0 except that M3 lags M0 by one residue. Because the contribution to M3 in the iteration-performing branch of the last residue is either 0 or 1, M3 is either equal to M0 or is one less than M0.

The result-producing branch is equivalent to

$$\frac{M_3^3}{M_0(M_0 + M_3)(L + 0.53)}.$$

The subexpression (- LEN -0.53) is always positive and therefore can be ignored in determining whether the result-producing branch is positive or nonpositive. Because of the close relationship between M0 and M3, analysis shows that the result-producing branch identifies a protein segment as a transmembrane domain whenever the running sum of the differences, M0, is greater than 0, except for the special case when M0 = 1 and M3 = 0. This special case occurs only when the running values of M0 and M3 are tied at 0 and when the very last residue of the protein segment is I or L (i.e., ADF1 returns 1).

Ignoring this special case, we can summarize the operation of this overall best-of-all program from generation 20 of run 3 as follows: If the number of occurrences of I and L in a given protein segment exceeds the number of occurrences of D, E, K, R, Q, N, and P, classify the segment as a transmembrane domain; otherwise, classify it as non-transmembrane.

Figure 18.9 shows that the out-of-sample correlation closely tracks the in-sample correlation in the neighborhood of generation 20 of run 3. At generation 20, the out-of-sample correlation is 0.968 and the in-sample correlation is 0.976.

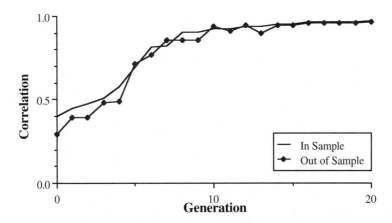

Figure 18.9 Comparison of values of in-sample and out-of-sample correlation for run 3 of the subset-creating version of the transmembrane problem.

Table 18.10 Statistics for the best-of-all program from run 3 for the subset-creating version of the transmembrane problem.

Out-of-sample statistics	Best-of-run from generation 20
Number of fitness cases N_{fc}	250
Number of true positives N_{tp}	123
Number of true negatives N_{tn}	123
Number of false positives N_{fp}	2
Number of false negatives N_{fn}	2
In-sample correlation C	0.976
Out-of-sample correlation C	0.968
Standardized fitness	0.16
Hits	98
Accuracy Q_3	98.4%
Error rate	1.6%
Percentage of agreement c_a	98.4%
Percentage of overprediction c_{na}	98.4%

Table 18.11 Comparison of five methods for the subset-creating version of the transmembrane problem.

Method	Error rate
von Heijne 1992	2.8%
Engelman, Steitz, and Goldman 1986	2.7%
Kyte-Doolittle 1982	2.5%
Weiss, Cohen, and Indurkhya 1993	2.5%
Best-of-all genetically evolved program from run 3 of the set-creating version	1.6%

Table 18.10 summarizes the measures of out-of-sample statistics for the best-of-all program for the subset-creating version of the transmembrane problem (i.e., the best of generation 20 of run 3).

For the reasons stated above, we prefer correlation for evolving prediction programs and for measuring their performance. However, many papers on predicting algorithms in the biological literature (particularly older papers) use other measures, such as accuracy, percentage agreement, and error rate. Weiss, Cohen, and Indurkhya (1993) use the common yardstick of error rate to compare three methods in the biological literature with a new algorithm of their own created using the SWAP-1 induction technique (Weiss and Indurkhya 1991; Arikawa et al. 1992). Therefore, we present the comparison below using error rate.

Table 18.11 shows the error rates for the four algorithms for recognizing transmembrane domains reviewed by Weiss, Cohen, and Indurkhya (1993) as well as the out-of-sample error rate of the best-of-all genetically-evolved program from generation 20 from run 3 for the subset-creating version of the transmembrane problem. As can be seen, the error rate of the genetically evolved program is the best of the five.

In fact, our second best genetically evolved program (from generation 11 of run 1) also outscores the other four methods (with an out-of-sample error rate of 2.0%).

We wrote a computer program to test the solution discovered by the SWAP-1 induction technique used in the first experiment of Weiss, Cohen, and Indurkhya (1993). Our implementation of their solution produced an error rate on our test data identical to the error rate reported by them on their own test data (i.e., the 2.5% of row 4 of table 18.11). Weiss, Cohen, and Indurkhya reported that the error rate for their method was superior to the error rate of two of the other three methods (rows 1 and 2 of table 18.11) on their test data and was equal to the error rate of one of the other three methods (row 3 of the table 18.11) on their test data.

We did not write a computer programs for the other three methods and therefore cannot say, with certainty, that our best genetically evolved program is the best of the five methods on our test data. In any event, the genetically evolved program clearly compares favorably to the other methods.

As mentioned above, after making 11 runs of this problem without automatically defined functions, we noted that all the values of out-of-sample correlation achieved in all but one of the runs are clustered at relatively low values of correlation. We therefore retrospectively defined the success predicate for this problem as the attainment of an out-of-sample correlation C of 0.94. On the basis of this retrospective success predicate, only one of the 11 runs of this problem without automatically defined functions is deemed successful and six of the 22 runs with automatically defined functions are deemed successful.

Table 18.12 shows, in ascending order, the out-of-sample correlation attained by the best-of-run individual from the six successful runs (out of 22) and the generation on which the best value was attained.

Table 18.12 Values of out-of-sample correlation for six successful runs (out of 22) of the subset-creating version of the transmembrane problem with ADFs.

Generation	Out-of-sample correlation
12	0.944
16	0.945
7	0.945
13	0.952
11	0.960
20	0.968

With Defined Functions

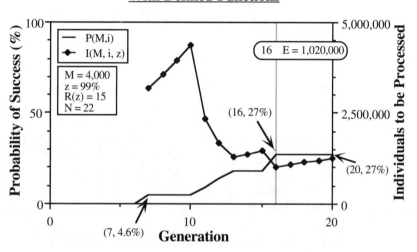

Figure 18.10 Performance curves for the subset-creating version of the transmembrane problem showing that E_{with} = 1,020,000 with ADFs.

Table 18.13 Comparison table for the subset-creating version of the transmembrane problem.

	Without ADFs	With ADFs
Average structural complexity $\bar{S}$	71	122.0
Computational effort E	3,724,000	1,020,000

The average structural complexity, $\bar{S}_{without}$, of the best-of-run programs from the six successful runs (out of 22 runs) of the subset-creating version of the transmembrane problem without automatically defined functions is 122.0 points.

Figure 18.10 presents the performance curves based on the 22 runs of the transmembrane problem with automatically defined functions. The cumulative probability of success, $P(M,i)$, is 27% by generation 16 and is 27% by generation 20. The two numbers in the oval indicate that if this problem is run through to generation 16, processing a total of $E_{with} = 1{,}020{,}000$ individuals (i.e., $4{,}000 \times 17$ generations $\times 15$ runs) is sufficient to yield a satisfactory result for this problem with 99% probability.

18.9   SUMMARY FOR THE SUBSET-CREATING VERSION

Table 18.13 compares the average structural complexity, $\bar{S}_{without}$ and $\bar{S}_{with}$, and the computational effort, $E_{without}$ and E_{with}, for the transmembrane problem with automatically defined functions and without them. Note that the value of 71 for $\bar{S}_{without}$ and the value of $E_{without}$ of 3,724,000 without automatically defined functions are based on only one run that satisfies the retrospectively-created success predicate.

In summary, automatically defined functions reduce the computational effort necessary to yield a satisfactory result for this problem.

The error rate produced by the genetically evolved program for the subset-creating version of the transmembrane problem described here is better than the error rates reported for the four algorithms for recognizing transmembrane domains reviewed in Weiss, Cohen, and Indurkhya (1993).

18.10   THE ARITHMETIC-PERFORMING VERSION

In the foregoing set-creating version of the transmembrane problem, the automatically defined functions were used for the purpose of set formation. The only function in the function set of the function-defining branches is the two-argument numerically-valued disjunctive function ORN. This approach constrained the nature of the detectors that could be evolved in two ways. First, an automatically defined function could return only +1 or –1. Second, all the amino acid residues in any one automatically defined function were given equal weight in the decision made by the ORN function.

We used this set-creating approach because our interest in the transmembrane problem was motivated by the set-creating approach presented by Weiss, Cohen, and Indurkhya (1993) at the First International Conference on Intelligent Systems for Molecular Biology. However, the question naturally arises as to whether genetic programming can solve this same problem without predetermining that the automatically defined functions would be used solely for the purpose of set formation.

In this section, we enable each automatically defined function to perform arbitrary arithmetic operations as well as conditional operations and to

Table 18.14 Partial tableau with ADFs for the arithmetic-performing version of the transmembrane problem.

Terminal set for the function-defining branches ADF0, ADF1, and ADF2:	Random constants $\Re_{\text{bigger-reals}}$ and 20 zero-argument functions (A?), (C?), ..., (Y?).
Function set for the function-defining branches ADF0, ADF1, and ADF2:	IFGTZ, +, −, *, %, and ORN.
Types of points:	• The IFGTZ operator (which is always at the root). • Point in first argument (condition part) of IFGTZ. • The IFGTZ operator when positioned other than at the root. • Point in an arithmetic expression.
Rules of construction:	• The root node must be an IFGTZ. • The condition (first) argument of an IFGTZ may contain any composition of ORN and the residue-detecting functions (A?), (C?), ..., (Y?). • The second (then) and third (else) arguments of an IFGTZ may be only other IFGTZs or compositions of the arithmetic functions +, −, *, %, and the random constants $\Re_{\text{bigger-reals}}$. •An arithmetic function can have as its arguments only random floating-point constants or arithmetic functions.

return a potentially more discriminating floating-point value (rather than just +1 or −1).

This increase in flexibility is achieved by adding the four arithmetic operations (+, −, *, and %) and the conditional decision-making operator IFGTZ (If Greater Than Zero) to the function set of the function-defining branches. The two-argument numerically-valued disjunctive function ORN is retained.

IFGTZ (If Greater Than Zero) is a three-argument conditional decision-making operator that returns the result of evaluating its second argument if its first argument is greater than zero, but otherwise returns the result of evaluating its third argument. Since there are side effecting functions in this problem (i.e., the four setting functions), IFGTZ must be implemented as a macro as described in section 12.2.

Experience indicates that we can increase our ability to understand the genetically evolved expressions arising from hierarchies of conditional decision-making operations such as IFGTZ by imposing a constrained syntactic structure on the branches that use the conditional operation. The rules of construction for the constrained syntactic structure require that the root node of each function-defining branch must always be IFGTZ. The program typically contains additional IFGTZs; however, the first (condition) argument of every IFGTZ must be a composition only of ORNs and the 20 residue-detecting

Prediction of Transmembrane Domains in Proteins

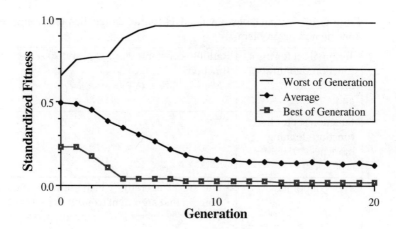

Figure 18.11 Fitness curves for one run of the arithmetic-performing version of the transmembrane problem

functions (A?), (C?),…, (Y?). In particular, the first argument of an IFGTZ never contains another IFGTZ. The second (then) and third (else) arguments of each IFGTZ consist only of compositions of other IFGTZ operators, the arithmetic operations (+, −, *, and %), and random floating-point constants. The effect of these constraints is that the condition (antecedent) part of each IFGTZ is truly a condition and the consequent parts of each IFCTZ are truly consequents (i.e., another IFGTZ or an expression that evaluates to a floating-point value). In this problem, the effect of nesting an IFGTZ in either the then-part or the else-part of another IFGTZ is to create a hierarchy.

Table 18.14 is a partial tableau with ADFs that contains only the differences between this arithmetic-performing version of the transmembrane problem and the subset-creating versions (tables 18.6 and 18.8).

Figure 18.11 shows the fitness curves for one run. At generation 0, the in-sample correlation of the best-of-generation program is 0.532 and the standardized fitness is 0.234.

The out-of-sample error rate for the best of generation 5 of this run of the arithmetic-performing version of the transmembrane problem equals the out-of-sample error rate of 1.6% for the best-of-all program from the subset-creating version of the transmembrane problem.

The best of generation 5 has an in-sample correlation of 0.912 resulting from getting 114 true positives, 121 true negatives, 2 false positive, and 9 false negatives over the 246 in-sample fitness cases. Its out-of-sample correlation of 0.968 is the result of getting 123 true positives, 123 true negatives, 2 false positives, and 2 false negatives over the 250 out-of-sample fitness cases. It scores 98 hits.

```
(progn (defun ADF0 ()
          (values (IFGTZ (ORN (ORN (ORN (C?) (A?))
                               (ORN (L?) (V?)))
                          (ORN (ORN (S?) (I?))
                               (ORN (F?) (V?))))
```

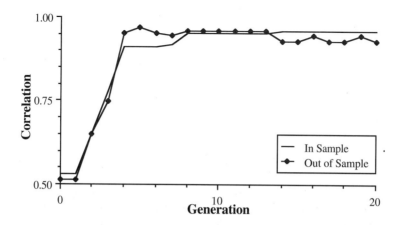

Figure 18.12 Comparison of values of in-sample and out-of-sample correlation for one run of the arithmetic-performing version of the transmembrane problem

```
(* (% (* 4.768 6.557) (- 0.138 2.525))
   (* (% 0.971 1.964) (+ -0.35 -6.054)))
(- (+ (* -1.795 -3.919) (+ 8.618 0.052))
   (+ (* -8.642 -9.429)
      (- -7.407 3.464))))))
(progn (looping-over-residues
        (SETM3 (+ (SETM1 (+ (ADF0) M3))
                  (SETM2 (% LEN M1)))))
       (values (+ M2 M2)))).
```

We have omitted the two branches defining ADF1 and ADF2 in the above program because they are ignored by the iteration-performing branch.

ADF0 tests whether the current residue is in the set {S, C, A, L, V, I, F}. S is a neutral residue. C, A, L, V, I, or F are six of the seven hydrophobic residues (according to the categories of table 18.1). Moreover, the omitted residue (M) is one of the least hydrophobic. If the current residue is in the specified set, the first argument of the IFGTZ evaluates to +1; otherwise, it evaluates to −1. The then-part and else-part of this particular IFGTZ are both merely compositions of the arithmetic operations and the random constants and do not contain any additional IFGTZs. The root IFGTZ returns either +41.47 (the result of evaluating the then-argument of the IFGTZ) or −54.91 (the result of evaluating its else-argument of the IFGTZ). Specifically,

$$adf\,0(r) = \begin{cases} +41.47 & \text{if residue} \in \{\text{S C A L V I F}\} \\ -54.91 & \text{Otherwise} \end{cases}$$

Interestingly, the −1.32 ratio of the two genetically evolved constants, +41.47 and −54.91, in ADF0 is close to the −1.43 ratio of the sum of the seven Kyte-Doolittle values for all seven hydrophobic residues in table 18.1 (i.e., +21.5) and the sum of the Kyte-Doolittle values for all six neutral and all seven hydrophilic residues (i.e., −30.8).

The iteration-performing branch uses M1, M2, and M3 to perform a somewhat complicated calculation which can be rewritten as

$$M_3(r) \leftarrow M_3(r-1) + adf\,0(r) + \frac{len}{adf\,0(r) + M_3(r-1)}$$

and

$$M_2(r) \leftarrow \frac{len}{adf\,0(r) + M_3(r-1)}$$

The result-producing branch doubles M2. The doubling can be ignored since the final classification decision is made by the wrapper based on whether the result-producing branch is positive or not (rather than on the magnitude of the value returned). M2 is almost equal to the running sum M3. The difference is that M2 lags M3 and that M2 does not contain the contribution of the last term. The effect of this difference is not large since the value of the length, LEN, of the protein segments in our fitness cases averages 23.0 and since ADF0 returns numbers with larger magnitudes (+41.47 and –54.91).

Figure 18.12 compares, by generation, the in-sample correlation and out-of-sample correlation for this run. As can be seen, out-of-sample correlation peaks at 0.968 on generation 5, but in-sample correlation increases from generation to generation. Overfitting is occurring after generation 5.

18.11 SUMMARY FOR THE ARITHMETIC-PERFORMING VERSION

The error rate produced by the genetically evolved program for the arithmetic-performing version of the transmembrane problem is equal to the error rate produced by the genetically evolved program for the subset-creating version. Thus, regardless of the choice for the function set for the function-defining branches, genetic programming improved on the error rate reported for the four algorithms for recognizing transmembrane domains reviewed in Weiss, Cohen, and Indurkhya (1993).

19 Prediction of Omega Loops in Proteins

This chapter uses genetic programming to evolve a program for predicting whether a given protein segment is, or is not, an omega loop. As in chapter 18, there are set-creating and arithmetic-performing versions of the problem.

19.1 BACKGROUND ON OMEGA LOOPS

One possible way to approach the difficult problem of predicting the .itertiary structure of a protein from its primary structure (i.e., the protein folding problem) is to first solve the seemingly simpler problem of predicting the secondary structure of a protein from its primary structure. If one could accurately predict a protein's secondary structure from its primary structure, one could presumably change the representation of the problem of predicting the tertiary structure from the primary structure into a problem of predicting the tertiary structure from the secondary structure. If one could then accurately predict a protein's tertiary structure from its secondary structure, one would presumably then have solved the protein folding problem.

Researchers have expended considerable effort on the problem of predicting the secondary structure of a protein from its primary structure both because of the considerable interest in secondary structure in its own right and because of this alluring idea of decomposing the more difficult tertiary-structure problem into the secondary-structure problem. However, since the secondary-structure problem is not even close to solution, it remains to be seen whether solving it will actually prove to be useful in solving the tertiary-structure problem.

The α-helices and β-strands are well defined, easily recognized, highly regular structures composed of a periodic pattern of hydrogen bonding and repeating dihedral angles along the backbone of the protein. Interestingly, the existence of these two regular secondary structures was correctly hypothesized from chemical principles (Pauling and Corey 1951; Pauling, Corey, and Branson 1951) years before the atomic structures of the first proteins and their α-helices and β-strands were actually observed (Kendrew 1958).

The α-helices and β-strands (each accounting for about a quarter of all the amino acid residues of a typical protein) represent an important component of protein structure. Prediction of secondary structures has traditionally involved the classification of continuous subsequences of the amino acid residues of a protein into three categories: α-helices, β-strands, and "other." This "other" category is also sometimes called ".random coil," a particularly confusing misnomer since the residues are neither random nor necessarily coiled (Leszcynski and Rose 1986). What is worse, this very large "other" category does not contain just one kind of structure. Nonetheless, since the structures that are contained in this "other" category are not as regular, symmetric, well-defined, or easily recognized as the α-helices and the β-strand, this three-way classification continues to receive considerable research attention.

A variety of technological approaches have been applied to the problem of predicting the secondary structure of a protein from its primary sequence of residues (Chou and Fasman 1974a, 1974b; Doolittle 1987; Lesk 1988; Argos 1989; Bell and Marr 1990; Doolittle 1990; Fasman 1990; Holbrook, Muskal and Kim 1990; Muskal, Holbrook, and Kim 1990; Lapedes et al. 1990; Muskal and Kim 1992; Wu et al. 1992; Hunter 1993; Hunter, Searls, and Shavlik 1993; Zhang et al. 1993). However, up to the end of 1993, these various predicting algorithms have had an accuracy of no better than about 65% and a correlation of no better than about 0.40 for the usual three-way classification.

Many reasons have been suggested as to why all of these efforts have not been highly successful. One explanation is simply that the problem is difficult and the right approach has yet to be found. Another possible explanation is that global considerations of tertiary structure have such a major effect on the formation of the secondary structure that it may not be possible to solve the secondary-structure problem without simultaneously solving the tertiary-structure problem. Yet another explanation is that the wrong question may be being asked in connection with secondary structure. Specifically, the usual three categories (and specifically the lack of refinement in the definition of the "other" category) may be the wrong targets for this prediction problem.

Thus, several researchers have attempted to substitute entirely different categories for the usual three, or to subdivide the "other" category into its disparate components.

For example, Zhang et al. (1993) found that when self-organizing clustering techniques using neural networks are employed to permit the residues to organize themselves into categories, six categories, rather than the usual three, emerge. These six structural building blocks may be better targets than the usual three categories.

Leszcynski and Rose (1986) have pursued the idea of devising different categories by subdividing the "other" category using a novel category called the omega loop. Omega loops account for about a quarter of the residues of all proteins. The omega loop is therefore a potentially significant and useful category. There would then presumably be four major categories: α-helices, β-strands, omega loops, and a new category of "other" representing the remaining quarter of the residues. However, the omega loop is not as attractive as the α-helix and β-strand because it does not have a regular structure and because its definition is derivative.

An omega loop is a non-regular secondary structure that consists of a relatively short continuous segment of the main chain of the protein in three-dimensional space that resembles the Greek letter Ω (when viewed from the right direction). An omega loop is defined in terms of segment length, distance between the ends of the segment, and the absence of other regular secondary structure (i.e., α-helices and β-strands). Specifically, the segment length must be between six and 16 residues. The lower limit of six on segment length eliminates the inverse turn, a known structure. The upper limit eliminates most compound loops. The end-to-end distance between the α-carbons of the first and the last residue of the segment must be within 10 Å. In addition, this end-to-end distance may not exceed two-thirds of the maximum distance between any two α-carbons within the segment. The absence of other secondary structures is based on the Kabsch and Sander dictionary of protein secondary structure (Kabsch and Sander 1983), thus linking the definition of the omega loop to the absence of α-helices and β-strands.

The residues constituting an omega loop are usually exposed to a watery milieu and consequently have a tendency to be hydrophilic or neutral. Since residues lying on the surface of a folded protein also face a watery milieu, a tendency toward hydrophobicity and neutrality is not uniquely associated with omega loops.

Figure 19.1 shows the primary sequence of cobra neurotoxin venom (identified as 1CTX in the April 1993 release of the Brookhaven Protein Data Bank). The 10 residues C, D, A, F, C, S, I, R, G, and K between positions 26 and 35 of this 71-residue protein form an omega loop and are boxed.

Figure 19.2 shows the general structure of cobra neurotoxin venom (1CTX) highlighting the omega loop at residues 26–35. The a-carbon of residue 26 at the beginning of the omega loop and the α-carbon of residue 35 at the end of the omega loop are within 5.321 Å of each other; the backbone of the intervening residues resembles the Greek letter Ω and protrudes away from the main body of the protein and into the surrounding solvent.

19.2 PREPARATORY STEPS WITH ADFs

We now apply genetic programming to the problem of predicting whether a given protein segment is an omega loop. Based on our experience without automatically defined functions for the transmembrane problem (chapter 18), we only consider the case in this chapter where automatically defined functions are being used.

IRCFITPDIT SKDCPNGHVC YTKTWCDAFC SIRGKRVDLG CAATCPTVKT   50

GVDIQCCSTD NCNPFPTRKR P   71

Figure 19.1 Primary sequence of cobra neurotoxin venom 1CTX.

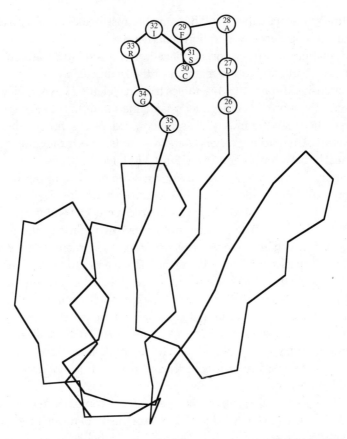

Figure 19.2   General structure of cobra neurotoxin venom (1CTX) highlighting an omega loop at residues 26–35.

Except for differences in the fitness cases and the success predicate, the tableaux for the subset-creating version of the transmembrane problem (tables 18.6 and 18.8) and the partial tableau for the arithmetic-performing version (table 18.14) apply to the omega-loop problem.

Note that the function set and terminal set used ignore the distance criterion that is part of the definition of an omega loop. Because of this limitation, we do not expect to get a satisfactory solution to this problem.

Leszcynski and Rose (1986) listed 270 omega loops among 61 proteins. Since 1986, the Brookhaven Protein Data Bank has become available on CD-ROM. However, the exact versions of only 45 of the 67 proteins cited in the 1986 article are present in the current April 1993 release of the Brookhaven Protein Data Bank. We included all of these versions of proteins to create our in-sample set of fitness cases; however, we excluded 17 proteins with anomalies (e.g., gaps in numbering, ambiguous residues, nonstandard residues, etc.). Negative cases were created, where possible, from the 28 non-excluded proteins by randomly choosing equally long segments not contained in any of the protein's omega loops.

Table 19.1 In-sample fitness cases for the omega-loop problem.

PDB protein code	Chain	Length of protein	Number of omega loops	Locations of omega loops (positive fitness cases)
351C		82	2	16-26, 51-62
1ABP		306	6	93-99, 142-148, 203-208, 236-248, 289-294, 299-304
2ACT		218	8	8-13, 58-64, 89-103, 139-144, 141-156, 182-192, 198-205, 203-209
1BP2		123	3	23-30, 25-39, 56-66
2BP2		130	3	30-37, 32-46, 68-75
2C2C		112	4	18-33, 30-43, 41-56, 74-89
3CNA		237	8	13-21, 97-104, 116-123, 147-155, 160-165, 199-209, 222-235, 229-237
3CPA		307	7	128-141, 142-156, 156-166, 205-213, 231-237, 244-250, 272-285
1CRN		46	1	33-44
1CTX		71	2	1-15, 26-35
1CYC		103	4	18-32, 30-43, 40-54, 70-84
1ECD		136	2	33-42, 41-49
3FXN		138	1	54-61
1HIP		85	4	20-26, 28-41, 43-49, 44-59
1LH1		153	2	41-53, 47-54
1MBN		153	1	40-47
1MBS		153	3	37-50, 49-54, 78-84
1NXB		62	1	6-13
2PAB	B	123	1	49-54
1PCY		99	4	6-13, 41-56, 63-68, 84-92
3PGM		230	6	11-25, 98-109, 109-120, 123-130, 132-145, 209-224
1REI	B	107	1	91-96
1RHD		293	9	34-43, 43-57, 60-73, 85-90, 99-105, 185-191, 193-199, 216-223, 284-293
1RNS		104	2	16-21, 67-76
1SBT		275	7	17-22, 37-44, 74-86, 96-101, 157-164, 181-187, 257-266
2SNS		141	3	43-52, 114-119, 136-141
2SSI		113	1	19-25
3TLN		316	11	24-31, 32-38, 44-53, 55-70, 91-97, 125-130, 188-203, 204-213, 214-219, 221-233, 248-255

Table 19.2 Out-of-sample fitness cases for the omega-loop problem.

PDB protein code	Chain	Length of protein	Number of omega loops	Locations of omega loops (positive fitness cases)
351C		82	2	16-26, 51-62
155C		135	3	22-29, 48-55, 84-96
1ABP		306	6	93-99, 142-148, 203-208, 236-248, 289-294, 299-304
2ACT		218	8	8-13, 58-64, 89-103, 139-144, 141-156, 182-192, 198-205, 203-209
8ADH		374	5	14-21, 100-112, 115-122, 122-128, 282-287
3ADK		195	1	134-143
3APP		323	4	42-56, 130-137, 141-151, 184-192
1AZU		127	6	8-14, 34-45, 66-71, 72-82, 83-91, 111-117
3B5C		88	1	32-47
1BP2		123	3	23-30, 25-39, 56-66
2BP2		130	3	23-30, 25-39, 61-68
2C2C		112	4	18-33, 30-43, 41-56, 74-89
3CNA		237	8	13-21, 97-104, 116-123, 147-155, 160-165, 199-209, 222-235, 229-237
3CPA		307	7	128-141, 142-156, 156-166, 205-213, 231-237, 244-250, 272-285
5CPV		109	2	19-24, 65-78
1CRN		46	1	33-44
1CTX		71	2	1-15, 26-35
1CYC		103	4	18-32, 30-43, 40-54, 70-84
3CYT	I	104	4	19-33, 35-44, 41-55, 71-85
3CYT	O	104	4	19-33, 35-44, 41-55, 71-85
1ECD		136	2	33-42, 41-49
3FAB	H	220	3	72-77, 99-105, 132-140
1FDX		54	3	12-23, 30-41, 39-50
3FXN		138	1	54-61
1HIP		85	4	20-26, 28-41, 43-49, 44-59
1LH1		153	2	41-53, 47-54
2LHB		149	2	46-59, 55-64
7LYZ		129	4	18-25, 36-42, 44-52, 60-75
7LZM		162	1	134-139
1MBN		153	1	40-47
1MBS		153	3	37-50, 49-54, 78-84
2MHB	B	146	2	39-54, 47-57

PDB protein code	Chain	Length of protein	Number of omega loops	Locations of omega loops (positive fitness cases)
2MHB	A	141	1	40-48
1NXB		62	1	6-13
2PAB	A	114	1	40-45
9PAP		212	7	8-13, 60-67, 86-100, 138-153, 175-185, 191-198, 198-203
1PCY		99	4	6-13, 41-56, 63-68, 84-92
3PGM		230	6	11-25, 98-109, 109-120, 123-130, 132-145, 209-224
1REI	B	107	1	91-96
1REI	A	107	1	91-96
1RHD		293	9	34-43, 43-57, 60-73, 85-90, 99-105, 185-191, 193-199, 216-223, 284-293
1RNS		104	2	36-41, 87-96
1SBT		275	7	17-22, 37-44, 74-86, 96-101, 157-164, 181-187, 257-266
2SNS		141	3	43-52, 114-119, 136-141
2SOD	G	152	5	51-59, 68-79, 104-110, 123-138, 133-138
2SOD	B	152	5	51-59, 68-79, 104-110, 123-138, 133-138
2SOD	Y	152	5	51-59, 68-79, 104-110, 123-138, 133-138
2SOD	O	152	5	51-59, 68-79, 104-110, 123-138, 133-138
2SSI		113	1	19-25
3TLN		316	11	24-31, 32-38, 44-53, 55-70, 91-97, 125-130, 188-203, 204-213, 214-219, 221-233, 248-255

Table 19.1 shows the 28 proteins from which the in-sample set of fitness cases was created. A total of 212 fitness cases was created from these 28 proteins (107 positive and 105 negative).

In every case where the exact version of a protein cited in the 1986 article was not present in the April 1993 release of the Brookhaven Protein Data Bank, a later version of the same protein was present (typically because the earlier study was replaced with a later study with better resolution). We used the most recent version of such proteins to create the out-of-sample set of fitness cases. In each instance, we created a three-dimensional kinemage of each of the newer versions using the PREKIN software (Richardson and Richardson 1992) and visually verified that the residue numbers cited in the 1986 article still corresponded to an apparent omega loop. We excluded any omega loop where this was not the case. Negative cases were created in the same manner as described above.

Table 19.2 shows the 44 proteins from which the out-of-sample set of fitness cases were created. A total of 356 fitness cases were created from these proteins (181 positive and 175 negative).

19.3 RESULTS FOR THE SUBSET-CREATING VERSION WITH ADFs

Except for the fitness cases and the success predicate, the tableaux for the subset-creating version of the transmembrane problem (tables 18.6 and 18.8) apply to this version of the omega-loop problem.

Figure 19.3 shows the fitness curves for one run of the subset-creating version of the omega-loop problem. At generation 0, the in-sample correlation of the best-of-generation program is 0.302 and the standardized fitness is 0.349.

The best-of-generation predicting program from generation 11 has an in-sample correlation of 0.52 as a result of getting 75 true positives, 86 true negatives, 19 false positives, and 32 false negatives over the 212 in-sample fitness cases. When tested on the out-of-sample set, this program has an out-of-sample correlation of 0.57 as a result of getting 57 true positives, 55 true negatives, 15 false positives, and 16 false negatives over the 143 out-of-sample fitness cases. It scores 78 hits.

```
(progn (defun ADF0 ()
          (values (ORN (ORN (ORN (A?) (I?)) (ORN (V?) (Q?)))
                       (ORN (M?) (I?))))))
       (defun ADF1 ()
         (values (ORN (H?) (T?))))
       (defun ADF2 ()
         (values (ORN (ORN (N?) (W?)) (ORN (I?) (W?)))))
       (progn (looping-over-residues
                (SETM0 (- (SETM1 M0) (ADF0))))
              (values (+ (IFLTE M0 (+ LEN -5.805)
                            (* (IFLTE M0 LEN LEN M0)
                               (IFLTE LEN 5.006 2.078 M3))
                            (IFLTE M1 LEN M3 M3))
                         (+ (IFLTE M2 M3 M2 M2)
                            (+ (- (* (+ (IFLTE (+ 5.17 M1)
                                               LEN M3 LEN) M1)
                                     (% -4.02 M2))
                                  (- 5.654 LEN))
                               M1)))))).
```

This program can be simplified to the program shown below. Since ADF1 and ADF2 are ignored, they are deleted below. The two-argument numerically valued disjunctive operator ORN is replaced by ORN* that takes multiple arguments.

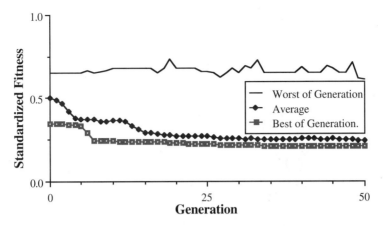

Figure 19.3 Fitness curves for one run of the subset-creating version of the omega-loop problem.

```
(progn  (defun ADF0 ()
            (values (ORN* (A?) (I?) (V?) (Q?) (M?))))
        (progn (looping-over-residues
                (SETM0 (- (SETM1 M0) (ADF0))))
            (values (+ (IFLTE M0 (+ LEN -5.805)
                            (* LEN (IFLTE LEN 5.006 2.078 0))
                 0)
                (IFLTE (+ 5.17 M1) LEN 0 LEN)
                -5.654
                LEN
                (* 2 M1))))).
```

In this program ADF0 returns +1 when the current residue is A, I, V, Q, or M and to –1 otherwise.

The iteration-performing branch uses memory cell M0 to compute a negative running sum of the values returned by ADF0. For residues 26–35 of cobra neurotoxin venom (1CTX), namely C, D, A, F, C, S, I, R, G, and K, ADF0 evaluates to +1 two times out of 10 and evaluates to –1 eight times out of ten. Thus, M0 equals +8. Memory cell M1 lags the accumulated value of memory cell M0 by one residue so M1 is the negative running sum of all but the last value returned by ADF0. The result is that M1 equals +7.

The result-producing branch computes the five-term sum shown above in which the first two terms are IFLTEs. This expression returns a positive value so the wrapper classifies this protein segment as being an omega loop.

Figure 19.4 compares, by generation, the in-sample correlation and out-of-sample correlation for this run. As can be seen, out-of-sample correlation peaks at 0.57 for generations 11–14, but in-sample correlation increases relentlessly over the entire range of generations. After generation 14, the evolved predicting programs are not getting better at predicting and overfitting is occurring. Instead, they are being fitted more and more to the idiosyncrasies of the

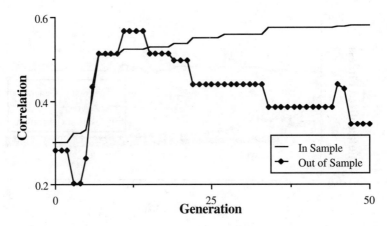

Figure 19.4 Comparison of values of in-sample and out-of-sample correlation for one run of the subset-creating version of the omega-loop problem

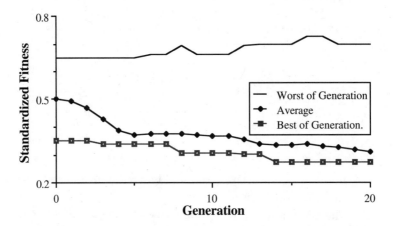

Figure 19.5 Fitness curves for one run of the arithmetic-performing version of the omega-loop problem.

particular available in-sample fitness cases. When this run was extended to generation 50, the peak at generations 11–14 continued to be the high point for out-of-sample correlation.

19.4 RESULTS FOR THE ARITHMETIC-PERFORMING VERSION WITH ADFs

The arithmetic-performing version of the omega-loop problem is similar to the arithmetic-performing version of the transmembrane problem in that the function-defining branch is changed so that arithmetic and conditional operations can be performed.

Except for the fitness cases and the success predicate, the original tableaux for the subset-creating version of the transmembrane problem (tables 18.6

and 18.8), as modified by the partial tableau for the arithmetic-performing version of the transmembrane problem (table 18.14), apply to the arithmetic-performing version of the omega-loop problem.

Figure 19.5 shows the fitness curves for one run. At generation 0, the in-sample correlation of the best-of-generation program is 0.30 and the standardized fitness is 0.35.

The best of generation 14 has an in-sample correlation of 0.453 resulting from getting 78 true positives, 76 true negatives, 29 false positive, and 29 false negatives over the 212 in-sample fitness cases. Its out-of-sample correlation of 0.449 is the result of getting 134 true positives, 124 true negatives, 51 false positives, and 47 false negatives over the 356 out-of-sample fitness cases. It scores 72 hits.

```
(progn (defun ADF0 ()
        (values (IFGTZ (H?) 4.172 1.591)))
      (defun ADF1 ()
        (values (IFGTZ (ORN (ORN (R?) (K?)) (ORN (N?) (K?)))
          (- (- -8.842 5.865) (% (% -6.399 3.942) (% -5.531
          8.623))) (IFGTZ (ORN (E?) (F?)) (- (* -4.17 4.843)
          6.434) (% 0.798004 4.244)))))
      (defun ADF2 ()
        (values (IFGTZ (ORN (ORN (M?) (I?)) (V?)) (+ (% (+
          1.726 0.0620003) (- 8.783 1.476)) (% -8.943 7.316))
          (% (% -8.943 7.316) (- -7.393 2.183)))))
      (progn (looping-over-residues
              (% (SETM1 (+ M1 (ADF2)))
                (+ (* M2 M0) (* -2.037 LEN))))
            (values (IFLTE (- (IFLTE (- (IFLTE 6.061 M2 M0
              M1) (* M1 1.677)) (% (% M0 M0) (IFLTE M3 M3
              -7.51 0.0160007)) (% (- M0 M1) (+ M1 -
              5.334)) (* (IFLTE LEN 6.771 4.685 -2.358) (+
              M3 LEN))) (* M1 1.677)) (% (% M0 M0) (* 9.91
              M3)) (% (- M0 M1) (+ M1 -5.334)) (* (IFLTE
              LEN 6.771 4.685 -2.358) (+ M3 LEN)))))).
```

In this program ADF0 and ADF1 are ignored by the iteration-performing branch. M0, M2, and M3 all remain at zero throughout.

ADF2 returns the numerical value of –0.9777 if the current residue is M, I, or V (all of which are hydrophobic) but otherwise returns +0.1277.

The iteration-performing branch, IPB0, uses M1 to create a running sum of the numerical values returned by ADF2. Note that the subsequent division by (* -2.037 LEN) plays no role in the accumulated values in M1.

The operation of the result-producing branch, RPB, can be illustrated with residues 26–35 of cobra neurotoxin venom (1CTX), namely C, D, A, F, C, S, I, R, G, and K. There is only one I among these 10 residues so M1 acquires the value of 0.1712 in the iteration-performing branch, IPB0. The result-producing branch, RPB, then evaluates to 0.0332. Because this value is positive, the wrapper classifies the protein segment as an omega loop.

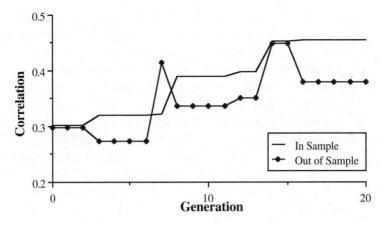

Figure 19.6 Comparison of values of in-sample and out-of-sample correlation for one run of the arithmetic-performing version of the omega-loop problem.

Had there been two occurrences, of M, I, or V among the 10 residues (instead of one), M1 would have been –0.9341 and the result-producing branch, RPB, would have evaluated to –0.1490. Because this value is negative, the wrapper would have classified the protein segment as an omega loop.

Figure 19.6 compares, by generation, the in-sample correlation and out-of-sample correlation for this run. As can be seen, out-of-sample correlation peaks at 0.449 for generations 14 and 15, although in-sample correlation increases monotonically over the entire range of generations.

19.5 SUMMARY FOR OF THE OMEGA-LOOP PROBLEM

The in-sample correlation of 0.52 for the subset-creating version of the omega-loop problems corresponds to an accuracy of 76% and the out-of-sample correlation of 0.57 corresponds to an accuracy of 78%. We are not aware of any published efforts at predicting omega loops using machine learning techniques; however, as previously mentioned, efforts at predicting other secondary structures (employing different techniques and a distinctly non-comparable statement of the predicting problem) have yielded values of out-of-sample correlation and accuracy that are somewhat smaller, but in the same general neighborhood as 76% and 78%.

For the arithmetic-performing version of the omega-loop problem, the in-sample correlation of 0.458 corresponds to an accuracy of 73% and the out-of-sample correlation of 0.476 corresponds to an accuracy of 74%. Thus, for the small number of runs involved here, the arithmetic-performing version did somewhat less well than the subset-creating version.

20 Lookahead Version of the Transmembrane Problem

This chapter considers a more difficult version of the transmembrane problem (first considered in chapter 18).

20.1 THE PROBLEM

The version of the transmembrane problem of section 18.2 corresponds to the first experiment reported in Weiss, Cohen, and Indurkhya 1993 in which the protein sequence is pre-parsed into segments such that each segment is either an entire transmembrane domain or an entirely non-membrane area of the sequence. The goal of the classifying program is to classify the entire segment into one of the two classes.

In the third and most difficult experiment of Weiss, Cohen, and Indurkhya (1993), the entire protein sequence is presented and the goal of the classifying program is to classify each individual residue of the sequence as to whether it belongs to a transmembrane domain or to a non-transmembrane area of the protein.

Transmembrane domains contain mostly hydrophobic residues and non-transmembrane areas contain mostly hydrophilic residues; however, transmembrane domains and non-transmembrane areas cannot be recognized by examining any single residue. There are many hydrophobic residues in non-transmembrane areas and many hydrophilic residues in transmembrane domains. Thus, the classification of an individual residue requires a calculation based on the characteristics of the neighborhood of the residue. However, one cannot compute the characteristics of a neighborhood until one knows where the neighborhood begins and ends. The beginning and the end of a neighborhood is determined by the fact that the members of a neighborhood share the overall characteristics of the neighborhood while the members of the adjacent neighborhoods share different overall characteristics. Yet one cannot determine the characteristics of a neighborhood, the previous neighborhood, or the next neighborhood until one knows where the neighborhood itself begins and ends.

It is necessary to parse the entire protein sequence in order to resolve this problem. Moreover, it is necessary to tentatively parse at least part of the sequence in order to decide where actually to parse the sequence (i.e., lookahead or backtracking is required in some form). After the parsing is successfully done, all the individual residues in each now-identified neighborhood are classified uniformly.

20.2 PARTIAL PARSING

Since we are attempting to identify two kinds of areas of the protein, it seems reasonable that the overall program for this version of the transmembrane problem should contain two separate running calculations in order to recognize the end of each kind of area of the protein and the beginning of the next.

The difficulty of the parsing version of this problem can be appreciated if one imagines scanning the residues (starting from the first residue at the N-terminal end of the protein) and attempting to perform one or two running calculations based on the hydrophobicity, neutrality, and hydrophilicity of the residues. What do such calculations actually do? How many residues should be included in the window for performing each calculation? How do we deal with the fact that each protein being considered has a different total number of residues? How do we deal with the fact that we do not know the total number of transmembrane domains, if any, in the protein? How do we deal with our lack of foreknowledge of the number of residues in each transmembrane domain? And each non-transmembrane area? What is the condition for deciding that one kind of area has ended and the other kind of area has started? How do we identify the boundary between a first area and a second area, if the boundary between the areas is defined by a change in the value of some calculation that depends on information about residues outside and beyond the first area?

Parsing calls for nested iterations. We can tolerate an iteration, multiple iterations, or even nested iterations in a genetically evolved program provided there is a cap on the computer time available to any one program. In both the set-creating and arithmetic-performing versions of the transmembrane problem in chapter 18, the cap was ensured by not permitting evolutionary modification of the termination predicate of the iteration. This was accomplished by restricting the iteration to one iterative pass over the finite, known set of residues of each protein segment. The parsing required by this new version of the transmembrane problem requires multiple iterative calculations at points that cannot be specified in advance. That is, we must evolve termination predicates while we evolve various iterative calculations. Because this problem involves a finite, known sequence, we can continue to enjoy the benefits of an overall cap on computer time while evolving various termination predicates and various iterative calculations if we again restrict all activity of the evolved overall program to a single pass over the residues of the protein sequence.

Figure 20.1 shows the various kinds of branches that might appear in an overall computer program to solve this problem. One function-defining branch is shown on the left side of the figure, but, in general, there could be many

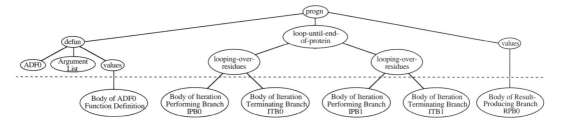

Figure 20.1   Hypothetical six-branch overall program.

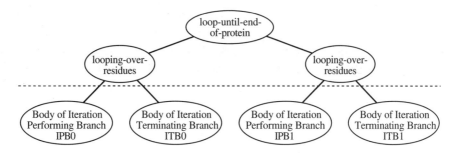

Figure 20.2.   Four-branch overall program actually used in the lookahead version of the transmembrane problem.

such branches or none. Then, two pairs of branches are shown in the middle of the figure. Each pair contains one iteration-performing branch and one *iteration-terminating branch*. Finally, one result-producing branch, RPB, is shown on the right side of the figure; however, this final branch may possibly be deleted. In any event, the bodies of all branches are subject to evolution.

We will actually use only a subset of these six branches in our approach to the lookahead version of the transmembrane problem. Figure 20.2 shows the four branches actually used; there are no explicit function-defining branches and there is no separate result-producing branch.

An overall behavior called `loop-until-end-of-protein` governs the execution of the four branches.

When the two groups of two iterative branches are executed, a pointer identifying the current residue of the protein is started at the first residue at the N-terminal (i.e., the beginning of the protein sequence). Control then passes to a behavior called `looping-over-residues` that encompasses the first pair of branches, IPB0 and ITB0. The first of the four iterative branches is an iteration-performing branch, IPB0, and the second is an iteration-terminating branch, ITB0. Initially, the body of iteration-performing branch, IPB0, is executed. Each time the body of IPB0 is executed, the pointer identifying the current residue is advanced one residue along the protein toward the C-terminal (i.e., the end of the protein sequence). Then the body of iteration-terminating branch, ITB0, is executed. An iteration-terminating branch is deemed to be satisfied when it returns a numerical value greater than 0. The process of executing the pair, ITB0 and IPB0, is iterated until ITB0 becomes satisfied (if ever). When ITB0 is satisfied, control passes to the second pair of branches, IPB1 and ITB1.

The third of the four iterative branches is a second iteration-performing branch, IPB1, and the fourth branch is a second iteration-terminating branch, ITB1. Initially, the body of iteration-performing branch, IPB1, is executed. Each time the body of IPB1 is executed, the pointer is advanced one residue. Then ITB1 is executed. If ITB1 is not satisfied, then ITB1 and IPB1 are iteratively executed until ITB1 becomes satisfied (if ever).

Since the number of transmembrane domains will vary among the different proteins represented by the set of fitness cases and is not known in advance for any particular protein, these four branches are placed inside an outer loop. This outer loop permits toggling between the two pairs of branches. Thus, when iteration-terminating branch, ITB1, is satisfied (if ever), control passes back to the first pair of branches, IPB0 and ITB0.

At the instant when the pointer identifying the current residue reaches the C-terminal of the protein, the iteration is terminated. Thus, regardless of the imperfections of the two iteration-terminating branches (ITB0 and ITB1), execution of the overall program is always limited to exactly one pass over the finite, known set of residues of the protein sequence.

The four iterative branches are embedded in a wrapper that makes the final decision as to whether to classify an individual residue as belonging to a transmembrane domain or to a non-transmembrane area. The wrapper toggles in synchrony with the satisfaction of the termination predicates of the iteration-terminating branches, ITB0 and ITB1. Specifically, the wrapper begins by classifying all residues as being in a non-transmembrane area until the first iteration-terminating branch, ITB0, is satisfied. The wrapper then classifies all residues as being in a transmembrane domain until the second iteration-terminating branch, ITB1, is satisfied. The wrapper then toggles back to a non-transmembrane classification.

Let us consider some of the possibilities that may occur. If the first iteration-terminating branch, ITB0, does not cause termination before the entire protein is examined, the second pair of iterative branches (IPB1 and ITB1) will never be executed. If the second iteration-terminating branch, ITB1, does not cause termination before the entire protein is fully examined, execution of the overall program will be limited to only one completed series of executions of the pair, IPB0 and ITB0, and only one interrupted series of executions of the pair, IPB1 and ITB1. On the other hand, if ITB1 causes termination before the entire protein is fully examined, then a second series of executions of the pair, IPB0 and ITB0, will be possible. Similarly, if ITB0 causes the termination of the second series of executions of the pair, IPB0 and ITB0, before the entire protein is fully examined, then a second series of executions of the pair, IPB1 and ITB1, will be possible. If the entire protein is still not fully examined, both the pair, IPB0 and ITB0, and the pair, IPB1 and ITB1, will have additional opportunities to be executed.

The following code employing the LOOP macro of Common LISP (Steele 1990) specifies the overall loop-until-end-of-protein behavior and the `looping-over-residues` behavior for one protein for the lookahead version of the transmembrane problem.

```
1    (loop with residue-index = 0
2         until (>= residue-index (length protein-sequence)
3         do (loop initially (progn (setf M0 0.0) (setf M1 0.0)
4                                   (setf M2 0.0) (setf M3 0.0))
5               for res from residue-index
6                    below (length protein-sequence)
7               for residue = (aref protein-sequence res)
8               do (eval IPB0)
9               until (> (eval ITB0) 0.0)
10              finally (progn (mark-as-non-transmembrane
11                                 residue-index res)
12                             (setf residue-index res)))
13         (loop initially (progn (setf J0 0.0) (setf J1 0.0)
14                                   (setf J2 0.0) (setf J3 0.0))
15              for res from residue-index
16                    below (length protein-sequence)
17              for residue = (aref protein-sequence res)
18              do (eval IPB1)
19              until (> (eval IPT1) 0.0)
20              finally (progn (mark-as-transmembrane
21                                 residue-index res)
22                             (setf residue-index res)))
23        finally (return (wrapper (compute-correlation))))).
```

The outer loop starts on line 1 with `residue-index` initialized to 0 and runs until `residue-index` is determined on line 2 to equal or exceed the length of the `protein-sequence`. The scope of this outer loop goes until the `finally` clause on line 23. The body of this outer loop contains two similar inner loops running between lines 3–12 and 13–22 (the first being associated with areas that will become marked as non-transmembrane areas and the second associated with areas that will become marked as transmembrane domains).

The first inner loop running between lines 3–12 initializes four settable variables, `M0`, `M1`, `M2`, and `M3` to 0 on lines 3 and 4.

Line 5 starts a local loop counter called `res` that starts at the current residue (i.e., `residue-index`) and terminates the loop if `res` reaches the end of the protein.

On line 7 the residue whose index is `residue-index` is extracted by the array-referencing function `aref` from the array `protein-sequence` and assigned to `residue`.

Line 8 evaluates the iteration-performing branch `IPB0` until the result of evaluating the iteration-terminating branch, `ITB0`, on line 9 is greater than 0. The whole loop iterates the evaluation of `IPB0` and the testing of `ITB0` until either is satisfied (i.e., becomes greater than zero) or the loop runs off the end of the protein.

The `finally` clause of the first inner loop uses a `progn` to do two things on lines 10–12. Lines 10 and 11 cause the entire area to be marked as being a non-transmembrane area. These identifications are retained in a hidden vector of length (`length protein-segment`) and are compared in line 23 to the correct classifications for each residue of the protein. Line 12 ends the first inner loop; it sets `residue-index` to the value of `res` on which the first inner loop ends.

The second inner loop running between lines 13–22 operates in a similar manner, except that the settable variables are `J0`, `J1`, `J2`, and `J3`; `IPB1` and `ITB1` are the iteration-performing and iteration-terminating branches; and the delineated area is marked as a transmembrane domain, instead of a non-transmembrane area.

The `finally` clause of the outer loop on line 23 causes the areas marked as being non-transmembrane areas on lines 10 and 11 and the areas marked as being transmembrane domains on lines 20 and 21 to be passed to the fitness calculation. The `compute-correlation` calculation computes the correlation between the identification made by the individual program for each residue of the protein and the correct classification of the residue. The `wrapper` then converts the correlation into the standardized fitness of the individual program.

If the calculation performed by the first iteration-performing branch, `IPB0`, evolves in such a way as to become relevant to recognizing a non-transmembrane area, and if the first iteration-terminating branch, `ITB0`, evolves to become relevant to recognizing the end of a non-transmembrane area, and if the second iteration-performing branch, `IPB1`, evolves to become relevant to recognizing a transmembrane domain, and if the second iteration-terminating branch, `ITB1`, evolves to become relevant to recognizing the end of a transmembrane domain, then the overall program will be able to identify an arbitrary number of transmembrane domains within a protein sequence and correctly classify each residue in the protein sequence.

Presumably, the iteration-performing branches, `IPB0` and `IPB1`, make some calculation based on the characteristics of the area involved. However, recognizing the boundary for one kind of area requires recognizing that the characteristics of the area just beyond the yet-to-be-determined boundary are the characteristics of the other kind of area.

True parsing requires nested iterations or recursion. Nested iterations would have entailed more computer time than was available. We therefore compromised by using a form of partial parsing. This partial parsing uses a one-argument lookahead function, called `LOOK`, and the already-described unnested iterative structure involving the four branches. The `LOOK` provides a way to examine the characteristics of the part of the protein sequence just beyond a yet-to-be-determined boundary. Execution of a `LOOK` does not change the index of the current residue on which the overall program is operating. However, if the argument to a `LOOK` contains a residue-examining function, the residue referred to by that residue-examining function within the argument of the `LOOK` is the residue one ahead of what it would otherwise be.

Since the argument of a LOOK may contain other LOOKs, it is possible for a program to look ahead as far as it likes (subject only to the limit on program size and depth common to all programs in a run). The looking is, of course, inherently biased in favor of relatively short lookaheads because it takes one additional occurrence of the LOOK function in the program tree to achieve each additional increment of lookahead. The argument to the LOOK function is executed after entering the LOOK and is implemented as a macro in LISP.

20.3 PREPARATORY STEPS

The fitness cases for this version of the problem are based on the same mouse transmembrane proteins as before; however, in order to save computer time, we include only proteins with either at least two transmembrane domains or no more than 200 residues. The 47 qualifying in-sample proteins contain a total of 22,981 residues (5,630 positive in-sample fitness cases and 17,351 negative in-sample cases). That is, about a quarter of all residues of the qualifying proteins are in transmembrane domains. The 38 qualifying out-of-sample proteins contain a total of 17,158 residues (4,572 positive out-of-sample fitness cases and 12,586 negative out-of-sample cases).

The set of 22,981 in-sample fitness cases is very large in comparison to other problems in this book and in comparison to the set-creating and arithmetic-performing versions of the transmembrane problem (chapter 18). We have already demonstrated that genetic programming is capable of evolving biochemically relevant subsets of amino acids using automatically defined functions (chapters 18 and 19). Since the lookahead version of the transmembrane problem (with its huge number of fitness cases) is clearly going to be exceedingly time-consuming, we decided to supply, on a silver platter, the same sort of detectors for hydrophobic and hydrophilic amino acids that were evolved in previous problems. That is, we decided to directly insert functions in the function set that ascertain whether the current residue belongs to certain subsets of amino acids. This approach has the advantage of concentrating the available computer resources on the new and difficult aspect of partial parsing and lookahead, rather than on the already-demonstrated evolution of detectors. However, even after eliminating the need to evolve the detectors, a run of this problem to generation 20 requires a week of computer time.

The following five residue-detecting functions are used:

PHOBIC is a zero-argument function that returns +1 if the current residue belongs to the hydrophobic category as defined in table 18.1 (i.e., it's either I, V, L, F, C, M, or A) and returns –1 otherwise.

PHILIC is a zero-argument function that returns +1 if the current residue belongs to the hydrophilic category (i.e., H, Q, N, E, D, K, or R) and returns –1 otherwise.

NEUTRAL is a zero-argument function that returns +1 if the current residue belongs to the neutral category (i.e., G, T, S, W, Y, or P) and returns –1 otherwise.

`VERY-PHOBIC` is a zero-argument function that returns +1 if the current residue is one of the four residues with the highest numerical value of hydrophobicity on the Kyte-Doolittle hydrophobicity scale of table 18.1 (i.e., I, V, L, or F) and returns –1 otherwise.

`CHARGED` is a zero-argument function that returns +1 if the current residue is one of the four electrically charged residues (i.e., D, E, K, or R) and returns –1 otherwise. These residues include the most hydrophilic residues in table 18.1.

As usual, these five zero-argument functions are treated as terminals.

Because we are not evolving detectors for hydrophobicity and other categories of amino acids, the 20 zero-argument functions `(A?)`, `(C?)`, ... for detecting a particular amino acid at the current residue are not used in this version of the problem.

The terminal set, $\mathcal{T}_{ipb0}$, for the first iteration-performing branch, `IPB0`, contains the five zero-argument numerically-valued residue-classifying functions, the settable variables `M0`, `M1`, `M2`, and `M3`, and the random constants. That is,

$$\mathcal{T}_{ipb0} = \{ \, (\text{PHOBIC}), (\text{PHILIC}), (\text{NEUTRAL}), (\text{CHARGED}), (\text{VERY-PHOBIC}), \text{M0}, \text{M1}, \text{M2}, \text{M3}, \mathfrak{R}_{\text{bigger-reals}} \}.$$

The terminal set, $\mathcal{T}_{ipb1}$, for the second iteration-performing branch `IPB1` is similar, but contains the settable variables `J0`, `J1`, `J2`, and `J3`.

$$\mathcal{T}_{ipb1} = \{ \, (\text{PHOBIC}), (\text{PHILIC}), (\text{NEUTRAL}), (\text{CHARGED}), (\text{VERY-PHOBIC}), \text{J0}, \text{J1}, \text{J2}, \text{J3}, \mathfrak{R}_{\text{bigger-reals}} \}.$$

The function set, $\mathcal{F}_{ipb0}$, for the first iteration-performing branch, `IPB0`, contains the four one-argument setting functions `SETM0`, `SETM1`, `SETM2`, and `SETM3`, the lookahead function `LOOK` (described in the previous section), the conditional `IFLTE` operator, the four arithmetic functions, and the numerically valued disjunctive function `ORN`.

$$\mathcal{F}_{ipb0} = \{\text{SETM0}, \text{SETM1}, \text{SETM2}, \text{SETM3}, \text{LOOK}, \text{IFLTE}, +, -, *, \%, \text{ORN}\}.$$

The function set, $\mathcal{F}_{ipb1}$, for the second iteration-performing branch, `IPB1`, is similar, but contains the four one-argument setting functions, `SETJ0`, `SETJ1`, `SETJ2`, and `SETJ3`.

$$\mathcal{F}_{ipb1} = \{ \text{SETJ0}, \text{SETJ1}, \text{SETJ2}, \text{SETJ3}, \text{LOOK}, \text{IFLTE}, +, -, *, \%, \text{ORN}\}.$$

The terminal set, $\mathcal{T}_{itb0}$, for the first iteration-terminating branch, `ITB0`, contains the five zero-argument numerically-valued residue-classifying functions, the settable variables, `M0`, `M1`, `M2`, and `M3`, and the random constants. That is,

$$\mathcal{T}_{itb0} = \{ \, (\text{PHOBIC}), (\text{PHILIC}), (\text{NEUTRAL}), (\text{CHARGED}), (\text{VERY-PHOBIC}), \text{M0}, \text{M1}, \text{M2}, \text{M3}, \mathfrak{R}_{\text{bigger-reals}} \}.$$

The terminal set, $\mathcal{T}_{itb1}$, for the second iteration-terminating branch, `ITB1`, is similar, but contains the settable variables, `J0`, `J1`, `J2`, and `J3`.

$$\mathcal{T}_{itb1} = \{ \, (\text{PHOBIC}), (\text{PHILIC}), (\text{NEUTRAL}), (\text{CHARGED}), (\text{VERY-PHOBIC}), \text{J0}, \text{J1}, \text{J2}, \text{J3}, \mathfrak{R}_{\text{bigger-reals}} \}.$$

Since the iteration-terminating branch uses the settable variables, but does not change them, the function set, $\mathcal{F}_{itb0}$, for the first iteration-terminating branch, ITB0, is the same as $\mathcal{F}_{ipb0}$, except for the deletion of the four setting functions, SETM0, SETM1, SETM2, and SETM3.

$\mathcal{F}_{itb0} = \{\text{LOOK, IFLTE, +, -, *, \%, ORN}\}.$

The function set, $\mathcal{F}_{itb1}$, for the second iteration-terminating branch, ITB1, is the same as $\mathcal{F}_{ipb1}$, except for the deletion of the four setting functions, SETJ0, SETJ1, SETJ2, and SETJ3, so that

$\mathcal{F}_{itb1} = \mathcal{F}_{itb0}.$

There is no explicit result-producing branch in this problem.

The fitness measure and other aspects of the lookahead version of the transmembrane problem are the same as for the set-creating and arithmetic-performing versions of this problem (section 18.10).

Table 20.1 summarizes the key features of the lookahead version of the transmembrane problem.

20.4   RESULTS

We first examine the run that produced the best-of-all individual (called run 1 herein).

As one would expect, the vast majority of the randomly generated programs in generation 0 have a correlation C of 0.0 indicating that they are no better than random in predicting whether a residue belongs to a transmembrane domain. Many of these programs achieve their poor performance because the result-producing branch returns the same value regardless of the composition of the protein segment presented.

The best-of-generation predicting program from generation 0 of run 1 has an in-sample correlation of 0.42 and a standardized fitness of 0.29 as a result of getting 3,201 true positives, 14,723 true negatives, 2,948 false positives, and 2,109 false negatives over the 22,981 in-sample fitness cases. When tested on the out-of-sample set, this program has an out-of-sample correlation of 0.48 and an out-of-sample standardized fitness of 0.26 as a result of getting 2,853 true positives, 10,824 true negatives, 1,792 false positives, and 1,689 false negatives over the 17,158 out-of-sample fitness cases. It scores 74 hits.

```
(loop-until-end-of-protein
  (looping-over-residues
    (SETM1 (SETM0 M0))
    (+ (LOOK (VERY-PHOBIC)) (- (VERY-PHOBIC) M1))
  (looping-over-residues
    (SETJ1 (SETJ0 (CHARGED)))
    (% (* (PHOBIC) (NEUTRAL)) (% (PHOBIC) J2))).
```

The first iteration-performing branch, IPB0, of this program repeatedly sets M0 and M1 to M0's original value of 0.

Table 20.1 Tableau for the lookahead transmembrane problem.

Objective:	Find a program to classify each individual residue of a protein sequence as to whether it lies in a transmembrane domain or a non-transmembrane area.
Architecture of the overall program:	Two iteration-performing branches (IPB0, IPB1) and two iteration-terminating branches (ITB0, ITB1).
Parameters:	Branch typing.
Terminal set for the iteration-performing branch IPB0:	(PHOBIC), (PHILIC), (NEUTRAL), (CHARGED), (VERY-PHOBIC), M0, M1, M2, M3, and the random constants $\Re_{\text{bigger-reals}}$.
Terminal set for the iteration-performing branch IPB1:	(PHOBIC), (PHILIC), (NEUTRAL), (CHARGED), (VERY-PHOBIC), J0, J1, J2, J3, and the random constants $\Re_{\text{bigger-reals}}$.
Function set for the iteration-performing branch IPB0:	SETM0, SETM1, SETM2, SETM3, LOOK, IFLTE, +, -, *, %, and ORN.
Function set for the iteration-performing branch IPB1:	SETJ0, SETJ1, SETJ2, SETJ3, LOOK, IFLTE, +, -, *, %, and ORN.
Terminal set for the iteration-terminating branch ITB0:	(PHOBIC), (PHILIC), (NEUTRAL), (CHARGED), (VERY-PHOBIC), M0, M1, M2, M3, and the random constants $\Re_{\text{bigger-reals}}$.
Terminal set for the iteration-terminating branch ITB1:	(PHOBIC), (PHILIC), (NEUTRAL), (CHARGED), (VERY-PHOBIC), J0, J1, J2, J3, and the random constants $\Re_{\text{bigger-reals}}$.
Function set for the iteration-terminating branch ITB0:	LOOK, IFLTE, +, -, *, %, and ORN.
Function set for the iteration-performing branch ITB1:	Same as ITB0.
Fitness cases:	Set of 22,981 in-sample residues from 47 mouse transmembrane proteins and 17,158 out-of-sample residues from 38 mouse transmembrane proteins.
Raw fitness:	Correlation C (ranging from −1.0 to +1.0).
Standardized fitness:	Standardized fitness is $$\frac{1-C}{2}.$$
Hits:	100 times the difference of 1.0 minus standardized fitness for the *out-of-sample* set.
Wrapper:	Labels each individual residue as being in a transmembrane domain or non-transmembrane area.
Parameters:	$M = 4,000$. $G = 21$.
Success predicate	A program scores an out-of-sample correlation of 1.00.

The first iteration-terminating branch, ITB0, uses (LOOK (VERY-PHOBIC)) to look ahead to see if the next residue is very hydrophobic. It also uses (VERY-PHOBIC) to determine if the current residue is very hydrophobic. Thus, ITB0 can evaluate to –2, 0, or +2 and can be positive only when both the current residue and the next residue are very hydrophobic. Thus, two consecutive very hydrophobic residues will terminate execution of the first iteration-performing branch, IPB0. Even though transmembrane domains do not necessarily begin with two consecutive very hydrophobic residues and non-transmembrane areas can sometimes contain two consecutive very hydrophobic residues, two consecutive very hydrophobic residues does better than random in predicting the onset of a transmembrane domain.

The second iteration-performing branch, IPB1, of the best of generation 0 sets J0 and J1 to –1 or +1 according to whether the current residue is electrically charged; however, no use is ever made of J0 or J1.

The second iteration-terminating branch, ITB1, can be simplified to the product of (PHOBIC) and (NEUTRAL) for the current residue. Since (PHOBIC) and (NEUTRAL) cannot simultaneously be +1, ITB1 can be positive only if (PHOBIC) and (NEUTRAL) are both –1. This occurs when the current residue is neither hydrophobic nor neutral (i.e., when the current residue is hydrophilic). Thus, the putative transmembrane domain predicted by ITB0 is ended by the occurrence of the first hydrophilic residue.

Figure 20.3 shows the 446 residues of D3DR_MOUSE. This 446-residue protein has seven transmembrane domains (boxed in the figure) at positions 33–55, 67–92, 105–126, 150–172, 186–209, 375–399, and 413–434. As it happens, D3DR_MOUSE is not included in the set of fitness cases because its length is greater than 200.

Figure 20.4 is an analysis of the behavior of the best of generation 0 of run 1 on the 446 residues of D3DR_MOUSE. The seven transmembrane domains are boxed in the figure. The residues responsive to the (VERY-PHOBIC) detector are underlined in boldface in this particular figure. The solid areas denote the correctly classified residues. Specifically, the solid black areas denote true positives and the solid gray areas denote true negatives. The hatched areas denote incorrectly classified residues. Northeasterly hatching denotes false negatives and northwesterly hatching denotes false positives.

The best of generation 0 of run 1 misclassifies 81 of the 446 residues of D3DR_MOUSE. This program starts by classifying residues 1–38 as a non-transmembrane area. The first transmembrane domain actually starts at residue 33, so this program misses the actual starting point by six residues and misclassifies residues 33–38. The first 32 residues are shown in solid gray since they are true negatives and residues 33–38 are given a northeasterly hatching since they are false negatives. Residues 39 and 40 (L and l) are both very hydrophobic (indicated by the underlined boldface type), so ITB0 is satisfied and the residues starting at position 39 are correctly classified as being in a transmembrane domain. Residue 47 is hydrophilic (i.e., not neutral and not hydrophobic), so ITB1 is satisfied and residue 48 is misclassified as

```
MAPLSQISSH INSTCGAENS TGVNRARPHA YYALSYCALI LAIIFGNGLV    50

CAAVIRERAL QTTTNYLVVS LAVADLLVAT LVMPWVVYLE VTGGVWNFSR    100

ICCDVFVTLD VMMCTASILN LCAISIDRYT AVVMPVHYQH GTGQSSCRRV    150

ALMITAVWVL AFAVSCPLLF GFNTTGDPSI CSISNPDFVI YSSVVSFYV     200

FGVTVLVYAR IYMVLRQRRR KRILTRQNSQ CISIRPGFPQ QSSCLRLHPI    250

RQFSIRARFL SDATGQMEHI EDKPYPQKCQ DPLLSHLQPL SPGQTHGELK    300

RYYSICQDTA LRHPNFEGGG GMSQVERTRN SLSPTMAPKL SLEVRKLSNG    350

RLSTSLKLGP LQPRGVPLRE KKATQMVVIV LGAFIVCWLP FFLTHVLNTH    400

CQACHVSPEL YRATTWLGYV NSALNPVIYT TFNIEFRKAF LKILSC        446
```

Figure 20.3   The 446 residues of D3DR_MOUSE.

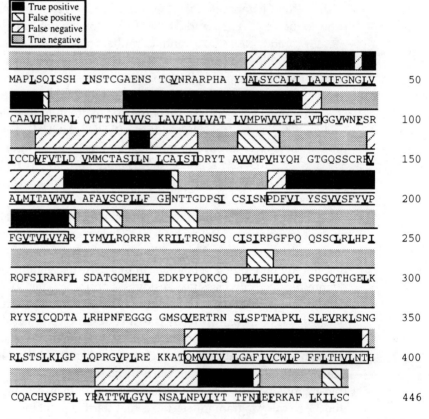

Figure 20.4   Analysis of the behavior of the best of generation 0 of run 1 for the lookahead version of the transmembrane problem.

non-transmembrane (and is given northeasterly hatching showing that it is a false negative). Residues 39–47 are shown in solid black since they are true positives. Control then toggles back to the first pair of branches, IPB0 and ITB0. The misclassification is immediately corrected because of the fortuitous occurrence in this particular protein of two consecutive very hydrophobic residues at positions 48 and 49 thereby satisfying ITB0. The residues starting at position 49 are correctly classified as being in a transmembrane domain. Residues 49 and 50 (and beyond) are therefore shown in solid black since they are true positives.

Residue 57 is hydrophilic, so ITB1 is satisfied and the residues starting at position 57 are correctly classified as non-transmembrane (and are solid gray denoting true negatives). However, the first transmembrane domain actually ends at residue 55, so this program misses the actual ending and misclassifies residue 56 (given a northwesterly hatching showing that it is a false positive). A total of eight errors have been made up to this point in this protein. The second transmembrane domain actually starts at residue 67. Because this particular protein happens to have two consecutive very hydrophobic residues at positions 67 and 68, this program correctly identifies the exact beginning of this transmembrane domain.

The presence of two consecutive very hydrophobic residues is not a very good indicator of the beginning of a transmembrane domain. However, it is sometimes correct (as at the beginning of the second transmembrane domain at residue 67). Moreover, since a transmembrane domain does contain a preponderance of hydrophobic residues, it often harbors two consecutive very hydrophobic residues. Thus, the correct beginning of the first transmembrane domain at residue 33 is missed by this imperfect trigger; however, the domain is belatedly detected when the L and I appear at positions 39 and 40.

The above best random program is somewhat better than certain similar programs present in generation 0. For example, when the first iteration-terminating branch, ITB0, uses (PHOBIC) instead of (VERY-PHOBIC), the resulting hypothetical program makes 93 errors, instead of 81 errors.

The best-of-generation predicting program from generation 6 of run 1 has an in-sample correlation of 0.48 as a result of getting 4,004 true positives, 15,255 true negatives, 2,416 false positives, and 1,306 false negatives over the 22,981 in-sample fitness cases. When tested on the out-of-sample set, this program has an out-of-sample correlation of 0.63 as a result of getting 3,500 true positives, 11,135 true negatives, 1,481 false positives, and 1,042 false negatives over the 17,158 out-of-sample fitness cases. It scores 81 hits.

```
(loop-until-end-of-protein
 (looping-over-residues
  (% (ORN (% (VERY-PHOBIC) (PHILIC)) (SETM1 (PHILIC)))
     (LOOK (% (NEUTRAL) (PHOBIC))))
  (LOOK (IFLTE (ORN M1 (PHILIC))
              (IFLTE M1 (PHOBIC) M2 (PHOBIC))
```

```
(LOOK (* (LOOK (IFLTE (PHOBIC) M1 M3 (NEUTRAL)))
          (* (IFLTE (PHOBIC) (NEUTRAL) M3 (PHILIC))
             (ORN (PHOBIC) 2.632)))))
    (% M0 (CHARGED)))))
(looping-over-residues
 (+ (SETJ2 (PHOBIC)) (+ J2 J0))
 (LOOK (CHARGED))).
```

Figure 20.5 is an analysis of the behavior of the best of generation 6 of run 1 on D3DR_MOUSE. The underlined boldfaced type is used in this particular figure to denote the residues responsive to the (CHARGED) detector in this figure.

The best of generation 6 misclassifies 67 of the 446 residues of the D3DR_MOUSE protein.

The first iteration-terminating branch, ITB0, of the best of generation 6 of run 1 is not very good at detecting the beginnings of transmembrane domains of this protein. It belatedly identifies the beginning of five of the seven actual transmembrane domains (three domains by two residues and two domains by six residues). It correctly identifies the exact beginning of one of the seven actual transmembrane domains. It totally misses the seventh transmembrane domain at 413–434 (this large false negative area being indicated by the large northeasterly hatched area at the bottom of figure 20.5).

The (LOOK (CHARGED)) of ITB1 of the best of generation 6 does a reasonably good job of detecting the ends of the seven actual transmembrane domains of this protein. ITB1 correctly identifies the exact ending of three of the seven actual transmembrane domains; it prematurely terminates one transmembrane domain by three residues; it belatedly terminates two transmembrane domains by four and nine residues. It also incorrectly terminates the second transmembrane domain at residue 75.

Figure 20.6 shows the fitness curves for run 1 of the lookahead version of the transmembrane problem.

The best-of-generation predicting program from generation 19 of run 1 has an in-sample correlation of 0.68 as a result of getting 4,121 true positives, 16,162 true negatives, 1,509 false positives, and 1,189 false negatives over the 22,981 in-sample fitness cases. When tested on the out-of-sample set, this program has an out-of-sample correlation of 0.6988 as a result of getting 3,549 true positives, 11,593 true negatives, 1,023 false positives, and 993 false negatives over the 17,158 out-of-sample fitness cases. This corresponds to an out-of-sample error rate of 11.7%. It scores 84 hits.

```
(loop-until-end-of-protein
 (looping-over-residues
  (% (ORN (% (VERY-PHOBIC) (PHILIC)) (% (ORN (% (VERY-
     PHOBIC) (PHILIC)) (SETM1 (PHILIC))) (LOOK (% 6.636
     M3)))) (LOOK (% (LOOK (% (% (ORN (% (VERY-PHOBIC)
     (PHILIC)) (SETM1 (PHILIC))) (LOOK (% 6.636 M3)))
     (PHOBIC))) (LOOK (% 6.636 M3)))))
```

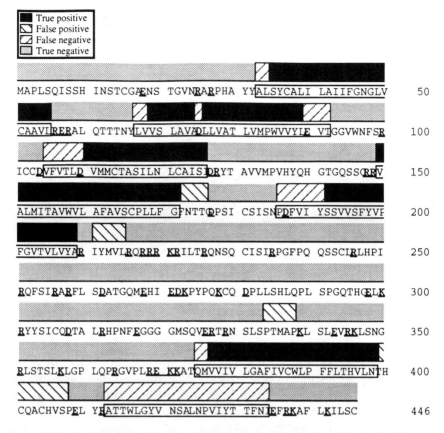

Figure 20.5 Analysis of the behavior of the best of generation 6 of run 1 for the lookahead version of the transmembrane problem.

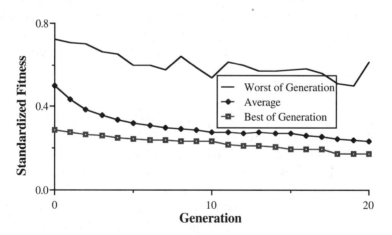

Figure 20.6 Fitness curves for run 1 of the lookahead version of the transmembrane problem.

```
(LOOK (IFLTE (ORN M1 (PHILIC)) (IFLTE M1 (PHOBIC) M2
  (PHOBIC)) (LOOK (IFLTE (ORN M1 (PHILIC)) (* (% M0
  (CHARGED)) -5.229) (LOOK (IFLTE (ORN M1 (PHILIC))
  (IFLTE (ORN M1 (PHILIC)) (* (LOOK (IFLTE (PHOBIC) M1
  M3 (NEUTRAL))) (* (% M0 (CHARGED)) -5.229)) (LOOK (*
  (LOOK (IFLTE (PHOBIC) M1 M3 (NEUTRAL))) (* (IFLTE
  (PHOBIC) (NEUTRAL) M3 (PHILIC)) (* (NEUTRAL) -
  5.229)))) (* (IFLTE (PHOBIC) (NEUTRAL) M3 (PHILIC))
  (* (NEUTRAL) -5.229))) (LOOK (LOOK (IFLTE (ORN M1
  (PHILIC)) (IFLTE (PHOBIC) M1 M3 (NEUTRAL)) (LOOK (*
  (LOOK (IFLTE (PHOBIC) M1 M3 (NEUTRAL))) (* (IFLTE
  (PHOBIC) (NEUTRAL) M3 (PHILIC)) (ORN (PHOBIC)
  2.632)))) (% M0 (CHARGED))))) (% M0 (CHARGED)))) (%
  M3 (CHARGED)))) (% M0 (CHARGED))))
(looping-over-residues
 (ORN (SETJ2 (CHARGED))
     (+ (ORN (NEUTRAL) J1) (* J0 (CHARGED)))))
 (LOOK (CHARGED))).
```

Figure 20.7 is an analysis of the behavior of the best of generation 19 of run 1 on D3DR_MOUSE.

The best of generation 19 of run 1 misclassifies only 30 of the 446 residues of the D3DR_MOUSE protein. The first iteration-terminating branch, ITB0, of the best of generation 19 belatedly identifies the beginning of four of the seven actual transmembrane domains (by between one and four residues); it correctly identifies the exact beginning of one of the seven actual transmembrane domains; it prematurely identifies the beginning of two transmembrane domains (by one residue each). Unlike the program from generation 6, this program does not miss the seventh transmembrane domain. In turn, ITB1 correctly identifies the exact ending of the seventh transmembrane domain. This program found the correct number of transmembrane domains (but for the incorrect interruption of the third transmembrane domain at residues 110–111).

Figure 20.8 compares, by generation, the in-sample correlation and out-of-sample correlation for run 1.

The fact that neither the out-of-sample correlation nor the in-sample correlation had peaked by generation 20 in figure 20.8 suggests that running this problem for additional generations might be productive.

Figure 20.9 shows the fitness curves for the third best run (called run 2 here) of this problem.

In run 2 of this problem, the best-of-generation predicting program from generation 20 has an in-sample correlation of 0.6343 as a result of getting 4,226 true positives, 15,516 true negatives, 2,155 false positives, and 1,084 false negatives over the 22,981 in-sample fitness cases. When tested on the out-of-sample set, this program has an out-of-sample correlation of 0.6638 as a result of getting 3,655 true positives, 11,150 true negatives, 1,466 false positives, and 887 false negatives over the 17,158 out-of-sample fitness

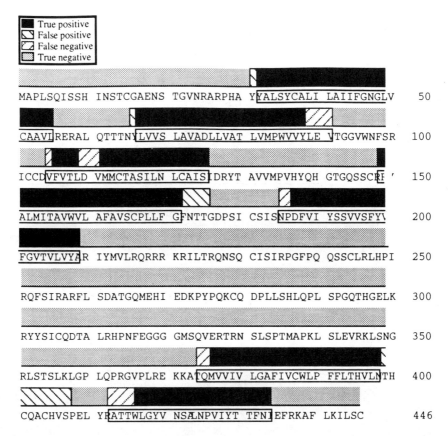

Figure 20.7 Analysis of the behavior of the best of generation 19 of run 1 for the lookahead version of the transmembrane problem.

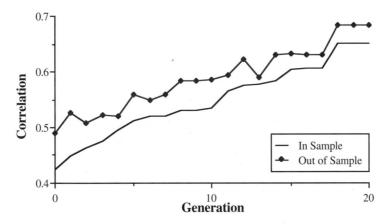

Figure 20.8 Comparison of values of in-sample and out-of-sample correlation for the run 1 of the lookahead version of the transmembrane problem.

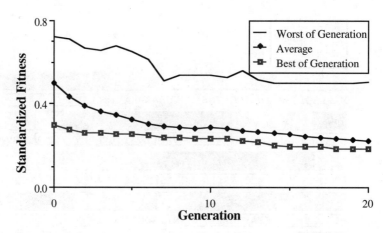

Figure 20.9 Fitness curves for run 2 of the lookahead version of the transmembrane problem.

cases. This corresponds to an out-of-sample error rate of 13.7%. It scores 83 hits.

```
(loop-until-end-of-protein
  (looping-over-residues
    (SETI2 I2)
    (IFLTE (* I1 (VERY-PHOBIC)) (LOOK (PHOBIC)) (+ (LOOK (LOOK
      (+ (LOOK (LOOK (LOOK (PHOBIC)))) (+ (LOOK (LOOK (PHO-
      BIC))) (+ (LOOK (LOOK (LOOK (LOOK (+ (LOOK (PHOBIC))
      (IFLTE (PHILIC) (PHOBIC) (VERY-PHOBIC) (NEUTRAL)))))))
      (ORN (LOOK (ORN (ORN I1 (PHOBIC)) (PHOBIC))) (+ I0 (VERY-
      PHOBIC)))))))) (ORN (+ (VERY-PHOBIC) 0.517) (* I2 I2)))
      (LOOK I2)))
  (looping-over-residues
    (* (LOOK J2) (- (PHILIC) (VERY-PHOBIC)))
    (ORN J0 (LOOK (CHARGED))))))).
```

Figure 20.10 is an analysis of the behavior of the best of generation 20 of run 2 on D3DR_MOUSE.

Figure 20.11 compares, by generation, the in-sample correlation and out-of-sample correlation for run 2.

Run 2 was actually extended to generation 33 where in-sample correlation improved to 0.6652 and out-of-sample correlation improved to 0.6881. However, this value is not as good as the value obtained on generation 19 of run 1. Nonetheless, the operation of the program here is very similar to the best of run 1. Notice, for example, the same error at residues 110–111 in the third transmembrane domain.

Table 20.2 shows the best values of out-of-sample correlation for five runs of the lookahead version of the transmembrane problem.

Weiss, Cohen, and Indurkhya (1993) wrote a program that did a full parse (rather than the partial parsing with lookahead used here) and achieved a superior error rate of about 8%. Thus, the genetically evolved partial parser did almost as well as a full parser written by a human researcher.

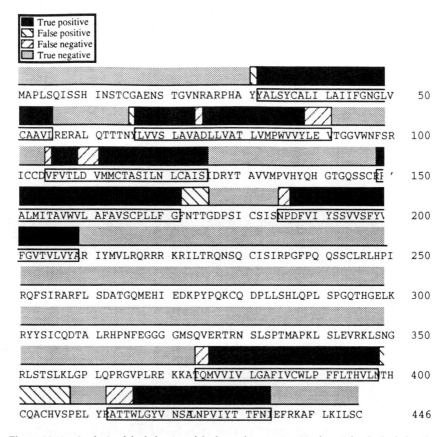

Figure 20.10 Analysis of the behavior of the best of generation 20 of run 2 for the lookahead version of the transmembrane problem.

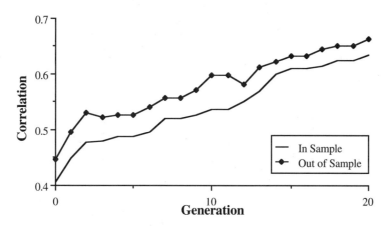

Figure 20.11 Comparison of values of in-sample and out-of-sample correlation for run 2 of the lookahead version of the transmembrane problem.

Table 20.2 Best values of out-of-sample correlation for five runs of the lookahead version of the transmembrane problem.

Run	Generation	Out-of-sample correlation	Error
1	19	0.6988	11.7%
2	20	0.6844	12.3%
3	20	0.6638	13.7%
4	17	0.6556	13.2%
5	20	0.6541	13.5%

Our goal in this chapter and chapters 18 and 19 was to illustrate how genetic programming can be used to evolve complicated multi-branch programs capable of solving problems from the real world. Our goal was not actually to produce the best possible solution for any particular problem. Performance can be improved for many problems by using various post-processing techniques. The outputs produced by neural networks for practical problems are frequently wrapped in a filter that applies various simple rules to eliminate manifest errors. These post-processing techniques are, of course, equally applicable to the programs evolved by genetic programming. For example, whenever one or two isolated residues in a protein are classified differently from numerous neighboring residues, then the isolated residues can be reclassified to conform to their neighborhood. The second transmembrane domain of D3DR_MOUSE runs from positions 67–92; however, there are two isolated false negatives at positions 77–78 in figure 20.10. Those two residues are, in fact, clearly part of the transmembrane domain.

21 Evolutionary Selection of the Architecture of the Program

So far in this book, whenever we have applied genetic programming with automatically defined functions to a problem, we first made a group of architectural choices for the yet-to-be-evolved overall programs. We called these architectural choices the sixth major step in preparing to use genetic programming. As previously mentioned, the sixth major step involves determining

(a) the number of function-defining branches,

(b) the number of arguments possessed by each function-defining branch, and

(c) if there is more than one function-defining branch, the nature of the hierarchical references (if any) allowed between the function-defining branches.

Four different ways of making these architectural choices have been previously described (chapter 7):

- prospective analysis of the nature of the problem,
- seemingly sufficient capacity,
- affordable capacity, and
- retrospective analysis of the results of actual runs.

We saw in sections 7.4 and 7.5 that, regardless of which of 15 architectures were employed, genetic programming with automatically defined functions was still capable of solving the even-5-parity problem. Moreover, regardless of the architectural choice, less computational effort was required with automatically defined functions than without them for that problem.

The above facts are comforting in the sense that they offer four ways to perform the sixth major step and that they suggest that genetic programming can solve some problems in spite of a bad architectural choice (albeit more slowly).

But suppose one is unable or unwilling to make these architectural choices. This chapter and chapters 22–25 demonstrate a way by which the architecture of the overall program can be evolutionarily selected in a competitive fitness-driven process during a run of genetic programming at the same time as the problem is being solved. That is, the solution to the problem will consist of a yet-to-be-evolved result-producing branch that can call a yet-to-be-determined number of yet-to-be-evolved automatically defined functions (each taking a yet-to-be-chosen number of arguments).

The function set of the result-producing branch of the overall program that solves the problem will consist of the primitive functions of the problem along with a yet-to-be-determined number of yet-to-be-evolved automatically defined functions. The function set of each function-defining branch will consist of the primitive functions of the problem along with whatever other automatically defined functions, if any, that function-defining branch is entitled to reference hierarchically (in accordance with our usual convention for numbering the automatically defined functions from left to right). The terminal set of the result-producing branch will consist of the actual variables of the problem. The terminal set of each function-defining branch will consist of the now-chosen number of dummy variables appropriate for that branch.

Implementation of this evolutionary method of selecting the architecture of the overall program is accomplished by making the following two changes from the general method of implementing genetic programming with automatically defined functions described in chapter 4 and used heretofore in this book:

- The initial random population is created so as to be architecturally diverse (rather than architecturally uniform).
- The way of assigning types to noninvariant points of an overall program is point typing (rather than branch typing). This has a concomitant impact on the way of performing crossover.

In this chapter and chapters 22–25, the architecture of the eventual solution to the problem is not preordained by the user during the preparatory steps. Instead, it emerges from a competitive fitness-driven process that occurs during the run at the same time as the problem is being solved. The architecture of each offspring produced by crossover will be the architecture of the receiving parent of the pair of parents. The evolutionary fitness-driven process will cause certain suitably configured individuals to prosper in the population; at the same time, individuals in the population with architectures that are less suitable for the problem environment will tend to wither away in the population.

When the initial random population is created in this evolutionary method, generation 0 contains programs with different architectures. That is, the number of automatically defined functions and the number of arguments that they each possess can differ from program to program within the population. The different architectures range over various potentially useful architectures. Each program is evaluated for fitness and selected to participate in the genetic operations, such as crossover, on the basis of its fitness in the usual way.

Because the population is architecturally diverse, the parents selected to participate in the crossover operation will usually possess different numbers of automatically defined functions. Moreover, an automatically defined function with a certain name (e.g., ADF2) belonging to one parent will often possess a different number of arguments than the same-named automatically defined function belonging to the other parent (if indeed ADF2 is present at all).

If, hypothetically, branch-typing were to be used on an architecturally diverse population, the crossover operation would be virtually hamstrung; hardly any crossovers could occur. Point typing (described below in section 21.3) cures this potential difficulty.

Structure-preserving crossover with point typing permits robust recombination while simultaneously guaranteeing that any pair of architecturally different parents will produce syntactically and semantically valid offspring. When genetic material is inserted into the receiving parent during structure-preserving crossover with point typing, the offspring inherits its architecture from the receiving parent and is guaranteed to be syntactically and semantically valid.

21.1   CREATION OF THE INITIAL RANDOM POPULATION

When we are using the evolutionary method of determining the architecture while solving a problem, the creation of an individual program in the initial random population begins with a random choice of the number of automatically defined functions, if any, that will belong to the program. Then a series of independent random choices is made for the number of arguments possessed by *each* automatically defined function, if any, in the program. All of these random choices are made within a wide (but limited) range that includes every number that might reasonably be thought to be useful for the problem at hand. Zero is included in the range of choices for the number of automatically defined functions, so the initial random population also includes some programs without any automatically defined functions.

Once the number of automatically defined functions is chosen for a particular overall program, the automatically defined functions, if any, are systematically named in the usual sequential manner from left to right. For example, if a particular newly created program has three automatically defined functions, they are named ADF0, ADF1, and ADF2.

We first use the Boolean even-5-parity problem to illustrate the evolution of architecture.

The range of possibly useful numbers of arguments for the automatically defined functions cannot, in general, be predicted with certainty for an arbitrary problem. One can conceive of hypothetical problems involving only a few actual variables for which it might be useful to have an automatically defined function that takes a much larger number of arguments. However, our focus is primarily on solving problems by decomposing them into problems of lower dimensionality. Accordingly, it is reasonable to cap the range of the number of probably-useful arguments for each automatically defined function by the number of actual variables of the problem. There is no guarantee that this cap (motivated by our desire to decompose problems) is necessarily optimal, desirable, or sufficient to solve a given problem. Conceivably, a wider range may be necessary for a particular problem. (If this were the case, there is no reason not to use a wider range).

In any event, practical considerations concerning computer resources play an important role in setting the upper bound on the number of arguments to be permitted. In the case of the even-5-parity problem, there are five actual variables for the problem, D0, D1, D2, D3, and D4. When we apply the above cap, the range of the number of arguments for each automatically defined function for the even-5-parity problem is from zero to five.

The range of potentially useful numbers of automatically defined functions cannot, in general, be predicted with certainty for an arbitrary problem. The number of automatically defined functions does not necessarily bear any relation to the dimensionality of the problem. However, once again, considerations of computer resources again play a controlling role in setting the upper bound on the number of automatically defined functions to be permitted. A range of between zero and five automatically defined functions provides seemingly sufficient capacity to solve the even-5-parity problem.

Of course, if no consideration need be given to computer resources, one might permit automatically defined functions with more arguments than there are actual variables for the problem and one might permit still more automatically defined functions than just specified.

In practice, a zero-argument automatically defined function may not be a meaningful option. If an automatically defined function has no access to the actual variables of the problem (consistent with the convention used throughout this book), has no dummy variables, does not contain any side-effecting primitive functions, and does not contain any random constants, nothing is available to serve as terminals (leaves) of the program tree in the body of such a zero-argument automatically defined function. In the floating-point, integer, and certain other domains, it may be useful to include random constants because a zero-argument automatically defined function can be used to create an evolvable constant that can then be repeatedly called from elsewhere in the overall program (i.e., a let, as described in section 5.4). However, for the special case of the Boolean domain, the two possible Boolean constants (T or NIL) have limited usefulness because all compositions of these two constants merely evaluate to one of these two values. Consequently, we have started the range of the number of arguments for each automatically defined function for a Boolean problems at one, instead of zero.

If we adopt the ranges described above for the even-5-parity problem, there are six possibilities for the number of automatically defined functions and five possibilities for the number of arguments for each automatically defined function. When there are no automatically defined functions, there is only one possible argument map for the automatically defined functions, namely the map {}. When there is exactly one automatically defined function in the overall program, there are five possible argument maps for that automatically defined function, namely {1}, {2}, {3}, {4}, and {5}. When there are exactly two automatically defined functions, there are 25 possible argument maps for the automatically defined functions. In all, there are 3,906 possible argument maps for programs subject to the constraints described above.

A population size of 4,000 is used throughout this chapter. Given this choice, not all of the 3,906 possible argument maps for the ADFs will, as a practical matter, be represented in the initial random generation. If the population were significantly larger than 4,000, virtually all of the 3,906 possible argument maps for the ADFs would likely be represented in generation 0. In a population of 4,000, there are about 666 initial random programs with each of the six possible numbers of automatically defined functions (between zero and five). Approximately a fifth of the automatically defined functions have each of the five possible numbers of arguments (between one and five).

The terminal set for the result-producing branch, T_{rpb}, for a program in the population for the Boolean even-5-parity problem is

$$T_{rpb} = \{\text{D0, D1, D2, D3, D4}\}.$$

The terminal set for each automatically defined function is derived from the argument map of the overall program.

For example, if the argument map is {3, 5}, there are two automatically defined functions in the overall program. The terminal set for ADF0 is

$$T_{adf0} = \{\text{ARG0, ARG1, ARG2}\},$$

and the terminal set for ADF1 is

$$T_{adf1} = \{\text{ARG0, ARG1, ARG2, ARG3, ARG4}\}.$$

The function set for the result-producing branch, F_{rpb}, is the union of {AND, OR, NAND, NOR} and whatever automatically defined functions are present in that particular program. Thus, when there are no automatically defined functions,

$$F_{rpb} = \{\text{AND, OR, NAND, NOR}\}$$

with an argument map for this function set of

$$\{2, 2, 2, 2\}.$$

However, when there are five automatically defined functions, the function set for the result-producing branch is

$$F_{rpb} = \{\text{ADF0, ADF1, ADF2, ADF3, ADF4, AND, OR, NAND, NOR}\}$$

with an argument map for this function set of

$$\{k_0, k_1, k_2, k_3, k_4, 2, 2, 2, 2\},$$

where k_0, k_1, k_2, k_3, and k_4 are the number of arguments possessed by ADF0, ADF1, ADF2, ADF3, and ADF4, respectively, in that particular individual.

The function set, F_{adf0}, for ADF0 (if present in a particular program in the population) consists merely of the primitive functions of the problem.

Table 21.1 Tableau without ADFs for the even-5-parity problem with evolution of architecture.

Objective:	Find a program that produces the value of the Boolean even-5-parity function as its output when given the values of the five independent Boolean variables as input.
Terminal set without ADFs:	D0, D1, D2, D3, and D4.
Function set without ADFs:	AND, OR, NAND, and NOR.
Fitness cases:	All $2^5 = 32$ combinations of the five Boolean arguments D0, D1, D2, D3, and D4.
Raw fitness:	The number of fitness cases for which the value returned by the program equals the correct value of the even-5-parity function.
Standardized fitness:	The standardized fitness of a program is the sum, over the $2^5 = 32$ fitness cases, of the Hamming distance (error) between the value returned by the program and the correct value of the Boolean even-5-parity function.
Hits:	Same as raw fitness.
Wrapper:	None.
Parameters:	$M = 4,000$. $G = 51$.
Success predicate:	A program scores the maximum number of hits.

$\mathcal{F}_{adf0} = \{\text{AND, OR, NAND, NOR}\}$

with an argument map for this function set of

$\{2, 2, 2, 2\}$.

Each automatically defined function can refer hierarchically to any already-defined function-defining branches belonging to the program. For example, the function set, $\mathcal{F}_{adf1}$, for ADF1 (if present) is

$\mathcal{F}_{adf1} = \{\text{ADF0, AND, OR, NAND, NOR}\}$

with an argument map for this function set of

$\{k_0, 2, 2, 2, 2\}$,

where k_0 is the number of arguments possessed by ADF0.

Similarly, the function set for each successive automatically defined function (if present) is the union of the function set of the previous automatically defined function and the name of the previous automatically defined function. For example, the function set, $\mathcal{F}_{adf4}$, for ADF4 (if present) is

$\mathcal{F}_{adf4} = \{\text{ADF0, ADF1, ADF2, ADF3, AND, OR, NAND, NOR}\}$

with an argument map for this function set of

$\{k_0, k_1, k_2, k_3, 2, 2, 2, 2\}$,

Table 21.2 Tableau with ADFs for the even-5-parity problem with evolution of architecture.

Objective:	Find a program that produces the value of the Boolean even-5-parity function as its output when given the values of the five independent Boolean variables as input.
Architecture of the overall program with ADFs:	One result-producing branch and between zero and five ADFs, each taking between one and five arguments. Each ADF may hierarchically refer to a lower numbered ADF (if any).
Parameters:	Point typing (section 21.2).
Terminal set for the result-producing branch:	D0, D1, D2, D3, and D4.
Function set for the result-producing branch:	AND, OR, NAND, NOR, and whatever ADFs are present (if any) in the program.
Terminal set for the function-defining branch of each ADF (if any):	Each ADF takes a variable number of dummy variables between one and five.
Function set for the function-defining branch of each ADF (if any):	AND, OR, NAND, NOR, and each lower numbered ADF (if any).

where k_0, k_1, k_2, and k_3, are the number of arguments possessed by ADF0, ADF1, ADF2, and ADF3, respectively.

The random method of creating the initial population determines whether the body of any particular function-defining branch of any particular program in the population actually calls all, none, or some of the automatically defined functions which it is theoretically permitted to call hierarchically. Subsequent crossovers may change the body of a particular function-defining branch and thereby change the set of other automatically defined functions that the branch actually calls hierarchically. Thus, the function-defining branches have the ability to organize themselves into arbitrary disjoint hierarchies of dependencies among the automatically defined functions. For example, within an overall program with five automatically defined functions at generation 0, ADF4 might actually refer only to ADF2 and ADF3, with ADF2 and ADF3 not referring at all to either ADF0 or ADF1; and ADF1 might refer only to ADF0. In this situation, there would be two disjoint hierarchies of dependencies. A subsequent crossover might change this organization so that ADF3 might then refer to ADF0 (but still not to ADF1). After this crossover, a different hierarchy of dependencies would exist. Any allowable (i.e., noncircular) hierarchy of dependencies may thus be created in generation 0 or created by crossover during the evolutionary process.

Tables 21.1 and 21.2 summarize the key features of the even-5-parity problem with evolution of architecture. The tableau without ADFs provides general information about the problem and applies to those individuals in the population that happen to have no automatically defined functions. The tableau with ADFs applies to multi-branch individuals.

21.2 Point typing for Structure-Preserving Crossover

The basic idea of structure-preserving crossover is that any noninvariant point anywhere in the overall program is randomly chosen, without restriction, as the crossover point of the first parent; however, once the crossover point of the first parent has been chosen, the crossover point of the second parent is randomly chosen from among points of the same type. The typing of the noninvariant points of an overall program is done so that the structure-preserving crossover operation will always produce valid offspring.

Point typing is used when the architecture of the overall program is being evolutionarily selected while the problem is being solved. The crossover point of the first (contributing) parent is chosen, without restriction, in the usual manner for structure-preserving crossover. The types produced by branch typing are insufficiently descriptive and overly constraining in an architecturally diverse population. Note that after a crossover is performed, each call to an automatically defined function actually appearing in the crossover fragment from the contributing parent will no longer refer to the automatically defined function of the contributing parent, but instead will refer to the same-named automatically defined function of the receiving parent. Consequently, the restriction on the choice for the crossover point of the receiving (second) parent must be different for point typing. The crossover point of the receiving (second) parent (called the *point of insertion*) must be chosen from the set of points such that the crossover fragment from the contributing (first) parent "has meaning" if the crossover fragment from the contributing parent were to be inserted at the chosen point of insertion.

Point typing is governed by three general principles.

First, every terminal and function actually appearing in the crossover fragment from the contributing parent must be in the terminal set or function set of the branch of the receiving parent containing the point of insertion. This first general principle applies to actual variables of the problem, dummy variables, random constants, primitive functions, and automatically defined functions.

Second, the number of arguments of every function actually appearing in the crossover fragment from the contributing parent must equal the number of arguments specified for the same-named function in the argument map of the branch of the receiving parent containing the insertion point. This second general principle governing point typing applies to all functions. However, the emphasis is on the automatically defined functions because the same function name is used to represent entirely different functions with differing number of arguments for different individuals in the population.

Third, all other syntactic rules of construction of the problem must be satisfied.

For clarity and ease of implementation, the three general principles above governing point typing can be restated as the following seven conditions. A crossover fragment from a contributing parent is said to *have meaning* at a chosen crossover point of the receiving parent if the following seven conditions are satisfied:

(1) All the actual variables of the problem, if any, actually appearing in the crossover fragment from the contributing parent must be in the terminal set of the branch of the receiving parent containing the point of insertion.

(2) All the dummy variables, if any, actually appearing in the crossover fragment from the contributing parent must be in the terminal set of the branch of the receiving parent containing the point of insertion.

(3) All the automatically defined functions, if any, actually appearing in the crossover fragment from the contributing parent must be in the function set of the branch of the receiving parent containing the point of insertion.

(4) All the automatically defined functions, if any, actually appearing in the crossover fragment from the contributing parent must have exactly the number of arguments specified for that automatically defined function for the branch of the receiving parent containing the point of insertion.

(5) All functions (other than automatically defined functions) must also satisfy conditions (3) and (4).

(6) All terminals (other than dummy variables and actual variables of the problem already mentioned in conditions (1) and (2), if any, actually appearing in the crossover fragment from the contributing parent must be in the terminal set of the branch of the receiving parent containing the point of insertion.

(7) All other syntactic rules of construction of the problem must be satisfied.

We now comment on these seven conditions.

The first condition will usually be satisfied if both crossover points are from the result-producing branch of their respective parents. For the even-5-parity problem, the actual variables of the problem, D0, D1, D2, D3, and D4, appear in the result-producing branch. Moreover, they appear only in the result-producing branch in accordance with the convention used throughout this book that the actual variables of the problem do not appear in function-defining branches. To the extent that this convention is observed, this first condition applies only to result-producing branches. However, if the actual variables of the problem appear in the function-defining branches, this condition must also be satisfied in such function-defining branches.

The second condition requires that the argument list of the branch of the receiving parent into which the crossover fragment from the contributing parent is being inserted must contain all the dummy variables, if any, contained in the crossover fragment. Since dummy variables may not appear in the result-producing branch, this second condition applies only to crossovers between function-defining branches.

There are several implications of the third condition which requires that all automatically defined functions in the crossover fragment must be in the function set of the branch in which they are to be inserted. This condition specifies that it is only permissible to have an automatically defined function in a crossover fragment if that automatically defined function has already been defined at the point of insertion of the receiving parent. In the context of the even-5-parity problem where each function-defining branch is allowed to refer hierarchically to every already-defined (i.e., lower numbered) automatically defined function, this means that the number of every automatically defined function referenced from within a crossover fragment must be lower than the number of the automatically defined function being defined by the branch of the receiving parent containing the point of insertion. For example, a crossover fragment containing a reference to ADF1 may be inserted into the branch defining ADF2 of the receiving parent, but may not be inserted into branches defining ADF0 (or ADF1) of the receiving parent.

The fourth condition requires that the number of arguments taken by each automatically defined function in a crossover fragment from the contributing parent exactly match the number of arguments in the argument list of the branch of the receiving parent that defines the same-named automatically defined function. For example, a crossover fragment from a contributing parent containing a four-argument call to ADF0 cannot be inserted into any branch of a receiving parent unless the branch of the receiving parent that defines ADF0 specifies that ADF0 can take exactly four arguments.

The fifth condition merely restates the omnipresent requirement that a non-ADF function cannot be imported into a branch unless it is permitted to be included in that branch by the function set of that branch. This condition (and the sixth condition) are presented separately in order to highlight the issues related to automatically defined functions.

The sixth condition similarly restates the general requirement that any other type of terminal (e.g., random constants, zero-argument primitive functions being treated as terminals) cannot be imported into a branch unless it is permitted to be included in that branch by the terminal set of that branch.

The seventh condition covers the fact that all of the other syntactic rules of construction of the problem must always continue to be satisfied. Although there are no syntactic constraints in the even-5-parity problem beyond those required to implement the automatically defined functions themselves, other problems, such as those involving decision trees, have additional syntactic constraints.

Figure 21.1 shows an illustrative program, called parent A. Parent A has two function-defining branches and one result-producing branch. The first function-defining branch of parent A defines a three-argument function (ADF0) and its second function-defining branch defines a two-argument function

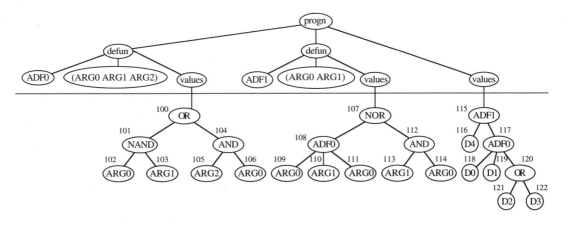

Figure 21.1   Parent A with an argument map of {3, 2} for its automatically defined functions.

(ADF1). The argument map for the automatically defined functions belonging to this overall program is {3, 2}. ADF1 can refer hierarchically to ADF0. If we were planning to perform structure-preserving crossover using branch typing, there would only be three types of points in the overall program. The points of the body of the three-argument ADF0 would be of type 7a; the points of the two-argument ADF1 would be of type 7b; and the points of the result-producing branch would be of type 8.

Figure 21.2 shows another illustrative program, called parent B, with an argument map of {3, 2, 2} for its automatically defined functions. Parent B has three function-defining branches and one result-producing branch. The first function-defining branch defines a three-argument function (ADF0); the second function-defining branch defines a two-argument function (ADF1); and the third function-defining branch defines a two-argument function (ADF2). The usual hierarchy of dependencies applies here in that ADF1 can refer hierarchically to ADF0 and ADF2 can refer hierarchically to both ADF0 and ADF1. If we were planning to perform structure-preserving crossover using branch typing, the points of ADF0, ADF1, ADF2, and the result-producing branch would be of different types.

We now illustrate structure-preserving crossover with point typing using parents A and B.

Suppose point 101 (labeled NAND) from ADF0 is chosen as the crossover point from contributing parent A (figure 21.1). The crossover fragment rooted at point 101 is (NAND ARG0 ARG1). Now suppose we consider the eligibility of a point such as 207 (labeled NAND) of ADF1 of parent B (figure 21.2) to be a point of insertion. The eligibility of point 207 is determined by examining the terminal set, the function set, and the ordered set containing the number of arguments associated with each function in the function set of the receiving parent.

The terminal set for ADF1 of the receiving parent (parent B) is

$$\mathcal{T}_{adf1} = \{\text{ARG0, ARG1}\}$$

Evolutionary Selection of the Architecture of the Program

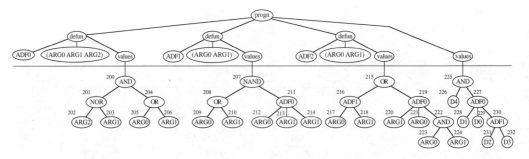

Figure 21.2   Parent B has an argument map of {3, 2, 2} for its automatically defined functions.

The function set for ADF1 of the receiving parent (parent B) is

$$\mathcal{F}_{adf1} = \{\text{ADF0, AND, OR, NAND, NOR}\}$$

with an argument map for this function set of

$$\{3, 2, 2, 2, 2\}.$$

Point 207 is eligible to be a crossover point in parent B to receive the crossover fragment (NAND ARG0 ARG1) rooted at point 101 of parent A because both ARG0 and ARG1 are in the terminal set, $\mathcal{T}_{adf1}$, of ADF1 of receiving parent B, because NAND is in the function set, $\mathcal{F}_{adf1}$, of ADF1 of receiving parent B, and because the NAND function from contributing parent A takes the same number of arguments (two) as the same-named function, NAND, takes in receiving parent B.

In fact, all eight points (points 207 through 214) are eligible to be chosen as the point of insertion of parent B because the crossover fragment (NAND ARG0 ARG1) is valid throughout ADF1 of parent B. In addition, all ten points of ADF2 of parent B (points 215 through 224) are also eligible to be chosen as the point of insertion of parent B because the crossover fragment chosen in parent A is also valid throughout ADF2. All seven points of ADF0 of parent B (200 through 206) are also acceptable points of insertion for this crossover fragment. Thus, when point typing is being used and the crossover fragment rooted at point 101 of parent A is chosen, a total of 25 points of parent B are eligible to receive this crossover fragment.

If point 104 labeled AND from ADF0 is chosen as the crossover point of parent A, no point within ADF1 or ADF2 of parent B is eligible to be chosen. The reason is that the crossover fragment (AND ARG2 ARG0) that is rooted at point 104 contains the dummy variable ARG2. ADF1 and ADF2 of parent B both take only two dummy variables, ARG0 and ARG1. ARG2 is not in the argument list of either ADF1 or ADF2 of parent B. The terminal set of ADF1 (shown above) does not contain ARG2. The terminal set of ADF2 of parent B happens to be the same as that of ADF1 and also does not contain ARG2. The second condition above would be violated for such a choice. In fact, the only points of parent B that are eligible as points of insertion are the seven points (200 through 206) of ADF0 of parent B.

If point 112 labeled AND from ADF1 is chosen as the crossover point of parent A, then all seven points of ADF0 of parent B (200 through 206), all eight points of ADF1 of parent B (points 207 through 214), and all ten points of ADF2 of parent B (points 215 through 224) are now eligible to be chosen as the point of insertion of parent B because the crossover fragment (AND ARG1 ARG0) is valid throughout ADF0, ADF1, and ADF2 in parent B.

However, if point 108 labeled ADF0 from ADF1 is chosen from parent A as the crossover point, no point within ADF0 of the second parent may be chosen. The function set for ADF0 of parent B, the receiving parent, is

$\mathcal{F}_{adf0}$ = {AND, OR, NAND, NOR}

with an argument map for this function set of

{2, 2, 2, 2}

and this function set does not contain ADF0 (i.e., recursion is not permitted here). The third condition above would be violated for such a choice. The same applies to point 107 labeled NOR because ADF0 appears within the crossover fragment rooted at this point.

In contrast, all ten points of ADF2 of parent B (points 215 through 224) are eligible since ADF2 is permitted to refer hierarchically to ADF0. The function set for ADF2 of parent B is

$\mathcal{F}_{adf2}$ = {ADF0, ADF1, AND, OR, NAND, NOR}

with an argument map for this function set of

{3, 2, 2, 2, 2, 2}.

The second condition is illustrated by considering points 225 through 232 from the result-producing branch of parent B. None of these points is eligible to be chosen as the point of insertion for any of the above cases because all of the crossover fragments contain dummy variables which are not in the terminal set of the result-producing branch.

The first condition can be illustrated by considering points 115 through 122 from the result-producing branch of parent A. If any point from the result-producing branch of parent A is chosen as the crossover point of parent A, then only points in the result-producing branch of parent B (points 225 through 232) may be chosen as the point of insertion of the second parent because the actual variables of the problem, D0, D1, D2, D3, and D4, are, for this problem, in the terminal set of only the result-producing branch of the overall program.

Point typing imposes a directionality on structure-preserving crossover that does not arise with branch typing. For example, when point 101 from ADF0 is chosen as the crossover point of parent A, a point such as 211 of ADF1 of parent B is eligible to be chosen as the point of insertion of parent B because the crossover fragment (NAND ARG0 ARG1) is valid anywhere in ADF1 of parent B. However, crossover is not possible from parent B to parent A, given the selection of these two points. The subtree (ADF0 ARG0 ARG1 ARG1) rooted at point 211 of parent B is not eligible for insertion at point 101 of ADF0 of parent A because ADF0 is not yet defined at point 101 of parent A. Because of this asymmetry, the simplest approach to implementing point typing is to produce only one offspring each time two parents are selected to participate in crossover. Consequently, if crossover is being performed on 90% of the population, 3,600 structure-preserving crossover operations with point typing (each involving the selection of two parents on the basis of their fitness, with reselection allowed) are required to produce 3,600 offspring for a given generation (rather than the 1,800 structure-preserving crossover operations with branch typing).

Now suppose that the roles of parents A and B are reversed and parent B (figure 21.2) becomes the contributing parent while parent A (figure 21.1) becomes the receiving parent. There are three different possibilities for the ten points of the branch defining ADF2 of parent B when they are chosen as the crossover point.

First, if the point 216 labeled ADF1 from ADF2 of parent B is chosen as the crossover point of the contributing parent, none of the eight points (107 through 114) of ADF1 of parent A and none of the seven points (100 through 106) of ADF0 of parent A may be chosen because ADF1 is not allowed in ADF0 or ADF1. The same applies to point 215 (labeled OR) because point 216 (labeled ADF1) appears within the crossover fragment rooted at point 215. After selecting the two parents to participate in crossover and choosing the crossover point from the contributing parent, an attempt is made to choose a valid crossover point from the receiving parent. If the set of eligible points in the second parent proves to be empty, the second parent is discarded and a new selection is made for the second parent to mate with the first parent. Note that no crossover ever fails completely due to the constraints imposed by point typing because there is always at least one eligible point of insertion (e.g., when a program mates with itself).

Second, if the point 219 labeled ADF0 from ADF2 of parent B is chosen as the crossover point of the contributing parent, any point of the eight points (107 through 114) of ADF1 of parent A can now be chosen as the point of insertion since the entire crossover fragment rooted at point 219 is allowed in ADF1 of the receiving parent; however, it is still true that none of the seven points (100 through 106) of ADF0 of parent A may be chosen because a reference to ADF0 is not permitted in ADF0.

Third, if points such as 217, 218, 220, 221, 222, 223, or 224 from ADF2 of parent B are chosen, the constraints imposed by point typing permit any point of ADF0 or ADF1 of parent A to be chosen. The unrelated convention used throughout this book of never choosing a root as the point of insertion for a crossover fragment consisting only of a single terminal would have the effect of preventing points 100 and 107 of parent A from being chosen for terminal points 217, 218, 220, 221, 223, or 224 (but they could be chosen for point 222).

Figure 21.3 shows parent C with an argument map of {4, 2} for its automatically defined functions. Parent C has two function-defining branches and one

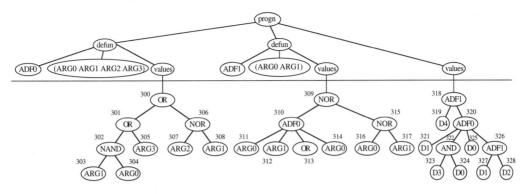

Figure 21.3   Parent C has an argument map of {4, 2} for its automatically defined functions.

result-producing branch. The first function-defining branch defines a four-argument function (ADF0); and the second function-defining branch defines a two-argument function (ADF1).

New situations arise when parent B (figure 21.2) is chosen to be the first (contributing) parent while parent C (figure 21.3) is chosen to be the second (receiving) parent.

If either point 211 (labeled ADF0) from ADF1 of contributing parent B or point 219 (also labeled ADF0) from ADF2 of parent B is chosen as a crossover point of the contributing parent, then the crossover fragment contains a reference to a three-argument ADF0. No point in receiving parent C is eligible to be chosen as the point of insertion for this fragment because ADF0 takes four arguments in parent C and the occurrences of ADF0 in these crossover fragments from parent B take only three arguments. That is, the fourth condition above would be violated by either of these choices. The same applies to points 207 and 215. Note that this ineligibility arises only in relation to a particular receiving parent; these same points are eligible to be crossover points when the ADF0 belonging to the receiving parent takes three arguments.

Similarly, points such as 227 (labeled ADF0) and 225 (labeled AND) from the result-producing branch of parent B cannot find a home in parent C because a crossover fragment rooted at those points would contain a three-argument reference to ADF0.

Point typing enables genetic recombination to occur in an architecturally diverse population. The architecture of an offspring produced by crossover is always same as the architecture of the receiving parent participating in the crossover. However, it is possible that an individual with an architecture appropriate for solving the problem and bodies that actually solve the problem can emerge during a run involving such a architecturally diverse population. We now demonstrate that this potential for the simultaneous evolution of the architecture while solving a problem can be realized in connection with the Boolean even-parity problems of orders five, four, and three.

21.3 Results for the Even-5-Parity Problem

We made 41 runs of the even-5-parity problem using the evolutionary method of determining the architecture of the overall program. Twenty-six of these runs (64%) produced a 100%-correct solution (scoring 32 hits) by generation 50, thus demonstrating that is indeed possible to solve this problem without prespecifying the architecture.

All of the 26 solutions employed one or more automatically defined functions even though it is, of course, possible to solve this problem without automatically defined functions.

Table 21.3 Distribution of architectures of the ADFs of 26 solutions to the even-5-parity problem with evolution of architecture.

Run number	Number of ADFs	Generation when solved	Argument map of ADFs
1	1	19	{2}
2	1	16	{3}
3	2	27	{3, 3}
4	2	5	{3, 5}
5	2	10	{3, 5}
6	2	9	{4, 2}
7	2	18	{4, 3}
8	2	23	{4, 4}
9	2	33	{5, 3}
10	3	13	{2, 1, 3}
11	3	18	{2, 4, 3}
12	3	37	{3, 1, 4}
13	3	16	{4, 3, 5}
14	3	17	{5, 2, 2}
15	3	9	{5, 5, 1}
16	3	10	{5, 5, 2}
17	4	13	{2, 4, 3, 5}
18	4	40	{3, 2, 2, 3}
19	4	19	{3, 4, 5, 5}
20	4	9	{4, 3, 1, 1}
21	4	19	{5, 3, 3, 5}
22	4	9	{5, 4, 2, 1}
23	4	13	{5, 5, 2, 5}
24	5	22	{2, 4, 5, 1, 5}
25	5	7	{3, 1, 2, 2, 2}
26	5	20	{3, 2, 3, 3, 3}

Table 21.3 shows the distribution of the number of automatically defined functions and the number of arguments they each possess among 26 solutions to the even-5-parity problem. The average number of automatically defined functions for these 26 solutions is 3.08.

There is considerable variation among these 26 solutions as to their number of automatically defined functions and the number of arguments they each possess. In fact, only one of the argument maps for the automatically defined functions of these 26 solutions is repeated.

In addition, an examination of the 451 best-of-generation individuals among these 26 successful runs showed that every one of these best intermediate programs employed automatically defined functions. In other words, when the number of automatically defined functions is open to evolutionary determination, all of the solutions and all of the best-of-generation programs produced along the way employ automatically defined functions. The reason for this is apparently that programs lacking automatically defined functions tend, on average, to be at a selective disadvantage throughout the run because their fitness, at any given generation, tends to lag that of competitors with automatically defined functions. Consequently, the programs lacking automatically defined functions are crowded out by the selective pressure exerted by the competitive evolutionary process throughout the run. This observation adds further support to main point 3 that automatically defined functions improve the performance of genetic programming.

The average structural complexity, $\overline{S}_{with}$, of solutions from the 26 successful runs (out of 41 runs) of the even-5-parity problem with evolution of architecture is 150.1 points.

Figure 21.4 presents the performance curves based on the 41 runs of the even-5-parity function with evolution of architecture. The cumulative probability of success, $P(M,i)$, is 54% by generation 23 and 64% by generation 50.

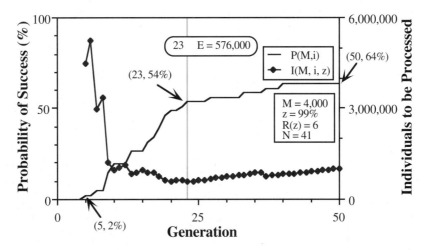

Figure 21.4 Performance curves for the even-5-parity problem with evolution of architecture showing that $E_{with} = 576,000$ with ADFs.

Evolutionary Selection of the Architecture of the Program

The two numbers in the oval indicate that if this problem is run through to generation 23, processing a total of $E_{with} = 576{,}000$ (i.e., $4{,}000 \times 24$ generations $\times 6$ runs) individuals is sufficient to yield a solution to this problem with 99% probability.

The 576,000 individuals required to yield a solution to the even-5-parity problem with 99% probability with the evolution of the architecture is about twice the 272,000 individuals shown in table 7.2 to be required with either two two-argument automatically defined functions or three three-argument automatically defined functions. Although not as low as the optimal number of 272,000, the 576,000 individuals is smaller than four of the 12 numbers in table 7.2. It is only 63% of 912,000, the worst number in table 7.2.

However, because of point typing, implementation of the evolutionary method of determining the architecture takes considerably more wallclock time (about three times as much for this problem). Thus, simultaneously evolving the architecture along with solving the even-5-parity problem takes about six times as much wallclock time as the evolution of the solution alone when compared to the optimal value of 272,000 in table 7.2. Simultaneously evolving the architecture along with solving the problem takes about twice as much wallclock time when compared to the worst value in table 7.2.

An examination of seven of the 26 successful runs illustrates several points about the evolution of architecture.

We first examine the run that yields a solution on the earliest generation (row 4 in table 21.3).

Generation 0 consists of randomly generated programs. The distribution of the number of automatically defined functions among the 4,000 programs of generation 0 of this run is, as expected, reasonably flat. There are 760 programs with no automatically defined functions, 646 with one, 652 with two, 652 with three, 658 with four, and 632 with five arguments.

The best of generation 0 scores 18 hits and contains two automatically defined functions. ADF0 takes four arguments and ADF1 takes three arguments so this program has an argument map for its ADFs of {4, 3}.

```
(progn  (defun ADF0 (ARG0 ARG1 ARG2 ARG3)
          (values (NAND (OR (NAND ARG3 ARG1) ARG1) (AND (NAND
            ARG0 ARG2) (AND ARG2 ARG1))))))
        (defun ADF1 (ARG0 ARG1 ARG2)
          (values (NOR (ADF0 (AND ARG2 ARG1) (NOR ARG0 ARG1)
            (ADF0 ARG1 ARG2 ARG0 ARG0) (NOR ARG0 ARG0)) (NOR ARG1
            ARG2))))
        (values (ADF0 (ADF1 (OR D1 D3) (ADF1 D1 D4 D1) (NAND D0
          D2)) (NAND (NAND D4 D0) (NAND D1 D4)) (NAND (AND D3 D2)
          (OR D1 D4)) (ADF1 (NAND D2 D0) (OR D4 D0) (OR D2
          D0)))))) .
```

The best of generation program in generation 1 scores 19 hits. Both ADF0 and ADF1 take four arguments so this program has an argument map for its ADFs of {4, 4}.

```
(progn (defun ADF0 (ARG0 ARG1 ARG2 ARG3)
          (values (NAND (OR (OR ARG3 ARG0) (OR ARG2 ARG2)) (OR
             (NAND ARG0 ARG3) (NOR ARG1 ARG0)))))
       (defun ADF1 (ARG0 ARG1 ARG2 ARG3)
          (values (NOR (OR (AND ARG3 ARG1) (AND ARG0 ARG0)) (ADF0
             (NAND ARG2 ARG0) (OR ARG2 ARG2) (ADF0 ARG1 ARG0 ARG3
             ARG2) (OR ARG2 ARG1)))))
       (values (NAND (AND (OR D2 D3) (ADF0 D3 D4 D0 D3)) (OR
          (AND D2 D3) (ADF0 D4 D1 D0 D1)))))).
```

The best of generation program in generation 2 scores 20 hits and has three, instead of only two, automatically defined functions. It has an argument map for its ADFs of {3, 4, 4} and is shown below:

```
(progn (defun ADF0 (ARG0 ARG1 ARG2)
          (values (AND (NAND (OR ARG2 ARG1) (NOR ARG1 ARG1))
             (NAND (NAND ARG1 ARG0) (AND ARG1 ARG1)))))
       (defun ADF1 (ARG0 ARG1 ARG2 ARG3)
          (values (OR (OR (AND ARG1 ARG1) (AND ARG1 ARG2)) (NOR
             (OR ARG0 ARG3) (NOR (NAND ARG3 ARG1) (OR ARG0
             ARG2))))))
       (defun ADF2 (ARG0 ARG1 ARG2 ARG3)
          (values (ADF0 (ADF1 (AND ARG3 ARG1) (NAND ARG2 ARG1)
             (AND ARG2 ARG3) (NOR ARG2 ARG3)) (NAND (ADF0 ARG3
             ARG2 ARG0) (ADF1 ARG3 ARG2 ARG2 ARG0)) (ADF0 (OR ARG0
             ARG1) (OR ARG2 ARG3) (ADF0 ARG0 ARG0 ARG1)))))
       (values (ADF2 (AND (NAND D3 D3) (NOR D4 D1)) (AND (NOR D2
          D2) (ADF1 D4 D4 D0 D3)) (NOR (AND D2 D2) (ADF2 D2 D0 D4
          D3)) (NAND (AND D1 D1) (NAND D3 D2)))))).
```

The best of generation 3 is a different program that also scores 20 hits and has the same argument map for its ADFs.

The best of generation 4 scores 26 hits and has an argument map for its ADFs of {3, 5}.

The problem is solved on generation 5 of this run with the following program with an argument map for its ADFs of {3, 5}:

```
(progn (defun ADF0 (ARG0 ARG1 ARG2)
          (values (NOR (NOR (AND ARG2 ARG1) (NOR ARG0 ARG2)) (AND
             (NOR ARG0 ARG2) (OR ARG2 ARG1)))))
       (defun ADF1 (ARG0 ARG1 ARG2 ARG3 ARG4)
          (values (NOR (AND ARG0 ARG2) (NOR (AND ARG3 ARG2) (OR
          ARG0 ARG2)))))
       (values (ADF0 (NOR D0 D4) (ADF1 (ADF0 D3 D1 D3) (OR D1
          D1) (ADF1 D4 D0 D2 D1 D3) (NAND D0 D3) (ADF0 D1 D4 D4))
          (AND (NAND (OR D3 D3) (NOR (NAND D2 D2) (OR (NAND (AND
          D2 D4) (OR D1 D1)) (OR (NAND D4 D3) (NAND D0 D2)))))
          (NOR D0 D0)))))).
```

In this 100%-correct solution, ADF0 is three-argument Boolean rule 195 which performs the even-2-parity function on two of the three arguments available to it (ARG1 and ARG2). It is equivalent to

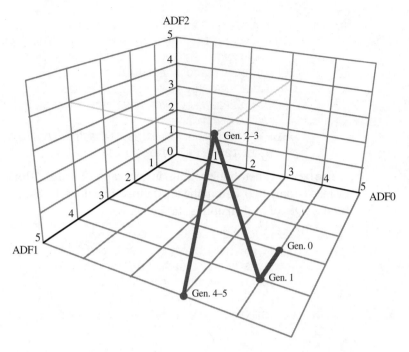

Figure 21.5 Argument trajectory of the number of arguments in ADFs for the best-of-generation programs between generations 0 and 5 of the {3, 5} run of the even-5-parity problem with evolution of architecture.

(EVEN-2-PARITY ARG1 ARG2).

ADF1 is five-argument Boolean rule 1,437,226,410 and is equivalent to

(ODD-2-PARITY ARG0 ARG3).

Rule 1,437,226,410 performs the odd-2-parity function on two of the five arguments available to it (ARG0 and ARG3).

Thus, this 100%-correct solution is a composition of two parity functions of order two (one odd-parity and one even-parity).

Figure 21.5 is a three-dimensional trajectory, called the *argument trajectory*, for this run showing, by generation, the number of arguments of ADF0, ADF1, and ADF2 (if present) of the best-of-generation programs. It is possible to visualize this trajectory in three dimensions only because the number of automatically defined functions for the best-of-generation program does not exceed three for this particular run. As can be seen, the trajectory begins on the floor of the three-dimensional region at generation 0 with a best-of-generation program that has only two automatically defined functions and an argument map for its ADFs of {4, 3}. The trajectory is on the floor of the three-dimensional region because the best of generation 0 does not possess an ADF2. The trajectory continues along the floor in generation 1, but rises from the floor in generations 2 and 3 when ADF2 is present. The trajectory falls back to the floor with {3, 5} in generations 4 and 5. We call this run the "{3, 5} run"

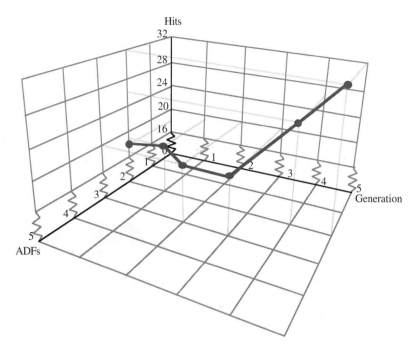

Figure 21.6 Fitness-branch trajectory showing the number of ADFs and hits for the best of generations 0 through 5 of the {3, 5} run of the even-5-parity problem with evolution of architecture.

because {3, 5} is the argument map for the ADFs of the 100%-correct best-of-run individual on the final generation of the run.

Figure 21.6 shows the trajectory, by generation, of the best-of-generation programs according to their raw fitness (hits) and the number of automatically defined functions for the {3, 5} run. This type of figure is called a *fitness-branch trajectory*.

Figure 21.7 is a three-dimensional histogram (called the *branch histogram*) showing, by generation, the number of programs in the population of 4,000 of the {3, 5} run with a specified number (from 0 to 5) of automatically defined functions. For generation 0 there is approximate equality in the number of programs in the population with zero, one, two, three, four, or five automatically defined functions. However, by generation 5, the number of programs with no automatically defined functions drops from an initial value of 760 at generation 0 to only 200 at generation 5. Similarly, the number of programs with only one automatically defined function drops from 646 to only 197, and the number of programs with four automatically defined functions decreases from 658 to 180. By generation 5, most of the programs have two, three or five automatically defined functions.

This run is unique among the 26 successful runs in that it is the only run where the programs with no automatically defined functions did not become extinct in the population before a solution was found. However, even in this run, only 5% of the individuals in the population had no automatically

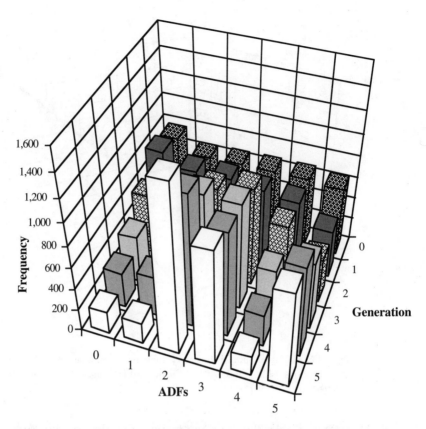

Figure 21.7 Branch histogram between generations 0 and 5 showing the number of programs in the population with various numbers of ADFs for the {3, 5} run of the even-5-parity problem with evolution of architecture.

defined functions by generation 5. The poor performance of programs with no automatically defined functions (relative to the programs with automatically defined functions) causes their near-extinction in the competitive environment in which evolution is being used to determine the architecture of the overall program while the solution to the problem is being found.

The population sometimes converges to a particular configuration of automatically defined functions and number of arguments. The {3} run (row 2 of table 21.3) produces a solution on generation 16. Starting with generation 3, the best-of-generation programs all consist of one three-argument automatically defined function.

Figure 21.8 shows the three-dimensional trajectory, by generation, of the number of arguments of ADF0 and ADF1 of the best-of-generation programs for the {3} run. Since none of the best-of-generation programs in this run employ ADF2, the trajectory begins on the floor of the three-dimensional region at generation 0 with a best-of-generation program having an argument map for its ADFs of {4, 3}, moves to the point {3} on the ADF0 axis on generation 1, returns to {4, 3} for generation 2, returns to {3} on generation 3, and then stays there until the problem is solved at generation 16.

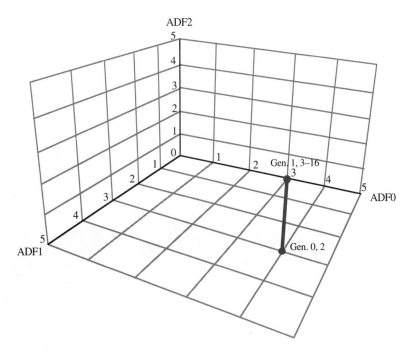

Figure 21.8 Argument trajectory between generations 0 and 16 for the {3} run of the even-5-parity problem with evolution of architecture.

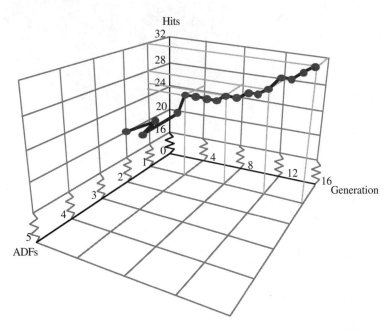

Figure 21.9 Fitness-branch trajectory between generations 0 and 16 of the {3} run of the even-5-parity problem with evolution of architecture.

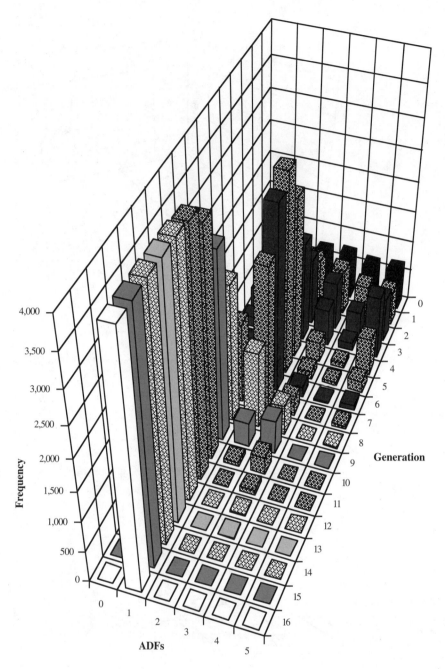

Figure 21.10 Branch histogram between generations 0 and 16 for the {3} run of the even-5-parity problem.

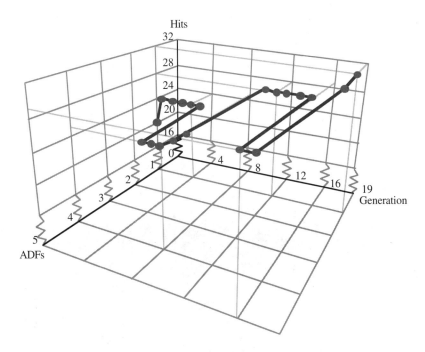

Figure 21.11 Fitness-branch trajectory between generations 0 and 19 of the {2} run of the even-5-parity problem with evolution of architecture.

Figure 21.9 shows the trajectory, by generation, of the best-of-generation programs according to their raw fitness (hits) and the number of automatically defined functions for the {3} run.

Figure 21.10 is a three-dimensional histogram for the {3} run showing, by generation, the number of programs in the population of 4,000 with a specified number (from 0 to 5) of automatically defined functions. As can be seen, programs with one automatically defined function quickly start to dominate the population. By generations 15 and 16, 100% of the population has one automatically defined function.

This run produced the following solution on generation 16:

```
(progn (defun ADF0 (ARG0 ARG1 ARG2)
           (values (NOR (AND (NAND (NAND (NOR (NAND (NAND (NAND
           ARG0 ARG0) (NAND (NOR ARG2 ARG0) (NOR ARG0 ARG0)))
           (NOR ARG1 ARG1)) (NOR ARG0 ARG0)) (NOR ARG1 ARG1))
           (NOR ARG1 ARG1)) (AND (NOR ARG0 ARG0) (NOR ARG0
           ARG2))) (NOR (AND (NOR ARG1 ARG2) (NOR ARG0 ARG2))
           (AND (NAND (AND ARG0 ARG2) ARG1) (NAND (NAND ARG2
           ARG0) (NOR ARG1 ARG1)))))))
        (values (ADF0 (OR D1 D4) (NAND (ADF0 (ADF0 D2 D1 D0) (NAND
           D4 D1) (OR D1 D3)) (NAND (ADF0 D2 D1 D0) (AND D3 D0)))
           (AND (OR (NAND (NAND D3 D2) D0) (NAND D4 D1)) (AND (OR D1
           D4) (AND D3 D1)))))))).
```

In this 100%-correct solution, the one automatically defined function `ADF0` performs the even-3-parity function (Boolean rule 105),

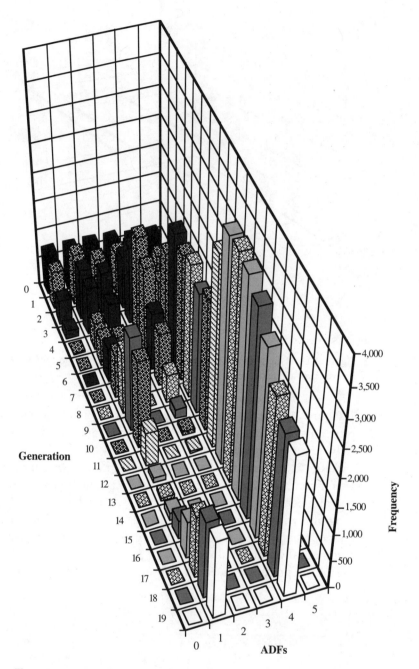

Figure 21.12 Branch histogram between generations 0 and 19 for the {2} run of the even-5-parity problem.

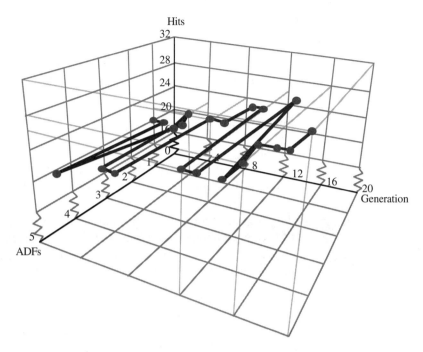

Figure 21.13 Fitness-branch trajectory between generations 0 and 20 of the {3, 2, 3, 3, 3} run of the even-5-parity problem with evolution of architecture.

```
(EVEN-3-PARITY ARG0 ARG1 ARG2),
```

Thus, this solution to the even-5-parity problem is built up from the even-3-parity function.

In the {2} run (row 1 in table 21.3), the population became dominated by programs with one and four automatically defined functions.

Figure 21.11 shows the trajectory, by generation, of the best-of-generation programs according to their raw fitness (hits) and the number of automatically defined functions for the {2} run.

Figure 21.12 is a three-dimensional histogram for the {2} run showing, by generation, the number of programs in the population with a specified number (from 0 to 5) of automatically defined functions. As can be seen, by generation 12, 100% of the population has converged to programs with either one-argument or four-argument automatically defined functions. The number of programs in the population with only one automatically defined function is very small at generation 12; however, these programs proliferate and the solution to the problem at generation 19 turns out to have only automatically defined function.

The best of generations 6, 7, 8, 9, 10, 16, and 17 have an argument map of their ADFs of {1, 3, 3, 4} and the best of all other generations have an argument map of their ADFs of {2}.

The following 100%-correct program with an argument map for its ADFs of {2} emerged on generation 19:

Evolutionary Selection of the Architecture of the Program

```
(progn (defun ADF0 (ARG0 ARG1)
          (values (NOR (AND (AND (AND ARG1 ARG0) ARG0) ARG1) (AND
             (AND (NAND ARG1 ARG1) (NAND ARG0 ARG0)) (NAND (OR ARG1
             ARG0) (NOR ARG1 (NOR ARG1 ARG0)))))))
       (values (ADF0 (NAND (OR D2 D1) (ADF0 D4 (ADF0 D3 D0))) (AND
          (NAND D1 D2) (OR (OR D2 D1) (ADF0 D4 (ADF0 D3 D0)))))))
```

ADF0 of this 100%-correct program performs

```
(ODD-2-PARITY ARG0 ARG1),
```

which is the two-argument Boolean rule 6. This solution to the even-5-parity problem is composed of four invocations of the odd-2-parity function.

In the {3,2,3,3,3} run (row 26 of table 21.3), the population quickly became dominated by programs with one and five automatically defined functions.

Figure 21.13 shows the trajectory, by generation, of the best-of-generation programs according to their raw fitness (hits) and the number of automatically defined functions. This zigzagging trajectory shows that programs with one and five automatically defined functions are battling it out for supremacy within this run.

Figure 21.14 is a three-dimensional histogram for the {3, 2, 3, 3, 3} run showing, by generation, the number of programs in the population with a specified number (from 0 to 5) of automatically defined functions. Programs with five automatically defined functions are almost extinct in generation 6. The battle for supremacy shown in figure 21.13 is reflected here by the dominance of the programs with either one or five automatically defined functions in the later generations of this run. As can be seen, 100% of the population in generation 20 has either one or five automatically defined functions.

The best of generations 0, 1, 3, 4, 10, and 11 have an argument map for their ADFs of {4} and the best of all other generations have an argument map for their ADFs of {3, 2, 3, 3, 3}.

The following 100%-correct program with an argument map for its ADFs of {3, 2, 3, 3, 3} emerged on generation 20:

```
(progn (defun ADF0 (ARG0 ARG1 ARG2)
          (values (OR (NOR (AND (NAND ARG1 ARG0) (OR ARG0 ARG1))
             (NAND (OR ARG2 ARG2) (NOR ARG0 ARG0))) (OR (NOR (NAND
             ARG1 ARG0) (NOR ARG2 ARG1)) (AND (NOR ARG0 ARG0) (AND
             ARG0 ARG1))))))
       (defun ADF1 (ARG0 ARG1)
          (values (OR (ADF0 (OR (NOR ARG1 ARG1) (NAND ARG1 ARG1))
             (AND ARG0 ARG1) (AND ARG0 ARG1)) (ADF0 (ADF0 (AND ARG1
             ARG0) (OR ARG1 ARG1) (AND ARG0 ARG1)) (ADF0 (AND ARG0
             ARG1) (NAND ARG1 ARG0) (NOR ARG1 ARG1)) (OR (AND ARG0
             ARG1) (OR ARG0 ARG1))))))
       (defun ADF2 (ARG0 ARG1 ARG2)
          (values (NAND (NAND (NOR (OR ARG0 ARG2) (ADF0 ARG1 ARG2
             ARG0)) (AND (ADF1 ARG1 ARG1) (OR (NAND ARG0 ARG1) (AND
             (NOR ARG0 ARG1) ARG1)))) (NAND (NOR (OR ARG1 ARG0)
```

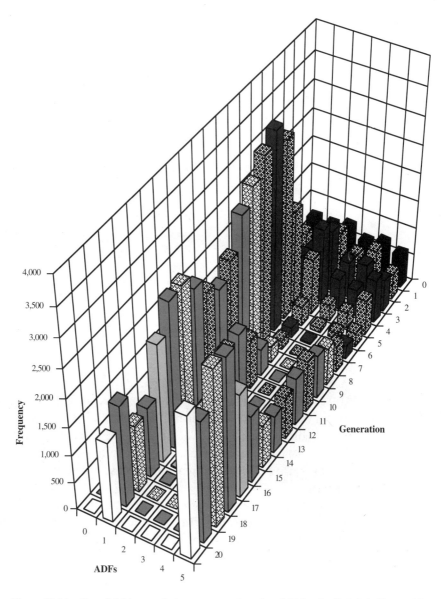

Figure 21.14   Branch histogram between generations 0 and 20 for the {3, 2, 3, 3, 3} run of the even-5-parity problem

Evolutionary Selection of the Architecture of the Program

```
            (ADF0 ARG2 ARG2 ARG1)) (ADF1 (NAND ARG1 ARG2) (AND
            ARG2 ARG0))))))
      (defun ADF3 (ARG0 ARG1 ARG2)
         (values (ADF0 (OR (OR (NAND ARG1 ARG2) (NOR ARG0 ARG2))
            (OR (OR ARG1 (NAND ARG0 ARG1)) (AND ARG0 ARG1))) (NOR
            (ADF1 (AND ARG0 ARG0) (NOR ARG2 ARG1)) (OR (NOR ARG1
            ARG1) (ADF2 ARG2 ARG0 ARG0))) (ADF1 (AND (ADF2 ARG0
            ARG0 ARG0) (AND ARG0 ARG0)) (ADF1 (AND ARG1 ARG2)
            (ADF2 ARG1 ARG2 ARG2))))))
      (defun ADF4 (ARG0 ARG1 ARG2)
         (values (OR (OR (ADF0 (AND ARG2 ARG0) (ADF3 ARG1 ARG0
            ARG0) (ADF0 ARG2 ARG0 ARG2)) (ADF2 (ADF0 ARG2 ARG2
            ARG2) (AND ARG1 ARG1) (OR ARG2 ARG0))) (OR (ADF0 (ADF0
            ARG0 ARG1 ARG0) (NAND ARG2 ARG2) (ADF3 ARG0 ARG1
            ARG1)) (OR (ADF1 ARG2 ARG2) (ADF2 ARG2 (NAND ARG1
            ARG0) ARG1))))))
      (values (ADF4 (ADF4 (ADF0 (NAND D4 D0) (NAND D0 D3) (NOR D3
         D3)) (AND D1 D1) (ADF1 (ADF2 D2 D2 D0) (NAND D4 D0)))
         (ADF0 (ADF4 (NOR D3 D4) (NAND D2 D0) (NOR D3 D2)) (AND
         (NOR D3 D3) (ADF1 D2 D3)) (OR (ADF3 D0 D0 D2) (OR D0
         D4))) (NAND (AND (NAND D2 D3) (NOR D3 D3)) (NOR (OR D4
         D0) (OR D2 D2)))))))).
```

In this solution, ADF0 is equivalent to three-argument Boolean rule 152; ADF1 is equivalent to (ODD-2-PARITY ARG0 ARG1); ADF2 is equivalent to three-argument Boolean rule 1; ADF3 is equivalent to three-argument Boolean rule 64; and ADF3 is equivalent to (EVEN-3-PARITY ARG0 ARG1 ARG2). That is, two of the five automatically defined functions here are parity rules and three of the five automatically defined functions are not.

In the {4,2} run (row 6 of table 21.3), the population quickly becomes dominated by programs with one and two automatically defined functions, although a few programs with four and five automatically defined functions remain.

Figure 21.15 is a three-dimensional trajectory showing, by generation, the number of arguments of ADF0 and ADF1 of the best-of-generation programs for the {4, 2} run. As can be seen, the trajectory begins on the floor of the three-dimensional region at generations 0 and 1 with a best-of-generation program having an argument map for its ADFs of {4, 2}, moves along the floor to {2, 5} on generation 2, returns to {4, 2} for generation 3 and then stays there until the problem is solved at generation 9.

Figure 21.16 shows the trajectory, by generation, of the best-of-generation programs according to their raw fitness (hits) and the number of automatically defined functions for the {4, 2} run.

Figure 21.17 is a three-dimensional histogram for the {4, 2} run showing, by generation, the number of programs in the population with a specified number (from 0 to 5) of automatically defined functions.

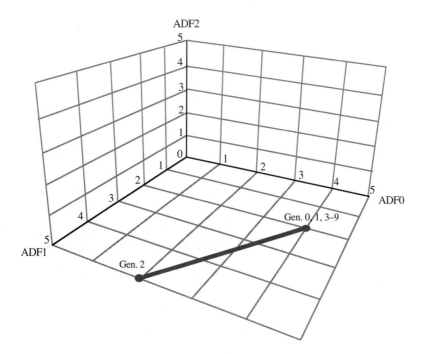

Figure 21.15 Argument trajectory between generations 0 and 9 of the {4, 2} run of the even-5-parity problem with evolution of architecture.

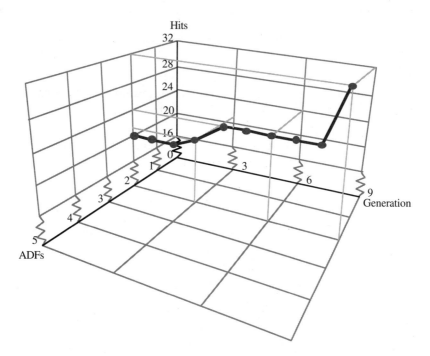

Figure 21.16 Fitness-branch trajectory between generations 0 and 9 of the {4, 2} run of the even-5-parity problem with evolution of architecture.

Evolutionary Selection of the Architecture of the Program

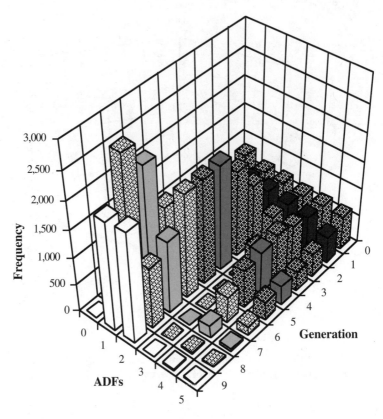

Figure 21.17 Branch histogram between generations 0 and 9 for the {4, 2} run of the even-5-parity problem.

The best of generation 2 has an argument map for its ADFs of {2, 5}. The best of all other generations have argument maps for their ADFs of {4, 2}.

The following 100%-correct program with an argument map for its ADFs of {4, 2} emerged on generation 9:

```
(progn (defun ADF0 (ARG0 ARG1 ARG2 ARG3)
          (values (OR (AND (NOR (NAND (OR (OR (AND ARG2 ARG2) (NOR
              ARG3 ARG2)) (NOR ARG1 ARG3)) (NAND (NAND ARG1 ARG3)
              (AND ARG1 ARG1))) (AND (NOR (AND ARG0 ARG1) (OR ARG3
              ARG3)) (OR (AND ARG2 ARG2) (NAND ARG3 ARG1)))) ARG1)
              (OR (NOR ARG3 ARG2) (NOR ARG1 ARG0)))))
       (defun ADF1 (ARG0 ARG1)
          (values (AND (NAND (AND ARG1 ARG1) (AND ARG1 ARG0)) (OR
              (OR ARG1 ARG0) (OR ARG1 ARG0)))))
       (values (ADF1 (ADF0 (OR D0 D1) (NOR D3 D3) (NAND D3 D0)
          (ADF1 D1 D0)) (ADF1 (AND D4 D4) (NAND D2 D2))))) .
```

ADF0 is equivalent to four-argument Boolean rule 53,535 and ADF1 is equivalent to (ODD-2-PARITY ARG0 ARG1). In other words, this solution

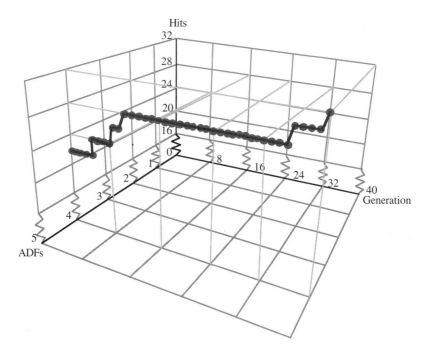

Figure 21.18   Fitness-branch trajectory between generations 0 and 40 of the {3, 2, 2, 3} run of the even-5-parity problem with evolution of architecture.

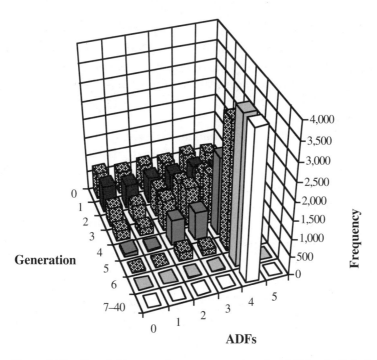

Figure 21.19   Branch histogram between generations 0 and 40 for the {3, 2, 2, 3} run of the even-5-parity problem.

Evolutionary Selection of the Architecture of the Program

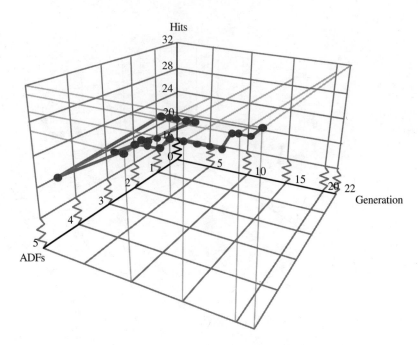

Figure 21.20 Fitness-branch trajectory between generations 0 and 22 of the {2, 4, 5, 1, 5} run of the even-5-parity problem with evolution of architecture.

is built up from one lower-order parity function and one Boolean function that is not a parity rule.

In the {3,2,2,3} run (row 18 of table 21.3), the population quickly converged completely to programs with four automatically defined functions.

Figure 21.18 shows the trajectory, by generation, of the best-of-generation programs according to their raw fitness (hits) and the number of automatically defined functions. The best of generation 40 has an argument map for its ADFs of {3, 2, 2, 3}.

Figure 21.19 is a three-dimensional histogram for the {3, 2, 2, 3} run showing, by generation, the number of programs in the population with a specified number (from 0 to 5) of automatically defined functions. By generation 7, all 4,000 programs in the population have four automatically defined functions.

The following 100%-correct program with an argument map for its ADFs of {3, 2, 2, 3} emerged on generation 40:

```
(progn  (defun ADF0 (ARG0 ARG1 ARG2)
           (values (OR (OR (NAND (NAND ARG0 ARG1) (NOR ARG1 ARG0))
              (AND (AND ARG1 ARG1) (NOR ARG1 ARG2))) (NOR (AND (OR
              ARG0 ARG2) (OR (NAND ARG1 (NAND ARG0 ARG1)) (OR ARG0
              ARG1))) (OR (NAND ARG0 ARG1) (NOR ARG0 ARG0))))))
        (defun ADF1 (ARG0 ARG1)
           (values (OR (NAND (OR (ADF0 ARG1 ARG0 ARG1) (AND ARG0
              ARG1)) (NAND (AND ARG0 ARG1) (ADF0 ARG0 ARG0 ARG1)))
              (AND (OR (ADF0 ARG1 ARG1 ARG1) (ADF0 ARG0 ARG1 ARG0))
              (NOR (NAND ARG1 ARG1) (NOR ARG0 ARG0))))))
```

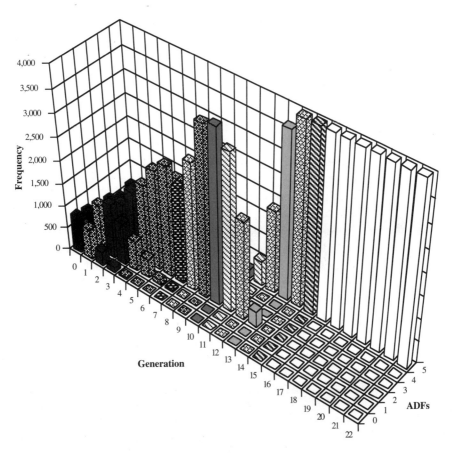

Figure 21.21 Branch histogram between generations 0 and 22 for the {2, 4, 5, 1, 5} run of the even-5-parity problem.

```
(defun ADF2 (ARG0 ARG1)
   (values (ADF1 (AND (AND (ADF1 ARG1 ARG0) (AND ARG0
    ARG0)) ARG1) (ADF0 (NOR (OR ARG0 ARG1) (OR ARG0 ARG0))
    (NOR (NAND ARG1 ARG0) (ADF0 ARG1 (NAND ARG1 ARG1)
    ARG0)) (NAND ARG1 ARG0)))))
(defun ADF3 (ARG0 ARG1 ARG2)
   (values (NAND (NAND (NAND (NAND ARG1 ARG0) (NAND ARG0
    ARG1)) (ADF1 (ADF2 ARG2 ARG1) (ADF1 ARG1 ARG2))) (ADF2
    (OR (NOR (AND (NAND ARG0 ARG1) (NAND ARG1 ARG0)) (OR
    (NOR ARG1 ARG0) (NOR ARG1 ARG0))) (NAND (OR ARG0 ARG2)
    (NOR ARG0 ARG0))) (ADF0 (NAND ARG1 ARG0) (ADF1 ARG2
    ARG0) (ADF1 ARG2 ARG2))))))
   (values (ADF1 (NOR (AND D0 D3) (NOR D1 D3)) (ADF1 (ADF1
    (NOR D2 D4) (OR D3 D0)) (ADF3 (NAND D2 D4) (OR D2 D3)
    (ADF0 (NOR D1 D3) D1 D3)))))) .
```

ADF0 is equivalent to three-argument Boolean rule 238; ADF1 is equivalent to (EVEN-2-PARITY ARG0 ARG1); ADF2 is equivalent to (ODD-2-PAR-ITY ARG0 ARG1); and ADF3 is equivalent to three-argument Boolean rule

167. This solution is composed of two parity functions of order two (one odd and one even) and two other Boolean functions that are not parity rules.

The solution produced by the {2,4,5,1,5} run (row 24 of table 21.3) is one of only three solutions (of the 26 solutions) where no automatically defined function is a lower-order parity function.

Figure 21.20 shows the trajectory, by generation, of the best-of-generation programs according to their raw fitness (hits) and the number of automatically defined functions for the {2, 4, 5, 1, 5} run.

Figure 21.21 is a three-dimensional histogram for the {2, 4, 5, 1, 5} run showing, by generation, the number of programs in the population with a specified number (from 0 to 5) of automatically defined functions. The best of generation 0 of the {2, 4, 5, 1, 5} run has an argument map for its ADFs of {4}. The best of several early generations have an argument map for their ADFs of {3, 2}. However, starting at generation 9, all 4,000 programs in the population converge to an argument map for ADFs of {2, 4, 5, 1, 5} involving five automatically defined functions.

The following 100%-correct program with an argument map for its ADFs of {2, 4, 5, 1, 5} emerges on generation 22:

```
(progn (defun ADF0 (ARG0 ARG1)
         (values (NOR (AND (AND ARG1 ARG1) (NOR ARG1 ARG1)) (AND
           (NOR ARG1 ARG1) (NOR ARG1 ARG1)))))
       (defun ADF1 (ARG0 ARG1 ARG2 ARG3)
         (values (OR (NAND (OR ARG0 ARG3) (NAND ARG0 ARG2)) (NOR
           (NAND ARG1 ARG3) (NAND ARG0 ARG0)))))
       (defun ADF2 (ARG0 ARG1 ARG2 ARG3 ARG4 )
         (values (NAND (OR (AND ARG0 ARG1) (NAND ARG3 ARG1))
           (ADF0 (NOR ARG2 (NAND (NAND ARG1 ARG0) ARG0)) (OR (AND
           (OR (OR ARG0 ARG2) ARG1) (NAND (OR ARG0 ARG2) (NAND
           ARG2 ARG0))) (NAND (NAND ARG1 (OR (NOR ARG1 ARG1)
           ARG0)) ARG0))))))
       (defun ADF3 (ARG0)
         (values (ADF2 (ADF2 (NOR ARG0 ARG0) (NAND ARG0 ARG0)
           (ADF0 ARG0 ARG0) (AND ARG0 ARG0) (NAND ARG0 ARG0))
           (AND (AND ARG0 ARG0) (ADF2 ARG0 ARG0 ARG0 ARG0 ARG0))
           (ADF0 (AND ARG0 ARG0) (OR ARG0 ARG0)) (OR (ADF2 ARG0
           ARG0 ARG0 ARG0 ARG0) (NOR (AND ARG0 ARG0) ARG0)) (OR
           (ADF0 ARG0 ARG0) (ADF1 ARG0 ARG0 ARG0 ARG0)))))
       (defun ADF4 (ARG0 ARG1 ARG2 ARG3 ARG4)
         (values (OR (NAND (NAND ARG0 ARG0) (NAND ARG0 ARG2))
           (NAND (OR ARG0 ARG3) (NAND ARG0 ARG2)))))
       (values (ADF1 (ADF1 (ADF1 D3 D3 D1 D2) (AND D1 D1) (AND D1
         D2) (ADF1 D2 D3 D1 D3)) (OR D0 (NAND D4 D0)) (ADF2 (NOR
         D3 D4) (ADF2 D1 D4 D3 D3 D2) (ADF0 D0 D2) (NOR D1 D3)
         (NAND (NAND (OR D3 D0) (OR D2 D3))) (OR D2 D3))) (ADF0
         (ADF0 D0 D1) (ADF2 D0 D4 D4 D4 D3)))))) .
```

ADF0 of this 100%-correct program performs two-argument Boolean rule 12; ADF1 performs four-argument Boolean rule 43,253; ADF2 performs five-argument Boolean rule 1,174,554,114; `ADF3` performs one-argument Boolean rule 0 (always false); and `ADF4` performs five-argument Boolean rule 2,868,882,175.

Table 21.4 shows, in its first two columns, the run number and the argument map for the ADFs of the 26 solutions to the even-5-parity problem. Each pair of the 10 remaining columns relates to each of the five automatically defined functions that may appear in a particular solution. The Boolean rule number appears in the first column of each such pair. If the Boolean rule is a parity rule, the second column identifies it. As can be seen, only runs 7, 22, and 24 of these 26 successful runs solve the problem without using at least one parity rule. That is, 88% of these runs invoke lower-order parity functions (of orders two and three). In contrast, only 42% of the 19 solutions shown in table 6.6 invoke lower-order parity functions.

21.4   Results for the even-4-Parity Problem

We made 25 runs of the even-4-parity problem to further test the evolutionary method of determining the number of automatically defined functions and the number of arguments they each possess. All of these runs produced a 100%-correct solution (scoring 16 hits).

All of the 25 solutions employed one or more automatically defined functions, even though it is, of course, possible to solve this problem without automatically defined functions. An examination of the 258 best-of-generation individuals among these 25 successful runs showed that 254 of these 258 intermediate best-of-generation programs employed automatically defined functions. That is, when the number of automatically defined functions is open to evolutionary determination, almost all of the best-of-generation programs produced along the way employ automatically defined functions for this problem.

As with the even-5-parity problem, there is no convergence of architecture among the various runs of the even-4-parity problem. Instead, there is a wide variation among the argument maps of these 25 overall programs (with only two argument maps being repeated). The average number (3.08) of automatically defined functions for these 25 solutions happens to be the same as for the even-5-parity problem.

Figure 21.22 shows the trajectory, by generation, of the best-of-generation programs of the {2, 4, 4, 3, 5} run (row 22 of table 21.5) of the even-4-parity problem according to their raw fitness (hits) and the number of automatically defined functions.

Figure 21.23 is a three-dimensional histogram for the {2, 4, 4, 3, 5} run of the even-4-parity problem showing, by generation, the number of programs in the population of 4,000 with a specified number (from 0 to 5) of automatically defined functions. As can be seen, programs with five automatically defined functions quickly start to dominate the population and by generation 14, almost all of the population has five automatically defined functions.

Table 21.4 Characteristics of the ADFs of 26 solutions to the even-5-parity problem with evolution of architecture.

Run	Argument map for ADFs	Rule number for ADF0	Is ADF0 a parity rule?	Rule number for ADF1	Is ADF1 a parity rule?	Rule number for ADF2	Is ADF2 a parity rule?
1	{2}	6	(ODD-2-PARITY RULE?ARG0 ARG1)				
2	{3}	105	(EVEN-3-PARITY ARG0 ARG1 ARG2)				
3	{3, 3}	1	No	150	(ODD-3-PARITY ARG0 ARG1 ARG2)		
4	{3, 5}	193	No	1,515,870,810	(ODD-2-PARITY ARG0 ARG2)		
5	{3, 5}	195	(EVEN-2-PARITY ARG1 ARG2)	1,437,226,410	(ODD-2-PARITY ARG0 ARG3)		
6	{4, 2}	53,535	No	6	(ODD-2-PARITY ARG0 ARG1)		
7	{4, 3}	34,952	No	147	No		
8	{4, 4}	26,214	(ODD-2-PARITY ARG0 ARG1)	55,253	No		
9	{5, 3}	56,034,135	No	150	(ODD-3-PARITY ARG0 ARG1 ARG2)		
10	{2, 1, 3}	9	(EVEN-2-PARITY ARG0 ARG1)	3	No	102	(ODD-2-PARIT ARG0 ARG1)
11	{2, 4, 3}	6	(ODD-2-PARITY ARG0 ARG1)	7,395	No	150	(ODD-3-PARITY ARG0 ARG1 ARG2)
12	{3, 1, 4}	165	(EVEN-2-PARITY ARG0 ARG2)	0	No	13,260	(ODD-2-PARITY ARG1 ARG3)
13	{4, 3, 5}	26,214	(ODD-2-PARITY ARG0 ARG1)	103	No	4,294,770,684	No
14	{5, 2, 2}	547,889,320	No	9	(EVEN-2-PARITY ARG0 ARG1)	9	(EVEN-2-PARITY ARG0 ARG1)
15	{5, 5, 1}	4,294,967,295	No	267,390,960	(ODD-2-PARITY ARG2 ARG3)	2	No
16	{5, 5, 2}	2,947,526,575	No	3,284,386,755	(EVEN-2-PARITY ARG1 ARG2)	15	No
17	{2, 4, 3, 5}	6	(ODD-2-PARITY ARG0 ARG1)	31,354	No	156	No
18	{3, 2, 2, 3}	238	No	9	(EVEN-2-PARITY ARG0 ARG1)	6	(ODD-2-PARITY ARG0 ARG1)
19	{3, 4, 5, 5}	63	No	43,605	(EVEN-2-PARITY ARG0 ARG3)	2,700,452,085	No
20	{4, 3, 1, 1}	13,076	No	195	(EVEN-2-PARITY ARG1 ARG2)	0	No
21	{5, 3, 3, 5}	1,717,986,918	(ODD-2-PARITY ARG0 ARG1)	0	No	105	(EVEN-3-PARITY ARG0 ARG1 ARG2)
22	{5, 4, 2, 1}	1,441,420,778	No	43,690	No	11	No
23	{5, 5, 2, 5}	2,779,620,781	No	2,778,768,800	No	12	No
24	{2, 4, 5, 1, 5}	12	No	43,253	No	1,174,554,114	No
25	{3, 1, 2, 2, 2}	95	No	0	No	9	(EVEN-2-PARITY ARG0 ARG1)
26	{3, 2, 3, 3, 3}	152	No	6	(ODD-2-PARITY ARG0 ARG1)	1	No

Run	Is ADF3 a parity rule?	Rule number for ADF3	Is ADF4 a parity rule?	Rule number for ADF4
1				
2				
3				
4				
5				
6				
7				
8				
9				
10				
11				
12				
13				
14				
15				
16				
17	818,884,815	No		
18	167	No		
19	2,857,740,885	(EVEN-2-PARITY ARG0 ARG3)		
20	0	No		
21	809,250,876	No		
22	0	No		
23	2,857,740,885	(EVEN-2-PARITY ARG0 ARG3)		
24	2,868,882,175	No		
25	9	(EVEN-2-PARITY ARG0 ARG1)	3	No
26	64	No	105	(EVEN-3-PARITY ARG0 ARG1 ARG2)

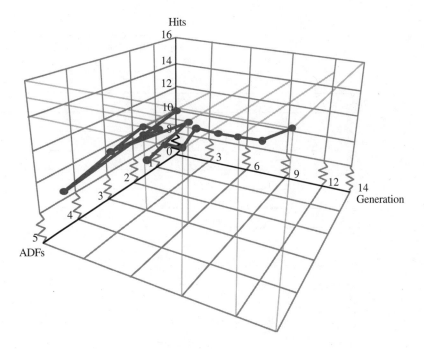

Figure 21.22 Fitness-branch trajectory between generations 0 and 14 of the {2, 4, 4, 3, 5} run of the even-4-parity problem with evolution of architecture.

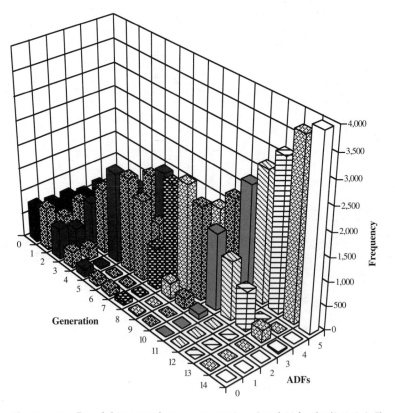

Figure 21.23 Branch histogram between generations 0 and 14 for the {2, 4, 4, 3, 5} run of the even-4-parity problem

With Defined Functions

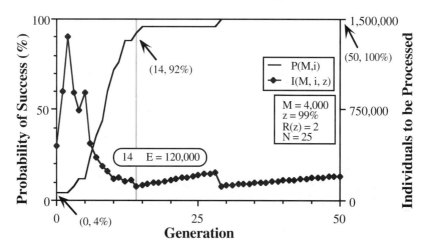

Figure 21.24 Performance curves for the even-4-parity problem with evolution of architecture showing that E_{with} = 120,000 with ADFs.

The average structural complexity, $\overline{S}_{with}$, of the solutions of the even-4-parity problem over 25 successful runs (out of 25 runs) is 130.9 points using the evolutionary method of determining the architecture.

Figure 21.24 presents the performance curves based on the 25 runs of the even-4-parity problem with the evolutionary selection of architecture. The cumulative probability of success, $P(M,i)$, is 92% by generation 14 and is 100% by generation 50. The two numbers in the oval indicate that if this problem is run through to generation 14, processing a total of E_{with} = 120,000 individuals (i.e., 4,000 × 15 generations × 2 runs) is sufficient to yield a solution to this problem with 99% probability.

For the purpose of comparing the above value of E_{with} of 120,000 with the evolution of architecture for the even-4-parity problem, we made three series of runs with the same population size of 4,000 without the evolution of architecture. For comparison, we made two series of runs with automatically defined functions employing fixed argument maps for their ADFs of {3} and {3, 3}, respectively. We obtained values of E_{with} of 76,000 and 80,000 for these two series of runs. We then made an additional series of runs without automatically defined functions and obtained the value of $E_{without}$ of 276,000. Thus, for the even-4-parity problem, the evolutionary method of determining the architecture requires more computational effort, E, than the two particular tested fixed argument maps, but less than if automatically defined functions are not used at all.

The details of these three series of runs follow.

Figure 21.25 presents the performance curves based on 30 runs of the even-4-parity problem using automatically defined functions with a fixed argument map for the ADFs of {3}. The cumulative probability of success, $P(M,i)$, is 100% by generation 18. The two numbers in the oval indicate that if this

With Defined Functions

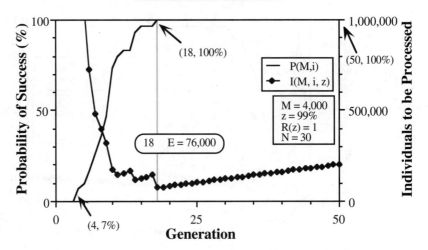

Figure 21.25 Performance curves for the even-4-parity problem showing that $E_{with} = 76,000$ with ADFs having a fixed argument map of {3}.

With Defined Functions

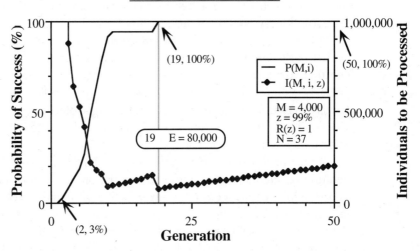

Figure 21.26 Performance curves for the even-4-parity problem showing that $E_{with} = 80,000$ with ADFs having a fixed argument map of {3, 3}.

problem is run through to generation 18, processing a total of $E_{with} = 76,000$ individuals (i.e., $4,000 \times 19$ generations $\times 1$ run) is sufficient to yield a solution to this problem with 99% probability.

Figure 21.26 presents the performance curves based on 37 runs of the even-4-parity problem using automatically defined functions with a fixed argument map for the ADFs of {3, 3}. The cumulative probability of success, $P(M, i)$, is 100% by generation 19. The two numbers in the oval indicate that if this

Without Defined Functions

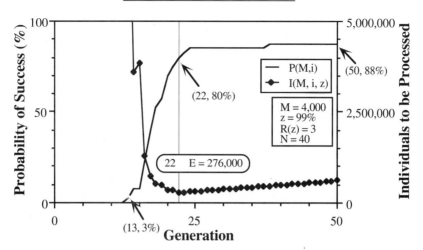

Figure 21.27 Performance curves for the even-4-parity problem showing that $E_{without} = 276,000$ without ADFs.

With Defined Functions

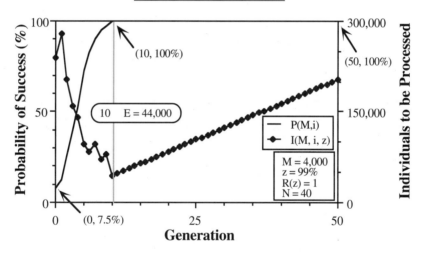

Figure 21.28 Performance curves for the even-3-parity problem with evolution of architecture showing that $E_{with} = 44,000$ with ADFs.

problem is run through to generation 19, processing a total of $E_{with} = 80,000$ individuals (i.e., $4,000 \times 20$ generations $\times 1$ run) is sufficient to yield a solution to this problem with 99% probability.

Figure 21.27 presents the performance curves based on 40 runs of the even-4-parity problem without automatically defined functions. That is, the argument map for the ADFs is fixed and is the empty map {}. The cumulative probability of success, $P(M, i)$, is 100% by generation 22. The two numbers in

Table 21.5 Characteristics of the ADFs of the 25 solutions to the even-4-parity problem with evolution of architectu

Run	Argument map for ADFs	Rule number for ADF0	Is ADF0 a parity rule?	Rule number for ADF1	Is ADF1 a parity rule?	Rule number for ADF2	Is ADF2 a parity rule?
1	{2}	6	(ODD-2-PARITY ARG0 ARG1)				
2	{4}	20,235	No				
3	{2, 5}	8	No	4,027,576,335	(EVEN-2-PARITY ARG2 ARG3)		
4	{2, 5}	6	(ODD-2-PARITY ARG0 ARG1)	3,996,380,723	No		
5	{4, 4}	40,975	No	4,573	No		
6	{4, 4}	35,779	No	17,488	No		
7	{5, 2}	511,319,674	No	15	No		
8	{5, 4}	267,390,960	(ODD-2-PARITY ARG2 ARG3)	56,729	No		
9	{5, 5}	100,599,295	No	4,233,362,515	No		
10	{1, 1, 4}	3	No	3		0	No
11	{1, 5, 2}	3	No	1,437,226,410	(ODD-2-PARITY ARG0 ARG3)	9	(EVEN-2-PARI ARG0 ARG1)
12	{2, 1, 4}	6	(ODD-2-PARITY ARG0 ARG1)	3	No	65,535	No
13	{2, 1, 5}	6	(ODD-2-PARITY ARG0 ARG1)	1	No	2,852,497,925	No
14	{2, 3, 2}	9	(EVEN-2-PARITY ARG0 ARG1)	148	No	10	No
15	{2, 4, 4}	9	(EVEN-2-PARITY ARG0 ARG1)	11,822	No	40	No
16	{4, 4, 3}	61,030	No	38,058		17	No
17	{5, 5, 4}	3,755,991,007	No	3,284,386,755	(EVEN-2-PARITY ARG1 ARG2)	0	No
18	{2, 2, 5, 4}	6	(ODD-2-PARITY ARG0 ARG1)	6	(ODD-2-PARITY ARG0 ARG1)	4,283,826,005	No
19	{3, 4, 4, 3}	9	No	57,054	No	7,501	No
20	{3, 4, 5, 3}	155	No	53,110	No	3,539,718,907	No
21	{1, 3, 1, 2, 3}	0	No	102	(ODD-2-PARITY ARG0 ARG1)	3	No
22	{2, 4, 4, 3, 5}	3	No	13,090	No	11,835	No
23	{2, 4, 5, 5, 2}	6	(ODD-2-PARITY ARG0 ARG1)	50,634	No	3,547,583,347	No
24	{4, 2, 3, 3, 4}	68	No	9	(EVEN-2-PARITY ARG0 ARG1)	134	No
25	{5, 3, 5, 5, 4}	2,779,096,485	(EVEN-2-PARITY ARG0 ARG2)	181	No	1,195,853,639	No

Run	Is ADF3 a parity rule?	Rule number for ADF3	Is ADF4 a parity rule?	Rule number for ADF4
1				
2				
3				
4				
5				
6				
7				
8				
9				
10				
11				
12				
13				
14				
15				
16				
17				
18	43,622	No		
19	90	(ODD-2-PARITY ARG0 ARG2)		
20	93	No		
21	6	(ODD-2-PARITY ARG0 ARG1)	60	(ODD-2-PARITY ARG1 ARG2)
22	163	No	3,423,718,417	No
23	2,863,311,530	No	6	(ODD-2-PARITY ARG0 ARG1)
24	51	No	0	No
25	3,805,274,831	No	9,260	No

Evolutionary Selection of the Architecture of the Program

Table 21.6 Characteristics of the ADFs of 40 solutions to the even-3-parity problem with evolution of architectur

Run	Argument map for ADFs	Rule number for ADF0	Is ADF0 a parity rule?	Rule number for ADF1	Is ADF1 a parity rule?	Rule number for ADF2	Is ADF2 a parity rule?
1	{2}	6	(ODD-2-PARITY ARG0 ARG1)				
2	{3}	90	(ODD-2-PARITY ARG0 ARG2)				
3	{3}	122	No				
4	{3}	165	(EVEN-2-PARITY ARG0 ARG2)				
5	{5}	1,179,010,630	No				
6	{2, 2}	3	No	6	(ODD-2-PARITY ARG0 ARG1)		
7	{3, 2}	112	No	6	(ODD-2-PARITY ARG0 ARG1)		
8	{3, 3}	47	No	90	(ODD-2-PARITY ARG0 ARG2)		
9	{4, 1}	64,504	No	1	No		
10	{4, 2}	20,563	No	2	No		
11	{4, 3}	28,704	No	104	No		
12	{5, 3}	4,285,529,967	No	45	No		
13	{5, 4}	2,576,980,377	(EVEN-2-PARITY ARG0 ARG1)	0	No		
14	{5, 4}	526,131,036	No	32,639	No		
15	{2, 1, 4}	11	No	2	No	4,080	(ODD-2-PARITY ARG2 ARG3)
16	{2, 3, 4}	9	(EVEN-2-PARITY ARG0 ARG1)	64	No	16,464	No
17	{3, 2, 5}	22	No	13	No	657,336,110	No
18	{3, 3, 2}	193	No	127	No	6	(ODD-2-PARITY ARG0 ARG1)
19	{3, 4, 2}	0	No	24,415	No	9	(EVEN-2-PARIT ARG0 ARG1)
20	{4, 2, 5}	40,112	No	7	No	2,013,231,103	No
21	{4, 3, 5}	61,690	No	153	(EVEN-2-PARITY ARG0 ARG1)	2,688,852,036	No
22	{5, 2, 2}	1,996,846,853	No	2	No	6	(ODD-2-PARITY ARG0 ARG1)
23	{5, 3, 3}	983,055	No	90	(ODD-2-PARITY ARG0 ARG2)	238	No
24	{5, 3, 5}	2,013,231,103	No	61	No	536,879,104	No
25	{1, 1, 2, 4}	2	No	2	No	6	(ODD-2-PARITY ARG0 ARG1)
26	{2, 4, 1, 2}	9	(EVEN-2-PARITY ARG0 ARG1)	30,855	No	3	No
27	{2, 4, 4, 3}	3	No	61,695	No	8,738	No
28	{3, 2, 2, 2}	64	No	9	(EVEN-2-PARITY ARG0 ARG1)	15	No
29	{3, 2, 5, 4}	184	No	6	(ODD-2-PARITY ARG0 ARG1)	2,476,512,156	No
30	{3, 3, 1, 2}	38	No	255	No	2	No
31	{3, 5, 5, 4}	250	No	1,712,416,273	No	1,432,966,505	No
32	{4, 1, 5, 4}	30,207	No	1	No	269,488,144	No
33	{5, 1, 3, 3}	2,694,881,440	No	0	No	61	No
34	{5, 2, 3, 1}	4,008,636,142	No	6	(ODD-2-PARITY ARG0 ARG1)	9	No
35	{2, 3, 4, 2, 2}	13	No	116	No	29,571	No
36	{2, 5, 5, 2, 2}	6	(ODD-2-PARITY ARG0 ARG1)	2,523,305,574	No	3,435,973,836	No
37	{3, 3, 5, 4, 4}	195	(EVEN-2-PARITY ARG1 ARG2)	248	No	96,142,779	No
38	{4, 3, 4, 3, 1}	21,845	No	185	No	46,026	No
39	{5, 1, 4, 1, 3}	1,515,870,810	(ODD-2-PARITY ARG0 ARG2)	0	No	23,130	(ODD-2-PARITY ARG0 ARG2)
40	{5, 4, 3, 4, 2}	1,414,812,756	No	13,260	(ODD-2-PARITY ARG1 ARG3)	0	No

Run	Is ADF3 a parity rule?	Rule number for ADF3	Is ADF4 a parity rule?	Rule number for ADF4
1				
2				
3				
4				
5				
6				
7				
8				
9				
10				
11				
12				
13				
14				
15				
16				
17				
18				
19				
20				
21				
22				
23				
24				
25	11,565	No		
26	8	No		
27	90	(ODD-2-PARITY ARG0 ARG2)		
28	6	(ODD-2-PARITY ARG0 ARG1)		
29	63,479	No		
30	8	No		
31	55,048	No		
32	34,048	No		
33	109	No		
34	3	No		
35	14	No	4	No
36	7	No	11	No
37	56,540	No	27,246	No
38	172	No	0	No
39	2	No	0	No
40	43,516	No	8	No

the oval indicate that if this problem is run through to generation 22, processing a total of $E_{without} = 276,000$ individuals (i.e., $4,000 \times 23$ generations $\times 3$ runs) is sufficient to yield a solution to this problem with 99% probability.

Table 21.5 summarizes the 25 solutions to the even-4-parity problem in the same manner as table 21.4. There is a wide variation among the argument maps of these 25 solutions (with only two argument maps being repeated). The average number (3.08) of automatically defined functions for these 25 solutions happens to be the same as for the even-5-parity problem. Of these 25 successful runs, 40% solve the problem without using a lower-order parity function and 60% invoke a parity function of order two. No parity functions of order higher than two are invoked in solving this parity problem of order four.

21.5   RESULTS FOR THE EVEN-3-PARITY PROBLEM

Finally, we made 40 runs of the even-3-parity problem, all of which produced a 100%-correct solution (scoring 8 hits).

All of the 40 solutions employed one or more automatically defined functions. An examination of the 210 best-of-generation individuals among these 40 successful runs showed that 195 of these 210 intermediate best-of-generation programs employed automatically defined functions.

The average structural complexity, $\overline{S}_{with}$, of the solutions of the even-3-parity problem over these 40 successful runs (out of 40 runs) is 125.1 points with the evolution of architecture.

Figure 21.28 presents the performance curves based on these 40 runs of the even-3-parity problem with the evolutionary selection of architecture. The cumulative probability of success, $P(M,i)$, is 100% by generation 10. The two numbers in the oval indicate that if this problem is run through to generation 10, processing a total of $E_{with} = 44,000$ individuals (i.e., $4,000 \times 11$ generations $\times 1$ run) is sufficient to yield a solution to this problem with 99% probability.

Table 21.6 summarizes the 40 solutions to the even-3-parity problem in the same manner as tables 21.4 and 21.6. There is a wide variation among the argument maps of these 40 solutions (with only two argument maps appearing more than once). The average number (3.08) of automatically defined functions for these 40 solutions again happens to be the same as for the even-5-parity and the even-4-parity problem. Of these 40 successful runs, 40% solve the problem without using a lower-order parity function and 60% invoke a lower-order (i.e., order two) parity function.

21.6   SUMMARY

In this chapter we showed that it is possible to use the competitive fitness-driven evolutionary process to determine the architecture of the overall program to be evolved while solving the problem. This simultaneous evolution takes more computer resources than the solution of the problem where the architecture is prespecified for the Boolean even-5-parity problem.

Thus, this chapter and additional examples in subsequent chapters provide evidence to support main point 8:

Main point 8: Genetic programming is capable of simultaneously solving a problem and evolving the architecture of the overall program.

22 Evolution of Primitives and Sufficiency

As previously mentioned, the second preparatory step in applying genetic programming to a problem is to determine the set of primitive functions of which the yet-to-be-evolved programs are composed. For example, the set of primitive functions used throughout this book for the Boolean even-5-parity problem has consisted of AND, OR, NAND, and NOR. As mentioned earlier, we chose this particular set of four primitive functions because we knew that it satisfies both the sufficiency and closure requirements. Indeed, NAND alone, NOR alone, the set {AND, NOT}, and the set {OR, NOT} all satisfy both the sufficiency and closure requirements for any problem of Boolean symbolic regression.

Suppose that we did not know what set of primitive functions is sufficient to solve a problem of symbolic regression for the Boolean even-5-parity function or, for some reason, did not want to make the decision of determining the set of primitive functions for this problem.

One approach would be to choose a set of primitive functions from a large, presumably sufficient superset. Experiments in *Genetic Programming* (section 24.3) showed that genetic programming is generally capable of selecting a useful subset of primitive functions from a superset replete with extraneous functions.

But suppose we wanted to evolve a set of primitive functions, rather than merely home in on a subset of primitive functions within a prespecified superset. We have already seen how genetic programming is capable of evolving automatically defined functions for various problems. The question arises as to whether it is possible for genetic programming to evolve a set of primitive functions during a run at the same time that it is solving the problem and evolving the architecture of the overall program. Presumably, primitive functions can be evolved in the same manner as automatically defined functions are evolved. In other words, primitive functions can be viewed as automatically defined functions composed of very primitive ingredients. Of course, before embarking on an attempt to evolve a set of primitive functions, one must be clear that every representation ultimately comes down to some kind of primitive. Thus, when we talk here about evolving a set of primitive functions, we are necessarily talking about a class of problems for which the usual primitive functions have a yet more elementary representation.

In this chapter we demonstrate that genetic programming can, in fact, evolve a sufficient set of primitive functions (in the sense described above) at the same time as it solves the problem and evolves the architecture of the overall program.

The idea is to start with at least one primitive function (called a PF) in an overall program. The PFs would then be used to define the ADFs (if any are present in the particular overall program). Then, both the PFs and the ADFs (if present) are typically used in the result-producing branch.

In other words, the function set for the result-producing branch, $\mathcal{F}_{rpb}$, will consist of a yet-to-be-determined number of yet-to-be-evolved primitive functions (each taking an as-yet-to-be-chosen number of arguments) along with a yet-to-be-determined number of yet-to-be-evolved automatically defined functions (each taking an as-yet-to-be-chosen number of arguments). The function set for each function-defining branch, if any, will consist of a yet-to-be-determined number of yet-to-be-evolved primitive functions (each taking an as-yet-to-be-chosen number of arguments) along with whatever other automatically defined functions each function-defining branch is entitled to reference hierarchically.

The function set for the result-producing branch, $\mathcal{F}_{rpb}$, is

$$\mathcal{F}_{rpb} = \{\text{ADF0}, \dots\} \cup \{\text{PF0}, \dots\}.$$

where the PFs are primitive functions (described in detail in section 22.1) that will be evolved during the run of genetic programming. There is at least one PF in $\mathcal{F}_{rpb}$, but there need not be any ADFs in $\mathcal{F}_{rpb}$.

The function set, $\mathcal{F}_{adf0}$, for the first function-defining branch (defining ADF0), if ADF0 is indeed present in a particular program, is

$$\mathcal{F}_{adf0} = \{\text{PF0}, \dots\}.$$

There is at least one PF in $\mathcal{F}_{adf0}$.

Given that the second function-defining branch (defining ADF1) is entitled to refer hierarchically to ADF0, the function set for the second function-defining branch, if ADF1 is present, is

$$\mathcal{F}_{adf1} = \{\text{ADF0}\} \cup \{\text{PF0}, \dots\}.$$

The function sets for any subsequent function-defining branches, if present in a particular program, are progressively defined in a similar way.

A population size of 4,000 is used throughout this chapter. The techniques of structure-preserving crossover with point typing (chapter 21) are used throughout this chapter.

Of course, in order to evolve a primitive function, it must be represented in some more elementary way that permits us to define its behavior.

22.1 PRIMITIVE DEFINING BRANCHES

Boolean primitive functions (e.g., AND, OR, NAND, NOR) admit of an elementary representation (the *truth table*) that gives us access to the definition of the function. A primitive-defining branch for defining a `PF` may be viewed as a truth table whose entries come from the set of the constants, $\Re_{Boolean}$, of the Boolean domain (i.e., `T` and `NIL`).

For example, suppose, as a consequence of some evolutionary process, primitive function `PF0` came to have two arguments and came to be equivalent to the Boolean function we usually call `NAND`, then the primitive-defining branch for `PF0` would be the truth table with four rows shown in table 22.1. `NAND` is two-argument Boolean rule 7 and is one of the 16 possible two-argument Boolean functions.

In addition, suppose, as a consequence of some evolutionary process, that a second primitive function, `PF1`, is evolved within the same overall program. `PF1` might be the one-argument Boolean function that we usually call `NOT`. In that event, the primitive-defining branch for `PF1` would be the truth table with two rows shown in table 22.2. `NOT` is one of four possible one-argument Boolean functions and is one-argument Boolean rule 1.

Similarly, suppose that yet another primitive function, `PF2`, is evolved within the same overall program. Table 22.3 has eight rows and defines a three-argument function `PF2` that is equivalent to (`IF ARG0 ARG1 ARG2`). The `IF` function is three-argument Boolean rule 216 and is one of 256 possible three-argument Boolean functions.

When the initial random population is created, each overall program contains a randomly chosen number of primitive-defining branches (where this random number is greater than or equal to one and less than or equal to some maximum number of primitive-defining branches). Each primitive-defining branch possesses a randomly chosen number of arguments; this random choice being made independently for each primitive-defining branch (in the same way as these choices were made for the number of arguments for each `ADF` in chapter 21). Then, for each primitive-defining branch, a random constant (either `T` or `NIL`) is randomly chosen and associated with each of the 2^k possible combinations of the now-known number of arguments, k, of that branch. These random choices are made independently for each of the 2^k possible combinations of arguments. In other words, we construct the last column (the output) of the truth table by randomly inserting the constants `T` or `NIL`.

During the run, structure-preserving crossover with point typing will be performed on the various branches of the overall program. When neither crossover point is in a primitive-defining branch, the structure-preserving crossover proceeds in the same manner as in section 21.2. However, from time to time, one or both crossover points will fall within a primitive-defining branch.

If both crossover points are in primitive-defining branches, then only the terminals in the truth table are non-invariant points. In this case, the crossover operation simply inserts the constant (`T` or `NIL`) residing at the crossover point in the truth table of the contributing parent into the receiving parent (at the point of insertion in its truth table).

Table 22.1 Truth table representing the primitive-defining branch for two-argument PF0 equivalent to NAND.

	ARG1	ARG0	PF0
0	NIL	NIL	T
1	NIL	T	T
2	T	NIL	T
3	T	T	NIL

Table 22.2 Truth table representing the primitive-defining branch for one-argument PF1 equivalent to NOT.

	ARG0	PF1
0	NIL	T
1	T	NIL

Table 22.3 Truth table representing the primitive-defining branch for three-argument PF2 equivalent to (IF ARG0 ARG1 ARG2).

	ARG2	ARG1	ARG0	PF2
0	NIL	NIL	NIL	NIL
1	NIL	NIL	T	NIL
2	NIL	T	NIL	NIL
3	NIL	T	T	T
4	T	NIL	NIL	T
5	T	NIL	T	NIL
6	T	T	NIL	T
7	T	T	T	T

If the crossover point in the contributing parent is in a primitive-defining branch but the crossover point in the receiving parent is not in a primitive-defining branch, then we must consider whether the random constants, $\Re_{Boolean}$, were included in the terminal set of the non-primitive-defining branch involved. For the remainder of this book, the random constants, $\Re_{Boolean}$, will always be included in the terminal sets of all branches. Given that this is the case, point typing then permits a random constant from a primitive-defining branch to be inserted into any branch. Conversely, point typing also permits a random constant (but nothing else) from a non-primitive-defining branch to be inserted as an entry in the truth table of a primitive-defining branch.

If the random constants, $\Re_{Boolean}$, were not included in the terminal sets of the non-primitive-defining branches, then the choice of a crossover point from the contributing parent from within a primitive-defining branch would mandate that the crossover point of the receiving parent be a point lying in one of its primitive-defining branches.

Primitive-defining branches are implemented using a constrained syntactic structure. The following LISP code precisely defines the operation of the two-argument PF0 for NAND shown in table 22.1:

```
1   (defun PF0 (arg0 arg1)
2    (values (IF arg1 (IF arg0 NIL
3                                 T)
4                    (IF arg0 T
5                               T)
6              )
7    )
8   )
```

In this definition for PF0, nested IFs are used to implement the truth table. Line 2, for example, deals with the case where both ARG0 and ARG1 are T and says that PF0 returns NIL for that case.

Figure 22.1 shows the above defun for PF0 as a rooted, point-labeled tree with ordered branches. The points above the upper dotted line (i.e., the defun; the function name, PF0; the argument list, (arg0 arg1); and the values) are the usual invariant points of the constrained syntactic structure common to all function definitions in this book. The six points between the two dotted lines (i.e., the three IFs, the two arg0s, and the one arg1) constitute the invariant points of the constrained syntactic structure for implementing a two-argument truth table. The only variable points in this figure are the four points below the lower dotted line. These four points are the entries of the truth table and correspond to the four Boolean constants (i.e., NIL, T, T, and T) that appear at the far right of lines 2, 3, 4, and 5 of the program above.

The above LISP code and figure precisely specify the operation of this primitive-defining branch. For presentation purposes, the truth table is abbreviated with a function called TRUTH-TABLE as follows:

(TRUTH-TABLE T T T NIL).

This expression is then interpreted as if all of the structure described above were present.

Since the primitive-defining branches are created at random at the initial random generation, there is no guarantee that the particular set of primitive functions belonging to an overall program will be sufficient to solve the problem. The potential insufficiency is automatically dealt with in two ways. First, some individual overall programs in the initial random population may contain a sufficient set of primitive functions. They may consequently be more fit and enjoy a differential advantage in the competitive evolutionary process. Second, the primitive-defining branches are subject to crossover and are therefore subject to modification during the run.

Figure 22.2 shows an illustrative five-branch overall program for the even-5-parity problem. The first branch is a primitive-defining branch PF0 for the one-argument NOT function; the second branch is a primitive-defining branch

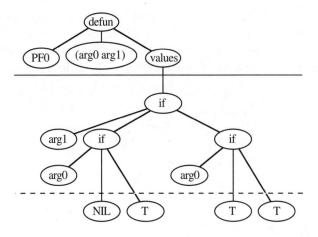

Figure 22.1 Primitive-defining branch PF0 for implementing NAND.

PF1 for the two-argument OR function; and the third branch is a primitive-defining branch PF2 for the two-argument AND function. The fourth branch is a function-defining branch ADF0 for the two-argument odd-2-parity function. Finally, the fifth branch is a result producing branch that invokes ADF0 four times and PF0 once in order to create the even-5-parity function. The points above the upper dotted line (i.e., the defun; the function names, PF0, PF1, PF2, and ADF0; the argument lists, (ARG0), (ARG0 ARG1), (ARG0 ARG1), and (ARG0 ARG1); and the five values functions) are the usual invariant points of the constrained syntactic structure common to all function-defining branches and all result-producing branches in this book. The points between the two dotted lines (i.e., the IFs, the ARG0s, and the ARG1s) constitute the invariant points of the constrained syntactic structure for implementing truth tables. The only noninvariant points associated with PF0, PF1, and PF2 are the ten points below the lower dotted line. The body of ADF0 and the result-producing branch also appear below the lower dotted line for those branches (indicating that they too are noninvariant points).

22.2.   RESULTS FOR THE EVEN-5-PARITY PROBLEM

All of the 14 runs of the even-5-parity problem using the evolutionary method of determining a sufficient set of primitive functions produced a 100%-correct solution (scoring 32 hits) by generation 50.

Table 22.4 shows the wide variation among these 14 solutions in both the number of primitive-defining branches, the number of arguments each PF possesses, the number of function-defining branches, and the number of arguments each automatically defined function possesses. The average number of PFs is 3.00 and the average number of automatically defined functions is 1.43 for the 14 solutions.

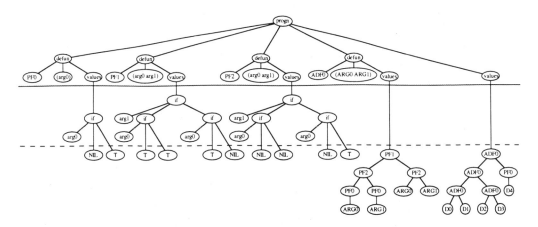

Figure 22.2 Illustrative five-branch overall program with three primitive-defining branches, one function-defining branch, and one result-producing branch.

Table 22.4 Distribution of architectures of the PFs and ADFs of 14 solutions to the even-5-parity problem with evolution of primitives and sufficiency.

Run	Generation when solved	Number of PFs	Argument map for PFs	Number of ADFs	Argument map for ADFs
1	4	3	{2, 3, 1}	1	{1}
2	6	4	{2, 1, 3, 3}	0	{}
3	3	3	{3, 2, 2}	2	{3, 4}
4	1	4	{1, 1, 3, 1}	0	{}
5	2	1	{2}	4	{3, 2, 4, 3}
6	4	3	{3, 1, 3}	1	{3}
7	1	1	{3}	3	{4, 2, 4}
8	7	4	{3, 3, 1, 2}	0	{}
9	10	2	{2, 3}	0	{}
10	7	4	{1, 3, 3, 2}	3	{1, 2, 1}
11	4	3	{3, 3, 1}	3	{2, 4, 3}
12	6	4	{1, 3, 3, 2}	0	{}
13	1	2	{2, 2}	0	{}
14	7	4	{3, 1, 3, 3}	3	{4, 1, 2}

With Defined Functions

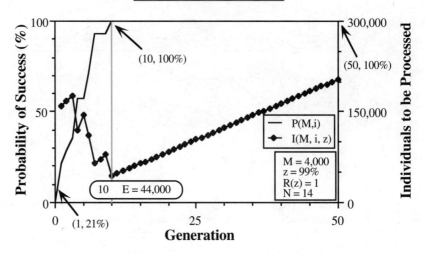

Figure 22.3 Performance curves for the even-5-parity problem showing that E_{with} = 44,000 with evolution of primitives and sufficiency.

The average structural complexity, $\bar{S}_{with}$, of the 100%-correct program from the 14 successful runs (out of 14 runs) of the even-5-parity problem is 156.8 points with evolution of primitives and sufficiency.

Figure 22.3 presents the performance curves based on these 14 runs of the even-5-parity function with evolution of primitives and sufficiency. The cumulative probability of success, $P(M,i)$, is 100% by generation 10. The two numbers in the oval indicate that if this problem is run through to generation 10, processing a total of E_{with} = 44,000 (i.e., 4,000 × 11 generations × 1 run) individuals is sufficient to yield a solution to this problem with 99% probability.

An examination of one of the 14 successful runs illustrates several points about the evolutionary method of determining a sufficient set of primitive functions. 97% of the 4,000 programs from generation 0 of run 1 from table 22.4 score 16 hits (out of 32). The best of generation 0 of this run scores 24 hits and consists of three primitive-defining branches and one function-defining branch. The argument map for the three PFs is {2, 3, 1} and the argument map for the one ADF is {1}.

```
(progn (defun PF0 (ARG0 ARG1)
          (truth-table T T T NIL))
       (defun PF1 (ARG0 ARG1 ARG2)
          (truth-table NIL T T NIL T NIL NIL T))
       (defun PF2 (ARG0)
          (truth-table NIL T))
       (defun ADF0 (ARG0)
          (values (PF2 (PF2 (PF1 (PF1 T ARG0 ARG0) (PF2 T) (PF2
          NIL))))))
       (values (PF1 (PF1 (PF0 (ADF0 D3) (PF2 D3)) (PF0 (PF2 D1)
          (ADF0 D3)) (PF1 (PF1 D1 D1 D0) (PF0 D1 D3) (PF0 D2 D3)))
          (PF1 (PF1 (PF1 NIL D0 D1) (PF1 D0 T D1) (PF0 D3 D0)) (PF0
```

```
(ADF0 NIL) (ADF0 D1)) (PF1 (ADF0 D1) (PF1 D1 D2 D2) (PF1
T D2 D4))) (PF0 (PF2 (PF1 D4 D4 D3)) (ADF0 (PF0 D2
T)))))).
```

In this program the two-argument PF0 is the NAND function (rule 7) and corresponds to the truth table shown in table 22.1. The three-argument PF1 is the odd-3-parity function (rule 150). The one-argument PF2 is the identity function (rule 2).

Although ADF0 contains 11 points and seems to be doing some work, it proves to be the "Always False" function (one-argument Boolean rule 0). In other words, ADF0 has recreated the already-available Boolean constant NIL.

The result-producing branch invokes the "Always False" ADF0 six times, PF0 eight times, PF1 12 times, and the identity function PF2 three times.

The best of generation 1 scores 26 hits. Although there are three primitive-defining branches in this individual, the argument map for the primitive-defining branches is {1, 3, 3} as opposed to {2, 3, 1} for the best of generation 0. Like the best of generation 0, the best of generation 1 has one function-defining branch, but the argument map for its function-defining branch is {3}, instead of {1}.

```
(progn (defun PF0 (ARG0)
          (truth-table NIL NIL))
       (defun PF1 (ARG0 ARG1 ARG2)
          (truth-table NIL NIL NIL T T T T NIL))
       (defun PF2 (ARG0 ARG1 ARG2)
          (truth-table T NIL NIL NIL NIL NIL NIL T))
       (defun ADF0 (ARG0 ARG1 ARG2)
          (values (PF2 (PF1 (PF2 ARG2 ARG2 ARG2) (PF1 ARG2 ARG0
            ARG0) (PF0 ARG0)) (PF1 (PF0 ARG0) (PF1 ARG2 NIL ARG0)
            (PF1 ARG0 ARG2 ARG2)) (PF0 (PF0 ARG1)))))
       (values (PF2 (ADF0 (ADF0 D1 D3 D3) (PF0 D0) (ADF0 D4 D4 T))
          (ADF0 (PF0 NIL) (ADF0 NIL D0 D2) (ADF0 D2 D1 D0)) (PF2
          (PF2 D3 D2 D0) (ADF0 T D2 D0) (PF0 T))))).
```

In this program PF0 is one-argument Boolean rule 0 (i.e., it has recreated the already-available Boolean constant NIL). Here PF1 is the three-argument Boolean rule 120. Three-argument PF2 is rule 129. This program scores better than the best of generation 0 even though it does not have the seemingly valuable odd-3-parity function.

ADF0 is three-argument Boolean rule 165 which is equivalent to

```
(EVEN-2-PARITY ARG0 ARG2).
```

The best of generation 2 scores 28 hits. The three PFs and one ADF are identical to the best of generation 1; however, the result-producing branch has changed to

```
(values (PF2 (ADF0 (ADF0 D1 D3 D3) (PF0 D0) (ADF0 D4 D4 T))
          (ADF0 (PF0 NIL) (ADF0 NIL D0 D2) (ADF0 D2 D1 D0))
          (PF2 (PF2 D3 D2 D0) (PF0 NIL) (PF0 T)))).
```

This 28-scoring program remains the best for generation 3.

The problem is solved on generation 4 by a program scoring 32 hits. Compared to the best of the previous generation, this program has a different argument map for its primitive-defining branches, {2, 3, 1}, and a different argument map for its function-defining branches, {1}. The three PFs and one ADF in this solution are the same as the best of generation 0. This program's 100%-correct performance derives from differences in the result-producing branch from that seen in generation 0:

```
(values (PF1 (PF1 D1 D0 D1)
             (PF1 (PF1 (PF1 NIL D0 D1) (PF1 D0 T D1) (PF0 T D3))
                  (PF0 (ADF0 NIL) (ADF0 D1))
                  (PF1 (ADF0 D1) (PF1 D1 D2 D2) (PF1 T D2 D4)))
             (PF0 (PF2 (PF1 D4 D4 D3)) (ADF0 (PF0 D2 T))))).
```

If we substitute NAND for the four occurrences of PF0, ODD-3-PARITY for the 10 occurrences of PF1, the constant NIL for the four occurrences of ADF0, and delete the one occurrence of PF2 (the one-argument identity function), this result-producing branch becomes

```
(values (ODD-3-PARITY
          (ODD-3-PARITY D1 D0 D1)
          (ODD-3-PARITY (ODD-3-PARITY (ODD-3-PARITY NIL D0 D1)
                                      (ODD-3-PARITY D0 T D1)
                                      (NAND T D3))
                        (NAND NIL NIL)
                        (ODD-3-PARITY NIL
                                      (ODD-3-PARITY D1 D2 D2)
                                      (ODD-3-PARITY T D2 D4)))
          (NAND (ODD-3-PARITY D4 D4 D3) NIL))).
```

This can be further simplified to the following

```
(values (EVEN-2-PARITY
          D0
          (EVEN-2-PARITY
            (ODD-3-PARITY (ODD-3-PARITY D0 D1)
                          (EVEN-2-PARITY D0 D1)
                          (NOT D3))
            (ODD-2-PARITY (ODD-3-PARITY D1 D2 D2)
                          (EVEN-2-PARITY D2 D4))))),
```

which is a composition of ODD-3-PARITY, ODD-2-PARITY and EVEN-2-PARITY functions that correctly mimics the behavior of the even-5-parity function.

Table 22.5 shows, by generation, the characteristics of the best-of-generation programs of run 1 from table 22.4.

Figure 22.4 depicts two three-dimensional trajectories showing, by generation, the number of arguments of the primitive-defining branches and the number of arguments of the function-defining branches in the best-of-generation programs of this run of the even-5-parity problem. The three

Table 22.5 Characteristics of the best of generation program for generations 0 through 4 of run 1 of the even-5-parity problem with evolution of primitives and sufficiency.

Gener-ation	Hits	Number of PFs	Argument map of PFs	Rule number for PF0	Rule number for PF1	Rule number for PF2	Number of ADFs	Argument map of ADFs	Rule num-ber of ADF0	Rule num-ber of ADF1	Rule num-ber of ADF2	Rule num-br of ADF3
0	24	3	{2, 3, 1}	7	150	000	1	{1}	000			
1	26	3	{1, 3, 3}	0	120	129	1	{3}	165			
2	28	3	{1, 3, 3}	0	120	129	1	{3}	165			
3	28	3	{1, 3, 3}	0	120	129	1	{3}	165			
4	32	3	{2, 3, 1}	7	150	000	1	{1}	000			

axes are labeled "F0," "F1," and "F2" and these labels refer to the number of arguments of PF0, PF1, and PF2 in connection with the primitive-defining branches. The first trajectory (shown with a broken line) traces, by generation, the number of arguments of PF0, PF1 (if present), and PF2 (if present). Since the number of primitive-defining branches does not exceed three for this particular run, it is possible to visualize this trajectory using a three-dimensional graph. For generation 0, this first trajectory starts at the point {2, 3, 1} in this three-dimensional space. For generation 1–3, the trajectory goes to the point {1, 3, 3}. For generation 4, the trajectory returns to the point {2, 3, 1}.

The second trajectory (shown with a solid line in figure 22.4) traces, by generation, the number of arguments of ADF0, ADF1 (if present), and ADF2 (if present). We can similarly visualize this trajectory provided the number of function-defining branches does not exceed three (as is the case for this run). The three labels F0, F1, and F2 refer to ADF0, ADF1, and ADF2 in connection with the solid line representing the function-defining branches. The values of F1 and F2 are zero for generations 0–4 of this run. This second trajectory starts with a value for ADF0 of 1 for generation 0. The trajectory goes to a value for ADF0 of 3 for generations 1–3, and returns to a value for ADF0 of 1 for generation 4.

Figure 22.5 depicts two three-dimensional trajectories, by generation, showing the raw fitness (hits) and the number of primitive-defining branches and function-defining branches in the best-of-generation programs of this run. The axis labeled "branches" refers to both the number of primitive-defining branches and the number of function-defining branches. The first trajectory (shown with a broken line) traces, by generation, the number of primitive-defining branches. As it happens, the number of primitive-defining branches is three for generations 0–4 of this particular run. The second trajectory (shown with a solid line) traces, by generation, the number of function-defining branches which is 1 for generations 0 through 4 of this run.

Figure 22.6 is a three-dimensional histogram for run 1 of the even-5-parity problem with evolution of primitives and sufficiency. This histogram

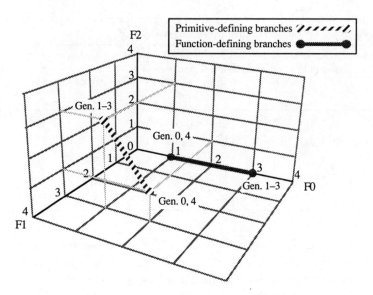

Figure 22.4 Argument trajectory of the number of arguments of the primitive-defining branches and the number of arguments of the function-defining branches between generations 0 and 4 for the best-of-generation programs of run 1 of the even-5-parity problem with evolution of primitives and sufficiency.

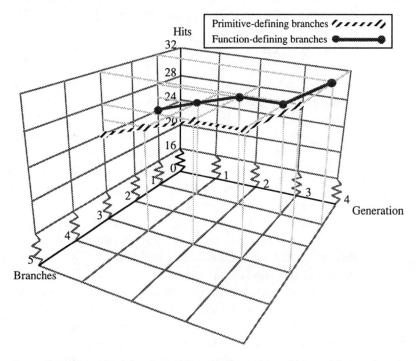

Figure 22.5 Fitness-branch trajectory showing the number of hits and the number of primitive-defining branches and the number of function-defining branches between generations 0 and 4 for the best-of-generation programs of run 1 of the even-5-parity problem with evolution of primitives and sufficiency.

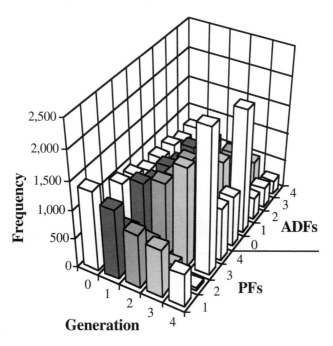

Figure 22.6 Branch histogram between generations 0 and 4 of the number of programs in the population with various numbers of primitive-defining branches and function-defining branches for run 1 of the even-5-parity problem with evolution of primitives and sufficiency.

shows, by generation, the number of programs in the population of 4,000 with a specified number of primitive-defining branches (from 1 to 3) and a specified number of function-defining branches (from 0 to 4). As can be seen, there is approximate equality at generation 0 in the number of programs with one, two, and three primitive-defining branches and with zero, one, two, three, and four function-defining branches. However, by generation 4, the most common configuration has three primitive-defining branches and one function-defining branch.

Table 22.6 shows, in its first two columns, the run number and the argument map of the primitive-defining branches for the 14 solutions to the even-5-parity problem with evolution of primitives and sufficiency. Each of the next four pairs of columns relates to each of the four possible PFs that appear in that solution. The Boolean rule number appears in the first column of each such pair. If the rule is a parity rule of any kind, the second column of each pair identifies the parity function.

Table 22.7 shows, in its first two columns, the run number and the argument map of the function-defining branches for the 14 solutions to the even-5-parity problem with evolution of primitives and sufficiency. Each of the next four pairs of columns relates to each of the four possible ADFs that appear in that solution in the same manner as the previous table.

Table 22.6 Characteristics of the PFs of 14 solutions to the even-5-parity problem with evolution of primitives and sufficiency.

Run	Argument map for	Rule number for PF0	Is PF0 a parity rule?	Rule number for PF1	Is PF1 a parity rule?
1	{2, 3, 1}	7	No	150	Yes
2	{2, 1, 3, 3}	9	(EVEN-2-PARITY ARG0 ARG1)	3	No
3	{3, 2, 2}	124	No	5	No
4	{1, 1, 3, 1}	1	No	1	No
5	{2}	6	(ODD-2-PARITY ARG0 ARG1)		
6	{3, 1, 3}	150	(ODD-3-PARITY ARG0 ARG1 ARG2)	1	No
7	{3}	90	(ODD-2-PARITY ARG0 ARG2)		
8	{3, 3, 1, 2}	214	No	90	(ODD-2-PARITY ARG0 ARG2)
9	{2, 3}	7	No	129	No
10	{1, 3, 3, 2}	1	No	57	No
11	{3, 3, 1}	36	No	150	(ODD-3-PARITY ARG0 ARG1 ARG2)
12	{1, 3, 3, 2}	3	No	162	No
13	{2, 2}	0	No	9	(EVEN-2-PARITY ARG0 ARG1)
14	{3, 1, 3, 3}	176	No	0	No

Run	Rule number for PF2	Is PF2 a parity rule?	Rule number for PF3	Is PF3 a pairty rule?
1	0	No		
2	57	No	177	No
3	9	(EVEN-2-PARITY ARG0 ARG1)		
4	105	(EVEN-2-PARITY ARG0 ARG1 ARG2)		
5				
6	108	No		
7				
8	1	No	10	No
9				
10	154	No	10	No
11	2	No		
12	05	(EVEN-3-PARITY ARG0 ARG1 ARG2)	15	No
13				
14	94	No	156	No

Table 22.7 Characteristics of the ADFs of 14 solutions to the even-5-parity problem with evolution of primitives and sufficiency.

Run	Argument map for ADFs	Rule number for ADF0	Is ADF0 a parity rule?	Rule number for ADF1	Is ADF1 a parity rule?
1	{1}	0	No		
2	{}				
3	{3, 4}	170	No	38505	(EVEN-4-PARITY ARG0 ARG1 ARG2 ARG3))
4	{}				
5	{3, 2, 4, 3}	195	(EVEN-2-PARITY ARG1 ARG2))	5	No
6	{3}	123	No		
7	{4, 2, 4}	118	No	9	(EVEN-2-PARITY ARG0 ARG1)
8	{}				
9	{}				
10	{1, 2, 1}	0	No	10	No
11	{2, 4, 3}	10	No	0	No
12	{}				
13	{}				
14	{4, 1, 2}	13,107	No	0	No

Run	Rule number for ADF2	Is ADF2 a parity rule?	Rule number for ADF3	Is ADF3 a pairty rule?
1				
2				
3				
4				
5	39270	(ODD-3-PARITY ARG0 ARG1 ARG3)	165	(EVEN-2-PARITY ARG0 ARG2))
6				
7	54,191	No		
8				
9				
10	2	No		
11	0	No		
12				
13				
14	0	No		

22.3 Results for the Boolean 6-Multiplexer Problem

The inputs to the Boolean *N-multiplexer* function consist of k *address bits* a_i and 2^k *data bits* d_i, where $N = k + 2^k$. That is,

$$a_{k-1}, \ldots, a_1, a_0, \ d_{2^k-1}, \ldots, d_1, \ d_0.$$

Its output is the Boolean value of the particular data bit that is singled out by the k address bits of the multiplexer. For example, if the two address bits, a_1 and a_0, of a Boolean 6-multiplexer (where $k = 2$) are 1 and 0, respectively, the multiplexer singles out data bit d_2 (out of the 4) to be the output of the multiplexer because $10_2 = 2$. For example, for an input of 100100, the output of the multiplexer is 1; for an input of 101011, the output of the multiplexer is 0.

Genetic programming can, of course, solve the problem of symbolic regression of the 6-multiplexer function using a computationally complete set of primitive functions such as

$$\mathcal{F}_1 = \{\text{AND}, \text{OR}, \text{NOT}\}.$$

However, the solution to a higher-order multiplexer problem is facilitated (*Genetic Programming*, subsection 24.3.1) when the function IF is added to $\mathcal{F}_1$ so that the set of primitive functions becomes

$$\mathcal{F}_2 = \{\text{IF}, \text{AND}, \text{OR}, \text{NOT}\}.$$

The reason for the improved performance by generation with $\mathcal{F}_2$ versus $\mathcal{F}_1$ is that a higher-order Boolean multiplexer function can very naturally be decomposed into lower-order multiplexers. The three-argument IF function is the lowest-order multiplexer.

For example, the 6-multiplexer problem can be decomposed into three instances of the 3-multiplexer subproblem. The 6-multiplexer is equivalent to

```
(3-MULTIPLEXER A1 (3-MULTIPLEXER A0 D3 D2)
               (3-MULTIPLEXER A0 D1 D0)),
```

or, as it would more commonly be written,

```
(IF A1 (IF A0 D3 D2) (IF A0 D1 D0)).
```

Thus, the IF function is especially useful in solving a higher-order multiplexer problem.

Figure 22.7 shows this decomposition.

Suppose that we do not know what set of primitive functions is sufficient (or helpful) in solving the problem of symbolic regression of the Boolean multiplexer or, for some reason, did not want to make the decision of choosing the set of primitive functions for this problem. Genetic programming can, in fact, evolve a sufficient set of primitive functions for the multiplexer problem at the same time as it solves the problem and evolves the architecture of the overall program.

In one run of the 6-multiplexer problem, the best of generation 0 scores 46 (out of 64) hits and has an argument map of {2, 3} for its primitive-defining

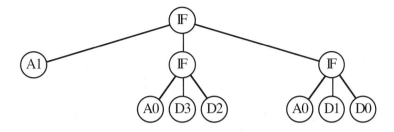

Figure 22.7 Decomposition of the 6-multiplexer function into three calls to the 3-multiplexer (IF) function.

branches and the empty argument map of {} for its function-defining branches (i.e., it has no ADFs).

```
(progn (defun PF0 (ARG0 ARG1)
          (truth-table T NIL NIL NIL))
       (defun PF1 (ARG0 ARG1 ARG2)
          (truth-table T NIL NIL NIL T T NIL NIL))
       (values (PF0 (PF1 D5 D1 D0) (PF0 D4 D2)))).
```

In this program PF0 is the two-argument NOR function and PF1 is three-argument Boolean rule 49. NOR alone is, of course, computationally complete.

The following 100%-correct program with an argument map of {1, 1, 3} for its primitive-defining branches and an argument map of {} for its function-defining branches emerged on generation 14 of this run:

```
(progn (defun PF0 (ARG0)
          (truth-table T NIL))
       (defun PF1 (ARG0)
          (truth-table NIL T))
       (defun PF2 (ARG0 ARG1 ARG2)
          (truth-table T T NIL NIL T NIL T NIL))
       (values (PF0 (PF2 (PF0 (PF2 D3 D1 D5)) (PF0 (PF2 (PF0 (PF2
          D3 D0 D5)) (PF0 (PF2 D1 D2 D4)) (PF2 (PF2 D4 D0 D5) D5
          (PF2 D0 D2 D5)))) D4)))).
```

Here, PF0 is the one-argument NOT function and PF1 is the one-argument identity function.

Table 22.8 is a truth table for PF2 which is equivalent to three-argument rule 83 and (IF ARG2 (NOT ARG0) (NOT ARG1)). This doubly negative IF rule, in conjunction with NOT, enables the result-producing branch to produce the desired behavior of the 6-multiplexer function.

In a second run, a solution emerged on generation 20 with an argument map of {3, 2} for its primitive-defining branches and an argument map of {4} for its function-defining branches. Since this solution occupies an entire page, we do not show it here. However, the important point is that PF0 in this solution is the familiar three-argument IF function (rule 216) shown in table 22.3. In addition, PF1 is the two-argument NOR function and ADF0 is four-argument rule 29,490.

Table 22.8 Truth table representing the primitive-defining branch for three-argument PF2 equivalent to (IF ARG2 (NOT ARG0) (NOT ARG1)).

	ARG2	ARG1	ARG0	PF2
0	NIL	NIL	NIL	T
1	NIL	NIL	T	T
2	NIL	T	NIL	NIL
3	NIL	T	T	NIL
4	T	NIL	NIL	T
5	T	NIL	T	NIL
6	T	T	NIL	T
7	T	T	T	NIL

Thus, in both runs, some variant of the IF function evolved in one of the primitive-defining branches of the solution to the 6-multiplexer problem. It is, of course, possible to represent the multiplexer function without the IF function. However, this convergence apparently occurs because the IF function is inherently so useful and helpful in constructing the behavior of a multiplexer.

22.4 RESULTS FOR A SINGLE PRIMITIVE FUNCTION

In the foregoing two sections, we allowed genetic programming to dynamically discover the number of primitive-defining branches. Suppose, however, that we are specifically interested in discovering a single primitive function that is sufficient to solve a problem (assuming this is possible for the problem domain involved).

Genetic programming may be used to solve the problem of identifying a single primitive function sufficient to solve a given problem by restricting the number of primitive functions to exactly one and then proceeding in the same manner as the previous section.

The number of arguments possessed by the single primitive-defining branch is not predetermined (unless that, too, is a goal of the effort). In any event, the number of function-defining branches and the number of arguments they each possess is not predetermined.

22.4.1 Boolean 6-Multiplexer Problem

In one run of the 6-multiplexer problem, the following 100%-correct solution employing exactly one PF emerged in generation 11:

```
(progn (defun PF0 (ARG0 ARG1 ARG2)
         (truth-table NIL NIL NIL T T NIL T T))
       (defun ADF0 (ARG0)
         (values (PF0 T ARG0 ARG0))))
```

```
(defun ADF1 (ARG0 ARG1 ARG2 ARG3)
  (values (PF0 T ARG1 NIL)))
(values (PF0 (PF0 T D4 D5) (PF0 (PF0 D0 D4 D4) (PF0 D5 D3
  D1) (PF0 D5 D2 D0)) (PF0 D5 D2 D0)))).
```

In this program PF0 is (IF D0 D1 D2). Indeed, as previously discussed, we would expect some variant of the IF function to emerge as the single building block for constructing the multiplexer function.

22.4.2   Even-5-Parity Problem

In two runs of the even-5-parity problem (out of three runs made), a 100%-correct solution employing exactly one PF emerged wherein the lone PF possesses two arguments and is equivalent to EVEN-2-PARITY (two-argument rule 9).

In contrast, in the third run, a corpulent 100%-correct solution employing exactly one PF emerged in generation 2. In this solution, the single PF possesses three arguments and is equivalent to rule 103. Rule 103 is not a parity rule. The result-producing branch, in conjunction with this program's ADF, produce the desired behavior of the even-5-parity function.

Evolutionary Selection of Terminals

The first preparatory step in applying genetic programming to a problem is to determine the set of terminals from which the yet-to-be-evolved programs will be composed.

In order to evolve a computer program capable of producing the desired output for a given problem, it is necessary to have access to a set of inputs that are at least a superset of the inputs necessary to solve the problem (that is, the terminals must be sufficient for the problem). For example, if one is trying to evolve a model for the quarterly price level of an economy, it may be necessary to have access to independent variables such as the quarterly gross national product and the quarterly money supply of the economy (since these variables suffice to establish the price level). The yields of three-month U.S. Treasury Bills is not correlated to the price level of the economy. However, given the gross national product, the money supply, and the short-term T-bill yields, genetic programming is capable of evolving the well-known econometric exchange equation for the price level of the economy by identifying and using the subset of inputs that are relevant to the problem (*Genetic Programming*, sections 10.3 and 24.1) while ignoring rainfall.

The question arises as to whether it is possible for genetic programming to evolve the terminal set of a problem (in the sense of enabling genetic programming to select the inputs of the yet-to-be evolved program from a sufficient superset of available inputs) during a run at the same time that genetic programming is evolving a sufficient set of primitive functions, evolving the architecture, and solving the problem.

In this chapter we demonstrate that genetic programming can, in fact, evolve a terminal set in the above sense. The techniques of chapter 21 involving structure-preserving crossover with point typing are used to accomplish this.

23.1 PREPARATORY STEPS

A terminal set containing the five actual variables, D0, D1, D2, D3, and D4, is sufficient to solve the even-5-parity problem. In the absence of one or more of these five relevant variables, genetic programming cannot compose a 100%-correct computer program to perform the behavior of the even-5-parity function. However, suppose the terminal set were enlarged and became the superset

$T_1 = \{$NOISE, D0, D1, D2, D3, D4, $\Re_{\text{Boolean}}\}$,

NOISE is an extraneous noise variable that is not correlated in any way to the five actual variables of the problem (i.e., D0, D1, D2, D3, and D4) or to the value of the even-5-parity function associated with these five actual variables. On each instance when the terminal NOISE is encountered in any branch of any program, NOISE is randomly set to either T or NIL by a call to a randomizer. The random choice for the value of NOISE is made independently and anew on each instance when NOISE is encountered.

As before, $\Re_{\text{Boolean}}$ is the random Boolean constant ranging over the values T and NIL.

A population size of 4,000 and the techniques of structure-preserving crossover with point typing (chapter 21) are used throughout this chapter.

23.2 RESULTS FOR THE EVEN-5-PARITY PROBLEM

The fitness of a program in the even-5-parity problem is the sum, over the 32 fitness cases, of the errors between the value returned by the program and the correct value of the even-5-parity function for that fitness case. If NOISE is present in a part of a program that contributes to the eventual value returned by the program for a fitness case, the effect is usually that the value returned is not correlated to the correct value of the target even-5-parity function for that fitness case.

In one run, 85% of the programs in generation 0 had a fitness of 16 and an additional 7% of the programs had a fitness of either 15 or 17.

In generation 0 of one run of the even-5-parity problem with the noise variable, the best of generation 0 scores 23 hits (out of 32) and has an argument map for its primitive-defining branches of {3} and an argument map for its function-defining branches of {2, 1}. PF0 is three-argument rule 85; ADF0 is two-argument rule 10; ADF1 is one-argument rule 1 (NOT); and the result-producing branch contains one reference to NOISE.

Between generations 1 and 7, the number of hits for the best-of-generation program is 25, 27, 28, 28, 30, 30, and 30 and the number of occurrences of NOISE in the best-of-generation programs is 5, 3, 3, 5, 1, 3, and 3.

On generation 8, the following 100%-correct program emerged with an argument map for its primitive-defining branches of {3} and an argument map for its function-defining branches of {}:

```
(progn (defun PF0 (ARG0 ARG1 ARG2)
          (truth-table NIL NIL T T T NIL NIL NIL))
       (values (PF0 (PF0 (PF0 NOISE D3 D0) (PF0 D2 D4 D0)
          (PF0 D2 D4 D0)) (PF0 D0 D0 D4) (PF0 (PF0 D3 D0 D3)
          (PF0 NIL T D3) (PF0 NIL D2 D1)))))).
```

Even in this 100%-correct program, NOISE appears once (in boldface) in the result-producing branch.

In this program, PF0 is rule 28. When the entire program is rewritten by expanding rule 28 and, for convenience, using NOT, EVEN-2-PARITY, and ODD-2-PARITY, it becomes

```
(OR (AND (NOT (OR (AND (EVEN-2-PARITY d1 d2) (NOT D3))
                  (AND (ODD-2-PARITY d1 d2) d3)))
         (ODD-2-PARITY d0 d4))
    (AND (OR (AND (EVEN-2-PARITY d1 d2) (NOT D3))
             (AND (ODD-2-PARITY d1 d2) d3))
         (NOT (OR (AND (OR (AND (NOT D0) D4)
                           (AND D0 (NOT (OR D2 D4))))
                       (NOT (OR (OR (AND (NOT D0) D3)
                                    (AND D0
                                         (NOT (OR NOISE D3)))))
                            (OR (AND (NOT D0) D4)
                                (AND D0
                                     (NOT (OR D2 D4)))))))
         (ODD-2-PARITY d0 d4))))).
```

The entire section in boldface above (containing NOISE) is equivalent to NIL, so this expression can be simplified to

```
(OR (AND (NOT (OR (AND (EVEN-2-PARITY D1 D2) (NOT D3))
                  (AND (ODD-2-PARITY D1 D2) D3)))
         (ODD-2-PARITY D0 D4))
    (AND (OR (AND (EVEN-2-PARITY D1 D2) (NOT D3))
             (AND (ODD-2-PARITY D1 D2) D3))
         (EVEN-2-PARITY D0 D4))),
```

which, in turn, is equivalent to the even-5-parity function.

24 Evolution of Closure

Every function in the function sets of all the foregoing problems in this book has satisifed the closure requirement in that it been able to accept, as its arguments, any value that it may possibly encounter as the return value of any function in the function set and any value that it may possibly encounter as the value of any terminal in the terminal set. This closure requirement has previously been identified (section 2.3) as being desirable when applying genetic programming to a problem. All automatically defined functions herein have also satisfied the closure requirement.

In chapter 22, we saw that it is possible to evolve a set of primitive functions (in terms of a yet more elementary representation). Chapter 23 shows that it is possible to evolve a set of terminals (from a sufficient superset of terminals).

The question arises as to whether it is possible for genetic programming to discover solutions to problems in the absence of a prior guarantee that the closure requirement is satisfied. That is, can closure be dynamically achieved during a run at the same time that genetic programming is simultaneously evolving a sufficient set of primitive functions, evolving the architecture of the overall program, and solving the problem. This question is answered in the affirmative in this chapter.

We use the Boolean even-4- and 5-parity problems to illustrate this process.

24.1 UNDEFINED VALUES

When the primitive-defining branches are created for the initial random generation, the set of possible entries in the truth tables is expanded from NIL and T to the following three possibilities:

{NIL, T, :UNDEFINED},

where :UNDEFINED denotes an undefined value.

In defining a primitive function, it is necessary to specify a return value for every combination of arguments to the PF. When one (or more) arguments to a PF can be :UNDEFINED, it becomes necessary to specify the value that the PF returns in that situation.

Table 24.1 presents the definition in the form of a truth table of the two-argument OR function whose arguments can assume the values NIL, T, or :UNDEFINED. Since either or both arguments (arg0 or arg1) can each assume one of three possible values, the truth table has nine rows. The function returns NIL or T for the four rows of the truth table for which both arg0 and arg1 assume the values NIL or T; however, the function returns :UNDEFINED for the five rows for which one or both of its arguments are :UNDEFINED.

In defining an automatically defined function, it is necessary to specify a return value for every combination of arguments to the ADF. When an argument to an ADF can assume the value :UNDEFINED, it is necessary to specify the value that the function should return when any of its arguments are undefined.

An ADF is a composition of PFs, ADFs, and terminals. The root of an ADF here is always a PF or an ADF. The reasons for this are that our conventions require that the root of each branch of a program in the initial random generation be a function and that our conventions require that the crossover fragment cannot be a terminal if the root of a branch is chosen as the point of insertion.

24.2 PREPARATORY STEPS

When the result-producing branch returns :UNDEFINED, the fitness measure must penalize the undefined value. Whether the penalty is moderate or severe is a matter of choice. For simplicity in this discussion, we will choose a severe penalty such that if, during the evaluation of the fitness of a program, :UNDEFINED is returned for any fitness case, the fitness of the program is worse than the worst possible value of fitness for a program whose value is defined for every fitness case. For the even-4-parity problem, standardized fitness ordinarily varies between 0 and 16, with 16 being the worst. Thus, the fitness of a program that returns :UNDEFINED for any fitness case should be at least 17. To provide additional information for analysis purposes, we decided to increment standardized fitness by 17 for each fitness case for which the program returns :UNDEFINED. Thus, a program with one :UNDEFINED fitness case has a standardized fitness of 17 plus whatever contribution comes from the other 15 fitness cases; a program with 16 :UNDEFINED fitness cases has a standardized fitness of 272. All of these values (between 17 and 272) are worse than the worst possible value (16) of fitness for a program whose value is defined, but wrong, for every fitness case. Since tournament selection is the default method of selection for both parents in this book (appendix D), the effect is that a program with as few as one :UNDEFINED fitness case never wins a tournament with a program whose standardized fitness varies between 0 and 16. Occasionally, when the operation being performed is reproduction and when a tournament consists of a group of seven programs each with a standardized fitness of 17 or worse, the program that is

Table 24.1 Nine-row truth table for the primitive-defining branch PF0 for the two-argument OR function whose arguments may assume the values NIL, T, or :UNDEFINED.

	ARG1	ARG0	PF0
0	NIL	NIL	NIL
1	NIL	T	T
2	NIL	:UNDEFINED	:UNDEFINED
3	T	NIL	T
4	T	T	T
5	T	:UNDEFINED	:UNDEFINED
6	:UNDEFINED	NIL	:UNDEFINED
7	:UNDEFINED	T	:UNDEFINED
8	:UNDEFINED	:UNDEFINED	:UNDEFINED

copied into the next generation will have a standardized fitness of 17 or worse. Such a program will, of course, have a very low probability of remaining in the population thereafter. Thus, even if the initial random population contains numerous primitive-defining branches that do not satisfy the closure requirement, genetic programming should rather rapidly select in favor primitive-defining branches that do satisfy the closure requirement.

A population size of 4,000 is used throughout this chapter. The function sets and terminal sets for the function-defining branches and the result-producing branches are the same as in chapter 23, except that the random constants, $\Re_{\text{ternary}}$, ranging over the values T, NIL, and :UNDEFINED are used. The techniques of structure-preserving crossover with point typing (chapter 21) are used throughout this chapter.

24.3 RESULTS FOR THE EVEN-4-PARITY PROBLEM

As one would expect, many of the primitive-defining branches in the initial random generation do not satisfy the closure requirement. In fact, in one run, 21% of the overall programs return :UNDEFINED for all 16 fitness cases and have a standardized fitness of 272. An additional 31% return :UNDEFINED for between one and 15 of the 16 fitness cases. However, 48% of the programs in the initial random population satisfy the closure requirement for all 16 fitness cases.

The median program from generation 0 of run 1 scores 41, has {2, 2, 1, 1} as the argument map for its four primitive-defining branches, and has {4, 2, 3, 4} as the argument map for its four function-defining branches.

The best of generation 0 of run 1 (shown below) has a standardized fitness of 4 (i.e., scores 12 out of 16 hits), has an argument map of {2, 2} for its primitive-defining branches, and has an argument map of {1} for its function-defining branch.

```
(progn (defun PF0 (ARG0 ARG1)
          (truth-table T :UNDEFINED :UNDEFINED :UNDEFINED T
            NIL NIL NIL NIL))
       (defun PF1 (ARG0 ARG1)
          (truth-table :UNDEFINED T NIL T NIL :UNDEFINED T NIL
            :UNDEFINED))
       (defun ADF0 (ARG0)
          (values (PF0 (PF0 ARG0 :UNDEFINED) (PF0 T
            :UNDEFINED))))
       (values (PF0 (PF0 D0 D2) (PF0 D3 D1))))).
```

In this program PF0 appears in the result-producing branch, but PF1 and ADF0 do not.

Table 24.2 shows the truth table for PF0 from the best of generation 0 of run 1.

The fact that three of the nine rows of the truth table for PF0 contain :UNDEFINED seems highly unfavorable; however, the result-producing branch of the best of generation 0 contains only the terminals D0, D1, D2, and D3 and does not contain any occurrences of the random constant :UNDEFINED. Thus, we need not be concerned about the :UNDEFINED value appearing in row 2 of the truth table. In fact, the two inner PF0s in the result-producing branch return either T or :UNDEFINED, but never NIL. The two inner PF0s of the result-producing branch each return T whenever their two arguments agree (rows 0 and 4), so the outer PF0 returns T (from row 4) whenever D0 matches D2, and D3 matches D1. Thus, for a few fitness cases, the result-producing branch has the behavior of the even-4-parity function. The two inner PFs of the result-producing branch each return :UNDEFINED (rows 1 and 3) whenever their two arguments disagree. The outer PF0 can return NIL (from row 8) if both inner PFs return :UNDEFINED or it can return NIL (from rows 5 or 7) if exactly one inner PF returns :UNDEFINED. Thus, this particular program from generation 0 never returns :UNDEFINED and its behavior bears some resemblance to the target even-4-parity function.

Table 24.2 Nine-row truth table for two-argument PF0 from the best of generation 0 of run 1 of the even-4-parity problem.

	ARG1	ARG0	PF0
0	NIL	NIL	T
1	NIL	T	:UNDEFINED
2	NIL	:UNDEFINED	:UNDEFINED
3	T	NIL	:UNDEFINED
4	T	T	T
5	T	:UNDEFINED	NIL
6	:UNDEFINED	NIL	NIL
7	:UNDEFINED	T	NIL
8	:UNDEFINED	:UNDEFINED	NIL

We now consider a second run.

In generation 4, the following 100%-correct program emerges with an argument map of {2, 1} for its two primitive-defining branches and an argument map of {4, 2, 2, 2} for its four function-defining branches:

```
(progn (defun PF0 (ARG0 ARG1)
          (truth-table T NIL NIL NIL T T :UNDEFINED :UNDEFINED
           :UNDEFINED))
       (defun PF1 (ARG0)
         (truth-table :UNDEFINED NIL :UNDEFINED))
       (defun ADF0 (ARG0 ARG1 ARG2 ARG3)
         (values (PF1 (PF0 (PF1 ARG0) (PF0 ARG1 ARG1)))))
       (defun ADF1 (ARG0 ARG1)
         (values (PF0 NIL ARG0)))
       (defun ADF2 (ARG0 ARG1)
         (values (PF0 (PF0 (PF0 ARG0 NIL) (PF0 NIL ARG1))
           (PF0 (PF0 ARG1 ARG0) (PF0 ARG0 ARG0)))))
       (defun ADF3 (ARG0 ARG1)
         (values (ADF1 (ADF1 (ADF2 ARG0 ARG1) (PF1 ARG0))
           (PF0 (PF0 NIL NIL) (PF1 ARG0)))))
       (values (PF0 (PF0 D2 D3) (PF0 D1 D0)))).
```

In this program PF0 (but no ADF0s) appear in the result-producing branch. Table 24.3 shows the definition of PF0 for the result-producing branch of this best-of-run program from generation 4.

Here PF0 returns :UNDEFINED only when its first argument is :UNDEFINED. When both of its arguments are defined, this new PF0 is equivalent to the EVEN-2-PARITY function. Since the result-producing branch contains only the four actual variables of the problem (D0, D1, D2, and D3) and does not contain any occurrences of the random constant :UNDEFINED, the result-producing branch becomes

```
(EVEN-2-PARITY (EVEN-2-PARITY D2 D3) (EVEN-2-PARITY D1 D0)),
```

which, in turn, is equivalent to the even-4-parity function.

Table 24.3 Nine-row truth table for two-argument PF0 from the solution from generation 4 of run 1 of the even-4-parity problem.

	ARG1	ARG0	PF0
0	NIL	NIL	T
1	NIL	T	NIL
2	NIL	:UNDEFINED	NIL
3	T	NIL	NIL
4	T	T	T
5	T	:UNDEFINED	T
6	:UNDEFINED	NIL	:UNDEFINED
7	:UNDEFINED	T	:UNDEFINED
8	:UNDEFINED	:UNDEFINED	:UNDEFINED

In generation 7 of run 2, the following 100%-correct program emerges with an argument map of {2} for its one primitive-defining branch and an argument map of {2, 4, 2} for its three function-defining branches:

```
(progn (defun PF0 (ARG0 ARG1)
          (truth-table T NIL NIL :UNDEFINED T NIL T NIL :UNDE-
            FINED))
       (defun ADF0 (ARG0 ARG1)
          (values (PF0 (PF0 (PF0 (PF0 T ARG1) (PF0 ARG0 T)) (PF0
            (PF0 :UNDEFINED ARG1) (PF0 ARG1 ARG1))) (PF0 (PF0
              (PF0 :UNDEFINED ARG1) (PF0 ARG1 ARG0)) (PF0 (PF0 NIL
            ARG0) (PF0 ARG0 ARG1))))))
       (defun ADF1 (ARG0 ARG1 ARG2 ARG3)
          (values (ADF0 ARG1 T)))
       (defun ADF2 (ARG0 ARG1)
          (values (PF0 (ADF1 (ADF1 (ADF1 ARG1 ARG1 ARG1 ARG1)
            (ADF0 ARG1 ARG1) (ADF0 ARG1 ARG1) (ADF0 ARG1 T))
            (PF0 (ADF1 ARG1 :UNDEFINED NIL ARG0) (ADF0 ARG0
            :UNDEFINED)) (ADF0 (PF0 ARG1 ARG1) (PF0 T :UNDE-
            FINED)) (PF0 (ADF1 ARG0 ARG1 ARG0 :UNDEFINED) (PF0
            NIL ARG1))) (ADF0 NIL (ADF1 (ADF0 T :UNDEFINED)
            (ADF0 ARG0 ARG1) (PF0 ARG1 ARG0) (ADF0 ARG1 T))))))
       (values (ADF0 (ADF0 (ADF0 (ADF2 D1 D3) (PF0 NIL D2))
         (ADF1 (ADF1 D3 D1 T D1) (ADF1 T D1 D1 D2) T (ADF0 D2
         NIL))) (ADF0 (ADF0 (ADF1 D1 :UNDEFINED D1 D0) (ADF2 D3
         D0)) (ADF2 (ADF2 D3 D0) (PF0 :UNDEFINED D1)))))).
```

In this program PF0, ADF0, ADF1, and ADF2, along with the random constants NIL, T, and :UNDEFINED all appear in the result-producing branch. Moreover, :UNDEFINED appears twice in the definition of PF0, as shown in table 24.4. Nonetheless, the result-producing branch never

Table 24.4   Truth table for two-argument PF0 from the best-of-run program from generation 7 of run 2.

	ARG1	ARG0	PF0
0	NIL	NIL	T
1	NIL	T	NIL
2	NIL	:UNDEFINED	NIL
3	T	NIL	:UNDEFINED
4	T	T	T
5	T	:UNDEFINED	NIL
6	:UNDEFINED	NIL	T
7	:UNDEFINED	T	NIL
8	:UNDEFINED	:UNDEFINED	:UNDEFINED

returns :UNDEFINED and has the desired behavior of the target even-4-parity function.

24.4 RESULTS FOR THE EVEN-5-PARITY PROBLEM

This section considers the even-5-parity problem using the evolutionary method of determining the architecture, a sufficient set of primitive functions, and closure.

The best of generation 0 of one run scores 17 hits (out of 32), has {1, 2} as the argument map for its two primitive-defining branches, and has {2} as the argument map for its one function-defining branch.

On generation 27, the following 100%-correct program scores 32 hits, has {1, 2} as the argument map for its two primitive-defining branches, and has {3, 4, 4} as the argument map for its three function-defining branches:

```
(progn (defun PF0 (ARG0)
          (truth-table T :UNDEFINED T))
        (defun PF1 (ARG0 ARG1)
          (truth-table NIL NIL :UNDEFINED T :UNDEFINED NIL NIL T
           NIL))
        (defun ADF0 (ARG0 ARG1 ARG2)
          (values (PF1 (PF0 NIL) (PF1 (PF0 ARG2) (PF1 NIL
           ARG1)))))
        (defun ADF1 (ARG0 ARG1 ARG2 ARG3)
          (values (PF1 (PF1 (PF1 ARG0 ARG3) (ADF0 ARG0 ARG0
           ARG2)) (PF0 T))))
        (defun ADF2 (ARG0 ARG1 ARG2 ARG3)
          (values (ADF0 (PF1 (PF0 ARG2) (PF0 T)) (PF0 (PF0 (PF0
           T))) (PF1 (PF0 (PF1 ARG0 ARG0)) (PF1 (PF0 ARG2) (PF1
           ARG1 :UNDEFINED))))))
        (values (ADF1 (PF1 (PF1 (ADF0 D2 NIL NIL) (PF1 (ADF0 D2
         NIL NIL) (ADF2 D3 D4 D4 D3))) D1) (PF1 (PF1 (ADF2 T D0
         D4 NIL) (ADF2 D3 D4 D4 D3)) (ADF1 D4 NIL D1 D4)) (PF1
         (ADF2 T D0 D3 NIL) (PF1 (ADF2 D3 D2 D4 :UNDEFINED)
         (PF0 (PF0 T)))) (PF1 (ADF0 :UNDEFINED NIL NIL) (ADF2
         D3 D4 D4 D3))))).
```

Table 24.5 Three-row truth table for one-argument PF0 from the solution from generation 27 of the even-5-parity problem.

	ARG0	PF0
0	NIL	T
1	T	:UNDEFINED
2	:UNDEFINED	T

Table 24.6   Nine-row truth table for two-argument PF1 from the solution from generation 27 of the even-5-parity problem.

	ARG1	ARG0	PF0
0	NIL	NIL	NIL
1	NIL	T	NIL
2	NIL	:UNDEFINED	:UNDEFINED
3	T	NIL	T
4	T	T	:UNDEFINED
5	T	:UNDEFINED	NIL
6	:UNDEFINED	NIL	NIL
7	:UNDEFINED	T	T
8	:UNDEFINED	:UNDEFINED	NIL

With Defined Functions

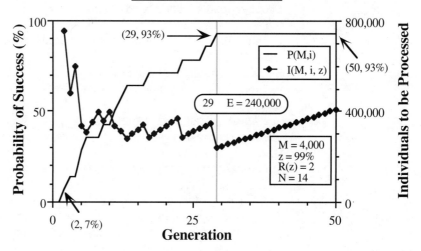

Figure 24.1   Performance curves for the even-5-parity problem showing that E_{with} = 240,000 with evolution of closure.

Table 24.5 is a three-row truth table for the one-argument PF0 from the best of generation 27 of the even-5-parity problem.

Table 24.6 is a nine-row truth table for the two-argument PF1 from the best of generation 27 of the even-5-parity problem.

This three-argument ADF0 has the behavior of (ODD-2-PARITY ARG1 ARG2) for the eight of its 27 combinations of arguments that contain no occurrences of :UNDEFINED.

Even though the result-producing branch of this 100% correct program contains two occurrences of the random constant :UNDEFINED, it nonetheless has the behavior of the even-5-parity function.

Figure 24.1 presents the performance curves based on the 14 runs of the even-5-parity problem with the evolutionary method of simultaneously determining the architecture, a sufficient set of primitive functions, and closure. The cumulative probability of success, $P(M,i)$, is 93% by generation 29 and is still 93% at generation 50. The two numbers in the oval indicate that if this problem is run through to generation 29, processing a total of $E_{with} = 240{,}000$ individuals (i.e., $4{,}000 \times 30$ generations $\times 2$ runs) is sufficient to yield a solution to this problem with 99% probability.

25 Simultaneous Evolution of Architecture, Primitive Functions, Terminals, Sufficiency, and Closure

The sixth major preparatory step in applying genetic programming with automatically defined functions to a problem is to determine the architecture of the yet-to-be-evolved programs.

The second major preparatory step in applying genetic programming to a problem is to determine the set of primitive functions from which the programs to be evolved will be composed.

The first major preparatory step in applying genetic programming to a problem is to determine the set of terminals from which the programs to be evolved will be composed.

The set of primitive functions and the set of terminals should satisfy both the sufficiency requirement and the closure requirement.

Chapters 21 through 24 demonstrated that genetic programming is capable of evolving (selecting), in various separate combinations, the solution to a problem, the architecture, the primitive functions, and the terminals while satisfying the sufficiency requirement and the closure requirements. In this chapter we demonstrate that genetic programming is capable of solving a problem while simultaneously evolving *all five* of these attributes together.

25.1 PREPARATORY STEPS

The process proceeds in the same manner as in chapter 24.

If the problem is the even-4-parity problem, then the terminal set is

$$T = \{\text{NOISE, D0, D1, D2, D3}, \Re_{\text{ternary}}\},$$

where NOISE is an extraneous noise variable (described in section 23.1) and where $\Re_{\text{ternary}}$ is the random constant ranging over the values T, NIL, :UNDEFINED.

A population size of 4,000 and the techniques of structure-preserving crossover with point typing (chapter 21) are used throughout this chapter.

25.2 Results for Even-4-Parity Problem

The best of generation 0 has a standardized fitness of 4 (i.e., scores 12 out of 16 hits), has an argument map of {2, 2} for its two primitive-defining branches, and has no function-defining branches. It is shown below:

```
(progn (defun PF0 (ARG0 ARG1)
          (truth-table NIL NIL T T NIL NIL NIL T :UNDEFINED))
       (defun PF1 (ARG0 ARG1)
          (truth-table :UNDEFINED T :UNDEFINED NIL T :UNDEFINED
            :UNDEFINED :UNDEFINED :UNDEFINED))
       (values (PF0 (PF0 (PF1 (PF0 D1 D1) (PF1 D2 D0)) (PF0 (PF0
          NOISE :UNDEFINED) (PF0 D2 D1))) (PF1 (PF1 (PF1 NOISE
          NOISE) (PF0 D2 D3)) (PF0 (PF1 D0 D3) (PF1 D3 D1)))))))).
```

The noise variable, NOISE, appears three times in the result-producing branch of this program.

A 100% correct solution to the even-4-parity problem emerges on generation 8 with a standardized fitness of 0 (i.e., scores 16 out of 16 hits), an argument map of {2} for its one primitive-defining branch, and an argument map of {4, 1} for its two function-defining branches:

```
(progn (defun PF0 (ARG0 ARG1)
          (truth-table T NIL NIL NIL T NIL T T :UNDEFINED))
       (defun ADF0 (ARG0 ARG1 ARG2 ARG3)
          (values (PF0 (PF0 ARG1 ARG1) (PF0 T T))))
       (defun ADF1 (ARG0)
          (values (PF0 T ARG0)))
       (values (PF0 (PF0 NIL NIL) (PF0 (PF0 D3 D1) (PF0 D2 D0))))).
```

NOISE does not appear in the result-producing branch of this program.

Table 25.1 is the truth table for the primitive-defining branch PF0 for best-of-run program from generation 8 of run 1.

According to the truth table, (PF0 NIL NIL) is T. Since the actual variables of the problem (D0, D1, D2, and D3) can assume only defined values, PF0 is equivalent to EVEN-2-PARITY. The result-producing branch can be simplified to

```
(values (EVEN-2-PARITY T
              (EVEN-2-PARITY (EVEN-2-PARITY D3 D1)
                             (EVEN-2-PARITY D2 D0))))).
```

Since (EVEN-2-PARITY T «X») is equivalent to «X», for all «X», the result-producing branch can be further simplified to

```
(values (EVEN-2-PARITY (EVEN-2-PARITY D3 D1)
              (EVEN-2-PARITY D2 D0)))),
```

which is equivalent to the even-4-parity function.

25.3 RESULTS FOR EVEN-5-PARITY PROBLEM

The previous section established that it is possible to simultaneously evolve the solution to a problem, the architecture, the primitive functions, and the terminals while satisfying the sufficiency requirement and the closure requirement for the even-4-parity problem. We now apply this process to a series of runs of the even-5-parity problem.

Table 25.1 Nine-row truth table for the primitive-defining branch PF0 for the solution from generation 8.

	ARG1	ARG0	PF0
0	NIL	NIL	T
1	NIL	T	NIL
2	NIL	:UNDEFINED	NIL
3	T	NIL	NIL
4	T	T	T
5	T	:UNDEFINED	NIL
6	:UNDEFINED	NIL	T
7	:UNDEFINED	T	T
8	:UNDEFINED	:UNDEFINED	:UNDEFINED

Table 25.2 Distribution of architectures of the PFs and ADFs of 14 solutions to the even-5-parity problem with evolution of architecture, primitive functions, sufficiency, terminals and closure.

Run	Generation when solved	Number of PFs	Argument map for PFs	Number of ADFs	Argument map for ADFs
1	4	1	{2}	3	{4, 3, 4}
2	12	3	{2, 1, 2}	4	{4, 4, 1, 3}
3	11	3	{2, 2, 2}	0	{}
4	12	1	{2}	2	{4, 4}
5	3	1	{2}	0	{}
6	21	4	{1, 2, 1, 2}	3	{4, 2, 1}
7	10	4	{2, 2, 2, 2}	1	{4}
8	6	2	{1, 2}	3	{2, 4, 4}
9	6	1	{2}	4	{4, 3, 3, 3}
10	21	3	{2, 1, 2}	4	{3, 4, 2, 4}
11	14	2	{2, 2}	0	{}
12	9	3	{2, 2, 2}	3	{4, 4, 3}
13	11	2	{2, 2}	2	{4, 4}
14	5	1	{2}	0	{}

We made 22 runs of which 14 (64%) produced a 100%-correct solution by generation 50.

There was no convergence to any particular architecture for this particular problem. Table 25.2 shows the variation among the 14 solutions in both the number of primitive-defining branches, the number of arguments each PF possesses, the number of function-defining branches, and the number of arguments each automatically defined function possesses. The average number of PFs is 2.21 and the average number of automatically defined functions is 2.07 for the 14 solutions. Four of these 14 solutions did not employ automatically defined functions.

Figure 25.1 presents the performance curves based on the 22 runs of the even-5-parity problem with the evolution of the architecture, primitive functions, sufficiency, terminals and closure. The cumulative probability of success, $P(M,i)$, is 55% by generation 14 and 64% by generation 50. The two numbers in the oval indicate that if this problem is run through to generation 14, processing a total of $E_{with} = 360{,}000$ individuals (i.e., $4{,}000 \times 15$ generations $\times$ 6 runs) is sufficient to yield a solution to this problem with 99% probability.

In run 1 from table 25.2, the even-5-parity problem is solved on generation 4. The solution has {2} as the argument map for its primitive-defining branches and {4, 3, 4} as the argument map for its function-defining branches.

```
(progn (defun PF0 (ARG0 ARG1)
          (truth-table T NIL NIL NIL T T T NIL :UNDEFINED))
       (defun ADF0 (ARG0 ARG1 ARG2 ARG3)
          (values (PF0 (PF0 (PF0 (PF0 ARG3 ARG1) (PF0 ARG1 ARG2))
            (PF0 (PF0 ARG1 ARG3) (PF0 ARG1 ARG1))) (PF0 ARG1
            ARG1))))
       (defun ADF1 (ARG0 ARG1 ARG2)
          (values (PF0 (PF0 (ADF0 (PF0 ARG1 ARG1) (PF0 :UNDEFINED
            ARG2) (PF0 ARG0 ARG1) (PF0 NIL ARG1)) (ADF0 (ADF0 ARG0
            :UNDEFINED ARG0 ARG0) (PF0 ARG0 ARG0) (ADF0 ARG2
            :UNDEFINED ARG0 ARG1) (ADF0 T ARG2 ARG1 ARG0))) (PF0
            ARG0 T))))
       (defun ADF2 (ARG0 ARG1 ARG2 ARG3)
          (values (PF0 (PF0 (ADF0 (ADF0 ARG2 ARG2 ARG0 ARG0) (ADF1
            ARG0 ARG2 ARG3) (PF0 ARG0 ARG3) (PF0 ARG0 T)) (PF0
            (ADF0 ARG1 ARG1 ARG3 ARG3) (ADF1 ARG1 T ARG1))) (ADF1
            (PF0 (ADF0 T ARG0 T ARG3) (ADF1 ARG3 ARG0 ARG3)) (ADF1
            (ADF0 ARG3 ARG3 :UNDEFINED T) (ADF1 :UNDEFINED ARG3
            ARG1) (PF0 ARG2 ARG2)) (ADF0 (ADF1 T NIL ARG3) (ADF0
            ARG1 T ARG2 ARG0) (ADF0 :UNDEFINED :UNDEFINED ARG3 T)
            (ADF1 ARG3 ARG0 ARG3))))))
       (values (PF0 (ADF1 (ADF2 (PF0 D4 D1) (ADF0 D4 NOISE D3 D0)
         (ADF2 D2 NOISE NIL NOISE) (ADF0 D3 NOISE D1 D1)) (ADF1
         (PF0 D3 D3) (ADF2 D4 D0 NOISE D0) (PF0 D0 NIL)) (PF0
         (ADF0 D3 D3 D4 D4) (ADF2 D4 D4 D2 T))) (PF0 (PF0 (ADF0
         NOISE D2 D2 D3) (ADF2 NIL D4 T :UNDEFINED)) (ADF0 (ADF1
         :UNDEFINED D3 D1) (PF0 D1 D4) (PF0 D2 D4) (PF0 D3
         D4)))))))).
```

Table 25.3 shows that PF0 from this program has the behavior of the even-2-parity function whenever both of its arguments are defined. The three automatically defined functions are defined in terms of PF0 and the result-producing branch is then defined in terms of PF0, ADF0, ADF1, and ADF2.

Figure 25.2 depicts two three-dimensional trajectories, by generation, showing the hits and the number of primitive-defining branches and function-defining branches in the best-of-generation programs of this run with the evolutionary method of simultaneously determining the architecture, primi-

With Defined Functions

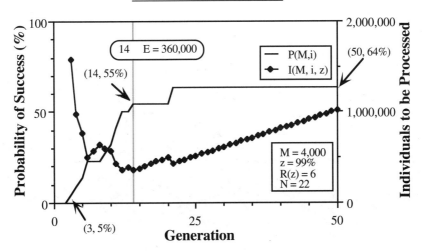

Figure 25.1 Performance curves for the even-5-parity problem showing that $E_{with} = 360,000$ with evolution of architecture, primitive functions, sufficiency, terminals and closure.

Table 25.3 Nine-row truth table for the primitive-defining branch PF0 from solution from run 1 to the even-5-parity problem with the evolution of architecture, primitive functions, sufficiency, terminals and closure.

	ARG1	ARG0	PF0
0	NIL	NIL	T
1	NIL	T	NIL
2	NIL	:UNDEFINED	NIL
3	T	NIL	NIL
4	T	T	T
5	T	:UNDEFINED	T
6	:UNDEFINED	NIL	T
7	:UNDEFINED	T	NIL
8	:UNDEFINED	:UNDEFINED	:UNDEFINED

tive functions, sufficiency, terminals and closure. The axis labeled "branches" refers to both the number of primitive-defining branches and the number of function-defining branches. The first trajectory (shown with a broken line) traces, by generation, the number of primitive-defining branches. The second trajectory (shown with a solid line) traces, by generation, the number of function-defining branches.

Figure 25.3 is a three-dimensional histogram for run 1 of the even-5-parity problem with the evolutionary method of simultaneously determining the architecture, primitive functions, sufficiency, terminals and closure. This histogram shows, by generation, the number of programs in the population of 4,000 with a specified number of primitive-defining branches (from 1 to 3)

Simultaneous Evolution of Architecture, Primitive Functions, Terminals, Sufficiency, and Closure

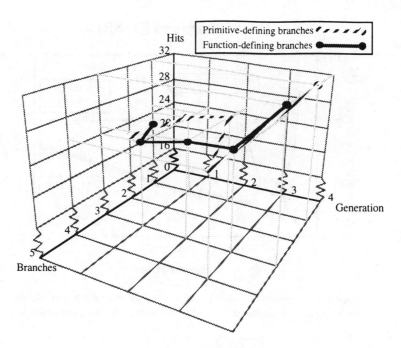

Figure 25.2 Fitness-branch trajectory of hits and the number of primitive-defining branches and the number of function-defining branches between generations 0 and 4 for the best-of-generation programs of run 1 of the even-5-parity problem with evolution of architecture, primitive functions, sufficiency, terminals closure.

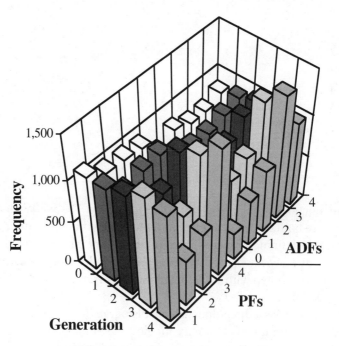

Figure 25.3 Branch histogram between generations 0 and 4 of the number of programs in the population with various numbers of primitive-defining branches and function-defining branches for run 1 of the even-5-parity problem with evolution of architecture, primitive functions, sufficiency, terminals closure.

and a specified number of function-defining branches (from 0 to 4). As can be seen, there is approximate equality at generation 0 in the number of programs with one, two, and three primitive-defining branches and with zero, one, two, three, and four function-defining branches. However, by generation 4, the most common configuration consists of four primitive-defining branches and three function-defining branches.

25.4 SUMMARY

We have demonstrated that genetic programming is capable of simultaneously solving a problem while separately evolving the architecture, the primitive functions, and the terminals and while satisfying the sufficiency requirement and the closure requirement.

The fifth major preparatory step in applying genetic programming involves only the administrative matter of determining the termination predicate and the method of result designation. The fourth major preparatory step involves selecting parameters, of which the population size, M, and the maximum number of generations to be run, G, are the most important. One can envisage allowing the population size to evolve to its own best level on the basis of fitness; however, I believe that the best choice of population size for any non-trivial and interesting problem that one is likely to encounter in the foreseeable future is the largest possible population size that is supported by the available computing machinery. Of course, in nature, there is no artificial limit on G since populations reproduce themselves indefinitely.

Since the first, second, fourth, fifth, and sixth major preparatory steps as well as the sufficiency requirement and the closure requirement can either be replaced by a competitive evolutionary process or can be said to be of secondary importance, the third major step appears (based on the limited number of problems considered) to be the irreducible requirement for genetic programming.

Fitness need not always be explicit (as it is in this book). Instead, it can be implicit as it is when two or more populations co-evolve in a common ecology (*Genetic Programming*, chapter 16) or as it is when the members of a single population merely interact with one another and either survive and reproduce or die. Implicit fitness is often used in simulations in the field of artificial life. However, whether explicit or implicit, the conclusion is that the irreducible requirement for genetic programming is the fitness measure and that structure arises from fitness.

26 The Role of Representation and the Lens Effect

Representation plays a key role in facilitating or thwarting the solution of problems by means of artificial intelligence and machine learning. This chapter explores the question of how a representation employing automatically defined functions differs from a representation without automatically defined functions.

The focus in this chapter is solely on the role of representation, not on the role of genetic programming in solving problems. This chapter considers only populations of random individuals (i.e., the initial random generation in genetic programming). The initial random generation of a run of genetic programming is, of course, an exercise in blind random search in the search space of permissible structures for possible solutions to the problem. Given an initial random population of computer programs, any one of many different parallel adaptive methods could potentially be used to modify the individuals in an initial random population. For example, one might define a modifying operator that mutates a single point in the parse tree of the program to a different value having the same arity (number of branches radiating away from the point) and then employ parallel hill climbing, parallel simulated annealing, or some other adaptive method to create a new generation of programs. However, at the time when the initial random population is created, no commitment has yet been made as to which adaptive method might be used to try to discover better points in the search space of the problem.

The Boolean even-3-parity problem (section 6.1) can be used to illustrate how representation can facilitate or thwart the solution of a problem. For example, if a three-argument Boolean function is represented as a truth table (such as table 6.1), then the search space of the problem consists of $2^{2^3} = 256$ possible eight-row truth tables. A blind random search procedure that fills in the value of the Boolean function for the eight rows of the truth table with either T or NIL has a probability of 1:256 of finding an arbitrary three-argument Boolean function. Thus, when a three-argument Boolean function is represented by means of a truth table, a blind random search has a probability of success of 1:256. This probability is independent of which of the 256 three-argument Boolean functions is being sought.

On the other hand, suppose that the search space of the problem consists of compositions of the terminals from the terminal set

$\mathcal{T} = \{\text{D0, D1, D2}\}$

and the functions from the function set

$\mathcal{F} = \{\text{AND, OR, NAND, NOR}\}$

with an argument map for this function set of

$\{2, 2, 2, 2\}$.

A blind random search has a very different probability of success when three-argument Boolean functions are represented as such compositions (i.e., as parse trees or LISP S-expressions). Moreover, in contrast to the representation employing truth tables, the probability of success in the blind random search is dependent on the particular three-argument Boolean function chosen.

Consider, for example, the Boolean even-3-parity function (three-argument Boolean rule 105). The probability of success of a blind random search in the space of compositions of functions from the function set, $\mathcal{F}$, and terminals from the terminal set, $\mathcal{T}$, is so low that, after 10,000,000 tries, we never found even a single random program that performed the even-3-parity function (*Genetic Programming*, table 9.3). In other words, in the space of computer programs (over $\mathcal{F}$ and $\mathcal{T}$), the even-3-parity function is extremely difficult to find by means of a blind random search. The representation of Boolean functions as computer programs makes the learning of the even-3-parity problem decidedly more difficult than a representation based on a truth table. The extreme difficulty of solving the even-3-parity problem by blind random search is reflected by the fact that the cumulative probability of success, $P(M,i)$, is 0% for generation 0 in the performance curve in figure 6.2 for the even-3-parity function without automatically defined functions. The minimum number of individuals required to be processed to yield a solution to the even-3-parity problem (figure 6.2) was only 544,000 individuals (i.e., 34 runs with a population of 16,000). This is considerably smaller than 10,000,000.

In contrast, three-argument Boolean rule 000 ("Always Off") is randomly generated with a probability of 1:6.76 in the space of compositions of functions from the same function set, $\mathcal{F}$, and terminals from the same terminal set, $\mathcal{T}$, so rule 000 is much easier to find in the space of programs than in the space of truth tables.

The reader may have noticed that the cumulative probability of success, $P(M,i)$, is 39% for generation 0 in the performance curve in figure 6.10 for the even-3-parity function *with automatically defined functions* for a population of 16,000. That is, in approximately two out of five runs, there is at least one solution in generation 0 among the 16,000 programs. In fact, there are 15 such programs in the 528,000 individuals contained in the 33 runs involved, so the probability of solving this problem by means of blind random search with automatically defined functions is about 1:35,200.

A probability of success of 1:35,200 is a considerable improvement over a failure to find a single solution in 10,000,000 tries. Representation is the reason for this difference in probability of success of these two blind random searches. When automatically defined functions are not being used, the elements of the search space are computer programs consisting only of a result-producing branch. However, when automatically defined functions are being used, the elements of the search space are computer programs consisting of two function-defining branches and one result-producing branch. The availability of automatically defined functions provides a significantly different way of representing Boolean functions and a dramatically different way of viewing the space of Boolean functions.

This chapter explores the way automatically defined functions change the way of looking at problem spaces for several different problems from this book. To do this, this chapter compares the distribution of values of fitness for 1,000,000 randomly generated programs without automatically defined functions with the distribution of values of fitness for 1,000,000 randomly generated programs with automatically defined functions. The distributions are examined in tabular form, visualized as histograms, quantified by their means and standard deviations, and further quantified by the values of their outliers. For each problem, the 1,000,000 random programs are generated in the same manner in which the programs were generated when the problem was first treated herein. Specifically, the programs were generated with the same function set, the same terminal set, the same arrangement of defined functions (if any), and the same limitations on program size or depth. The programs were generated as if they belonged to generation 0 of a population of 5,000 and then consolidated into a group of 1,000,000.

26.1   EVEN-3-, 4-, 5-, AND 6-PARITY PROBLEMS

We start with the even-3-, 4-, 5-, and 6-parity problems.

26.1.1   Even-3-Parity Problem

Table 26.1 shows the distribution of values of raw fitness for the even-3-parity function for 1,000,000 randomly created programs with automatically defined functions and 1,000,000 randomly created programs without automatically defined functions. Two two-argument automatically defined functions are used. Raw fitness (hits) ranges between 0 and 8 for this problem.

As can be seen, no programs out of the 1,000,000 without automatically defined functions achieve a perfect score of eight hits. This result is consistent with the experiment cited above involving 10,000,000 random programs. In contrast, 33 programs out of the 1,000,000 with automatically defined functions score eight hits. These 33 100%-correct solutions suggest a probability of 1:30,303 (which is close to the probability of 1:35,200 computed above with the different sample of size of 528,000).

There are no programs that score zero hits without automatically defined functions, whereas there are 49 programs that do so with them.

In addition, there are only 33 near-perfect programs scoring seven hits without automatically defined functions, whereas there are 55 such near-perfect

Table 26.1 Distribution of raw fitness (hits) for the even-3-parity problem with and without ADFs.

Raw fitness (hits)	Without ADFs	With ADFs
0	0	49
1	46	57
2	5,803	2,022
3	156,227	63,545
4	675,629	869,656
5	156,495	62,587
6	5,767	1,996
7	33	55
8	0	33

programs with them. Similarly, only 46 programs score one hit without automatically defined functions; 57 do so with them.

In other words, when the even-3-parity problem environment is viewed through the lens of automatically defined functions, a blind random search is more likely to find outliers scoring extreme values (such as zero and eight hits) with automatically defined functions than without them. We call this difference the *lens effect*.

The means of the two distributions are, of course, each four.

The distribution with automatically defined functions has a lesser variance than without automatically defined functions for this particular problem. There are 869,656 programs scoring four hits (the mean) with automatically defined functions versus 675,629 without them. There are only 62,587 programs scoring five hits (i.e., the mean plus one) with automatically defined functions versus 156,495 without them. Similarly, as one would expect because of the symmetry of this problem, there are only 63,545 programs scoring three hits (i.e., the mean minus one) with automatically defined functions versus 156,227 without them. There are only about a third as many programs scoring six hits (and two hits) with automatically defined functions than without them. The standard deviations of the distributions are 0.60 without automatically defined functions and 0.38 with them.

Figure 26.1 shows the hits histograms for 1,000,000 randomly generated programs for the even-3-parity problem, with and without automatically defined functions. The vertical axis for these histograms (and all the other histograms in this chapter) employs a logarithmic scale running between 1 (10^0) and 1,000,000 (10^6). The bars of the histogram start somewhat below the dotted line at 1 (10^0), so as to highlight the absence of any programs scoring a particular value of fitness. For example, in the upper histogram applying to the 1,000,000 programs without automatically defined functions, there are no

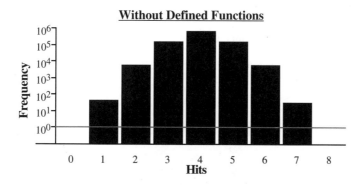

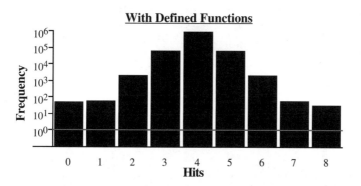

Figure 26.1 Hits histograms for the even-3-parity problem for 1,000,000 randomly generated programs with and without ADFs.

programs scoring either zero or eight. The logarithmic scale highlights the difference in the distributions of the outliers.

In summary, the distribution with automatically defined functions has more extreme outliers, but less variance, than the distribution without them.

If the points in the search space of three-argument Boolean functions are represented as truth tables, there is a 1:256 probability of solving the even-3-parity problem by means of blind random search. If the points in the search space of three-argument Boolean functions are represented as three-branch computer programs consisting of one result-producing branch and two function-defining branches (over the function and terminal sets being used here), there is a probability of about 1:30,303 of solving the even-3-parity problem by means of blind random search. But if the points in the search space of three-argument Boolean functions are represented as single-branch computer programs (consisting only of one result-producing branch), then the probability of solving the even-3-parity problem by means of blind random search is very small (smaller than 1:10,000,000).

Of course, when automatically defined functions are involved in randomly generated programs, the defined functions are simply random defined functions. Since no Darwinian reproduction and no genetic crossover has yet occurred, the fitness measure plays no role in this random generative process.

The Role of Representation and the Lens Effect

Table 26.2 Distribution of raw fitness (hits) for the even-4-parity problem with and without ADFs.

Raw fitness (hits)	Without ADFs	With ADFs
0	0	1
1	0	0
2	0	2
3	0	7
4	7	52
5	62	191
6	3,023	2,099
7	84,604	37,702
8	824,910	920,273
9	84,401	37,424
10	2,906	2,025
11	78	154
12	9	60
13	0	10
14	0	0
15	0	0
16	0	0

The generation of the two sets of 1,000,000 programs described above does not involve either the Darwinian operation of reproduction or the genetic operation of crossover. The difference in success of finding 100%-correct solutions to the even-3-parity function reflects only the way points in the search space of the problem are represented.

The representation chosen to view the points in the search space of the problem (i.e., the three-argument Boolean function) is a kind of lens through which the system views the world. It appears that a computer program incorporating automatically defined functions provides a different lens for viewing a highly regular, symmetric, and homogeneous function such as the even-3-parity function than does a computer program composed of similar ingredients without automatically defined functions.

Solutions to problems are outliers. If the goal is finding solutions to problems, this different lens may be a better lens. As we will see in the remainder of this chapter, this lens effect appears in other problems.

26.1.2 Even-4-Parity Problem

The lens effect also appears in the even-4-parity problem.

Table 26.2 shows the distribution of values of raw fitness (between 0 and 16) for the even-4-parity function with or without automatically defined functions. Two three-argument automatically defined functions are used. There

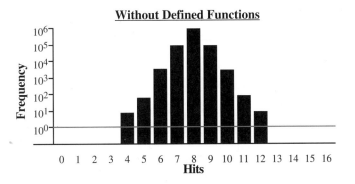

Without Defined Functions

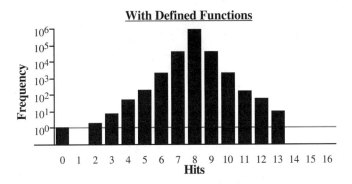

With Defined Functions

Figure 26.2 Hits histograms for the even-4-parity problem for 1,000,000 randomly generated programs with and without ADFs.

are no 100%-correct solutions to this problem among the 1,000,000 randomly generated programs either with or without automatically defined functions. As before, the two distributions are different. For example, the distribution with automatically defined functions has 10 outliers scoring 13 hits and 60 outliers scoring 12 hits and also has seven outliers scoring three hits. In contrast, there are no programs scoring 13 or three hits without automatically defined functions. In addition, one program out of the 1,000,000 scores zero hits and two programs score two hits with automatically defined functions. Thus, there is evidence of the lens effect for this problem.

The means of the two distributions are each eight. The distribution shown in this table with automatically defined functions has a lower variance than the distribution without automatically defined functions. There are only 37,424 programs scoring nine hits (i.e., the mean plus one) with automatically defined functions, versus 84,401 without them. Similarly, as one would expect from symmetry, there are only 37,702 programs scoring seven hits (i.e., the mean minus one) with automatically defined functions, versus 84,604 without them. There are only about two-thirds as many programs scoring ten hits and six hits with automatically defined functions as without them. The standard deviation of the distribution is 0.44 without automatically defined functions and 0.31 with them.

Table 26.3 Distribution of raw fitness (hits) for the even-5-parity problem with and without ADFs.

Raw fitness (hits)	Without ADFs	With ADFs
0–7	0	0
8	0	1
9	0	0
10	0	3
11	0	8
12	3	65
13	33	253
14	1,003	2,088
15	25,956	23,134
16	946,015	948,678
17	25,986	23,236
18	980	2,153
19	21	306
20	3	62
21	0	10
22	0	2
23	0	0
24	0	1
25–32	0	0

Figure 26.2 shows the hits histograms for 1,000,000 randomly generated programs for the even-4-parity problem with and without automatically defined functions. The figure shows the presence of outliers farther from the mean when automatically defined functions are involved.

26.1.3 Even-5-Parity Problem

We again see the lens effect for the even-5-parity problem employing two four-argument defined functions.

Table 26.3 shows the distribution of values of raw fitness (between 0 and 32) for the even-5-parity function. The first and last six rows of this table are omitted since none of the 1,000,000 randomly generated programs, with or without automatically defined functions, scores a value of fitness in these ranges. As with the even-4-parity problem there are no 100%-correct solutions to this problem among the 1,000,000 randomly generated programs either with or without automatically defined functions. There are programs scoring 24, 22, and 21 (and 8, 10, and 11) hits with automatically defined functions whereas there are no programs achieving those scores without automatically defined functions. Moreover, there are considerably more programs scoring 20, 19, and 18 (and 12, 13, and 14) hits with automatically defined

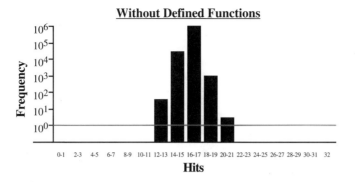

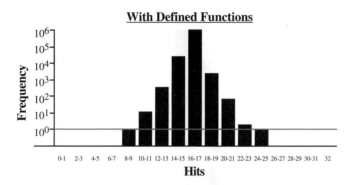

Figure 26.3 Hits histograms for the even-5-parity problem for 1,000,000 randomly generated programs with and without ADFs.

functions than without them. Thus, there is again evidence of the lens effect for this problem.

The means of the two distributions are each 16. The standard deviation of the distribution without automatically defined functions is 0.25 and 0.27 with them.

Figure 26.3 shows the hits histograms for 1,000,000 randomly generated programs for the even-5-parity problem with and without automatically defined functions.

26.1.4 Even-6-Parity Problem

Figure 26.4 shows the hits histograms for 1,000,000 randomly generated programs for the even-6-parity problem with and without two five-argument automatically defined functions. As before, the figure shows the presence of outliers farther from the mean when automatically defined functions are involved.

26.1.5 Summary for the Parity Problems

Table 26.4 shows the mean and standard deviations of distributions for the even-3-, 4-, 5-, and 6-parity problems of 1,000,000 randomly generated

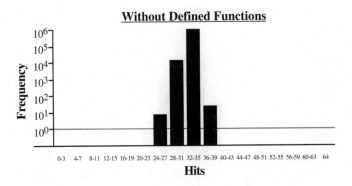

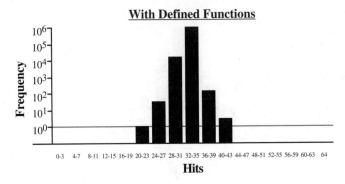

Figure 26.4 Hits histograms for the even-6-parity problem for 1,000,000 randomly generated programs with and without ADFs.

programs, with and without automatically defined functions. The table also shows the highest value of raw fitness (hits) and the number of occurrences of that outlying value of raw fitness. For example, the highest number of hits for the 1,000,000 initial random individuals for the even-3-parity function with automatically defined functions is 8; there are 33 such 8-scoring outliers in the 1,000,000 programs with automatically defined functions.

26.2   THE LAWNMOWER PROBLEM

This section shows evidence of the lens effect for the lawnmower problem for lawn sizes of 32, 48, 64, 80, and 96.

26.2.1   Lawnmower Problem with Lawn Size of 32

Table 26.5 shows that there are no 100%-correct solutions to this problem among the 1,000,000 randomly generated programs for the lawnmower problem (section 8.1) with a lawn size of 32 without automatically defined functions, but there are 60 among the 1,000,000 randomly generated programs with automatically defined functions. There are no programs scoring in the range between 12 and 32 hits without automatically defined functions; however, there are 120,532 programs (about 12% of the 1,000,000) in this range

Table 26.4 Summary for distributions for the even-3-, 4-, 5-, and 6-parity problems of 1,000,000 randomly generated programs with and without ADFs.

Arity	3	3	4	4	5	5	6	6
	Without ADFs	With ADFs	Without ADFs	With ADFs	Without ADFs	With ADFs	Without ADFs	With ADFs
Mean	4.00	4.00	8.00	8.00	16.0	16.0	32.0	32.0
Standard deviation	0.600	0.380	0.441	0.312	0.246	0.267	0.188	0.226
Best outlier	7	8	12	13	20	24	39	42
Outlier frequency	33	33	9	10	3	1	1	1

with automatically defined functions. There is again evidence of the lens effect for this problem.

Figure 26.5 shows the hits histograms for 1,000,000 randomly generated programs for the 32-square lawnmower problem, with and without automatically defined functions. The mean of the distribution is 2.0 without automatically defined functions and 5.3 with them. The standard deviation is 1.3 without automatically defined functions and 5.4 with automatically defined functions.

26.2.2   Lawnmower Problem with Lawn Size of 48

There are no 100%-correct solutions to this problem among the 1,000,000 randomly generated programs without automatically defined functions, but there are 11 among the 1,000,000 randomly generated programs with automatically defined functions. The largest number of hits scored by a program without automatically defined functions among 1,000,000 randomly generated programs for the 48-square lawnmower problem is 11. There are no programs scoring between 12 and 48 hits without automatically defined functions, but there are 133,579 programs (about 13% of the 1,000,000) having between 12 and 48 hits with automatically defined functions. There is again evidence of the lens effect for this problem.

Figure 26.6 shows the hits histograms for 1,000,000 randomly generated programs for the 48-square lawnmower problem with and without automatically defined functions. The mean of the distribution is 2.06 without automatically defined functions and 5.8 with them. The standard deviation is 1.29 without automatically defined functions and 6.81 with them.

26.2.3   Lawnmower Problem with Lawn Size of 64

There are no 100%-correct solutions to the 64-square lawnmower problem among the 1,000,000 randomly generated programs without automatically defined functions, but there is one 100%-correct solution among the 1,000,000

Table 26.5 Distribution of raw fitness (hits) for the 32-square lawnmower problem with and without ADFs.

Raw fitness (hits)	Without ADFs	With ADFs
0	44,173	20,068
1	335,318	147,189
2	349,385	211,186
3	150,315	142,631
4	70,261	107,549
5	30,674	66,564
6	13,357	51,547
7	4,839	37,900
8	1,368	35,128
9	248	23,394
10	55	19,928
11	7	16,384
12	0	14,592
13	0	11,758
14	0	11,410
15	0	9,379
16	0	9,572
17	0	8,263
18	0	7,902
19	0	7,021
20	0	7,223
21	0	6,242
22	0	5,900
23	0	4,921
24	0	4,773
25	0	3,791
26	0	3,148
27	0	2,053
28	0	1,384
29	0	696
30	0	359
31	0	85
32	0	60

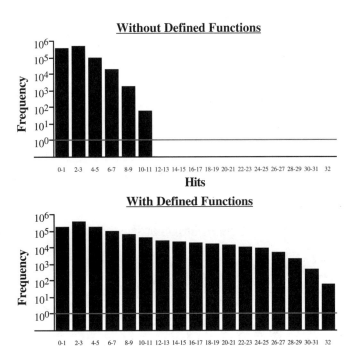

Figure 26.5 Hits histograms for the 32-square lawnmower problem for 1,000,000 randomly generated programs with and without ADFs.

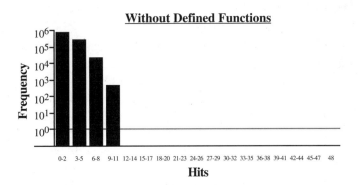

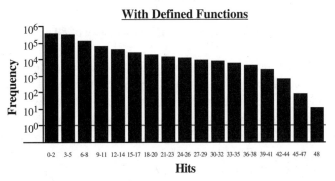

Figure 26.6 Hits histograms for the 48-square lawnmower problem for 1,000,000 randomly generated programs with and without ADFs.

The Role of Representation and the Lens Effect

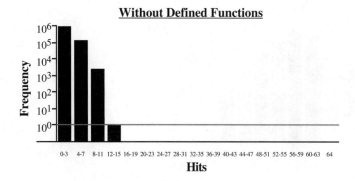

Without Defined Functions

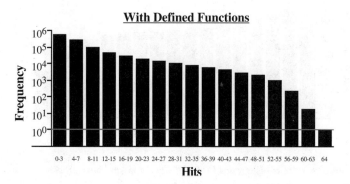

With Defined Functions

Figure 26.7 Hits histograms for the 64-square lawnmower problem for 1,000,000 randomly generated programs with and without ADFs.

randomly generated programs with automatically defined functions. There is a complete absence of programs scoring between 13 and 64 hits without automatically defined functions; however, there are 124,915 programs (over 12% of the 1,000,000) in this range with automatically defined functions.

Figure 26.7 shows the hits histograms for 1,000,000 randomly generated programs for the lawnmower problem with and without automatically defined functions. The means of the distributions are 2.07 without automatically defined functions and 6.19 with them. The standard deviations are 1.31 without automatically defined functions and 7.71 with them.

26.2.4 Lawnmower Problem with Lawn Size of 80

The largest number of hits scored among 1,000,000 randomly generated programs for the 80-square lawnmower problem without automatically defined functions is 12, but the largest number of hits scored by a program among 1,000,000 randomly generated programs with automatically defined functions is 77. There are no programs scoring between 13 and 17 hits without automatically defined functions, but there are 127,101 programs (about 13% of the 1,000,000) having between 13 and 77 hits with automatically defined functions. Thus, there is again evidence of the lens effect for this problem.

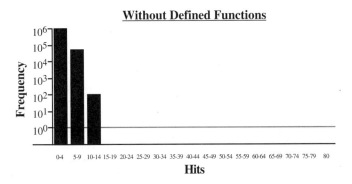

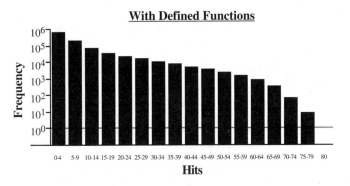

Figure 26.8 Hits histograms for the 80-square lawnmower problem for 1,000,000 randomly generated programs with and without ADFs.

Figure 26.8 shows the hits histograms for 1,000,000 randomly generated programs for the 80-square lawnmower problem with and without automatically defined functions. The means of the distributions are 2.06 without automatically defined functions and 6.35 with them. The standard deviations are 1.31 without automatically defined functions and 8.29 with them.

26.2.5 Lawnmower Problem with Lawn Size of 96

The largest number of hits scored among 1,000,000 randomly generated programs for the 96-square lawnmower problem without automatically defined functions is 12, but the largest number of hits scored by a program among 1,000,000 randomly generated programs with automatically defined functions is 88. There are no programs scoring between 13 and 88 hits without automatically defined functions, but there are 128,088 programs (about 13% of the 1,000,000) having between 13 and 88 hits with automatically defined functions. This problem also shows evidence of the lens effect.

Figure 26.9 shows the hits histograms for 1,000,000 randomly generated programs for the 96-square lawnmower problem with and without automatically defined functions. The mean of the distribution is 2.07 without automatically defined functions and 6.43 with them. The standard

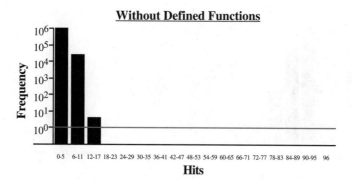

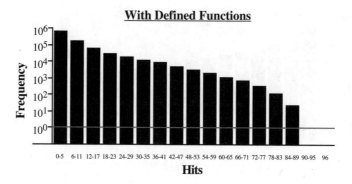

Figure 26.9 Hits histograms for the 96-square lawnmower problem for 1,000,000 randomly generated programs with and without ADFs.

deviation is 1.31 without automatically defined functions and 8.60 with them.

26.2.6 Summary for the Lawnmower Problem

Table 26.6 shows the mean and standard deviations of distributions for the lawnmower problem with lawn sizes of 32, 48, 64, 80, and 96 of 1,000,000 randomly generated programs, with and without automatically defined functions. The table also shows the highest value of raw fitness (hits) and the number of occurrences of that outlying value of raw fitness.

26.3 THE BUMBLEBEE PROBLEM

This section shows evidence of the lens effect for the bumblebee problem with 10, 15, 20, and 25 flowers.

26.3.1 Bumblebee Problem with 10 Flowers

Figure 26.10 shows the hits histograms for 1,000,000 randomly generated programs for the bumblebee problem with 10 flowers, with and without automatically defined functions.

Table 26.6 Summary of distributions for the lawnmower problem with a lawn size of 32, 48, 64, 80, and 96 and 1,000,000 randomly generated programs with and without ADFs.

Lawn size	32	32	48	48	64	64	80	80	96	96
	Without ADFs	With ADFs	Without ADFs	With ADFs	Without ADFs	With ADFs	Without ADFs	With ADFs	Without ADFs	With ADFs
Mean	2.05	5.34	2.06	5.88	2.07	6.19	2.07	6.35	2.07	6.43
Standard deviation	1.27	5.41	1.29	6.81	1.31	7.71	1.31	8.29	1.31	8.60
Best outlier	11	32	11	48	12	64	12	77	12	88
Outlier frequency	7	60	10	11	1	1	1	3	4	2

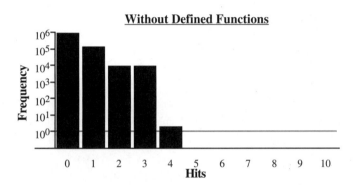

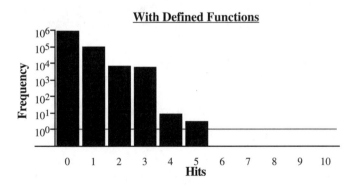

Figure 26.11 Hits histograms for the bumblebee problem with 15 flowers for 1,000,000 randomly generated programs with and without ADFs.

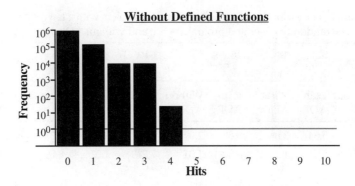

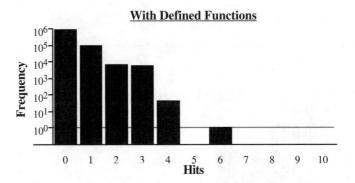

Figure 26.12 Hits histograms for the bumblebee problem with 20 flowers for 1,000,000 randomly generated programs with and without ADFs.

26.3.2 Bumblebee Problem with 15 Flowers

Figure 26.11 shows the hits histograms for 1,000,000 randomly generated programs for the bumblebee problem with 15 flowers, with and without automatically defined functions.

26.3.3 Bumblebee Problem with 20 Flowers

Figure 26.12 shows the hits histograms for 1,000,000 randomly generated programs for the bumblebee problem with 20 flowers, with and without automatically defined functions.

26.3.4 Bumblebee Problem with 25 Flowers

Figure 26.13 shows the hits histograms for 1,000,000 randomly generated programs for the bumblebee problem with 25 flowers, with and without automatically defined functions.

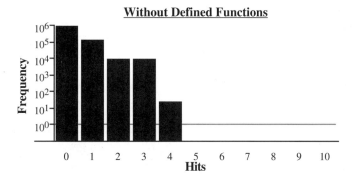

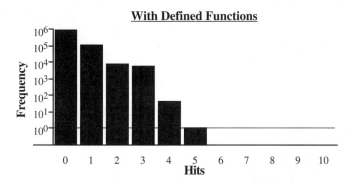

Figure 26.13 Hits histograms for the bumblebee problem with 25 flowers for 1,000,000 randomly generated programs with and without ADFs.

26.3.5 Summary for Bumblebee Problem

Table 26.7 shows the mean and standard deviations of distributions for the bumblebee problem with 10, 15, 20, and 25 flowers of 1,000,000 randomly generated programs with and without automatically defined functions. The table also shows the highest value of raw fitness (hits) and the number of occurrences of that outlying value of raw fitness.

26.4 OBSTACLE-AVOIDING-ROBOT PROBLEM

This section shows that the obstacle-avoiding-robot problem (chapter 13) also shows evidence of the lens effect. Raw fitness (hits) ranges between 0 and 116 for this problem. There are no programs scoring 19 or more hits without automatically defined functions, but there are 36,094 programs (3.6% of the 1,000,000) scoring between 19 and 91 hits with automatically defined functions.

Figure 26.14 shows the hits histograms for 1,000,000 randomly generated programs for the obstacle-avoiding-robot problem with and without automatically defined functions. The mean of the distribution is 2.83 without automatically defined functions and 5.47 with them. The standard deviation is 1.98 without automatically defined functions and 5.78 with them.

Table 26.7 Summary for distributions for the bumblebee problem with 10, 15, 20, and 25 flowers of 1,000,000 randomly generated programs with and without ADFs.

Number of flowers	10	10	15	15	20	20	25	25
	Without ADFs	With ADFs	Without ADFs	With ADFs	Without ADFs	With ADFs	Without ADFs	With ADFs
Mean	0.0402	0.0329	0.161	0.131	0.162	0.133	0.162	0.133
Standard deviation	0.268	0.235	0.451	0.402	0.453	0.406	0.453	0.405
Best outlier	3	4	4	5	4	6	4	5
Outlier frequency	4	8	2	3	25	1	24	1

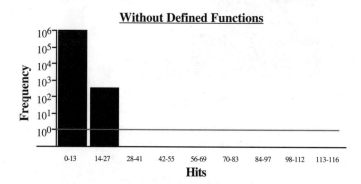

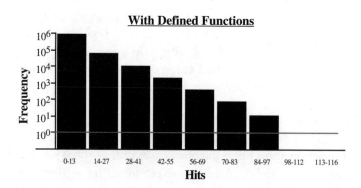

Figure 26.14 Hits histograms for the obstacle-avoiding-robot problem for 1,000,000 randomly generated programs with and without ADFs.

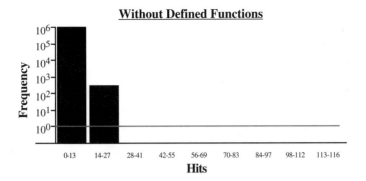

Without Defined Functions

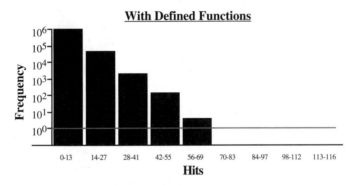

With Defined Functions

Figure 26.15 Hits histograms for the minesweeper problem for 1,000,000 randomly generated programs with and without ADFs.

26.5 MINESWEEPER PROBLEM

The minesweeper problem (chapter 14) also shows evidence of the lens effect. Raw fitness (hits) ranges between 0 and 116. There are no programs scoring 21 or more hits without automatically defined functions, but there are 14,453 programs (1.4% of the 1,000,000) scoring between 21 and 58 hits with automatically defined functions.

Figure 26.15 shows the hits histograms for 1,000,000 randomly generated programs for the minesweeper problem with and without automatically defined functions. The mean of the distribution is 2.81 without automatically defined functions and 4.85 with them. The standard deviation is 1.96 without automatically defined functions and 4.23 with them.

26.6 ARTIFICIAL ANT PROBLEM

There is evidence of a slight lens effect for the artificial ant problem (chapter 12). Raw fitness (hits) ranges between 0 and 96 for this problem. There are no programs scoring between 88 and 92 hits without automatically defined functions, but there are four programs in this range with automatically defined functions. Moreover, between 57 and 87 hits, every entry in the table for

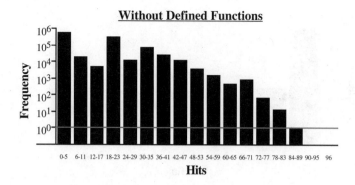

Without Defined Functions

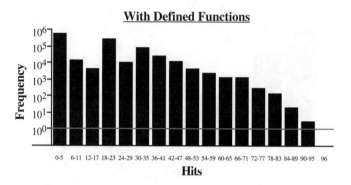

With Defined Functions

Figure 26.16 Hits histograms for the artificial ant problem for 1,000,000 randomly generated programs with and without ADFs.

automatically defined functions is higher than the corresponding entry without automatically defined functions. There are only 1,839 programs (0.18% of the 1,000,000) without automatically defined functions between 57 and 87 hits, whereas there are 4,007 programs (0.40% of the 1,000,000) without automatically defined functions.

The mean of the distribution is 10.08 without automatically defined functions and 10.06 with them. The standard deviation is 12.64 without automatically defined functions and 13.17 with them.

Figure 26.16 shows the hits histograms for 1,000,000 randomly generated programs for the artificial ant problem with and without automatically defined functions.

26.7 DISCUSSION

We have observed, for the problems reviewed in this chapter, that when the representation of problem environments employs automatically defined functions, a blind random search yields higher scoring outliers than when the representation does not employ automatically defined functions. The possible contribution of this lens effect to the operation of genetic programming with automatically defined functions warrants further investigation.

Reynolds (1994c) considers three versions of a problem calling for the discovery of a controller for a corridor-following robot (subsection F.3.4 in appendix F). The robot had a roving sensor, an arbitrary static sensor, and a predetermined static sensor in the three versions. The histograms of fitness in the initial random generation of Reynold's runs were distinctly different for the three versions. The version of Reynold's problem with the best outlier proved to be the easiest to solve. These differences foreshadowed the difficulty of solving the problem in the actual full runs of genetic programming and are another the existence of the lens effect.

27 Conclusion

Main point 1 was stated as follows in chapter 1:

Main point 1: Automatically defined functions enable genetic programming to solve a variety of problems in a way that can be interpreted as a decomposition of a problem into subproblems, a solving of the subproblems, and an assembly of the solutions to the subproblems into a solution to the overall problem (or which can alternatively be interpreted as a search for regularities in the problem environment, a change of representation, and a solving of a higher level problem).

The numerous illustrative problems in this book provide evidence in support of this conclusion that genetic programming with ADFs does indeed work.

Main point 2 was stated as follows:

Main point 2: Automatically defined functions discover and exploit the regularities, symmetries, homogeneities, similarities, patterns, and modularities of the problem environment in ways that are very different from the style employed by human programmers.

This point has, of course, been repeatedly made throughout this book in the many examples.

Main point 3 was stated as follows:

Main point 3: For a variety of problems, genetic programming requires less computational effort to solve a problem with automatically defined functions than without them, provided the difficulty of the problem is above a certain relatively low problem-specific breakeven point for computational effort.

Table 27.1 summarizes the efficiency ratio, R_E, and the structural complexity ratio, R_S, for various problems covered in this book.

An examination of the rightmost column of the first five rows of the table indicates that the efficiency ratio, R_E, is less than 1 (indicating that a greater number of fitness evaluations is required to yield a solution of the problem with automatically defined functions than without them). These five rows correspond to the simple two-boxes problem (chapter 4) and the simpler versions of the four problems in chapter 5 that straddle the breakeven point for computational effort. However, starting with the scaled-up versions of the four problems in chapter 5 and continuing all the way down the rightmost column of the table, we see that all the other problems in this book have an efficiency ratio of greater than 1 (indicating that fewer fitness evaluations are required to yield a solution to the problem with automatically defined functions than without them).

Main point 4 was stated as follows:

Main point 4: For a variety of problems, genetic programming usually yields solutions with smaller overall size (lower average structural complexity) with automatically defined functions than without them, provided the difficulty of the problem is above a certain problem-specific breakeven point for average structural complexity.

Starting with the even-4-parity problem on the ninth row of the table and continuing down the rightmost column of the table, we see that the structural complexity ratio is greater than 1 (indicating a smaller average size for successful runs of the problem with automatically defined functions than without them) except for the three isolated exceptions. The exceptions occur for the two extreme values of the architectural parameters for the even-5-parity problem (out of 15 combinations considered) and the subset-creating version of the transmembrane problem (where the "average" structural complexity comes from only one successful run).

Main point 5 was stated as follows:

Main point 5: For the three problems herein for which a progression of several scaled-up versions is studied, the average size of the solutions produced by genetic programming increases as a function of problem size at a lower rate with automatically defined functions than without them.

Main point 6 was stated as follows:

Main point 6: For the three problems herein for which a progression of several scaled-up versions is studied, the computational effort increases as a function of problem size at a lower rate with automatically defined functions than without them.

The evidence reported in sections 6.15 (parity problems), 8.15 (lawnmower problems), and 9.13 (bumblebee problems) supports main points 5 and 6.

Main point 7 is closely related to main points 5 and 6 and was stated as follows:

Main point 7: For the three problems herein for which a progression of several scaled-up versions is studied, the benefits in terms of computational effort and average structural complexity conferred by automatically defined functions increase as the problem size is scaled up.

Specifically, table 27.1 shows that the efficiency ratios for the group of even-parity problems are 1.50, 2.18, 14.07, and 52.2 as the problem is scaled up from three, to four, to five, and to six arguments, respectively. The efficiency ratios for the group of lawnmower problems are 3.80, 6.22, 9.09, 33.0, and 283.7, as the lawn size is scaled up from 32, to 48, to 64, to 80, and to 96, respectively. The efficiency ratios for the group of bumblebee problems are 1.20, 1.21, 1.24, and 3.2, as the number of flowers is scaled up from 10, to 15, to 20, and to 25, respectively. These monotonically increasing efficiency ratios exhibited within all three groups of problems suggest that the facilitating benefits of automatically defined functions increase as problems are scaled up.

Table 27.1 Summary table of the structural complexity ratio, R_S, and the efficiency ratio, R_E, for various problems.

Problem	Reference	Structural Complexity R_S	Efficiency ratio R_E
Two boxes	Chapter 4	0.53	0.53
Quintic polynomial $x^5 - 2x^3 + x$	5.1.2	1.07	0.33
Boolean 5-symmetry	5.2.2	0.80	0.56
Three-sines $\sin x + \sin 2x + \sin 3x$	5.3.1	1.09	0.89
Two-term $x / \pi + x^2 / \pi^2$	5.4.2	0.82	0.38
Sextic polynomial $x^6 - 2x^4 + x^2$	5.1.1	0.98	1.22
Boolean 6-symmetry	5.2.1	1.82	1.82
Four-sines $\sin x + \sin 2x + \sin 3x + \sin 4x$	5.3.2	1.30	1.28
Three-term $x / \pi + x^2 / \pi^2 + 2\pi x$	5.4.1	0.92	1.32
Even-3-parity $- M = 16,000$	6.3, 6.10	0.92	1.50
Even-4-parity $- M = 16,000$	6.4, 6.11	1.87	2.18
Even-5-parity $- M = 16,000$	6.5, 6.12	1.91	14.07
Even-6-parity $- M = 16,000$	6.6, 6.13	1.77	52.20
Even-5-parity $- M = 4,000 -$ one two-argument ADF	7.4.2	3.64	5.44
Even-5-parity $- M = 4,000 -$ one three-argument ADF	7.4.3	2.51	4.25
Even-5-parity $- M = 4,000 -$ one four-argument ADF	7.4.4	1.81	2.76
Even-5-parity $- M = 4,000 -$ two two-argument ADFs	7.4.5	3.01	6.00
Even-5-parity $- M = 4,000 -$ two three-argument ADFs	7.4.6	1.97	4.08
Even-5-parity $- M = 4,000 -$ two four-argument ADFs	7.4.7	1.32	2.49
Even-5-parity $- M = 4,000 -$ three two-argument ADFs	7.4.8	2.51	4.29
Even-5-parity $- M = 4,000 -$ three three-argument ADFs	7.4.9	1.70	6.00
Even-5-parity $- M = 4,000 -$ three four-argument ADFs	7.4.10	1.11	2.43
Even-5-parity $- M = 4,000 -$ four two-argument ADFs	7.4.11	2.29	4.53
Even-5-parity $- M = 4,000 -$ four three-argument ADFs	7.4.12	1.38	3.88
Even-5-parity $- M = 4,000 -$ four four-argument ADFs	7.4.13	0.77	1.79
Even-5-parity $- M = 4,000 -$ five two-argument ADFs	7.4.14	2.01	4.53
Even-5-parity $- M = 4,000 -$ five three-argument ADFs	7.4.15	1.21	3.18
Even-5-parity $- M = 4,000 -$ five four-argument ADFs	7.4.16	0.69	2.22
Lawnmower $-$ lawn size 32	8.4, 8.10	2.19	3.80
Lawnmower $-$ lawn size 48	8.5, 8.11	3.15	6.22
Lawnmower $-$ lawn size 64	8.3, 8.9	3.65	9.09
Lawnmower $-$ lawn size 80	8.6, 8.12	4.65	33.00
Lawnmower $-$ lawn size 96	8.7, 8.13	5.06	234.60
Bumblebee $-$ 10 flowers	9.10, 9.11	1.49	1.20
Bumblebee $-$ 15 flowers	9.8, 9.9	1.72	1.21
Bumblebee $-$ 20 flowers	9.6, 9.7	1.72	1.24
Bumblebee $-$ 25 flowers	9.3, 9.5	1.84	3.20
Impulse response	Chapter 11	1.81	1.46
Artificial ant	Chapter 12	1.27	2.00
Obstacle-avoiding robot	Chapter 13	2.71	3.27
Minesweeper	Chapter 14	2.86	6.87

Chapters 21 through 25 provide evidence in support of main point 8 which is as follows:

Main point 8: Genetic programming is capable of simultaneously solving a problem and evolving the architecture of the overall program.

The problems of chapters 15 through 20 were so time-consuming that we were unable to make enough successful runs to make meaningful performance curves (and therefore do not appear in table 27.1). Nonetheless, the results of experiments with these problems provide additional evidence supporting the main points of this book. For the letter-recognition problem (chapter 15), the three-way classification of flushes and fours-of-a-kind (chapter 16), the set-creating and arithmetic-performing versions of the transmembrane problem (chapter 18), the omega-loop problem (chapter 19), and the lookahead version of the transmembrane problem (chapter 20), there was evidence based on a small number of runs that automatically defined functions do indeed facilitate solution to these problems. The evidence took the form that the problem was solved with apparent ease when automatically defined functions were used, but only rarely when they were not used. In other cases, genetic programming was only able to come close to a solution when automatically defined functions were not used, but was able to solve the problem one or more times when they were used.

Finally, when the architecture was evolved in chapters 21 through 25, we repeatedly saw that architectures employing automatically defined functions consistently won the competitive battle within the population. This fact further supports the proposition that automatically defined functions are generally beneficial in genetic programming.

In summary, the evidence from this book supports the proposition that automatically defined functions should become a standard part of the genetic programmer's toolkit. Automatically defined functions work so well for so many different problems that anyone using genetic programming should also try automatically defined functions on their problem.

Appendix A: List of Special Symbols

Table A.1 shows the definition and a reference (chapter or section) for each of the special symbols defined and used in multiple places in this book.

Table A.1   Special symbols.

Symbol	Definition	Reference
ADF0	Automatically defined function 0 (the function defined by the first function-defining branch of an overall program).	4.6
C	Correlation	16.2, 18.5.2
E	Computational effort as measured by the minimum value of $I(M, i, z)$ over all the generations between 0 and G. $E = I(M, i^*, z) = (i^* + 1)MR(z)$. E is one of the two numbers appearing in the oval of the performance curves.	4.11
E_{with}	Computational effort with automatically defined functions	4.11
$E_{without}$	Computational effort without automatically defined functions	4.11
G	Maximum number of generations to be run	2.1
$\mathcal{F}_{adf0}$	Function set for automatically defined function ADF0.	4.6
$\mathcal{F}_{rpb}$	Function set for the result-producing branch RPB.	4.6
$\mathcal{F}$	Function set	4.2
i	Current generation number	2.1
i^*	The best generation number (i.e., the number of the first generation for which the minimum value of $I(M, i, z)$ is achieved). i^* is one of the two numbers appearing in the oval of the performance curves.	4.11
$I(M, i, z)$	Total number of individuals that must be processed to yield a solution (or satisfactory result) by generation i with probability z using a population of size M	4.11

Symbol	Definition	Reference
IPB0	Iteration-performing branch.	18.4
ITB0	Iteration-terminating branch.	20.2
K	Number of characters in alphabet	2.1
L	Length of string	2.1
M	Population size	2.1
NIL	The Boolean constant denoting false	2.2
$P(M,i)$	Cumulative probability of success by generation i with population size M	4.11
$R(z)$	The value of $R(M,i,z)$ for the best generation $i*$	4.11
$R(M,i,z)$	Number of independent runs required to yield a solution (or satisfactory result) by generation i, for a population size of M, with a probability of z. $R(M,i,z)$ is computed from $P(M,i)$ and z.	4.11
R_E	Efficiency ratio between the value of $E_{without}$ without automatically defined functions to the value of E_{with} with ADFs	4.11
R_S	Structural complexity ratio between the value of $\overline{S}_{without}$ without automatically defined functions to the value of $\overline{S}_{with}$ with ADFs	4.10
R_W	Wallclock ratio between the value of $W_{without}$ without automatically defined functions to the value of W_{with} with ADFs	8.16
$\Re_{bigger\text{-}reals}$	Floating-point random constants ranging between −10.000 and +10.000 (with a granularity of 0.001)	11.2
$\Re_{Boolean}$	Random Boolean constants (T or NIL)	22.1
$\Re_{reals}$	Floating-point random constants ranging between −1.000 and +1.000 (with a granularity of 0.001)	5.1.1.1
$\Re_{real\text{-}vector}$	Vector random constants ranging between −5.0000 and +5.0000 with floating-point numbers as components.	9.2
$\Re_{ternary}$	Ternary random constants from the set {T, NIL, :UNDEFINED}	24.2
$\Re_{v8}$	Vector random constants ranging between (0,0) and (7,7) with integers modulo 8 as components	8.2
RPB	Result-producing branch (the last branch of an overall program).	4.6
$\overline{S}$	Average structural complexity (number of functions and terminals) in a set of programs (usually the set of successful runs)	4.10
$\overline{S}_{with}$	Average structural complexity with ADFs	4.10

Symbol	Definition	Reference
$\overline{S}_{without}$	Average structural complexity without ADFs	4.10
T	The Boolean constant denoting true	2.2
$\mathcal{T}$	Terminal set	4.2
$\mathcal{T}$adf0	Terminal set for automatically defined function ADF0.	4.6
$\mathcal{T}$rpb	Terminal set for the result-producing branch RPB.	4.6
:UNDEFINED	The ternary constant denoting an undefined value	24.1
$W(M,i,z)$	Average elapsed wallcock time in order to yield a solution (or satisfactory result) by generation i, for a population size, M, with a probability of z.	8.16
W_{with}	Wallclock time with ADFs	8.16
$W_{without}$	Wallclock time without ADFs	8.16
$Y(M,i)$	Observed instantaneous probability that a run yields in a population of size M, for the first time, at least one program that satisfies the success predicate of the problem *on* generation i.	4.11
z	Probability threshold desired for finding at least one successful run in a series of run. z is 99% throughout this book.	4.11
*	"Don't care" symbol in a schema or in rule of a genetic classifier system	2.1, 4.5

Appendix B: List of Special Functions

Table B.1 shows the name, number of arguments, and a reference for certain special functions used in this book.

Table B.1 Special functions used in this book.

Function	Name	Number of argument	Reference
%	Protected division	2	4.2, 11.2
IF	If	3	15.2
IFGTZ	If Greater Than Zero	3	18.10
IFLTE	If Less Than or Equal	4	11.2, 18.5.1
EXPP	Protected exponentiation	1	11.2
ORN	Numerically valued disjunction (OR)	2	18.5.1

Appendix C: List of Fonts

Table C.1 shows the usage of each of the type fonts used in this book.

Table C.1 Fonts used in this book.

Example	Usage of Font
ADF0	Parts of computer programs
A, C, G, T, U	Nucleiotide bases in DNA or RNA
A, C, D, ...	The 20 amino acid residues used in proteins
H, C, O, N, S	Chemical elements: Hydrogen, carbon, oxygen, nitrogen, sulfur
N, C	The N-terminal end and the C-terminal end of a protein

Appendix D: Default Parameters for Controlling Runs of Genetic Programming

Runs of genetic programming are controlled by 21 control parameters, including two major numerical parameters and 19 minor parameters. The 19 minor parameters consist of 11 numerical parameters and eight qualitative variables that control various alternative ways of executing a run. Two of the minor variables discussed below were not included in the list of parameters in *Genetic Programming* (section 6.9) and are new to this volume.

Except as otherwise specifically indicated, the values of all 21 control parameters are fixed at the default values specified below throughout this book. The default values are used in the vast majority of cases.

The two major numerical parameters are the population size, M, and the maximum number of generations to be run, G.

- The default population size, M, is 4,000. (Populations of 1,000, 8,000, or 16,000 are used for certain problems herein).

- The default value for the maximum number of generations to be run, G, is 51 (an initial random generation, called generation 0, plus 50 subsequent generations). (A value of 21 is used occasionally).

Because of their importance, these two major parameters are explicitly mentioned in the tableau of every problem even when the default values are being used.

Many of the 19 minor parameters are direct analogs of parameters that are used in connection with the conventional genetic algorithm; some are specific to genetic programming.

We have intentionally made the same choices for the default values for the various minor parameters as in *Genetic Programming* (section 6.9) with two exceptions. One exception is that the selection method is tournament selection (with a group size of seven) as opposed to fitness-proportionate reproduction for every run herein (except those in section 6.16). The second exception concerns the method of randomization of fitness cases (a variable that was not specifically identified as a control variable in *Genetic Programming*).

Table D.1 Default values of the 21 control parameters for genetic programming.

Two major parameters
- Population size M = 4,000.
- Maximum number of generations to be run G = 51.

Eleven minor numerical parameters
- Probability p_c of crossover = 90%.
- Probability p_r of reproduction = 10%.
- Probability p_{ip} of choosing internal points for crossover = 90%.
- Maximum size $D_{created}$ for programs created during the run = 17.
- Maximum size $D_{initial}$ for initial random programs = 6.
- Probability p_m of mutation = 0.0%.
- Probability p_p of permutation = 0.0%.
- Frequency f_{ed} of editing = 0.
- Probability p_{en} of encapsulation = 0.0%.
- Condition for decimation = NIL.
- Decimation target percentage p_d = 0.0%.

Eight minor qualitative variables
- The generative method for initial random population is ramped half-and-half.
- The basic selection method is tournament selection with a group size of seven.
- Spousal selection method is tournament selection with a group size of seven.
- Adjusted fitness is not used.
- Over-selection is not used.
- The elitist strategy is not used.
- The randomization, if any, involved in the creation of the fitness cases for a problem is fixed for all runs of the problem.
- In structure-preserving crossover, the way of assigning types to the noninvariant points of a program is branch typing.

The eleven minor numerical parameters used to control the process are described below:

- The probability of crossover, p_c, is 0.90. That is, crossover is performed such that the number of individuals produced as offspring by the crossover operation is equal to 90% of the population size on each generation. For example, if the population size is 16,000, then 14,400 individuals are produced as offspring by the crossover operation on each generation.

- The probability of reproduction, p_r, is 0.10. That is, for each generation, reproduction is performed on a number of individuals equal to 10% of the population size. For example, if the population size is 16,000, 1,600 individuals are selected (with reselection allowed) to participate in reproduction on each generation.

- In choosing crossover points, we use a probability distribution that allocates $p_{ep} = 90\%$ of the crossover points equally among the internal points of each tree and $p_{ep} = 1 - p_{ip} = 10\%$ of the crossover points equally among the external points of each tree (i.e., the terminals). The choice of crossover points are further restricted so that if the root of any branch is chosen as the point of insertion for a parent, then the crossover point of the other parent may not be merely a terminal.

- A maximum size (measured by depth), $D_{created}$, is 17 for programs created by the crossover operation for all runs not using the array method of representation. (The array method is described below; it is used only for the 3-, 4-, 5-, and 6-parity problems in chapter 6 and the comparative study of the 15 architectures of the even-5-parity problem of chapter 7). If a particular offspring created by crossover exceeds the applicable limit, the crossover is aborted as to that particular offspring. If offspring 1 is unacceptable, parent 1 becomes offspring 1. Similarly, if offspring 2 is unacceptable, parent 2 becomes offspring 2.

- A maximum size (measured by depth), $D_{initial}$, is 6 for the random individuals generated for the initial population.

- The probability of mutation, p_m specifying the frequency of performing the operation of mutation is 0.

- The probability of permutation, p_p, specifying the probability of performing the operation of permutation is 0.

- The parameter specifying the frequency, f_{ed}, of applying the operation of editing is 0.

- The probability of encapsulation, p_{en}, specifying the probability of performing the operation of encapsulation is 0.

- The condition for invoking the decimation operation is set to NIL. That is, decimation is not used.

- The decimation percentage, p_d (which is irrelevant if the condition for invoking the decimation operation is NIL) is arbitrarily set to 0.

Eight minor qualitative variables control the way a run of genetic programming is executed. The first six of these variables were included in *Genetic Programming* (section 6.9); the last two are new to this volume.

- The generative method for the initial random population is ramped half-and-half .

- The method of selection for reproduction and for the first parent in crossover is tournament selection (with a group size of seven). This choice differs from *Genetic Programming* where the method of selection was fitness-proportionate reproduction (and where greedy over-selection was used for larger population sizes). In *tournament selection*, a specified group of individuals is chosen with a uniform random probability distribution from the population and the one with the best fitness (i.e., the lowest standardized fitness) is then selected (Goldberg and Deb 1991). If two individuals are to be selected (say, for participation in crossover), a second group of the specified size is chosen at random and the one with the best fitness is selected. Tournament selection with a group size of two is illustrated when two bulls fight over the right to mate with a given cow. We use a group size of seven for tournament selection because it lessens the probability that the current best-of-generation individual will not be selected to participate in at least one operation. All individuals remain in the population while selection is performed for the entire current generation. That is, the selection is always done with replacement (i.e., reselection). Tournament selection is used throughout this book, except for the runs in section 6.16 which were done prior to our decision to switch to tournament selection. Therefore, if the goal is to replicate the results reported in this book, tournament selection should be used as indicated. In retrospect, it is not clear that the decision to use tournament selection was beneficial, so we do not necessarily recommend this choice for future work.

- The method of selecting the second parent for a crossover is the same as the method for selecting the first parent (i.e., tournament selection with a group size of seven).

- The optional adjusted fitness measure (usually used in *Genetic Programming*) is irrelevant in the context of tournament selection.

- The technique of greedy over-selection (used in *Genetic Programming* for certain population sizes) is irrelevant in the context of tournament selection.

- The elitist strategy is not used.

The last two of these eight minor variables were not included in the list of parameters in *Genetic Programming* (section 6.9).

- If there is any randomization involved in the creation of the fitness cases for the problem, the randomization occurs once and is fixed for all runs of the problem. The alternatives to this default choice are to randomize the fitness cases anew at the beginning of each run (used in tables 4.2 and 5.15), to randomize the fitness cases anew from generation to generation within the run (not used at all in this book), and to randomize the fitness cases anew for each fitness evaluation (not used at all in this book).

- The way of assigning types to the noninvariant points of an overall program is branch typing. The alternatives to this default choice are point typing (used in chapters 21 through 25) and like-branch typing (not used in this book, but considered in section 25.11 of *Genetic Programming*).

The 19 minor parameters are generally not specifically mentioned in the tableau unless there is deviation from the default value. However, because automatically defined functions are central to this book, we do explicitly mention the choice of the way of assigning types to noninvariant points in each tableau with ADFs even when the default value (i.e., branch typing) is being used.

Note that the default value of 17 for the maximum permissible depth, $D_{created}$, for a program created by crossover is not a significant or relevant constraint on program size. In fact, this choice permits potentially enormous programs. For example, the largest permissible LISP program consisting of entirely two-argument functions would contain $2^{17} = 131{,}072$ functions and terminals. If four LISP functions and terminals are roughly equivalent to one line of a program written in a conventional programming language, then this largest permissible program corresponds to about 33,000 lines of code.

We do not use LISP S-expressions to represent the programs in the populations for three purposes in this book: when the population size is 16,000 (as it is only for the even-3-, 4-, 5-, and 6-parity problems in chapter 6), for the runs of the even-5-parity problem with the 15 different architectures (chapter 7), and for the runs of 1,000,000 programs in chapter 26. Instead, we use the *array method* of representation for programs in which the tree structure of individual programs in the population is represented as a table. With the array method, the size limit for the random individuals generated for the initial random population is expressed in terms of the total number of points, rather than in terms of the depth of the tree. (This is in contrast to our usual practice throughout this book, where the limits on program size are applied separately to each branch of an overall program). For example, for an overall program consisting of two function-defining branches and one result-producing branch, there is an overall limit of 500 points for all the branches, a separate limit of 200 on the result-producing branch, and a separate limit of 150 on each function-defining branch. These same limits are imposed on each potential offspring of the crossover operation. If a particular offspring created by crossover exceeds the applicable limit, the crossover is aborted as to that particular offspring. If offspring 1 is unacceptable, parent 1 becomes offspring 1. Similarly, if offspring 2 is unacceptable, parent 2 becomes offspring 2. When these size limits are applied separately to each branch, the average size of programs in generation 0 with automatically defined functions are much larger (by a multiple approximately equal to the total number of branches in the overall program) than the average size without automatically defined functions.

Table D.1 summarizes the default values used in this book for the numerical parameters and qualitative variables for controlling runs of genetic programming.

Many problems described herein undoubtedly could be solved better or faster by means of different choices of these parameters and variables. No detailed studies of the optimal choice for the control parameters, with or without automatically defined functions, have been made. Instead, the focus in this book is on the demonstration of the main points stated in chapter 1. In my view, the optimal choices for the control parameters become relevant only after one has been persuaded of the basic usefulness of genetic programming with automatically defined functions. In the present volume, this process of persuasion would be undermined by frequent variation of the various control parameters; the reader might come to attribute any demonstrated success of automatically defined functions to the fortuitous choice of the parameters. Of course, parameters are occasionally changed for certain specific reasons for illustrative purposes, for historical reasons, and when necessary.

Appendix E: Computer Implementation of ADFs

In order to further explore the potential of genetic programming with automatically defined functions and to replicate the experimental results reported herein, it is necessary to implement genetic programming with automatically defined functions on a computer.

Common LISP code for implementing genetic programming appears in appendixes B and C of *Genetic Programming* (Koza 1992a). That code and the code in this appendix (along with such updates as may from time to time be added) can be obtained on-line via anonymous FTP (file transfer protocol) from the `pub/genetic-programming` directory at the FTP site `ftp.cc.utexas.edu` as described in appendix G.

Automatically defined functions can be implemented by modifying the code in appendixes B and C of *Genetic Programming* in light of the following five considerations.

First, since each overall program in the population consists of one or more function-defining branches as well as a result-producing branch, a constrained syntactic structure must be created to accommodate the multi-branch overall program.

Second, the terminal and function sets differ among the branches. One difference is that the function set of the result-producing branch contains at least one automatically defined function, whereas at least one of the function-defining branches does not refer to any automatically defined function. Another difference is that there are no dummy variables in the result-producing branch. It is frequently (but not necessarily) true that the terminal set of the function-defining branches contains dummy variables (formal parameters), although the artificial ant problem of chapter 12 using side-effecting functions illustrates that function-defining branches do not necessarily have any dummy variables. It is also frequently (but not necessarily) true that the terminal set of the function-defining branches does not contain any of the actual variables of the problem. The terminal set of the result-producing branch frequently (but not necessarily) contains the actual variables of the problem.

Third, generation 0 of the population must be created in conformity with the desired constrained syntactic structure. Specifically, each branch of each overall program in the population must be composed of the functions and terminals appropriate to that branch.

Fourth, crossover must be performed so as to preserve the syntactic validity of all offspring. Crossover is limited to the work-performing bodies of the various branches. Structure-preserving crossover is implemented by allowing any point in the work-performing body of any branch of the overall program to be chosen, without restriction, as the crossover point of the first parent. Once the crossover point of the first parent has been chosen in structure-preserving crossover, the choice of the crossover point of the second parent is restricted to points of the same type. Types are assigned to the noninvariant points of an overall program in one of three ways (branch typing, point typing, and like-branch typing) described in section 4.8.

Fifth, when the result-producing branch is being evaluated, it must be able to invoke the appropriate automatically defined functions within the overall program.

This appendix contains Common LISP code (Steele 1990) for a simple version of genetic programming with automatically defined functions. This code is based as closely as possible on the LISP code from appendixes B and C of *Genetic Programming*. Since our experience with that code has been that most users used the code as a guide to write their own code (often in another programming language), the LISP code in this appendix is written in an intentionally very simple style so that it can be easily understood by a user who has only minimal knowledge of LISP. The user will find many opportunities to optimize this code and make it more general and flexible in the process of using it or translating it to another language. The code is divided into a problem specific part and a problem independent kernel. Implementation of automatically defined functions requires changes to both the problem-specific part and the kernel. We have tested the code in this appendix on the Texas Instruments Explorer™ II⁺ computer using its Common LISP environment.

The code in this appendix illustrates the problem of symbolic regression of the Boolean even-5-parity problem (chapters 6 and 7) using two three-argument automatically defined functions.

In order to run a different problem, the user need only modify a relatively small amount of code. If the user's new problem involves two three-argument automatically defined functions, only the problem specific part of the code here need be modified. Techniques for modifying the problem specific code to handle different problems were illustrated in *Genetic Programming* (appendix B) with three different problems, so our focus here will be on the aspects of the code that differ depending on whether or not automatically defined functions are being used.

The potential user of this code should be alert to the fact that almost all the problems in this book require considerably more computer resources to run than a typical problem described in *Genetic Programming*. The reason is that problems that contain a sufficient amount of internal regularity to benefit from automatically defined functions are inherently more complex. Very simple problems do not need, and do not benefit from, automatically defined functions. The most common population size in this book is 4,000 versus only 500 in *Genetic Programming*. The size of the population, of course, impacts both computer time and memory. In addition, the number of fitness cases is also generally higher in this book because more complex problems usually require more fitness cases. Moreover, many of the problems herein use random constants and successful runs with random constants generally require larger population sizes. In addition, because we chose to apply the depth restrictions independently to the body of each branch (for all population sizes below 16,000), the programs in this book tend to much larger and hence more demanding of computer time and memory than those without automatically defined functions. Finally, the interpretation and execution of programs with automatically defined functions takes more time than programs without them.

The Texas Instruments Explorer™ II$^+$ computer that we used to run all the problems of this book was of late 1980s vintage. Except for the simple problems in early chapters, a single run of most problems described in this book took between a half day to several days each on one processor of this excellent, but now-outdated, machine. Comparing machines is always uncertain. Comparisons are especially uncertain when one machine is a LISP machine and the other is not. The overall performance of our machine is, roughly, comparable to a Sun IPX™ when running a commercial software version of LISP.

The user should also keep in mind the fact that a sufficient population size is absolutely essential in genetic methods. Genetic methods start to perform only when a sufficient population size with a sufficient variety of genetic material is available. If an insufficient population size is used, virtually no results are produced.

E.1 PROBLEM SPECIFIC CODE FOR BOOLEAN EVEN-5-PARITY PROBLEM

As previously mentioned, there are six major steps in preparing to use genetic programming with automatically defined functions, namely determining

(1) the set of terminals for each branch,

(2) the set of functions for each branch,

(3) the fitness measure,

(4) the parameters and variables for controlling the run,

(5) the method for designating a result and the criterion terminating a run, and

(6) the architecture of the overall program.

The problem specific part of the LISP code in this appendix closely parallels these six major steps. It is relatively straightforward to adapt the problem specific part of the code in this appendix to a new problem by visualizing a problem in terms of these steps.

The sixth major step is peculiar to automatically defined functions and should be performed first.

The sixth major step involves determining

(a) the number of function-defining branches,

(b) the number of arguments possessed by each function-defining branch, and

(c) if there is more than one function-defining branch, the nature of the hierarchical references (if any) allowed between the function-defining branches.

For the Boolean even-5-parity problem, the sixth major step, for this example, consists of deciding that there will be two function-defining branches (for automatically defined functions ADF0 and ADF1); that ADF0 and ADF1 will each take three arguments; and that the second automatically defined function, ADF1, is permitted to refer hierarchically to the first automatically defined function, ADF0. The fact that there are two function-defining branches and one result-producing branch in each overall program in the population means that the terminal set and the function set must be specified for each of these three branches.

Having performed the sixth major step, we can proceed to the other five major steps.

The problem specific part of the LISP code requires writing code for the following 12 types of items:

(1) `defvar` declaration(s),

(2) a group of functions whose names begin `define-terminal-set-for-EVEN-5-PARITY` for each function-defining branch and the result-producing branch of the overall program,

(3) a group of functions whose names begin `define-function-set-for-EVEN-5-PARITY` for each function-defining branch and the result-producing branch of the overall program,

(4) if applicable, user-defined problem specific function(s),

(5) `defstruct EVEN-5-PARITY-fitness-case`,

(6) `define-fitness-cases-for-EVEN-5-PARITY`,

(7) `EVEN-5-PARITY-wrapper`,

(8) `evaluate-standardized-fitness-for-EVEN-5-PARITY`,

(9) `define-parameters-for-EVEN-5-PARITY`,

(10) `define-termination-criterion-for-EVEN-5-PARITY`,

(11) the function `EVEN-5-PARITY`, and

(12) the invocation using `run-genetic-programming-system`.

The first major step in preparing to use genetic programming is to identify the set of terminals and the second major step is to identify the function set. When automatically defined functions are involved, these two steps must be applied to each branch of the overall program. That is, items (2) and (3) require that code be written for each branch of the overall program. For this problem, each of the three branches is composed of different ingredients.

The terminal set, T_{rpb}, for the result-producing branch consists of the five actual variables of the problem, namely the five Boolean variables D0, D1, D2, D3, and D4.

$T_{rpb} = \{$D0, D1, D2, D3, D4$\}$.

The function set, F_{rpb}, of the result-producing branch for this problem will contain four primitive Boolean functions and two automatically defined functions, ADF0 and ADF1.

$F_{rpb} = \{$ADF0, ADF1, AND, OR, NAND, NOR$\}$

with an argument map for this function set of

$\{3, 3, 2, 2, 2, 2\}$.

The terminal set, T_{adf0}, for the first function-defining branch that defines automatically defined function, ADF0, consists of three dummy variables.

$T_{adf0} = \{$ARG0, ARG1, ARG2$\}$.

The function set, F_{adf0}, for ADF0 consists of the following set of four primitive Boolean functions:

$F_{adf0} = \{$AND, OR, NAND, NOR$\}$

with an argument map for this function set of

$\{2, 2, 2, 2\}$.

The terminal set, T_{adf1}, for the second function-defining branch defining, ADF1, consists of two dummy variables (i.e., is the same as ADF0).

$T_{adf1} = \{$ARG0, ARG1, ARG2$\}$.

The function set, F_{adf1}, for ADF1 consists of the set of four primitive Boolean functions and the already-defined function ADF0. That is, the function-defining branch for ADF1 is capable of hierarchically calling the already-defined function ADF0.

$F_{adf1} = \{$ADF0, AND, OR, NAND, NOR$\}$

with an argument map for this function set of

$\{3, 2, 2, 2, 2\}$.

Note that the actual variables of the problem, D0, D1, D2, D3, and D4, do not appear in either function-defining branch of this problem and that the result-producing branch does not contain any dummy variables, such as ARG0, ARG1, and ARG2. Also, note that although we use the names ARG0, ARG1, and ARG2 for the dummy variables of both ADF0 and ADF1, these dummy variables only have a defined value locally within a particular automatically defined function.

We start by declaring each variable in the terminal set of the result-producing branch and the function-defining branches as global variables. Thus, the first of the 12 items that we must write in the problem specific part of the code consist of the following eight declarations:

```
(defvar d0)
(defvar d1)
(defvar d2)
(defvar d3)
(defvar d4)
(defvar arg0)
(defvar arg1)
(defvar arg2)
```

In addition, we need two additional global variables, *ADF0* and *ADF1* associated with the two automatically defined functions and definitions for them.

```
(defvar *adf0*)

(defun adf0 (arg0 arg1 arg2)
  (eval *adf0*))

(defvar *adf1*)

(defun adf1 (arg0 arg1 arg2)
  (eval *adf1*))
```

We place these declarations and definitions at the beginning of the file containing the LISP code for this problem.

Since there are multiple branches to each overall program in the population, we now create a LISP function to define the terminal set for each function-defining branch and the result-producing branch of the overall program. Each overall program here consists of ADF0, ADF1, and one result-producing branch, RPB. Each of the functions for defining a terminal set returns the list of the terminals used in a particular branch of the overall program. Thus, the second group of items in the problem specific part of the LISP code that we must write consists of three functions for defining the terminal sets of the three branches of the overall program.

The function for defining the terminal set of the single result-producing branch, RPB, is as follows:

```
(defun define-terminal-set-for-EVEN-5-PARITY-RPB ()
  (values '(d4 d3 d2 d1 d0))
)
```

The function for defining the terminal set of the function-defining branch ADF0 is as follows:

```
(defun define-terminal-set-for-EVEN-5-PARITY-ADF0 ()
  (values '(arg0 arg1 arg2))
)
```

The function for defining the terminal set of the function-defining branch ADF1 is as follows:

```
(defun define-terminal-set-for-EVEN-5-PARITY-ADF1 ()
```

```
  (values '(arg0 arg1 arg2))
)
```

Note that, for clarity, we explicitly highlight the value(s) returned by each function by using a `values` form.

The third group of items in the problem specific part of the LISP code that we must write consists of three functions for specifying the function sets and the argument maps of the three branches of the overall program.

The function for defining the function set and the argument map of the result-producing branch, RPB, is as follows:

```
(defun define-function-set-for-EVEN-5-PARITY-RPB ()
  (values '(and or nand nor ADF0 ADF1)
          '(  2  2    2  2    3    3)
  )
)
```

The function for defining the function set and the argument map of the first function-defining branch, ADF0, is as follows:

```
(defun define-function-set-for-EVEN-5-PARITY-ADF0 ()
  (values '(and or nand nor)
          '(  2  2    2  2)
  )
)
```

Since ADF1 is permitted to refer hierarchically to ADF0, ADF0 appears in the function set of the second function-defining branch, ADF1. Thus, the function for defining the function set and the argument map of the second function-defining branch, ADF1, is as follows:

```
(defun define-function-set-for-EVEN-5-PARITY-ADF1 ()
  (values '(and or nand nor ADF0)
          '(  2  2    2  2    3)
  )
)
```

For purposes of programming, we treat all zero-argument functions as terminals. Note that, for purposes of exposition in the text of this book, we treat zero-argument side-effecting functions as terminals, but treat zero-argument ADFs as functions.

Many of the 12 items that we must write in the problem specific part of the code for a problem when using automatically defined functions are written in much the same way as when automatically defined functions are not being used. We include them here for completeness; however, we describe some of them briefly.

The fourth item in the problem specific part of the LISP code that we must write consists of writing the definition of any problem specific functions (if any) peculiar to the problem. For this problem, the primitive functions, NAND and NOR, appearing in the function sets of all three branches require definition. The multi-argument ODD-PARITY function (used later to compute the target even-5-parity function) is also defined here.

```
(defun NAND (a b)
  (not (and a b))
)

(defun NOR (a b)
  (not (or a b))
)

(defun ODD-PARITY (&rest args)
  (let ((result nil))
    (dolist (value args result)
      (when value (setf result (not result)))))
)
```

The third major step in preparing to use genetic programming is identifying the fitness measure for evaluating how good a given computer program is at solving the problem at hand. The even-5-parity problem is typical of most problems in that fitness is computed using a number of fitness cases. We establish the fitness cases at the beginning of the run. The kernel then loops over each individual program in the population calling on the user-specified fitness function to evaluate the fitness of each individual. If the fitness measure requires fitness cases, the fitness function loops over the fitness cases in order to evaluate the fitness of each particular S-expression from the population.

We store the fitness cases in an array, each element of which corresponds to one fitness case. Each fitness case is implemented as a record structure. It is convenient to store the values of all the independent variables for a given fitness case in the record for that fitness case along with any dependent variables (the "answer") for that fitness case. Since the Boolean even-5-parity problem is a problem of symbolic regression involving five independent variables and one dependent variable, there are six variables for this problem.

The fifth item in the problem specific part of the LISP code that we must write is the `defstruct` record structure declaration for the fitness cases of this problem:

```
(defstruct EVEN-5-PARITY-fitness-case
  d0
  d1
  d2
  d3
  d4
  target
)
```

The sixth item in the problem specific part of the LISP code that we must write is the function called `define-fitness-cases-for-EVEN-5-PARITY` for this problem. The fitness cases for this problem consist of all $2^5 = 32$ possible combinations of the five Boolean arguments, d0, d1, d2, d3, and d4, so the `*number-of-fitness-cases*` is 32. These fitness cases are created with five nested `dolist` functions, each looping over the list (t nil). Maximum raw fitness is 32 matches.

Standardized fitness is 32 minus raw fitness. The `target` is defined by using the negation of the multi-argument ODD-PARITY function.

```
(defun define-fitness-cases-for-EVEN-5-PARITY ()
  (let (fitness-case fitness-cases index)
    (setf fitness-cases (make-array *number-of-fitness-cases*))
    (format t "~%Fitness cases")
    (setf index 0)
    (dolist (d4 '(t nil))
     (dolist (d3 '(t nil))
      (dolist (d2 '(t nil))
       (dolist (d1 '(t nil))
        (dolist (d0 '(t nil))
            (setf fitness-case
                  (make-EVEN-5-PARITY-fitness-case)
            )
            (setf (EVEN-5-PARITY-fitness-case-d0 fitness-case)
                  d0)
            (setf (EVEN-5-PARITY-fitness-case-d1 fitness-case)
                  d1)
            (setf (EVEN-5-PARITY-fitness-case-d2 fitness-case)
                  d2)
            (setf (EVEN-5-PARITY-fitness-case-d3 fitness-case)
                  d3)
            (setf (EVEN-5-PARITY-fitness-case-d4 fitness-case)
                  d4)
            (setf (EVEN-5-PARITY-fitness-case-target
                    fitness-case)
                  (not (ODD-PARITY d4 d3 d2 d1 d0))
            )
            (setf (aref fitness-cases index) fitness-case)
            (incf index)
            (format t
                    "~% ~3D   ~10S~10S~10S~10S~10S~15S"
                    index d4 d3 d2 d1 d0
                    (EVEN-5-PARITY-fitness-case-target
                      fitness-case
                    )
            )
        )
       )
      )
     )
    )
    (values fitness-cases)
  )
)
```

The seventh item in the problem specific part of the code that we must write for this problem is the function EVEN-5-PARITY-wrapper. In this problem, the wrapper (output interface) merely returns what it is produced by the result-producing branch of the program, namely `result-from-program`.

```
(defun EVEN-5-PARITY-wrapper (result-from-program)
  (values result-from-program)
)
```

The eighth item in the problem specific part of the LISP code that we must write is the function called `evaluate-standardized-fitness-for-EVEN-5-PARITY`. This function receives two arguments from the kernel, namely the individual computer program from the population which is to be evaluated (called `program`) and the set of fitness cases (called `fitness-cases`). This function returns two values, namely the standardized fitness of the individuals and the number of hits. Note that prior to the evaluation (via `eval`) of the result-producing branch of `program`, it is necessary to set each of the five independent variables of this problem (represented by the global variables `d0`, `d1`, `d2`, `d3`, and `d4`). The Boolean flag `match-found` is defined as a result of testing `value-from-program` for equality (i.e., `eq`) with `target-value`.

```
(defun evaluate-standardized-fitness-for-EVEN-5-PARITY
            (program fitness-cases)
  (let (raw-fitness hits standardized-fitness target-value
        match-found value-from-program fitness-case rpb
        )
    (setf raw-fitness 0.0)
    (setf hits 0)
    (setf rpb (ADF-program-RPB program))
    (setf *adf0* (ADF-program-ADF0 program))
    (setf *adf1* (ADF-program-ADF1 program))
    (dotimes (index *number-of-fitness-cases*)
      (setf fitness-case (aref fitness-cases index))
      (setf d0 (EVEN-5-PARITY-fitness-case-d0 fitness-case))
      (setf d1 (EVEN-5-PARITY-fitness-case-d1 fitness-case))
      (setf d2 (EVEN-5-PARITY-fitness-case-d2 fitness-case))
      (setf d3 (EVEN-5-PARITY-fitness-case-d3 fitness-case))
      (setf d4 (EVEN-5-PARITY-fitness-case-d4 fitness-case))
      (setf target-value
            (EVEN-5-PARITY-fitness-case-target fitness-case))
      (setf value-from-program
            (EVEN-5-PARITY-wrapper (eval rpb)))
      (setf match-found (eq target-value value-from-program))
      (incf raw-fitness (if match-found 1.0 0.0))
      (when match-found (incf hits))
    )
    (setf standardized-fitness (- 32 raw-fitness))
    (values standardized-fitness hits)
  )
)
```

Except for very simple problems, the bulk of computer time is consumed during the execution of the `evaluate-standardized-fitness-for-EVEN-`

`5-PARITY` function. Thus, the user should focus his optimization efforts on the fitness measure and any functions that may be called when a program from the population is measured for fitness.

For Boolean problems, the user can save an enormous amount of computer time with one of two possible optimization techniques. One technique involves identifying the particular three-argument Boolean functions that are performed by the bodies of `ADF0` and `ADF1`; creating two eight-row lookup tables for `ADF0` and `ADF1`; and thereafter using the lookup tables in lieu of evaluating the entire bodies `ADF0` and `ADF1` for each fitness case. A second technique involves converting the Boolean expressions in `ADF0` and `ADF1` to disjunctive normal form (DNF) and compiling the resulting program. Both techniques are especially valuable when there is one or more hierarchical reference between the function-defining branches because the hierarchical reference is, in effect, eliminated.

The fourth major step in preparing to use genetic programming is determining the values of certain parameters for controlling the run.

The ninth item in the problem specific part of the code that we must write is the `define-parameters-for-EVEN-5-PARITY` function. This function is used to assign the values to ten parameters that control the run.

```
(defun define-parameters-for-EVEN-5-PARITY ()
  (setf *number-of-fitness-cases* 32)
  (setf *max-depth-for-new-individuals* 5)
  (setf *max-depth-for-new-subtrees-in-mutants* 4)
  (setf *max-depth-for-individuals-after-crossover* 17)
  (setf *reproduction-fraction* 0.1)
  (setf *crossover-at-any-point-fraction* 0.2)
  (setf *crossover-at-function-point-fraction* 0.7)
  (setf *method-of-selection* :tournament)
  (setf *tournament-size* 7)
  (setf *method-of-generation* :ramped-half-and-half)
  (values)
)
```

The `*number-of-fitness-cases*`, which depends on the problem, is set in the second line. The remaining lines contain the values of the numerical parameters and the qualitative parameters for controlling the run shown as default values in appendix D. The `*tournament-size*` is set to 7 here.

Finally, the fifth major step in preparing to use genetic programming involves determining the criterion for terminating a run and the method for designating the result of a run.

The tenth item in the problem specific part of the code is the `define-termination-criterion-for-EVEN-5-PARITY` function.

```
(defun define-termination-criterion-for-EVEN-5-PARITY
        (current-generation
        maximum-generations
        best-standardized-fitness
        best-hits)
```

```
(declare (ignore best-standardized-fitness))
(values  (or (>= current-generation maximum-generations)
             (>= best-hits *number-of-fitness-cases*)
    )
  )
)
```

The eleventh item in the problem specific part of the LISP code that we must write is a function called EVEN-5-PARITY which informs the kernel about the various functions we have just written for this problem. The name of this function establishes the name of the problem.

```
(defun EVEN-5-PARITY ()
  (values 'define-function-set-for-EVEN-5-PARITY-ADF0
          'define-function-set-for-EVEN-5-PARITY-ADF1
          'define-function-set-for-EVEN-5-PARITY-RPB
          'define-terminal-set-for-EVEN-5-PARITY-ADF0
          'define-terminal-set-for-EVEN-5-PARITY-ADF1
          'define-terminal-set-for-EVEN-5-PARITY-RPB
          'define-fitness-cases-for-EVEN-5-PARITY
          'evaluate-standardized-fitness-for-EVEN-5-PARITY
          'define-parameters-for-EVEN-5-PARITY
          'define-termination-criterion-for-EVEN-5-PARITY
  )
)
```

We now illustrate a run of genetic programming by calling a function called run-genetic-programming-system. This function takes four mandatory arguments, namely

(1) the name of the problem (e.g., EVEN-5-PARITY),
(2) the randomizer seed (which should be greater than 0.0 and less than or equal to 1.0),
(3) the maximum number G of generations to be run, and
(4) the population size M.

Thus, the twelfth and final item in the problem specific part of the code that we must write is the one line required to execute this problem by invoking the function run-genetic-programming-system, with four mandatory arguments as follows:

```
(run-genetic-programming-system 'EVEN-5-PARITY 1.0 51 4000)
```

Evaluation of the above would result in a run of the EVEN-5-PARITY problem, using the randomizer seed of 1.0 with a maximum number G of generations of 51 (i.e., generation 0 plus 50 additional generations) with a population size, M, of 4,000.

The randomizer seed is an explicit argument to this function in order to give the user direct control over the randomizer. By re-using a seed, the user can obtain the same results (e.g., for debugging or so that interesting runs can be replicated). By using different seeds on different runs, the user will obtain different results.

After the above four mandatory arguments, this function can take up to M additional optional arguments. Each optional argument represents a primed individual that will be seeded into the initial population. If fewer than M such primed individuals are provided, the initial population will contain all the primed individuals that are provided and will then be filled out with randomly created individuals.

One useful test that the user can perform is to verify that the correct fitness is computed for a single primed individual consisting of a correct program for the even-5-parity function.

```
(run-genetic-programming-system
  'EVEN-5-PARITY 1.0 1 1
  (make-ADF-program
    :adf0 '(or (and arg0 arg1)
               (and (nand arg0 arg0)
                    (nand arg1 arg1)))
    :adf1 '(nand (or (and arg0 arg1)
                     (and (nand arg0 arg0) (nand arg1 arg1)))
                 (or (and arg0 arg1)
                     (and (nand arg0 arg0)
                          (nand arg1 arg1))))
    :rpb '(adf1 (adf0 (adf0 d0 d1 d0) (adf0 d2 d3 d0) d0)
                d4 d0)))
```

ADF0 here is equivalent to the even-2-parity and ADF1 is equivalent to the odd-2-parity.

The user can verify the correct operation of his program by running this problem a number of times.

We have verified the computer code in this appendix by comparing its operation with our computer code on our Texas Instruments Explorer II$^+$ computer. We made 32 runs of the even-5-parity problem using the computer code in this appendix.

Figure E.1 shows the performance curves generated from these 32 runs with the computer code contained in this appendix for the even-5-parity problem with two three-argument automatically defined functions. The population size, M, of 4,000. The cumulative probability of success is 62% at generation 19 and 78% at generation 50. The numbers 19 and 400,000 in the oval indicate that, if this problem is run through to generation 19, processing a total of E_{with} = 400,000 individuals (i.e., 4,000 × 20 generations × 5 runs) is sufficient to yield a solution to this problem with 99% probability.

Figure 7.6 summarizes the results of 96 runs of this problem with our computer code on our Texas Instruments Explorer II$^+$ computer. A comparison of figures 7.6 and E.1 indicates that the rising cumulative probability curve is virtually the same. Moreover, figure 7.6 reports that the computational effort, E_{with}, for the 96 runs is also 400,000.

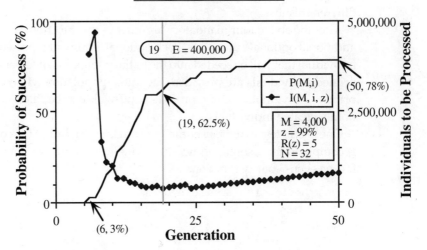

With Defined Functions

Figure E.1 Performance curves generated from 32 runs using the computer code in this appendix for the even-5-parity problem showing that E_{with} = 400,000 with ADFs having a fixed argument map of {3, 3}.

E.2 KERNEL

The kernel is the generic part of the simple LISP code for genetic programming. In this appendix, we briefly provide an overview of how the kernel works and some basic information to the user who may want to modify the kernel.

The discussion of the kernel is divided into 12 parts.

First, the kernel contains a `defstruct` declaration to declare the data structure representing each individual in the population. The `defstruct` form in LISP is similar to declarations of record types in other programming languages. The `program` slot in this record type is the individual in the population. There are four additional slots in this record type, namely for the `standardized-fitness`, `adjusted-fitness`, `normalized-fitness`, and `hits` of the individual `program` in question.

```
(defstruct individual
  program
  (standardized-fitness 0)
  (adjusted-fitness 0)
  (normalized-fitness 0)
  (hits 0))
```

The following is a record structure declaration for the programs. The print method below allows the user to print out a `program` in the form used throughout this book.

```
(defstruct
  (adf-program
    (:print-function
      (lambda (instance stream depth)
```

```
         (declare (ignore depth))
         (format stream
           "(progn (defun ADF0 (ARG0 ARG1 ARG2)~
         ~%         (values ~S))~
         ~%       (defun ADF0 (ARG0 ARG1 ARG2)~
         ~%         (values ~S))~
         ~%         (values ~S))"
         (adf-program-adf0 instance)
         (adf-program-adf1 instance)
         (adf-program-rpb instance)))))
  adf0
  adf1
  rpb)
```

Second, the kernel contains ten `defvar` declarations for 10 global variables and binds each of them to `:unbound`. These are the 10 parameters that the user is expected to set in the `define-parameters-for-«*»` function described in the previous section.

```
(defvar *number-of-fitness-cases* :unbound
  "The number of fitness cases")
```

```
(defvar *max-depth-for-new-individuals* :unbound
  "The maximum depth for individuals of the initial
   random generation")
```

```
(defvar *max-depth-for-individuals-after-crossover* :unbound
  "The maximum depth of new individuals created by crossover")
```

```
(defvar *reproduction-fraction* :unbound
  "The fraction of the population that will experience fitness
   proportionate reproduction (with reselection)
   during each generation")
```

```
(defvar *crossover-at-any-point-fraction* :unbound
  "The fraction of the population that will experience
   crossover at any point in the tree (including terminals)
   during each generation")
```

```
(defvar *crossover-at-function-point-fraction* :unbound
  "The fraction of the population that will experience
   crossover at a function (internal) point in the tree
   during each generation.")
```

```
(defvar *max-depth-for-new-subtrees-in-mutants* :unbound
  "The maximum depth of new subtrees created by mutation")
```

```
(defvar *method-of-selection* :unbound
  "The method of selecting individuals in the population.
   Either :fitness-proportionate, :tournament or
   :fitness-proportionate-with-over-selection.")
```

```
(defvar *tournament-size* :unbound
  "The group size to use when doing tournament selection.")
```

```
(defvar *method-of-generation* :unbound
  "Can be any one of :grow, :full, :ramped-half-and-half")
```

Third, the kernel defines three variables used by the randomizer and for bookkeeping purposes.

```
(defvar *seed* :unbound
  "The seed for the Park-Miller congruential randomizer.")
```

```
(defvar *best-of-run-individual* :unbound
  "The best individual found during this run.")
```

```
(defvar *generation-of-best-of-run-individual* :unbound
  "The generation at which the best-of-run individual was found.")
```

Fourth, the kernel contains the top level function run-genetic-programming-system that controls the genetic programming system. This is the function that the user uses to invoke the kernel. It has four mandatory arguments.

The first mandatory argument to this function is problem-function. When the kernel calls problem-function, this function delivers to the kernel the functions that are needed by the kernel to define a specific problem.

The second mandatory argument to the run-genetic-programming-system function is the seed to the randomizer.

The third mandatory argument is the maximum-generations, G, to be run.

The fourth mandatory argument is the size-of-population, M.

After the four mandatory arguments, there may be any number (up to M) of optional seeded-program arguments.

This function calls the problem-function (using funcall) and thereby obtains the problem specific functions that the user has defined in the problem specific part of the code.

This function does some cursory checking of the validity of arguments to this function using four assert clauses.

```
(defun run-genetic-programming-system
          (problem-function
           seed
           maximum-generations
           size-of-population
           &rest seeded-programs)
;; Check validity of some arguments
  (assert (and (integerp maximum-generations)
               (not (minusp maximum-generations)))
          (maximum-generations)
          "Maximum-generations must be a non-negative ~
           integer, not ~S" maximum-generations)
  (assert (and (integerp size-of-population)
               (plusp size-of-population))
          (size-of-population)
          "Size-Of-Population must be a positive integer, ~
           not ~S" size-of-population)
```

```
      (assert (or (and (symbolp problem-function)
                        (fboundp problem-function))
                  (functionp problem-function))
              (problem-function)
              "Problem-Function must be a function.")
      (assert (numberp seed) (seed)
              "The randomizer seed must be a number")
;; Set the global randomizer seed.
      (setf *seed* (coerce seed 'double-float))
;; Initialize best-of-run recording variables
      (setf *generation-of-best-of-run-individual* 0)
      (setf *best-of-run-individual* nil)
;; Get the problem-specific functions needed to
;; specify this problem as returned by a call to
;; problem-function
      (multiple-value-bind (adf0-function-set-creator
                            adf1-function-set-creator
                            rpb-function-set-creator
                            adf0-terminal-set-creator
                            adf1-terminal-set-creator
                            rpb-terminal-set-creator
                            fitness-cases-creator
                            fitness-function
                            parameter-definer
                            termination-predicate)
          (funcall problem-function)
;; Get the function sets and associated
;; argument maps
        (multiple-value-bind (adf0-function-set adf0-argument-map)
            (funcall adf0-function-set-creator)
          (multiple-value-bind (adf1-function-set adf1-argument-map)
              (funcall adf1-function-set-creator)
            (multiple-value-bind (rpb-function-set rpb-argument-map)
                (funcall rpb-function-set-creator)
;; Set up the parameters using parameter-definer
              (funcall parameter-definer)
;; Print out parameters report
              (describe-parameters-for-run
              maximum-generations size-of-population)
;; Set up the terminal-set using terminal-set-creator
              (let ((adf0-terminal-set
                      (funcall adf0-terminal-set-creator))
                    (adf1-terminal-set
                      (funcall adf1-terminal-set-creator))
                    (rpb-terminal-set
                      (funcall rpb-terminal-set-creator)))
;; Create the population
                (let ((population
                        (create-population
                          size-of-population
```

```
                        adf0-function-set adf0-argument-map
                        adf0-terminal-set
                        adf1-function-set adf1-argument-map
                        adf1-terminal-set
                        rpb-function-set rpb-argument-map
                        rpb-terminal-set
                        seeded-programs)))
;; Define the fitness cases using the
;; fitness-cases-creator function
            (let ((fitness-cases
                    (funcall fitness-cases-creator))
                ;; New-Programs is used in the breeding of
                ;; the new population. Create it here to
                ;; reduce consing.
                (new-programs
                    (make-array size-of-population)))
;; Now run the Genetic Programming Paradigm using
;; the fitness-function and termination-predicate provided
            (execute-generations
                population new-programs fitness-cases
                maximum-generations fitness-function
                termination-predicate
                adf0-function-set adf0-argument-map
                adf0-terminal-set
                adf1-function-set adf1-argument-map
                adf1-terminal-set
                rpb-function-set rpb-argument-map
                rpb-terminal-set)
;; Finally print out a report
            (report-on-run)
;; Return the population and fitness cases
;; (for debugging)
            (values population fitness-cases)))))))))
```

Fifth, the kernel contains four functions for printing out various reports.

```
(defun report-on-run ()
  "Prints out the best-of-run individual."
  (let ((*print-pretty* t))
    (format t "~5%The best-of-run individual program ~
            for this run was found on ~%generation ~D and ~
            had a standardized fitness measure ~
            of ~D and ~D hit~P. ~%It was:~%~S"
        *generation-of-best-of-run-individual*
        (individual-standardized-fitness
          *best-of-run-individual*)
        (individual-hits *best-of-run-individual*)
        (individual-hits *best-of-run-individual*)
        (individual-program *best-of-run-individual*))))
```

```lisp
(defun report-on-generation (generation-number population)
  "Prints out the best individual at the end of each generation"
  (let ((best-individual (aref population 0))
        (size-of-population (length population))
        (sum 0.0)
        (*print-pretty* t))
    ;; Add up all of the standardized fitnesses to get average
    (dotimes (index size-of-population)
      (incf sum (individual-standardized-fitness
                  (aref population index))))
    (format t "~2%Generation ~D:  Average standardized-fitness ~
              = ~S. ~%~
              The best individual program of the population ~
              had a ~%standardized fitness measure of ~D ~
              and ~D hit~P. ~%It was: ~%~S"
            generation-number (/ sum (length population))
            (individual-standardized-fitness best-individual)
            (individual-hits best-individual)
            (individual-hits best-individual)
            (individual-program best-individual))))

(defun print-population (population)
  "Given a population, this prints it out (for debugging) "
  (let ((*print-pretty* t))
    (dotimes (index (length population))
      (let ((individual (aref population index)))
        (format t "~&~D   ~S    ~S"
                index
                (individual-standardized-fitness individual)
                (individual-program individual))))))

(defun describe-parameters-for-run
    (maximum-generations size-of-population)
  "Lists the parameter settings for this run."
  (format t "~2%Parameters used for this run.~
            ~%==============================")
  (format t "~%Maximum number of Generations:~50T~D"
          maximum-generations)
  (format t "~%Size of Population:~50T~D" size-of-population)
  (format t "~%Maximum depth of new individuals:~50T~D"
          *max-depth-for-new-individuals*)
  (format t "~%Maximum depth of new subtrees for mutants:~50T~D"
          *max-depth-for-new-subtrees-in-mutants*)
  (format t
          "~%Maximum depth of individuals after crossover:~50T~D"
          *max-depth-for-individuals-after-crossover*)
  (format t "~%Reproduction fraction:~50T~D"
          *reproduction-fraction*)
  (format t "~%Crossover at any point fraction:~50T~D"
          *crossover-at-any-point-fraction*)
```

```
(format t "~%Crossover at function points fraction:~50T~D"
        *crossover-at-function-point-fraction*)
(format t "~%Number of fitness cases:~50T~D"
        *number-of-fitness-cases*)
(format t "~%Selection method: ~50T~A" *method-of-selection*)
(format t "~%Tournament group size: ~50T~A" *tournament-size*)
(format t "~%Randomizer seed: ~50T~D" *seed*))
(format t
  "~%Fitness-proportionate reproduction fraction:~50T~D"
  *fitness-proportionate-reproduction-fraction*)
(format t "~%Crossover at any point fraction:~50T~D"
        *crossover-at-any-point-fraction*)
(format t "~%Crossover at function points fraction:~50T~D"
        *crossover-at-function-point-fraction*)
(format t "~%Number of fitness cases:~50T~D"
        *number-of-fitness-cases*)
(format t "~%Selection method: ~50T~A" *method-of-selection*)
(format t "~%Generation method: ~50T~A"
  *method-of-generation*)
(format t "~%Randomizer seed: ~50T~D" *seed*))
```

Sixth, the kernel contains a group of six functions for creating the individual programs for generation 0. These same functions are also used for creating tree fragments if we happen to be using the mutation operation. The function `create-population` causes the population of individuals to be created in a form specified by the variable `*method-of-generation*`, which can be `:full`, `:grow` or `:ramped-half-and-half`, these being the methods described in *Genetic Programming* (section 6.2). Small changes to this function allow different generative methods, such as a ramped, full, or grow method. The `choose-from-terminal-set` function in this group creates the random constants (if any) for the initial random programs. Small changes to this function permit different ranges and granularity for the random constants. We use the `do` macro of Common LISP in `create-population` and throughout the kernel, rather than the more convenient `loop` macro, because `loop` may not be supported in some generally available, older implementations of Common LISP.

```
(defvar *generation-0-uniquifier-table*
        (make-hash-table :test #'equal)
  "Used to guarantee that all generation 0 individuals
  are unique")

(defun create-program-branch
       (function-set argument-map terminal-set
        minimum-depth-of-trees maximum-depth-of-trees
        individual-index full-cycle-p)
  "Creates a complete branch for an ADF-containing program."
  (create-individual-subtree
    function-set argument-map
    terminal-set
```

```
      (ecase *method-of-generation*
        ((:full :grow) maximum-depth-of-trees)
        (:ramped-half-and-half
         (+ minimum-depth-of-trees
            (mod individual-index
                 (- maximum-depth-of-trees
                    minimum-depth-of-trees)))))
      t
      (ecase *method-of-generation*
        (:full t)
        (:grow nil)
        (:ramped-half-and-half full-cycle-p))))

(defun create-new-program (individual-index full-cycle-p
                           minimum-depth-of-trees
                           maximum-depth-of-trees
                           adf0-function-set adf0-argument-map
                           adf0-terminal-set
                           adf1-function-set adf1-argument-map
                           adf1-terminal-set
                           rpb-function-set rpb-argument-map
                           rpb-terminal-set)
  "Creates a new individual with ADF structure."
  (make-adf-program
    :adf0
    (create-program-branch
      adf0-function-set adf0-argument-map
      adf0-terminal-set minimum-depth-of-trees
      maximum-depth-of-trees individual-index full-cycle-p)
    :adf1
    (create-program-branch
      adf1-function-set adf1-argument-map
      adf1-terminal-set minimum-depth-of-trees
      maximum-depth-of-trees individual-index full-cycle-p)
    :rpb
    (create-program-branch
      rpb-function-set rpb-argument-map
      rpb-terminal-set minimum-depth-of-trees
      maximum-depth-of-trees individual-index full-cycle-p)))

(defun create-population (size-of-population
                          adf0-function-set adf0-argument-map
                          adf0-terminal-set
                          adf1-function-set adf1-argument-map
                          adf1-terminal-set
                          rpb-function-set rpb-argument-map
                          rpb-terminal-set
                          seeded-programs)
  "Creates the population. This is an array of size
   size-of-population that is initialized to contain individual
   records. The Program slot of each individual is initialized
```

to a suitable random program except for the first N programs,
where N = (length seeded-programs). For these first N
individuals the individual is initialized with the respective
seeded program. This is very useful in debugging."

```lisp
(let ((population (make-array size-of-population))
      (minimum-depth-of-trees 1)
      (attempts-at-this-individual 0)
      (full-cycle-p nil))
  (do ((individual-index 0))
      ((>= individual-index size-of-population))
    (when (zerop
            (mod individual-index
                 (max 1 (- *max-depth-for-new-individuals*
                           minimum-depth-of-trees))))
      (setf full-cycle-p (not full-cycle-p)))
    (let ((new-program
            (if (< individual-index (length seeded-programs))
                ;; Pick a seeded individual
                (nth individual-index seeded-programs)
                ;; Create a new random program.
                (create-new-program
                  individual-index full-cycle-p
                  minimum-depth-of-trees
                  ;; We count one level of depth for the
                  ;; root above all of the branches that
                  ;; get evolved.
                  (- *max-depth-for-new-individuals* 1)
                  adf0-function-set adf0-argument-map
                  adf0-terminal-set
                  adf1-function-set adf1-argument-map
                  adf1-terminal-set
                  rpb-function-set rpb-argument-map
                  rpb-terminal-set))))
      ;; Check if we have already created this program.
      ;; If not then store it and move on.
      ;; If we have then try again.
      (let ((program-as-list
              (list (adf-program-adf0 new-program)
                    (adf-program-adf1 new-program)
                    (adf-program-rpb new-program))))
        ;; Turn the defstruct representation of the
        ;; program into a list so that it can be
        ;; compared using an EQUAL hash table.
        ;; defstruct instances have to be compared with EQUALP
        (cond ((< individual-index (length seeded-programs))
               (setf (aref population individual-index)
                     (make-individual :program new-program))
               (incf individual-index))
              ((not (gethash program-as-list
                             *generation-0-uniquifier-table*))
```

```
                (setf (aref population individual-index)
                      (make-individual :program new-program))
                (setf (gethash program-as-list
                               *generation-0-uniquifier-table*)
                      t)
                (setf attempts-at-this-individual 0)
                (incf individual-index))
               ((> attempts-at-this-individual 20)
                ;; Then this depth has probably filled up, so
                ;; bump the depth counter.
                (incf minimum-depth-of-trees)
                ;; Bump the max depth too to keep in line with
                ;; new minimum.
                (setf *max-depth-for-new-individuals*
                      (max *max-depth-for-new-individuals*
                           minimum-depth-of-trees)))
               (:otherwise
                (incf attempts-at-this-individual))))))
  ;; Flush out uniquifier table to that no pointers
  ;; are kept to generation 0 individuals.
  (clrhash *generation-0-uniquifier-table*)
  ;; Return the population that we've just created.
  population))

(defun choose-from-terminal-set (terminal-set)
  "Chooses a random terminal from the terminal set.
   If the terminal chosen is the ephemeral
   :Floating-Point-Random-Constant,
   then a floating-point single precision random constant
   is created in the range -5.0->5.0.
   If :Integer-Random-Constant is chosen then an integer random
   constant is generated in the range -10 to +10."
  (let ((choice (nth (random-integer (length terminal-set))
                     terminal-set)))
    (case choice
      (:floating-point-random-constant
       ;; pick a random number in the range -5.0 —> +5.0.
       ;; Coerce it to be single precision floating-point.
       ;; Double precision is more expensive
       ;; A similar clause to this could be used to coerce it
       ;; to double prevision if you really need
       ;; double precision.
       ;; This is also the place to modify if you need a range
       ;; other than -5.0 —> +5.0.
       (coerce (- (random-floating-point-number 10.0) 5.0)
               'single-float))
      (:integer-random-constant
       ;; pick a random integer in the range -10 —> +10.
       (- (random-integer 21) 10))
      (otherwise choice))))
```

```
(defun create-individual-subtree
        (function-set argument-map terminal-set
        allowable-depth top-node-p full-p)
  "Creates a subtree recursively using the specified functions
   and terminals. Argument map is used to determine how many
   arguments each function in the function set is supposed to
   have if it is selected. Allowable depth is the remaining
   depth of the tree we can create, when we hit zero we will
   only select terminals. Top-node-p is true only when we
   are being called as the top node in the tree. This allows
   us to make sure that we always put a function at the top
   of the tree. Full-p indicates whether this individual
   is to be maximally bushy or not."
  (cond ((<= allowable-depth 0)
         ;; We've reached maxdepth, so just pack a terminal.
         (choose-from-terminal-set terminal-set))
        ((or full-p top-node-p)
         ;; We are the top node or are a full tree,
         ;; so pick only a function.
         (let ((choice (random-integer (length function-set))))
           (let ((function (nth choice function-set))
                 (number-of-arguments
                   (nth choice argument-map)))
             (cons function
                   (create-arguments-for-function
                     number-of-arguments function-set
                     argument-map terminal-set
                     (- allowable-depth 1) full-p)))))
        (:otherwise
         ;; choose one from the bag of functions and terminals.
         (let ((choice (random-integer
                         (+ (length terminal-set)
                            (length function-set)))))
           (if (< choice (length function-set))
               ;; We chose a function, so pick it out and go
               ;; on creating the tree down from here.
               (let ((function (nth choice function-set))
                     (number-of-arguments
                       (nth choice argument-map)))
                 (cons function
                       (create-arguments-for-function
                         number-of-arguments function-set
                         argument-map terminal-set
                         (- allowable-depth 1) full-p)))
               ;; We chose an atom, so pick it out.
               (choose-from-terminal-set terminal-set))))))
```

```
(defun create-arguments-for-function
          (number-of-arguments function-set
           argument-map terminal-set allowable-depth
           full-p)
  "Creates the argument list for a node in the tree.
   Number-Of-Arguments is the number of arguments still
   remaining to be created. Each argument is created
   in the normal way using Create-individual-subtree."
  (if (= number-of-arguments 0)
      nil
      (cons (create-individual-subtree
              function-set argument-map terminal-set
              allowable-depth nil full-p)
            (create-arguments-for-function
              (- number-of-arguments 1) function-set
              argument-map terminal-set
              allowable-depth full-p))))
```

Seventh, the kernel contains a group of five functions to execute the main parts of the genetic programming system.

```
(defun execute-generations
    (population new-programs fitness-cases maximum-generations
     fitness-function termination-predicate
     adf0-function-set adf0-argument-map
     adf0-terminal-set
     adf1-function-set adf1-argument-map
     adf1-terminal-set
     rpb-function-set rpb-argument-map
     rpb-terminal-set)
  "Loops until the user's termination predicate says to stop."
  (do ((current-generation 0 (+ 1 current-generation)))
      ;; loop incrementing current generation until
      ;; termination-predicate succeeds.
      ((let ((best-of-generation (aref population 0)))
         (funcall
           termination-predicate current-generation
           maximum-generations
           (individual-standardized-fitness best-of-generation)
           (individual-hits best-of-generation))))
    (when (> current-generation 0)
      ;; Breed the new population to use on this generation
      ;; (except gen 0, of course).
      (breed-new-population population new-programs
                           adf0-function-set adf0-argument-map
                           adf0-terminal-set
                           adf1-function-set adf1-argument-map
                           adf1-terminal-set
                           rpb-function-set rpb-argument-map
                           rpb-terminal-set))
```

```
;; Clean out the fitness measures.
(zeroize-fitness-measures-of-population population)
;; Measure the fitness of each individual. Fitness values
;; are stored in the individuals themselves.
(evaluate-fitness-of-population
  population fitness-cases fitness-function)
;; Normalize fitness in preparation for crossover, etc.
(normalize-fitness-of-population population)
;; Sort the population so that the roulette wheel is easy.
(sort-population-by-fitness population)
;; Keep track of best-of-run individual
(let ((best-of-generation (aref population 0)))
  (when (or (not *best-of-run-individual*)
            (> (individual-standardized-fitness
                  *best-of-run-individual*)
               (individual-standardized-fitness
                  best-of-generation)))
    (setf *best-of-run-individual*
          (copy-individual best-of-generation))
    (setf *generation-of-best-of-run-individual*
          current-generation)))
;; Print out the results for this generation.
(report-on-generation current-generation population)))

(defun zeroize-fitness-measures-of-population (population)
  "Clean out the statistics in each individual in the
   population. This is not strictly necessary, but it helps to
   avoid confusion that might be caused if, for some reason, we
   land in the debugger and there are fitness values associated
   with the individual records that actually matched the program
   that used to occupy this individual record."
  (dotimes (individual-index (length population))
    (let ((individual (aref population individual-index)))
      (setf (individual-standardized-fitness individual) 0.0)
      (setf (individual-adjusted-fitness individual) 0.0)
      (setf (individual-normalized-fitness individual) 0.0)
      (setf (individual-hits individual) 0))))

(defun evaluate-fitness-of-population (population fitness-cases
                                       fitness-function)
  "Loops over the individuals in the population evaluating and
   recording the fitness and hits."
  (dotimes (individual-index (length population))
    (let ((individual (aref population individual-index)))
      (multiple-value-bind (standardized-fitness hits)
          (funcall fitness-function
                   (individual-program individual)
                   fitness-cases)
        ;; Record fitness and hits for this individual.
        (setf (individual-standardized-fitness individual)
              standardized-fitness)
```

```
           (setf (individual-hits individual) hits)))))
(defun normalize-fitness-of-population (population)
  "Computes the normalized and adjusted fitness of each
   individual in the population."
  (let ((sum-of-adjusted-fitnesses 0.0))
    (dotimes (individual-index (length population))
      (let ((individual (aref population individual-index)))
        ;; Set the adjusted fitness.
        (setf (individual-adjusted-fitness individual)
              (/ 1.0 (+ 1.0 (individual-standardized-fitness
                              individual))))
        ;; Add up the adjusted fitnesses so that we can
        ;; normalize them.
        (incf sum-of-adjusted-fitnesses
              (individual-adjusted-fitness individual))))
    ;; Loop through population normalizing the adjusted fitness.
    (dotimes (individual-index (length population))
      (let ((individual (aref population individual-index)))
        (setf (individual-normalized-fitness individual)
              (/ (individual-adjusted-fitness individual)
                 sum-of-adjusted-fitnesses))))))

(defun sort-population-by-fitness (population)
  "Sorts the population according to normalized fitness.
   The population array is destructively modified."
  (sort population #'> :key #'individual-normalized-fitness))
```

Eighth, the kernel contains six functions for controlling the breeding of the new population. This involves executing the appropriate genetic operation (e.g., crossover, reproduction, or mutation) with the appropriate probability. The *method-of-selection* may be either :fitness-proportionate or :tournament.

```
(defun breed-new-population
       (population new-programs
        adf0-function-set adf0-argument-map adf0-terminal-set
        adf1-function-set adf1-argument-map adf1-terminal-set
        rpb-function-set rpb-argument-map rpb-terminal-set)
  "Controls the actual breeding of the new population.
   Loops through the population executing each operation
   (e.g., crossover, fitness-proportionate reproduction,
   mutation) until it has reached the specified fraction.
   The new programs that are created are stashed in new-programs
   until we have exhausted the population, then we copy the new
   individuals into the old ones, thus avoiding consing a new
   bunch of individuals."
  (let ((population-size (length population)))
    (do ((index 0)
         (fraction 0 (/ index population-size)))
        ((>= index population-size))
```

```
           (let ((individual-1
                   (find-individual population)))
              (cond ((and (< index (- population-size 1))
                          (< fraction
                             (+ *crossover-at-function-point-fraction*
                                *crossover-at-any-point-fraction*)))
                      (multiple-value-bind (new-male new-female)
                        (funcall
                          (if (< fraction
                                 *crossover-at-function-point-fraction*)
                              'crossover-at-function-points
                              'crossover-at-any-points)
                           individual-1
                           (find-individual population))
                         (setf (aref new-programs index) new-male)
                         (setf (aref new-programs (+ 1 index))
                               new-female))
                       (incf index 2))
                     ((< fraction
                        (+ *reproduction-fraction*
                           *crossover-at-function-point-fraction*
                           *crossover-at-any-point-fraction*))
                      (setf (aref new-programs index) individual-1)
                      (incf index 1))
                     (:otherwise
                      (setf (aref new-programs index)
                            (mutate individual-1
                                     adf0-function-set adf0-argument-map
                                     adf0-terminal-set
                                     adf1-function-set adf1-argument-map
                                     adf1-terminal-set
                                     rpb-function-set rpb-argument-map
                                     rpb-terminal-set))
                      (incf index 1)))))
        (dotimes (index population-size)
          (setf (individual-program (aref population index))
                (aref new-programs index)))))

(defun find-individual (population)
  "Finds an individual in the population according to the
   defined selection method."
  (ecase *method-of-selection*
    (:tournament (find-individual-using-tournament-selection
                   population))
    (:fitness-proportionate-with-over-selection
      (find-fitness-proportionate-individual
        (random-floating-point-number-with-over-selection
          population)
        population))
```

```
      (:fitness-proportionate
        (find-fitness-proportionate-individual
          (random-floating-point-number 1.0) population))))

(defun random-floating-point-number-with-over-selection
         (population)
  "Picks a random number between 0.0 and 1.0 biased using the
  over-selection method."
  (let ((pop-size (length population)))
    (when (< pop-size 1000)
      (error "A population size of ~D is too small ~
              for over-selection." pop-size))
    (let ((boundary (/ 320.0 pop-size)))
      ;; The boundary between the over and under selected parts.
      (if (< (random-floating-point-number 1.0) 0.8)
          ;; 80% are in the over-selected part
          (random-floating-point-number boundary)
          (+ boundary
             (random-floating-point-number
               (- 1.0 boundary)))))))

(defun pick-k-random-individual-indices (k max)
  "Returns a list of K random numbers between 0 and (- max 1)."
  (let ((numbers nil))
    (loop for number = (random-integer max)
          unless (member number numbers :test #'eql)
          do (push number numbers)
          until (= (length numbers) k))
    numbers))

(defun find-individual-using-tournament-selection (population)
  "Picks *tournament-size* individuals from the population at
  random and returns the best one."
  (let ((numbers (pick-k-random-individual-indices
                   *tournament-size* (length population))))
    (loop with best = (aref population (first numbers))
          with best-fitness
            = (individual-standardized-fitness best)
          for number in (rest numbers)
          for individual = (aref population number)
          for this-fitness
            = (individual-standardized-fitness individual)
          when (< this-fitness best-fitness)
          do (setf best individual)
             (setf best-fitness this-fitness)
          finally (return (individual-program best)))))

(defun find-fitness-proportionate-individual
    (after-this-fitness population)
```

```
"Finds an individual in the specified population whose
normalized fitness is greater than the specified value.
All we need to do is count along the population from the
beginning adding up the fitness until we get past the
specified point."
(let ((sum-of-fitness 0.0)
      (population-size (length population)))
  (let ((index-of-selected-individual
          (do ((index 0 (+ index 1)))
              ;; Exit condition
              ((or (>= index population-size)
                   (>= sum-of-fitness after-this-fitness))
               (if (>= index population-size)
                   (- (length population) 1)
                   (- index 1)))
            ;; Body. Sum up the fitness values.
            (incf sum-of-fitness
                  (individual-normalized-fitness
                    (aref population index))))))
    (individual-program
      (aref population index-of-selected-individual)))))
```

**Ninth, the kernel contains a group of 10 functions for performing struc-
ture-preserving crossover at any point.**

```
(defun select-branch (within-program)
  "Returns two values:
    - A keyword in {:ADF0, :ADF1, :RPB} to denote a
      branch selected at random. The selection of the
      branch is biased according to the number of
      points in that branch.
    - The subtree for the branch selected."
  (let ((adf0 (adf-program-adf0 within-program))
        (adf1 (adf-program-adf1 within-program))
        (rpb (adf-program-rpb within-program)))
    (let ((adf0-points (count-crossover-points adf0))
          (adf1-points (count-crossover-points adf1))
          (rpb-points (count-crossover-points rpb)))
      (let ((selected-point
              (random-integer
                (+ adf0-points adf1-points rpb-points))))
        (cond ((< selected-point adf0-points)
               (values :adf0 adf0))
              ((< selected-point (+ adf1-points adf0-points))
               (values :adf1 adf1))
              (t (values :rpb rpb)))))))

(defun adf-program-branch (branch program)
  "Returns a branch from Program selected by the keyword
Branch."
```

```
(ecase branch
  (:adf0 (adf-program-adf0 program))
  (:adf1 (adf-program-adf1 program))
  (:rpb (adf-program-rpb program)))))

(defun copy-individual-substituting-branch
       (branch new-branch-subtree program-to-copy)
  "Makes a copy of Program-To-Copy only substituting
   the branch selected by Branch with the new branch
   subtree created by crossover."
  (make-adf-program
    :adf0 (if (eq :adf0 branch)
              new-branch-subtree
              (copy-tree (adf-program-adf0 program-to-copy)))
    :adf1 (if (eq :adf1 branch)
              new-branch-subtree
              (copy-tree (adf-program-adf1 program-to-copy)))
     :rpb (if (eq :rpb branch)
              new-branch-subtree
              (copy-tree (adf-program-rpb program-to-copy))))))

(defun crossover-selecting-branch
       (how-to-crossover-function male female)
  "Performs crossover on the programs Male and Female by calling
   the function How-To-Crossover-Function, which will cause it
   to perform crossover at either function points or at any
   point.
   The crossover happens between a compatible pair of branches
   in the two parents.
   Once the crossover has happened the function returns two new
   individuals to insert into the next generation."
  (let ((branch (select-branch male)))
    (multiple-value-bind (new-male-branch new-female-branch)
        (funcall how-to-crossover-function
                 (adf-program-branch branch male)
                 (adf-program-branch branch female))
      (values (copy-individual-substituting-branch
                branch new-male-branch male)
              (copy-individual-substituting-branch
                branch new-female-branch female)))))

(defun crossover-at-any-points (male female)
  "Performs crossover on the programs at any point
   in the trees."
  (crossover-selecting-branch
    #'crossover-at-any-points-within-branch male female))

(defun crossover-at-any-points-within-branch (male female)
  "Performs crossover on the program branches at any point
   in the subtrees."
  ;; Pick points in the respective trees
  ;; on which to perform the crossover.
```

```lisp
    (let ((male-point
            (random-integer (count-crossover-points male)))
          (female-point
            (random-integer (count-crossover-points female))))
     ;; First, copy the trees because we destructively modify the
     ;; new individuals to do the crossover. Reselection is
     ;; allowed in the original population. Not copying would
     ;; cause the individuals in the old population to
     ;; be modified.
     (let ((new-male   (list (copy-tree male)))
           (new-female (list (copy-tree female))))
      ;; Get the pointers to the subtrees indexed by male-point
      ;; and female-point
      (multiple-value-bind (male-subtree-pointer male-fragment)
          (get-subtree (first new-male) new-male male-point)
        (multiple-value-bind
          (female-subtree-pointer female-fragment)
            (get-subtree
              (first new-female) new-female female-point)
          ;; Modify the new individuals by smashing in the
          ;; (copied) subtree from the old individual.
          (setf (first   male-subtree-pointer) female-fragment)
          (setf (first female-subtree-pointer) male-fragment)))
     ;; Make sure that the new individuals aren't too big.
     (validate-crossover male new-male female new-female))))

(defun count-crossover-points (program)
  "Counts the number of points in the tree (program).
   This includes functions as well as terminals."
  (if (consp program)
      (+ 1 (reduce #'+ (mapcar #'count-crossover-points
                               (rest program))))
      1))

(defun max-depth-of-tree (tree)
  "Returns the depth of the deepest branch of the
   tree (program)."
  (if (consp tree)
      (+ 1 (if (rest tree)
               (apply #'max
                      (mapcar #'max-depth-of-tree (rest tree)))
               0))
      1))

(defun get-subtree (tree pointer-to-tree index)
  "Given a tree or subtree, a pointer to that tree/subtree and
   an index return the component subtree that is numbered by
   Index. We number left to right, depth first."
  (if (= index 0)
      (values pointer-to-tree (copy-tree tree) index)
      (if (consp tree)
```

```
                 (do* ((tail (rest tree) (rest tail))
                       (argument (first tail) (first tail)))
                      ((not tail) (values nil nil index))
                   (multiple-value-bind
                       (new-pointer new-tree new-index)
                       (get-subtree argument tail (- index 1))
                     (if (= new-index 0)
                         (return
                           (values new-pointer new-tree new-index))
                         (setf index new-index)))))
                 (values nil nil index))))

(defun validate-crossover (male new-male female new-female)
  "Given the old and new males and females from a crossover
   operation check to see whether we have exceeded the maximum
   allowed depth. If either of the new individuals has exceeded
   the maxdepth then the old individual is used."
  (let ((male-depth   (max-depth-of-tree (first new-male)))
        (female-depth (max-depth-of-tree (first new-female))))
    (values
      (if (or (= 1 male-depth)
              (>= male-depth ;; >= counts 1 depth for root above
                  ;; branches.
                  *max-depth-for-individuals-after-crossover*))
          male
          (first new-male))
      (if (or (= 1 female-depth)
              (>= female-depth.
                  *max-depth-for-individuals-after-crossover*))
          female
          (first new-female)))))
```

Tenth, the kernel contains a group of four functions for performing cross-over restricted to function (internal) points.

```
(defun crossover-at-function-points (male female)
  "Performs crossover on the two programs at a function
   (internal) point in a randomly selected branch of the trees."
  (crossover-selecting-branch
    #'crossover-at-function-points-within-branch male female))

(defun crossover-at-function-points-within-branch (male female)
  "Performs crossover on the two program branches at a function
   (internal) point in the trees."
  ;; Pick the function (internal) points in the respective trees
  ;; on which to perform the crossover.
  (let ((male-point
          (random-integer (count-function-points male)))
        (female-point
          (random-integer (count-function-points female))))
    ;; Copy the trees because we destructively modify the new
```

```
               ;; individuals to do the crossover and Reselection is
               ;; allowed in the original population. Not copying would
               ;; cause the individuals in the old population to
               ;; be modified.
               (let ((new-male   (list (copy-tree male)))
                     (new-female (list (copy-tree female))))
                 ;; Get the pointers to the subtrees indexed by male-point
                 ;; and female-point
                 (multiple-value-bind (male-subtree-pointer male-fragment)
                     (get-function-subtree
                       (first new-male) new-male male-point)
                   (multiple-value-bind
                     (female-subtree-pointer female-fragment)
                       (get-function-subtree
                         (first new-female) new-female female-point)
                     ;; Modify the new individuals by smashing in
                     ;; the (copied) subtree from the old individual.
                     (setf (first   male-subtree-pointer) female-fragment)
                     (setf (first female-subtree-pointer) male-fragment)))
                 ;; Make sure that the new individuals aren't too big.
                 (validate-crossover male new-male female new-female))))

(defun count-function-points (program)
  "Counts the number of function (internal) points
   in the program."
  (if (consp program)
      (+ 1 (reduce #'+ (mapcar #'count-function-points
                              (rest program))))
      0))

(defun get-function-subtree (tree pointer-to-tree index)
  "Given a tree or subtree, a pointer to that tree/subtree and
   an index return the component subtree that is labeled with
   an internal point that is numbered by Index. We number left
   to right, depth first."
  (if (= index 0)
      (values pointer-to-tree (copy-tree tree) index)
      (if (consp tree)
          (do* ((tail (rest tree) (rest tail))
                (argument (first tail) (first tail)))
               ((not tail) (values nil nil index))
            (multiple-value-bind
              (new-pointer new-tree new-index)
                (if (consp argument)
                    (get-function-subtree
                      argument tail (- index 1))
                    (values nil nil index))
              (if (= new-index 0)
                  (return
                    (values new-pointer new-tree new-index))
```

```
                              (setf index new-index))))
            (values nil nil index)))))
```

Eleventh, the kernel contains a function for performing the mutation operation.

```
(defun mutate
        (program
          adf0-function-set adf0-argument-map adf0-terminal-set
          adf1-function-set adf1-argument-map adf1-terminal-set
          rpb-function-set rpb-argument-map rpb-terminal-set)
        "Mutates the argument program by picking a random point in
         the tree and substituting in a brand new subtree created in
         the same way that we create the initial random population."
        ;; Pick the mutation point.
        (multiple-value-bind (branch branch-tree)
            (select-branch program)
          (let ((mutation-point
                  (random-integer
                    (count-crossover-points branch-tree)))
                ;; Create a brand new subtree.
                (new-subtree
                  (create-individual-subtree
                    (case branch
                      (:adf0 adf0-function-set)
                      (:adf1 adf1-function-set)
                      (:rpb rpb-function-set))
                    (case branch
                      (:adf0 adf0-argument-map)
                      (:adf1 adf1-argument-map)
                      (:rpb rpb-argument-map))
                    (case branch
                      (:adf0 adf0-terminal-set)
                      (:adf1 adf1-terminal-set)
                      (:rpb rpb-terminal-set))
                    *max-depth-for-new-subtrees-in-mutants* t nil)))
            (let ((new-branch (list (copy-tree branch-tree))))
              (multiple-value-bind (subtree-pointer fragment)
                  ;; Get the pointer to the mutation point.
                  (get-subtree (first new-branch)
                               new-branch mutation-point)
                ;; Not interested in what we're snipping out.
                (declare (ignore fragment))
                ;; Smash in the new subtree.
                (setf (first subtree-pointer) new-subtree))
              (values (copy-individual-substituting-branch
                        branch (first new-branch) program)
                      new-subtree)))))
```

Twelfth, the kernel contains a group of three functions for generating random numbers needed by the genetic programming system. The first is the Park-Miller multiplicative congruential randomizer (Park and Miller 1988).

```
(defun park-miller-randomizer ()
  "The Park-Miller multiplicative congruential randomizer
   (Communications of the ACM, October 88, Page 1195).
   Creates pseudo random floating point numbers in the range
   0.0 < x <= 1.0. The seed value for this randomizer is
   called *seed*, so you should record/set this if you want
   to make your runs reproducible."
  (assert (not (zerop *seed*)) () "*seed* cannot be zero.")
  (let ((multiplier 16807.0d0);16807 is (expt 7 5)
        (modulus 2147483647.0d0))
            ;2147483647 is (- (expt 2 31) 1)
    (let ((temp (* multiplier *seed*)))
      (setf *seed* (mod temp modulus))
      ;;Produces floating-point number in the range
      ;;  0.0 < x <= 1.0
      (/ *seed* modulus))))
```

The Park-Miller randomizer can then be used to create random floating-point numbers as follows:

```
(defun random-floating-point-number (n)
  "Returns a pseudo random floating-point number
            in range 0.0 <= number < n"
  (let ((random-number (park-miller-randomizer)))
    ;; We subtract the randomly generated number from 1.0
    ;; before scaling so that we end up in the range
    ;; 0.0 <= x < 1.0, not 0.0 < x <= 1.0
    (* n (- 1.0d0 random-number))))
```

The Park-Miller randomizer can then be used to create random integers as follows:

```
(defun random-integer (n)
  "Returns a pseudo-random integer in the range 0 -> n-1."
  (let ((random-number (random-floating-point-number 1.0)))
    (floor (* n random-number))))
```

The user can test the correctness of his Park-Miller randomizer by starting with a seed of 1.0 and running it 10,000 times. At that point, the seed should be 1.043618065×10^9. We believe that the code for the Park-Miller randomizer above is very nearly machine independent and LISP implementation independent.

The programs, procedures, and applications presented in this book have been included for their instructional value. The publisher and author offer NO WARRANTY OF FITNESS OR MERCHANTABILITY FOR ANY PARTICULAR PURPOSE or accept any liability with respect to these programs, procedures, and applications. U.S. patent numbers 4,935,877, 5,136,686, 5,148,513, Canadian patent number 1,311,561, Australian patent number 611,350, and U. S. and foreign patents pending.

Appendix F: Annotated Bibliography of Genetic Programming

One hundred papers have been published on the subject of genetic programming in the 15 months since the publication of *Genetic Programming* in December, 1992. This group of papers does not include 49 papers of which I am author or co-author.

Many of these 100 papers were published in the proceedings of various conferences, including the International Conference on Simulation of Adaptive Behavior, the IEEE International Conference on Neural Networks, the International Workshop on Artificial Life, the International Conference on Genetic Algorithms, the International Simulation Technology Multiconference, and the National Conference on Artificial Intelligence.

The largest existing concentration of papers on genetic programming is the recently published book *Advances in Genetic Programming* edited by Kenneth E. Kinnear, Jr. (Kinnear 1994a). In addition, the proceedings of the IEEE World Conference on Computational Intelligence in Florida on June 26 to July 2, 1994, contain another large group of papers on genetic programming.

Many papers (including not-yet-published papers) are announced over the genetic programming electronic mailing list or are deposited in the on-line public repository for genetic programming as described in appendix G.

This appendix briefly reviews these 100 publications (each of which is flagged with a ≈ in the bibliography). The publications in this appendix are rather arbitrarily divided into the following groups:

• Design,

• Pattern recognition and classification,

• Robotic control and planning,

• Neural networks,

• Induction and regression,

• Financial,

• Art,

• Databases,

• Algorithms,

• Natural language,

• Modules,

- Programming methods,
- Variations in genetic operations,
- Memory, state, and mental models, and
- Theoretical foundations.

F.1 DESIGN

F.1.1 Design of Stack Filters and Fitting Chaotic Data

Howard Oakley (1994) of the Institute of Naval Medicine in the United Kingdom considers two scientific applications of genetic programming.

In the first, Oakley compares a heuristic search method, the conventional genetic algorithm, and genetic programming for developing a filter to remove noise from experimental data. The stack filter evolved by genetic programming appeared as the fittest answer and is in current use in a laser Doppler rheometer system.

Oakley also used genetic programming to evolve equations to fit chaotic time series data produced by the Mackey-Glass equations and certain physiological data.

F.2 PATTERN RECOGNITION AND CLASSIFICATION

F.2.1 Feature Discovery and Image Discrimination

Tackett (1993a, 1993b) of Hughes Missile Systems applied genetic programming to a difficult induction problem using data taken from the real world. A comparative performance study was conducted against other well-known methods of machine learning. Fitness cases comprised features computed from a U.S. Army database of 512-by-640 pixel infrared images containing tracked and wheeled vehicles, fixed- and rotary-wing aircraft, and air defense units in a cluttered terrain. The features could be computed from subregions containing either targets (e.g., tanks, aircraft) or clutter (e.g., rocks and bushes). The fitness of an individual was based on its ability to discriminate between these two categories. Fitness was computed using an in-sample set of 2,000 fitness cases. The fitness of the best-of-generation program was reported using a larger out-of-sample set of 7,000 fitness cases in order to determine the ability of the evolved program to generalize with respect to data it has not encountered in training.

In a first experiment, genetic programming was used to construct classifiers that processed feature vectors produced by a preexisting algorithm. In a second experiment, genetic programming was allowed to form its own feature set directly from the primitive intensity measurements. Against the same data sets, the results produced by genetic programming achieved better performance than the results produced by an ID3-like decision tree classifier and a multilayer perceptron trained using back propagation.

F.2.2 Pattern Recognition using Automatically Defined Features

Andre's (1994a) approach to a two-dimensional pattern recognition problem involved evolving hit-or-miss feature-detecting matrices (using a two-dimensional version of the conventional genetic algorithm) while simultaneously evolving a computer program (using genetic programming) to act on the hit-or-miss results reported by the feature detectors. The feature-detecting matrices were evolved using a crossover operator that exchanges randomly chosen sub-matrices.

F.2.3 Upgrading Rules for an OCR System

One approach to optical character recognition involves writing detailed rules for recognizing each possible character and each possible font. Andre (1994c) successfully used genetic programming to upgrade handwritten rules when new characters and new fonts must be processed.

F.2.4 Prediction of Secondary Structure of Proteins

Handley (1993a) used genetic programming to attempt to predict α-helices in globular proteins. Each program was executed once for each residue along a protein sequence. Each program was required to predict whether or not the current residue was part of an α-helix. The programs had access to the Kyte-Doolittle hydrophobicity values (Kyte and Doolittle 1982) and a measure of the bulk of the current residue. A turtle operation enabled an inspecting head to wander to the left or right of the current residue and thereby obtain the hydrophobicity and bulk values for neighboring residues. Many other efforts at prediction of features of proteins inspect residues in a window of fixed size around the current residue. In this approach, the extent of inspection of neighboring residues was not specified in advance, but was, instead, evolved.

Handley (1994c) evolved a program for detecting whether or not a protein segment is an α-helix. The evolved program achieved an out-of-sample correlation of 0.48 on this version of the secondary structure prediction problem.

F.2.5 The Donut Problem

Tackett and Carmi (1994a) studied a classification problem involving two stochastic donuts interlocked like two links of a chain. The problem was to classify a given point in three-dimensional space as to the donut to which it belonged. This classification problem is pathological for a number of reasons. The mean of each probability distribution lies in the densest part of the other; the distributions cannot be linearly separated by a perceptron rule; the distributions cannot be covered by cones or hypercones; and they cannot be enclosed by a pair of radial basis functions. Moreover, class membership is inherently ambiguous because outlying points of each probability distribution intermingle with points of the other.

The donut problem has the advantage that its difficulty can be scaled in a controlled manner in several ways. Tackett and Carmi genetically evolved classification programs for versions of the donut problem with different degrees of ambiguity of class membership, with different degrees of sparseness of data to test generalization, and with different "bites" removed from the donut.

Tackett and Carmi also compared the effect of different breeding policies, comparing *demes* (spatially distributed local breeding groups) with *panmictic breeding* (where each individual is equally likely to breed with any other equally fit individual). They also compared the effects of the *steady state* approach to genetic algorithms (where the offspring produced by one application of one genetic operation are immediately available to participate in subsequent genetic operations) with the *generational approach* (where offspring produced by a large number of genetic operations are held aside until an entire new population is ready to replace the entire old population).

F.2.6 Evolution of a Model for a Jetliner

Nguyen and Huang (1994) evolved three-dimensional models for jetliners designed for use in an object recognition system employing an interactive fitness measure provided by the user.

F.3 ROBOTIC CONTROL

F.3.1 Crawling and Walking of a Six-Legged Creature

Beer (1990) demonstrated that it was possible for a human to design a neural network involving a surprisingly modest number of neurons to enable a simulated cockroach to crawl and walk. Brooks (1989) demonstrated that a human could design a controller written in the style of the subsumption architecture to enable a similar six-legged artificial creature to perform similar tasks.

Spencer (1993, 1994) used genetic programming to automatically generate a program that enables a six-legged creature to crawl and walk. Three progressively more difficult versions of the problem were solved. The performance of the programs was analyzed using the gait of the walk of the robot in terms of leg-dragging, balancing, and forward motion.

Spencer introduces a new *constant perturbation operation* which perturbs random constants by a small, bounded, random percentage during a run of genetic programming.

F.3.2 Evolution of Herding Behavior

Craig Reynolds, developer of the famous *Boids* video (Reynolds 1991), studied the question of whether coordinated group motion could evolve among a population of critters using genetic programming (Reynolds 1993). A simulated two-dimensional environment contained critters, static obstacles, and a predator. In order to survive, the critters had to steer a safe course through a dynamic environment and avoid collisions with obstacles and each other. The predator preferentially targeted stragglers, thus encouraging aggregation and herding behavior.

F.3.3 Obstacle-Avoiding Behavior

Reynolds (1994a) showed how noise can be used to promote robust solutions to the problem of obstacle-avoiding behavior for a robot. Reynolds (1994b) presented a vision-based model of obstacle-avoiding behavior for a robot.

F.3.4 Corridor-Following and the Lens Effect

In "The Difficulty of Roving Eyes," Reynolds (1994c) considered three versions of a problem calling for the discovery of a controller for a corridor-following robot. The robot had a roving sensor, an arbitrary static sensor, and a predetermined static sensor in the three versions. The histograms of fitness in the initial random generation were distinctly different for the three versions. These differences foreshadowed the difficulty of solving the problem in the actual full runs of genetic programming and validate the existence of the lens effect (chapter 26) for another problem domain.

F.3.5 Control of Autonomous Robots

Ghanea-Hercock and Fraser (1994) discussed the evolution of behavior-based controllers for autonomous robot agents. Complex emergent behavior can arise as a result of the interactions among low-level behaviors. As agents attempt more complex problems, the number of interactions can increase beyond the capacity of manual design. Ghanea-Hercock and Fraser used evolution to automate the process of designing controllers.

F.3.6 Evolution of Co-Operation among Autonomous Robots

Complex tasks can be performed either by a single very sophisticated device or by a distributed collection of co-operating simpler devices. Rush, Fraser, and Barnes (1994) discussed how to automate the design of a control architecture for complex tasks. They evolved a solution to a co-operative object relocation task that previously had been designed manually with a behavior synthesis architecture.

F.3.7 Incorporating Domain Knowledge into Evolution

Fraser and Rush (1994) discussed ways of evolving artificial nervous systems using the genetic algorithm and genetic programming. The aim was to produce control systems for multiple autonomous devices called BIRos (Biologically Inspired Robots), without explicit design. They discussed the ways in which intelligent knowledge (INK) of the problem domain, as seen by the designer could be incorporated into the evolutionary mechanism. A co-operative relocation task previously designed using manual methods was used.

F.3.8 Monitoring Strategy for Independent Agents

Independent agents, such as robots, need to acquire information about their environment in order to perform their assigned tasks. Atkin and Cohen (1993a, 1993b, 1994) applied genetic programming to enable an independent agent to learn a monitoring strategy for monitoring its environment.

F.3.9 Genetic Planner for Robots

Planning is the creation of computer programs that will be executed in the future to control an independent agent, such as a robot. Handley (1993b, 1993c, 1994a) successfully applied genetic programming with automatically defined functions to the creation of plans for the task of pushing three boxes together and moving the robot to a specified location in another room. Handley achieved an efficiency ratio, R_E, of 6.0 for performing the task of moving the robot to a specified location in another room.

F.3.10 AI Planning Systems

Spector (1994) described a series of illustrative experiments in which genetic programming was applied to traditional blocks-world planning problems from the field of artificial intelligence. Spector discussed genetic planning in the context of traditional artificial intelligence planning systems and commented on the costs and benefits to be expected from further work.

F.4 NEURAL NETWORKS

F.4.1 Cellular Encoding of Neural Networks
There are, of course, numerous effective algorithms for training a neural network to solve a problem. Back propagation (Rumelhart, Hinton, and Williams 1986) is the most widely used such algorithm.

Neural networks are complex structures that can be represented by line-labeled, point-labeled, directed graphs. The points may be input points, output points, or neural processing units within the network. The lines are labeled with weights to represent the weighted connections between two points. The neural processing units are labeled with numbers indicating the threshold and bias of the unit.

The conventional genetic algorithm operating on fixed-length character strings has been used to discover the weights for neural nets (Miller, Todd, and Hegde 1989; Belew, McInerney, and Schraudolph 1991; Whitley, Starkweather and Bogart 1990; Wilson 1990). Typically, the weights (and perhaps also the thresholds and biases) in the network are concatenated into a long string (chromosome) of bits (or sometimes floating-point numbers); the genetic algorithm then operates on this linear structure in the usual way. Superficially, the conventional genetic algorithm provides an attractive approach for searching the highly nonlinear multidimensional search space of weight vectors. The genetic algorithm seems especially appropriate when recurrent neural networks (i.e., non-feed-forward networks with memory and state) are involved (Jefferson et al. 1991) because of the scarcity of methods for discovering the weights of a recurrent neural network.

Simultaneous discovery of both the architecture and weights of a neural network has also been attempted using genetic programming (*Genetic Programming*, section 19.9).

However, the continuing difficulty in applying genetic methods for designing neural networks has centered on the problem of finding a manipulable representation for the line-labeled, point-labeled, directed graph representing the neural network that is crossover-friendly and congenial to the neural net problem domain.

Gruau (1992a, 1992b, 1993a, 1993b, 1994a, 1994b) and Gruau and Whitley (1993a, 1993b) dealt with this difficulty. Instead of applying genetic methods to entities that attempt to directly represent the identifiable parts of the neural network, Gruau's clever and innovative cellular encoding technique applied genetic programming to program trees that specify how the neural net was to be constructed.

In Gruau's scheme, each individual (program tree) in the genetic population is a composition of network-constructing, neuron-creating, and neuron-adjusting functions and terminals. Each of Gruau's program trees in the population is one step removed from the actual neural network. The program tree is the genotype and the neural network constructed in accordance with the tree's instructions is the phenotype. The fitness of an individual program tree in the population is measured in terms of how well the neural network that is constructed in accordance with the instructions contained in the program tree performs the desired task. Genetic programming then breeds the population of program trees in the usual manner.

The construction process for a neural network starts from an embryonic neural network consisting of a single neuron. This embryonic neuron has a threshold of 0; its input is connected to all of the network's input nodes with connections with weights of +1; its output is connected to all of the network's output nodes.

The network-constructing functions in the program tree then specify how to grow the single embryonic neuron into the full neural network. Certain network-constructing functions permit a particular neuron to be subdivided in a parallel or sequential manner. Other neuron-adjusting functions can change the threshold of a neuron, the weight of a connection, or the bias on a neuron. A pointer links the current operation in the program tree to a current point in the developing neural network so as to give specificity to the current operation.

In addition, Gruau extends his basic scheme to permit recursions which, in turn, permit neural networks to be generated for high-order parity, symmetry, and other functions.

F.4.2   Synthesis of Sigma-Pi Neural Networks

Zhang and Muhlenbein (1994) described the breeder genetic programming method incorporating parsimony (Occam's razor) in its fitness measure. They applied this method to the synthesis of sigma-pi neural networks which contain multiplicative processing elements in addition to the usual additive processing elements.

F.4.3   New Learning Rules for Neural Networks

Learning mechanisms for neural networks adjust the synaptic weights of a neural network according to some rule. Bengio, Bengio, and Cloutier (1994) used genetic programming to discover the form as well as the numerical parameters for such rules. Their experiments involving 20 two-dimensional classification problems (half linearly separable problems) suggested that genetic programming found a better learning rule for the particular problems tested than simulated annealing, the conventional genetic algorithm, or backpropagation. The genetically evolved learning rule bore some resemblance to backpropagation. The evolved rule generalized to the seven-input LED identification task.

F.5   INDUCTION AND REGRESSION

F.5.1   Induction of Regular Languages

Dunay, Petry, and Buckles (1994) considered the problem of discovering a regular language from examples of sentences known to be in an unknown language and sentences known not to be in that language. They proceeded by translating deterministic finite automata to binary trees and binary trees to S-expressions.

F.5.2   Levenberg-Marquardt Regression

Jiang (1992, 1993) and Jiang and Wright (1992) described a system for symbolic regression that combined the Levenberg-Marquardt regression algorithm with genetic programming.

F.5.3 Multiple Steady States of a Dynamical System

Lay (1994) used genetic programming to analyze the multiple steady states of a dynamical system for a continuously stirred tank reactor.

F.5.4 Inverting and Co-Evolving Randomizers

Jannink (1994) attempted to unravel the structure of several random number generators by using co-evolution in which their previous outputs were used to predict their future outputs. He also co-evolved populations of randomizing programs to play a game similar to the penny matching game.

F.5.5 Adaptive Learning using Structured Genetic Algorithms

Hitoshi Iba and his colleagues at the Electrotechnical Laboratory in Japan have published a number of papers on structured genetic algorithms and genetic programming.

Iba and Sato (1992) discussed meta-level strategy learning for structured genetic algorithms. Iba, de Garis, and Higuchi (1993) described the adaptive learning of structured classifiers for foraging using structured genetic algorithms.

F.5.6 Minimum Description Length and Group Method of Data Handling

In addition to the work described above, Iba and his colleagues at the Electrotechnical Laboratory in Japan have published three papers on solving system identification (symbolic regression) problems.

Iba, Kurita, de Garis, and Sato (1993) introduced STROGANOFF (Structured Representation On Genetic Algorithms for Non-linear Function Fitting) for solving system identification (symbolic regression) problems. Fitness was measured using the minimum description length (MDL) principle. The Group Method of Data Handling (GMDH), developed by Ivakhnenko (1971), was used as a basis for their technique. Genetic programming was used to efficiently explore the space of possible GMDH solutions. This is an interesting example of genetic programming being used to tie together several existing powerful techniques.

This approach was applied to the Mackey-Glass equations and a pattern recognition problem.

Iba, deGaris, and Sato (1994) also applied the minimum description length (MDL) principle to the problem of finding a decision tree for the Boolean multiplexer function. The results were again compared with the results produced by GMDH.

Further work involving minimum description length was reported in Iba, Sato, and de Garis (1994) and Iba and Sato (1994).

F.5.7   Sequence Induction

Jones (1991) described the induction of mathematical formulae representing observed sequences produced by single-parameter numeric functions. His program had a feature permitting an additional example (a pair of values of the independent variable and dependent variable) to be presented after it had evolved a formula. His program would then either confirm that the new example was consistent with the evolved program or would restart the evolutionary process using the enlarged set of examples.

F.6   FINANCIAL

F.6.1   Horse Race Prediction

Programs for making predictions in the real world typically have an enormous number of inputs. Perry (1994) described work on the prediction of horse races using genetic programming. Evolution of such predicting programs was facilitated by enriching the population with individuals bred off-line in preliminary runs.

F.6.2   Double Auction Market Strategies

Since 1990, the Santa Fe Institute has run a double auction tournament using a mechanism similar to that used in the minute-by-minute trading of commodity and futures exchanges. The participants in this market are strategies embodied in computer programs written and submitted by economists, mathematicians, and computer scientists from around the world. In addition, human players have been competing against automated players over the Internet on the Arizona Token Exchange. Andrews and Prager (1994) used genetic programming to create strategies for such double auction tournaments. The strategies were compared to those created by simulated annealing.

F.6.3   C++ Implementation

Andrew Singeton of Creation Mechanics Inc. in Dublin, New Hampshire is applying genetic programming to financial analysis. Singeton (1994) described his GPQUICK implementation of genetic programming in C++.

F.7   ART

F.7.1   Interactive Evolution of Equations of Images

Karl Sims, developer of the famous *Panspermia* video (Sims 1991b), has shown that a spectacular variety of color images can be produced by selecting images from a large number of randomly created and mutated programs displayed by an interactive workstation (Sims 1991a, 1992a, 1992b, 1993a, 1993b).

In this approach employing interactive fitness, the human evaluates the current images and interactively selects the preferred image.

Sims (1993b) interactive method has recently been displayed in the Georges Pompidou museum in Paris. Sims interactively produced the genetic art that appears on the cover of *Genetic Programming* and this book.

1.7.1.1 Genetic Art in Virtual Reality

Das et al. (1994) extend Sims' work by evolving genetic art which the viewer can walk around, examine, and manipulate using virtual reality.

F.7.2 Jazz Melodies from Case-Based Reasoning and Genetic Programming

Spector and Alpern (1994) apply case-based reasoning and genetic programming in a system that produces new bebop jazz melodies from a case-base of melodies. Genetic programming was driven by user-provided evaluation.

F.8 DATABASES

F.8.1 News Story Classification by Dow Jones

Editors at Dow Jones must assign one or more of about 350 codes daily to thousands of news stories originating from newspapers, magazines, news wires, and press releases. Brij Massand (1994) of Thinking Machines Corporation used the massively parallel Connection Machine to implement a memory-based reasoning (MBR) system for encoding news stories. Genetic programming was used to evolve a program which predicted the classification accuracy of the memory-based reasoning approach.

F.8.2 Building Queries for Information Retrieval

Kraft et al. (1994) viewed Boolean queries for information retrieval as a parse tree and used genetic programming to improve the formulation of Boolean queries by means of relevance feedback.

F.9 ALGORITHMS

F.9.1 Evolution of the Schedule for Simulated Annealing

Simulated annealing (Kirkpatrick, Gelatt, and Vecchi 1983; Aarts and Korst 1989; van Laarhoven and Aarts 1987) is a probabilistic optimization technique that is often applied to highly nonlinear multidimensional search spaces. Simulated annealing attempts to find the global optimum for the energy level (fitness) among all the points of the search space.

Simulated annealing operates over a series of discrete time steps (generations). The process is controlled by an annealing schedule which changes the temperature parameter, T, in a specified way as a function of the time step.

Simulated annealing starts with a single initial user-defined domain-specific structure. The energy (a zero-based measure comparable to standardized fitness) is measured for the current structure.

There is a user-defined probabilistic method for modifying (mutating) the current structure. At each step of the process, a modification is probabilistically created from the existing structure and the energy level of the single new structure is determined.

The Metropolis algorithm is used to select between the new modified structure and the old structure. One of the two will be retained for the next time step. If the energy level of the modification is an improvement, the modification is always greedily accepted. However, if the energy level of the modification is not an improvement, the modification may still be accepted with a certain probability determined by the Boltzmann equation. This probability of acceptance is greater if the energy difference is small and the probability of acceptance is greater if the temperature parameter, T, is high. Simulated annealing differs from hillclimbing in that the observed better alternative is not always adopted as the next point in the search space.

The temperature specified by the annealing schedule plays a very important role in the process. If the annealing schedule is monotonically decreasing, a non-improving modification will be less likely to be accepted in a later generation of the process.

A monotonically decreasing annealing schedule is conventionally used in applying simulated annealing to specific problems. This practice appears to be a consequence of the fact that an exponentially decreasing annealing schedule is used in the mathematical proof of an important existence theorem in the field of simulated annealing. However, the theorem involved does not address the question of whether a monotonically decreasing annealing schedule is either best or required for a practical problem. In spite of almost universal conventional practice of using a monotonically decreasing annealing schedules, the nature of the optimal annealing schedule is, in fact, an open question. There is no mathematical justification for requiring the use of a monotonically decreasing annealing schedule for a practical problem.

Thonemann (1992, 1994) applied genetic programming to finding an optimal annealing schedule for controlling runs of simulated annealing for benchmark examples of the quadratic assignment problem (QAP). Thonemann found that a variety of evolved oscillatory annealing schedules are superior to the usual monotonically decreasing annealing schedule.

F.9.2 Sorting Programs

Kinnear (1993a, 1993b) used genetic programming to successfully evolve general iterative sorting algorithms employing various sets of primitive functions. He also explored the differences in difficulty created by the use of different primitive functions.

O'Reilly and Oppacher (1992) applied genetic programming to the task of evolving generalized sorting algorithms and explored the difficulty of this task in some detail.

Ryan (1994) used the problem of evolving a minimal sorting network to show the advantages of disassortative mating in reducing premature convergence in genetic algorithms and genetic programming.

F.10 NATURAL LANGUAGE

F.10.1 Word Sense Disambiguation

Siegel (1994) used genetic programming to induce decision trees that determine the meaning of a word by looking at the context in which it is used (word sense disambiguation). He developed a method for evolving decision trees that had sets of values on each arc; the sets were represented using bit strings; and bit-string crossover was intermingled with the subtree-swapping of genetic programming.

Siegel showed that genetic programming benefited from the competitive co-evolution of training data, as first developed by Hillis (1990, 1991). In particular, he developed a method by which a fixed set of training examples (collected empirically) could competitively co-adapt against the decision trees.

F.10.2 Classification of Swedish Words

Nordin (1994) developed an extremely fast version of genetic programming in which the programs were composed of low-level binary machine code. He applied it to the problem of classifying spelled-out Swedish words as nouns or pronouns.

F.11 MODULES

F.11.1 Module Acquisition and the Genetic Library Builder

Angeline and Pollack (1992, 1994) have developed a tree compression operation that begins by choosing a point in a program tree and identifying the portion of the tree lying within a specified distance below the chosen point. If all branches of the portion of the program tree thus identified terminate with a terminal within the specified distance, the portion is defined as a newly acquired module taking no arguments, and the portion is replaced by a zero-argument call to the newly acquired module. This process is identical to the encapsulation operation (*Genetic Programming*, subsection 6.5.4). In the more interesting case, if there are terminals or subtrees "hanging out" below the portion of the program tree thus identified that lie outside the specified distance, the portion is defined as a newly acquired module taking as many arguments as there are terminals or subtrees below the portion of the program tree thus identified, and the portion is replaced by a parameterized call to the newly acquired module. The newly acquired modules are collected by a genetic library builder (GLib). This module acquisition (MA) operation provides a means to create subroutines with arguments that are defined dynamically during a run of genetic programming. Angeline and Pollack then applied genetic programming to tasks such as Tic-Tac-Toe.

Angeline and Pollack (1993a, 1993b) explored the advantages of competitive fitness measures for handling complex tasks. Co-evolution can be implemented where each individual in the population competes with every other individual, where there is bipartite competition between pairs of individuals, and where there is a multi-level tournament in which the winner of the competition between pairs of individuals at one level of the tournament competes with other winners at the next higher level of the tournament.

Angeline (1994a, 1994b) explored how the concept of emergent intelligence could be implemented using a number of evolutionary algorithms, including genetic algorithms, genetic programming, evolution strategies, and evolutionary programming. Knowledge-based symbolic artificial intelligence relies on internal representations of the task environment. The fact that these internal representations are inside the independent agents leads to the well-known problems of AI, including brittleness, learnability, knowledge acquisition, memory indexing, and credit allocation. These problems may be reduced or eliminated if the agent is allowed to interact directly with its task environment. In what Angeline calls "emergent intelligence," task-specific knowledge emerges from the interaction of the agent and the task environment.

Angeline (1994c) is an overview of genetic programming that describes genetic programming's flexibility to tailor the representation language to the problem being solved, and how its specially designed crossover operator provides a robust tool for evolving problem solutions. This paper provides an introduction to genetic programming, a short review of dynamic representations used in other evolutionary systems and their relation to genetic programming, and a description of some of genetic programming's inherent properties.

F.11.2 Modules and Automatically Defined Functions

Kinnear (1994b) compared automatically defined functions (such as are described in this book) with module acquisition (described in subsection F.11.1) using the even-4-parity problem. He explored why automatically defined functions yielded significant speedup for this problem while the approach using module acquisition did not. Kinnear determined that the speedup was due to a particular form of structural regularity in even-parity problems that was exploited by automatically defined functions, but was not exploited by module acquisition. Kinnear invented a novel crossover operator, called modular crossover, that provided much of the speedup provided by automatically defined functions on the even-4-parity problem without the use of automatically defined functions.

F.11.3   Learning by Adapting Representations

Rosca and Ballard (1994a) demonstrated how genetic programming could take advantage of its own search traces and thereby discover useful genetic material to accelerate the search process. The newly discovered genetic material could be used to restructure the search space so that solutions could be more easily found.

Rosca and Ballard (1994b) discussed constructive induction, minimum description length, and learning. Their approach to automatic discovery of functions in genetic programming was based on the discovery of useful building blocks by analyzing the evolution trace, generalizing blocks to define new functions, and finally adapting the problem representation on-the-fly. Adaptation of the representation determined a hierarchical organization of the extended function set which enabled a restructuring of the search space so that solutions could be found more easily. Measures of complexity of solution trees were defined for an adaptive representation framework (e.g., structural, evaluational, descriptional and expanded structural complexity). The minimum description length principle was applied to justify the feasibility of approaches based on a hierarchy of discovered functions and to suggest alternative ways of defining a problem's fitness function.

F.12   PROGRAMMING METHODS

F.12.1   Directed Acyclic Graphs for Representing Populations of Programs

Handley (1994b) presented a technique that reduced the time and space requirements for representing the programs in the population. The population of parse trees was stored as a directed acyclic graph (DAG), rather than as a forest of trees. Space was saved by not duplicating the storage of structurally identical subtrees. Time was also saved because the contribution toward fitness of each subtree could be cached both within a generation and between generations.

F.12.2   Co-Routine Execution Model

Maxwell (1994) expanded the methodology of genetic programming with a co-routine model for the synchronous, parallel execution of the individual programs in the population. Maxwell's approach allowed the removal of arbitrary time-out limits on execution time for problems that permit monitoring of progress (change in fitness) during the execution of programs working toward a solution.

F.12.3 Stack-Based Virtual Machine

Perkis (1994) described a new and more efficient implementation of genetic programming using a stack-based virtual machine.

F.13 VARIATIONS IN GENETIC OPERATIONS

F.13.1 Context-Preserving Crossover

D'haeseleer (1994) described two versions of a new context-preserving crossover operation and tested their performance on four problems: the obstacle-avoiding robot problem (chapter 13), the Boolean 11-multiplexer, the central place food-foraging problem, and an iterated version of the obstacle-avoiding robot problem. He found that a mix of strong context-preserving crossover with ordinary crossover was superior to ordinary crossover alone in this testbed of problems.

F.13.2 Brood Selection and Soft Selection

In nature it is common for organisms to produce many offspring and then neglect or eat some of them or allow them to eat each other. This brood selection (soft selection) reduces the parent's investment of resources in offspring that are potentially less fit than others. Tackett and Carmi (1994b) showed that brood selection could benefit genetic programming by conserving computer time and memory during runs. Altenberg (1994) argues that brood selection benefits the evolvability under recombination in genetic programming.

F.13.3 Implementation in C++

Keith and Martin (1994) discussed how to maximize efficiency and flexibility in an implementation of genetic programming in C++.

F.13.4 Effect of Locality

D'haeseleer and Bluming (1994) demonstrated the beneficial effect of isolation, based on distance, on the performance of genetic programming on a game involving simulated robot tanks. In other work, the structure of the demes (isolated group of individuals in the population) was predetermined in advance, whereas the demes spontaneously emerged in the work of D'haeseleer and Bluming.

F.13.5 Biologically Motivated Representation of Programs

Banzhaf (1993) described a method of representing programs employing binary strings and a set of biologically motivated operations (transcription, repair, editing, and linking) for such strings.

F.13.6 Niches

Abbott (1991) evolved partial solutions to a problem. These partial solutions defined niches which could then be combined to yield complete solutions to the overall problem. This approach yielded significant speedup.

F.13.7 Recombination and Selection

Tackett (1994) studied the effects of recombination and selection in genetic programming, performed significant testing of genetic programming in the context of induction, and introduced several new methods and operators.

Tackett characterized genetic programming as a search of the space of computer programs and compared it to alternative methods such as Tierra and FOIL. Tackett compared genetic programming to other methods of machine learning using a problem of image discrimination.

Many natural organisms overproduce zygotes and subsequently cull the offspring at some later stage of development. This brood selection is done in order to reduce parental resource investment in inferior offspring. Tackett introduced a brood recombination operator which was parameterized by the brood size and a brood culling function. Tackett characterized the computational investment of CPU and memory resources in terms of brood size, brood fitness evaluation cost, and the fitness evaluation cost for full-fledged population members. Tackett showed that the brood recombination operator performs a greedy search of potential recombination sites (as opposed to the random search of recombination sites performed in standard genetic programming). Subsequent tests of the brood recombination operator demonstrated that by using smaller population sizes with large broods, equivalent or improved performance could be achieved using the brood recombination operator, while reducing the CPU and memory requirements relative to genetic programming with standard (random) recombination.

Tackett also presented a new class of constructional problems in which fitness was based strictly on the syntactic form of expressions rather than semantic evaluation: a certain target expression was assigned perfect fitness while those subexpressions resulting from its hierarchical decomposition had intermediate fitness values. This problem allowed precise control over the structure of the search space thereby providing a mechanism with which to test the search properties of operators. Four problems were constructed, analogous to the Royal Road and deceptive problems previously applied to binary-string genetic algorithms. Greedy and random recombination methods were tested in combination with several selection methods.

A criticism of connectionist learning by the symbolic AI community is that neural methods are opaque with respect to providing insight into what they have learned about a problem. Machine learning has successfully produced alternative systems which can learn parsimonious symbolic rules of induction through hill climbing. Other work has shown how such learning may be readily integrated with preexisting expert knowledge. Genetic programming is likewise a symbolic method of induction, and so has potential to feed symbolic knowledge about what it has learned back into the user environment. Among the potential advantages are that the genetic search may be more powerful than other methods applied in symbolic learning to date. It has been observed that genetically induced programs do not yield readily to inspection for many problems. Tackett introduced a "genebankers algorithm" that hashes all expressions and subexpressions (traits) occuring in the population in a time linearly proportional to the number of functions and terminals in the population. A variety of statstics including conditional (schema) fitness of each trait was computed and tracked over time. After a run completed, the collection of traits could be mined in order to try and determine which traits and relationships were salient. For the purpose of this simple experiment, traits were primarily extracted by sorting on conditional fitness and on frequency of occurrence. It is demonstrated that for simple problems the extraction of salient expressions was readily achievable, while for more difficult induction problems it was problematic. Hitchhiking (which Tackett defines as the artificial inflation of fitness estimates for useless expressions which embed themselves among salient expressions) was shown to be a primary confounding factor in this analysis. Tackett concluded by discussing how more advanced methods of analysis could be applied to the mining of genetic traits.

F.13.8 Strongly Typed Genetic Programming

Montana (1993) addressed the requirement of genetic programming that all the variables, constants, arguments for functions, and values returned from functions must be of the same data type. Montana dealt with the difficulties imposed by the closure requirement by introducing a variation of genetic programming called *strongly typed* genetic programming (STGP). In STGP, variables, constants, arguments, and returned values can be of any data type with the provision that the data type for each such value be specified beforehand. Consequently, the initialization process and the genetic operators only generate syntactically correct parse trees. Generic functions and generic data types are key concepts for STGP. Generic functions are not true strongly typed functions, but rather are templates for classes of such functions. Generic data types are analogous. To illustrate STGP, Montana presented four examples involving vector and matrix manipulation and list manipulation. The first was a multi-dimensional least-squares regression problem; the second was a multi-dimensional Kalman filter problem; the third was the list manipulation function NTH; and the fourth was the list manipulation function MAPCAR.

F.14 MEMORY, STATE, AND MENTAL MODELS

F.14.1 Evolution of Indexed Memory

An independent agent can effectively perform some simple tasks merely by reacting to information provided by its sensors about the current state of its world. However, complex tasks generally require the acquisition, storage, and retrieval of information in addition to the mere processing of information. The question arises as to whether genetic programming can evolve programs that use state (memory) in addition to sensory inputs in order to solve problems.

Teller (1993, 1994a) constructed a task that could not possibly be successfully performed without the use of state. In this task the independent agent had to push several boxes to the edges of a grid. Teller gave the agent access to an indexed memory capable of storing 20 numbers. Teller used a two-argument WRITE operator for writing a particular value into a designated memory cell and a one-argument READ operator for reading the value stored in a designated memory cell. Thus, both WRITE and READ accessed memory in an indexed way.

By writing and reading information to memory, the genetically evolved program created a mental model of the environment. The genetically evolved mental model was not the kind of iconic or sentential model envisaged by practitioners of symbolic artificial intelligence. The sequence of information processing steps performed in the memory was not readily comprehensible. However, the usefulness of the genetically evolved mental model was demonstrated by the otherwise unattainable high scores achieved in performing the task. When Teller introduced lesions to certain parts of the memory, the agent's success in performing the task was degraded. Lesions to other parts of the memory had no effect.

Teller compared solutions to his box-pushing problem both with and without automatically defined functions and reported that automatically defined functions improved the performance on this task.

F.14.2 Map-Making and Map-Using

Andre (1994b) described a task involving the search for buried gold. Each program in the population had two branches, called the map-maker and the map-user. The map-maker could examine the environment for buried gold and could store information in an indexed memory; however, it had no tools for digging up the gold. The map-user was incapable of sensing gold; but it had access to the information stored in the indexed memory and has the tools to dig up gold. A mental model of the environment stored in an indexed memory enabled the map-user to find the gold.

F.15 THEORETICAL FOUNDATIONS

F.15.1 Evolution of Evolvability

Altenberg (1994) has explored the notion of evolvability, by which he means the ability of a population to produce variants that are fitter than any yet existing. Altenberg used Price's theorem on covariance and selection to clarify the relationship between the fitness measure, the representation scheme, and the genetic operators in genetic programming. Altenberg analyzed the relationship of evolvability to the observed proliferation of common blocks of code within programs evolved using genetic programming. This important theoretical analysis points the way to several intriguing ways to improve the power of a genetic programming system.

F.15.2 Fitness Landscapes and Difficulty

The concept of fitness landscape, introduced by the biologist Sewell Wright, refers to the mapping from the genome of the population to their fitnesses. Kinnear (1994c) compared various measures for the fitness landscapes for a range of problems to the difficulty of the problems as perceived by genetic programming. He found that the autocorrelation of the fitness values of the result of random walks was only a weak indicator of the difficulty, and that some measures determined from adaptive walks appeared to offer greater predictive value.

F.15.3 Schema in Genetic Programming

O'Reilly and Oppacher (1994) defined a schema, the order of a schema, and the defining length of a schema and accounted for the variable length and the non-homologous nature of the representation in genetic programming. They formulated a schema theorem for genetic programming. Their schema theorem, in turn, leads to a testable hypothetical account of how genetic programming searches by hierarchically combining building blocks.

F.15.4 Turing Completeness

Teller (1994b, 1994c) showed that when genetic programming is combined with indexed memory (described in subsection F.14.1), the resulting system is Turing complete.

Appendix G: Electronic Mailing List and Public Repository

Additional information on genetic programming can be obtained from the mailing list and the on-line public repository and FTP site described below.

G.1 ELECTRONIC MAILING LIST

A mailing list on genetic programming has been established and is currently maintained by James P. Rice of the Knowledge Systems Laboratory of Stanford University. You may subscribe to this on-line mailing list, at no charge, by sending a subscription request on the Internet consisting of the message `subscribe genetic-programming` to `genetic-programming-REQUEST@cs.stanford.edu` by electronic mail.

G.2 PUBLIC REPOSITORY AND FTP SITE

An on-line public repository and FTP (file transfer protocol) site containing computer code, papers on genetic programming, and frequently asked questions has been established on the Internet and is currently maintained by James McCoy of the Computation Center at the University of Texas at Austin.

This repository may be accessed on the Internet by anonymous FTP from the site `ftp.cc.utexas.edu` and the `pub/genetic-programming` directory.

This FTP site contains

- the Common LISP computer code appearing in appendix E of this book for implementing automatically defined functions,

- the original "Little LISP" computer code written in Common LISP for genetic programming as contained in appendixes B and C of *Genetic Programming: On the Programming of Computers by Means of Natural Selection* (Koza 1992a),

- various computer implementations of for genetic programming written by others in C, and C++, and other programming languages,

- various papers on genetic programming (often including some not-yet published papers),
- answers to frequently asked questions about genetic programming, and
- back issues of the GP mailing list.

Bibliography

The symbol ≈ indicates that the reference is discussed in the annotated bibliography of appendix F.

Aarts, E. and Korst, J. 1989. *Simulated Annealing and Boltzmann Machines*. Wiley.

≈Abbott, R. J. 1991. Niches as a GA divide-and-conquer strategy. In Chapman, Art and Myers, Leonard (editors). *Proceedings of the Second Annual AI Symposium for the California State University*. California State University.

Albrecht, R. F., Reeves, C. R., and Steele, N. C. 1993. *Artificial Neural Nets and Genetic Algorithms*. Springer-Verlag.

≈Altenberg, L. 1994. The evolution of evolvability in genetic programming. In Kinnear, K. E. Jr. (editor). *Advances in Genetic Programming*. The MIT Press.

≈Andre, D. 1994a. Automatically defined features: The simultaneous evolution of 2-dimensional feature detectors and an algorithm for using them. In Kinnear, K. E. Jr. (editor). *Advances in Genetic Programming*. The MIT Press.

≈Andre, D. 1994b. Evolution of map making: Learning, planning, and memory using genetic programming. *Proceedings of the 1994 IEEE World Congress on Computational Intelligence*. IEEE Press.

≈Andre, D. 1994c. Learning and upgrading rules for an OCR system using genetic programming. *Proceedings of the 1994 IEEE World Congress on Computational Intelligence*. IEEE Press.

≈Andrews, M. and Prager, R. 1994. Genetic programming for the acquisition of double auction market strategies. In Kinnear, K. E. Jr. (editor). *Advances in Genetic Programming*. The MIT Press.

Anfinsen, C. B. 1973. Principles that govern the folding of protein chains. *Science* 81: 223-230.

≈Angeline, P. J. 1994a. *Evolutionary Algorithms and Emergent Intelligence*. Ph.D. dissertation. Computer Science Department. The Ohio State University.

≈Angeline, P. J. 1994b. Genetic programming and the emergence of intelligence. In Kinnear, K. E. Jr. (editor). *Advances in Genetic Programming*. The MIT Press.

≈Angeline, P. J. 1994c. Genetic programming: A current snapshot. In Fogel, D. B. and Atmar, W. (editors). *Proceedings of the Third Annual Conference on Evolutionary Programming*. Evolutionary Programming Society 1994.

≈Angeline, P. J. and Pollack, J. B. 1992. The evolutionary induction of subroutines. *Proceedings of the Fourteenth Annual Conference of the Cognitive Science Society*. Lawrence Earlbaum.

≈Angeline, P. J. and Pollack, J. B. 1993a. *Coevolving High-Level Representations*. Technical report 92-PA-COEVOLVE. Laboratory for Artificial Intelligence. The Ohio State University. July 1993.

≈Angeline, P. J. and Pollack, J. B. 1993b. Competitive environments evolve better solutions for complex tasks. In Forrest, S. (editor). *Proceedings of the Fifth International Conference on Genetic Algorithms*. Morgan Kaufmann.

≈Angeline, P. J. and Pollack, J. B. 1994. Coevolving high-level representations. In Langton, C. G. (editor). *Artificial Life III, SFI Studies in the Sciences of Complexity*. Volume XVII. Addison-Wesley.

Argos, P. 1989. Predictions of protein structure from gene and amino acid sequences. In Creighton, T. (editor). *Protein Structure: A Practical Approach*. IRL Press.

Arikawa, S., Kuhara, S., Miyano, S., Shinohara, A., and Shinohara, T. 1992. A learning algorithm for elementary formal systems and its experiments on identification of transmembrane domains. In Shriver, B. D. (editor). *Proceedings of the Twenty-Fifth Hawaii International Conference on System Sciences 1992*. The IEEE Computer Society Press. Volume I.

≈Atkin, M. and Cohen, P. R. 1993a. Genetic programming to learn an agent's monitoring strategy. *Proceedings of the AAAI-93 Workshop on Learning Action Models*. AAAI Press.

≈Atkin, M. and Cohen, P. R. 1993b. *Genetic programming to learn an agent's monitoring strategy*. Technical report TR-93-26, Computer Science Department, University of Massachusetts, Amherst.

≈Atkin, M. and Cohen, P. R. 1994. Learning monitoring strategies: A difficult genetic programming application. *Proceedings of the 1994 IEEE World Congress on Computational Intelligence*. IEEE Press.

Bairoch, A. and Boeckmann, B. 1991. The SWISS PROT protein sequence data bank. *Nucleic Acids Research* 19: 2247–2249.

≈Banzhaf, W. 1993. Genetic programming for pedestrians. In Forrest, S. (editor). *Proceedings of the Fifth International Conference on Genetic Algorithms*. Morgan Kaufmann.

Barr, A., Cohen, P. R. and Feigenbaum, E. A. 1989. *The Handbook of Artificial Intelligence*. Addison-Wesley. Volume IV.

Bauer, R. J. 1994. *Genetic Algorithms and Investment Strategies*. Wiley.

Bell, G. I. and Marr, T. G. (editors). 1990. *Computers and DNA*. Addison-Wesley.

Beer, R. D. 1990. *Intelligence as Adaptive Behavior: Experiments in Computational Neuroethology*. Academic Press.

Belew, R., and Booker, L. (editors). 1991. *Proceedings of the Fourth International Conference on Genetic Algorithms*. Morgan Kaufmann.

Belew, R., McInerney, J., and Schraudolph, N. N. 1991. Evolving networks: Using the genetic algorithm with connectionist learning. In Langton, Christopher, et al. (editors). *Artificial Life II, SFI Studies in the Sciences of Complexity*. Volume X. Addison-Wesley.

≈Bengio, S., Bengio, Y., and Cloutier, J. 1994. Use of genetic programming for the search of a new learning rule for neutral networks. *Proceedings of the 1994 IEEE World Congress on Computational Intelligence*. IEEE Press.

Bernstein, F. C., Koetzle, T. F., Williams, G. J. B., Meyer, E.J., Jr., Brice, M. D., Rodgers, J. R., Kennard, O., Shimamouchi, T., and Tasumi, M. 1977. The protein data bank: A computer based archival file for macromolecular structures. *Journal of Molecular Biology*. 112: 535-542.

Branden, C. and Tooze, J. 1991. *Introduction to Protein Structure*. Garland Publishing.

Brooks, R. 1989. A robot that walks: Emergent behaviors from a carefully evolved network. *Neural Computation* 1(2): 253-262.

Buckles B. P. and Petry, F. E. 1992. *Genetic Algorithms*. The IEEE Computer Society Press.

Cantor, C., C., R. and Lim, H. A. (editors). 1991. *The First International Conference on Electrophoresis, Supercomputing, and the Human Genome*. World Scientific.

Cedeno, W. and Vemuri, V. 1993. An investigation of DNA mapping with genetic algorithms: Preliminary results. *Proceedings of the Fifth Workshop on Neural Networks: An International Conference on Computational Intelligence: Neural Networks, Fuzzy Systems, Evolutionary Programming, and Virtual Reality.* The Society for Computer Simulation.

Charniak, E. and McDermott, D. 1985. *Introduction to Artificial Intelligence.* Addison-Wesley.

Chou, P. Y. and Fasman, G. D. 1974a. Conformational parameters for amino acids in helical, b-sheet, and random coil regions calculated from proteins. *Biochemistry.* 13: 211-222.

Chou, P. Y. and Fasman, G. D. 1974b. Prediction of protein conformation. *Biochemistry.* 13: 222-245.

Collins, R. and Jefferson, D. 1991. Representations for artificial organisms. In Meyer, J-A, and Wilson, S. W. *From Animals to Animats: Proceedings of the First International Conference on Simulation of Adaptive Behavior.* The MIT Press.

Creighton, T. E. 1993. *Proteins: Structures and Molecular Properties.* Second Edition. W. H. Freeman.

≈Das, S., Franguiadakis, T., Papka, M., DeFanti, T. A., and Sandin, D. J. 1994. A genetic programming application in virtual reality. *Proceedings of the 1994 IEEE World Congress on Computational Intelligence.* IEEE Press.

Davidor, Y. 1991. *Genetic Algorithms and Robotics.* World Scientific.

Davis, L. (editor). 1987. *Genetic Algorithms and Simulated Annealing.* Pittman.

Davis, L. 1991. *Handbook of Genetic Algorithms.* Van Nostrand Reinhold.

DeJong, G. 1981. Generalization based on explanations. *Proceedings of the Seventh International Joint Conference on Artificial Intelligence.* Morgan Kaufmann.

DeJong, G. 1983. Acquiring schemata through understanding and generalizing plans. *Proceedings of the Eighth International Joint Conference on Artificial Intelligence.* Morgan Kaufmann.

≈D'haeseleer, P. and Bluming, J. 1994. Effects of locality in individual and population evolution. In Kinnear, K. E. Jr. (editor). *Advances in Genetic Programming.* The MIT Press.

≈D'haeseleer, P. 1994. Context preserving crossover in genetic programming. *Proceedings of the 1994 IEEE World Congress on Computational Intelligence.* IEEE Press.

Doolittle, R. F. (editor). 1990. *Methods in Enzymology — Volume 183 – Molecular Evolution: Computer Analysis of Protein and Nucleic Acid Sequences.* Academic Press.

Doolittle, R. F. 1987. *Of Urfs and Orfs: A Primer on How to Analyze Derived Amino Acid Sequences.* University Science Books.

≈Dunay, B. D., Petry, F. E., and Buckles, W. P. 1994. Regular language induction with genetic programming. *Proceedings of the 1994 IEEE World Congress on Computational Intelligence.* IEEE Press.

Engelman, D., Steitz, T., and Goldman, A. 1986. Identifying nonpolar transbilayer helices in amino acid sequences of membrane proteins. *Annual Review of Biophysics and Biophysiological Chemistry.* Annual Reviews. Volume 15.

Fasman, G. D. 1990. *Prediction of Protein Structure and the Principles of Protein Conformation.* Plenum Press.

Fickett, J. W. and Cinkosky, M. J. 1993. A genetic algorithm for assembling chromosome physical maps. In Lim, H. A., Fickett, J. W., Cantor, C. R., and Robbins, R. J. (editors). *The Second International Conference on Bioinformatics, Supercomputing, and Complex Genome Analysis.* World Scientific.

Fikes, R. E., Hart, P. E., and Nilsson, N. J. 1972. Learning and executing generalized robot plans. *Artificial Intelligence*, 3:251–288.

Fisher, R. A. 1958. *Statistical Methods for Research Workers*. 13th Edition. Hafner.

Fogel, D. B. 1991. *System Identification through Simulated Evolution*. Ginn Press.

Fogel, D. B. and Atmar, W. (editors). 1992. *Proceedings of the First Annual Conference on Evolutionary Programming*. Evolutionary Programming Society.

Fogel, D. B. and Atmar, W. (editors). 1993. *Proceedings of the Second Annual Conference on Evolutionary Programming*. Evolutionary Programming Society.

Forrest, S. (editor). 1990. Emergent Computation: Self-Organizing, Collective, and Cooperative Computing Networks. The MIT Press.

Forrest, S. 1991. *Parallelism and Programming in Classifier Systems*. Pittman.

Forrest, S. (editor). 1993. *Proceedings of the Fifth International Conference on Genetic Algorithms*. Morgan Kaufmann.

≈Fraser, A. P. and Rush, J. R. 1994. Putting INK into a BIRo: A discussion of problem domain knowledge for evolutionary robotics. *Proceedings of the Workshop on Artificial Intellingence and Simulation of Behaviour Workshop on Evolutionary Computing, April 11-13, 1994*.

Fukushima, K. and Miyake, S. 1982. Neocognitron: A new algorithm for pattern recognition tolerant of deformations and shifts in position. *Pattern Recognition*, 15(6): 455-469.

Fukushima, K., Miyake, S., and Takatuki, I. 1983. *IEEE Transactions on Systems, Man, and Cybernetics*. 13(5): 826-834.

Fukushima, K. 1989. Analysis of the process of visual pattern recognition by neocognitron. *Neural Networks*, 2: 413-420.

≈Ghanea-Hercock, R. and Fraser, A. P. 1994. Evolution of autonomous robot control architectures. *Proceedings of the Workshop on Artificial Intellingence and Simulation of Behaviour Workshop on Evolutionary Computing, April 11-13, 1994*.

Gierasch, L. M. and King, J. 1990. *Protein Folding: Deciphering the Second Half of the Genetic Code*. American Association for the Advancement of Science.

Goldberg, D. E. 1989. *Genetic Algorithms in Search, Optimization, and Machine Learning*. Addison-Wesley.

Goldberg, D. E. and Deb, K. 1991. A comparative analysis of selection schemes used in genetic algorithms. In Rawlins, G. (editor). *Foundations of Genetic Algorithms*. Morgan Kaufmann.

Grefenstette, J. J. (editor). 1985. *Proceedings of an International Conference on Genetic Algorithms and Their Applications*. Erlbaum.

Grefenstette, J. J. (editor). 1987. *Genetic Algorithms and Their Applications: Proceedings of the Second International Conference on Genetic Algorithms*. Erlbaum.

≈Gruau, F. 1992a. Genetic synthesis of Boolean neural networks with a cell rewriting developmental process. In Schaffer, J. D. and Whitley, D. (editors). *Proceedings of the Workshop on Combinations of Genetic Algorithms and Neural Networks 1992*. The IEEE Computer Society Press.

≈Gruau, F. 1992b. *Cellular encoding of Genetic Neural Networks*. Technical report 92-21. Laboratoire de l'Informatique du Parallélisme. Ecole Normale Supérieure de Lyon.

≈Gruau, F. 1993a. Genetic synthesis of modular neural networks. In Forrest, S. (editor). *Proceedings of the Fifth International Conference on Genetic Algorithms*. Morgan Kaufmann.

≈Gruau, F. 1993b. Grammatical inference with genetic search using cellular encoding. In Lucas, Simon (editor). *Proceedings of the International Conference on Grammatical Inference*. The Institution of Electrical Engineers, London.

≈Gruau, F. 1994a. *Neural Network Synthesis using Cellular Encoding and the Genetic Algorithm.* PhD thesis. Laboratoire de l'Informatique du Parallélisme, Ecole Normale Supèrieure de Lyon.

≈Gruau, F. 1994b. Genetic micro programming of neural networks. In Kinnear, K. E. Jr. (editor). *Advances in Genetic Programming.* The MIT Press.

≈Gruau, F and Whitley, D. 1993a. *The cellular development of neural networks: The interaction of learning and evolution.* Technical report 93-04. Laboratoire de l'Informatique du Parallélisme, Ecole Normale Supèrieure de Lyon.

≈Gruau, F and Whitley, D. 1993b. Adding learning to the cellular development process: a comparative study. *Evolutionary Computation.* 1(3):213–233.

Hamaguchi, K. 1992. *The Protein Molecule: Conformation, Stability, and Folding.* Japan Scientific Societies Press.

≈Handley, S. 1993a. Automated learning of a detector for α-helices in protein sequences via genetic programming. In Forrest, S. (editor). *Proceedings of the Fifth International Conference on Genetic Algorithms.* Morgan Kaufmann.

≈Handley, S. 1993b. The genetic planner: The automatic generation of plans for a mobile robot via genetic programming. *Proceedings of the Eighth IEEE International Symposium on Intelligent Control.* The IEEE Control System Society.

≈Handley, S. 1993c. The automatic generation of plans for a mobile robot via genetic programming with automatically defined functions. *Proceedings of the Fifth Workshop on Neural Networks: An International Conference on Computational Intelligence: Neural Networks, Fuzzy Systems, Evolutionary Programming, and Virtual Reality.* The Society for Computer Simulation.

≈Handley, S. 1994a. The automatic generation of plans for a mobile robot via genetic programming with automatically defined functions. In Kinnear, K. E. Jr. (editor). *Advances in Genetic Programming.* The MIT Press.

≈Handley, S. 1994b. On the use of a directed acyclic graph to represent a population of computer programs. *Proceedings of the 1994 IEEE World Congress on Computational Intelligence.* IEEE Press.

≈Handley, S. 1994c. Automated learning of a detector for the cores of α-helices in protein sequences via genetic programming. *Proceedings of the 1994 IEEE World Congress on Computational Intelligence.* IEEE Press.

Hibbert, D. B. 1993. Display of chemical structures in two dimensions and the evolution of molecular recognition. In Forrest, S. (editor). *Proceedings of the Fifth International Conference on Genetic Algorithms.* Morgan Kaufmann.

Hillis, W. D. 1990. Co-evolving parasites improve simulated evolution as an optimization procedure. In Forrest, S. (editor). *Emergent Computation: Self-Organizing, Collective, and Cooperative Computing Networks.* The MIT Press.

Hillis, W. D. 1991. Co-evolving parasites improve simulated evolution as an optimization procedure. In Langton, Christopher, et al. (editors). *Artificial Life II, SFI Studies in the Sciences of Complexity.* Volume X. Addison-Wesley.

Hinton, G. 1989. Connectionist learning procedures. *Artificial Intelligence.* 40: 185–234.

Holbrook, S. R., Muskal, S. M., and Kim, S. H. 1990. Predicting surface exposure of amino acids from protein sequence. *Protein Engineering.* 3(8): 659-665.

Holland, J. H. 1975. *Adaptation in Natural and Artificial Systems: An Introductory Analysis with Applications to Biology, Control, and Artificial Intelligence.* University of Michigan Press. Also second edition, The MIT Press 1992.

Holland, J. H. 1986. Escaping brittleness: The possibilities of general-purpose learning algorithms applied to parallel rule-based systems. In Michalski, Ryszard S. et al. (editors). *Machine Learning: An Artificial Intelligence Approach, Volume II*. Morgan Kaufmann.

Holland, J. H, Holyoak, K.J., Nisbett, R.E., and Thagard, P.A. 1986. *Induction: Processes of Inference, Learning, and Discovery*. The MIT Press.

Hopp, T. P. and Woods, K. R. 1981. *Proceedings of the National Academy of Sciences USA*. 78: 3824-3828.

Hunter, L. (editor). 1993. *Artificial Intelligence and Molecular Biology*. AAAI Press.

Hunter, L., Searls, D., and Shavlik, J. (editors). 1993. *Proceedings of the First International Conference on Intelligent Systems for Molecular Biology*. AAAI Press.

≈Iba, H., de Garis, H., and Higuchi, T. 1993. Evolutionary learning of predatory behaviors based on structured classifiers. In Meyer, J. A., Roitblat, H. L. and Wilson, S. W. (editors). *From Animals to Animats 2: Proceedings of the Second International Conference on Simulation of Adaptive Behavior*. The MIT Press.

≈Iba, H., deGaris, H., and Sato, T. 1993. *Solving identification problems by structured genetic algorithms*. Technical report ETL-TR-93-17. Japan Electrotechnical Laboratory.

≈Iba, H., deGaris, H., and Sato, T. 1994. Genetic programming using a minimum description length principle. In Kinnear, K. E. Jr. (editor). *Advances in Genetic Programming*. The MIT Press.

≈Iba, H., Kurita, T., de Garis, H., and Sato, T. 1993. System identification using structured genetic algorithms. In Forrest, S. (editor). *Proceedings of the Fifth International Conference on Genetic Algorithms*. Morgan Kaufmann.

≈Iba, H. and Sato, T. 1992. Meta-level strategy learning for GA based on structured representation. In *Proceedings of the Second Pacific Rim International Conference on Artificial Intelligence*. Center for Artificial Intelligence Research, Kaist.

≈Iba, H. and Sato, T. 1994. *Extension of STROGANOFF for symbolic problems*. Technical report ETL-TR-94-1. Japan Electrotechnical Laboratory.

≈Iba, H., Sato, T., and deGaris, H. 1994. System identification approach to genetic programming. *Proceedings of the 1994 IEEE World Congress on Computational Intelligence*. IEEE Press.

Ioerger, T R., Rendell, L., and Subramaniam, S. 1993. Constructive induction and protein tertiary structure prediction. In Searls, D., and Shavlik, J. (editors). 1993. *Proceedings of the First International Conference on Intelligent Systems for Molecular Biology*. AAAI Press.

Ishikawa, M., Toya, T., Totoki, Y., and Konagaya, A. 1993. Parallel iterative aligner with genetic algorithm. In Takagi, T., Imai, H., Miyano, S. Mitaku, S., and Kanehisa, M. (editors). *Genome Informatics Workshop IV*. Universal Academy Press.

Ivakhnenko, A. G. 1971. Polynomial theory of complex systems. *IEEE Transactions on Systems, Machines, and Cybernetics*. 1(4): 364–378.

≈Jannink, J. 1994. Cracking and co-evolving randomizers. In Kinnear, K. E. Jr. (editor). *Advances in Genetic Programming*. The MIT Press.

Jefferson, D., Collins, R., Cooper, C., Dyer, M., Flowers, M., Korf, R., Taylor, C., and Wang, A. 1991. Evolution as a theme in artificial life: The genesys/tracker system. In Langton, C., et al. (editors). *Artificial Life II, SFI Studies in the Sciences of Complexity*. Volume X. Addison-Wesley.

≈Jiang, M. 1992. *A hierarchical genetic system for symbolic function identification*. Master's thesis. University of Montana.

≈Jiang, M. 1993. An adaptive function identification system. *Proceedings of the IEEE/ACM Conference on Developing and Managing Intelligent System Projects, Vienna, Virginia, March 1993*.

≈Jiang, M. and Wright, A. H. 1992. A hierarchical genetic system for symbolic function identification. *Proceedings of the 24th Symposium on the Interface: Computing Science and Statistics, College Station, Texas, March 1992.*

≈Jones, A. 1991. *Writing Programs Using Genetic Algorithms.* M.Sc. thesis, Department of Computer Science, University of Manchester, United Kingdom.

Jones, G., Brown, R. D., Clark, D. E., Willett, P., and Glen, R. C. 1993. Searching databases of two-dimensional and three-dimensional chemical structures using genetic algorithms. In Forrest, S. (editor). *Proceedings of the Fifth International Conference on Genetic Algorithms.* Morgan Kaufmann.

Kabsch, W. and Sander, C. 1983. Dictionary of protein secondary structure: Pattern recognition of hydrogen-bonded and geometrical features. *Biopolymers.* 22: 2577–2637.

Keane, M. A., Koza, J. R., and Rice, J. P. 1993. Finding an impulse response function using genetic programming. *Proceedings of the 1993 American Control Conference.* American Automatic Control Council. Volume III.

≈Keith, M. J. and Martin, M. C. Genetic programming in C++: Implementation issues. In Kinnear, K. E. Jr. (editor). *Advances in Genetic Programming.* The MIT Press.

Kendrew, J. C. 1958. A three-dimensional model of the myoglobin molecule obtained by x-ray analysis. *Nature.* 181: 662-666.

≈Kinnear, K. E., Jr. 1993a. Evolving a sort: Lessons in genetic programming. *1993 IEEE International Conference on Neural Networks, San Francisco.* IEEE Press. Volume 2.

≈Kinnear, K. E., Jr. 1993b. Generality and difficulty in genetic programming: Evolving a sort. In Forrest, S. (editor). *Proceedings of the Fifth International Conference on Genetic Algorithms.* Morgan Kaufmann.

≈Kinnear, K. E. ,Jr. (editor). 1994a. *Advances in Genetic Programming.* Cambridge: The MIT Press.

≈Kinnear, K. E., Jr. 1994b. Alternatives in automatic function definition: A comparison of performance. In Kinnear, K. E., Jr. (editor). *Advances in Genetic Programming.* Cambridge: The MIT Press.

≈Kinnear, K. E., Jr. 1994c. Fitness landscapes and difficulty in genetic programming. *Proceedings of the 1994 IEEE World Congress on Computational Intelligence.* IEEE Press.

Kirkpatrick, S., Gelatt, C. D., and Vecchi, M. P. 1983. Optimization by simulated annealing. *Science* 220: 671–680.

Konagaya, A. and Kondou, H. 1993. Stochastic motif extraction using a genetic algorithm with the MDL principle. In Mudge, T. N., Milutinovic, V., and Hunter, L. (editors). *Proceedings of the Twenty-Sixth Annual Hawaii International Conference on Systems Science 1993.* The IEEE Computer Society Press. Volume I.

Korf, R. E. 1980. Toward a model of representation changes. *Artificial Intelligence,* 14, 4178.

Korf, R. E. 1985a. Macro-operators: A weak method for learning. *Artificial Intelligence,* 26, 35–77.

Korf, R. E. 1985b. Depth-first iterative-deepening: An optimal admissible tree search. *Artificial Intelligence,* 27, 97–110.

Koza, J. R. 1972. On Inducing a Non-Trivial, Parsimonious, Hierarchical Grammar for a Given Sample of Sentences. Ph.D. dissertation, Department of Computer Science, University of Michigan.

Koza, J. R. 1988. *Non-Linear Genetic Algorithms for Solving Problems.* U.S. Patent Application filed May 20, 1988.

Koza, J. R. 1989. Hierarchical genetic algorithms operating on populations of computer programs. In *Proceedings of the 11th International Joint Conference on Artificial Intelligence.* Morgan Kaufmann. Volume I.

Koza, J. R. 1990a. *Genetic Programming: A Paradigm for Genetically Breeding Populations of Computer Programs to Solve Problems.* Stanford University Computer Science Department technical report STAN-CS-90-1314.

Koza, J. R. 1990b. A genetic approach to econometric modeling. Paper presented at Sixth World Congress of the Econometric Society, Barcelona, Spain. August 27, 1990.

Koza, J. R. 1990c. Genetically breeding populations of computer programs to solve problems in artificial intelligence. In *Proceedings of the Second International Conference on Tools for AI.* The IEEE Computer Society Press.

Koza, J. R. 1990d. *Non-Linear Genetic Algorithms for Solving Problems.* Filed May 20, 1988. U.S. Patent 4,935,877. Issued June 19, 1990.

Koza, J. R. 1990e. *Non-Linear Genetic Algorithms for Solving Problems by Finding a Fit Composition of Functions.* U.S. Patent Application filed March 28, 1990.

Koza, J. R. 1991a. Evolution and co-evolution of computer programs to control independent-acting agents. In Meyer, J-A., and Wilson, S. W. *From Animals to Animats: Proceedings of the First International Conference on Simulation of Adaptive Behavior.* The MIT Press.

Koza, J. R. 1991b. Concept formation and decision tree induction using the genetic programming paradigm. In Schwefel, H. P. and Maenner, R. (editors). *Parallel Problem Solving from Nature.* Springer-Verlag.

Koza, J. R. 1991c. Genetic evolution and co-evolution of computer programs. In Langton, Christopher, et al. (editors). *Artificial Life II, SFI Studies in the Sciences of Complexity.* Volume X. Addison-Wesley.

Koza, J. R. 1991d. A hierarchical approach to learning the Boolean multiplexer function. In Rawlins, G. (editor). *Foundations of Genetic Algorithms.* Morgan Kaufmann.

Koza, J. R. 1991e. Evolving a computer program to generate random numbers using the genetic programming paradigm. In Belew, R. and Booker, L. (editors). *Proceedings of the Fourth International Conference on Genetic Algorithms.* Morgan Kaufmann.

Koza, J. R. 1991f. A genetic approach to econometric modeling. In Bourgine, P. and Walliser, B. (editors). *Economics and Cognitive Science.* Pergamon.

Koza, J. R. 1992a. *Genetic Programming: On the Programming of Computers by Means of Natural Selection.* The MIT Press.

Koza, J. R. 1992b. Hierarchical automatic function definition in genetic programming. In Whitley, D. (editor). *Proceedings of the Workshop on the Foundations of Genetic Algorithms and Classifier Systems, Vail, Colorado 1992.* Morgan Kaufmann.

Koza, J. R. 1992c. The genetic programming paradigm: Genetically breeding populations of computer programs to solve problems. In Soucek, B. and the IRIS Group (editors). *Dynamic, Genetic, and Chaotic Programming.* Wiley.

Koza, J. R. 1992d. A genetic approach to finding a controller to back up a tractor-trailer truck. In *Proceedings of the 1992 American Control Conference.* American Automatic Control Council.

Koza, J. R. 1992e. A genetic approach to the truck backer upper problem and the inter-twined spirals problem. In *Proceedings of International Joint Conference on Neural Networks, Baltimore, June 1992.* IEEE Press.

Koza, J. R. 1992f. Evolution of subsumption using genetic programming. In Varela, F. J., and Bourgine, P. (editors). *Toward a Practice of Autonomous Systems: Proceedings of the First European Conference on Artificial Life.* The MIT Press.

Koza, J. R. 1992g. *Non-Linear Genetic Algorithms for Solving Problems by Finding a Fit Composition of Functions.* U.S. Patent 5,136,686. Filed March 28, 1990. Issued August 4, 1992.

Koza, J. R. 1992h Genetic evolution and co-evolution of game strategies. Paper presented at the International Conference on Game Theory and Its Applications, Stony Brook, New York. July 15, 1992.

Koza, J. R. 1992i. *Non-Linear Genetic Algorithms for Solving Problems*. Canadian Patent 1,311,561. Issued December 15, 1992.

Koza, J. R. 1992j. *Non-Linear Genetic Algorithms for Solving Problems*. Australian Patent 611,350. Issued September 21, 1991.

Koza, J. R. 1993a. Simultaneous discovery of detectors and a way of using the detectors via genetic programming. *1993 IEEE International Conference on Neural Networks, San Francisco*. IEEE 1993. Volume III.

Koza, J. R. 1993b. Simultaneous discovery of reusable detectors and subroutines using genetic programming. In Forrest, S. (editor). *Proceedings of the Fifth International Conference on Genetic Algorithms*. Morgan Kaufmann.

Koza, J. R. 1993c. Discovery of a main program and reusable subroutines using genetic programming. 1993. *Proceedings of the Fifth Workshop on Neural Networks: An International Conference on Computational Intelligence: Neural Networks, Fuzzy Systems, Evolutionary Programming, and Virtual Reality*. The Society for Computer Simulation.

Koza, John R. (editor) 1993d. *Artificial Life at Stanford 1993*. Stanford University Bookstore.

Koza, John R. (editor) 1993e. *Genetic Algorithms at Stanford 1993*. Stanford University Bookstore.

Koza, J. R. 1994a. Scalable learning in genetic programming using automatically defined functions. In Kinnear, K. E. Jr. (editor). *Advances in Genetic Programming*. The MIT Press.

Koza, J. R. 1994b. Introduction to genetic programming. In Kinnear, K. E. Jr. (editor). *Advances in Genetic Programming*. The MIT Press.

Koza, J. R. 1994c. Spontaneous emergence of self-replicating and evolutionarily self-improving computer programs. In Langton, C. G. (editor). 1994. *Artificial Life III, SFI Studies in the Sciences of Complexity*. Volume XVII. Addison-Wesley.

Koza, J. R. 1994d. Recognizing patterns in protein sequences using iteration-performing calculations in genetic programming. *Proceedings of the 1994 IEEE World Congress on Computational Intelligence*. IEEE Press.

Koza, J. R. 1994e. Evolution of a subsumption architecture that performs a wall following task for an autonomous mobile robot via genetic programming. In Petsche, T. (editor). *Computational Learning Theory and Natural Learning Systems, Volume 2*. The MIT Press.

Koza, John R. 1994f. Automated discovery of detectors and iteration-performing calculations to recognize patterns in protein sequences using genetic programming. *Proceedings of the Conference on Computer Vision and Pattern Recognition*. IEEE Computer Society Press.

Koza, J. R., and Keane, M. A. 1990a. Cart centering and broom balancing by genetically breeding populations of control strategy programs. In *Proceedings of International Joint Conference on Neural Networks, Washington, January 15-19, 1990*. Volume I, Erlbaum.

Koza, J. R., and Keane, M. A.1990b. Genetic breeding of non-linear optimal control strategies for broom balancing. In *Proceedings of the Ninth International Conference on Analysis and Optimization of Systems, Antibes, France*. Springer-Verlag.

Koza, J. R., Keane, M. A., and Rice, J. P. 1993. Performance improvement of machine learning via automatic discovery of facilitating functions as applied to a problem of symbolic system identification. *1993 IEEE International Conference on Neural Networks, San Francisco*. IEEE 1993. Volume I.

Koza, J. R., and Rice, J. P. 1990. *A Non-Linear Genetic Process for Use with Co-Evolving Populations*. U.S. Patent Application filed September 18, 1990.

Koza, J. R., and Rice, J. P. 1991a. Genetic generation of both the weights and architecture for a neural network. In *Proceedings of International Joint Conference on Neural Networks, Seattle, July 1991*, volume II. IEEE Press.

Koza, J. R., and Rice, J. P. 1991b. A genetic approach to artificial intelligence. In Langton, C. G. (editor). *Artificial Life II Video Proceedings*. Addison-Wesley.

Koza, J. R., and Rice, J. P. 1992a. *Genetic Programming: The Movie*. The MIT Press.

Koza, J. R., and Rice, J. P. 1992b. *A Non-Linear Genetic Process for Data Encoding·and for Solving Problems Using Automatically Defined Functions*. U.S. Patent Application filed May 11, 1992.

Koza, J. R., and Rice, J. P. 1992c. Automatic programming of robots using genetic programming. In *Proceedings of Tenth National Conference on Artificial Intelligence*. AAAI Press.

Koza, J. R., and Rice, J. P. 1992c. *A Non-Linear Genetic Process for Problem Solving Using Spontaneously Emergent Self-Replicating and Self-Improving Entities*. U.S. Patent Application filed June 16, 1992.

Koza, J. R., and Rice, J. P. 1992d. *A Non-Linear Genetic Process for Use with Plural Co-Evolving Populations*. U.S. Patent 5,148,513. Filed September 18, 1990. Issued September 15, 1992.

Koza, J. R., and Rice, J. P. *A Non-Linear Genetic Process for Problem Solving Using Spontaneously Emergent Self-Replicating and Self-Improving Entities*. U.S. Patent Application filed June 16, 1992.

Koza, J. R., and Rice, J. P. 1994. *Genetic Programming II Videotape: The Next Generation*. The MIT Press.

Koza, J. R., Rice, J. P., and Roughgarden, J. 1992a. *Evolution of Food Foraging Strategies for the Caribbean Anolis Lizard Using Genetic Programming*. Santa Fe Institute Working Paper 92-06-028.

Koza, J. R., Rice, J. P., and Roughgarden, J. 1992b. Evolution of food foraging strategies for the Caribbean *Anolis* lizard using genetic programming. *Adaptive Behavior*. 1(2): 47-74.

≈Kraft, D. H., Petry, F. E., Buckles, W. P., and Sadasivan, T. 1994. The use of genetic programming to build queries for information retrieval. *Proceedings of the 1994 IEEE World Congress on Computational Intelligence*. IEEE Press.

Kyte, J. and Doolittle, R. 1982. A simple method for displaying the hydropathic character of proteins. *Journal of Molecular Biology*. 157: 105-132.

Laird, J. E., Rosenbloom, P. S., and Newell, A. 1986a. *Universal Subgoaling and Chunking*. Kluwer Academic.

Laird, J. E., Rosenbloom, P. S., and Newell, A. 1986b. Chunking in Soar: The anatomy of a general learning mechanism. *Machine Learning*, 1(1) 11–46.

Langton, C. G. (editor). 1989. *Artificial Life, Santa Fe Institute Studies in the Sciences of Complexity*. Volume VI. Addison-Wesley.

Langton, C. G., Taylor, C., Farmer, J. D., and Rasmussen, S. (editors). 1991. *Artificial Life II, SFI Studies in the Sciences of Complexity*. Volume X. Addison-Wesley.

Langton, C. G. (editor). 1994. *Artificial Life III, SFI Studies in the Sciences of Complexity*. Volume XVII. Addison-Wesley.

Lapedes, A. Barnes, C., Burks, C., Farber, R., and Sirotkin, K.M. 1990. Application of neural networks and other machine learning algorithms to DNA sequence analysis. In Bell, G. I. and Marr, T. G. (editors). *Computers and DNA*. Addison-Wesley.

≈Lay, M-Y. 1994. Application of genetic programming in analyzing multiple steady states of dynamical systems. *Proceedings of the 1994 IEEE World Congress on Computational Intelligence.* IEEE Press.

Le Cun, Y., Boser, B. Denker, J. S., Henderson, R. E., Howard, H., W., and Jackel, L.D. 1990. Handwritten digit recognition with a back-propagation network. In Touretzky, D. S. (editor) *Advances in Neural Information Processing Systems 2.* Morgan Kaufmann.

Le Grand, S. M. 1993. *The Application of the genetic algorithm to protein tertiary structure prediction.* Ph.D. dissertation, Department of Chemistry, Biochemistry The Pennsylvania State University..

Lesk, A. M. (editor). 1988. *Computational Molecular Biology: Sources and Methods for Sequence Analysis.* Oxford University Press.

Lesk, A. M. 1991. *Protein Architecture: A Practical Approach.* Oxford University Press.

Leszcynski, J. F. and Rose, G. D. 1986. Loops in globular proteins: A novel category of secondary structure. *Science.* 234: 849-855. November 14, 1986.

Lim, H. A., Fickett, J. W., Cantor, C. R., and Robbins, R. J. (editors). 1993. *The Second International Conference on Bioinformatics, Supercomputing, and Complex Genome Analysis.* World Scientific.

Lucasius, C. B. and Kateman, G. 1989. Application of genetic algorithms to chemometrics. In Schaffer, J. D. (editor). *Proceedings of the Third International Conference on Genetic Algorithms.* Morgan Kaufmann.

Lucasius, C. B., Blommers, M. J. J., Buydens, L. M. C., and Kateman, G. 1991. In Davis, L. (editor). *Handbook of Genetic Algorithms.* Van Nostrand Reinhold.

Maenner, R. and Manderick, B. (editors). 1992. *Proceedings of the Second International Conference on Parallel Problem Solving from Nature.* North Holland.

Marcel, J. J., Blommers, M. J., Lucasius, C. B., Kateman, G, and Kaptein, R. 1992. Conformational analysis of a dinucleotide photodimer with the aid of the genetic algorithm. *Biopolymers* 32:45-52.

≈Massand, B. 1994. Optimizing confidence of text classification by evolution of symbolic expressions. In Kinnear, K. E. Jr. (editor). *Advances in Genetic Programming.* The MIT Press.

Matthews, B. W. 1975. Comparison of the predicted and observed secondary structure of T4 phage lysozyme. *Biochemica et Biophysica Acta.* 405:442-451.

≈Maxwell, S. R.,III. 1994. Experiments with a coroutine execution model for genetic programming. *Proceedings of the 1994 IEEE World Congress on Computational Intelligence.* IEEE Press.

Meyer, J. A., and Wilson, S. W. *From Animals to Animats: Proceedings of the First International Conference on Simulation of Adaptive Behavior.* Paris. September 24-28, 1990. The MIT Press 1991.

Meyer, J. A., Roitblat, H. L. and Wilson, S. W. (editors). 1993. *From Animals to Animats 2: Proceedings of the Second International Conference on Simulation of Adaptive Behavior.* The MIT Press.

Michalewicz, Z. 1992. *Genetic Algorithms + Data Structures = Evolution Programs.* Springer-Verlag.

Miller, G. F., Todd, P. M., and Hegde, S. U. 1989. Designing Neural Networks using Genetic Algorithms. In Schaffer, J. D. (editor). *Proceedings of the Third International Conference on Genetic Algorithms.* Morgan Kaufmann.

Minton S. 1990. Quantitative results concerning the utility of explanation-based learning. In Shavlik, J. W., and Dietterich, T. G. *Readings in Machine Learning.* Morgan Kaufmann.

Mitchell, T. M., Keller, R. M., and Kedar-Cabelli, S.T. 1986. Explanation-based generalization: A unifying view. *Machine Learning,* 1(1): 47–80.

≈Montana, D. J. 1993. *Strongly Typed Genetic Programming.* Bolt, Beranek, and Newman technical report 7866. May 7, 1993.

Muskal, S. M., Holbrook, S R. and Kim, S. H. 1990. Prediction of the disulfide-bonding state of cysteine in proteins. *Protein Engineering*. 3(8): 667-672.

Muskal, S. M. and Kim. S. H. 1992. Predicting protein secondary structure content – a tandem neural network approach. *Journal of Molecular Biology*. 225: 713-727.

≈Nguyen, T. and Huang, T. 1994. Evolvable modeling: Structural adaptation through hierarchical evolution for 3-D model-based vision. In Kinnear, K. E. Jr. (editor). *Advances in Genetic Programming*. The MIT Press.

Nilsson, N. J. 1980. *Principles of Artificial Intelligence*. Morgan Kaufmann.

≈Nordin, P. 1994. A compiling genetic programming system that directly manipulates the machine code. In Kinnear, K. E. Jr. (editor). *Advances in Genetic Programming*. The MIT Press.

≈Oakley, E. H. N. 1994. Two scientific applications of genetic programming: Stack filters and non-linear equation fitting to chaotic data. In Kinnear, K. E. Jr. (editor). *Advances in Genetic Programming*. The MIT Press.

≈O'Reilly, U. M. and Oppacher, F. 1992. An experimental perspective on genetic programming. In Maenner, R. and Manderick, B. (editors). *Proceedings of the Second International Conference on Parallel Problem Solving from Nature*. North Holland.

≈O'Reilly, U. M. and Oppacher, F. 1994. *The Troubling Aspects of a Building Block Hypothesis for Genetic Programming*. Santa Fe Institute Working Paper 94-02-001.

Park, S. K., and Miller, K. W. 1988. Random number generators: Good ones are hard to find. *Communications of the ACM*. 31: 1192-1201.

Pauling, L. and Corey, R. B. 1951. Configurations of polypeptide chains with favored orientations around single bonds: Two new pleated sheets. *Proceedings of the National Academy of Science USA*. 37: 729–740.

Pauling, L., Corey, R. B., and Branson, H. R. 1951. The structure of proteins: Two hydrogen-bonded helical configurations of the polypeptide chain. *Proceedings of the National Academy of Science USA*. 37: 205–211.

≈Perkis, T. 1994. Stack-based genetic programming. *Proceedings of the 1994 IEEE World Congress on Computational Intelligence*. IEEE Press.

≈Perry, J. E. 1994. The effect of population enrichment in genetic programming. *Proceedings of the 1994 IEEE World Congress on Computational Intelligence*. IEEE Press.

Platt, D. M. and Dix, T. I. 1993. Construction of restriction maps using a genetic algorithm. In Mudge, T. N., Milutinovic, V., and Hunter, L. (editors). *Proceedings of the Twenty-Sixth Annual Hawaii International Conference on Systems Science 1993*. The IEEE Computer Society Press. Volume I.

Prusinkiewicz, P. and Lindenmayer, A. 1990. *The Algorithmic Beauty of Plants*. Springer-Verlag.

Quinlan, J. R. Induction of decision trees. *Machine Learning* 1 (1): 81–106. 1986.

Ragavan, H. and Rendell, L. 1993. Lookahead feature construction for learning hard concepts. In *Machine Learning; Proceedings of the Tenth International Conference*. Morgan Kaufmann.

Rawlins, G. (editor). 1991. *Foundations of Genetic Algorithms*. Morgan Kaufmann.

Rendell, L. and Seshu, R. 1990. Learning hard concepts through constructive induction: Framework and rationale. *Computational Intelligence*. 6: 247-270.

Reynolds, C. W. 1991. *Boids*. In Langton, C. G. (editor). *Artificial Life II Video Proceedings*. Addison-Wesley.

≈Reynolds, C. W. 1993. An evolved vision-based behavioral model of coordinated group motion. In Meyer, J-A., Roitblat, H. L. and Wilson, S. W. (editors). *From Animals to Animats 2: Proceedings of the Second International Conference on Simulation of Adaptive Behavior*. The MIT Press.

≈Reynolds, C. W. 1994a. Evolution of obstacle avoidance behavior: Using noise to promote robust solutions. In Kinnear, K. E. Jr. (editor). *Advances in Genetic Programming*. The MIT Press.

≈Reynolds, C. W. 1994b. An evolved vision-based model of obstacle avoidance behavior. In Langton, C. G. (editor). *Artificial Life III, SFI Studies in the Sciences of Complexity*. Volume XVII. Addison-Wesley.

≈Reynolds, C. W. 1994c. The difficulty of roving eyes. *Proceedings of the 1994 IEEE World Congress on Computational Intelligence*. IEEE Press.

Rich, E. 1983. *Artificial Intelligence*. McGraw-Hill.

Richardson, D. C. and Richardson, J. S. 1992. The kinemage: A tool for scientific communication. *Protein Science* 1(1): 3–9.

≈Rosca, J. P. and Ballard, D. H. 1994a. Learning by adpating representations in genetic programming. *Proceedings of the 1994 IEEE World Congress on Computational Intelligence*. IEEE Press.

≈Rosca, J. P. and Ballard, D. H. 1994b. *Genetic Programming with Adaptive Representations*. Department of Computer Science technical report 489, University of Rochester, Feburary 1994.

Rosenbloom, P. S., Laird, J. E. 1986. Mapping explanation-based generalization onto Soar. *Proceedings of the Fifth National Conference on Artificial Intelligence*. Volume 1. Morgan Kaufmann.

Rosenbloom, P. S., Laird, J. E., and Newell, A. (editors). 1993. *The Soar Papers*. The MIT Press. Volumes I and II.

Rumelhart, D. E., Hinton, G. E., and Williams, R. J. 1986. Learning internal representations by error propagation. In Rumelhart, D. E., McClelland, J. L., and the PDP Research Group (editors). *Parallel Distributed Processing*, Volume 1. The MIT Press.

≈Rush, J. R., Fraser, A. P., and Barnes D. P. 1994. Evolving co-operation in autonomous robotic systems. *Proceeedings of the IEE International Conference on Control, March 21-24, 1994*. Institute of Electrical Engineers. London.

≈Ryan, C. 1994. Pygmies and civil servants. In Kinnear, K. E. Jr. (editor). *Advances in Genetic Programming*. The MIT Press.

Samuel, A. L. 1959. Some studies in machine learning using the game of checkers. *IBM Journal of Research and Development*, 3(3): 210–229. July 1959.

Schaffer, J. D. (editor). 1989. *Proceedings of the Third International Conference on Genetic Algorithms*. Morgan Kaufmann.

Schaffer, J. D. and Whitley, D (editors). 1992. *Proceedings of the Workshop on Combinations of Genetic Algorithms and Neural Networks 1992*. The IEEE Computer Society Press.

Schulz, G. E. and Schirmer, R. H. 1979. *Principles of Protein Structure*. Springer-Verlag.

Schulze-Kremer, S. 1993. Genetic algorithms for protein tertiary structure prediction. In Brazdil, P. B. (editor). *Machine Learning: European Conference on Machine Learning, Vienna, Austria, April 5–7, 1993, Proceedings*. Springer-Verlag.

Schwefel, H. P. and Maenner, R. (editors). 1991. *Parallel Problem Solving from Nature*. Springer-Verlag.

Schirmer, T. and Cowan, S. W. 1993. Prediction of membrane-spanning b-strands and its application to maltoporin. *Protein Science*. 2: 1361-1363. August 1993.

Shirai, Y. and Tsujii, J. 1982. *Artificial Intelligence: Concepts, Techniques, and Applications*. Wiley.

≈Siegel, E. 1994. Competitively evolving decision trees against fixed training cases for natural language processing. In Kinnear, K. E. Jr. (editor). *Advances in Genetic Programming*. The MIT Press.

≈Sims, K. 1991a. Artificial evolution for Computer Graphics. *Computer Graphics*. 25(4): 319–328. July 1991.

≈Sims, K. 1991b. *Panspermia*. In Langton, Christopher G. (editor). *Artificial Life II Video Proceedings*. Addison-Wesley.

≈Sims, K. 1992a. Interactive evolution of dynamical systems. In Varela, F. J., and Bourgine, P. (editors). *Toward a Practice of Autonomous Systems: Proceedings of the First European Conference on Artificial Life*. The MIT Press.

≈Sims, K. 1992b. Interactive evolution of equations for procedural models. *Proceedings of IMAGINA conference, Monte Carlo, January 29-31, 1992*.

≈Sims, K. 1993a. Interactive evolution of equations for procedural models. *The Visual Computer*. 9: 466-476.

≈Sims, K. 1993b. Evolving Images. Lecture presented at Centre George Pompidou, Paris on March 4, 1993. *Notebook*. Number 5.

≈Singleton, A. Genetic programming with C++. 1994. *Byte*, 19(2): 171–176.

≈Spencer, G. 1993. Automatic generation of programs for crawling and walking. In Forrest, S. (editor). *Proceedings of the Fifth International Conference on Genetic Algorithms*. Morgan Kaufmann.

≈Spencer, G. 1994. Automatic generation of programs for crawling and walking. In Kinnear, K. E. Jr. (editor). *Advances in Genetic Programming*. The MIT Press.

≈Spector, L. 1994. Genetic programming and AI planning systems. *Proceedings of Twelfth National Conference on Artificial Intelligence*.. AAAI Press / The MIT Press.

≈Spector, L. and Alpern, A. 1994. Criticism, culture, and the automatic generation of artworks. *Proceedings of Twelfth National Conference on Artificial Intelligence*. AAAI Press / The MIT Press.

Steele, G. L. Jr. 1990.*Common LISP: The Language*. Digital Press. Second Edition.

Stender, J. (editor). 1993. *Parallel Genetic Algorithms*. IOS Publishing.

Stryer, Lubert. 1988. *Biochemistry*. W. H. Freeman   Third Edition.

Sun, S. 1993. Reduced representation model of protein structure prediction: Statistical potential and genetic algorithms. *Protein Science*. 2(5): 762-785. May 1993.

≈Tackett, W. A. 1993a. Genetic programming for feature discovery and image discrimination. In Forrest, S. (editor). *Proceedings of the Fifth International Conference on Genetic Algorithms*. Morgan Kaufmann.

≈Tackett, W. A. 1993b. Genetic generation of dendritic trees for image classification. *Proceedings of the World Conference on Neural Networks, Portland, Oregon, July 1993*. IEEE Press.

≈Tackett, W. A. 1994. *Recombination, Selection, and the Genetic Construction of Computer Programs*. Ph.D. dissertation, University of Southern California, Department of Electrical Engineering Systems.

≈Tackett, W. A. and Carmi, A. 1994a. Scalability, generalization, and breeding schemes in genetic programming: The donut problem. In Kinnear, K. E. Jr. (editor). *Advances in Genetic Programming*. The MIT Press.

≈Tackett, W. A. and Carmi, A. 1994b. The unique implications of brood selection for genetic programming. *Proceedings of the 1994 IEEE World Congress on Computational Intelligence*. IEEE Press.

Tajima, K. 1993. Multiple sequence alignment using parallel genetic algorithms. In Takagi, T., Imai, H., Miyano, S. Mitaku, S., and Kanehisa, M. (editors). *Genome Informatics Workshop IV*. Universal Academy Press.

Takagi, T., Imai, H., Miyano, S. Mitaku, S., and Kanehisa, M. (editors). 1993. *Genome Informatics Workshop IV*. Universal Academy Press.

Tanimoto, S. L. 1987. *The Elements of Artificial Intelligence*. Computer Science Press.

≈Teller, A. 1993. Learning mental models. *Proceedings of the Fifth Workshop on Neural Networks: An International Conference on Computational Intelligence: Neural Networks, Fuzzy Systems, Evolutionary Programming, and Virtual Reality*. The Society for Computer Simulation.

≈Teller, A. 1994a. The evolution of mental models. In Kinnear, K. E. Jr. (editor). *Advances in Genetic Programming*. The MIT Press.

≈Teller, A. 1994b. Genetic programming, indexed memory, the halting problem, and other curiosities. *Proceedings of the Seventh Florida Artificial Intelligence Research Symposium*.

≈Teller, A. 1994c. Turing completeness in the language of genetic programming with indexed memory. *Proceedings of the 1994 IEEE World Congress on Computational Intelligence*. IEEE Press.

Teufel, M., Pompejus, M., Humbel, B., Friedrich, K., and Fritz, H. J. 1993. Properties of bacteriorhodopsin derivatives constructed by insertion of an exogenous epitope into extra-membrane loops. *The EMBO Journal*. 12(9): 3399-3408.

≈Thonemann, U. W. 1992. *Verbesserung des Simulated Annealing unter Anwendung Genetischer Programmierung am Beispiel des Diskreten Quadratischen Layoutproblems*. Master's thesis, University of Paderborn, Germany.

≈Thonemann, U. W. 1994. Finding improved simulated annealing schedules with genetic programming. *Proceedings of the 1994 IEEE World Congress on Computational Intelligence*. IEEE Press.

Uhr, L. and Vossler, C. 1966. A pattern recognition program that generates, evaluates, and adjusts its own operators. In Uhr, Leonard (editor). *Pattern Recognition*. Wiley.

Unger, R. and Moult, J. 1993a. On the applicability of genetic algorithms to protein folding. In Mudge, T. N., Milutinovic, V., and Hunter, L. (editors). *Proceedings of the Twenty-Sixth Annual Hawaii International Conference on Systems Science 1993*. The IEEE Computer Society Press. Volume I.

Unger, R. and Moult, J. 1993b. A genetic algorithm for 3D protein folding simulations. In Forrest, S. (editor). *Proceedings of the Fifth International Conference on Genetic Algorithms*. Morgan Kaufmann.

Unger, R. and Moult, J. 1993c. Genetic algorithms for protein folding simulations. *Journal of Molecular Biology*. 231: 75–81.

van Laarhoven, P. J. M., and Aarts, E. H. 1987. *Simulated Annealing; Theory and Applications*. Reidel.

von Heijne, G. 1992. Membrane protein structure prediction: Hydrophobicity analysis and the positive-inside rule. *Journal of Molecular Biology*. 225: 487–494.

Weiss, S. M. and Indurkhya, N. 1991. Reduced complexity rule induction. *Proceedings of the Twelfth International Joint Conference on Artificial Intelligence*.

Weiss, S. M., Cohen, D. M., and Indurkhya, N. 1993. Transmembrane segment prediction from protein sequence data. In Hunter, L., Searls, D., and Shavlik, J. (editors). *Proceedings of the First International Conference on Intelligent Systems for Molecular Biology*. AAAI Press.

Whitley, D (editor). 1992. *Proceedings of Workshop on the Foundations of Genetic Algorithms and Classifier Systems, Vail, Colorado 1992*. Morgan Kaufmann.

Whitley, D., Starkweather, T., and Bogart, C. 1990. Genetic algorithms and neural networks: Optimizing connections and connectivity. *Parallel Computing*. 14(3): 347–361.

Wilson, S. W. 1990. Perceptron redux: emergence of structure. In Forrest, S. (editor). *Emergent Computation: Self-Organizing, Collective, and Cooperative Computing Networks*. The MIT Press.

Winston, P. H. 1981. *Artificial Intelligence*. Addison-Wesley.

Winston, P. H., Binford, T. O., Katz, B. and Lowry, M. 1983. Learning physical descriptions from functional definitions, examples, and precedents. *Proceedings of the National Conference on Artificial Intelligence*. William Kaufmann.

Wu, C., Whitson, G., McLarty, J., Ermongkonchai, A., and Chang, T. C. 1992. Protein classification artificial neural system. *Protein Science*. 1(5): 667-677. May 1992.

Yeagle, P. L. 1993. *The Membranes of Cells*. Second edition. Academic Press.

≈Zhang, B-T. and Muhlenbein, H. Synthesis of sigma-pi neural networks by the breeder genetic programming. *Proceedings of the 1994 IEEE World Congress on Computational Intelligence*. IEEE Press.

Zhang, X., Fetrow, J. S., Rennie, W. A., Waltz, D. L., and Berg, G. 1993. Automatic derivation of substructures yields novel structural building blocks in globular proteins. In Hunter, L., Searls, D., and Shavlik, J (editors). *Proceedings of the First International Conference on Intelligent Systems for Molecular Biology*. AAAI Press.

Index